Lecture Notes in Computer Science 16431

The series Lecture Notes in Computer Science (LNCS), including its subseries Lecture Notes in Artificial Intelligence (LNAI) and Lecture Notes in Bioinformatics (LNBI), has established itself as a medium for the publication of new developments in computer science and information technology research, teaching, and education.

LNCS enjoys close cooperation with the computer science R & D community, the series counts many renowned academics among its volume editors and paper authors, and collaborates with prestigious societies. Its mission is to serve this international community by providing an invaluable service, mainly focused on the publication of conference and workshop proceedings and postproceedings. LNCS commenced publication in 1973.

Tianyong Hao · Juan Velásquez · Qing Li ·
Bin Hu · Guandong Xu
Editors

Behavioural and Social Computing

12th International Conference, BESC 2025
Hong Kong SAR, China, October 16–18, 2025
Proceedings, Part I

Springer

Editors
Tianyong Hao
South China Normal University
Guangzhou, China

Juan Velásquez
University of Chile
Santiago, Chile

Qing Li
The Hong Kong Polytechnic University
Hong Kong, China

Bin Hu
Beijing Institute of Technology
Beijing, China

Guandong Xu
The Education University of Hong Kong
Hong Kong, China

ISSN 0302-9743 ISSN 1611-3349 (electronic)
Lecture Notes in Computer Science
ISBN 978-981-95-7137-6 ISBN 978-981-95-7138-3 (eBook)
https://doi.org/10.1007/978-981-95-7138-3

This Springer imprint is published by the registered company Springer Nature Singapore Pte Ltd.
The registered company address is: 152 Beach Road, #21-01/04 Gateway East, Singapore 189721, Singapore

Preface

These three volumes contain papers from the 12th International Conference on Behavioural and Social Computing (BESC 2025), held October 16–18, 2025, at The Education University of Hong Kong, Hong Kong SAR, China. The conference program featured 2 workshops, 4 tutorials, 1 doctoral consortium, 1 demo session, and 15 technical sessions. These sessions covered topics including social computing, applied psychology, behaviour pattern learning, text and sentiment analysis, graph learning, AI in education, and AI for social good. The event also included four keynote addresses by world-class speakers specializing in social computing, explainable AI, trustworthy AI, and AI ethics and safety, as well as a panel discussion that stimulated insightful dialogue among participants.

BESC 2025 received 149 eligible submissions from 12 countries, including 63 research track papers. Each submission underwent a rigorous double-blind review process, with an average of 3.32 reviews per paper. Following detailed evaluation and discussion, the Program Committee accepted 18 full papers (28.6% acceptance rate), 23 regular papers, 41 special session papers, 5 doctoral consortium papers, 14 demo papers, and 10 workshop papers. This strong international response underscores the growing importance and vitality of behavioural and social computing research. The BESC conference brings together researchers and practitioners from artificial intelligence, information systems, psychology, and social sciences, fostering collaboration and accelerating scientific exchange in this rapidly evolving domain.

The papers included in these volumes reflect the interdisciplinary nature and innovative scope of the conference. Topics span behavioural analysis, social computing, text and sentiment analysis, behavioural pattern learning, trust and privacy, and applications of artificial intelligence in social and organizational contexts, in Behavioural and Social Computing, which has emerged as a vital interdisciplinary field that integrates computational methods with behavioural and social sciences. The field aims to model, analyse, and interpret human behaviours and social dynamics using data-driven approaches. This enables more effective solutions in governance, business intelligence, security, and community management.

We extend our sincere gratitude to the Program Committee members for their diligent efforts in ensuring a high-quality review process. We are deeply thankful to the Organizing Committee and volunteers, whose dedication was essential to the success of BESC 2025. We acknowledge the generous support of our sponsors. Finally, we thank all authors and participants for contributing to a vibrant and intellectually rich conference. We believe these proceedings will serve as a valuable resource for the research community and inspire further innovations in behavioural and social computing.

October 2025

Tianyong Hao
Juan Velásquez
Qing Li
Bin Hu
Guandong Xu

Organization

Honorary General Chair

John Lee Chi-Kin	Education University of Hong Kong, China

Steering Committee Chair

Guandong Xu	Education University of Hong Kong, China

General Chairs

Qing Li	Hong Kong Polytechnic University, China
Bin Hu	Beijing Institute of Technology, China

Program Chairs

Tianyong Hao	South China Normal University, China
Juan Velásquez	University of Chile, Chile

Special Session Track Chairs

Kaize Shi	University of Southern Queensland, Australia
Yongqing Sun	Nihon University, Japan

Interdisciplinary Track Chair

Hao Chen	Nankai University, China

Panel Chair

Jianquan Liu	NEC Corporation, Japan

Workshop Chairs

Jianwei Zhang	Iwate University, Japan
Konlakorn Wongpatikaseree	Mahidol University, Thailand
Wenxiu Xie	Guangdong Polytechnic Normal University, China

Tutorial Chair

Dan Lu	Harbin Engineering University, China

Extended Abstract Track Chairs

Raian Ali	Hamad Bin Khalifa University, Qatar
Ala Yankouskaya	Bournemouth University, UK

Demo Chairs

Xin Li	iFlyTek, China
Thittaporn Ganokratanaa	King Mongkut's University of Technology Thonburi, Thailand

Doctoral Consortium Chairs

Elena Vlahu-Gjorgievska	University of Wollongong, Australia
Lin Li	Wuhan University of Technology, China

Award Chairs

Jian Cao	Shanghai Jiao Tong University, China
Xiaohui Tao	University of Southern Queensland, Australia

Local Chairs

Yu Yang	Education University of Hong Kong, China
Zhiyuan Wen	Hong Kong Polytechnic University, China

Publicity Chairs

Dianer Yu	University of New South Wales, Australia
Waiman Pang	Hong Kong Polytechnic University, China

Finance Chair

Yakun Chen	Education University of Hong Kong, China

Proceeding Chair

Md Rafiqul Islam	Charles Darwin University, Australia

Web Chair

Shiqing Wu	City University of Macau, China

Program Committee

Sameha Alshakhsi	Hamad Bin Khalifa University, Qatar
Dena Althani	Hamad Bin Khalifa University, Qatar
Emily Arden-Close	Bournemouth University, UK
Gairui Bai	Xidian University, China
Debaditya Barman	Visva-Bharati University, India
Barbara Caci	University of Palermo, Italy
Yakun Chen	Education University of Hong Kong, China
Zhihong Cui	University of Oslo, Norway
Shizhuo Deng	Northeastern University, China
Khaldoon Dhou	Texas A&M University Central Texas, USA
Yinglan Feng	Shenzhen University, China
Eugene Yujun Fu	Education University of Hong Kong, China
Linjiang Guo	University of Technology Sydney, Australia
Huan Huo	University of Technology Sydney, Australia
Md Rafiqul Islam	Charles Darwin University, Australia
Mohammad Islam	Southern Connecticut State University, USA
Chyng-Yang Jang	University of Texas at Arlington, USA
Weiwei Jiang	Beijing University of Posts and Telecommunications, China

Baoshuo Kan	South China Normal University, China
Lingping Kong	VSB-Technical University of Ostrava, Czechia
Vivek Kumar	University of the Bundeswehr Munich, Germany
Lin Li	Wuhan University of Technology, China
Qian Li	Curtin University, Australia
Xin Li	University of Science and Technology of China, China
Yong Li	Guangdong University of Education, China
Rongjiao Liang	South China Normal University, China
Ying Liu	University of Chinese Academy of Sciences, China
Jing Long	University of Technology Sydney, Australia
Jinyi Long	Jinan University, China
Hao Miao	Hong Kong Polytechnic University, China
Georgios Mikros	Hamad Bin Khalifa University, Qatar
Hamid Mukhtar	University of Birmingham Dubai, United Arab Emirates
Steven Peng	Hong Kong University of Education, China
Xiuxiu Qi	Hong Kong Polytechnic University, China
Lin Qiu	Chinese University of Hong Kong, China
Ali Safa	Hamad Bin Khalifa University, Qatar
Mattia Salnitri	University of Bergamo, Italy
Zubair Shah	Hamad Bin Khalifa University, Qatar
Jiaxing Shen	Lingnan University, China
Kaize Shi	University of Southern Queensland, Australia
Yangyang Shu	University of New South Wales, Australia
Kullawadee Somboonviwat	Kasetsart University Sriracha Campus, Thailand
Xueyao Sun	University of Technology Sydney, Australia
Xiaohui Tao	University of Southern Queensland, Australia
Aleksandar Tomašević	University of Belgrade, Serbia
Elena Vlahu-Gjorgievska	University of Wollongong, Australia
Yao Wan	Huazhong University of Science and Technology, China
Hao Wang	University of Science and Technology of China, China
Xiangmeng Wang	Hong Kong Polytechnic University, China
Xinyi Wang	University of Malaya, Malaysia
Zhiyuan Wen	Hong Kong Polytechnic University, China
Runze Wu	NetEase Fuxi AI Lab, China
Shiqing Wu	City University of Macau, China
Guandong Xu	Education University of Hong Kong, China
Yiming Xu	Yanshan University, China

Ting Xue	Tianjin University of Chinese Traditional Medicine, China
Haoran Yang	Central South University, China
Xin Yang	Southwestern University of Finance and Economics, China
Yu Yang	Education University of Hong Kong, China
Dianer Yu	University of New South Wales, Australia
Jiayu Zhang	Suzhou University of Technology, China
Yong Zhang	Tsinghua University, China
Yuqing Zhao	Hong Kong Polytechnic University, China
Hengdong Zhu	South China Normal University, China

Contents

Early Detection of Fake News Based on Sequential Analysis of Social Context and Adaptive Thresholding ... 1
Jianwei Zhang, Soma Tani, and Lin Li

Accelerating High-Dimensional Expensive Multi-objective Optimization via Surrogate-Assisted Fuzzy Directed Sampling ... 16
Zihua Guo, Min-Rong Chen, Jixiang Zeng, Zeyan Zhang, and Songxiang Zhong

An Improved Large-Scale Multi-objective Competitive Swarm Optimizer Based on Harris Hawks Optimization ... 30
Jixiang Zeng, Min-Rong Chen, Zihua Guo, Zeyan Zhang, and Songxiang Zhong

Multimodal Multiobjective Optimization Algorithm Based on Two-Stage Proportional Selection ... 43
Zeyan Zhang, Min-Rong Chen, Jixiang Zeng, Zihua Guo, and Songxiang Zhong

A Multidimensional Sentiment Analysis Model for Experience Assessment ... 55
Wanwan Zheng, Yang Li, Koji Makino, Katsuhisa Yoshikawa, Kunihiko Hara, Hiroshi Shibata, and Hideki Ohira

Discrete-Time Sigma-Delta Modulator Coefficient Optimization via Soft Actor-Critic Reinforcement Learning ... 73
Wanli Zhao, Junpeng Zhang, Zhenyu Rao, Chen Yang, Minglei Tong, and Yongqing Sun

Anomaly Detection Method for Tabular Data Based on a Three-Phase Learning Paradigm ... 88
Yufei Li, Hongtao Song, and Qilong Han

GADM: Granularity-Aware Diffusion Model for Uncertainty Forecasting in Non-stationary Time Series ... 107
Zhuhua Wang, Rui Chen, Hongtao Song, and Qilong Han

SpiderGNN: Spatial-Aware Predictive Inference with Dynamic Edge Reasoning for In-building 5G Signal Estimation ... 123
Xingyi Gao, David Hason Rudd, Ziang Li, Yuming Guo, Huan Huo, and Guandong Xu

Contrastive Representation Learning of Floor Plan Images Using Human Annotated Attributed Graphs 141
Ibuki Uda and Tomonobu Ozaki

AgentLesson: LLM-Based Multi-agent System for Educational Lesson Plan Generation 155
Yakun Chen, Yu Yang, and Guandong Xu

Bridging Dependency Enhanced Counterfactual Supporting for Multi-hop Question Generation 171
Kaixi Hu, Lin Li, Haohan Zhang, Jianwei Zhang, and Xiaohui Tao

NLCC: Noisy Label Correction with CLIP for Robust Few-Shot Learning 188
Bowen Han, Shizhuo Deng, Jiaqi Chen, Zehua Gan, Dongyue Chen, and Yue Zhu

Quantifying Off-Ball Attacking Contribution in Football: A GCN-LSTM Approach Supervised by Expert Assessments 204
Daiki Yoshikawa and Tomonobu Ozaki

Optimizing Urban Commercial Landscapes with POI Strategic Group Analysis: A Meta-learning Hypergraph Approach 219
Jiaqi Jiang, Xin Lin, Jiahui Jin, Siyuan Huang, Haoyu Chen, and Xigang Sun

DCSN: Dynamic Calibration and Contrastive Sharpening for MultiModal Recommendation 236
Jicheng Sun, Shuai Xu, and Yicong Li

Echoes or Adversaries? Asymmetric Polarization in Elite Digital Communication 252
Meng-Jie Wang, Xiao-Cui Zhang, and Lin Qiu

Student Learning Engagement Recognition Method Based on Video Transformer 267
Wenhao Liao, Yuanyuan Wang, Xinwei Zhai, Sineng Yan, Kai Zhong, and Eugene Yujun Fu

Interpretable and Transparent Experimentation on Policy Ideas in a Social Simulation Environment 282
Nikitas M. Sgouros

Do You Tolerate System Failures? An Experimental Study on the Influence of Providing Prior Statements on Human Evaluation of System Failures 302
Masahide Yuasa

Classroom-Free Educational Experimentation: A Stochastic Learning-Design Simulation Framework with LLM Optimization 314
Da Gong

An Examination of Methods for Resolving Reviewer Dissatisfaction in Hotel Recommendation Systems 331
Yujiro Hayashi, Jianwei Zhang, Yukiko Kawai, and Shinsuke Nakajima

Developing a Novel Tag Cloud System for Optimized Visualization and Behavioural Analytics in Cosmetic Review Platforms 346
Shizuku Kitamura, Asaka Cheng Lan, Fumiya Yamaguchi, Mayumi Ueda, and Shinsuke Nakajima

Leveraging Comment Data for Enhanced Content Discovery Through Time Series Analysis of Impressive Scenes in Videos 362
Akito Sasahara, Asaka Cheng Lan, Da Li, Fumiya Yamaguchi, Mayumi Ueda, and Shinsuke Nakajima

Predicting Career Trajectories After Career Breaks: A Data-Driven Analysis Using LinkedIn Profiles 379
Kamila Kargabaeva, Yu Yang, Luka Anicin, Milos Stojmenovic, and Guandong Xu

Framework for Diverse Depression Patients Roleplaying and Cognitive Diagnosis of Scales Using LLMs Based on CoT Prompts 399
Shixin Peng, Kun Jiang, Yu Yang, Jingying Chen, and Guandong Xu

Using Topic Detection to Analyze Student Reflections in Service-Learning: A Text Mining Method for Understanding Learning Gains 415
Yuanyuan Wang, Grace Ngai, Hong Va Leong, Stephen C. F. Chan, and Eugene Yujun Fu

Modeling Rater Severity Drift in Single-Rater Performance Assessments Using Bayesian Hierarchical Methods 435
Yuichiro Yokouchi, Kuangzhe Xu, Shuichi Takaki, and Haruhiko Mitsunaga

Continuous Sub-sequence Denoising For Sequential Recommendation 452
Siying Wang, Rui Chen, Dan Lu, Chi Zhang, Yantong Du, and Qilong Han

ReCareer: Hybrid Graph Neural Networks for Post-Career-Break Job Recommendation 470
Yunqi Wang, Yu Yang, Longxiang Gao, Xiaoming Wu, and Guandong Xu

Two-Lane Local Optimality Driving Strategy for Enhancing Traffic Stability 488
Xuqian Qin, Zhengyuan Du, Shuanglin Wang, Jieyang Lin, Yuxi Sun, and Jinhua Tan

Multimodal Learning Analytics for Predicting Learning Gains in Online Service-Learning Programs 503
Kangzhong Wang, Eugene Yujun Fu, Grace Ngai, and Hong Va Leong

Beyond Words: Latent Profiles of Online Communication Styles and Their Association with Social Well-Being on Social Media 521
Asma Elfadl, Sameha Alshakhsi, Nan Jiang, Raian Ali, and Ala Yankouskaya

Author Index 539

Early Detection of Fake News Based on Sequential Analysis of Social Context and Adaptive Thresholding

Jianwei Zhang[1(✉)], Soma Tani[1], and Lin Li[2]

[1] Iwate University, Morioka, Japan
zhang@iwate-u.ac.jp
[2] Wuhan University of Technology, Wuhan, China
cathylilin@whut.edu.cn

Abstract. With the development and proliferation of social networking services, the widespread dissemination of false and misleading information—so-called fake news—has become a serious societal issue. Fake news can negatively affect various domains, including politics and economics, making early detection critical. Recent studies on automated fake news detection have primarily leveraged language models, with growing evidence that incorporating social context improves classification performance. However, as social context accumulates over time, a trade-off emerges between detection accuracy and timeliness. To address this challenge, we propose an early fake news detection method based on sequential analysis of social context and progressive threshold adjustment. Our method aims to enhance classification performance in the early stages of diffusion by removing news articles with high-confidence predictions from further analysis. By dynamically lowering the decision threshold as diffusion progresses, the method balances precision and recall—favoring confident early predictions while maintaining broader coverage later. Experimental results on two real-world datasets demonstrate that our method outperforms the baseline method in terms of F1 score during early detection stages, confirming its effectiveness in early-stage fake news identification.

Keywords: Text mining · Language model · Fake news detection · Social context · Ensemble learning

1 Introduction

With the widespread adoption of the Internet and smartphones, the number of users on social media and social networking services (SNS) has grown substantially. While these platforms serve as essential channels for information dissemination, they also enable the rapid spread of deliberately fabricated content, commonly referred to as fake news, which can significantly influence public opinion and behavior [18,22,23]. User-generated content—such as reposted articles and

T. Hao et al. (Eds.): BESC 2025, LNCS 16431, pp. 1–15, 2026.
https://doi.org/10.1007/978-981-95-7138-3_1

online discussions—amplifies this diffusion effect [30]. Since the global outbreak of the novel coronavirus in December 2019, the prevalence of misinformation related to COVID-19 and vaccines has dramatically increased on social media, raising concerns about information credibility in digital environments [12].

Although expert fact-checking can reliably identify fake news [25], manually verifying the vast volume of content circulating on social platforms is both costly and impractical. Moreover, studies have shown that fake news tends to spread more rapidly and widely than true information [30], underscoring the need for automated and early detection mechanisms—an area that has received increasing research attention [19,28,31].

Fake news detection methods are broadly categorized based on two feature types: news content and social context [27,29]. The former refers to features derived from the textual content of the article, including headlines and body text, while the latter leverages information related to user interactions and the dissemination process. Prior research, such as that by Raza et al. [16], has demonstrated that combining these two feature types significantly improves detection accuracy. However, a fundamental trade-off exists: social context features require time to accumulate, potentially delaying detection.

In this study, we address this challenge by proposing a method that performs sequential analysis of social context while adaptively adjusting decision thresholds over time. By leveraging both news content and the temporally evolving social context, our method aims to achieve high classification performance in the early stages of news diffusion. To further enhance robustness, we integrate ensemble learning using multiple pre-trained language models. Experiments on two real-world datasets demonstrate that our method outperforms baseline methods, particularly in the early detection phase.

Our key contributions are as follows:

1. We propose a method that employs sequential analysis of social context, in combination with news content, to improve classification performance and enable early-stage fake news detection.
2. We introduce an adaptive thresholding mechanism that adjusts the decision boundary over time, allowing for the early identification of high-confidence fake news instances and broader coverage later.
3. We empirically demonstrate the effectiveness of the proposed method through experiments on two real-world datasets, showing superior performance over the baseline method.

2 Related Work

Zhou et al. [30] conducted a comprehensive cross-disciplinary survey on fake news, covering foundational theories from psychology and sociology. Their work compared various detection methods based on classical machine learning and deep learning models, evaluating their classification performance, robustness, and cost. They further categorized existing techniques from different perspectives—such as news dissemination patterns and user trust—and highlighted their respective strengths and limitations. Importantly, the authors identified key research challenges, including the need for early detection and cross-domain generalizability.

Several prior studies have focused specifically on early detection of fake news. Sun et al. [21] proposed a joint learning model that captures early spreading behavior through hypergraph interactions and self-attention mechanisms, without relying on content or user identity. Akdag et al. [1] introduced a weakly supervised framework that generates pseudo-labels for data and fine-tunes RoBERTa for emerging topics, reducing dependence on large labeled datasets. Fang et al. [5] developed a semantic-inconsistency framework that analyzes discrepancies between news articles and related social media posts using attention-guided graph networks. Esteban-Bravo et al. [4] explored early prediction of fake news virality based on text features, using non-parametric models to differentiate the spread patterns of true versus fake news. Similarly, Cavalcante et al. [2] proposed a time-aware detection model that leverages crowd signals and user reputation, achieving competitive results without requiring private user data. Some other studies [8,20,26] proposed multimodal frameworks for early detection and reported improvements over traditional baselines.

Zhang et al. [24] framed fake news detection as an event-based time-series classification task. They considered an event consisting of multiple related posts on X (formerly Twitter)[1], extracted features from associated posts that comprise the event, and applied a two-stage model to assign labels along diffusion timeline. Their method utilized both news content and social context, serving as an early attempt at temporally aware fake news classification based on classical machine learning models. Building on this foundation, our study employs sequential modeling combined with pre-trained language models and ensemble learning to enhance early-stage detection performance.

Raza et al. [16] proposed a detection method based on the BART (Bidirectional Auto-Regressive Transformer) [9] model, a pre-trained transformer architecture that incorporates characteristics of both BERT [3] and GPT [13], enabling sequence-to-sequence learning. Their method utilized the NELA-GT-2019 [6] dataset for news content and the Fakeddit [11] dataset for social context. They further introduced a user credibility estimation mechanism via transfer learning, and aggregated weak labels from multiple features to infer ground truth. Their experiments demonstrated that both the encoderâĂŞdecoder structure of BART and the integration of content and context significantly enhanced detection performance, including in early diffusion stages. Our method extends their method by introducing an adaptive thresholding mechanism to further improve confidence and timeliness in early classification.

Mahabub et al. [10] investigated ensemble-based fake news detection by combining multiple classifiers. Their experiments compared soft voting—using the average of prediction probabilities—with hard voting—based on majority label voting. Results showed that soft voting outperformed other strategies. In our

[1] https://www.x.com/.

work, we adopt soft voting to aggregate outputs from multiple models, enhancing robustness and mitigating model-specific biases.

Building upon these prior studies, our method utilizes language models and integrates sequential analysis of social context with adaptive thresholding and ensemble learning, aiming to improve both classification performance and timeliness in fake news detection, particularly in the early stages of information diffusion.

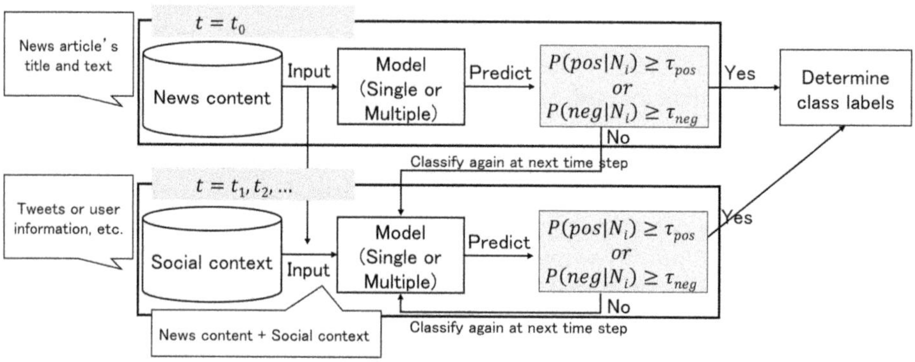

Fig. 1. Overview of the proposed method.

3 Proposed Method

3.1 Overview of the Proposed Method

The proposed method employs language models to classify whether a given news article is fake or true. The input consists of the news content (e.g., title and body text) and its social context (e.g., replies or reactions on social media). The output is a binary label indicating the veracity of the news. Multiple language models are trained independently and combined via ensemble learning during inference.

An overview of the inference process is shown in Fig. 1, and the classification flow with an example is illustrated in Fig. 2. Let N_i denote the i-th news article, and let $P(pos|N_i)$ and $P(neg|N_i)$ represent the predicted probabilities that N_i is fake (positive) and true (negative), respectively, where $P(pos|N_i) + P(neg|N_i) = 1$. The decision thresholds for positive and negative labels are denoted by τ_{pos} and τ_{neg}, and the detection stages are represented at time steps t_j (where $j = 0, 1, 2, \ldots$). In Fig. 2, solid lines represent classification targets, whereas dashed lines indicate no need to classify again. Gray rectangles denote finalized classifications, while white ones indicate deferred decisions.

At the initial time step t_0, classification is based solely on news content. From t_1 onward, social context is incrementally incorporated. At each time step, if either $P(pos|N_i) \geqq \tau_{pos}$ or $P(neg|N_i) \geqq \tau_{neg}$, a label is assigned and no further

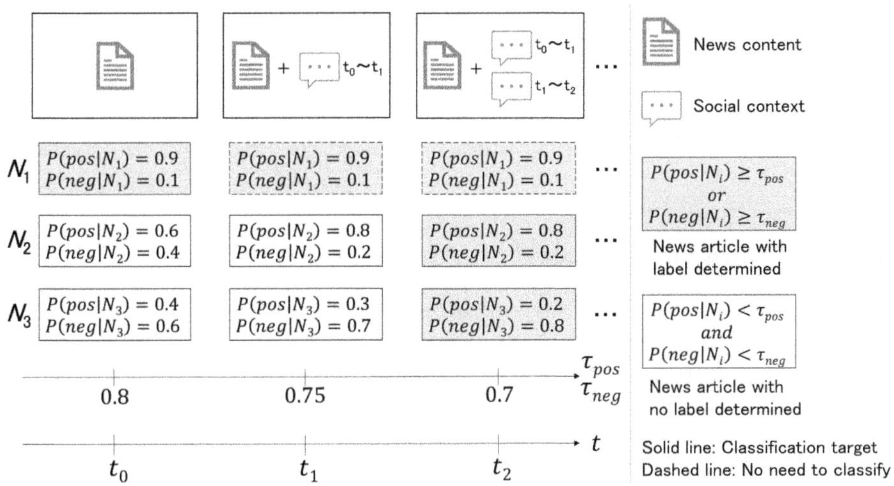

Fig. 2. Detection flow: An example for τ_{pos} and τ_{neg} with initial threshold $\tau_0 = 0.8$ and decrement value $\alpha = 0.05$.

classification is performed again for that article. Otherwise, the article is deferred to the next time step, allowing for additional social context to be included. The thresholds τ_{pos} and τ_{neg} are initialized to high values and gradually decreased over time to strike a balance between precision and recall.

3.2 Use of Social Context over Time

Detection at $t = t_0$ assumes the immediate publication of a news article, thus only the news content is used. For subsequent time steps $t = t_1, t_2, \ldots$, social context is added incrementally to simulate the diffusion process.

Let c_j be the j-th piece of social context collected between t_0 and t_m, and let $C_m = \{c_1, c_2, \ldots, c_j, \ldots, c_m\}$ represent the chronologically ordered set of social context up to time t_m. Let A denote the original news content, and $I_m = \{A, C_m\}$ be the model input at detection time t_m. This input is used to make a classification decision at each time step t_m.

3.3 Time-Dependent Threshold Adjustment

While binary classifiers typically use a probability threshold of 0.5 to separate positive and negative classes, our method adopts dynamic thresholding to prioritize confident decisions early. The threshold τ_j at time t_j is defined by:

$$\tau_j = \begin{cases} \tau_0 - \alpha j & \text{if } \tau_0 - \alpha j \geq 0.5 \\ 0.5 & \text{if } \tau_0 - \alpha j < 0.5 \end{cases}$$

Here, τ_0 is the initial threshold and α is the decrement value. For example, if $\tau_0 = 0.8$ and $\alpha = 0.05$, the thresholds for t_0 through t_7 are $\tau = 0.8, 0.75, 0.7, 0.65, 0.6, 0.55, 0.5, 0.5$.

This strategy allows the model to focus on high-confidence classifications early (favoring precision), and gradually increase coverage (favoring recall) in later stages.

3.4 Label Assignment Based on Predicted Probabilities

To ensure high reliability in early decisions, a news article is assigned a definitive label if either $P(pos|N_i) \geqq \tau_{pos}$ or $P(neg|N_i) \geqq \tau_{neg}$. Once labeled, the article is removed from further classification. If both probabilities are below the thresholds, the article is deferred to the next time step, where additional social context will be available.

To reduce the effect of abrupt changes in prediction confidence, the decision at time t_m is based on the average of probabilities at times t_m and t_{m-1}. For instance, in Fig. 2, even if $P(pos|N_2) = 0.8$ at time t_1, the label for N_2 is not finalized since the average (0.7) of its probabilities at times t_0 and t_1 does not exceed τ_1 (0.75).

3.5 Ensemble Learning

To improve classification robustness and reduce model-specific biases, we adopt ensemble learning. Specifically, we use soft voting, where the final prediction probability is obtained by averaging the outputs of multiple independently trained language models. This strategy leverages complementary strengths across models and enhances generalization performance.

4 Experimental Setup

4.1 Datasets

We evaluate our proposed method using two publicly available datasets: FakeNewsNet[2] [17] and Fakeddit[3] [11]. Experiments are conducted independently on each dataset.

FakeNewsNet. FakeNewsNet provides both news content and corresponding social context. The news content comprises articles from two fact-checking websites: PolitiFact[4] and GossipCop[5], where PolitiFact focuses on political news and GossipCop focuses on entertainment. The associated social context consists of posts on X (formerly Twitter) that shared these articles.

[2] https://github.com/KaiDMML/FakeNewsNet.
[3] https://github.com/entitize/Fakeddit.
[4] https://www.politifact.com.
[5] https://www.gossipcop.com.

We collected relevant data using the FakeNewsNet repository and the TwitterAPI[6]. For our experiments, we use the titles and full text of articles as news content. Due to the high similarity among the original sharing posts (a result of X's platform structure), we instead utilize the text of reply posts as the source of social context.

Fakeddit. Fakeddit is a Reddit[7]-based dataset that includes both posts and their replies. We treat posts referencing specific events as news content, and the text of replies as the corresponding social context.

The training and test data distributions for both datasets are summarized in Table 1 and Table 2. Due to imbalances in the number of replies per news item, we partition the datasets with an 80:20 split while preserving a similar distribution of reply counts. To mitigate the impact of sampling bias, we generate 10 different trainâĂŞtest splits and report the average evaluation metrics across these runs.

Table 1. Dataset summary (FakeNewsNet).

	Politifact		Gossipcop		Total
	True	Fake	True	Fake	
Train (with reply post)	172	109	259	682	1,222
Train (no reply post)	116	175	3,298	2,874	7,685
Test (with reply post)	44	28	66	171	309
Test (no reply post)	74	72	890	891	1,927

Table 2. Dataset summary (Fakeddit).

	True	Fake	Total
Train	1,891	2,230	4,121
Test	473	558	1,031

4.2 Verification Settings

We conduct experiments under two settings:

1. Single model classification, where each language model is used independently.
2. Ensemble classification, where outputs from multiple models are combined using soft voting.

[6] https://help.twitter.com/ja/rules-and-policies/twitter-api.
[7] https://www.reddit.com/?rdt=37392.

Due to the wide variability in the posting times of reply comments, we define detection stages every five reply posts. At each stage, five additional replies (in chronological order) are added to the input along with the news content. This setting emulates a time-dependent detection scenario.

In the proposed method, the classification thresholds τ_{pos} and τ_{neg} are dynamically adjusted using combinations of the initial threshold $\tau_0 \in \{0.7, 0.8, 0.9\}$ and decrement value $\alpha \in \{0.05, 0.1\}$. The baseline method uses a fixed threshold of 0.5 and re-evaluates all articles at each detection stage.

4.3 Language Models

For single-model experiments, we use the following pre-trained language models: DeBERTa (microsoft/deberta-v3-base[8] [7]), BART (facebook/bart-large-mnli[9] [9]), T5 (google-t5/t5-base[10] [15]), and GPT-2 (openai-community/gpt2[11] [14]). Then, the best-performing model (DeBERTa) is combined with each of other three models in the ensemble classification setting.

4.4 Evaluation Metrics

We use the F1 score as the main evaluation metric, computed as the harmonic mean of precision and recall.

In the baseline, all news articles are classified at every detection stage using a fixed threshold of 0.5. In contrast, the proposed method assigns labels only when the predicted probability exceeds an adaptive threshold. Articles that do not meet this criterion are deferred to the next stage.

Because of this selective classification, the proposed method is expected to achieve higher precision in early stages but lower recall due to fewer samples being classified. The trade-off between precision and recall is controlled by the threshold adjustment mechanism.

5 Experimental Results

5.1 Single Model Results

The results of single-model experiments are presented in Table 3, Table 4, Table 5 and Table 6, which report F1 scores across two datasets (FakeNewsNet and Fakeddit) and two threshold settings: $\tau_0 = 0.7$ or 0.8 with $\alpha = 0.05$. Similar trends were observed across other threshold configurations. In each table, higher scores between the proposed method and the baseline are highlighted in bold, while the overall best F1 score across all models is underlined.

Among the tested models, DeBERTa achieved the highest F1 scores for both datasets. Our proposed method with DeBERTa outperformed the baseline in the

[8] https://huggingface.co/microsoft/deberta-v3-base.
[9] https://huggingface.co/facebook/bart-large-mnli.
[10] https://huggingface.co/google-t5/t5-base.
[11] https://huggingface.co/openai-community/gpt2.

early detection stages—specifically from $t = 0$ to 15 for FakeNewsNet, and from $t = 0$ to 10 for Fakeddit. This improvement is attributed to the higher precision of the proposed method, as detailed in Table 7, Table 8, Table 9, and Table 10, which list precision and recall values for DeBERTa. Although recall is lower due to fewer samples being classified early, the precision gain compensates for this, resulting in improved F1 performance. These findings support the effectiveness of the proposed method in early-stage fake news detection.

In later detection stages (after 20 replies for FakeNewsNet and 15 replies for Fakeddit), the baseline method outperforms the proposed method. This is likely because the baseline reclassifies all news at each stage, allowing it to leverage accumulated social context, whereas the proposed method does not revise previously assigned labels.

A similar trend was observed with BART, where the proposed method showed better F1 scores in early stages. For T5 and GPT-2, however, the proposed method did not outperform the baseline, suggesting that the benefit of our method depends on the underlying model's capacity to capture social signals.

Table 3. F1 for experiment with single model (dataset: FakeNewsNet, initial threshold: 0.7, decrement value: 0.05).

Model \ # of Replies	0	5	10	15	20	25	30
1pt DeBERTa (Ours)	<u>**0.798**</u>	<u>**0.819**</u>	<u>**0.831**</u>	<u>**0.836**</u>	0.838	0.838	0.838
DeBERTa (Baseline)	0.772	0.783	0.823	0.830	<u>**0.849**</u>	<u>**0.852**</u>	<u>**0.854**</u>
1pt BART (Ours)	**0.753**	**0.783**	**0.806**	0.810	0.818	0.818	0.818
BART (Baseline)	0.729	0.775	0.798	**0.812**	**0.822**	**0.826**	**0.829**
1pt T5 (Ours)	0.747	0.777	0.786	0.799	0.812	0.812	0.812
T5 (Baseline)	**0.749**	**0.782**	**0.798**	**0.814**	**0.821**	**0.823**	**0.823**
1pt GPT-2 (Ours)	0.712	0.725	0.739	0.751	0.755	0.755	0.755
GPT-2 (Baseline)	**0.722**	**0.755**	**0.776**	**0.782**	**0.789**	**0.791**	**0.792**

5.2 Assemble Classification Results

Ensemble learning experiments combine DeBERTa, the top-performing single model, with one additional language model. The F1 scores are summarized in Table 11, Table 13, Table 12 and Table 14, corresponding to the same datasets and threshold settings used in the single-model experiments. As before, higher scores between the proposed method and the baseline are shown in bold, and ensemble results that surpass single DeBERTa are underlined.

The results indicate that ensemble learning with DeBERTa and BART achieves higher F1 scores than DeBERTa alone across both datasets and settings.

Table 4. F1 for experiment with single model (dataset: FakeNewsNet, initial threshold: 0.8, decrement value: 0.05).

Model \ # of Replies	0	5	10	15	20	25	30
1pt DeBERTa (Ours)	**0.791**	**0.810**	**0.825**	**0.835**	0.839	0.841	0.841
DeBERTa (Baseline)	0.772	0.783	0.823	0.830	**0.849**	**0.852**	**0.854**
1pt BART (Ours)	**0.749**	0.771	0.790	0.808	0.819	0.820	0.820
BART (Baseline)	0.729	**0.775**	**0.798**	**0.812**	**0.822**	**0.826**	**0.829**
1pt T5 (Ours)	0.738	0.759	0.774	0.790	0.806	0.809	0.809
T5 (Baseline)	**0.749**	**0.782**	**0.798**	**0.814**	**0.821**	**0.823**	**0.823**
1pt GPT-2 (Ours)	0.704	0.717	0.731	0.742	0.748	0.751	0.752
GPT-2 (Baseline)	**0.722**	**0.755**	**0.776**	**0.782**	**0.789**	**0.791**	**0.792**

Table 5. F1 for experiment with single model (dataset: Fakeddit, initial threshold: 0.7, decrement value: 0.05).

Model \ # of Replies	0	5	10	15	20	25	30
1pt DeBERTa (Ours)	**0.734**	**0.745**	**0.758**	0.766	0.773	0.773	0.773
DeBERTa (Baseline)	0.721	0.734	0.755	**0.768**	**0.774**	**0.776**	**0.776**
1pt BART (Ours)	**0.710**	**0.724**	**0.734**	**0.744**	0.749	0.749	0.749
BART (Baseline)	0.702	0.721	0.733	0.741	**0.749**	**0.750**	**0.750**
1pt T5 (Ours)	**0.706**	0.712	0.729	0.736	0.737	0.737	0.737
T5 (Baseline)	0.704	**0.718**	**0.731**	**0.739**	**0.742**	**0.743**	**0.743**
1pt GPT-2 (Ours)	**0.682**	**0.690**	0.697	0.702	0.704	0.704	0.704
GPT-2 (Baseline)	0.676	0.689	**0.700**	**0.707**	**0.709**	**0.709**	**0.709**

Table 6. F1 for experiment with single model (dataset: Fakeddit, initial threshold: 0.8, decrement value: 0.05).

Model \ # of Replies	0	5	10	15	20	25	30
1pt DeBERTa (Ours)	**0.728**	**0.741**	**0.756**	0.767	0.772	0.774	0.774
DeBERTa (Baseline)	0.721	0.734	0.755	**0.768**	**0.774**	**0.776**	**0.776**
1pt BART (Ours)	**0.706**	**0.723**	**0.734**	**0.742**	0.748	0.749	0.749
BART (Baseline)	0.702	0.721	0.733	0.741	**0.749**	**0.750**	**0.750**
1pt T5 (Ours)	0.701	0.711	0.724	0.733	0.738	0.739	0.739
T5 (Baseline)	**0.704**	**0.718**	**0.731**	**0.739**	**0.742**	**0.743**	**0.743**
1pt GPT-2 (Ours)	**0.677**	0.686	0.692	0.699	0.703	0.705	0.705
GPT-2 (Baseline)	0.676	**0.689**	**0.700**	**0.707**	**0.709**	**0.709**	**0.709**

Table 7. Precision for experiment with DeBERTa (dataset: FakeNewsNet, initial threshold: 0.7, decrement value: 0.05).

Model \ # of Replies	0	5	10	15	20	25	30
1pt DeBERTa (Ours)	0.963	0.962	0.962	0.961	0.962	0.962	0.962
DeBERTa (Baseline)	0.843	0.868	0.878	0.885	0.889	0.892	0.893
1pt Difference	0.120	0.094	0.084	0.076	0.073	0.070	0.069

Table 8. Recall for experiment with DeBERTa (dataset: FakeNewsNet, initial threshold: 0.7, decrement value: 0.05).

Model \ # of Replies	0	5	10	15	20	25	30
1pt DeBERTa (Ours)	0.681	0.713	0.731	0.740	0.742	0.742	0.742
DeBERTa (Baseline)	0.712	0.713	0.774	0.781	0.812	0.815	0.818
1pt Difference	0.031	0.000	0.043	0.041	0.070	0.073	0.076

Table 9. Precision for experiment with DeBERTa (dataset: Fakeddit, initial threshold: 0.7, decrement value: 0.05).

Model \ # of Replies	0	5	10	15	20	25	30
1pt DeBERTa (Ours)	0.912	0.908	0.909	0.909	0.908	0.908	0.908
DeBERTa (Baseline)	0.792	0.807	0.818	0.826	0.832	0.834	0.834
1pt Difference	0.120	0.101	0.091	0.083	0.076	0.074	0.074

Table 10. Recall for experiment with DeBERTa (dataset: Fakeddit, initial threshold: 0.7, decrement value: 0.05).

Model \ # of Replies	0	5	10	15	20	25	30
1pt DeBERTa (Ours)	0.614	0.632	0.650	0.662	0.673	0.673	0.673
DeBERTa (Baseline)	0.662	0.673	0.701	0.718	0.724	0.726	0.726
1pt Difference	0.048	0.041	0.051	0.056	0.051	0.053	0.053

This demonstrates that ensemble learning can effectively improve classification performance by reducing the influence of individual model biases.

However, we also observed that when lower-performing models (T5 and GPT-2) are included in the ensemble, the overall performance may degrade. This suggests that model selection in ensemble construction is critical, and simply increasing the number of models does not guarantee improvement.

Table 11. F1 for experiment with ensemble model (dataset: FakeNewsNet, initial threshold: 0.7, decreasing value: 0.05).

Model \ # of Replies	0	5	10	15	20	25	30
1pt DeBERTa (Ours)	**0.798**	**0.819**	**0.831**	**0.836**	0.838	0.838	0.838
DeBERTa (Baseline)	0.772	0.783	0.823	0.830	**0.849**	**0.852**	**0.854**
1pt DeBERTa+BART (Ours)	<u>**0.807**</u>	<u>**0.831**</u>	<u>**0.846**</u>	0.851	0.853	0.853	0.853
DeBERTa+BART (Baseline)	0.782	0.792	0.843	<u>**0.857**</u>	<u>**0.860**</u>	<u>**0.863**</u>	<u>**0.865**</u>
1pt DeBERTa+T5 (Ours)	**0.782**	0.802	0.819	0.831	0.832	0.832	0.832
DeBERTa+T5 (Baseline)	0.780	**0.807**	**0.829**	**0.845**	**0.848**	**0.851**	**0.851**
1pt DeBERTa+GPT-2 (Ours)	**0.752**	0.771	0.788	0.795	0.797	0.797	0.797
DeBERTa+GPT-2 (Baseline)	0.747	**0.789**	**0.801**	**0.817**	**0.820**	**0.822**	**0.823**

Table 12. F1 for experiment with ensemble model (dataset: FakeNewsNet, initial threshold: 0.8, decreasing value: 0.05).

Model \ # of Replies	0	5	10	15	20	25	30
1pt DeBERTa (Ours)	**0.791**	**0.810**	**0.825**	**0.835**	0.839	0.841	0.841
DeBERTa (Baseline)	0.772	0.783	0.823	0.830	**0.849**	**0.852**	**0.854**
1pt DeBERTa+BART (Ours)	<u>**0.803**</u>	<u>**0.825**</u>	<u>**0.843**</u>	0.852	0.856	0.857	0.857
DeBERTa+BART (Baseline)	0.782	0.792	0.843	<u>**0.857**</u>	<u>**0.860**</u>	<u>**0.863**</u>	<u>**0.865**</u>
1pt DeBERTa+T5 (Ours)	0.776	0.795	0.814	0.829	0.834	0.837	0.837
DeBERTa+T5 (Baseline)	**0.780**	**0.807**	**0.829**	**0.845**	**0.848**	**0.851**	**0.851**
1pt DeBERTa+GPT-2 (Ours)	**0.749**	0.767	0.785	0.796	0.798	0.799	0.799
DeBERTa+GPT-2 (Baseline)	0.747	**0.789**	**0.801**	**0.817**	**0.820**	**0.822**	**0.823**

Table 13. F1 for experiment with ensemble model (dataset: Fakeddit, initial threshold: 0.7, decreasing value: 0.05).

Model \ # of Replies	0	5	10	15	20	25	30
1pt DeBERTa (Ours)	**0.734**	**0.745**	**0.758**	0.766	0.773	0.773	0.773
DeBERTa (Baseline)	0.721	0.734	0.755	**0.768**	**0.774**	**0.776**	**0.776**
1pt DeBERTa+BART (Ours)	<u>**0.738**</u>	<u>**0.749**</u>	<u>**0.759**</u>	0.768	0.774	0.774	0.774
DeBERTa+BART (Baseline)	0.725	0.739	0.757	<u>**0.770**</u>	<u>**0.776**</u>	<u>**0.777**</u>	<u>**0.777**</u>
1pt DeBERTa+T5 (Ours)	**0.713**	**0.726**	0.735	0.744	0.747	0.747	0.747
DeBERTa+T5 (Baseline)	0.708	0.725	**0.739**	**0.746**	**0.749**	**0.750**	**0.700**
1pt DeBERTa+GPT-2 (Ours)	**0.701**	**0.719**	0.730	0.738	0.740	0.740	0.740
DeBERTa+GPT-2 (Baseline)	0.695	0.714	**0.735**	**0.743**	**0.744**	**0.745**	**0.745**

Table 14. F1 for experiment with ensemble model (dataset: Fakeddit, initial threshold: 0.8, decreasing value: 0.05).

Model \ # of Replies	0	5	10	15	20	25	30
1pt DeBERTa (Ours)	**0.728**	**0.741**	**0.756**	0.767	0.772	0.774	0.774
DeBERTa (Baseline)	0.721	0.734	0.755	**0.768**	**0.774**	**0.776**	**0.776**
1pt DeBERTa+BART (Ours)	**0.732**	**0.747**	**0.763**	**0.771**	0.775	0.776	0.776
DeBERTa+BART (Baseline)	0.725	0.739	0.757	0.770	**0.776**	**0.777**	**0.777**
1pt DeBERTa+T5 (Ours)	0.707	0.723	0.736	0.745	0.747	0.748	0.748
DeBERTa+T5 (Baseline)	**0.708**	**0.725**	**0.739**	**0.746**	**0.749**	**0.750**	**0.700**
1pt DeBERTa+GPT-2 (Ours)	**0.697**	**0.716**	0.732	0.739	0.742	0.743	0.743
DeBERTa+GPT-2 (Baseline)	0.695	0.714	**0.735**	**0.743**	**0.744**	**0.745**	**0.745**

6 Conclusion and Future Work

In this study, we proposed an automatic fake news detection method that incorporates sequential analysis of social context and adaptive thresholding to improve classification performance during the early stages of news diffusion. By leveraging both static news content and temporally evolving social context, and adjusting decision thresholds over time, the proposed method aims to detect fake news earlier with higher confidence. Experiments conducted on two real-world datasets—FakeNewsNet and Fakeddit—demonstrated that our method using DeBERTa outperforms the baseline method in terms of F1 score during early detection stages. This result confirms the effectiveness of combining sequential context modeling with dynamic threshold adjustment for early-stage classification. Furthermore, our ensemble learning strategy, which combines DeBERTa and BART, achieved even higher F1 scores than DeBERTa alone, highlighting the value of multi-model integration in improving robustness. However, in the later stages of diffusion, the baseline method achieved higher F1 scores than the proposed method. This is likely due to the fact that, once a news article is classified in our method, it is excluded from further evaluation—even if additional social context becomes available. Thus, early misclassifications cannot be corrected, which may affect long-term performance.

While our method focuses on improving early-stage detection, further improvements are necessary to maintain high classification performance as more social context accumulates. In future work, we plan to:

1. Conduct a more detailed error analysis to better understand early misclassifications and reduce false positives and false negatives.
2. Explore adaptive re-evaluation mechanisms that allow reclassification under certain conditions without compromising early precision.
3. Investigate the impact of incorporating additional social context features such as sentiment, stance, or user credibility into the model.

Ultimately, our goal is to develop a detection framework that is both responsive in early stages and accurate over the full diffusion lifecycle.

Acknowledgments. This work was supported by JSPS KAKENHI Grant Number JP22K12271 and JSPS Invitational Fellowships for Research in Japan (Short-term).

References

1. Akdag, S.H., Cicekli, N.K.: Early detection of fake news on emerging topics through weak supervision. J. Intell. Inf. Syst. **62**(5), 1263–1284 (2024)
2. Cavalcante, A.A.B., Freire, P.M.S., Goldschmidt, R.R., Justel, C.M.: Early detection of fake news on virtual social networks: a time-aware approach based on crowd signals. Expert Syst. Appl. **247**, 123350 (2024)
3. Devlin, J., Chang, M., Lee, K., Toutanova, K.: BERT: pre-training of deep bidirectional transformers for language understanding. In: NAACL-HLT, pp. 4171–4186 (2019)
4. Esteban-Bravo, M., Jiménez-Rubido, L., Vidal-Sanz, J.M.: Predicting the virality of fake news at the early stage of dissemination. Expert Syst. Appl. **248**, 123390 (2024)
5. Fang, X., et al.: NSEP: early fake news detection via news semantic environment perception. Inf. Process. Manag. **61**(2), 103594 (2024)
6. Gruppi, M., Horne, B.D., Adali, S.: NELA-GT-2019: a large multi-labelled news dataset for the study of misinformation in news articles. CoRR arxiv:2003.08444 (2020)
7. He, P., Gao, J., Chen, W.: Debertav3: improving deberta using electra-style pre-training with gradient-disentangled embedding sharing. In: ICLR (2023)
8. Hu, W., Wang, Y., Jia, Y., Liao, Q., Zhou, B.: A multi-modal prompt learning framework for early detection of fake news. In: ICWSM, pp. 651–662 (2024)
9. Lewis, M., etal.: BART: denoising sequence-to-sequence pre-training for natural language generation, translation, and comprehension. In: ACL, pp. 7871–7880 (2020)
10. Mahabub, A.: A robust technique of fake news detection using ensemble voting classifier and comparison with other classifiers. SN Appl. Sci. **2** (2020)
11. Nakamura, K., Levy, S., Wang, W.Y.: Fakeddit: a new multimodal benchmark dataset for fine-grained fake news detection. In: LREC, pp. 6149–6157 (2020)
12. Pogorelov, K., Schroeder, D.T., Brenner, S., Langguth, J.: Fakenews: corona virus and conspiracies multimedia analysis task at mediaeval 2021. In: MediaEval 2021 Workshop (2021)
13. Radford, A., Narasimhan, K., Salimans, T., Sutskever, I.: Improving language understanding by generative pre-training. OpenAI Blog (2018)
14. Radford, A., Wu, J., Child, R., Luan, D., Amodei, D., Sutskever, I.: Language models are unsupervised multitask learners. OpenAI Blog (2019)
15. Raffel, C., et al.: Exploring the limits of transfer learning with a unified text-to-text transformer. J. Mach. Learn. Res. **21**, 140:1–140:67 (2020)
16. Raza, S., Ding, C.: Fake news detection based on news content and social contexts: a transformer-based approach. Int. J. Data Sci. Anal. **13**(4), 335–362 (2022)
17. Shu, K., Mahudeswaran, D., Wang, S., Lee, D., Liu, H.: Fakenewsnet: a data repository with news content, social context, and spatiotemporal information for studying fake news on social media. Big Data **8**(3), 171–188 (2020)

18. Shu, K., Sliva, A., Wang, S., Tang, J., Liu, H.: Fake news detection on social media: a data mining perspective. SIGKDD Explor. **19**(1), 22–36 (2017)
19. Song, C., Yang, C., Chen, H., Tu, C., Liu, Z., Sun, M.: CED: credible early detection of social media rumors. IEEE Trans. Knowl. Data Eng. **33**(8), 3035–3047 (2021)
20. Sormeily, A., Dadkhah, S., Zhang, X., Ghorbani, A.A.: Mefand: a multimodel framework for early fake news detection. IEEE Trans. Comput. Soc. Syst. **11**(4), 5337–5353 (2024)
21. Sun, L., Rao, Y., Lan, Y., Xia, B., Li, Y.: HG-SL: jointly learning of global and local user spreading behavior for fake news early detection. In: AAAI, pp. 5248–5256 (2023)
22. Vosoughi, S., Roy, D., Aral, S.: The spread of true and false news online. Science **359**(6380), 1146–1151 (2018)
23. Zafarani, R., Zhou, X., Shu, K., Liu, H.: Fake news research: theories, detection strategies, and open problems. In: SIGKDD, pp. 3207–3208 (2019)
24. Zhang, J., Yamanaka, J., Li, L.: Early automatic detection of false information in twitter event considering occurrence scale and time series. In: iiWAS, pp. 282–289 (2020)
25. Zhang, J., Dong, B., Yu, P.S.: Fakedetector: effective fake news detection with deep diffusive neural network. In: ICDE, pp. 1826–1829 (2020)
26. Zhang, L., et al.: Early detection of multimodal fake news via reinforced propagation path generation. IEEE Trans. Knowl. Data Eng. **37**(2), 613–625 (2025)
27. Zhou, X., Jain, A., Phoha, V.V., Zafarani, R.: Fake news early detection: a theory-driven model. DTRAP **1**(2), 12:1–12:25 (2020)
28. Zhou, X., Wu, J., Zafarani, R.: SAFE: similarity-aware multi-modal fake news detection. In: PAKDD, pp. 354–367 (2020)
29. Zhou, X., Zafarani, R.: Network-based fake news detection: a pattern-driven approach. SIGKDD Explor. **21**(2), 48–60 (2019)
30. Zhou, X., Zafarani, R.: A survey of fake news: fundamental theories, detection methods, and opportunities. ACM Comput. Surv. **53**(5), 109:1–109:40 (2021)
31. Zhou, X., Zafarani, R., Ferrara, E.: From fake news to #fakenews: mining direct and indirect relationships among hashtags for fake news detection. CoRR arxiv:2211.11113 (2022)

Accelerating High-Dimensional Expensive Multi-objective Optimization via Surrogate-Assisted Fuzzy Directed Sampling

Zihua Guo, Min-Rong Chen(✉), Jixiang Zeng, Zeyan Zhang, and Songxiang Zhong

School of Computer Science, South China Normal University, Guangzhou 510631, China
{2023023247,2023023216,2023023267,2023023300}@m.scnu.edu.cn, mrongchen@126.com

Abstract. Surrogate-assisted multi-objective evolutionary algorithms (SAEAs) have shown great performance in solving computationally expensive multi-objective optimization problems. However, when the dimensionality of the decision variables increases, the performance of these algorithms deteriorates drastically due to the curse of dimensionality and the interactions between the decision variables. In order to solve this problem, this paper proposes a fuzzy directed sampling assisted SAEA called FDSEMO. The use of directed sampling to obtain guiding solutions contributes to the rapid convergence of the population, and then using fuzzy operations to approximate the solutions in the population reduces the cumulative prediction error of the model and strengthens the global search capability. A comprehensive comparison of FDSEMO with six state-of-the-art algorithms on two standardized benchmarks shows that FDSEMO is capable of obtaining solution sets with better convergence and diversity.

Keywords: Expensive optimization · high-dimensional optimization · multi-objective optimization · evolutionary computation

1 Introduction

In practical production activities, many problems require multiple objectives to be simultaneously optimized, which are called multi-objective optimization problems (MOPs). The objectives in MOPs are usually conflicting, and it is impossible to find a solution that maximizes or minimizes multiple objectives. Therefore, it is only possible to optimize these objectives in the same problem by balancing and coordinating the relationship between them [22]. MOPs that people encounters in real life, e.g., in artificial intelligence [12], scheduling [23], economics, and many other fields of science and engineering, not only have multiple objectives to be optimized, but also come with computationally expensive

T. Hao et al. (Eds.): BESC 2025, LNCS 16431, pp. 16–29, 2026.
https://doi.org/10.1007/978-981-95-7138-3_2

function evaluations and hundreds of decision variables. Specific examples are automotive structural design [24], industrial power delivery [8], and neural network architecture search [13], to name a few. The computation of objective values for these problems is usually time or economically expensive, such as in neural network architecture search, where there are a large number of hyperparameters to be decided upon, and evaluating the performance of a network structure may require a huge time cost. Thus, solving this type of expensive multi-objective optimization problems (EMOPs) has considerable difficulty after the number of real evaluations has been limited. In order to handle this challenge, surrogate-assisted evolutionary algorithms (SAEAs) were proposed [14]. By replacing the expensive computational function with a surrogate model, the number of real evaluations can be reduced, which means that the optimization process can be extended and the solution space can be explored more fully. The existing SAEAs can be categorized into the following two groups.

Regression-based SAEAs: In this type of algorithm, the regression model is used as a surrogate model to predict the objective or fitness value of the solution, so the regression model is naturally adapted to multi-objective optimization evolutionary algorithms (MOEAs) [28]. The Kriging model [18] is widely used in SAEAs due to its small prediction error on low-dimensional problems and ability to provide error variance. In EMOPs with high-dimensional decision variables, the high dimensionality of the model inputs leads to a sharp increase in the training time and a decrease in the prediction accuracy of the Kriging model. In this case, RBF neural network [16] can be used as an alternative to the Kriging model. XGBoost [2], with its advantages of fast training speed and accurate fitting, can assist algorithms in obtaining high-quality solutions in EMOPs of low to medium dimensional decision variables. Regression-based SAEAs require high prediction accuracy from proxy models and require a large amount of data to ensure the generalization performance of the model.

Classification-based SAEAs: In classification-based SAEA, the surrogate models are classification models, where the solutions in the solution set are categorized into different classes according to different classification methods designed to represent the priority level of the solutions when they are selected. Currently there are three main classification methods: rank-based classification, relation-based classification and grid-based classification. In rank-based classification methods, each solution is usually labeled as good or poor, representing the relative priority level [27]. The idea of relation-based classification mainly relies on the dominance relation to predict the dominance relation between any pair of solutions [7]. Grid-based classification involves dividing the objective space into multiple fine grids and then replacing the specific locations of the solutions with grid coordinates and introducing grid dominance relation [25]. Classification-based SAEAs have good robustness to data and fast training speed for surrogate models, but provide limited information.

Many SAEAs can be applied to low-dimensional EMOPs, but it is more difficult to find PFs for high-dimensional EMOPs for two reasons. Firstly, the size of the search space grows exponentially as the dimension of decision variables increases linearly, so the algorithm needs to spend more function evaluations to find the PF. Secondly, high-dimensional inputs but only a small amount of training data make the model's prediction error larger, which can easily mislead the evolutionary direction of the population. We can consider using existing large-scale multi-objective optimization strategies and more robust models to solve these two problems. In recent years, researchers have proposed a series of methods for large-scale multi-objective optimization problems, which can be classified into three categories: i) cooperative coevolution [1]; ii) decision variable analysis [11]; iii) problem transformation [15]. In recent years, large-scale optimization techniques have been applied to solve high-dimensional EMOPs. TPSAEA [15] proposes an expensive multi-objective optimization method based on problem transformation, which uses Kriging to replace the function evaluation of the simplified single-objective optimization problem. AVGSEAEA [11] is an algorithm based on decision variable analysis, which proposes an adaptive variable grouping method and solves the problem that variable analysis needs to consume a large number of functions for evaluation.

However, the adaptability between large-scale optimization techniques and expensive optimization has not been fully studied at present. There are more efficient techniques that can be applied. For example, conducting random sampling in promising search directions and selecting non-dominated solutions to guide evolution [17]. This method can reduce the information loss caused by problem transformation and obtain a more comprehensive solution set. In addition, fuzzy mathematics is also applied in large-scale optimization [26], where the decision variables of the solution are fuzzified, which can blur similar solutions into the same solution and reduce the search range. If these methods are applied to high-dimensional expensive optimization, it can not only enhance the population search ability, but also reduce the number of model predictions and minimize the impact of cumulative errors. The ideas of sampling and fuzzing have not yet been applied to high-dimensional EMOPs at the same time. Therefore, this paper proposes a fuzzy directed sampling method, which first uses directed sampling to find solutions that have the ability to guide population evolution, and then fuzzifies the offspring of these solutions to reduce the number of model predictions and enhance the global search ability of the algorithm.

2 Background

2.1 The Mathematical Definition of MOPs

In terms of minimization, a multi-objective optimization problem can be described as [28]:

$$\begin{cases} minimize\ F(X) = (f_1(X), ..., f_M(X)) \\ subject\ to\ X \in \Omega \end{cases} \tag{1}$$

where $X = (x_1, ..., x_D)$ is an decision variable vector in decision space Ω, M is the number of objectives and D is the number of decision variables. Due to the trade-off between objectives, only a set of Pareto optimal solutions can be obtained. Let $X_a, X_b \in \Omega$ be two solutions of the MOP, X_a dominates X_b if and only if:

$$\begin{aligned} &\forall i \in \{1,...,M\}, f_i(X_a) \leq f_i(X_b) \\ &\exists j \in \{1,...,M\}, f_j(X_a) < f_j(X_b) \end{aligned} \tag{2}$$

A solution is called Pareto optimal solution if it is not dominated by any other solution in Ω. Pareto optimal set (PS) is the set of all Pareto optimal solutions in Ω, and its projection in the objective space is called Pareto optimal front (PF).

2.2 Fuzzy Set and Membership Function

A fuzzy set constitutes a collection of objects characterized by imprecisely defined attributes. Membership function serves as a formal mathematical representation of such sets, representing the true membership degree of objects to these sets. This function outputs values within the closed interval $[0,1]$, where 0 denotes complete non-membership and 1 indicates full inclusion. Intermediate values reflect partial membership, with higher values signifying stronger association with the set. Formally, let O be a set of objects represented by x, the fuzzy set A in X is defined by ordered pairs [26]:

$$A = \{(x, \mu_A(x) | x \in O)\} \tag{3}$$

where $\mu_A(x)$ is the membership function:

- $\mu_A(x) = 0$: x is excluded from A
- $\mu_A(x) = 1$: x is fully included in A
- $\mu_A(x) \in (0,1)$: x has partial membership in A

When applying fuzzy theory to solve optimization problems, assuming that each decision variable has two possible fuzzy sets, it is necessary to calculate the membership degree of the decision variable to the two fuzzy sets. Then the values of the decision variables can be updated to the values represented by fuzzy sets with higher membership degrees. When all decision variables of a solution have been updated, the fuzzy processing of the solution is achieved and the fuzzy solution composed of the fuzzy decision variables is obtained. At this point, the fuzzy solution replaces the original solution for subsequent operations.

3 Proposed Algorithm

The proposed FDSEMO is based on SAEA to save the overhead of real function evaluation. In order to improve the search ability of the algorithm in high-dimensional decision space, FDSEMO employs a directed guidance mechanism and fuzzy processing method in the surrogate-assisted evolution phase. Afterwards, an improved reference vector-based environmental selection strategy is used to select a sufficient number of high-quality convergent solutions from the offspring and the existing population to form a new population, while ensuring that these solutions are evenly distributed. Figure 1 shows the framework of FDSEMO. In addition, the number of iterations in the surrogate-assisted evolutionary phase is dynamically parameterized, and the number of iterations per round is dynamically adjusted according to the optimization process.

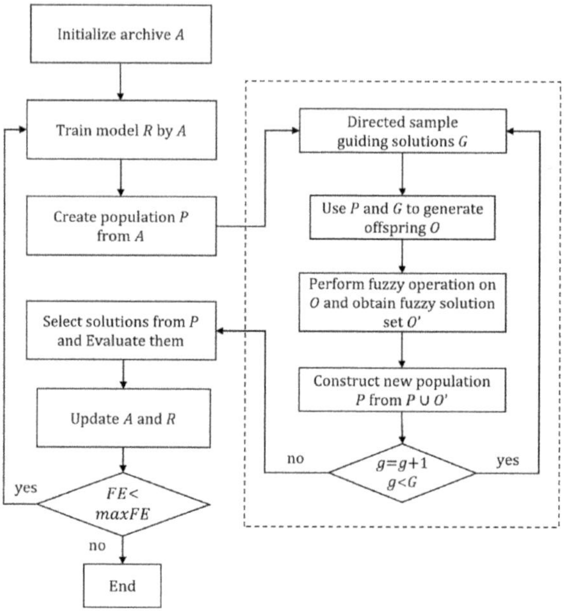

Fig. 1. Framework of FDSEMO

3.1 Adaptive Surrogate-Assisted Evolution

In the initialization phase, an equivalent number of real evaluations of the population size N are consumed to initialize N solutions for the archive A, which are then used to train the surrogate model. In the early stages of optimization, the surrogate model has limited prediction accuracy supported by the small amount of data in the archive A, so the surrogate-assisted evolution is iterated only once. When archive A contains more data in the later stages of optimization, the model learns more comprehensive data rules and is able to provide more accurate information for the evolution of the population, so the number of iterations can be increased.

Suppose that at the end of each surrogate-assisted evolution, k solutions are selected for true evaluation and added into archive A. At the end of the algorithm run, $c = (maxFE - N)/k$ surrogate-assisted evolutions can be performed, where $maxFE$ is the maximum number of function evaluations. Assuming the case that

$N = 100$, $maxFE = 500$ and $k = 5$, the total number of evolution iterations is $c = 80$ in the case of one constant round of iteration for each evolution phase. To enable faster accumulation of training data in the early stage of optimization and extend the surrogate-assisted evolution phase in the later stage, the number of iterations in each evolution phase can be dynamically adjusted according to the current number of consumed function evaluations (FE) using the following formula.

$$G = 1 + [\frac{N}{max\ (maxFE - FE, \frac{N}{\alpha})}] \tag{4}$$

where α ($\alpha >= 1$) is the parameter to control the total number of iterations. If the other parameters are kept constant as previously described, the total number of iterations is $c = 100$ when $\alpha = 1$ and $c = 122$ when $\alpha = 5$. The closer the end of the run, the more iterations in the evolution phase.

3.2 Directed Sampling

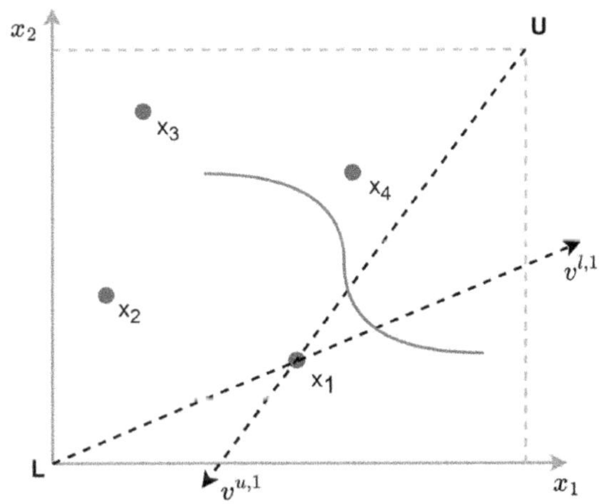

Fig. 2. Two direction generated by solution $\mathbf{x}_1$, points L and U

In order to quickly converge to the PF in high-dimensional EMOP, a directed sampling strategy [17] is used to generate guiding solutions that help accelerate the search process. First of all, efficient search directions on the decision space need to be determined so that we can sample solutions on these directions. For this purpose, solutions closest to the ideal point in the objective space will be selected first. Subsequently, sampling directions are determined by constructing lines between these solutions and the extreme boundary points L (lower bound) and U (upper bound) of the decision space. Based on the uniformly distributed

N_W reference vectors, N_W solutions close to the ideal point will be selected. Thus $2 \times N_W$ search directions can be obtained [17]:

$$v^{l,i} = S_i - L \tag{5}$$

$$v^{u,i} = S_i - U \tag{6}$$

where S_i is the solution closest to the ideal point along the i-th reference vector. $v^{l,i}$ and $v^{u,i}$ are two directions defined by S_i. Figure 2 shows the directions generated by a solution X_1.

Thereafter, random sample solutions along each direction with the sampling range is $[0, ||U - L||]$. For direction $v^{l,i}$ and $v^{u,i}$, the sampling formula are [17]:

$$X = L + r^l \frac{v^{l,i}}{||v^{l,i}||} \tag{7}$$

$$X = U + r^u \frac{v^{u,i}}{||v^{u,i}||} \tag{8}$$

where r^l and r^u are random numbers distributed in $[0, ||U - L||]$. Assuming that N_S solutions are sampled in each search direction, a total of $2 \times N_S \times N_W$ solutions are obtained. Then non-dominated sorting is applied to select guiding solutions from them, and offspring solutions are generated based on the current population and guiding solutions. Subsequent fuzzy operation is applied to the offspring solutions.

3.3 Fuzzy Operation

The fuzzy operation on the offspring solutions before the environmental selection is to reduce the cumulative error generated by the surrogate model evaluating different solutions, while narrowing down the search scope. Before introduce the fuzzy operation, the following notations are defined [26].

$$\Gamma_n^1 = \left\lfloor 10^i \cdot R_n^{-1} \cdot (X_n - X_n^l) \right\rfloor \cdot R_n \cdot 10^{-i} + X_n^l \tag{9}$$

$$\Gamma_n^2 = \left\lceil 10^i \cdot R_n^{-1} \cdot (X_n - X_n^l) \right\rceil \cdot R_n \cdot 10^{-i} + X_n^l \tag{10}$$

$$\mu_{\tilde{A}_1}(X_n) = \frac{1}{X_n - \Gamma_n^1} \tag{11}$$

$$\mu_{\tilde{A}_2}(X_n) = \frac{1}{\Gamma_n^2 - X_n} \tag{12}$$

$$\tilde{A}_1 = \left\{ \left(X_n, \mu_{\tilde{A}_1}(X_n) \mid n = 1, 2, \ldots, D\right) \right\} \tag{13}$$

$$\tilde{A}_2 = \left\{ \left(X_n, \mu_{\tilde{A}_2}(X_n) \mid n = 1, 2, \ldots, D\right) \right\} \tag{14}$$

where X represents the D-dimensional original solution vector and X' represents its fuzzified variant. X_n denotes the n-th decision variable in X, X_n^l denotes the

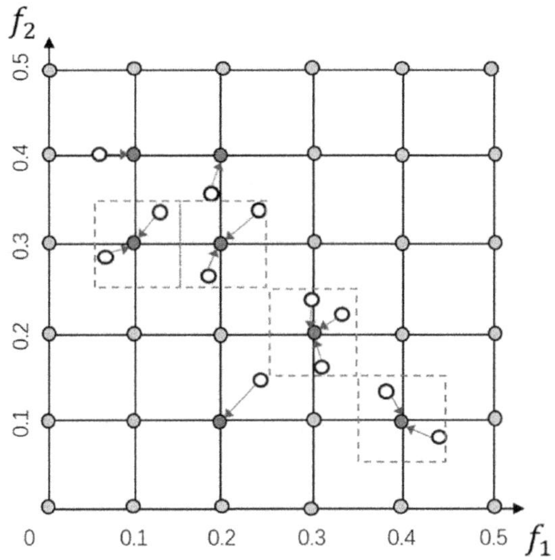

Fig. 3. Diagram of fuzzy operation

lower limit of the values of X_n, and R_n denotes the length of the value interval of X_n. X_n may be fuzzy as Γ_n^1 or Γ_n^2. These fuzzy values are characterized by the fuzzy sets $\tilde{A}_1$ and $\tilde{A}_2$, with their respective membership functions $\mu_{\tilde{A}_1}$ and $\mu_{\tilde{A}_2}$ quantifying the degree of membership for each variable value.

$$X_n' = \begin{cases} \Gamma_n^1, & \mu_{\tilde{A}_1}(X_n) > \mu_{\tilde{A}_2}(X_n) \\ \Gamma_n^2, & \mu_{\tilde{A}_1}(X_n) < \mu_{\tilde{A}_2}(X_n) \\ \text{rand}\left(\Gamma_n^1, \Gamma_n^2\right), & \mu_{\tilde{A}_1}(X_n) = \mu_{\tilde{A}_2}(X_n) \end{cases} \tag{15}$$

For solution X, first calculate the membership degree $\mu_{\tilde{A}_1}(X_n)$ and $\mu_{\tilde{A}_2}(X_n)$ of X_n to two fuzzy sets. Then decide whether X_n is fuzzified as Γ_n^1 or Γ_n^2. According to Eq. (15), the solution X is fuzzified as $X' = [0.4, 0.1]$. As shown in the Fig. 3, there are 12 example solutions (white points), which are finally blurred into 6 types of solutions (red points). Therefore, fuzzy operation can reduce the prediction burden of the model and simplify the subsequent evolutionary direction.

3.4 Environmental Selection

The reference vector-based selection method [4] uses a set of reference vectors uniformly distributed on the objective space to complete the clustering of individuals, and then selects best individual from each cluster. Since the clustering approach binds each individual to the cluster belonging to the closest reference vector to that individual, this approach does not guarantee that each reference vector cluster is not empty. This will result in not being able to stably select a sufficient number of individuals to form a new population into the next iteration.

Algorithm 1. Improved environmental selection

Input: P(Current population), W (Reference vector set)
Output: P' (New population)

$P' \leftarrow \emptyset$;
for $i = 1 : |P|$ **do**
  Compute dot product of P_i and each vector in W;
  Bind P_i to the cluster C_k associate with its the vector W_k that has minimum dot product with P_i;
end for
for $i = 1 : |W|$ **do**
  if $C_i \neq \emptyset$ **then**
    Compute the distance between each individual of C_i to the ideal point along W_i;
    Choose the individual that has the minimum distance to the ideal point and move it from P to P';
  end if
end for
for $i = 1 : |W|$ **do**
  if $C_i = \emptyset$ **then**
    Move the individual that has the minimum dot product with W_i from P to P';
  end if
end for
return P';

Therefore, in order to stably select a sufficient number of solutions while ensuring the convergence and diversity of the new population, this paper uses a quadratic binding reference vector selection method, which is inspired by the identification of search directions in [17]. The pseudo code is described in Algorithm 1. First, a round of reference vector binding will be performed on the solutions in the population, and then the solution with the smallest projection distance (i.e., the distance between the individual and the ideal point along vector) is selected from each cluster to be added to the new population. If there is a case where the cluster of reference vectors is an empty set, the closest solution from the remaining unselected solutions is bound and added to the new population.

4 Experimental Results

4.1 Experimental Settings

In this paper, the performance of the algorithms is tested using two benchmarks of multi-objective optimization problems, DTLZ [5] and LSMOP [3]. The DTLZ test set consists of DTLZ1-7, with a total of seven problems, and the LSMOP test set consists of LSMOP1-9, with a total of nine test problems. The algorithms involved in the comparison experiments include LDSAF [6], SFADE [9], PIEA [10], MCEA/D [20], AVG-SAEA [11], MOL2SMEA [19] and the proposed FDSEMO.

For fair comparison, all compared algorithms use the parameters recommended in their original papers. The population size of all algorithms is $N = 100$, the number of objectives of the DTLZ and LSMOP test sets is $M = 2$ and 3, the maximum number of function evaluations consumed by all algorithms on each problem is set to $maxFE = 500$, and all algorithms use simulated binary crossover (SBX) and polynomial mutation (PM) operators unless otherwise specified, where the crossover probability of SBX is 1 and the distribution index is 20, and the variance probability of PM is 1/D and the distribution index is 20. In the proposed FDSEMO, $N_W = 10$ and $N_S = 30$. The evaluation criterion of the output solution set adopts the Inverted Generational Distance (IGD) metric [29], which can evaluate the convergence and diversity of the solutions at the same time.

The experiment was conducted on the PlatEMO platform [21] using Matlab, version 2023b. All algorithms were run on a personal computer equipped with an Intel i5-14600KF CPU processor (3.50 GHz) and 32 GB 4800 MHz memory. Each algorithm was independently tested 20 times, and the IGD value was taken as the average of the algorithm's experimental results.

4.2 Comparison with State-of-the-Art Algorithms

Tables 1 and 2 show the average IGD values and standard deviations of the seven algorithms involved in the experiment on the DTLZ test set and LSMOP test set, respectively. At the significance level of 0.05, using the Wilcoxon rank sum test, the "+", "–", and "=" symbols in the tables indicate that the performance of the compared algorithms is superior, inferior, or close to the FDSEMO. Values with gray backgrounds in each row represent the corresponding algorithm performs best on that problem.

From Table 1, it can be seen that the proposed FDSEMO performs the best overall on DTLZ problems compared to other comparative algorithms. Among the 28 test cases of the DTLZ problems, FDSEMO performs significantly better than LDSAF, SFADE, PIEA, MCEAD, AVGSAEA, and MOL2SMEA, with test case ratios of 21/28, 19/28, 22/28, 24/28, 27/28, and 28/28, respectively. FDSEMO exhibits the best performance in all test dimensions of DTLZ1, 3, 6, and 7, with the best or near-best performance in DTLZ2, 4, and 5 at 100D (100-dimensions), and relatively poor performance only in DTLZ2, 4, and 5 at 200D.

In Table 2, the proposed FDSEMO also demonstrates superior performance in LSMOP problems. Among the 18 test cases of LSMOP, FDSEMO performed significantly better than LDSAF, SFADE, PIEA, MCEAD, AVGSAEA, and MOL2SMEA, with a proportion of 14/18, 14/18, 13/18, 14/18, 16/18, and 15/18, respectively. FDSEMO achieved the best results on both the 100D and 200D of LSMOP1, 3, 4, 5, 7, and performed the best or nearly the best on the 100D of LSMOP2, 8. FDSEMO performs worse than SFADE and LDSAF on LSMOP6. Based on the analysis of comparison results, the proposed FDSEMO demonstrates superior performance in high-dimensional expensive optimization problems compared to the six recently advanced algorithms, and can obtain solution

Table 1. Statistics of IGD results obtained by seven compared algorithms on 28 test instances from DTLZ test suite.

Problem	M	D	LDSAF	SFADE	PIEA	MCEA/D	AVGSAEA	MOL2SMEA	FDSEMO
DTLZ1	2	100	9.7283e+2 (3.04e+2) −	1.0849e+3 (1.33e+2) −	1.1585e+3 (1.36e+2) −	1.3255e+3 (2.63e+2) −	2.6040e+3 (1.65e+2) −	3.0013e+3 (1.53e+2) −	4.4953e+2 (7.14e+1)
		200	1.7396e+3 (3.83e+2) −	2.0317e+3 (3.03e+2) −	2.3331e+3 (3.03e+2) −	2.5812e+3 (5.94e+2) −	5.7792e+3 (1.74e+2) −	6.5976e+3 (2.08e+2) −	7.5603e+2 (9.14e+1)
	3	100	7.6460e+2 (2.56e+2) −	1.0653e+3 (1.34e+2) −	9.6017e+2 (1.76e+2) −	1.0630e+3 (2.98e+2) −	2.3179e+3 (1.56e+2) −	2.5195e+3 (1.21e+2) −	3.6112e+2 (7.16e+1)
		200	1.4013e+3 (4.47e+2) −	2.2044e+3 (2.08e+2) −	1.9117e+3 (3.39e+2) −	2.2850e+3 (7.41e+2) −	5.4681e+3 (2.16e+2) −	5.4522e+3 (2.06e+2) −	6.0476e+2 (8.98e+1)
DTLZ2	2	100	4.5625e-1 (3.35e-2) −	2.3405e-1 (4.47e-2) −	8.5929e-1 (1.96e-1) −	8.3549e-1 (2.06e-1) −	5.9278e-1 (3.58e-1) −	8.3424e-1 (1.01e-1) −	1.1472e-1 (5.81e-2)
		200	9.0470e-1 (2.66e-1) +	4.7468e-1 (6.89e-2) +	1.3746e+0 (2.46e-1) ≈	1.5516e+0 (3.79e-1) ≈	1.1039e+1 (1.19e+0) −	5.7651e+0 (3.16e-1) −	1.3841e+0 (3.11e-1)
	3	100	6.1988e-1 (9.12e-2) −	4.1075e-1 (7.85e-2) ≈	9.5075e-1 (1.01e-1) −	8.3801e-1 (1.02e-1) −	6.7055e-1 (1.48e-1) −	1.4373e+0 (1.76e-1) −	4.6259e-1 (1.53e-1)
		200	9.9989e-1 (2.00e-1) +	8.3118e-1 (1.68e-1) +	1.7869e+0 (2.74e-1) +	1.4213e+0 (2.45e-1) +	1.2133e+1 (1.06e+0) −	3.7981e+0 (3.91e-1) −	2.9283e+0 (6.53e-1)
DTLZ3	2	100	2.1460e+3 (4.04e+2) −	2.4531e+3 (1.99e+1) −	2.4713e+3 (2.56e+1) −	2.3900e+3 (6.28e+2) −	7.1284e+3 (4.91e+2) −	7.9251e+3 (4.08e+2) −	1.1193e+3 (1.05e+2)
		200	4.4611e+3 (1.51e+3) −	4.9686e+3 (2.11e+1) −	4.9749e+3 (6.44e+1) −	5.4435e+3 (1.53e+3) −	1.6385e+4 (7.06e+2) −	1.7502e+4 (7.44e+2) −	1.9550e+3 (1.25e+2)
	3	100	1.8812e+3 (4.71e+2) −	2.4599e+3 (9.31e+1) −	2.4326e+3 (1.99e+1) −	2.6638e+3 (4.39e+2) −	7.2897e+3 (5.16e+2) −	7.7984e+3 (3.83e+2) −	1.0192e+3 (1.32e+2)
		200	3.6961e+3 (1.00e+3) −	4.9152e+3 (7.44e+1) −	4.9440e+3 (2.42e+1) −	5.1863e+3 (1.49e+3) −	1.7838e+4 (4.97e+2) −	1.7567e+4 (8.08e+2) −	1.7948e+3 (1.69e+2)
DTLZ4	2	100	7.8987e-1 (2.76e-2) −	7.5217e-1 (1.95e-3) −	1.0070e+0 (5.03e-2) −	1.0879e+0 (2.18e-1) −	8.4025e-1 (3.72e-2) −	1.4300e+0 (1.65e-1) −	2.2458e-1 (1.93e-1)
		200	9.7008e-1 (1.50e-1) ≈	7.9071e-1 (8.13e-3) ≈	1.3755e+0 (1.02e-1) ≈	1.6872e+0 (3.10e-1) −	1.0603e+1 (1.29e+0) −	6.3286e+0 (6.09e-1) −	1.0258e+0 (6.25e-1)
	3	100	1.0703e+0 (5.34e-2) ≈	9.5404e-1 (2.29e-3) ≈	1.1640e+0 (5.24e-2) −	1.2027e+0 (6.47e-2) −	9.7959e-1 (5.31e-2) ≈	1.6152e+0 (1.39e-1) −	1.0514e+0 (2.91e-1)
		200	1.2483e+0 (1.31e-1) +	1.0271e+0 (1.24e-2) +	1.5838e+0 (1.88e-1) +	1.5756e+0 (1.69e-1) +	1.1127e+1 (1.11e+0) −	3.8285e+0 (3.62e-1) −	2.6246e+0 (7.10e-1)
DTLZ5	2	100	4.8800e-1 (7.11e-2) −	2.2517e-1 (2.76e-2) −	8.4182e-1 (1.78e-1) −	9.4121e-1 (1.85e-1) −	4.7329e-1 (8.55e-2) −	9.0729e-1 (1.43e-1) −	9.2408e-2 (4.14e-2)
		200	7.6071e-1 (1.01e-1) +	4.7284e-1 (5.16e-2) +	1.3930e+0 (2.14e-1) ≈	1.5400e+0 (2.35e-1) −	1.1759e+1 (8.04e-1) −	5.5969e+0 (3.76e-1) −	1.1667e+0 (3.42e-1)
	3	100	4.8683e-1 (1.24e-1) −	2.9202e-1 (5.20e-2) ≈	7.9735e-1 (1.57e-1) −	6.9753e-1 (1.09e-1) −	7.1026e-1 (3.91e-1) −	1.3100e+0 (1.75e-1) −	2.9832e-1 (1.05e-1)
		200	9.0293e-1 (3.57e-1) +	6.6044e-1 (1.47e-1) +	1.6895e+0 (3.42e-1) +	1.3777e+0 (2.72e-1) +	1.2094e+1 (1.01e+0) −	3.7237e+0 (3.64e-1) −	2.6421e+0 (5.44e-1)
DTLZ6	2	100	4.3410e+1 (4.37e+0) −	4.2440e+1 (4.38e+0) −	4.0317e+1 (6.81e+0) −	4.8975e+1 (3.06e+0) −	7.5582e+1 (3.55e+0) −	8.5108e+1 (7.15e-1) −	8.3075e-1 (1.11e+0)
		200	9.3816e+1 (6.21e+0) −	9.0930e+1 (6.20e+0) −	8.7876e+1 (6.83e+0) −	1.0769e+2 (7.23e+0) −	1.6332e+2 (2.18e+0) −	1.7373e+2 (2.25e+0) −	4.4702e+0 (3.68e+0)
	3	100	4.2151e+1 (3.39e+0) −	4.2751e+1 (4.74e+0) −	3.8926e+1 (3.48e+0) −	4.8284e+1 (2.55e+0) −	8.0444e+1 (4.72e+0) −	8.4564e+1 (1.45e+0) −	3.2647e+0 (3.97e+0)
		200	8.8898e+1 (6.16e+0) −	9.2328e+1 (8.89e+0) −	8.9600e+1 (6.22e+0) −	1.0062e+2 (5.97e+0) −	1.6860e+2 (3.23e+0) −	1.7460e+2 (1.29e+0) −	1.3761e+1 (9.47e+0)
DTLZ7	2	100	5.8093e+0 (5.11e-1) −	4.4330e+0 (4.65e-1) −	5.6619e+0 (5.51e-1) −	6.7080e+0 (4.07e-1) −	5.4006e+0 (7.64e-1) −	6.6568e+0 (1.96e-1) −	1.6505e-2 (1.42e-2)
		200	6.8416e+0 (3.08e-1) −	6.0464e+0 (4.83e-1) −	6.7392e+0 (4.31e-1) −	7.1365e+0 (2.26e-1) −	6.1151e+0 (4.02e-1) −	7.0476e+0 (2.02e-1) −	9.9347e-2 (3.73e-2)
	3	100	8.9259e+0 (4.52e-1) −	4.9219e+0 (7.52e-1) −	9.5399e+0 (6.81e-1) −	1.0165e+1 (4.59e-1) −	8.0008e+0 (8.44e-1) −	1.0368e+1 (3.50e-1) −	1.2383e-1 (3.96e-2)
		200	1.0037e+1 (5.51e-1) −	7.9271e+0 (7.37e-1) −	1.0318e+1 (1.10e+0) −	1.0543e+1 (4.27e-1) −	9.2092e+0 (4.77e-1) −	1.0719e+1 (2.44e-1) −	2.4485e-1 (4.42e-2)
+/−/≈			5/21/2	5/19/4	3/22/3	3/24/1	0/27/1	0/28/0	

Table 2. Statistics of IGD results obtained by seven compared algorithms on 18 test instances from LSMOP test suite.

Problem	M	D	LDSAF	SFADE	PIEA	MCEA/D	AVGSAEA	MOL2SMEA	FDSEMO
LSMOP1	3	100	1.9242e+0 (3.15e-1) −	1.6634e+0 (3.98e-1) −	2.3979e+0 (3.58e-1) −	2.1872e+0 (4.52e-1) −	2.0802e+0 (8.23e-1) −	2.6252e+0 (3.21e-1) −	1.3180e+0 (3.49e-1)
		200	2.1276e+0 (2.69e-1) −	2.1066e+0 (2.63e-1) −	2.7429e+0 (2.33e-1) −	2.4226e+0 (2.79e-1) −	9.2018e+0 (6.36e-1) −	3.8218e+0 (4.77e-1) −	1.7390e+0 (6.58e-1)
LSMOP2	3	100	2.0046e-1 (6.48e-3) −	2.0008e-1 (3.90e-3) −	1.7764e-1 (2.39e-3) −	1.9099e-1 (5.67e-3) −	2.0711e-1 (1.80e-3) −	1.7462e-1 (2.36e-3) −	1.5841e-1 (6.53e-3)
		200	1.1701e-1 (2.21e-3) −	1.1579e-1 (1.73e-3) −	1.0574e-1 (1.49e-3) +	1.1395e-1 (2.45e-3) ≈	1.1999e-1 (4.19e-4) −	1.1317e-1 (9.13e-4) ≈	1.1298e-1 (3.39e-3)
LSMOP3	3	100	1.3001e+1 (1.27e+0) −	1.7437e+1 (9.14e+0) −	4.0978e+1 (7.35e+1) −	1.4458e+1 (3.39e+0) −	1.2222e+1 (2.81e+0) −	3.4687e+1 (2.47e+1) −	4.3625e+0 (2.72e+0)
		200	1.3518e+1 (1.92e+0) −	1.8621e+1 (5.06e+0) −	2.2776e+1 (1.39e+1) −	1.7225e+1 (4.67e+0) −	2.9736e+1 (1.46e+1) −	3.4418e+1 (2.86e+1) −	9.6911e+0 (4.23e+0)
LSMOP4	3	100	5.3698e-1 (1.39e-2) −	5.3949e-1 (7.31e-3) −	5.0677e-1 (7.96e-3) −	5.2531e-1 (1.28e-2) −	5.5507e-1 (7.75e-3) −	4.9535e-1 (1.11e-2) −	4.4084e-1 (1.86e-2)
		200	3.5724e-1 (1.24e-2) −	3.4621e-1 (9.17e-3) −	3.2605e-1 (5.33e-3) −	3.4225e-1 (8.59e-3) −	3.7831e-1 (1.65e-3) −	3.5233e-1 (3.45e-3) −	3.1284e-1 (8.57e-3)
LSMOP5	3	100	3.7309e+0 (4.36e-1) −	3.5428e+0 (8.14e-1) −	5.3399e+0 (1.68e+0) −	4.5220e+0 (8.43e-1) −	4.6590e+0 (1.09e+0) −	5.1546e+0 (7.95e-1) −	2.0468e+0 (7.63e-1)
		200	4.3243e+0 (5.30e-1) −	4.2449e+0 (5.39e-1) −	6.3127e+0 (1.18e+0) −	5.1727e+0 (8.01e-1) −	1.4489e+1 (1.54e+0) −	7.5580e+0 (1.02e+0) −	3.4331e+0 (1.32e+0)
LSMOP6	3	100	1.1559e+3 (7.06e+2) ≈	3.2650e+2 (1.68e+2) +	1.0091e+3 (4.59e+2) ≈	1.3388e+3 (5.92e+2) −	1.3339e+3 (6.41e+2) −	3.2673e+3 (1.76e+3) −	7.7963e+2 (4.44e+2)
		200	1.9145e+3 (5.78e+2) +	1.2891e+3 (7.03e+2) +	2.6044e+3 (9.39e+2) ≈	2.7880e+3 (8.01e+2) ≈	1.8348e+4 (4.08e+3) −	1.0357e+4 (3.27e+3) −	2.8369e+3 (1.35e+3)
LSMOP7	3	100	2.7798e+0 (1.22e-1) −	2.5762e+0 (3.14e-1) −	3.7637e+1 (1.54e+2) −	2.9372e+0 (1.72e-1) −	1.3643e+1 (4.73e+1) −	4.9517e+2 (4.02e+2) −	2.3154e+0 (3.40e-1)
		200	1.7992e+0 (3.76e-2) −	1.7343e+0 (8.40e-2) −	1.1332e+1 (4.19e+1) −	1.8273e+0 (4.06e-2) −	6.1159e+1 (1.82e+2) −	1.4658e+2 (1.56e+2) −	1.5528e+0 (1.16e-1)
LSMOP8	3	100	9.6978e-1 (7.72e-2) ≈	8.5849e-1 (6.67e-2) ≈	9.5518e-1 (1.09e-1) ≈	8.8367e-1 (7.02e-2) ≈	9.6314e-1 (8.09e-2) ≈	8.3918e-1 (6.26e-2) ≈	8.9857e-1 (1.40e-1)
		200	6.7872e-1 (3.83e-2) +	7.4327e-1 (7.21e-2) +	8.5898e-1 (1.07e-1) ≈	7.2496e-1 (6.05e-2) +	8.5547e-1 (1.15e-1) ≈	7.0511e-1 (4.12e-2) +	9.1007e-1 (1.11e-1)
LSMOP9	3	100	1.6612e+1 (2.35e+0) −	8.1147e+0 (1.53e+0) −	5.2795e+1 (1.22e+1) −	2.4552e+1 (3.81e+0) −	2.9696e+1 (1.12e+1) −	3.7669e+1 (8.07e+0) −	1.3248e+0 (5.44e-1)
		200	2.4174e+1 (3.49e+0) −	1.4287e+1 (2.58e+0) −	7.2694e+1 (9.15e+0) −	2.9729e+1 (4.07e+0) −	9.7943e+1 (1.34e+1) −	5.3756e+1 (6.28e+0) −	2.0903e+0 (5.76e-1)
+/−/≈			2/14/2	3/14/1	1/13/4	1/14/3	0/16/2	1/15/2	

set with good convergence and diversity. But in concave problems, the effectiveness of FDSEMO still needs to be improved.

4.3 Ablation Experiment

In order to further demonstrate the effectiveness of fuzzy directed sampling, this paper also designed fuzzy-only variant called FEMO and directed sampling-only variant DSEMO. Table 3 shows the average IGD values and standard deviations obtained from 20 independent experiments of FEMO, DSEMO and FDSEMO on three-objectives and 100-dimensions DTLZ and LSMOP test sets. From Table 3, it can be seen that FDSEMO obtains better IGD values for 10 of 16 test instances, indicating that fuzzy directed sampling provides a more comprehensive search capability. Using the fuzzy processing mechanism significantly improves the ability of directed sampling to explore the solution space.

Table 3. Statistics of IGD results obtained by FEMO, DSEMO and FDSEMO.

Problem	FEMO	DSEMO	FDSEMO
DTLZ1	2.1329e+2 (1.65e+1) +	8.1455e+2 (8.82e+1) −	3.6112e+2 (7.16e+1)
DTLZ2	4.9889e+0 (3.12e-1) −	6.8033e-1 (8.40e-2) −	4.6259e-1 (1.53e-1)
DTLZ3	6.7717e+2 (3.84e+1) +	2.4576e+3 (1.02e+2) −	1.0192e+3 (1.32e+2)
DTLZ4	4.8463e+0 (3.29e-1) −	1.4057e+0 (2.60e-1) −	1.0514e+0 (2.91e-1)
DTLZ5	4.9348e+0 (4.57e-1) −	5.7644e-1 (1.60e-1) −	2.9832e-1 (1.05e-1)
DTLZ6	7.7182e+1 (1.39e+0) −	9.5544e+0 (4.40e+0) −	3.2647e+0 (3.97e+0)
DTLZ7	4.3225e+0 (5.61e-1) −	1.4115e-1 (5.03e-2) ≈	1.2383e-1 (3.96e-2)
LSMOP1	6.5796e+0 (9.48e-1) −	1.4394e+0 (6.93e-1) ≈	1.3180e+0 (3.49e-1)
LSMOP2	2.0980e-1 (1.58e-3) −	1.6045e-1 (9.80e-3) ≈	1.5841e-1 (6.53e-3)
LSMOP3	1.4886e+1 (1.14e+0) −	2.7073e+0 (2.45e+0) +	4.3625e+0 (2.72e+0)
LSMOP4	5.4973e-1 (6.43e-3) −	4.4648e-1 (2.02e-2) ≈	4.4084e-1 (1.86e-2)
LSMOP5	7.1401e+0 (1.22e+0) −	1.9019e+0 (5.57e-1) ≈	2.0468e+0 (7.63e-1)
LSMOP6	5.2560e+3 (2.38e+3) −	8.4248e+2 (3.71e+2) ≈	7.7963e+2 (4.44e+2)
LSMOP7	2.7196e+0 (1.42e-1) −	2.1286e+0 (3.03e-1) ≈	2.3154e+0 (3.40e-1)
LSMOP8	1.0206e+0 (2.48e-2) −	8.4804e-1 (1.59e-1) ≈	8.9857e-1 (1.40e-1)
LSMOP9	5.4873e+1 (8.19e+0) −	1.6086e+0 (5.51e-1) −	1.3248e+0 (5.44e-1)
+ / − / ≈	2/14/0	1/7/8	

5 Conclusion

The FDSEMO proposed in this article is a surrogate model assisted evolutionary algorithm used to solve expensive multi-objective optimization problems with high-dimensional decision variables. In the surrogate-assisted evolution process, the guiding solutions are first sampled from the promising search direction and the offspring solutions of guiding solutions are generated. Then the fuzzy operation is performed on the offspring solutions to obtain fewer but more representative solutions. Finally, an improved reference vector-based selection method is adopted to select competitive individuals for the next generation. The directed sampling strategy can accelerate the convergence of the population, while fuzzy operation are beneficial for reducing the cumulative prediction error of the model and enhancing the global search capability.

The effectiveness of FDSEMO in solving high-dimensional expensive multi-objective optimization problems has been verified through comprehensive experiments and comparisons with six state-of-the-art algorithms. However, there are still some shortcomings in FDSEMO, such as the algorithm's poor performance in solving concave problems, and some parameters in FDSEMO are still directly specified. In future research, the adaptive ability of FDSEMO will be improved to enable it to solve more types of problem and real-world problems.

Acknowledgments. This work was partially supported by the National Natural Science Foundation of China (Grant Nos. 62573201, U23A20303 and 62573326), and Zhejiang Provincial Natural Science Foundation of China (Grant No. LZ25F030007).

References

1. Antonio, L.M., Coello, C.A.C.: Use of cooperative coevolution for solving large scale multiobjective optimization problems. In: 2013 IEEE Congress on Evolutionary Computation, pp. 2758–2765 (2013)
2. Chen, T., Guestrin, C.: Xgboost: a scalable tree boosting system. In: Proceedings of 22nd ACM SIGKDD International Conference on Knowledge Discovery and Data Mining, pp. 785–794 (2016)
3. Cheng, R., Jin, Y., Olhofer, M., sendhoff, B.: Test problems for large-scale multiobjective and many-objective optimization. IEEE Trans. Cybern. **47**(12), 4108–4121 (2017)
4. Chugh, T., Jin, Y., Miettinen, K., Hakanen, J., Sindhya, K.: A surrogate-assisted reference vector guided evolutionary algorithm for computationally expensive many-objective optimization. IEEE Trans. Evol. Comput. **22**(1), 129–142 (2018)
5. Deb, K., Thiele, L., Laumanns, M., Zitzler, E.: Scalable test problems for evolutionary multiobjective optimization. In: Evolutionary Multiobjective Optimization: Theoretical Advances and Applications, pp. 105–145. Springer, Heidelberg (2005). https://doi.org/10.1007/1-84628-137-7_6
6. Gu, H., Wang, H., He, C., Yuan, B., Jin, Y.: Large-scale multiobjective evolutionary algorithm guided by low-dimensional surrogates of scalarization functions. Evol. Comput. 1–26 (10 2024)
7. Hao, H., Zhou, A., Qian, H., Zhang, H.: Expensive multiobjective optimization by relation learning and prediction. IEEE Trans. Evol. Comput. **26**(5), 1157–1170 (2022)
8. He, C., Cheng, R., Zhang, C., Tian, Y., Chen, Q., Yao, X.: Evolutionary large-scale multiobjective optimization for ratio error estimation of voltage transformers. IEEE Trans. Evol. Comput. **24**(5), 868–881 (2020)
9. Horaguchi, Y., Nishihara, K., Nakata, M.: Evolutionary multiobjective optimization assisted by scalarization function approximation for high-dimensional expensive problems. Swarm Evol. Comput. **86**, 101516 (2024)
10. Li, Y., Li, W., Li, S., Zhao, Y.: A performance indicator-based evolutionary algorithm for expensive high-dimensional multi-/many-objective optimization. Inf. Sci. **678**, 121045 (2024)
11. Li, Y., Feng, X., Yu, H.: Solving high-dimensional expensive multiobjective optimization problems by adaptive decision variable grouping. IEEE Trans. Evol. Comput. 1–1 (2024)
12. Liu, J., Sarker, R., Elsayed, S., Essam, D., Siswanto, N.: Large-scale evolutionary optimization: a review and comparative study. Swarm Evol. Comput. **85**, 101466 (2024)

13. Lu, Z., Cheng, R., Jin, Y., Tan, K.C., Deb, K.: Neural architecture search as multiobjective optimization benchmarks: problem formulation and performance assessment. IEEE Trans. Evol. Comput. **28**(2), 323–337 (2024)
14. Mao, F., Chen, M., Zhong, K., Zeng, J., Liang, Z.: An xgboost-assisted evolutionary algorithm for expensive multiobjective optimization problems. Inf. Sci. **666**, 120449 (2024)
15. Pan, L., Lin, J., Wang, H., He, C., Tan, K.C., Jin, Y.: Computationally expensive high-dimensional multiobjective optimization via surrogate-assisted reformulation and decomposition. IEEE Trans. Evol. Comput. (2024)
16. Park, J., Sandberg, I.W.: Universal approximation using radial-basis-function networks. Neural Comput. **3**(2), 246–257 (1991)
17. Qin, S., Sun, C., Jin, Y., Tan, Y., Fieldsend, J.: Large-scale evolutionary multiobjective optimization assisted by directed sampling. IEEE Trans. Evol. Comput. **25**(4), 724–738 (2021)
18. Rasmussen, C.E.: Gaussian processes in machine learning. In: Summer School on Machine Learning, pp. 63–71. Springer, Heidelberg (2003)
19. Si, L., Zhang, X., Tian, Y., Yang, S., Zhang, L., Jin, Y.: Linear subspace surrogate modeling for large-scale expensive single/multiobjective optimization. IEEE Trans. Evol. Comput. **29**(3), 697–710 (2025)
20. Sonoda, T., Nakata, M.: Multiple classifiers-assisted evolutionary algorithm based on decomposition for high-dimensional multiobjective problems. IEEE Trans. Evol. Comput. **26**(6), 1581–1595 (2022)
21. Tian, Y., Cheng, R., Zhang, X., Jin, Y.: Platemo: a matlab platform for evolutionary multi-objective optimization [educational forum]. IEEE Comput. Intell. Mag. **12**(4), 73–87 (2017)
22. Tian, Y., et al.: Evolutionary large-scale multi-objective optimization: a survey. ACM Comput. Surv. **54**(8) (2021)
23. Tian, Y., Yang, S., Zhang, L., Duan, F., Zhang, X.: A surrogate-assisted multiobjective evolutionary algorithm for large-scale task-oriented pattern mining. IEEE Trans. Emerg. Topics Comput. Intell. **3**(2), 106–116 (2019)
24. Wang, Y., Lin, J., Liu, J., Sun, G., Pang, T.: Surrogate-assisted differential evolution with region division for expensive optimization problems with discontinuous responses. IEEE Trans. Evol. Comput. **26**(4), 780–792 (2022)
25. Yang, Q.T., Zhan, Z.H., Liu, X.F., Li, J.Y., Zhang, J.: Grid classification-based surrogate-assisted particle swarm optimization for expensive multiobjective optimization. IEEE Trans. Evol. Comput. **28**(6), 1867–1881 (2024)
26. Yang, X., Zou, J., Yang, S., Zheng, J., Liu, Y.: A fuzzy decision variables framework for large-scale multiobjective optimization. IEEE Trans. Evol. Comput. **27**(3), 445–459 (2023)
27. Zhang, J., Zhou, A., Zhang, G.: A classification and pareto domination based multiobjective evolutionary algorithm. In: 2015 IEEE Congress on Evolution Computation, pp. 2883–2890. IEEE (2015)
28. Zhang, Q., Li, H.: MOEA/D: a multiobjective evolutionary algorithm based on decomposition. IEEE Trans. Evol. Comput. **11**(6), 712–731 (2007)
29. Zitzler, E., Thiele, L., Laumanns, M., Fonseca, C.M., Da Fonseca, V.G.: Performance assessment of multiobjective optimizers: an analysis and review. IEEE Trans. Evol. Comput. **7**(2), 117–132 (2003)

An Improved Large-Scale Multi-objective Competitive Swarm Optimizer Based on Harris Hawks Optimization

Jixiang Zeng, Min-Rong Chen(✉), Zihua Guo, Zeyan Zhang, and Songxiang Zhong

School of Computer Science, South China Normal University, Guangzhou 510631, China
{2023023216,2023023247,2023023267,2023023300}@m.scnu.edu.cn, mrongchen@126.com

Abstract. Large-scale multi-objective optimization problems (LSMOPs), characterized by their high-dimensional decision spaces, pose a formidable challenge to solving multi-objective optimization. This paper proposes LMOHHO, an enhanced Harris Hawks optimizer specifically adapted for LSMOPs. The core of LMOHHO integrates the distinct strengths of competitive swarm optimization (CSO) and Harris Hawks optimization (HHO). The algorithm employs CSO for the global search to maintain a diverse population and uses HHO to accelerate convergence. An adaptive switching strategy dynamically manages the balance between these exploration and exploitation phases. The efficacy of LMOHHO is validated by its strong performance in experiments conducted on standard test problems.

Keywords: Competitive Swarm Optimization · Large-Scale Multi-Objective Optimization · Harris Hawks Optimization

1 Introduction

In real life, the optimization tasks often involve optimizing multiple conflicting objectives simultaneously, termed multi-objective optimization problems (MOPs). When the dimensionality of the decision variables increases to more than hundreds, these MOPs evolve into LSMOPs. [1–4]. These include optimization of engineering design (seeking optimal performance), business decision making (maximizing profit margins), and optimization of the manufacturing process (achieving maximum production efficiency) [5]. Due to the conflict between objectives, the primary goal in solving such problems locate a set of trade-off solutions in the decision space, referred to as the Pareto optimal set (PS), and the objective space corresponding to these solutions is called the Pareto optimal front (PF). It has proposed a significant challenge for MOEAs in dealing with LSMOPs.

T. Hao et al. (Eds.): BESC 2025, LNCS 16431, pp. 30–42, 2026.
https://doi.org/10.1007/978-981-95-7138-3_3

To address the challenges posed by LSMOPs, many MOEAs are proposed and used to solve LSMOPs [6,7]. The MOEAs can be divided into four categories according to their technical characteristics. The first two categories focus on the decision variables themselves, either by partitioning them into smaller groups or by analyzing their contributions to the objective functions [8,9]. The third category of approaches involves problem transformation, using a transformation function to convert the original LSMOP into a lower-dimensional MOP. The fourth category of MOEAs for LSMOPs leverages learning-based strategies, which introduce efficient learning operators to accelerate the search process.

CSO [10] is an algorithm that focuses on large-scale continuous single-objective problems (SOPs). Inspired by CSO, Tian et al. proposed LMOCSO for LSMOPs. This algorithm employs a two-stage particle update strategy. First, a particle is preliminarily updated using its previous velocity. Then, this position is further refined by learning from a designated winner particle, which enhances the effectiveness of the algorithm for complex LSMOPs.

HHO [11] is proposed by Heidari, emulates the cooperative hunting behavior of hawks to effectively balance global exploration and local exploitation. Although HHO has shown significant effectiveness on SOPs [12], its potential for application to LSMOPs has not yet been explored. This paper develops and presents a novel algorithm to tackle the challenges of LSMOPs and thereby fill a notable research gap.

The remainder of this paper is organized as follows: the background of proposing LMOHHO is presented in Sect. 2. The framework of LMOHHO and the experiment results are presented in Sects. 3 and 4, respectively. Finally, Sect. 5 summarizes the paper and outlines future work.

2 Background

2.1 The Mathematical Definition of MOPs

The definition of MOP is as follows [13]:

$$\begin{aligned} \text{minimize} \quad & F = (f_1(x), f_2(x), ..., f_m(x)) \\ \text{subject to} \quad & x \in \Omega^D \end{aligned} \tag{1}$$

where D is the dimension within the feasible decision space Ω, $x = (x_1, x_2, ..., x_D)$ denotes decision vector. m is the number of conflicting objectives. Due to the conflict between the objective functions, it can only find a set of non-dominated solutions representing the best possible trade-offs. Let $(X_a, X_b) \in \Omega$ are two different solution for MOPs that describe as formula 1, define X_a as dominating X_b(denoted $(X_a \prec X_b)$) if two conditions hold: (a) X_a is not worse than X_b $(\forall i, f_i(X_a) \leq f_i(X_b))$, (b) X_a strictly outperforms X_b in at least one objective $(\exists j, f_j(X_a) < f_j(X_b))$. If no $X \in \Omega$ satisfies $X \prec X_a$, X_a is called a non-dominated solution.

2.2 CSO

In the particle swarm optimization (PSO) [14], each particle P_i characterized by a position x_i and velocity v_i, which are updated via the following formulas:

$$v_i^{(t+1)} = wv_i^{(t)} + c_1 r_1 (p_{best}^{(t)} - x_i^{(t)}) + c_2 r_2 (g_{best}^{(t)} - x_i^{(t)}) \tag{2}$$

$$x_i^{(t+1)} = x_i^{(t)} + v_i^{(t+1)} \tag{3}$$

where the inertia weight (w) is used to balance search behaviors between the global and local search, $r1$,$r2 \in$ [0,1]. The acceleration coefficients $c1$ and $c2$ scale the pull toward p_{best} (personal best position) and g_{best} (global best position). Iteration counter is denoted as t.

PSO relies on the information from p_{best} and g_{best} to search the decision space, which makes the population easily get into in a local optimum or converge early. To address these problems, CSO does not rely on p_{best} and g_{best} anymore. Particles in the population are paired for competition, with winners and losers determined. The losers update their positions by learning from both the positions of the winner and the average position of the population, while the winners undergo mutation-based updates. The loser updates by learning from the winner, and the formula is as follows:

$$v_l^{(t+1)} = r_1 v_i^{(t)} + r_2 (x_w^{(t)} - x_l^{(t)}) + \phi r_3 (\bar{x}^{(t)} - x_l^{(t)}) \tag{4}$$

where $x_w^{(t)}$ and $x_l^{(t)}$ represents winner and loser particles, respectively, and $\bar{x}^{(t)}$ means the mean position of the winner. $v_l^{(t)}$ represents the velocity of loser particles. r_1, r_2,r_3 $\in$[0,1]. ϕ is used to control the influence of $\bar{x}^{(t)}$.

To better adapt this mechanism for LSMOPs, LMOCSO has improved the update strategies, and the updated formulas are [15]:

$$v_l^{(t+1)} = r_1 v_l^{(t)} + r_2 (x_w^{(t)} - x_l^{(t)}) \tag{5}$$

$$x_l^{(t+1)} = x_l^{(t)} + v_l^{(t+1)} + r_1 (v_l^{(t+1)} - v_l^{(t)}) \tag{6}$$

This method uses the velocity ($v_l^{(t)}$) of the loser particles before the update, and learn from the winner to get information to enhance the efficiency of the updated process.

2.3 HHO

HHO is proposed by observing the cooperative hawks hunting behavior in nature [16]. The strategies of the HHO is primarily governed by the escaping energy (E) of the prey that controls the algorithm transition from global exploration to local exploitation phases. And energy (E) decreases throughout iterations according to the formula 7:

$$E = 2E_0(1 - t/T) \tag{7}$$

where E_0 is a random energy value at the beginning of the iteration, the total number of iterations is denoted as T.

At the beginning of HHO, the prey has high energy, denoted $E \geq 1$, and the hawks perform a global search to locate the prey that has high energy. They explore different areas using one of two strategies, selected based on a random number $q \in [0, 1]$. The position of hawks (x_h) can be calculated by the following:

$$x_h^{(t+1)} = \begin{cases} (x_{\mathrm{p}}^{(t)} - x_{\mathrm{avg}}^{(t)}) - r_1(L + r_2(U - L)) \text{ if } q < 0.5 \\ x_{\mathrm{r}}^{(t)} - r_3|x_{\mathrm{r}}^{(t)} - 2r_4 x_h^{(t)}| \text{ if } q \geq 0.5 \end{cases} \tag{8}$$

where $x_p^{(t)}$ and x_{avg}^t are the position of prey and average position of the hawks, respectively, and x_r^t represents a randomly selected hawk. $r_{1-4} \in [0, 1]$. The upper and lower bounds of Ω are denoted as U and L.

When the prey energy level diminishes ($E \leq 1$), the algorithm enters the exploitation phase. The r is a parameter that denotes the escape probability of the prey; successful escapes occur when $r < 0.5$, while $r \geq 0.5$ indicates failed escape attempts. Under conditions $r \geq 0.5$ and $|E| \geq 0.5$ are both met, the hawk population makes precise positional adjustments to locate the prey, as mathematically described in formulas 9 and 10:

$$x_h^{(t+1)} = x_p^(t) - x_h^{(t)} - E|J \cdot x_p^{(t)} - x_h^{(t)}| \tag{9}$$

$$J = 2(1 - rand) \tag{10}$$

where J represents the random jump distance of prey, $rand \in$ [0,1]. When the conditions $r \geq 0.5$ and $|E| < 0.5$ are simultaneously satisfied, the hawk flock closely surrounds the prey by formula 11:

$$x_h^{(t+1)} = x_p^{(t)} - E|x_p^{(t)} - x_h^{(t)}| \tag{11}$$

Overall, the HHO has a unique search mechanism and a powerful global optimization capability [17], and has achieved significant optimization performance in single-objective optimization.

3 Proposed LMOHHO

In this section, to apply the HHO to solve LSMOPs, we proposed an enhanced large-scale multi-objective Harris Hawks optimizer (LMOHHO) that combines with CSO to solve LSMOPs. In the remainder of this section, we present the procedure of LMOHHO.

3.1 The Framework of LMOHHO

As shown in Algorithm 1, the pseudo-code details the process of LMOHHO. Before the start of each population iteration, we calculate the fitness value of each particle in the population. The formula is as follows [18]:

Algorithm 1. Procedure of LMOHHO

1: **Input:** N(population size), T (maximum iterations), E (escape energy of the prey)
2: **Output:** P (final population)
3: $P \leftarrow$Initialization(N) ;
4: $R \leftarrow$ Reference_Vectors (N);
5: **while** not terminated **do**
6:     $Fit \leftarrow$ Calculate_Fitness(P) ;
7:     $(W, L) \leftarrow$ Tournament_Selection(p);
8:     **if** $|E| \geq 1$ **then**
9:         $Offspring \leftarrow$ CSO_Operator(W, L);
10:     **else**
11:         $Offspring \leftarrow$HHO_Operator(W, L, E);
12:     **end if**
13:     $P \leftarrow$ EnvironmentalSelection($Offspring \cup P, R$);
14: **end while**
15: **return** P;

$$fit = \min_{p_2 \in P/\{p_1\}} \sqrt{\sum_{i=1}^{m} (max\{0, f_i(p_2) - f_i(p_1)\}^2)} \tag{12}$$

where $f_i(p)$ represents the value of particle p on the ith objective and m is the dimension of objectives. The higher the fitness, the better the quality of the particle.

In line 7 of Algorithm 1, the population is divided into two distinct subgroups. Two particles are randomly selected from the population to compare the fitness values. The particle with a higher fitness value is placed in the winner group (W), and the particle with a lower fitness value is placed in the loser group (L). This procedure is repeated until all particles have been processed. After that, choosing the operators base on the value of E.

3.2 Particle Updating Strategies in LMOHHO

Algorithm 2. CSO Operator

Input: X_w(winner particles), X_l (loser particles)
Output: $Offspring$
$V_l \leftarrow$ Calculate the velocity of loser particles by Eq.5;
$X_{new} \leftarrow$ Update the position of loser particles by Eq.6;
Mutate X_l and X_w by polynomial mutation;
$Offspring \leftarrow$ Evaluate $(X_{new} \cup X_w \cup X_l)$
return $Offspring$;

Algorithm 3. HHO Operator

1: **Input:** X_w(winner particles), X_l (loser particles), E (energy)
2: **Output:** $Offspring$
3: $J \leftarrow$ Calculate the jump distance of the prey by Eq.10;
4: $\Delta X \leftarrow X_w - X_l$;
5: **if** $|E| \geq 0.5$ **then** ▷ Soft besiege
6: $\quad X_{new} \leftarrow X_l + r \odot \Delta X - E \odot |J \odot X_w - X_l|$;
7: **else** ▷ Hard besiege
8: $\quad X_{new} \leftarrow X_w - E \odot |\Delta X|$;
9: **end if**
10: $Offspring \leftarrow$ Evaluate (X_{new});
11: **return** $Offspring$;

LMOHHO selects different operators based on the value of E. When $|E| \geq 1$, it means that the prey has enough energy to escape from the hawks. At this time, the population needs to have a strong global search ability. The CSO operator has excellent global search capabilities and passes through competing machines, which can help catch the excellent particles and improve the quality of the solution. However, the CSO operator also has disadvantages, such as the loser update mechanism of CSO relying on random learning and having a relatively slow convergence speed, especially with low efficiency in the later fine-search stage. These defects can all be well compensated for by the HHO operator, HHO can formulate different precise attack strategies to accelerate the approach to high-quality particles. When optimizing the multi-modal problem, CSO may be confined to a local area due to competition, while HHO jumps out of the local optimum through the prey energy model. When the population stagnates, HHO triggers re-exploration through the prey energy model.

As shown in Algorithm 3, when $|E| < 1$, the prey begins to get tired, and a refined search is needed. Hawks have two strategies for hunting prey. In Line 6 of the Algorithm 3, when $0.5 < |E| \leq 1$, the prey still retains some energy and has a chance to escape. To hunt for the excellent particle (prey), we use a soft besiege strategy to search within a certain range near the prey, where J is calculated by formula 10 and $r \in [0, 1]$. When $|E| \leq 0.5$, it is time to catch the prey, so we use the hard besiege strategy to approximate the prey directly.

3.3 Environment Selection

The LMOHHO algorithm utilizes the RVEA environmental selection approach [19] to pick particles for the subsequent iteration from the merged population of $Offspring \cup P$. The selection mechanism works in two stages: initially, every particle in $Offspring \cup P$ is mapped to its closest reference vector in set R using an angular similarity measurement. Following this, for every reference vector in V, the algorithm picks the particle exhibiting the optimal angle penalty distance (APD) score among all particles linked to that specific reference vector. The APD metric is pivotal to this process and is defined as follows:

$$\mathrm{APD}(\mathbf{p}, \boldsymbol{v}) = \left(m \cdot \left(\frac{t}{T}\right)^{\alpha} \cdot \frac{\langle \boldsymbol{f}(\boldsymbol{p}), \boldsymbol{v}\rangle}{\min_{\boldsymbol{s} \in V, \boldsymbol{s} \neq \boldsymbol{v}} \langle \boldsymbol{s}, \boldsymbol{v}\rangle} + 1\right) \cdot \|\boldsymbol{f}(\boldsymbol{p})\| \tag{13}$$

where the objective vector of particle $\mathbf{p}$ denotes as $\boldsymbol{f}(\boldsymbol{p})$, m indicates the dimension of objectives, t stands for the current generation count, T defines the max-

Table 1. Statistics of IGD results (mean and standard deviation) for LMOHHO and six compared algorithms on the 100-D, 500-D, 800-D, and 1000-D two-objective LSMOP1–9 problems. The best mean result in each row is highlighted.

Problem	M	D	DGEA	LMOCSO	MOEA/D	PCPSO	RVEA	MOPSO	LMOHHO
LSMOP1	2	100	1.4841e-1 (3.65e-2) -	6.3826e-2 (8.22e-2) =	3.0984e-1 (1.61e-1) -	1.7883e-1 (1.53e-1) =	7.5865e-1 (2.65e-1) -	6.9283e-1 (1.38e-1) -	5.1892e-2 (8.09e-3)
		500	3.4555e-1 (4.49e-2) +	8.6902e-1 (6.97e-2) -	5.0465e-1 (1.17e-1) =	7.9552e-1 (1.36e-1) -	3.6320e+0 (5.33e-1) -	1.6145e+0 (1.35e-1) -	5.0318e-1 (8.67e-2)
		800	4.0676e-1 (1.41e-1) +	1.5061e+0 (1.45e-1) -	1.5199e+0 (4.22e-1) -	1.1550e+0 (1.18e-1) -	3.9367e+0 (5.31e-1) -	1.7932e+0 (1.06e-1) -	5.7710e-1 (2.82e-2)
		1000	3.6000e-1 (5.32e-2) +	1.7458e+0 (1.22e-1) -	2.1455e+0 (5.24e-1) -	1.2064e+0 (1.05e-1) -	4.2856e+0 (5.38e-1) -	1.9117e+0 (1.41e-1) -	5.7320e-1 (2.62e-2)
LSMOP2	2	100	5.9671e-2 (3.18e-2) -	1.0954e-1 (5.38e-3) -	1.3903e-1 (1.08e-2) -	1.0452e-1 (4.52e-3) -	1.6856e-1 (6.90e-3) -	1.7781e-1 (5.82e-3) -	4.0945e-2 (3.59e-3)
		500	1.6447e-2 (8.62e-4) +	4.3861e-2 (7.17e-4) -	6.5473e-2 (1.12e-3) -	4.4066e-2 (7.79e-4) -	6.0345e-2 (8.58e-4) -	5.0465e-2 (9.76e-4) -	1.9612e-2 (6.44e-4)
		800	1.2003e-2 (9.50e-4) +	2.9926e-2 (5.05e-4) -	4.3978e-2 (6.17e-4) -	3.0548e-2 (7.27e-4) -	4.3132e-2 (4.38e-4) -	3.5395e-2 (1.01e-3) -	1.3633e-2 (3.59e-4)
		1000	1.0423e-2 (5.83e-4) +	2.4788e-2 (6.09e-4) -	3.6620e-2 (3.35e-4) -	2.5427e-2 (6.60e-4) -	3.6486e-2 (3.58e-4) -	3.0215e-2 (8.75e-4) -	1.1514e-2 (3.31e-4)
LSMOP3	2	100	1.4071e+0 (1.16e-1) +	1.4329e+1 (1.94e+0) -	6.9365e-1 (3.80e-2) +	1.2327e+1 (5.36e+0) -	8.3912e-1 (2.51e-1) +	1.6332e+1 (2.37e+0) -	1.5210e+0 (2.18e-3)
		500	1.4454e+0 (2.70e-1) +	2.7633e+1 (3.92e+0) -	4.8823e+0 (2.62e+0) -	2.6369e+1 (9.63e-1) -	8.5206e+0 (2.99e+0) -	2.9837e+1 (2.32e+0) -	1.5790e+0 (3.21e-4)
		800	1.5259e+0 (1.51e-1) +	1.8225e+2 (4.66e+2) -	9.0501e+0 (4.37e+0) -	2.8265e+1 (1.28e+0) -	1.2194e+1 (3.06e+0) -	3.0413e+1 (2.73e+0) -	1.5843e+0 (9.35e-5)
		1000	1.8588e+0 (1.22e+0) -	7.6163e+1 (1.65e+2) -	1.0773e+1 (5.03e+0) -	2.8786e+1 (1.24e+0) -	1.2968e+1 (3.02e+0) -	3.7943e+1 (2.84e+1) -	1.5860e+0 (8.49e-5)
LSMOP4	2	100	4.6716e-2 (1.64e-2) -	3.4511e-2 (1.44e-3) =	1.5220e-1 (1.38e-2) -	3.2456e-2 (2.26e-3) =	3.7027e-1 (5.39e-2) -	2.3572e-1 (1.10e-2) -	3.3963e-2 (1.29e-2)
		500	4.8622e-2 (2.43e-3) +	8.6544e-2 (8.37e-4) -	1.0223e-1 (3.00e-3) -	8.5437e-2 (1.38e-3) -	9.6505e-2 (2.34e-3) -	9.8305e-2 (1.40e-3) -	6.5655e-2 (1.25e-3)
		800	3.2704e-2 (2.27e-3) +	6.2207e-2 (7.54e-4) -	7.3684e-2 (2.47e-3) -	6.1803e-2 (6.21e-4) -	6.9234e-2 (2.15e-3) -	6.8227e-2 (7.07e-4) -	4.7624e-2 (5.80e-4)
		1000	2.7267e-2 (1.75e-3) +	5.2018e-2 (4.30e-4) -	6.1284e-2 (2.33e-3) -	5.2028e-2 (4.23e-4) -	5.8262e-2 (6.59e-4) -	5.6995e-2 (9.07e-4) -	3.9628e-2 (5.35e-4)
LSMOP5	2	100	6.8665e-1 (1.54e-1) -	5.7862e-1 (1.40e-1) -	5.4015e-1 (1.46e-1) -	5.2713e-1 (6.19e-2) -	1.6990e+0 (7.07e-1) -	1.7148e+0 (3.24e-1) -	7.0590e-2 (3.19e-2)
		500	3.1299e+0 (1.45e+0) -	2.9078e+0 (4.60e-1) -	7.3230e-1 (1.62e-1) =	2.9410e+0 (4.20e-1) -	1.1422e+1 (1.11e+0) -	3.7281e+0 (3.20e-1) -	7.4209e-1 (2.28e-16)
		800	3.4629e+0 (1.58e+0) -	4.2463e+0 (5.65e-1) -	2.6402e+0 (5.14e-1) -	3.6288e+0 (3.69e-1) -	1.3202e+1 (7.71e-1) -	4.0998e+0 (3.03e-1) -	7.4209e-1 (2.28e-16)
		1000	2.6762e+0 (1.65e+0) -	4.4409e+0 (6.29e-1) -	4.3416e+0 (5.54e-1) -	3.8265e+0 (5.52e-1) -	1.3880e+1 (6.38e-1) -	4.2188e+0 (3.53e-1) -	7.4209e-1 (2.28e-16)
LSMOP6	2	100	6.1187e-1 (1.94e-1) +	1.0231e+0 (6.41e-2) -	7.4978e-1 (6.79e-3) +	9.0906e-1 (4.72e-1) =	9.7826e-1 (5.91e-2) -	4.6572e+0 (1.64e+1) -	9.0876e-1 (1.84e-1)
		500	3.9670e-1 (1.62e-1) +	1.0322e+2 (4.18e+2) =	7.9324e-1 (1.12e-2) =	1.1753e+2 (5.22e+2) =	7.5593e-1 (7.42e-2) +	6.3453e+2 (5.34e+2) -	1.1775e+0 (3.95e-1)
		800	4.4735e-1 (2.11e-1) +	2.2574e+2 (3.84e+2) -	7.7688e-1 (4.26e-3) =	7.7076e-1 (5.19e-3) =	7.2320e-1 (1.29e-1) +	6.7519e+2 (1.00e+3) -	1.0576e+0 (4.16e-1)
		1000	5.2227e-1 (2.30e-1) +	3.4413e+2 (9.19e+2) =	7.7185e-1 (3.08e-3) +	8.7111e+2 (3.07e+3) =	7.8993e-1 (1.58e-1) +	8.4658e+2 (1.27e+3) -	1.2627e+0 (3.87e-1)
LSMOP7	2	100	1.6339e+1 (8.47e+0) -	1.0942e+2 (1.26e+2) -	2.3744e+0 (2.14e+0) =	1.1487e+1 (9.04e+0) -	4.9324e+0 (1.87e+0) -	2.3275e+2 (9.73e+1) -	1.4573e+0 (2.92e-3)
		500	1.6161e+3 (6.57e+2) -	4.5748e+3 (1.25e+3) -	1.0412e+1 (6.60e+0) -	7.7797e+2 (1.33e+2) -	2.2651e+3 (6.09e+2) -	2.2428e+3 (6.99e+2) -	1.5128e+0 (2.14e-4)
		800	1.5653e+3 (1.61e+3) -	5.9870e+3 (1.39e+3) -	4.4177e+2 (6.41e+2) -	1.5274e+3 (4.89e+2) -	4.4097e+3 (5.18e+2) -	2.7720e+3 (4.43e+2) -	1.5178e+0 (1.61e-4)
		1000	2.0414e+3 (1.62e+3) -	6.7963e+3 (1.62e+3) -	1.4493e+3 (1.58e+3) -	1.6240e+3 (4.05e+2) -	5.5686e+3 (6.90e+2) -	3.1322e+3 (2.81e+2) -	1.5193e+0 (1.52e-4)
LSMOP8	2	100	3.7769e-1 (2.33e-1) -	6.1606e-1 (1.28e-1) -	4.8079e-1 (2.78e-1) -	1.3986e-1 (6.45e-2) =	1.5349e+0 (2.22e-1) -	1.5362e+0 (3.33e-1) -	1.2749e-1 (2.31e-2)
		500	8.1445e-1 (1.24e-1) -	3.0564e+0 (2.99e-1) -	9.5168e-1 (1.34e-1) -	2.0868e+0 (2.77e-1) -	3.5848e+0 (2.89e-1) -	2.7680e+0 (2.09e-1) -	7.4209e-1 (2.28e-16)
		800	1.0570e+0 (7.20e-1) -	3.6357e+0 (3.22e-1) -	2.1659e+0 (2.40e-1) -	2.6401e+0 (3.29e-1) -	4.5924e+0 (3.85e-1) -	3.1741e+0 (2.73e-1) -	7.4209e-1 (2.28e-16)
		1000	1.0315e+0 (4.12e-1) -	4.2770e+0 (5.59e-1) -	2.8904e+0 (2.87e-1) -	2.7783e+0 (3.62e-1) -	5.3186e+0 (3.73e-1) -	3.2074e+0 (1.61e-1) -	7.4209e-1 (2.28e-16)
LSMOP9	2	100	8.5877e-1 (3.20e-1) =	9.8882e-1 (5.94e-1) =	5.2011e-1 (1.80e-1) +	4.5567e-1 (1.44e-1) +	1.1322e+0 (2.34e-1) -	4.3286e+0 (1.13e+0) -	7.9428e-1 (7.05e-2)
		500	2.1169e+0 (8.37e-1) -	7.9531e+0 (6.79e+0) -	4.7885e-1 (3.13e-2) +	9.2120e-1 (4.36e-1) =	2.9045e+0 (6.34e-1) -	6.3244e+0 (1.04e+0) -	8.0743e-1 (3.26e-3)
		800	5.1799e+0 (1.95e+0) -	1.1016e+1 (6.88e+0) -	9.6852e-1 (3.15e-1) -	2.2723e+0 (4.54e-1) -	8.7279e+0 (1.87e+0) -	6.2048e+0 (1.11e+0) -	8.0552e-1 (4.72e-3)
		1000	6.0857e+0 (1.50e+0) -	1.5527e+1 (8.56e+0) -	2.7609e+0 (9.78e-1) -	2.7636e+0 (7.59e-1) -	1.1980e+1 (1.95e+0) -	6.1702e+0 (1.15e+0) -	8.0552e-1 (3.78e-3)
+/ − / =			16/19/1	0/31/5	5/26/5	1/27/8	4/32/0	0/36/0	

imum iteration limit, and α serves as a penalty coefficient. Additionally, $\langle \boldsymbol{s}, \boldsymbol{r} \rangle$ represents the angular separation between vectors $\boldsymbol{s}$ and $\boldsymbol{v}$.

4 Experimental Study

This section evaluates the performance of LMOHHO to optimize LSMOPs. We have compared LMOHHO with six state-of-the-art MOEAs, including DGEA [20], LMOCSO [15], MOEA/D [21], PCPSO [22], RVEA [19] and MOPSO [23]. The experiments utilize the LSMOP1-9 benchmark suite, specifically designed for LSMOPs, and the LSMOP suite adheres to established design principles [24, 25], ensuring problem generality and extensibility. These test problems include LSMOP1-4 for having linear PS within the decision space, and LSMOP5-9 for nonlinear PS. The features of these problems contain different PS geometries -linear, concave, and disconnected.

To assess scalability, LMOHHO is evaluated on a suite of LSMOPs with two- and three-objective decision variable dimensions scaling from 100 to 2000. For fairness of comparison and to ensure a standardized evaluation environment, all algorithm implementations and experimental runs are based on PlatEMO [26].

Table 2. Statistics of IGD results (mean and standard deviation) for LMOHHO and six compared algorithms on the 100-D, 500-D, 800-D, and 1000-D three-objective LSMOP1–9 problems. The best mean result in each row is highlighted.

Problem	M	D	DGEA	LMOCSO	MOEA/D	PCPSO	RVEA	MOPSO	LMOHHO
LSMOP1	2	100	1.4841e-1 (3.65e-2) -	6.3826e-2 (8.22e-2) =	3.0984e-1 (1.61e-1) -	1.7883e-1 (1.53e-1) =	7.5865e-1 (2.65e-1) -	6.9283e-1 (1.38e-1) -	5.1892e-2 (8.09e-3)
		500	3.4555e-1 (4.49e-2) +	8.6902e-1 (6.97e-2) -	5.0465e-1 (1.17e-1) =	7.9552e-1 (1.36e-1) -	3.6320e+0 (5.33e-1) -	1.6145e+0 (1.35e-1) -	5.0318e-1 (8.67e-2)
		800	4.0676e-1 (1.41e-1) +	1.5061e+0 (1.45e-1) -	1.5199e+0 (4.22e-1) -	1.1550e+0 (1.18e-1) -	3.9367e+0 (5.31e-1) -	1.7932e+0 (1.06e-1) -	5.7710e-1 (2.82e-2)
		1000	3.6000e-1 (5.32e-2) +	1.7458e+0 (1.22e-1) -	2.1455e+0 (5.24e-1) -	1.2064e+0 (1.05e-1) -	4.2856e+0 (5.38e-1) -	1.9117e+0 (1.41e-1) -	5.7320e-1 (2.62e-2)
LSMOP2	2	100	5.9671e-2 (3.18e-2) -	1.0954e-1 (5.38e-3) -	1.3903e-1 (1.08e-2) -	1.0452e-1 (4.52e-3) -	1.6856e-1 (6.90e-3) -	1.7781e-1 (5.82e-3) -	4.0945e-2 (3.59e-3)
		500	1.6447e-2 (8.62e-4) +	4.3861e-2 (7.17e-4) -	6.5473e-2 (1.12e-3) -	4.4066e-2 (7.79e-4) -	6.0345e-2 (8.58e-4) -	5.0465e-2 (9.76e-4) -	1.9612e-2 (6.44e-4)
		800	1.2003e-2 (9.50e-4) +	2.9926e-2 (5.05e-4) -	4.3978e-2 (6.17e-4) -	3.0548e-2 (7.27e-4) -	4.3132e-2 (4.38e-4) -	3.5395e-2 (1.01e-3) -	1.3633e-2 (3.59e-4)
		1000	1.0423e-2 (5.83e-4) +	2.4788e-2 (6.09e-4) -	3.6620e-2 (3.35e-4) -	2.5427e-2 (6.60e-4) -	3.6486e-2 (3.58e-4) -	3.0215e-2 (8.75e-4) -	1.1514e-2 (3.31e-4)
LSMOP3	2	100	1.4071e+0 (1.16e-1) +	1.4329e+1 (1.94e+0) -	6.9365e-1 (3.80e-2) +	1.2327e+1 (5.36e+0) -	8.3912e-1 (2.51e-1) +	1.6332e+1 (2.37e+0) -	1.5210e+0 (2.18e-3)
		500	1.4454e+0 (2.70e-1) +	2.7633e+1 (3.92e+0) -	4.8823e+0 (2.62e+0) -	2.6369e+1 (9.63e-1) -	8.5206e+0 (2.99e+0) -	2.9837e+1 (2.32e+0) -	1.5790e+0 (3.21e-4)
		800	1.5259e+0 (1.51e-1) +	1.8225e+2 (4.66e+2) -	9.0501e+0 (4.37e+0) -	2.8265e+1 (1.28e+0) -	1.2194e+1 (3.06e+0) -	3.0413e+1 (2.73e+0) -	1.5843e+0 (9.35e-5)
		1000	1.8588e+0 (1.22e+0) -	7.6163e+1 (1.65e+2) -	1.0773e+1 (5.03e+0) -	2.8786e+1 (1.24e+0) -	1.2968e+1 (3.02e+0) -	3.7943e+1 (2.84e+1) -	1.5860e+0 (8.49e-5)
LSMOP4	2	100	4.6716e-2 (1.64e-2) -	3.4511e-2 (1.44e-3) =	1.5220e-1 (1.38e-2) -	3.2456e-2 (2.26e-3) =	3.7027e-1 (5.39e-2) -	2.3572e-1 (1.10e-2) -	3.3963e-2 (1.29e-2)
		500	4.8622e-2 (2.43e-3) +	8.6544e-2 (8.37e-4) -	1.0223e-1 (3.00e-3) -	8.5437e-2 (1.38e-3) -	9.6505e-2 (2.34e-3) -	9.8305e-2 (1.40e-3) -	6.5655e-2 (1.25e-3)
		800	3.2704e-2 (2.27e-3) +	6.2207e-2 (7.54e-4) -	7.3684e-2 (2.47e-3) -	6.1803e-2 (6.21e-4) -	6.9234e-2 (2.15e-3) -	6.8227e-2 (7.07e-4) -	4.7624e-2 (5.80e-4)
		1000	2.7267e-2 (1.75e-3) +	5.2018e-2 (4.30e-4) -	6.1284e-2 (2.33e-3) -	5.2028e-2 (4.23e-4) -	5.8262e-2 (6.59e-4) -	5.6995e-2 (9.07e-4) -	3.9628e-2 (5.35e-4)
LSMOP5	2	100	6.8665e-1 (1.54e-1) -	5.7862e-1 (1.40e-1) -	5.4015e-1 (1.46e-1) -	5.2713e-1 (6.19e-2) -	1.6990e+0 (7.07e-1) -	1.7148e+0 (3.24e-1) -	7.0590e-2 (3.19e-2)
		500	3.1299e+0 (1.45e+0) -	2.9078e+0 (4.60e-1) -	7.3230e-1 (1.62e-1) =	2.9410e+0 (4.20e-1) -	1.1422e+1 (1.11e+0) -	3.7281e+0 (3.20e-1) -	7.4209e-1 (2.28e-16)
		800	3.4629e+0 (1.58e+0) -	4.2463e+0 (5.65e-1) -	2.6402e+0 (5.14e-1) -	3.6288e+0 (3.69e-1) -	1.3202e+1 (7.71e-1) -	4.0998e+0 (3.03e-1) -	7.4209e-1 (2.28e-16)
		1000	2.6762e+0 (1.65e+0) -	4.4409e+0 (6.29e-1) -	4.3416e+0 (5.54e-1) -	3.8265e+0 (5.52e-1) -	1.3880e+1 (6.38e-1) -	4.2188e+0 (3.53e-1) -	7.4209e-1 (2.28e-16)
LSMOP6	2	100	6.1187e-1 (1.94e-1) +	1.0231e+0 (6.41e-2) -	7.4978e-1 (6.79e-3) +	9.0906e-1 (4.72e-1) =	9.7826e-1 (5.91e-2) -	4.6572e+0 (1.64e+1) -	9.0876e-1 (1.84e-1)
		500	3.9670e-1 (1.62e-1) +	1.0322e+2 (4.18e+2) =	7.9324e-1 (1.12e-2) =	1.1753e+2 (5.22e+2) =	7.5593e-1 (7.42e-2) +	6.3453e+2 (5.34e+2) -	1.1775e+0 (3.95e-1)
		800	4.4735e-1 (2.11e-1) +	2.2574e+2 (3.84e+2) -	7.7688e-1 (4.26e-3) =	7.7076e-1 (5.19e-3) =	7.2320e-1 (1.29e-1) +	6.7519e+2 (1.00e+3) -	1.0576e+0 (4.16e-1)
		1000	5.2227e-1 (2.30e-1) +	3.4413e+2 (9.19e+2) =	7.7185e-1 (3.08e-3) +	8.7111e+2 (3.07e+3) =	7.8993e-1 (1.58e-1) +	8.4658e+2 (1.27e+3) -	1.2627e+0 (3.87e-1)
LSMOP7	2	100	1.6339e+1 (8.47e+0) -	1.0942e+2 (1.26e+2) -	2.3744e+0 (2.14e+0) =	1.1487e+1 (9.04e+0) -	4.9324e+0 (1.87e+0) -	2.3275e+2 (9.73e+1) -	1.4573e+0 (2.92e-3)
		500	1.6161e+3 (6.57e+2) -	4.5748e+3 (1.25e+3) -	1.0412e+1 (6.60e+0) -	7.7797e+2 (1.33e+2) -	2.2651e+3 (6.09e+2) -	2.2428e+3 (6.99e+2) -	1.5128e+0 (2.14e-4)
		800	1.5653e+3 (1.61e+3) -	5.9870e+3 (1.39e+3) -	4.4177e+2 (6.41e+2) -	1.5274e+3 (4.89e+2) -	4.4097e+3 (5.18e+2) -	2.7720e+3 (4.43e+2) -	1.5178e+0 (1.61e-4)
		1000	2.0414e+3 (1.62e+3) -	6.7963e+3 (1.62e+3) -	1.4493e+3 (1.58e+3) -	1.6240e+3 (4.05e+2) -	5.5686e+3 (6.90e+2) -	3.1322e+3 (2.81e+2) -	1.5193e+0 (1.52e-4)
LSMOP8	2	100	3.7769e-1 (2.33e-1) -	6.1606e-1 (1.28e-1) -	4.8079e-1 (2.78e-1) -	1.3986e-1 (6.45e-2) =	1.5349e+0 (2.22e-1) -	1.5362e+0 (3.33e-1) -	1.2749e-1 (2.31e-2)
		500	8.1445e-1 (1.24e-1) -	3.0564e+0 (2.99e-1) -	9.5168e-1 (1.34e-1) -	2.0868e+0 (2.77e-1) -	3.5848e+0 (2.89e-1) -	2.7680e+0 (2.09e-1) -	7.4209e-1 (2.28e-16)
		800	1.0570e+0 (7.20e-1) -	3.6357e+0 (3.22e-1) -	2.1659e+0 (2.40e-1) -	2.6401e+0 (3.29e-1) -	4.5924e+0 (3.85e-1) -	3.1741e+0 (2.73e-1) -	7.4209e-1 (2.28e-16)
		1000	1.0315e+0 (4.12e-1) -	4.2770e+0 (5.59e-1) -	2.8904e+0 (2.87e-1) -	2.7783e+0 (3.62e-1) -	5.3186e+0 (3.73e-1) -	3.2074e+0 (1.61e-1) -	7.4209e-1 (2.28e-16)
LSMOP9	2	100	8.5877e-1 (3.20e-1) =	9.8882e-1 (5.94e-1) =	5.2011e-1 (1.80e-1) +	4.5567e-1 (1.44e-1) +	1.1322e+0 (2.34e-1) -	4.3286e+0 (1.13e+0) -	7.9428e-1 (7.05e-2)
		500	2.1169e+0 (8.37e-1) -	7.9531e+0 (6.79e+0) -	4.7885e-1 (3.13e-2) +	9.2120e-1 (4.36e-1) =	2.9045e+0 (6.34e-1) -	6.3244e+0 (1.04e+0) -	8.0743e-1 (3.26e-3)
		800	5.1799e+0 (1.95e+0) -	1.1016e+1 (6.88e+0) -	9.6852e-1 (3.15e-1) -	2.2723e+0 (4.54e-1) -	8.7279e+0 (1.87e+0) -	6.2048e+0 (1.11e+0) -	8.0552e-1 (4.72e-3)
		1000	6.0857e+0 (1.50e+0) -	1.5527e+1 (8.56e+0) -	2.7609e+0 (9.78e-1) -	2.7636e+0 (7.59e-1) -	1.1980e+1 (1.95e+0) -	6.1702e+0 (1.15e+0) -	8.0552e-1 (3.78e-3)
+/ − / =			16/19/1	0/31/5	5/26/5	1/27/8	4/32/0	0/36/0	

Table 3. Statistics of IGD results (mean and standard deviation) for LMOHHO and six compared algorithms on the 1000-D, 1500-D, and 2000-D two-objective ZDT1–6 problems. The best mean result in each row is highlighted.

Problem	M	D	DGEA	LMOCSO	MOEA/D	PCPSO	RVEA	MOPSO	LMOHHO
LSMOP1	2	100	1.4841e-1 (3.65e-2) -	6.3826e-2 (8.22e-2) =	3.0984e-1 (1.61e-1) -	1.7883e-1 (1.53e-1) =	7.5865e-1 (2.65e-1) -	6.9283e-1 (1.38e-1) -	5.1892e-2 (8.09e-3)
		500	3.4555e-1 (4.49e-2) +	8.6902e-1 (6.97e-2) -	5.0465e-1 (1.17e-1) =	7.9552e-1 (1.36e-1) -	3.6320e+0 (5.33e-1) -	1.6145e+0 (1.35e-1) -	5.0318e-1 (8.67e-2)
		800	4.0676e-1 (1.41e-1) +	1.5061e+0 (1.45e-1) -	1.5199e+0 (4.22e-1) -	1.1550e+0 (1.18e-1) -	3.9367e+0 (5.31e-1) -	1.7932e+0 (1.06e-1) -	5.7710e-1 (2.82e-2)
		1000	3.6000e-1 (5.32e-2) +	1.7458e+0 (1.22e-1) -	2.1455e+0 (5.24e-1) -	1.2064e+0 (1.05e-1) -	4.2856e+0 (5.38e-1) -	1.9117e+0 (1.41e-1) -	5.7320e-1 (2.62e-2)
LSMOP2	2	100	5.9671e-2 (3.18e-2) -	1.0954e-1 (5.38e-3) -	1.3903e-1 (1.08e-2) -	1.0452e-1 (4.52e-3) -	1.6856e-1 (6.90e-3) -	1.7781e-1 (5.82e-3) -	4.0945e-2 (3.59e-3)
		500	1.6447e-2 (8.62e-4) +	4.3861e-2 (7.17e-4) -	6.5473e-2 (1.12e-3) -	4.4066e-2 (7.79e-4) -	6.0345e-2 (8.58e-4) -	5.0465e-2 (9.76e-4) -	1.9612e-2 (6.44e-4)
		800	1.2003e-2 (9.50e-4) +	2.9926e-2 (5.05e-4) -	4.3978e-2 (6.17e-4) -	3.0548e-2 (7.27e-4) -	4.3132e-2 (4.38e-4) -	3.5395e-2 (1.01e-3) -	1.3633e-2 (3.59e-4)
		1000	1.0423e-2 (5.83e-4) +	2.4788e-2 (6.09e-4) -	3.6620e-2 (3.35e-4) -	2.5427e-2 (6.60e-4) -	3.6486e-2 (3.58e-4) -	3.0215e-2 (8.75e-4) -	1.1514e-2 (3.31e-4)
LSMOP3	2	100	1.4071e+0 (1.16e-1) +	1.4329e+1 (1.94e+0) -	6.9365e-1 (3.80e-2) +	1.2327e+1 (5.36e+0) -	8.3912e-1 (2.51e-1) +	1.6332e+1 (2.37e+0) -	1.5210e+0 (2.18e-3)
		500	1.4454e+0 (2.70e-1) +	2.7633e+1 (3.92e+0) -	4.8823e+0 (2.62e+0) -	2.6369e+1 (9.63e-1) -	8.5206e+0 (2.99e+0) -	2.9837e+1 (2.32e+0) -	1.5790e+0 (3.21e-4)
		800	1.5259e+0 (1.51e-1) +	1.8225e+2 (4.66e+2) -	9.0501e+0 (4.37e+0) -	2.8265e+1 (1.28e+0) -	1.2194e+1 (3.06e+0) -	3.0413e+1 (2.73e+0) -	1.5843e+0 (9.35e-5)
		1000	1.8588e+0 (1.22e+0) -	7.6163e+1 (1.65e+2) -	1.0773e+1 (5.03e+0) -	2.8786e+1 (1.24e+0) -	1.2968e+1 (3.02e+0) -	3.7943e+1 (2.84e+1) -	1.5860e+0 (8.49e-5)
LSMOP4	2	100	4.6716e-2 (1.64e-2) -	3.4511e-2 (1.44e-3) =	1.5220e-1 (1.38e-2) -	3.2456e-2 (2.26e-3) =	3.7027e-1 (5.39e-2) -	2.3572e-1 (1.10e-2) -	3.3963e-2 (1.29e-2)
		500	4.8622e-2 (2.43e-3) +	8.6544e-2 (8.37e-4) -	1.0223e-1 (3.00e-3) -	8.5437e-2 (1.38e-3) -	9.6505e-2 (2.34e-3) -	9.8305e-2 (1.40e-3) -	6.5655e-2 (1.25e-3)
		800	3.2704e-2 (2.27e-3) +	6.2207e-2 (7.54e-4) -	7.3684e-2 (2.47e-3) -	6.1803e-2 (6.21e-4) -	6.9234e-2 (2.15e-3) -	6.8227e-2 (7.07e-4) -	4.7624e-2 (5.80e-4)
		1000	2.7267e-2 (1.75e-3) +	5.2018e-2 (4.30e-4) -	6.1284e-2 (2.33e-3) -	5.2028e-2 (4.23e-4) -	5.8262e-2 (6.59e-4) -	5.6995e-2 (9.07e-4) -	3.9628e-2 (5.35e-4)
LSMOP5	2	100	6.8665e-1 (1.54e-1) -	5.7862e-1 (1.40e-1) -	5.4015e-1 (1.46e-1) -	5.2713e-1 (6.19e-2) -	1.6990e+0 (7.07e-1) -	1.7148e+0 (3.24e-1) -	7.0590e-2 (3.19e-2)
		500	3.1299e+0 (1.45e+0) -	2.9078e+0 (4.60e-1) -	7.3230e-1 (1.62e-1) =	2.9410e+0 (4.20e-1) -	1.1422e+1 (1.11e+0) -	3.7281e+0 (3.20e-1) -	7.4209e-1 (2.28e-16)
		800	3.4629e+0 (1.58e+0) -	4.2463e+0 (5.65e-1) -	2.6402e+0 (5.14e-1) -	3.6288e+0 (3.69e-1) -	1.3202e+1 (7.71e-1) -	4.0998e+0 (3.03e-1) -	7.4209e-1 (2.28e-16)
		1000	2.6762e+0 (1.65e+0) -	4.4409e+0 (6.29e-1) -	4.3416e+0 (5.54e-1) -	3.8265e+0 (5.52e-1) -	1.3880e+1 (6.38e-1) -	4.2188e+0 (3.53e-1) -	7.4209e-1 (2.28e-16)
LSMOP6	2	100	6.1187e-1 (1.94e-1) +	1.0231e+0 (6.41e-2) -	7.4978e-1 (6.79e-3) +	9.0906e-1 (4.72e-1) =	9.7826e-1 (5.91e-2) -	4.6572e+0 (1.64e+1) -	9.0876e-1 (1.84e-1)
		500	3.9670e-1 (1.62e-1) +	1.0322e+2 (4.18e+2) =	7.9324e-1 (1.12e-2) =	1.1753e+2 (5.22e+2) =	7.5593e-1 (7.42e-2) +	6.3453e+2 (5.34e+2) -	1.1775e+0 (3.95e-1)
		800	4.4735e-1 (2.11e-1) +	2.2574e+2 (3.84e+2) -	7.7688e-1 (4.26e-3) =	7.7076e-1 (5.19e-3) =	7.2320e-1 (1.29e-1) +	6.7519e+2 (1.00e+3) -	1.0576e+0 (4.16e-1)
		1000	5.2227e-1 (2.30e-1) +	3.4413e+2 (9.19e+2) =	7.7185e-1 (3.08e-3) +	8.7111e+2 (3.07e+3) =	7.8993e-1 (1.58e-1) +	8.4658e+2 (1.27e+3) -	1.2627e+0 (3.87e-1)
LSMOP7	2	100	1.6339e+1 (8.47e+0) -	1.0942e+2 (1.26e+2) -	2.3744e+0 (2.14e+0) =	1.1487e+1 (9.04e+0) -	4.9324e+0 (1.87e+0) -	2.3275e+2 (9.73e+1) -	1.4573e+0 (2.92e-3)
		500	1.6161e+3 (6.57e+2) -	4.5748e+3 (1.25e+3) -	1.0412e+1 (6.60e+0) -	7.7797e+2 (1.33e+2) -	2.2651e+3 (6.09e+2) -	2.2428e+3 (6.99e+2) -	1.5128e+0 (2.14e-4)
		800	1.5653e+3 (1.61e+3) -	5.9870e+3 (1.39e+3) -	4.4177e+2 (6.41e+2) -	1.5274e+3 (4.89e+2) -	4.4097e+3 (5.18e+2) -	2.7720e+3 (4.43e+2) -	1.5178e+0 (1.61e-4)
		1000	2.0414e+3 (1.62e+3) -	6.7963e+3 (1.62e+3) -	1.4493e+3 (1.58e+3) -	1.6240e+3 (4.05e+2) -	5.5686e+3 (6.90e+2) -	3.1322e+3 (2.81e+2) -	1.5193e+0 (1.52e-4)
LSMOP8	2	100	3.7769e-1 (2.33e-1) -	6.1606e-1 (1.28e-1) -	4.8079e-1 (2.78e-1) -	1.3986e-1 (6.45e-2) =	1.5349e+0 (2.22e-1) -	1.5362e+0 (3.33e-1) -	1.2749e-1 (2.31e-2)
		500	8.1445e-1 (1.24e-1) -	3.0564e+0 (2.99e-1) -	9.5168e-1 (1.34e-1) -	2.0868e+0 (2.77e-1) -	3.5848e+0 (2.89e-1) -	2.7680e+0 (2.09e-1) -	7.4209e-1 (2.28e-16)
		800	1.0570e+0 (7.20e-1) -	3.6357e+0 (3.22e-1) -	2.1659e+0 (2.40e-1) -	2.6401e+0 (3.29e-1) -	4.5924e+0 (3.85e-1) -	3.1741e+0 (2.73e-1) -	7.4209e-1 (2.28e-16)
		1000	1.0315e+0 (4.12e-1) -	4.2770e+0 (5.59e-1) -	2.8904e+0 (2.87e-1) -	2.7783e+0 (3.62e-1) -	5.3186e+0 (3.73e-1) -	3.2074e+0 (1.61e-1) -	7.4209e-1 (2.28e-16)
LSMOP9	2	100	8.5877e-1 (3.20e-1) =	9.8882e-1 (5.94e-1) =	5.2011e-1 (1.80e-1) +	4.5567e-1 (1.44e-1) +	1.1322e+0 (2.34e-1) -	4.3286e+0 (1.13e+0) -	7.9428e-1 (7.05e-2)
		500	2.1169e+0 (8.37e-1) -	7.9531e+0 (6.79e+0) -	4.7885e-1 (3.13e-2) +	9.2120e-1 (4.36e-1) =	2.9045e+0 (6.34e-1) -	6.3244e+0 (1.04e+0) -	8.0743e-1 (3.26e-3)
		800	5.1799e+0 (1.95e+0) -	1.1016e+1 (6.88e+0) -	9.6852e-1 (3.15e-1) -	2.2723e+0 (4.54e-1) -	8.7279e+0 (1.87e+0) -	6.2048e+0 (1.11e+0) -	8.0552e-1 (4.72e-3)
		1000	6.0857e+0 (1.50e+0) -	1.5527e+1 (8.56e+0) -	2.7609e+0 (9.78e-1) -	2.7636e+0 (7.59e-1) -	1.1980e+1 (1.95e+0) -	6.1702e+0 (1.15e+0) -	8.0552e-1 (3.78e-3)
+/ − / =			16/19/1	0/31/5	5/26/5	1/27/8	4/32/0	0/36/0	

4.1 Experimental Setting

Parameters. To ensure a fair and consistent evaluation, each algorithm is configured using its recommended optimal parameters. Common settings are applied across all algorithms, including a population size ($|P| = 100$) for all experiments, and a termination criterion of 1000 iterations.

Problems. For LSMOP1-9, considering the two-objective and three-objective, the dimension range of $D$is from 100 to 1000. For ZDT1-6, the test suite has only two objectives, and the dimension range of D is from 1000 to 2000.

Performance Index. The inverted generational distance (IGD) [27] is selected as the main performance index to evaluate the quality of the particle. A lower IGD value indicates a closer approach to the true Pareto front, suggesting better overall performance. The calculation formula is as follows:

$$IGD(P, X) = \frac{1}{|P|} \sum_{p \in P} \min_{x \in X} \|p - x\| \tag{14}$$

where $\|p-x\|$ represents the minimal Euclidean distance between solution p and set X. P is a uniformly distributed reference set, which is sampled from the PF of the test suite, where $|P| = 10,000$.

For robust statistical analysis, every experiment is repeated 20 times. The mean and standard deviation of the IGD scores are then calculated. We use the Wilcoxon rank-sum test ($\alpha = 0.05$) to assess the significance of the performance differences. In the comparison tables, "+", "-", and "=" denote that the competitor is, respectively, superior to, inferior to, or statistically equivalent to LMOHHO.

4.2 Experiment Result

Table 1 summarizes the results for the seven competitors on two-objective LSMOP1-9 test suites with the dimension of feasible decision space from 100 to 1000, where the proposed LMOHHO shows a distinct performance advantage. It achieves the best results in more instances than any other competitor, including DGEA, MOEA/D, and PCPSO. Statistically, the Wilcoxon rank sum test confirms the superiority of LMOHHO, showing it significantly outperforms DGEA, LMOCSO, MOEA/D, PCPSO, RVEA, and MOPSO in 19/36, 31/36, 26/36, 27/36, 32/36, and 36/36 of cases, respectively. For further observation, LMOHHO shows its excellent optimization performance on LSMOP 5, LSMOP 7, LSMOP 8, and LSMOP 9. These demonstrate that LMOHHO has a more powerful search ability and convergence ability when optimizing complex two-objective problems. And at the simple two-objective problems like LSMOP 1, LSMOP 2, and LSMOP 4, LMOHHO also has great optimization performance.

For the three-objective problem sets, Table 2 presents the results of the seven competitors on the test suites LSMOP1-9. Echoing the results from the two-objective tests, LMOHHO again exhibited the most impressive performance among the experiments. It achieved the highest number of best results, followed by DGEA, MOEA/D, and RVEA. The experiment validates this superiority. The proportions of test instances where LMOHHO is significantly better than DGEA, LMOCSO, MOEA/D, PCPSO, RVEA, and MOPSO are 14/36, 35/36, 26/36, 36/36, 31/36, and 34/36, respectively. In contrast to the two-objective results, LMOHHO demonstrated particularly excellent performance on LSMOP 1, LSMOP 2, and LSMOP 6, showcasing its enhanced search and convergence capabilities for three-objective problems. On the other problems in this category, the performance of LMOHHO is highly competitive, proving to be at least as effective as DGEA.

To assess the scalability of LMOHHO, we have compared it with six other MOEAs on the test suite ZDT. The ZDT test suite is a classic benchmark problem set in the field of MOEAs, and its core characteristics are: By constructing Pareto fronts with different characteristics (including convex, concave, discontinuous) through carefully designed mathematical forms, and introducing complex characteristics such as variable coupling, multimodality, and non-uniform distribution at the same time, which enables the test suites to comprehensively evaluate the performance of the test algorithm in terms of convergence, diversity maintenance, and evasion of local optimum. This suite has advantages such as a real Pareto front, scalable variable dimensions, and visualizable results.

To explicitly test scalability, the algorithms are compared on the two-objective ZDT1-6 suite with dimensionality scaled to 1000, 1500, and 2000 variables. The IGD results for this analysis are presented in Table 3. The data shows that our method is superior to the other competitors. Specifically, across the 15 test instances, LMOHHO achieves the best result 12 times, while PCPSO secures two best results and MOEA/D secures one. The Wilcoxon rank sum test further reinforces this dominance, showing that LMOHHO performs significantly better than DGEA, LMOCSO, MOEA/D, PCPSO, RVEA, and MOPSO in 12/15, 15/15, 12/15, 12/15, 12/15, and 13/15 of cases, respectively. This highlights a crucial finding: as problem dimensions scale into the thousands, the effectiveness of many other MOEAs declines sharply, while LMOHHO maintains its strong search and convergence capabilities.

5 Conclusion

This paper introduced LMOHHO, an enhanced CSO-based optimizer that integrates HHO to solve LSMOPs. The proposed method combines the CSO and HHO operators, utilizing these approaches at different stages of the optimization procedure. The core strategy is to utilize the strengths of HHO to overcome the known deficiencies of the CSO algorithm. The experimental results confirmed that our method, LMOHHO, is capable of solving LSMOPs more effectively than several current state-of-the-art MOEAs.

Despite its strong overall performance, the experimental analysis indicates that the effectiveness of LMOHHO could be further improved on LSMOPs with optimization efficiency. Therefore, we will focus on enhancing the search ability of LMOHHO to solve the complex LSMOPs. Future research directions could explore improving the exploration capability of LMOHHO in challenging optimization landscapes. Potential enhancements might include integrating advanced variable processing methodologies, such as decision variable decomposition techniques, Variable grouping approaches, and dimensionality reduction strategies.

Acknowledgments. This work was partially supported by the National Natural Science Foundation of China (Grant Nos. 62573201, U23A20303, and 62573326), and Zhejiang Provincial Natural Science Foundation of China (Grant No. LZ25F030007).

References

1. Liu, Y., Wang, H., Ma, J.: Infill criterion ensemble in multi-objective evolutionary algorithm for mixed-variable problems. In: IEEE Congress on Evolutionary Computation, pp. 1–8 (2024)

2. Tian, Y., Liu, R., Zhang, X., Ma, H., Tan, K.C., Jin, Y.: A multipopulation evolutionary algorithm for solving large-scale multimodal multiobjective optimization problems. IEEE Trans. Evol. Comput. **25**(3), 405–418 (2021)
3. Kinoyama, R., Suryanarayanan, N.A.V., Iba, H.: Continual learning of lstm using ant colony optimization. In: IEEE Congress on Evolutionary Computation, pp. 1–8 (2023)
4. Yang, J.Q., Du, K.J., Chen, C.H., Wang, H., Zhang, J., Zhan, Z.H.: Evolutionary multitasking bi-directional particle swarm optimization for high-dimensional feature selection. In: IEEE Congress on Evolutionary Computation, pp. 1–8 (2023)
5. Zille, H., Mostaghim, S.: Comparison study of large-scale optimisation techniques on the lsmop benchmark functions. In: IEEE Symposium on Series Computer Intelligence, pp. 1–8 (2017)
6. Cai, X., Wu, L., Zhao, T., Wu, D., Zhang, W., Chen, J.: Dynamic adaptive multi-objective optimization algorithm based on type detection. Inf. Sci. **654**, 119867 (2024)
7. Zhuang, X., et al.: Multi-objective optimization of reservoir development strategy with hybrid artificial intelligence method. Expert Syst. Appl. **241**, 122707 (2024)
8. Bohrer, J.D.S., Dorn, M.: Enhancing classification with hybrid feature selection: a multi-objective genetic algorithm for high-dimensional data. Expert Syst. Appl. **255**, 124518 (2024)
9. Zheng, W., Li, M., Deng, R., Doerr, B.: How to use the metropolis algorithm for multi-objective optimization? In: Proceedings of the Genetic and Evolutionary Computation Conference Companion, pp. 71–72 (2024)
10. Cheng, R., Jin, Y.: A competitive swarm optimizer for large scale optimization. IEEE Trans. Cybern. **45**(2), 191–204 (2015)
11. Heidari, A.A., Mirjalili, S., Faris, H., Aljarah, I., Mafarja, M., Chen, H.: Harris hawks optimization: algorithm and applications. Future Gener. Comput. Syst. **97**, 849–872 (2019)
12. Bonyadi, M.R., Michalewicz, Z.: Particle swarm optimization for single objective continuous space problems: a review. Evol. Comput. **25**(1), 1–54 (2017)
13. Tian, Y., et al.: Evolutionary large-scale multi-objective optimization: a survey. ACM Comput. Surv. **54**(8), 1–34 (2021)
14. Wang, D., Tan, D., Liu, L.: Particle swarm optimization algorithm: an overview. Soft. Comput. **22**(2), 387–408 (2018)
15. Tian, Y., Zheng, X., Zhang, X., Jin, Y.: Efficient large-scale multiobjective optimization based on a competitive swarm optimizer. IEEE Trans. Cybern. **50**(8), 3696–3708 (2019)
16. Alabool, H.M., Alarabiat, D., Abualigah, L., Heidari, A.A.: Harris hawks optimization: a comprehensive review of recent variants and applications. Neural Comput. Appl. **33**, 8939–8980 (2021)
17. Fan, Q., Chen, Z., Xia, Z.: A novel quasi-reflected harris hawks optimization algorithm for global optimization problems. Soft. Comput. **24**, 14825–14843 (2020)
18. Li, M., Yang, S., Liu, X.: Shift-based density estimation for pareto-based algorithms in many-objective optimization. IEEE Trans. Evol. Comput. **18**(3), 348–365 (2013)
19. Cheng, R., Jin, Y., Olhofer, M., Sendhoff, B.: A reference vector guided evolutionary algorithm for many-objective optimization. IEEE Trans. Evol. Comput. **20**(5), 773–791 (2016)
20. He, C., Cheng, R., Yazdani, D.: Adaptive offspring generation for evolutionary large-scale multiobjective optimization. IEEE Trans. Syst. Man Cybern. Syst. **52**(2), 786–798 (2020)

21. Zhang, Q., Li, H.: Moea/d: a multiobjective evolutionary algorithm based on decomposition. IEEE Trans. Evol. Comput. **11**(6), 712–731 (2007)
22. Lu, Y., Li, B., Liu, S., Zhou, A.: A population cooperation based particle swarm optimization algorithm for large-scale multi-objective optimization. Swarm Evol. Comput. **83**, 101377 (2023)
23. Coello Coello, C., Lechuga, M.: Mopso: a proposal for multiple objective particle swarm optimization. In: Proceedings of the Genetic and Evolutionary Computation Conference Companion, vol. 2, pp. 1051–1056 (2002)
24. Deb, K., Thiele, L., Laumanns, M., Zitzler, E.: Scalable test problems for evolutionary multiobjective optimization. In: Evolutionary Multiobjective Optimization: Theoretical Advances and Applications, pp. 105–145. Springer, Heidelberg (2005). https://doi.org/10.1007/1-84628-137-7_6
25. Huband, S., Hingston, P., Barone, L., While, L.: A review of multiobjective test problems and a scalable test problem toolkit. IEEE Trans. Evol. Comput. **10**(5), 477–506 (2006)
26. Tian, Y., Cheng, R., Zhang, X., Jin, Y.: Platemo: a matlab platform for evolutionary multi-objective optimization [educational forum]. IEEE Comput. Intell. Mag. **12**(4), 73–87 (2017)
27. Bosman, P.A., Thierens, D.: The balance between proximity and diversity in multiobjective evolutionary algorithms. IEEE Trans. Evol. Comput. **7**(2), 174–188 (2003)

Multimodal Multiobjective Optimization Algorithm Based on Two-Stage Proportional Selection

Zeyan Zhang, Min-Rong Chen(✉), Jixiang Zeng, Zihua Guo, and Songxiang Zhong

School of Computer Science, South China Normal University, Guangzhou 510631, China
{2023023267,2023023216,2023023247,2023023300}@m.scnu.edu.cn, mrongchen@126.com

Abstract. In multimodal multiobjective optimization problems, the existence of multiple equivalent Pareto optimal sets poses a challenge for optimization algorithms to balance convergence and diversity. Existing algorithms still have room for performance improvement in handling such problems. Therefore, this paper proposes a novel multimodal multiobjective optimization algorithm. Its key innovation lies in the introduction of a proportional selection strategy during the environmental selection process. By rationally setting the proportion to screen individuals for the next generation, it effectively balances the diversity and convergence of the population. To verify the performance of the algorithm, comprehensive comparative experiments are conducted between it and seven advanced multimodal multiobjective optimization algorithms. The results show that the proposed algorithm performs excellently in terms of the comprehensive performance in both the decision space and the objective space, significantly outperforming the comparative algorithms.

Keywords: Multimodal multiobjective optimization · two-stage evolutionary algorithm · proportional selection

1 Introduction

Multiobjective optimization problems (MOPs) [1] are widely present in numerous areas of the real world, such as engineering design, resource allocation, and machine learning. In these practical application scenarios, it is often necessary to optimize multiple conflicting objectives simultaneously. For instance, in engineering design, there is a need to maximize product performance while minimizing costs; in resource allocation, it is essential to balance resource utilization efficiency and distribution fairness. The core goal of multiobjective optimization is to find the optimal solution set among these conflicting objectives. From a mathematical definition perspective, a typical minimized multiobjective optimization problem can be formally described as:

T. Hao et al. (Eds.): BESC 2025, LNCS 16431, pp. 43–54, 2026.
https://doi.org/10.1007/978-981-95-7138-3_4

$$\begin{aligned} \min F(\mathbf{x}) &= \{f_1(\mathbf{x}), f_2(\mathbf{x}), \ldots, f_m(\mathbf{x})\} \\ \text{s.t. } \mathbf{x} &= (x_1, x_2, \ldots, x_n) \in \Omega \end{aligned} \tag{1}$$

where $F(\mathbf{x})$ is an m-dimensional vector of objective functions, with each component $f_i(\mathbf{x})$ corresponding to the i-th optimization objective $(i = 1, 2, \ldots, m)$. Ω represents the decision space, and $\boldsymbol{x}$ denotes the n-dimensional decision variable.

In multiobjective optimization problems, the objective functions $f_i(\boldsymbol{x})$ $(i = 1, 2, \ldots, m)$ are typically in conflict with each other, making it impossible to simultaneously optimize all objectives. Specifically, for any two solutions $\boldsymbol{x}_1$ and $\boldsymbol{x}_2$ in the decision space Ω, $\boldsymbol{x}_1$ is said to dominate $\boldsymbol{x}_2$ (denoted as $\boldsymbol{x}_1 \prec \boldsymbol{x}_2$) if the following conditions hold: (1) $f_i(\boldsymbol{x}_1) \leq f_i(\boldsymbol{x}_2)$ for all objectives $i \in \{1, 2, \ldots, m\}$; (2) There exists at least one objective j such that $f_j(\boldsymbol{x}_1) < f_j(\boldsymbol{x}_2)$. A solution $\boldsymbol{x}^*$ undominated by any other solution is defined as a Pareto optimal solution. The collection of all such solutions forms the Pareto optimal set (PS), whose projection onto the objective space is termed the Pareto front (PF).

However, early research on multiobjective optimization has predominantly focused on single-modal scenarios, assuming that problems possess only a single PS. In practical applications, however, a significant number of multiobjective optimization problems exhibit multimodal characteristics, evolving into multimodal multiobjective optimization problems (MMOPs). According to the definition, an MOP is classified as an MMOP if it satisfies at least one of the following criteria [2]: (1) There exist at least two equivalent global PSs corresponding to the same PF; (2) There exists at least one local PS. This paper focuses on MMOPs with multiple global PSs. The research significance of such problems lies in the fact that when a particular optimal solution becomes infeasible due to constraint adjustments, decision-makers can rapidly switch to alternative equivalent solution sets without altering the target expectations, thereby maintaining the same objective performance. This capability significantly enhances the robustness and adaptability of decision-making systems.

In order to address MMOPs, numerous researchers have been dedicated to studying MMOPs more closely and have proposed various multimodal multiobjective evolutionary algorithms (MMEAs) designed specifically to handle such problems. Currently, common MMEAs can be mainly classified into the following categories [3]:

1) Pareto dominance-based MMEAs: This category of methods stratifies the population by defining dominance relationships among solutions, prioritizing non-dominated solutions to approximate the PF. For example, Omni-Optimizer [4] extends NSGAII [5] framework by incorporating both objective space crowding distance and decision space similarity metrics to identify distinct PS regions. DNEA [6] employs a dual-niching mechanism to maintain diversity in both spaces. However, its performance heavily relies on manually tuned niche radius, limiting its generality across different problem landscapes. Notably, traditional Pareto dominance focuses solely on objective space convergence, causing well-distributed individuals in the decision space to be deleted during non-dominated sorting.

2) Decomposition-based MMEAs: This category of methods decomposes the original problem into multiple scalar optimization sub-problems, approximating the Pareto front through collaborative optimization. MOEA/D-AD [7] introduces adaptive decomposition in the MOEA/D [8] framework, dynamically adjusting reference vectors and niche radius to preserve decision space diversity. MOEA/D-MM [9] assigns independent sub-populations to each weight vector and employs a greedy elimination strategy to ensure uniform sampling across different PSs.
3) Indicator-based MMEAs: This category of methods designs comprehensive indicators that quantify both objective and decision space characteristics to balance convergence and diversity. MMEA-WI [10] integrates the diversity of the decision space and the convergence of the objective space into a weighted indicator to optimize distribution in both spaces. FPITSEA [11] adopts a fuzzy preference indicator to guide the population evolution, aiming to detect both global and local PSs.
4) Other MMEAs: MMDE-SC [12] utilizes species conservation techniques to detect distinct PSs within established regions. HREA [13] introduces a multi-level convergence quality evaluation to safeguard decision space diversity. A notable breakthrough of HREA lies in its hierarchical ranking mechanism, which adeptly balances solution diversity and convergence, enhancing the algorithm's adaptability. CMMO [14] employs co-evolutionary strategies to balance convergence and diversity across objective and decision spaces. The convergence-prioritized population is tasked with identifying uniformly distributed solution sets on the PF and PS, whereas the convergence-relaxed population explores unexplored PSs to ensure comprehensive decision space coverage.

To effectively solve MMOPs, we propose a multimodal multiobjective optimization algorithm based on two-stage proportional selection. The algorithm comprehensively considers the distribution characteristics of individuals in both the decision space and the objective space. Given the characteristic that multiple independent PSs exist in the decision space, the algorithm first implements a decision-space sub-population partitioning strategy: the initial population is divided into multiple sub-populations, each of which evolves independently to produce offspring. This strategy helps to preserve and explore a greater number of distinct PSs. In the environmental selection phase, the algorithm employs a two-stage selection approach. The first stage is centered around preserving the population diversity within the decision space, preventing the elimination of individuals close to specific PSs. The second stage aims to retain as many different PSs as possible while guiding the population to converge towards the PF. Furthermore, the algorithm introduces a proportional selection strategy in environmental selection. The number of individuals to be retained at each level is determined according to specific ratios after non-dominated sorting. In the first stage, to ensure diversity, a large number of high-rank individuals are retained along with low-rank ones, as these individuals can facilitate the discovery of different PSs. In the second stage, with a focus on convergence, more low-rank individuals especially non-dominated ones are preserved.

The subsequent sections of this paper are arranged as follows. In Sect. 2, the detailed methodology of the proposed algorithm is presented. Results and discussion of the numerical experiments are provided in Sect. 3. Section 4 summarizes the paper and puts forward insights on potential future research directions.

2 Proposed Algorithm

2.1 General Framework of MMEA-TSPS

The framework of the proposed algorithm MMEA-TSPS is illustrated in Algorithm 1. The population is first initialized to form an initial set of N individuals (see Line 1). Subsequently, relevant parameters are initialized, including the current generation count (see Line 2), two-stage division parameters (see Line 3), and the number of sub-populations (see Line 4). When the current maximum number of generations is not reached, the following operations are performed: The population is partitioned into k sub-populations via the k-means algorithm to provide a basis for mutation operations (see Line 6). Offspring individuals are generated using a differential evolution (DE) [15] variant (see Line 7). The next-generation individuals are determined through an environmental selection mechanism (see Line 8). The DE variant and environmental selection operations will be described in detail in subsequent sections.

Algorithm 1. General Framework of MMEA-TSPS

Input: Population size N, maximum generations $MaxGen$, the number of the decision variables D

Output: Optimal population P

1: $P \leftarrow Initialization(N)$ /* Generate the population */
2: $gen \leftarrow 1$ /* gen indicates the number of current generations*/
3: $\alpha \leftarrow$ Set the proportion of the first evolutionary stage in the algorithm
4: $k \leftarrow$ Initialize the number of divided populations
5: **while** $gen \leq MaxGen$ **do**
6:     $cluster \leftarrow kmeans(P, k)$ /* $cluster$ stores the population category to which each individual belongs */
7:     $Off \leftarrow DE(P, k, cluster)$ /* Generate the offspring according to Algorithm 2*/
8:     $P \leftarrow ES(P, Off, N, MaxGen, gen, \alpha)$ /* Select individuals according to Algorithm 3*/
9:     $gen \leftarrow gen + 1$
10: **end while**
11: **return** P

2.2 Generation of Offspring

Algorithm 2 illustrates the detailed procedure for offspring generation. In this operation, the DE/rand-to-best/1 mutation is employed, but multiple individuals are selected as alternative guiding individuals to prevent the population from evolving in a single direction. Notably, offspring generation is performed based on sub-populations. For the pre-divided sub-populations, it is expected that they are distributed in different regions of the decision space as much as possible so that each sub-population can evolve toward the PS of its region during mutation, thereby facilitating the exploration of different PSs. First, all individuals of the corresponding sub-population are selected (see Line 3). Then, the number of guiding individuals is initialized and set to 1/10 of the number of individuals in the sub-population (see Line 4). Subsequently, guiding individuals are selected and stored in the population *guideP* (see Lines 5–8), where half of the individuals are filtered based on the crowding distance in the decision space (without considering the objective space, to retain diversity), and the other half are selected based on the crowding distance of non-dominated individuals in the decision space (to obtain convergent individuals). Thereafter, when each individual evolves, a guiding individual is randomly selected from the corresponding guiding population, and offspring are generated through DE/rand-to-best/1 mutation (see Lines 9–14).

Algorithm 2. Offspring Generation

Input: Population P, population division num k, group index *cluster*
Output: Offspring Off
1: $Off \leftarrow \emptyset$
2: **for** $i = 1 : k$ **do**
3:     $PickedPop \leftarrow$ Find the individual of the i-th population
4:     $guideNum \leftarrow$ Initialize the number of individuals used as guides
5:     $guideP \leftarrow \emptyset$
6:     $[FNo, MaxF] \leftarrow NDSort(PickedPop)$ /*Obtain the Pareto rank of the *PickedPop* and the max Pareto rank*/
7:     $guideP \leftarrow$ Select $guideNum/2$ individuals according the crowding distance of $FNo = 1$ in the *PickedPop*
8:     $guideP \leftarrow$ Select $guideNum/2$ individuals according the crowding distance of in the *PickedPop*
9:     **for** $j = 1 : sum(cluster == i)$ **do**
10:         $x \leftarrow$ select an individual randomly from *guideP*
11:         $v \leftarrow$ generate new mutation vector
12:         $offspring \leftarrow$ generate offspring using original vector and mutation vector
13:         $Off \leftarrow [Off; offspring]$
14:     **end for**
15: **end for**
16: **return** Off

To be specific, the crowding distance in the decision space of individual i can be calculated by the following:

$$CD_i = \sum_{j=1}^{N'/10} dist(i,j) \tag{2}$$

where N' is the corresponding population size, $dist(i,j)$ denotes the Euclidean distance from individual i to its j-th closest neighbor in the decision space.

In addition, at the mutation operation process, for one solution $\mathbf{x}_i$, first generate a mutation vector as follows:

$$\mathbf{v}_i = \mathbf{x}_i + F * (\mathbf{x} - \mathbf{x}_1) + F * (\mathbf{x}_2 - \mathbf{x}_3) \tag{3}$$

where $\mathbf{x}$ is selected randomly from the $guideP$. $\mathbf{x}_1$, $\mathbf{x}_2$ and $\mathbf{x}_3$ are selected randomly from the corresponding sub-population, F is the scaling factor which is usually 0.5.

Next, $\mathbf{v}_i$ and $\mathbf{x}_i$ make a crossover as follows:

$$\mathbf{u}_i^j = \begin{cases} \mathbf{v}_i^j, & \text{if rand(0,1) } \leq Cr \text{ or } j = randi([1, D]) \\ \mathbf{x}_i^j, & \text{otherwise} \end{cases} \tag{4}$$

where j is a random integer from 1 to D, Cr is the crossover rate(CR) and usually set to 0.5.

In this case, if the vector $\mathbf{u}_i^j$ exceeds the boundary of certain dimensions, it will be reinitialized within the range of the corresponding dimension.

2.3 Environmental Selection

In the environmental selection stage, a two-stage proportional selection method is adopted to select individuals for the next generation, with the specific operational procedure detailed in Algorithm 3. First, the original population and newly generated offspring are merged into a mixed population (see Line 2), followed by non-dominated sorting to partition individuals into different levels (see Line 3). Individuals are then selected from each level according to the corresponding selection strategy until the total number of selected individuals meets the population size requirement (see Lines 4–10). Specifically, the number of individuals selected from the i-th level num_i in the first stage is calculated by the following:

$$num_i = (1 - \frac{i+1}{MaxF}) * numtotal_i \tag{5}$$

And the number of individuals selected from the i-th level num_i in the second stage is calculated by the following:

$$num_i = (1 - \frac{i-1}{MaxF}) * numtotal_i \tag{6}$$

Algorithm 3. Environmental Selection

Input: Population P, offspring Off, population size N, maximum generations $MaxGen$, current algorithm generation num gen, two-stage control parameter α
Output: Selected population P'

$P' \leftarrow \emptyset$
$jointP \leftarrow P \cup Off$ /*Merge population P and offspring Off*/
$[FNo, MaxF] \leftarrow NDSort(jointP)$
for $i = 1 : MaxF$ **do**
  if $|P'| == N$ **then**
    break;
  end if
  $num_i \leftarrow$ Calculate the number of individuals selected at the Pareto rank i
  $P' \leftarrow$ Select num_i or $N - |P'|$ individuals according their crowding distance in the decision space when $gen/MaxGen \leq \alpha$ or according the truncation strategy of SPEA2 by using decision space when $gen/MaxGen > \alpha$
end for
return P'

Table 1. IGDX results of the compared algorithms on 28 test instances from CEC2019 and IDMP test suites, where the best mean for each test instance is highlighted.

Problem	CMMO	DNNSGAII	FPITSEA	HREA	MMEAWI	MO-Ring-PSO-SCD	TriMOEA-TA&R	MMEA-TSPS
MMF1	3.9133e-2 (1.61e-3) +	5.0904e-2 (4.90e-3) -	4.1767e-2 (1.66e-3) -	**3.8907e-2 (1.46e-3)** +	4.4351e-2 (2.21e-3) -	6.6166e-2 (8.77e-3) -	6.9760e-2 (9.53e-3) -	4.0473e-2 (1.76e-3)
MMF1_e	3.6737e-1 (9.61e-2) -	1.3155e+0 (7.06e-1) -	3.3861e-1 (7.46e-2) -	3.5024e-1 (4.63e-2) -	7.1307e-1 (2.34e-1) -	9.1878e-1 (4.37e-1) -	1.5010e+0 (8.63e-1) -	**2.4286e-1 (5.39e-2)**
MMF1_z	2.7713e-2 (1.32e-3) =	4.6555e-2 (1.08e-2) -	2.9852e-2 (1.33e-3) -	**2.7264e-2 (1.59e-3)** +	3.2804e-2 (2.17e-3) -	4.9010e-2 (9.60e-3) -	6.8176e-2 (1.11e-2) -	2.8085e-2 (1.38e-3)
MMF2	2.7485e-2 (5.35e-3) -	7.3368e-2 (4.00e-2) -	2.0482e-2 (7.77e-3) -	4.0821e-2 (1.38e-2) -	3.8961e-2 (2.07e-2) -	9.3584e-2 (5.54e-2) -	8.2635e-2 (4.78e-2) -	**1.0124e-2 (1.98e-3)**
MMF3	2.4655e-2 (6.99e-3) -	5.5507e-2 (2.82e-2) -	1.7082e-2 (4.75e-3) -	3.1817e-2 (7.24e-3) -	2.9123e-2 (8.37e-3) -	6.7581e-2 (2.88e-2) -	6.8870e-2 (3.49e-2) -	**1.0415e-2 (2.56e-3)**
MMF4	**1.9857e-2 (1.10e-3)** =	2.9533e-2 (2.97e-3) -	2.3503e-2 (1.52e-3) -	1.9930e-2 (8.67e-4) =	2.5425e-2 (2.35e-3) -	4.0873e-2 (6.05e-3) -	1.3526e-1 (1.74e-1) -	2.0190e-2 (1.35e-3)
MMF5	6.8574e-2 (3.03e-3) =	9.6882e-2 (8.98e-3) -	7.1352e-2 (3.14e-3) =	**6.4390e-2 (2.64e-3)** +	7.6723e-2 (4.18e-3) -	1.0747e-1 (9.39e-3) -	1.0951e-1 (9.52e-3) -	6.9974e-2 (3.33e-3)
MMF6	5.7461e-2 (2.44e-3) +	7.9306e-2 (7.10e-3) -	6.1297e-2 (2.12e-3) -	**5.5920e-2 (2.03e-3)** +	6.5638e-2 (2.16e-3) -	9.5028e-2 (1.35e-2) -	8.9398e-2 (1.33e-2) -	5.8361e-2 (1.81e-3)
MMF7	2.0009e-2 (1.46e-3) -	2.5587e-2 (3.62e-3) -	2.1798e-2 (2.36e-3) -	1.9862e-2 (7.40e-4) -	2.4708e-2 (2.20e-3) -	3.7405e-2 (6.19e-3) -	4.2179e-2 (1.93e-2) -	**1.9396e-2 (1.30e-3)**
MMF8	6.1662e-2 (1.32e-2) -	1.3361e-1 (3.74e-2) -	5.8161e-2 (4.70e-3) -	5.1724e-2 (5.10e-3) -	8.8463e-2 (1.90e-2) -	1.2060e-1 (3.98e-2) -	3.1147e-1 (9.89e-2) -	**4.8916e-2 (6.43e-3)**
MMF9	7.0454e-3 (3.88e-4) -	6.2429e-3 (1.05e-3) -	6.3923e-3 (3.75e-4) -	9.1371e-3 (5.39e-4) -	6.2680e-3 (2.15e-4) -	1.2344e-2 (1.86e-3) -	**3.1785e-3 (8.77e-5)** +	4.2082e-3 (1.12e-4)
MMF14	4.8655e-2 (6.42e-4) -	6.0045e-2 (1.77e-3) -	5.3036e-2 (1.14e-3) -	6.0078e-2 (2.76e-3) -	5.2551e-2 (7.89e-4) -	7.4133e-2 (4.11e-3) -	3.8593e-2 (5.88e-4) =	**3.8374e-2 (6.39e-4)**
MMF14_a	6.4462e-2 (1.41e-3) -	7.3192e-2 (3.43e-3) -	7.2690e-2 (2.74e-3) -	6.0722e-2 (9.88e-4) -	7.3217e-2 (2.18e-3) -	8.2999e-2 (4.65e-3) -	7.0764e-2 (1.82e-3) -	**4.7480e-2 (5.41e-4)**
Omni_test	1.0957e-1 (2.02e-2) -	2.7451e-1 (1.12e-1) -	1.3757e-1 (2.73e-2) -	1.3310e-1 (4.37e-2) -	5.4538e-1 (2.01e-1) -	7.6578e-1 (1.54e-1) -	4.6442e-1 (1.47e-1) -	**8.8353e-2 (2.60e-2)**
SYM_PART_rotated	8.5387e-2 (9.48e-3) -	9.3403e-1 (9.20e-1) -	8.1417e-2 (3.65e-3) -	7.0093e-2 (6.64e-3) -	1.7257e-1 (2.46e-1) -	2.8456e-1 (2.69e-1) -	1.5356e+0 (8.65e-1) -	**4.9740e-2 (2.49e-3)**
SYM_PART_simple	4.0140e-2 (3.07e-3) -	7.5072e-2 (2.20e-2) -	5.6981e-2 (2.99e-3) -	4.6586e-2 (1.97e-3) -	5.9452e-2 (4.24e-3) -	2.8841e-1 (3.09e-1) -	**2.0813e-2 (2.23e-3)** +	3.5172e-2 (1.89e-3)
IDMPM2T1	1.9185e-3 (4.79e-3) -	5.8385e-1 (2.32e-1) -	7.0555e-4 (7.04e-5) -	4.5874e-3 (9.11e-3) -	9.5760e-4 (1.11e-4) -	2.5878e-1 (3.21e-1) -	6.2983e-1 (1.65e-1) -	**5.3237e-4 (4.24e-6)**
IDMPM2T2	2.3541e-2 (1.23e-1) -	2.4926e-1 (3.28e-1) -	9.2071e-4 (6.86e-5) -	9.0626e-4 (3.75e-4) -	1.1147e-3 (1.12e-4) -	7.5713e-3 (4.77e-3) -	4.7278e-1 (3.12e-1) -	**7.5979e-4 (2.69e-5)**
IDMPM2T3	1.8092e-3 (2.56e-4) -	1.9228e-1 (2.95e-1) -	1.8378e-3 (2.60e-4) -	2.6496e-3 (1.02e-3) -	2.0585e-3 (2.44e-4) -	3.4765e-3 (5.41e-4) -	1.8319e-1 (2.76e-1) -	**1.0304e-3 (3.33e-5)**
IDMPM2T4	4.6148e-2 (1.71e-1) -	6.5106e-1 (1.21e-1) -	**6.5062e-4 (3.69e-5)** +	9.6157e-3 (1.38e-2) +	9.1437e-2 (2.32e-1) -	1.0483e-1 (2.27e-1) -	6.0835e-1 (1.98e-1) -	2.2954e-2 (1.23e-1)
IDMPM3T1	1.0734e-2 (2.54e-2) -	5.0356e-1 (2.05e-1) -	[illegible]	[illegible]	[illegible]	[illegible]	[illegible]	[illegible]
IDMPM3T2	4.3027e-2 (8.49e-2) -	5.0727e-1 (2.51e-1) -	9.3551e-3 (1.72e-4) -	1.0203e-2 (4.24e-3) -	2.5774e-2 (6.18e-2) -	1.6910e-1 (1.51e-1) -	5.7254e-1 (2.71e-1) -	**6.4228e-3 (6.83e-5)**
IDMPM3T3	3.0476e-2 (6.05e-2) -	2.9487e-1 (2.44e-1) -	1.4798e-2 (7.19e-3) -	1.4206e-2 (4.30e-3) -	4.3947e-2 (8.45e-2) -	2.4789e-2 (3.94e-3) -	4.4460e-1 (2.91e-1) -	**6.8191e-3 (7.20e-5)**
IDMPM3T4	5.4935e-2 (9.32e-2) -	7.2011e-1 (2.61e-1) -	9.3479e-3 (3.64e-4) -	1.6127e-2 (7.64e-3) -	2.3835e-1 (1.57e-1) -	4.2308e-1 (2.68e-1) -	8.0176e-1 (2.51e-1) -	**6.3577e-3 (4.78e-5)**
IDMPM4T1	4.1675e-1 (3.06e-1) -	1.1705e+0 (8.71e-2) -	6.3888e-2 (9.60e-2) -	4.1543e-1 (3.02e-1) -	1.0948e-1 (1.46e-1) -	9.0327e-1 (2.88e-1) -	1.1677e+0 (9.29e-2) -	**4.7709e-2 (1.42e-1)**
IDMPM4T2	1.5517e-1 (1.33e-1) -	1.0878e+0 (1.69e-1) -	**4.5425e-2 (7.62e-2)** =	6.9733e-1 (3.62e-1) -	5.4023e-1 (3.79e-1) -	8.6890e-1 (3.01e-1) -	1.0653e+0 (1.99e-1) -	1.4910e-1 (1.35e-1)
IDMPM4T3	1.3919e-1 (1.26e-1) -	9.2803e-1 (3.13e-1) -	5.6183e-2 (6.92e-2) -	6.7406e-1 (3.89e-1) -	5.3115e-1 (3.40e-1) -	2.0912e-1 (1.88e-1) -	7.9937e-1 (2.37e-1) -	**7.3612e-3 (9.86e-5)**
IDMPM4T4	1.2312e-1 (1.21e-1) -	1.1045e+0 (1.63e-1) -	8.8934e-2 (1.10e-1) -	8.2647e-1 (3.35e-1) -	8.4587e-1 (3.30e-1) -	7.7943e-1 (2.81e-1) -	1.0684e+0 (1.66e-1) -	**4.2603e-2 (9.27e-2)**
+/-/=	2/23/3	0/28/0	1/25/2	5/22/1	0/28/0	0/28/0	2/25/1	

where $MaxF$ is the maximum Pareto rank of the current population after non-dominated sorting, and $numtotal_i$ is the total number of individuals in the corresponding i-th level.

Notably, in the first stage, after determining the number of individuals to select per level, individuals are chosen by crowding distance in the decision space. It effectively maintains population diversity and preserves more individuals near different PSs. In the second stage, when $i = 1$, all non-dominated individuals are preferentially selected. The truncation operation of the SPEA2 [22] algorithm is applied to individual selection in the decision space, ensuring the population converges to the PF while maximizing the diversity of the decision space and guaranteeing the balanced distribution of individuals in both objective and decision spaces.

3 Experiment

3.1 Experimental Setting

In the experiments conducted in this work, 28 MMOPs from the CEC2019 test suite [16] and the IDMP test suite [17] are employed. In addition, seven state-of-the-art MMEAs are selected as competitor algorithms, including CMMO [14], DNNSGAII [18], FPITSEA [11], HREA [13], MMEA-WI [10], MO-Ring-PSO-SCD [16] and TriMOEA-TA&R [19]. For a fair comparison, all algorithms are configured with a population size of $N = 100 * D$, and the maximum generations $MaxGen$ is set to $5000 * D$. The remaining parameters are set as the values suggested in their respective original papers.

The IGDX [20] and IGD [21] are used to evaluate the performance in the decision and objective spaces respectively:

$$\mathrm{IGDX}(\mathbf{X}) = \frac{1}{|\mathbf{X}^*|} \sum_{\mathbf{y} \in \mathbf{X}^*} \min_{\mathbf{x} \in \mathbf{X}} \{ED(\mathbf{x}, \mathbf{y})\} \tag{7}$$

$$\mathrm{IGD}(\mathbf{X}) = \frac{1}{|\mathbf{X}^*|} \sum_{\mathbf{y} \in \mathbf{X}^*} \min_{\mathbf{x} \in \mathbf{X}} \{\mathrm{ED}(F(\mathbf{x}), F(\mathbf{y}))\} \tag{8}$$

where ED($\mathbf{x}$,$\mathbf{y}$) represents the Euclidean distance between $\mathbf{x}$ and $\mathbf{y}$. $\mathbf{X}$ and $\mathbf{X}^*$ represent the obtained solution set and a finite Pareto optimal solution set uniformly sampled from the true PS, respectively. Smaller IGDX and IGD values indicate that the obtained solutions are closer to the true PS or PF.

3.2 Results

This section presents the performance results of MMEA-TSPS and comparative algorithms. The results are tabulated in Tables 1 and 2, which present the mean and standard deviation derived from 30 independent trials. The Wilcoxon rank sum test is applied at a 0.05 significance level to assess statistical differences between results. In the last row of each table, the notations "+" and "-" denote the quantities of test problems where comparative algorithms exhibit significantly superior or inferior performance, respectively, relative to MMEA-TSPS. The symbol "=" indicates the number of test problems where no significant performance discrepancy is observed between MMEA-TSPS and the comparative algorithms.

Table 1 presents the results of the IGDX metric. The data reveals that among 28 test problems, the MMEA-TSPS algorithm achieves the best performance on 19 problems. When compared with algorithms such as DNNSGAII, MMEAWI, and MO-Ring-PSO-SCD, MMEA-TSPS demonstrates significantly superior performance across all test problems. In contrast to the remaining comparative

Table 2. IGD results of the compared algorithms on 28 test instances from CEC2019 and IDMP test suites, where the best mean for each test instance is highlighted.

Problem	CMMO	DNNSGAII	FPITSEA	HREA	MMEAWI	MO-Ring-PSO-SCD	TriMOEA-TA&R	MMEA-TSPS
MMF1	**2.9883e-3 (9.66e-5)** +	3.1744e-3 (1.08e-4) =	3.7477e-3 (1.40e-4) -	3.5870e-3 (2.18e-4) -	3.7657e-3 (3.86e-4) -	4.4767e-3 (2.86e-4) -	4.5435e-3 (8.74e-4) -	3.2236e-3 (1.87e-4)
MMF1_e	1.0107e-2 (1.76e-3) -	**6.3715e-3 (3.20e-3)** +	6.8005e-3 (1.11e-3) +	9.0035e-3 (2.17e-3) -	2.6261e-2 (7.43e-3) -	1.0840e-2 (1.57e-3) -	7.6690e-3 (3.25e-3) +	7.7845e-3 (8.90e-4)
MMF1_z	**2.9215e-3 (9.94e-5)** +	3.2241e-3 (2.26e-4) -	3.4756e-3 (4.45e-4) -	3.3310e-3 (1.75e-4) -	3.7061e-3 (2.77e-4) -	4.2579e-3 (2.60e-4) -	4.0691e-3 (5.48e-4) -	3.0353e-3 (1.26e-4)
MMF2	1.2196e-2 (1.63e-3) -	1.9928e-2 (7.17e-3) -	1.0450e-2 (3.33e-3) -	2.0082e-2 (8.60e-3) -	1.2518e-2 (2.27e-3) -	4.4826e-2 (1.55e-2) -	4.4914e-2 (7.19e-2) -	**7.8131e-3 (1.25e-3)**
MMF3	1.0422e-2 (1.50e-3) -	2.0275e-2 (1.93e-2) -	9.3270e-3 (1.56e-3) -	1.4830e-2 (5.87e-3) -	1.2209e-2 (4.02e-3) -	3.3513e-2 (1.04e-2) -	2.3162e-2 (1.77e-2) -	**7.1270e-3 (1.30e-3)**
MMF4	3.1531e-3 (1.46e-4) =	3.1076e-3 (1.26e-4) +	**2.9863e-3 (1.46e-4)** +	3.2926e-3 (1.26e-4) -	3.7114e-3 (2.47e-4) -	3.7613e-3 (2.08e-4) -	5.4186e-2 (8.61e-2) =	3.1864e-3 (1.04e-4)
MMF5	**3.2242e-3 (1.72e-4)** =	3.2272e-3 (1.48e-4) =	4.1013e-3 (2.40e-4) -	3.4868e-3 (1.18e-4) -	3.5934e-3 (2.22e-4) -	4.0181e-3 (2.60e-4) -	4.5748e-3 (1.88e-3) -	3.2549e-3 (1.45e-4)
MMF6	3.2296e-3 (1.76e-4) =	**3.0920e-3 (1.17e-4)** +	3.8627e-3 (2.16e-4) -	3.5174e-3 (1.95e-4) -	3.5225e-3 (2.29e-4) -	3.9655e-3 (3.12e-4) -	3.6340e-3 (6.84e-4) -	3.2976e-3 (1.44e-4)
MMF7	3.0523e-3 (1.09e-4) +	3.2495e-3 (1.50e-4) -	**3.0149e-3 (4.63e-4)** +	3.7461e-3 (2.76e-4) -	3.8881e-3 (2.36e-4) -	3.7140e-3 (2.14e-4) -	4.0293e-3 (1.39e-3) -	3.1541e-3 (1.30e-4)
MMF8	3.7092e-3 (1.44e-4) =	4.5203e-3 (4.29e-4) -	4.3179e-3 (2.57e-4) -	4.0550e-3 (2.35e-4) -	**3.6693e-3 (1.74e-4)** +	4.6531e-3 (2.76e-4) -	4.2528e-3 (4.63e-3) -	3.8460e-3 (2.74e-4)
MMF9	1.2203e-2 (5.53e-4) +	1.3750e-2 (9.81e-4) +	**1.0017e-2 (2.90e-4)** +	3.3738e-2 (3.95e-3) -	1.5746e-2 (1.14e-3) -	1.7556e-2 (2.19e-3) -	7.0682e-2 (5.08e-3) -	1.4527e-2 (1.26e-3)
MMF14	7.7876e-2 (1.38e-3) -	9.1271e-2 (2.20e-3) -	7.4884e-2 (1.56e-3) -	1.0651e-1 (6.19e-3) -	8.6858e-2 (2.08e-3) -	1.0491e-1 (3.17e-3) -	9.0955e-2 (1.11e-3) -	**6.5181e-2 (1.26e-3)**
MMF14_a	8.1993e-2 (1.31e-3) -	9.2488e-2 (3.19e-3) -	7.9640e-2 (2.20e-3) -	8.7273e-2 (2.12e-3) -	9.4065e-2 (2.65e-3) -	9.9420e-2 (4.19e-3) -	8.9133e-2 (2.12e-3) -	**6.6414e-2 (1.12e-3)**
Omni_test	1.3171e-2 (9.49e-4) -	1.3027e-2 (1.24e-3) -	2.4917e-2 (2.26e-3) -	1.4787e-2 (1.56e-3) -	1.4604e-2 (1.56e-3) -	4.2155e-2 (4.12e-3) -	2.0806e-2 (4.51e-3) -	**8.9162e-3 (6.34e-4)**
SYM_PART_rotated	1.5496e-2 (2.18e-3) =	1.8360e-2 (2.44e-3) -	2.0422e-2 (2.00e-3) -	1.6837e-2 (2.31e-3) -	1.9109e-2 (2.29e-3) -	4.2650e-2 (5.73e-3) -	2.7587e-2 (4.05e-3) -	**1.5012e-2 (1.37e-3)**
SYM_PART_simple	1.3884e-2 (1.91e-3) =	**1.3203e-2 (1.52e-3)** =	1.5394e-2 (1.69e-3) -	1.5155e-2 (1.50e-3) -	1.5149e-2 (1.79e-3) -	3.6526e-2 (4.45e-3) -	3.1448e-2 (3.62e-3) -	1.3665e-2 (1.53e-3)
IDMPM2T1	7.6504e-4 (1.98e-4) -	5.2032e-4 (3.72e-5) -	6.8898e-4 (1.13e-4) -	5.6575e-4 (1.02e-4) -	8.0260e-4 (9.83e-5) -	2.9369e-3 (2.81e-4) -	6.3631e-4 (1.38e-5) -	**4.7985e-4 (1.20e-5)**
IDMPM2T3	5.8668e-4 (4.24e-5) -	**4.7464e-4 (3.90e-5)** +	6.6103e-4 (1.40e-4) -	5.4632e-4 (2.63e-5) =	8.5700e-4 (8.16e-5) -	1.6036e-3 (1.69e-4) -	1.4869e-2 (3.12e-2) -	5.4224e-4 (1.60e-5)
IDMPM2T2	5.3755e-4 (3.67e-5) -	**5.0097e-4 (3.51e-5)** =	5.0471e-4 (3.66e-5) =	5.2474e-4 (2.31e-5) -	6.7341e-4 (4.58e-5) -	1.4748e-3 (1.51e-4) -	6.3723e-4 (3.65e-5) -	5.1028e-4 (1.32e-5)
IDMPM2T4	6.3340e-4 (1.33e-4) -	4.8568e-4 (1.54e-5) -	5.6553e-4 (1.39e-4) -	5.2274e-4 (1.24e-4) =	8.5735e-4 (3.05e-4) -	3.1107e-3 (6.00e-4) -	6.4401e-4 (2.26e-5) -	**4.7296e-4 (2.24e-5)**
IDMPM3T1	6.7958e-3 (4.76e-4) -	6.3473e-3 (1.92e-4) -	6.4787e-3 (5.58e-4) -	6.1406e-3 (3.04e-4) -	6.5092e-3 (2.72e-4) -	1.4475e-2 (1.40e-3) -	1.0075e-2 (5.96e-4) -	**4.4225e-3 (6.24e-5)**
IDMPM3T2	5.9390e-3 (3.04e-4) -	6.2653e-3 (1.80e-4) -	6.1033e-3 (4.22e-4) -	5.7669e-3 (2.29e-4) -	6.2247e-3 (2.21e-4) -	1.2366e-2 (1.25e-3) -	9.9981e-3 (7.94e-4) -	**4.3490e-3 (5.62e-5)**
IDMPM3T3	6.3588e-3 (4.85e-4) -	6.3182e-3 (2.16e-4) -	6.1391e-3 (2.22e-4) -	5.7575e-3 (1.69e-4) -	6.4002e-3 (2.64e-4) -	1.2912e-2 (1.13e-3) -	9.4896e-3 (9.51e-4) -	**4.4034e-3 (6.54e-5)**
IDMPM3T4	7.0045e-3 (9.40e-4) -	6.2190e-3 (1.41e-4) -	6.2943e-3 (5.15e-4) -	5.7628e-3 (2.94e-4) -	6.5583e-3 (6.17e-4) -	7.0806e-2 (2.47e-1) -	1.0139e-2 (5.76e-4) -	**4.3387e-3 (5.27e-5)**
IDMPM4T1	1.9560e-2 (4.63e-3) -	9.4551e-3 (3.75e-4) -	1.1225e-2 (1.15e-3) -	1.4320e-2 (5.80e-3) -	1.2458e-2 (2.03e-3) -	4.0801e-2 (4.09e-3) -	2.0787e-2 (1.84e-3) -	**6.0528e-3 (1.04e-4)**
IDMPM4T2	2.1130e-2 (5.68e-3) -	8.6622e-3 (3.35e-4) -	9.6665e-3 (8.05e-4) -	9.3934e-3 (2.00e-3) -	1.0839e-2 (2.71e-3) -	4.2634e-2 (8.14e-3) -	2.1601e-2 (1.74e-3) -	**5.4843e-3 (8.10e-5)**
IDMPM4T3	2.0753e-2 (4.29e-3) -	8.8307e-3 (4.06e-4) -	9.6922e-3 (8.96e-4) -	1.0937e-2 (2.97e-3) -	9.9174e-3 (9.11e-4) -	4.2438e-2 (8.03e-3) -	2.0364e-2 (9.17e-3) -	**5.6631e-3 (1.11e-4)**
IDMPM4T4	3.6802e-2 (1.09e-2) -	8.6496e-3 (3.91e-4) -	1.0325e-2 (1.16e-3) -	1.5846e-2 (1.28e-2) -	1.0204e-2 (1.60e-3) -	9.5094e-2 (5.27e-2) -	2.0293e-2 (2.10e-3) -	**5.4643e-3 (7.95e-5)**
+/-/=	4/18/6	5/19/4	4/23/1	0/26/2	1/27/0	0/28/0	1/26/1	

algorithms, MMEA-TSPS shows marginal inferiority only on a minimal number of problems while maintaining dominance in the vast majority of cases. The results strongly indicate that MMEA-TSPS can achieve excellent performance in the decision space, effectively identifying multiple PSs, and further validating its effectiveness and superiority in solving MMOPs.

Table 2 presents the performance results of the IGD metric. The data indicates that MMEA-TSPS achieves the best performance on 16 test problems. When compared individually with each competing algorithm, the proposed algorithm exhibits only slight inferiority on a minimal number of test problems while significantly outperforming others in the vast majority of cases. Further analysis reveals that MMEA-TSPS demonstrates excellent convergence ability in the objective space, effectively approximating the PF. Taken together, these results show that MMEA-TSPS achieves superior performance balance in both decision space and objective space compared to other algorithms, making it suitable for solving MMOPs.

3.3 Parameter Sensitive Analysis

During the population evolution phase, the population is divided into k subpopulations for independent evolution and offspring generation. Since the choice of k significantly impacts algorithm performance, a series of comparative experiments are designed to determine the optimal value. Specifically, we develop four modified algorithms with $k = 3$, 4, 6, and 7 compared with $k = 5$. These modified algorithms are tested on 28 benchmark problems and we record the results of a comparison of IGDX and IGD. As shown in Table 3, when $k = 3$, 4, or 7, the algorithm's comprehensive performance in both decision space and objective space is significantly inferior to that of $k = 5$. For $k = 6$, although the decision space performance is comparable to $k = 5$, there is a noticeable gap in objective space convergence. Based on these findings, $k = 5$ is selected as the optimal value in this study.

Additionally, the division ratio parameter α between the two stages is critical to algorithm performance and requires experimental optimization. We set different α values of 0.3, 0.4, 0.6 and 0.7 compared with $\alpha = 0.5$. As shown in Table 4, when $\alpha = 0.3$, 0.6, or 0.7, the algorithm's comprehensive performance in both spaces is significantly inferior to that of $\alpha = 0.5$. For $\alpha = 0.4$, the performance in both spaces is comparable to $\alpha = 0.5$. Based on these results, $\alpha = 0.5$ is determined as the optimal value in this study.

Table 3. Comparison results of MMEA-TSPS with different values of k on 28 test problems.

Algorithms	IGDX +/-/=	IGD +/-/=
MMEA-TSPS with k=3 vs MMEA-TSPS	0/16/12	1/5/22
MMEA-TSPS with k=4 vs MMEA-TSPS	0/5/23	0/2/26
MMEA-TSPS with k=6 vs MMEA-TSPS	2/2/24	1/4/23
MMEA-TSPS with k=7 vs MMEA-TSPS	3/5/20	1/5/22

Table 4. Comparison results of MMEA-TSPS with different values of α on 28 test problems.

Algorithms	IGDX +/-/=	IGD +/-/=
MMEA-TSPS with α=0.3 vs MMEA-TSPS	3/7/18	0/6/22
MMEA-TSPS with α=0.4 vs MMEA-TSPS	3/3/22	2/2/24
MMEA-TSPS with α=0.6 vs MMEA-TSPS	2/8/18	0/7/21
MMEA-TSPS with α=0.7 vs MMEA-TSPS	5/14/9	2/10/16

4 Conclusion

This paper proposes a novel multimodal multiobjective optimization algorithm based on two-stage proportional selection, which comprehensively considers the distribution characteristics of individuals in both decision space and objective space. Specifically, before population evolution, the main population is decomposed into several sub-populations. Each sub-population evolves independently to converge towards different PSs, thereby facilitating the discovery and preservation of diverse PSs. During offspring generation, the DE/rand-to-best/1 differential evolution strategy is employed. For each sub-population, a guide population is established to store candidate elite individuals, from which a guiding individual is randomly selected during mutation operations to generate differential vectors, thus avoiding offspring convergence. In the environmental selection phase, a two-stage hierarchical proportional selection mechanism is designed: the first stage proportionally selects individuals from each non-dominated level to retain potential PS approximators, while the second stage focuses on non-dominated individuals to ensure convergence to the global PF.

Experimental results demonstrate that MMEA-TSPS outperforms existing state-of-the-art algorithms in both decision space and objective space. Future work will explore optimization algorithms for multimodal multiobjective problems with local PS characteristics.

Acknowledgments. This work was partially supported by the National Natural Science Foundation of China (Grant Nos. 62573201,U23A20303 and 62573326), and Zhejiang Provincial Natural Science Foundation of China (Grant No. LZ25F030007).

References

1. Deb, K.: Multi-objective genetic algorithms: problem difficulties and construction of test problems. Evol. Comput. **7**(3), 205–230 (1999)
2. Yue, C.T., et al.: Differential evolution using improved crowding distance for multimodal multiobjective optimization. Swarm Evol. Comput. **62**, 100849 (2021)
3. Zhang, K., Shen, C., He, J., Yen, G.G.: Knee based multimodal multiobjective evolutionary algorithm for decision making. Inf. Sci. **544**, 39–55 (2021)
4. Deb, K., Tiwari, S.: Omni-optimizer: a generic evolutionary algorithm for single and multi-objective optimization. Eur. J. Oper. Res. **185**(3), 1062–1087 (2008)
5. Deb, K., Pratap, A., Agarwal, S., Meyarivan, T.: A fast and elitist multiobjective genetic algorithm: NSGA-II. IEEE Trans. Evol. Comput. **6**(2), 182–197 (2002)
6. Liu, Y., Ishibuchi, H., Nojima, Y., Masuyama, N., Shang, K.: A double-niched evolutionary algorithm and its behavior on polygon-based problems. In: Auger, A., Fonseca, C.M., Lourenço, N., Machado, P., Paquete, L., Whitley, D. (eds.) PPSN 2018. LNCS, vol. 11101, pp. 262–273. Springer, Cham (2018). https://doi.org/10.1007/978-3-319-99253-2_21
7. Tanabe, R., Ishibuchi, H.: A decomposition-based evolutionary algorithm for multimodal multi-objective optimization. In: Auger, A., Fonseca, C.M., Lourenço, N., Machado, P., Paquete, L., Whitley, D. (eds.) PPSN 2018. LNCS, vol. 11101, pp. 249–261. Springer, Cham (2018). https://doi.org/10.1007/978-3-319-99253-2_20
8. Zhang, Q., Li, H.: MOEA/D: a multiobjective evolutionary algorithm based on decomposition. IEEE Trans. Evol. Comput. **11**(6), 712–731 (2007)
9. Peng, Y., Ishibuchi, H.: A decomposition-based large-scale multimodal multi-objective optimization algorithm. In: 2020 IEEE Congress on Evolutionary Computation (CEC), pp. 1–8. IEEE (2020)
10. Li, W., Zhang, T., Wang, R., Ishibuchi, H.: Weighted indicator-based evolutionary algorithm for multimodal multiobjective optimization. IEEE Trans. Evol. Comput. **25**(6), 1064–1078 (2021)
11. Xie, Y., Li, J., Li, Y., Zhu, W., Dai, C.: Two-stage evolutionary algorithm with fuzzy preference indicator for multimodal multiobjective optimization. Swarm Evol. Comput. **85**, 101480 (2024)

12. Ji, J., Wu, T., Yang, C.: Multimodal multiobjective differential evolutionary optimization with species conservation. IEEE Trans. Syst. Man Cybern. Syst. **54**(2), 1299–1311 (2024)
13. Li, W., Yao, X., Zhang, T., Wang, R., Wang, L.: Hierarchy ranking method for multimodal multiobjective optimization with local pareto fronts. IEEE Trans. Evol. Comput. **27**(1), 98–110 (2023)
14. Ming, F., Gong, W., Wang, L., Gao, L.: Balancing convergence and diversity in objective and decision spaces for multimodal multi-objective optimization. IEEE Trans. Emerg. Topics Comput. Intell. **7**(2), 474–486 (2023)
15. Storn, R., Price, K.: Differential evolution-a simple and efficient heuristic for global optimization over continuous spaces. J. Global Optim. **11**(4), 341–359 (1997)
16. Yue, C., Qu, B., Liang, J.: A multi-objective particle swarm optimizer using ring topology for solving multimodal multiobjective Problems. IEEE Trans. Evol. Comput. **22**(5), 805–817 (2018)
17. Liu, Y., Ishibuchi, H., Yen, G.G., Nojima, Y., Masuyama, N.: Handling imbalance between convergence and diversity in the decision space in evolutionary multimodal multiobjective optimization. IEEE Trans. Evol. Comput. **24**(3), 551–565 (2019)
18. Liang, J.J., Yue, C., Qu, B.-Y.: Multimodal multi-objective optimization: a preliminary study. In: 2016 IEEE Congress on Evolutionary Computation (CEC), pp. 2454–2461. IEEE (2016)
19. Liu, Y., Yen, G.G., Gong, D.: A multimodal multiobjective evolutionary algorithm using two-archive and recombination strategies. IEEE Trans. Evol. Comput. **23**(4), 660–674 (2018)
20. Zhou, A., Zhang, Q., Jin, Y.: Approximating the set of pareto-optimal solutions in both the decision and objective spaces by an estimation of distribution algorithm. IEEE Trans. Evol. Comput. **13**(5), 1167–1189 (2009)
21. Coello Coello, C.A., Cortes, N.C.: Solving multiobjective optimization problems using an artificial immune system. Genet. Program Evolvable Mach. **6**(2), 163–190 (2005)
22. Zitzler, E., Laumanns, M., Thiele, L.: SPEA2: improving the Strength Pareto Evolutionary Algorithm. Technical Report 103 (2001)

A Multidimensional Sentiment Analysis Model for Experience Assessment

Wanwan Zheng[1(✉)], Yang Li[2,3], Koji Makino[4], Katsuhisa Yoshikawa[4], Kunihiko Hara[5], Hiroshi Shibata[3], and Hideki Ohira[3]

[1] Humanity Center for Anthropocenic Actors and Agency, Graduate School of Humanities, Nagoya University, Nagoya, Japan
zheng@nagoya-u.jp
[2] Faculty of Business Administration, Tohoku-gakuin University, Sendai, Japan
[3] Graduate School of Informatics, Nagoya University, Nagoya, Japan
[4] Advanced Vehicle Planning Department, Toyota Motor Corporation, Nagoya, Japan
[5] Education and Research Center for Future Value Creation, Nagoya University, Nagoya, Japan

Abstract. In recent years, the increasing advancement and homogenization of products and services have made differentiation solely based on functionality or price increasingly difficult. Within this context, emotional resonance—emotional responses evoked through user experiences—has gained increasing recognition as a critical factor in contemporary marketing strategies. This study aims to quantitatively assess experiential value by analyzing users' emotional responses during interactions with products or services. To this end, two multidimensional sentiment analysis models were proposed, which extend beyond the conventional binary classification of positive and negative sentiments. Experimental results demonstrated that the proposed models outperform existing sentiment analysis models in accurately reproducing and classifying human emotions within a multidimensional space. Moreover, the models' effectiveness was demonstrated not only in terms of predictive accuracy but also in its ability to capture and reproduce the latent structure of emotions.

Keywords: Experience interaction · Experiential value · Emotional resonance · Multidimensional sentiment analysis · Emotion structure modeling

1 Introduction

Traditional marketing has primarily focused on differentiating products and services based on functionality, price and utility. However, in the contemporary context—where consumers' decision-making criteria and value perceptions have undergone significant shifts—such strategies are no longer sufficient to meet the increasingly diverse demands of consumers. Modern consumers are now not only

T. Hao et al. (Eds.): BESC 2025, LNCS 16431, pp. 55–72, 2026.
https://doi.org/10.1007/978-981-95-7138-3_5

incline to view the functional attributes, benefits, and quality of products, but also perceive brand image as a source of positive association. Beyond these elements, there is a growing expectation for products, communications, and marketing campaigns that captivate the senses, resonate emotionally, and stimulate intellectual engagement [17]. In response to these emerging consumer needs, the concept of "experiential marketing" has been introduced.

In experiential marketing, the marketing process is not considered to conclude at the point of purchase. Instead, it is regarded as essential to evoke a sense of comfort in consumers prior to the act of consumption, to provide a satisfying experience during consumption, and to sustain that satisfaction even after consumption [7,19]. By emphasizing consumer agency and fostering the development of sensory and emotional connections, experiences perceived as pleasurable by consumers can be shaped, thereby contributing to the enhancement of brand value. This perspective was articulated nearly three decades ago by [4], who noted that *"in many situations, differentiation that is considered meaningless from the traditional perspectives is nonetheless appreciated by consumers, and the competitive advantage created by such seemingly meaningless attributes can be sustained."* This observation underscores the early recognition of the effectiveness of experiential marketing, which is fundamentally rooted in consumers' subjective experiences.

On the other hand, it has been well established that emotions exert a powerful, predictable, and pervasive influence on decision-making [12]. In the field of behavioral economics, it is widely recognized that decision-making processes can be more accurately understood by incorporating psychological factors into analysis [9,10]. Reference [1], after synthesizing recent studies that conceptualize emotions as antecedents to decision-making, emphasized that even incidental emotions—those elicited by unrelated prior experiences—can influence subsequent choices through carried-over appraisal tendencies. Accordingly, understanding the emotions that emerge through experiences is critical not only for cultivating long-term relationships between consumers and brands, but also for fostering product and service loyalty. Ultimately, such emotional insight contributes to effective differentiation from competitors.

However, the concept of "emotion" is inherently ambiguous and difficult to capture. For example, even when individuals undergo the same experience, their emotional responses may vary depending on the timing of inquiry. Moreover, when multiple emotions are experienced simultaneously, individuals may be unaware of their own emotional states. Even when awareness is achieved, it may be challenging to determine which emotion is most dominant (Fig. 1). Given the subjective and fluctuating nature of emotions, quantitative measurement approaches are essential for reliably capturing and recording emotional responses.

Sentiment analysis refers to the process of detecting the contextual polarity of textual content [6]. This analysis is typically conducted at three levels: the aspect level, the sentence level, and the document level [3]. Aspect-level analysis aims to identify sentiment associated with specific entities, thereby enabling the

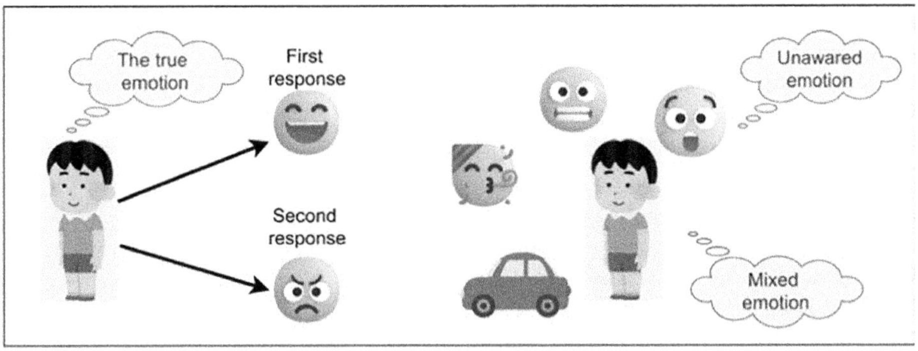

Fig. 1. Visualization of the complexity of human emotional responses, including temporal fluctuations, lack of self-awareness, and the coexistence of multiple emotions.

identification of what users like or dislike. In contrast, sentence- and document-level analyses focus on the overall sentiment expressed within the whole text. Because individual sentences or documents may contain multiple and potentially conflicting sentiments, a simple binary model—categorizing sentiment as either positive or negative—is often insufficient to capture the complexity of emotional experiences. Accordingly, recognizing the multidimensional nature of emotion is essential for both theoretical advancement and practical application [2,21].

Regarding to the computational approaches, current text-based sentiment analysis primarily relies on the construction of dictionaries and machine learning models trained on large text corpora [20]. With the advent and success of transformer architecture, a range of large language models (LLMs) has been developed with remarkable performance in capturing latent semantic meanings at the sentence and document levels. In addition, a growing body of research over the past half decade has enabled multimodal sentiment analysis to leverage complementary sources of information to enhance sentiment detection. Despite these advancements, most existing studies have focused on binary classification—such as positive versus negative [5,22]—or three-class classification involving positive, negative, and neutral categories [23,25]. Relatively few models have been developed for multidimensional sentiment analysis, largely due to the scarcity of suitable annotated datasets. Social media texts are frequently used as training data; however, they are often characterized by spelling errors, neologisms, and grammatical inconsistencies, which necessitate extensive preprocessing. In addition, the manual annotation of large-scale datasets remains a labor-intensive and time-consuming process. Most available resources are also limited to the English language [13]. Moreover, sentiment analysis approaches have been shown to be highly domain-dependent, thereby limiting their generalizability across different contexts [8].

In this study, two Japanese-language questionnaires were developed to assess product/service experiences and the diverse emotional responses elicited. The questionnaires were designed in collaboration with psychological researchers, and data collection was conducted through professional survey agencies, ensuring the acquisition of high-quality data. Based on the collected data, multidimensional sentiment analysis models were developed to assess experiential value by fine-tuning two existing state-of-the-art language models. The proposed models offer several key advantages: (1) they enable the quantification and precise identification of subjective and ambiguous emotional responses in terms of both emotional categories and intensities; and (2) to enhance practical applicability, they output a range of multidimensional emotions—namely “joy,” “anger,” “sadness,” “fear,” “surprise,” “disgust,” “expectation,” and “trust”—thereby enabling the measurement of both basic and mixed emotional states.

The remainder of this article is organized as follows. Section 2 describes the data collection process. Section 3 outlines the methodology, with a focus on the fine-tuning procedures and learning results. Section 4 presents the experimental evaluations. Finally, Sect. 5 summarizes the findings and discusses potential directions for future research.

2 Data Collection

2.1 Data 1

Participants were recruited from a market research company (Cross-Marketing; https://www.cross-m.co.jp/en/) panel. Data collection was conducted in March 2025. A total of 10,529 Japanese adults (mean age = 45.34, SD = 14.86) passed the attention-check questions and completed the questionnaire. Participants were evenly distributed across experimental conditions, age groups (approximately 10-year intervals), and gender. Participants received compensation through the market research company.

The study was conducted as a web-based survey. The entire survey took approximately 20 minutes to complete. At the beginning of the survey, participants reviewed an informed consent form outlining the study overview and only proceeded if they agreed to participate. After answering demographic questions, participants were randomly assigned to watch one of the two narrative conditions. Two attention-check questions were administered immediately after the movie, and only participants who passed both questions were allowed to continue with the remainder of the survey.

Two narrative conditions were used in this study. Both narratives depicted a protagonist driving a rental car to the airport who encounters traffic congestion along the way. During the traffic delay, the protagonist communicates with a friend who will meet them at the airport, discussing their upcoming travel plans to Thailand. In the new-tech condition, the rental car was equipped with autonomous driving capabilities that engaged during the traffic jam, and the protagonist interacted with their friend through an in-vehicle virtual reality system. In the control condition, the rental car lacked autonomous driving features, and the protagonist communicated with their friend via voice call using the car’s built-in speakers connected to a smartphone. The narratives were presented in an audio format through voice narration, accompanied by nine sequential static images that illustrated the story progression. Visual stimuli were synchronized with the corresponding narrative segments to provide contextual information for each scene. Each narrative lasted 7–8 minutes.

After the post-movie affect evaluation, participants provided their opinions on the story content and the product in free-text entry questions, each requiring at least 50 Japanese characters. Participants also evaluated the emotions in their text responses by indicating the percentage of each type of emotion from Plutchik's wheel of emotions (i.e., joy, anger, sadness, fear, surprise, disgust, expectation, trust) that was contained in the text. Participants then indicated their willingness to pay for the product from both customer and producer perspectives.

2.2 Data 2

Participants were recruited from a crowd-sourcing service (Lancers; https://www.lancers.jp/). Data collection was conducted in November 2024. A total of 541 Japanese adults (mean age = 45.12, SD = 10.00) completed the questionnaire. Participants were randomly allocated across experimental conditions. Each participant received compensation of 517 JPY through the site.

The study was conducted as a web-based survey. The entire survey took approximately 20 minutes to complete. Participants reviewed an informed consent form and only proceeded if they agreed to participate. After answering demographic questions, participants were randomly assigned to watch one of the two narrative conditions and answered the attention-check questions, which were identical to Data 1.

As in Data 1, we also measured participants' affect status, the favorability of the story and the products, the free-text format opinions on the story content and the product, and the emotion contained in the text. Accordingly, each participant submitted two separate text responses.

Participants also indicated their willingness to pay for the product from both customer and producer perspectives, randomly using the slider style, the binary-choices style, or the single-choice format. Those formats were designed to verify the willingness to pay measurement.

In this study, only the set of text responses and their corresponding annotated emotions were used. Within Data 1, 70% were utilized as training data and 30% as validation data. Data 2 was used as the test data (Table 1).

The study received ethical approval from the Ethics Review Committee, Nagoya University Graduate School of Medicine (approval no. 2023–0324). All participants provided informed consent online before participating in the survey.

Table 1. Overview of the online survey dataset used in this study.

	Data 1		**Data 2**
	Training Data	**Validation Data**	**Test Data**
Number of respondents	10,529		541
Number of text responses	14,741	6,317	1,082

3 Methodology

Figure 2 illustrates the construction process of the multidimensional sentiment analysis model developed in this study. In this model, the general-purpose language model was adopted as the base model, and fine-tuning was performed using the collected labeled dataset specifically designed for experience assessment. Each text response was annotated with eight emotion labels (e.g., joy: 0.34, sadness: 0.12), with the total sum of all emotion values normalized to 1.0. This procedure enabled the model to predict the intensity of each emotion in a multi-label classification setting. At the output layer, the Softmax activation function was employed to generate a probability distribution over the emotion labels, allowing for a quantitative representation of how strongly each emotion is expressed.

3.1 Pre-trained Language Model: Japanese-LUKE

In recent years, the application of LLMs to a wide range of natural language processing tasks has advanced rapidly; however, models tailored for sentiment analysis remain limited. This scarcity is particularly pronounced in the context of the Japanese language. As of June 4, 2025, 125 such models were available on Hugging Face, yet only eight had been downloaded more than 100 times. Moreover, only one of these models is capable of outputting eight emotions: a sentiment analysis model based on the Language Understanding with Knowledge-based Embeddings (LUKE, [24]), namely Luke-Japanese-large-sentiment-analysis (Japanese-LUKE). In this study, Japanese-LUKE (hereafter referred to as LUKE) was adopted as one of pre-trained language models.

LUKE is a language model that extends RoBERTa by incorporating an entity-aware self-attention mechanism. This mechanism enables the model to dynamically adjust attention scores—representing the relationships between words—based on specific word pairings within a given context. Such a design

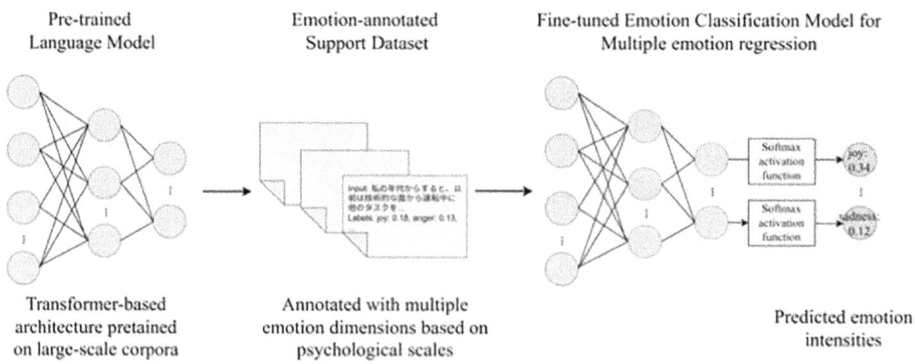

Fig. 2. Fine-tuning process of the multidimensional sentiment analysis model.

enables LUKE to capture word relationships with greater precision and contextual sensitivity. Reference [24] reported that LUKE achieved state-of-the-art performance across several benchmark tasks, including Open Entity (entity recognition), TACRED (relation extraction), CoNLL-2003 (named entity recognition), ReCoRD (reading comprehension with commonsense reasoning), and SQuAD 1.1 (Stanford question answering dataset).

During the fine-tuning process, the architecture of Japanese-LUKE was extended by incorporating a regression head designed to output an eight-dimensional vector, with each dimension corresponding to one of the target emotion values. The model was trained using the Mean Squared Error (MSE) loss function and optimized with the AdamW optimizer at a learning rate of 2e-5. The bath size was set to eight. During each training step, gradients were computed via backpropagation, and model parameters were updated accordingly by the optimizer. Training was conducted over five epochs, with the model being updated on the training data and evaluated on a validation data at the end of each epoch using the same MSE loss function. Finally, the average validation loss converged to 0.037.

3.2 Pre-trained Language Model: Gpt-3.5-Turbo

The other pre-trained model employed in this study was OpenAI's gpt-3.5-turbo (OpenAI, 2023). To align with OpenAI's fine-tuning protocol for chat-based models, the training data were converted into JSONL format, following the chat message structure. Specifically, each input text was framed as a user prompt requesting a psychological analysis of the emotional state within texts. The standardized prompt was *"You are one of the world's leading psychoanalysts, highly skilled at analyzing the psychological state of an author based on written text. Please analyze the following text and provide emotional scores based on your assessment:"* The assistant's response consisted of emotion scores across eight predefined categories, with the constraint that the sum of all emotion scores for each instance equaled 1.0. The resulting JSONL file was then uploaded to OpenAI's server via the Python API, specifying the purpose as "fine-tune". Finally, the training loss converged to 0.074.

This approach enabled the model to learn not only the distribution of emotional expressions but also the appropriate format for responding to open-ended prompts about human affect in a structured and informative manner. The fine-tuned model can subsequently be accessed via the OpenAI API to infer emotion scores from free-text Japanese inputs.

4 Experimental Evaluation

For model evaluation, comparative analyses were conducted among human annotations, the base models (LUKE and gpt-3.5-turbo), and the models developed in this study (emotion-fine-tuned LUKE and emotion-fine-tuned ChatGPT). These comparisons were performed using the test data to assess multiple aspects of model performance, including prediction accuracy, the distribution of emotion scores, and the representation performance of emotional opposition.

4.1 Prediction Accuracy

For the evaluation of prediction accuracy, human annotations were regarded as ground truth, and the model outputs were treated as predicted values. Three evaluation metrics were employed: MSE, which quantifies the difference between predicted and true values; Pearson correlation coefficient (r), which measures the strength of the linear relationship between them; and JensenâĂŞShannon Divergence (JS Divergence), which captures the dissimilarity between the probability distributions of the predicted and true values. The evaluation results for each metric are presented in Fig. 3.

Based on the results of MSE and r, the emotion-fine-tuned LUKE demonstrated the lowest prediction errors (MSE: 0.006–0.037; r: 0.356–0.662). In contrast, the emotion-fine-tuned ChatGPT achieved the smallest values in terms of JS divergence (0.015–0.052), indicating the highest similarity with human annotations. By comparison, the base ChatGPT model exhibited higher prediction errors (MSE: 0.010–0.053), weaker correlations (r: -0.310–0.642), and substantially higher JS divergence values (JS: 0.648–0.865). Similarly, the base LUKE model showed relatively high errors (MSE: 0.012–0.237), weaker correlations (r: -0.027–0.559), and higher JS divergence values (JS: 0.096–0.714). For both ChatGPT and LUKE, some emotions even exhibited negative correlations, suggesting unreliable alignment with human annotations.

Although minor variations were observed across evaluation metrics, both of the fine-tuned sentiment analysis models consistently produced predictions that closely aligned with human annotations, demonstrating their effectiveness in capturing nuanced emotional patterns.

4.2 Distribution of Emotion Scores

In this section, the distributional variability of emotion scores was examined by comparing human annotations with the predictions generated by each model. To minimize the impact of extreme values, outliers were removed using the interquartile range (IQR). Specifically, for each emotion, scores falling below the lower bound (Q1 - 1.5× IQR) or above the upper bound (Q3 + 1.5 × IQR) were excluded. Here, Q1 and Q3 denote the first and third quartiles, respectively.

Figure 4 illustrates the distributional spread of emotion scores across different emotions. Human annotations exhibited a wide range of score distributions for each emotion, reflecting the natural diversity and complexity of emotional intensity. In contrast, LUKE tended to output scores that were heavily skewed toward specific emotions, thereby limiting its ability to capture emotional multidimensionality. By comparison, the fine-tuned emotion analysis models generated score distributions that more closely resembled those of human annotation across multiple emotions, indicating their effectiveness in capturing both the balance and richness of emotional responses.

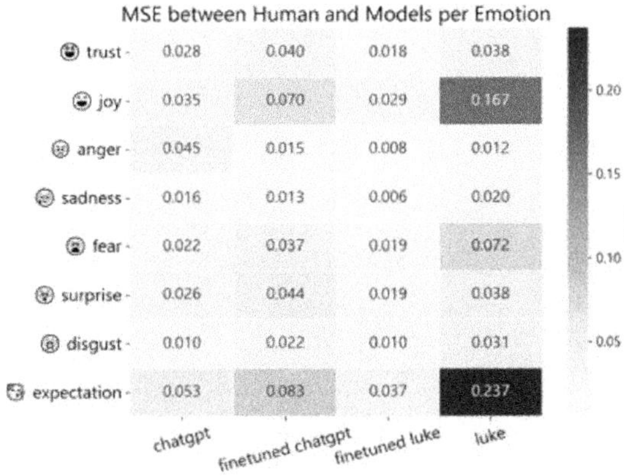

(a) MSE

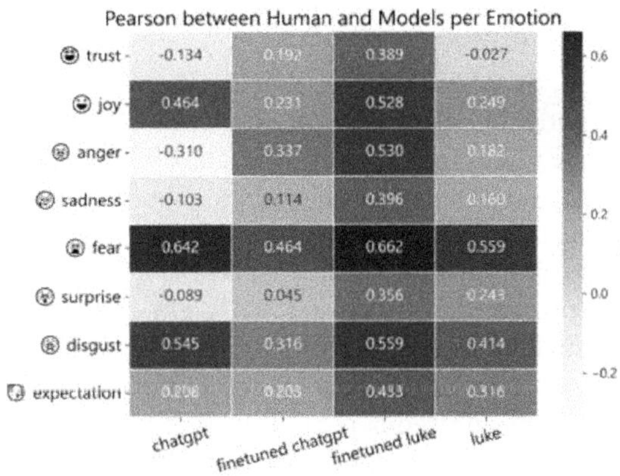

(b) r

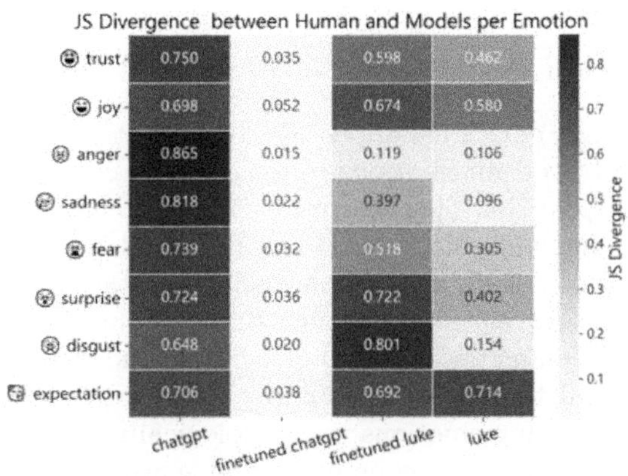

(c) JS Divergence

Fig. 3. The degree of similarity between human judgements and model-generated predictions.

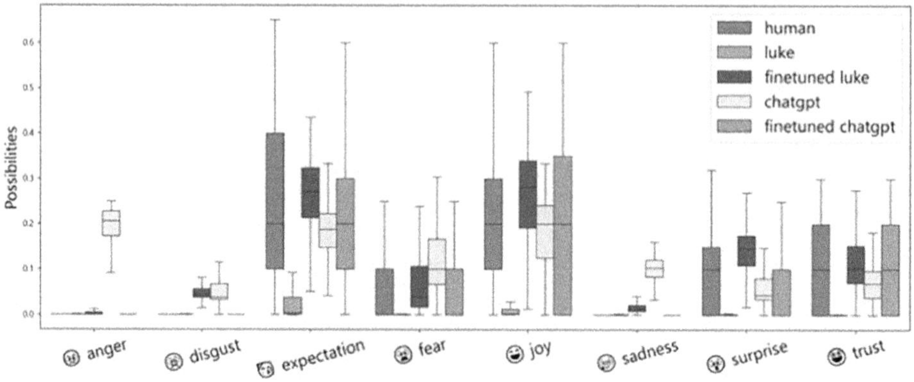

Fig. 4. Distribution of predicted emotion scores for each model and the human annotations.

Figure 5 presents a visual comparison of the distribution of emotional scores generated by each model, using Principal Component Analysis (PCA). Each data point represents a single text response, with different symbols denoting the corresponding model. The visualization reveals that the fine-tuned models not only produced distributions that closely aligns with human annotations, but also exhibited a wide dispersion of emotion scores, effectively capturing a broad spectrum of emotional expressions. In contrast, LUKE's outputs were concentrated within a narrow region, indicating limited emotional diversity. While ChatGPT demonstrated a moderate degree of variability, its outputs are densely clustered near the center, suggesting limited separability of strongly expressed emotions.

Overall, the PCA visualization confirmed that fine-tuning improves the spatial structure of the base models' emotional representations, resulting in closer alignment with human judgments.

4.3 Representation Performance of Emotional Opposition

In emotion psychology, emotional opposition refers to the phenomenon in which the intensification of a certain emotion is often accompanied by the attenuation of its opposing counterpart [14,15]. This concept is central to many influential theoretical frameworks, including Russell's circumplex model of affect and Plutchik's wheel of emotions, both of which posit that affective states are organized within a structured space where opposing emotions occupy opposite poles. For example, joy is typically regarded as the opposite of sadness, and trust as the opposite of disgust. Such antagonistic relationships imply that the simultaneous occurrence of strong levels of opposing emotions is psychologically improbable [11,16].

Recent advances in affective computing and sentiment analysis have led to the development of increasingly sentiment analysis models. However, most of these models are evaluated primarily based on their predictive accuracy for individual emotion labels, often overlooking the internal relational structure among

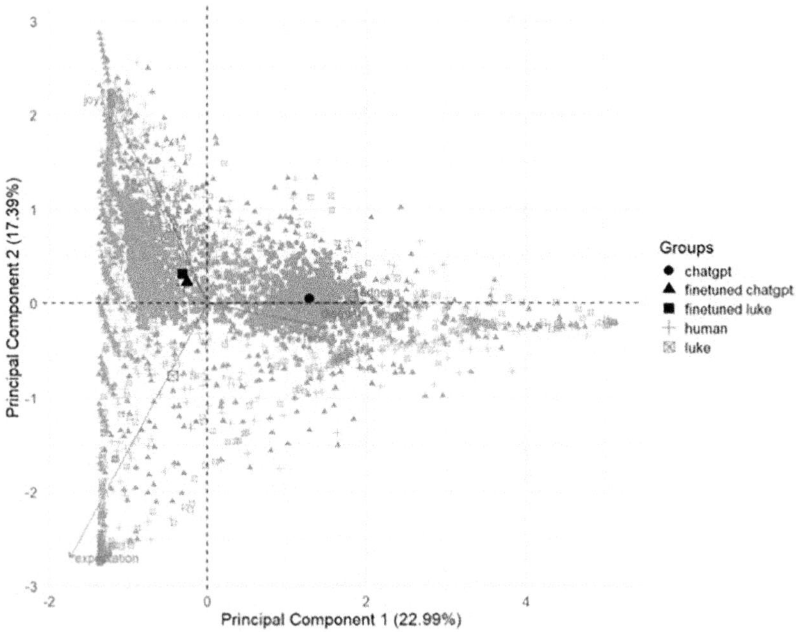

Fig. 5. A visual comparison of the distribution of emotional scores generated by each model using PCA.

emotions. Incorporating emotional opposition as an evaluation criterion provides a theoretically grounded method for assessing whether a model can reproduce the empirically observed structure of human affect, thereby enhancing its psychological plausibility and interpretability [18].

This section focuses on emotional opposition. Based on Plutchik's wheel of emotions, the analysis targeted mixed emotions formed through combinations of eight basic emotions: joy, anger, sadness, fear, surprise, disgust, expectation, and trust. The mixed emotions examined included *optimism* (joy + expectation), *admiration* (trust + surprise), *shame* (fear + disgust), and *resentment* (sadness + anger).

Figure 6 illustrates the smoothed variation in the scores of these mixed emotions, with texts arranged along the horizontal axis in ascending order of their optimism scores. In human annotations, increases in optimism were accompanied by decreases in shame and resentment scores, indicating a successful structural reproduction of emotional opposition, as predicted by emotion theory. In contrast, LUKE tended to produce either flat or highly polarized score distributions, failing to capture natural emotional transitions or oppositional dynamics. While ChatGPT exhibited smoother trends in score variation, it did not preserve the expected inverse relationship between optimism and resentment, highlighting limitations in its ability to model emotional opposition. By comparison, the emotion-fine-tuned models effectively reproduced the inverse pattern observed in

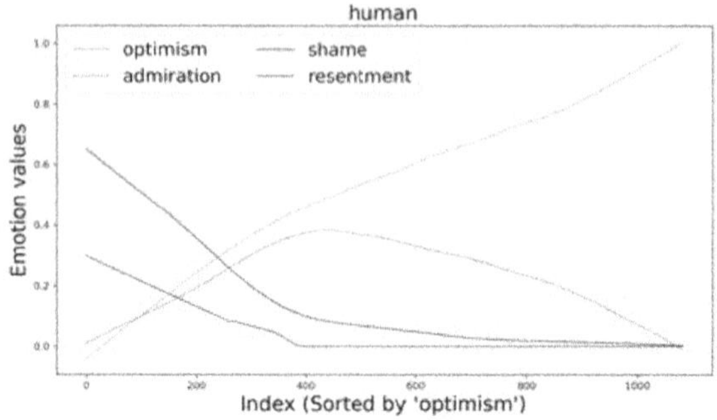

(a) Human annotations

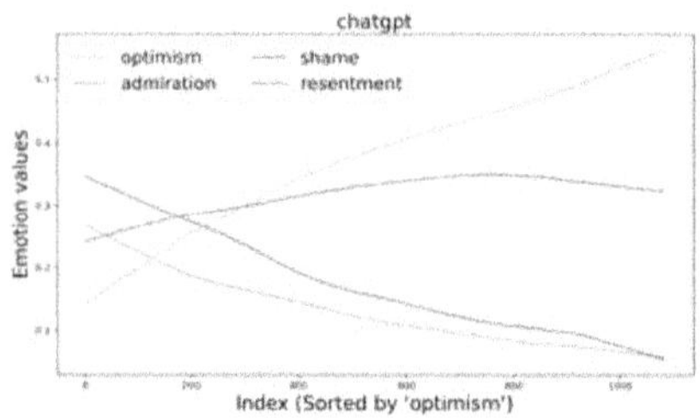

(b) ChatGPT

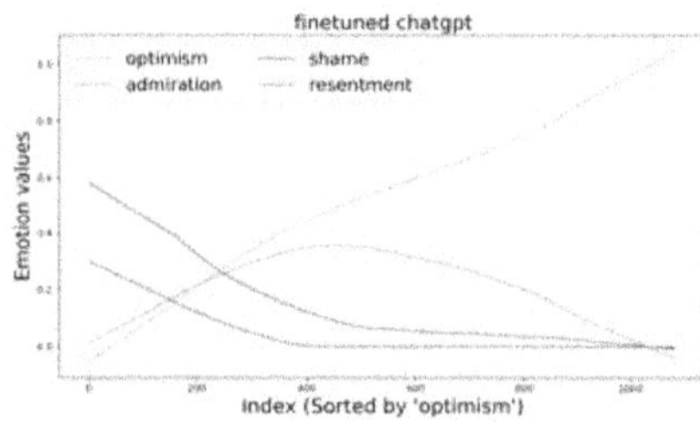

(c) Emotion-fine-tuned ChatGPT

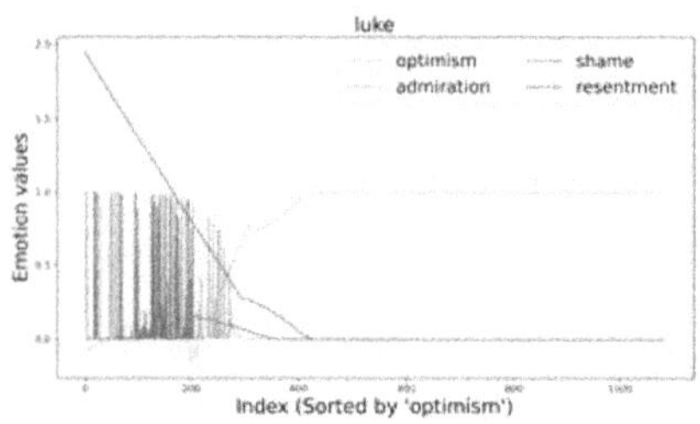

(d) LUKE

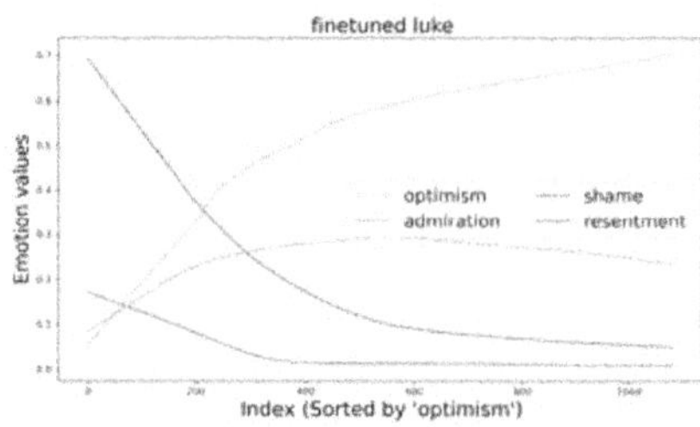

(e) Emotion-fine-tuned LUKE

Fig. 6. Comparison of the representation performance of emotional opposition in human annotations, existing models, and emotion-fine-tuned models (four types of mix emotions).

human annotations: as optimism increased, both shame and resentment declined. Importantly, the models also suppressed extreme outputs (i.e., 0 or 1), yielding more stable and balanced emotional representations.

To further assess alignment with human affective perception, Welch's t-tests were conducted to determine whether statistically significant differences existed between human annotations and model outputs (Fig. 7). The results revealed that both LUKE and ChatGPT significantly diverged from human ratings across all emotions. In contrast, the emotion-fine-tuned model exhibited greater consis-

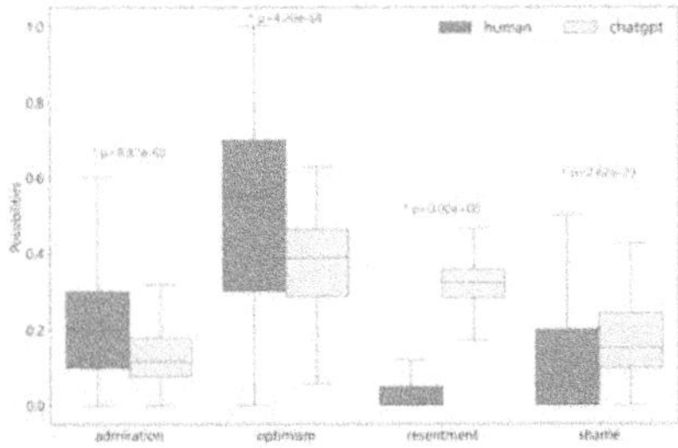

(a) Human annotations *vs.* ChatGPT

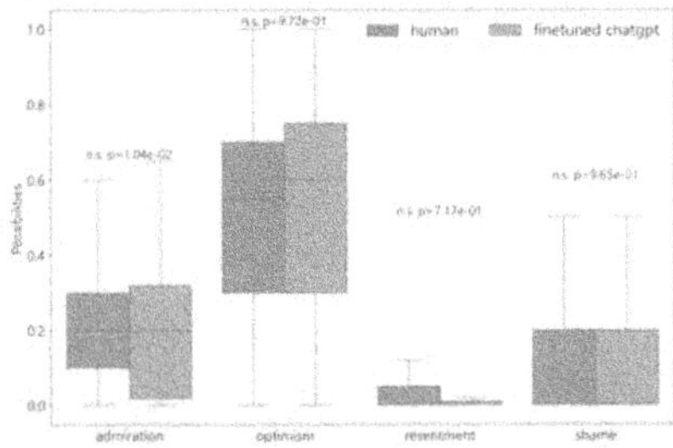

(b) Human annotations *vs.* Emotin-fine-tuned ChatGPT

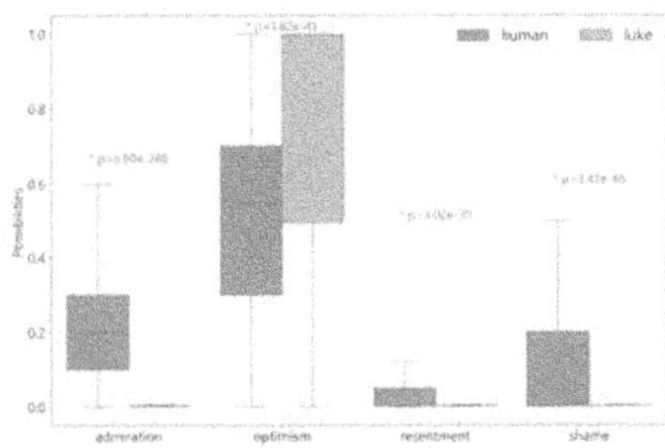

(c) Human annotations *vs.* LUKE

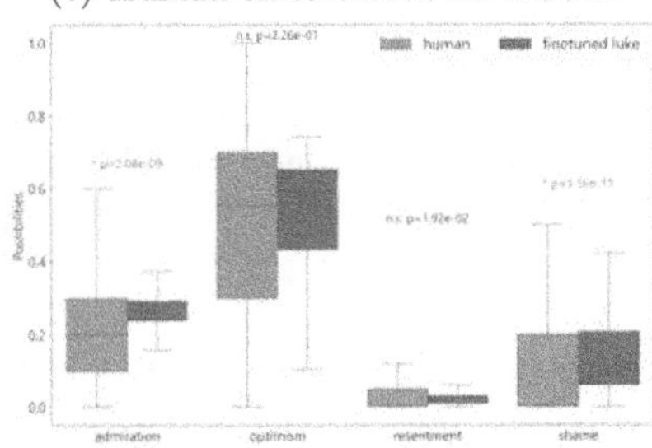

(d) Human annotations *vs.* Emotion-fine-tuned LUKE

Fig. 7. Comparison of emotion score distributions between human annotations, existing models, and emotion-fine-tuned models with the results of Welch's *t*-tests (four types of mix emotions).

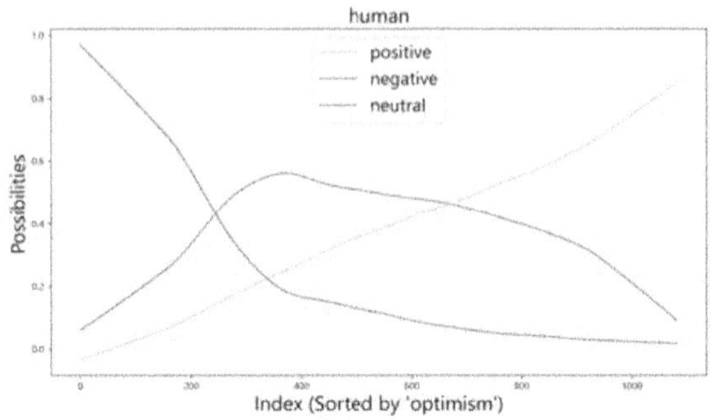

(a) Human annotations

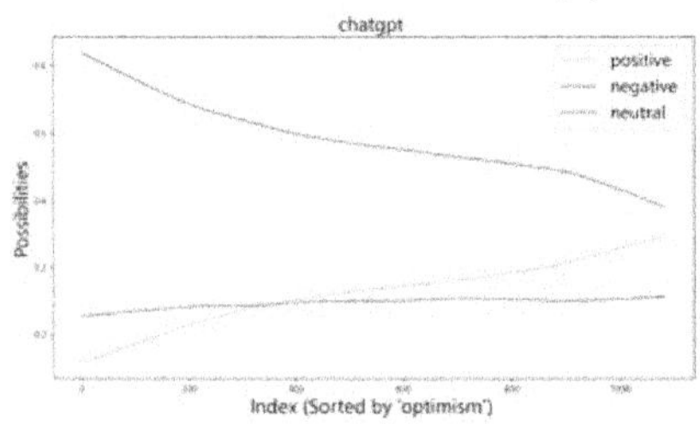

(b) ChatGPT

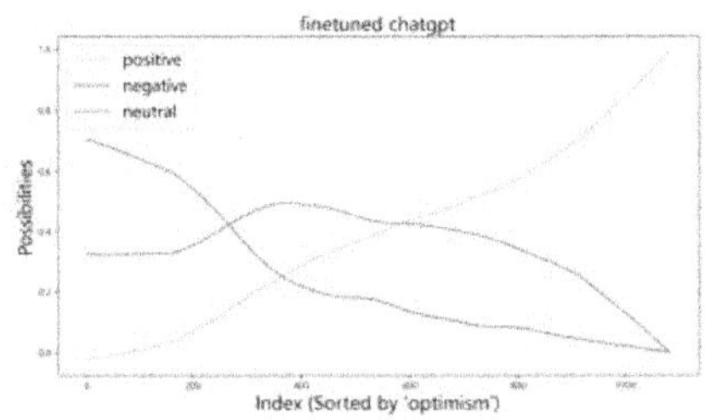

(c) Emotion-fine-tuned ChatGPT

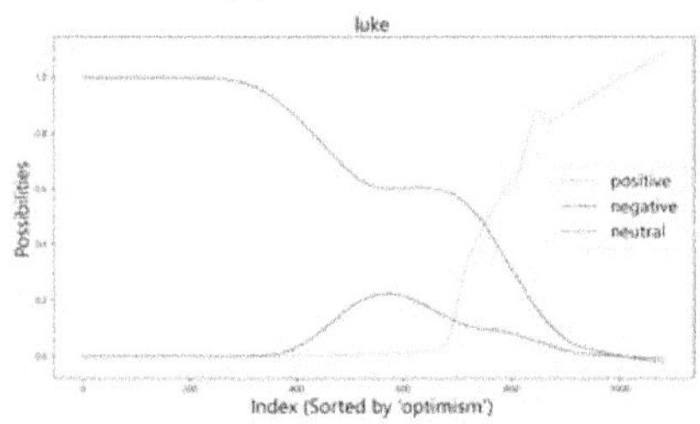

(c) LUKE

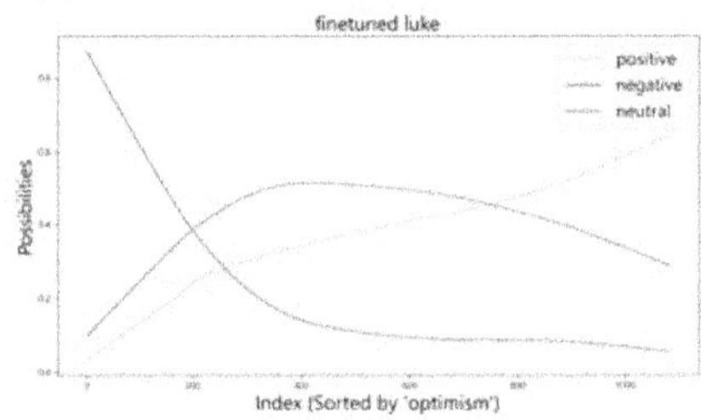

(c) Emotion-fine-tuned-LUKE

Fig. 8. Comparison of the representation performance of emotional opposition in human annotations, existing models, and emotion-fine-tuned models (three types of mix emotions).

tency with human annotations, with no significant differences observed for some or all emotion categories.

These findings indicated that the emotion-fine-tuned models not only achieved high predictive accuracy but also demonstrated superior capability in reproducing the structural property of emotional opposition, thereby confirming their improved alignment with human affective interpretation.

Moreover, emotions were reclassified into three categories: *positive* (joy + trust), *negative* (fear + disgust + sadness + anger), and *neutral* (expectation + surprise), and the same analyses were conducted (Figs. 8 and 9). In human

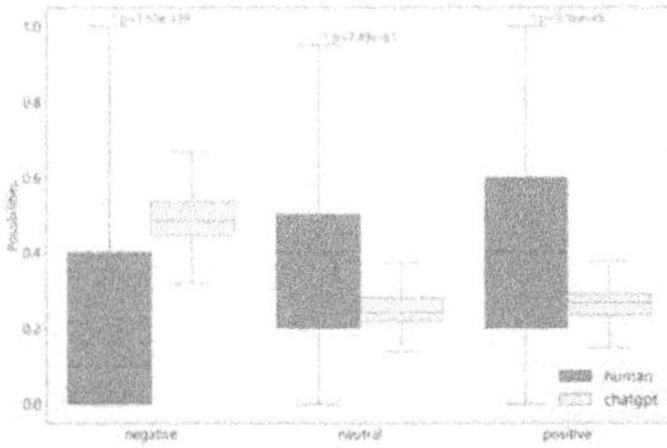

(a) Human annotations *vs.* ChatGPT

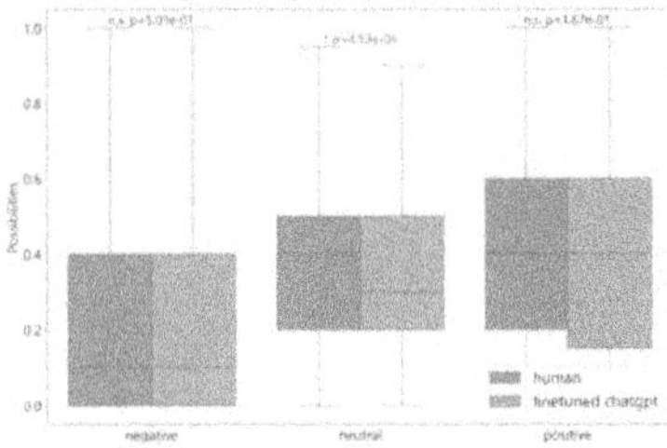

(b) Human annotations *vs.* emotin-fine-tuned ChatGPT

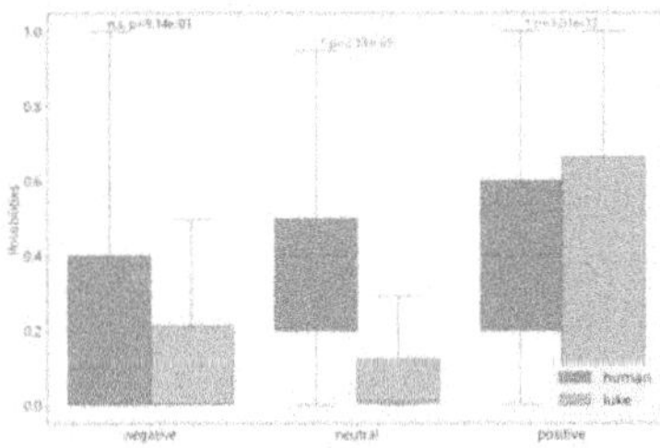

(c) Human annotations *vs.* LUKE

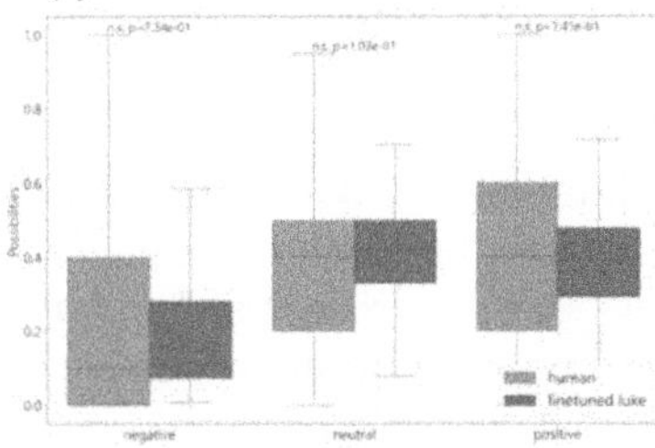

(d) Human annotations *vs.* emotion-fine-tuned LUKE

Fig. 9. Comparison of emotion score distributions between human annotations, existing models, and emotion-fine-tuned models with the results of Welch's t-tests (three types of mix emotions).

annotations, positive scores increased while negative scores decreased, and neutral scores fluctuated moderately in between, forming a natural and interpretable structure. In contrast, LUKE exhibited outputs that were strongly biased toward binary extremes (0 or 1), failing to reflect gradual emotional changes. ChatGPT showed a clear bias, with an excessively high proportion of negative outputs and almost no positive ones. The neutral scores remained nearly constant, suggesting that the model was effectively unable to predict neutral states. The fine-tuned models, on the other hand, produced distributions much closer to those of human annotations. Positive and negative scores changed symmetrically, while neutral scores remained in the middle range, successfully reproducing a more natural emotional structure.

Overall, these findings confirmed that the fine-tuned models exhibited a more human-like tendency in terms of emotional opposition and balance.

5 Conclusions

The necessity of advanced sentiment analysis in contemporary marketing is underscored by the increasing homogenization of products and services. In this context, the emotional resonance elicited through user experience has emerged as a critical source of differentiation. To address this need, this study proposed a multidimensional sentiment analysis model specifically tailored for the quantitative assessment of experiential value in consumer interactions. The experimental results underscored several key findings: (1) Existing models exhibited significant limitations, such as generating extreme outputs skewed toward 0 or 1 and failing to reproduce structures of emotional opposition, thereby rendering them inadequate for assessing experiential value; (2) The models developed in this study effectively captured the complexity and diversity of human emotional responses; and (3) Beyond achieving high predictive accuracy, the developed models demonstrated strong performance in reproducing structural properties of human affect, including emotional opposition and balance.

These findings were validated through both quantitative metrics and visualizations, confirming the models' suitability for sentiment analysis tasks. Moreover, the developed models showed greater alignment with human annotations and provided interpretable insights into emotional reactions, thereby enhancing their utility for experience-driven applications.

Future studies include cross-lingual transfer, extend baselines to recently released models, and incorporate both error and interpretation analyses.

Acknowledgements. This work was supported by Toyota Motor Corporation.

References

1. Achar, C., So, J., Agrawal, N., Duhachek, A.: What we feel and why we buy: the influence of emotions on consumer decision-making. Curr. Opin. Psychol. **10**, 166–170 (2016). https://doi.org/10.1016/j.copsyc.2016.01.009
2. Plaza-del Arco, F.M., Curry, A., Curry, A.C., Hovy, D.: Emotion analysis in NLP: trends, gaps and roadmap for future directions (2024). http://arxiv.org/abs/2403.01222
3. Birjali, M., Kasri, M., Beni-Hssane, A.: A comprehensive survey on sentiment analysis: approaches, challenges and trends. Knowl. Based Syst. **226** (2021). https://doi.org/10.1016/j.knosys.2021.107134
4. Carpenter, G.S., Glazer, R., Nakamoto, K.: Meaningful brands from meaningless differentiation: the dependence on irrelevant attributes. J. Mark. Res. **31**(3), 339–350 (1994). https://doi.org/10.2307/3152221
5. Chiny, M., Chihab, M., Chihab, Y., Bencharef, O.: LSTM, Vader and TF-IDF based hybrid sentiment analysis model. Int. J. Adv. Comput. Sci. Appl. **12**(7), 265–275 (2021)
6. Devika, M.D., Sunitha, C., Ganesh, A.: Sentiment analysis: a comparative study on different approaches. Procedia Comput. Sci. **87**, 44–49 (2016). https://doi.org/10.1016/j.procs.2016.05.124
7. Hirayama, H.: The creation of brand value: from the viewpoints of informational and experiential value. Koyoshobo (2007)
8. Hussein, D.M.E.D.M.: A survey on sentiment analysis challenges. J. King Saud Univ. Eng. Sci. **30**(4), 330–338 (2018). https://doi.org/10.1016/j.jksues.2016.04.002
9. Kahneman, D.: Thinking. Fast and Slow, Penguin UK (2012)
10. Kahneman, D., Tversky, A.: Prospect theory: an analysis of decision under risk. Econometrica **47**(2), 263–292 (1979). https://doi.org/10.2307/1914185
11. Larsen, J.T., McGraw, A.P., Cacioppo, J.T.: Can people feel happy and sad at the same time? J. Pers. Soc. Psychol. **81**(4), 648–696 (2001)
12. Lerner, J.S., Li, Y., Valdesolo, P., Kassam, K.S.: Emotion and decision making. Annu. Rev. Psychol. **66**, 799–823 (2015). https://doi.org/10.1146/annurev-psych-010213-115043
13. Nandwani, P., Verma, R.: A review on sentiment analysis and emotion detection from text. Soc. Netw. Anal. Min. **11**(1), 1–19 (2021). https://doi.org/10.1007/s13278-021-00776-6
14. Plutchik, R.: A general psychoevolutionary theory of emotion. In: Plutchik, R., Kellerman, H. (eds.) Emotion: Theory, Research, and Experience, pp. 3–33. Academic Press (1980)
15. Russell, J.: A circumplex model of affect. J. Pers. Soc. Psychol. **39**(6), 1161–1178 (1980)
16. Russell, J.: Core affect, prototypical emotional episodes, and other things called emotion: dissecting the elephant. J. Pers. Soc. Psychol. **76**(5), 805–819 (1999). https://doi.org/10.1037/0022-3514.76.5.805
17. Schmitt, B.H.: Experiential marketing: how to get customers to sense, feel, think, act. Free Press, Relate (1999)
18. Seyeditabari, A., Tabari, N., Gholizade, S., Takeda, H., Zadrozny, W.: Emotional embeddings: refining word embeddings to capture emotional content of words (2019). https://doi.org/10.48550/arXiv.1906.00112

19. Shahid, S., Paul, J., Gilal, F.G., Ansari, S.: The role of sensory marketing and brand experience in building emotional attachment and brand loyalty in luxury retail stores. Psychol. Mark. **39**(7), 1398–1412 (2022). https://doi.org/10.1002/mar.21661
20. Soleymani, M., Garcia, D., Jou, B., Schuller, B., Chang, S.F., Pantic, M.: A survey of multimodal sentiment analysis. Image Vis. Comput. **65**, 3–14 (2017). https://doi.org/10.1016/j.imavis.2017.08.003
21. Strapparava, C.: Emotions and NLP: future directions. In: Proceedings of the 7th Workshop on Computational Approaches to Subjectivity, Sentiment and Social Media Analysis, p. 180 (2016). https://aclanthology.org/W16-0430/
22. Taboada, M.: Sentiment analysis: an overview from linguistics. Ann. Rev. Linguistics **2**, 325–347 (2016). https://doi.org/10.1146/annurev-linguistics-011415-040518
23. Tan, K.L., Lee, C.P., Lim, K.M.: A survey of sentiment analysis: approaches, datasets, and future research. Appl. Sci. **13**(7) (2023). https://doi.org/10.3390/app13074550
24. Yamada, I., Asai, A., Shindo, H., Takeda, H., Matsumoto, Y.: Luke: deep contextualized entity representations with entity-aware self-attention. In: Proceedings of the 2020 Conference on Empirical Methods in Natural Language Processing (2020). https://doi.org/10.18653/v1/2020.emnlp-main.523
25. Zhang, L., Wang, S., Liu, B.: Deep learning for sentiment analysis: a survey. WIREs Data Min. Knowl. Discovery **8**(4), e1253 (2018). https://doi.org/10.1002/widm.1253

Discrete-Time Sigma-Delta Modulator Coefficient Optimization via Soft Actor-Critic Reinforcement Learning

Wanli Zhao[1], Junpeng Zhang[1], Zhenyu Rao[1], Chen Yang[1], Minglei Tong[1(✉)], and Yongqing Sun[2(✉)]

[1] School of Electronics and Information Engineering, Shanghai University of Electric Power, Shanghai, China
{suepzwl,zhangjunpeng33,raozhenyu2025,992914608}@mail.shiep.edu.cn, tongminglei@shiep.edu.cn

[2] School of Humanities and Sciences, Nihon University, Chiyoda, Japan
nakahara.eisei@nihon-u.ac.jp

Abstract. Coefficient optimization is critical for enhancing the performance of Sigma-Delta Modulator(SDMs), particularly in high-resolution analog-to-digital conversion. This paper proposes a reinforcement learning-based design framework using the Soft Actor-Critic (SAC) algorithm to optimize the key coefficients in discrete-time SDMs. The method autonomously adjusts feedforward, feedback, and integrator parameters to maximize signal-to-noise ratio (SNR) while ensuring loop stability. To validate the approach, a third-order single-bit CIFF-structured SDM was implemented and co-simulated using the Ngspice environment. Compared with conventional linearized model-based optimization, the proposed method achieves higher SNR and better stability margins with significantly reduced manual intervention. This approach enhances design efficiency, minimizes reliance on empirical parameter tuning, and demonstrates strong potential for integration into intelligent analog-digital co-design workflows.

Keywords: Sigma-Delta Modulator · Reinforcement Learning · Soft Actor-Critic · Coefficient Optimization · CIFF · SNR

1 Introduction

As a high-precision analog-to-digital converter (ADC), the SDM is widely employed in audio processing, sensor interfaces, and communication systems [1,2]. However, designing SDM involves several challenges, including accurately modeling non-idealities at the behavioral level, precisely determining optimal modulator coefficients, and ensuring stable and efficient circuit-level implementations [3]. Among these challenges, accurately determining the modulator coefficients–feedforward, feedback, and integrator gain terms—is particularly

T. Hao et al. (Eds.): BESC 2025, LNCS 16431, pp. 73–87, 2026.
https://doi.org/10.1007/978-981-95-7138-3_6

critical. These coefficients correspond directly to capacitor ratios within the circuit and significantly influence the noise shaping performance, stability, dynamic range, and signal distortion of the modulator [4,5]. Traditional design approaches typically rely on linearized modeling, approximating the inherently nonlinear modulator with a linear state-space representation. This approach facilitates the synthesis of the modulator's transfer function, from which the gain coefficients can be derived. Due to its theoretical clarity and computational efficiency, this linearized method is widely adopted. For example, the Delta Sigma Toolbox developed by Richard Schreier et al. represents a notable implementation of linearized noise transfer function (NTF) methodologies, enabling modeling of SDM structures, NTF synthesis, and coefficient realization [6]. Additionally, Mladenov et al. proposed a third-order modulator coefficient design procedure based on NTF zero-pole placement, which improves the SNR while ensuring system stability [7]. Similarly, Nowacki derived corresponding state-space coefficient matrices through linearized modeling techniques using the Delta Sigma Toolbox [8].

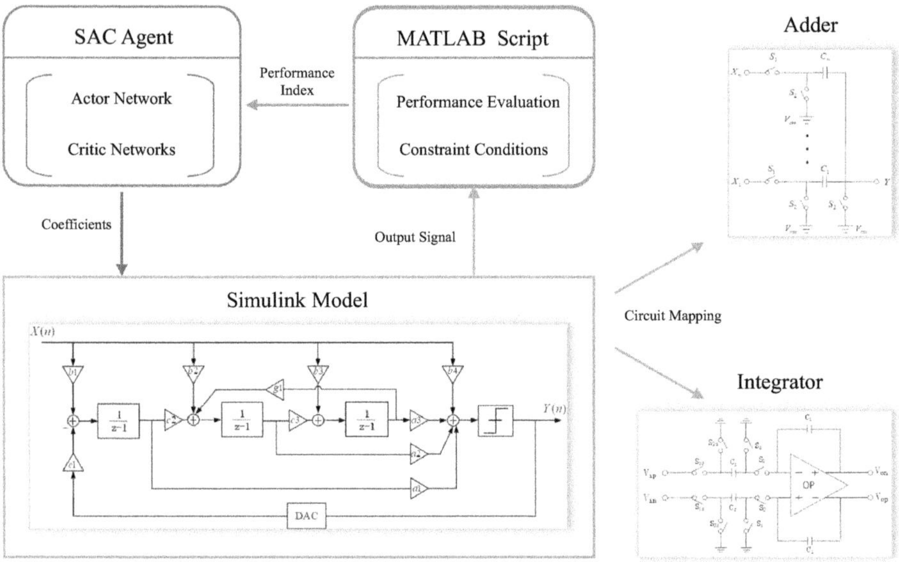

Fig. 1. Detailed Implementation Architecture Diagram

Despite the theoretical clarity and efficiency described above, traditional linearized methods still face substantial challenges when applied in real-world circuits [9]. Several factors contribute to these difficulties encountered when applying linearized modeling techniques to practical SDM implementations. Firstly, linearized models assume the modulator operates as an ideal linear system and therefore neglect critical non-idealities inherent in real circuits, such as quantizer nonlinearities, finite operational amplifier gain and bandwidth, capacitor mismatches, and switching errors. These non-ideal characteristics can significantly impair the stability and noise shaping performance of the modulator [10]. Secondly, coefficients derived from linearized models must be mapped onto capacitor ratios in practical circuits. However, some coefficient values may be either excessively small or large, exceeding process technology limitations or rendering the design overly sensitive to capacitor mismatches, thereby degrading overall system performance [11]. Furthermore, coefficients derived from traditional approaches often require manual iterative adjustments when translating to practical circuits, which introduces human error and can further diminish modulator performance. Most critically, improper coefficient configurations resulting from traditional linearized methods may lead to integrator overload due to the finite gain of practical operational amplifiers [12]. This issue particularly affects the first-stage integrator, which may saturate and lose linearity when processing large input signals or operating under high-gain conditions, ultimately undermining modulator stability [13]. Thus, for more efficient and reliable modulator design, non-idealities, dynamic range constraints, and overall system stability must be comprehensively considered during coefficient selection.

To address the limitations of traditional linearized methods in practical SDM design, reinforcement learning provides a data-driven alternative capable of handling nonlinear characteristics and complex constraints [14,15]. Among various RL algorithms, the SAC algorithm has demonstrated strong performance in continuous control tasks, making it highly suitable for optimizing analog circuit parameters [16]. As an off-policy, maximum entropy method that combines policy gradients and Q-learning, SAC ensures both sample efficiency and robustness by encouraging policy exploration and avoiding local optima [17]. In this work, SAC is applied to automatically optimize key coefficients of the SDM, such as feedforward, feedback, and integrator gains. The algorithm interacts with a behavioral-level Simulink model of the modulator through MATLAB scripts, using performance metrics such as SNR and stability margin as reward signals. This framework enables automatic exploration of high-performance coefficient combinations without relying on manual tuning or idealized assumptions. The system architecture is illustrated in Fig. 1.

2 The Proposed Method

2.1 SAC Algorithm

The SAC algorithm is a model-free, actor-critic reinforcement learning method based on the maximum entropy framework, proposed by Tuomas Haarnoja and colleagues in 2018. Its core idea is to encourage the agent to explore a diverse action space by maximizing not only the cumulative reward but also the entropy of the policy, thereby avoiding convergence to suboptimal local solutions. Unlike traditional reinforcement learning algorithms that focus solely on maximizing expected returns, SAC incorporates policy entropy as part of the optimization objective. This leads to greater stochasticity and robustness during exploration, improving both sample efficiency and convergence stability. The objective of the SAC algorithm is defined as maximizing the weighted sum of the expected cumulative reward and the policy entropy, as shown in Eq. (1).

$$J(\pi) = \sum_{t=0}^{T} \mathbb{E}_{(s_t,a_t)\sim\rho_\pi} \left[r(s_t, a_t) + \alpha\mathcal{H}(\pi(\cdot \mid s_t))\right] \tag{1}$$

Among them, the entropy term of the policy is defined in Eq. (2). ρ_π denotes the state-action distribution induced by the policy π, $r(s_t, a_t)$ represents the immediate reward, and α is the temperature coefficient used to balance the trade-off between reward and entropy. This objective encourages the policy not only to obtain high rewards but also to maintain sufficient exploratory behavior.

$$\mathcal{H}(\pi(\cdot|s_t)) = -\mathbb{E}_{a_t\sim\pi}[\log \pi(a_t|s_t)] \tag{2}$$

The neural network architecture of the SAC agent mainly consists of one Actor network, which generates the action distribution $\pi(a|s)$ given a state; two Critic networks that estimate $Q_1(s, a)$ and $Q_2(s, a)$ respectively, to mitigate overestimation bias in value estimation; and two target Critic networks, which are used to evaluate the current state. The SAC algorithm uses the Temporal-Difference error to evaluate the uncertainty of the expected reward of samples in the Critic networks. In addition, SAC employs experience replay and soft policy updates to train the agent. The experiential data obtained from agent-environment interactions are stored in a replay buffer. During training, the agent samples data from the replay buffer to perform network updates. The purpose of using the replay buffer mechanism in the SAC algorithm is to eliminate the correlation between experiential samples to achieve better training performance. The loss function minimized by the Actor network is defined as Eq. (3), and the Q-value function is updated by minimizing the mean squared error loss, as shown in Eqs. (4) and (5).

$$J_\pi = \mathbb{E}_{s_t\sim D, a_t\sim\pi} \left[\alpha \log \pi(a_t|s_t) - Q(s_t, a_t)\right] \tag{3}$$

$$J_Q = \mathbb{E}_{(s_t,a_t,r_t,s_{t+1})\sim D} \left[(Q(s_t, a_t) - y_t)^2\right] \tag{4}$$

$$y_t = r_t + \gamma \left[\underset{i=1,2}{min} Q_i\left(s_{t+1}, a_{t+1}\right) - \alpha \log \pi\left(a_{t+1}|s_{t+1}\right)\right] \tag{5}$$

where γ is the discount factor and D denotes the experience replay buffer. During the training process of SAC, the policy network and the two Q-networks are optimized simultaneously, and the target Q-networks are updated via a soft update mechanism to ensure smooth transitions. The architecture of the SAC algorithm is shown in Fig. 2.

2.2 Simulation Environment Based on SAC Algorithm

To achieve the optimized design of Sigma-Delta modulator coefficients, this work constructs a SAC-based optimization environment under Python 3.10 using the

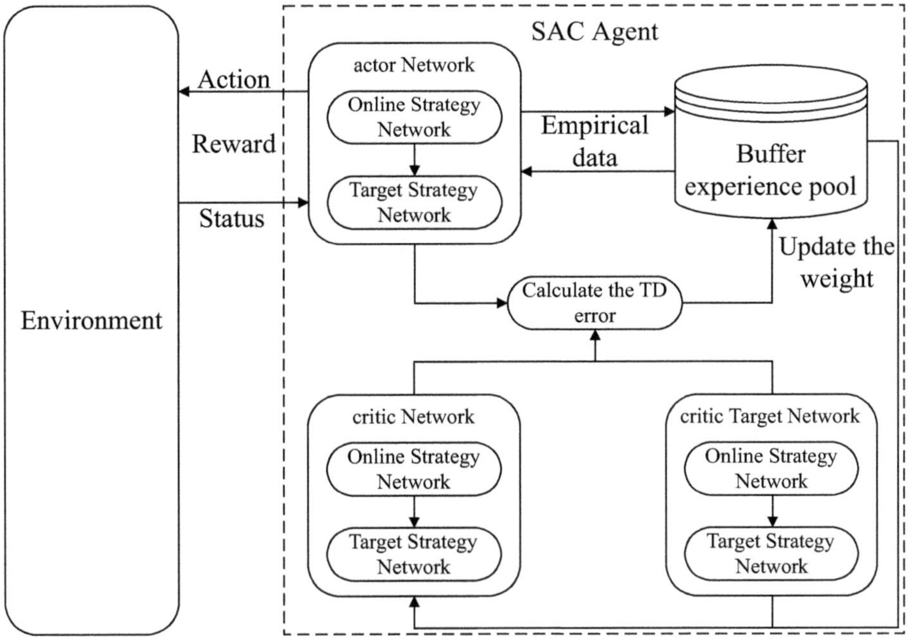

Fig. 2. SAC Architecture Diagram

Gym interface, and enables the invocation of the Simulink model by configuring the *MATLAB Engine for Python*. After the Python controller generates an action at each step, MATLAB is called to execute the simulation and return the results. In each round of interaction, the SAC agent generates an action based on the current state, and the environment model returns the new state and reward signal. The agent continuously optimizes the policy network through experience replay and policy update mechanisms, gradually learning the optimal mapping relationship between the modulator coefficient configuration and system performance. The specific steps are as follows:

- The modulator system to be designed is modeled in Simulink, with the modulator coefficients set as variable inputs to the model.
- Add stability constraints and integrator overload constraints. The stability constraint prevents invalid coefficient combinations that could lead to instability of the NTF, while the integrator overload constraint ensures that the integrators do not enter nonlinear regions, which would compromise the noise shaping characteristics and degrade the modulator's performance.
- Construct the SAC algorithm model for implementing coefficient optimization. SAC treats these coefficients as continuous variables within the action space, with their specific values output by the policy network. Each time the agent selects a set of parameters, the combination is dynamically passed into the Simulink-based modulator model for actual simulation execution.

The quantizer output signal generated by the model operation is analyzed in the frequency domain through a script, extracting SNR, stability, and the degree of integrator overload as performance indicators. The reward function uses this comprehensive assessment to evaluate the merits of each parameter combination, with SNR as a positive target and integrator overload and stability as negative targets. For parameter combinations that violate stability constraints or cause integrator overload, the reward function imposes penalty terms to suppress their selection probability, thereby guiding the SAC agent to focus on the parameter space with good performance and physical realizability during the training process. Through continuous iterative optimization, the algorithm can automatically explore the coefficient combinations that meet the system constraints and have high SNR and robustness. The flowchart of using SAC to optimize the coefficients of the Sigma-Delta modulator is shown in Fig. 3.

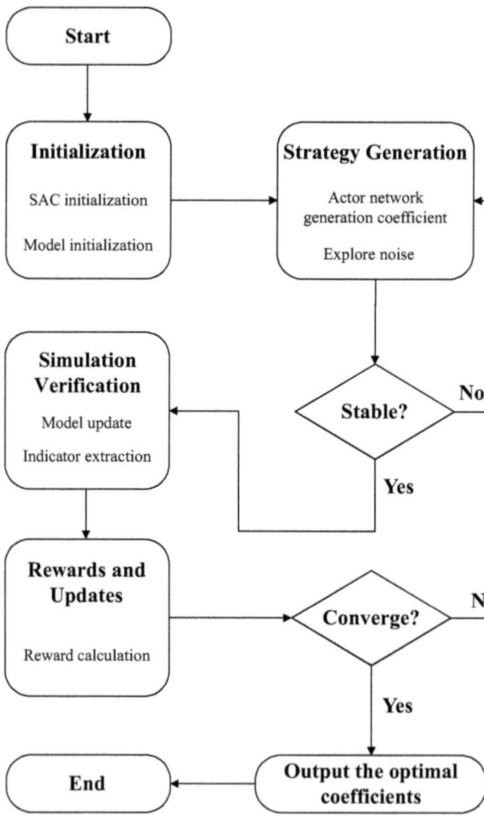

Fig. 3. Flowchart of SAC Optimizing SDM Coefficients

2.3 Markov Decision Process

In constructing the SAC algorithm, the design problem of the modulator's structural parameters is formulated as a Markov Decision Process (MDP). The state space s_t is defined as a vector of performance metrics obtained from the current simulation of the modulator, including the signal-to-noise ratio SNR_t, stability margin M_t, and integrator overload indicator O_t.Stability is quantified by the distance of the poles of the NTF from the unit circle, while integrator overload is evaluated based on the extent to which the output amplitude exceeds 1 V. This is expressed in Eq. (6).

$$s_t = [\text{SNR}_t, M_t, O_t] \tag{6}$$

The action space is defined as a vector a_t consisting of the modulator coefficients, representing the adjustments of parameters such as feedforward paths, feedback paths, and integrator gains, as shown in Eq. (7).

$$a_t = [a_i, b_i, c_i, g_i] \in \mathbb{R}^N \tag{7}$$

The reward function is formulated based on the performance metrics obtained from simulation results, comprehensively considering the signal-to-noise ratio, integrator overload, and stability margin. Its mathematical form is defined in Eq. (8), where α, β, and γ are weighting coefficients. In cases where the modulator is determined to be unstable, a large negative reward $-C$ is assigned to penalize such configurations and guide the policy away from unstable regions.

$$r(s_t, a_t) = \begin{cases} \alpha \cdot \text{SNR}_t - \beta \cdot M_t - \gamma \cdot O_t, & \text{stable} \\ -C, & \text{unstable} \end{cases} \tag{8}$$

2.4 Coefficient-to-Circuit Mapping

The Sigma-Delta modulator is a high-precision analog-to-digital conversion architecture based on integrators and feedback loops, whose performance largely depends on the proper configuration of its coefficients. As shown in Fig. 4, the third-order single-bit CIFF-structured Sigma-Delta modulator consists of three main parts:

- Three switched-capacitor integrators are used to implement high-order noise shaping.
- A single-bit quantizer module performs the nonlinear operation of analog-to-digital conversion.
- The feedback path and the feedforward summation path are implemented to achieve noise shaping and enhance system stability.

A total of 11 key coefficients are involved: a_1, a_2, and a_3 are the feedforward coefficients; b_1 to b_4 are the feedback coefficients; c_1, c_2, and c_3 are the integrator gain coefficients; and g_1 is the gain of the DAC output path. These coefficients

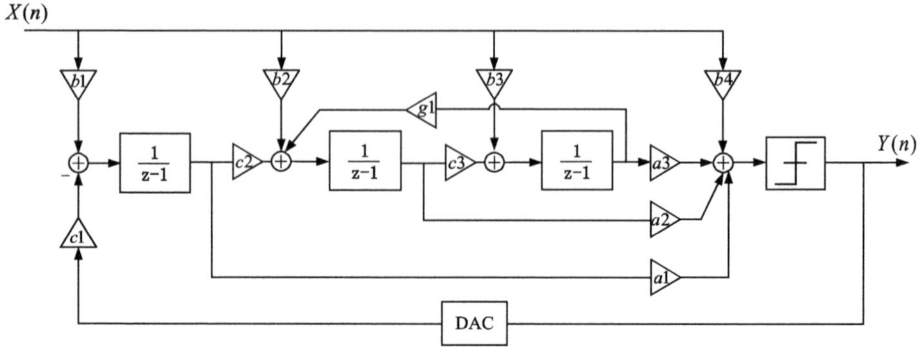

Fig. 4. Third-Order CIFF Structure SDM Schematic Diagram

are implemented by precisely configuring the sizes and ratios of capacitors. The corresponding modulator circuit structure is shown in Fig. 5, where each integrator stage consists of a sampling capacitor C_s, an integrating capacitor C_i, and an operational amplifier. The gain coefficient c_k is determined by the ratio of these two capacitors, as expressed in Eq. (9).

$$c_k = \frac{C_{sk}}{C_{ik}}, k = 1, 2, 3 \tag{9}$$

This implies that adjusting the size of either the sampling capacitor or the integrating capacitor directly changes the gain of the corresponding integrator. The feedforward coefficients a_1, a_2, and a_3 are implemented through the ratio of the feedforward capacitors $C_{\alpha 1}$, $C_{\alpha 2}$, and $C_{\alpha 3}$ to the reference capacitor $C_{\alpha 0}$, as expressed in Eq. (10). These capacitors are located between the outputs of each integrator and the input of the quantizer, enabling weighted summation of the feedforward signals. The feedback coefficients b_1 to b_4 are typically determined by the capacitor array in the feedback path, and their corresponding values are indirectly controlled by the capacitor distribution in the charge injection path. The DAC gain coefficient g_1 is implemented by adjusting the capacitor ratio in the digital feedback path before the first integrator.

$$a_k = \frac{C_{\alpha k}}{C_{\alpha 0}}, \quad k = 1, 2, 3 \tag{10}$$

3 System Simulation

3.1 Modulator Coefficients Estimation

Following the above method, the simulation environment for optimizing the coefficients of the third-order single-bit SDM was constructed. After training with the SAC algorithm, the set of coefficients corresponding to the highest reward

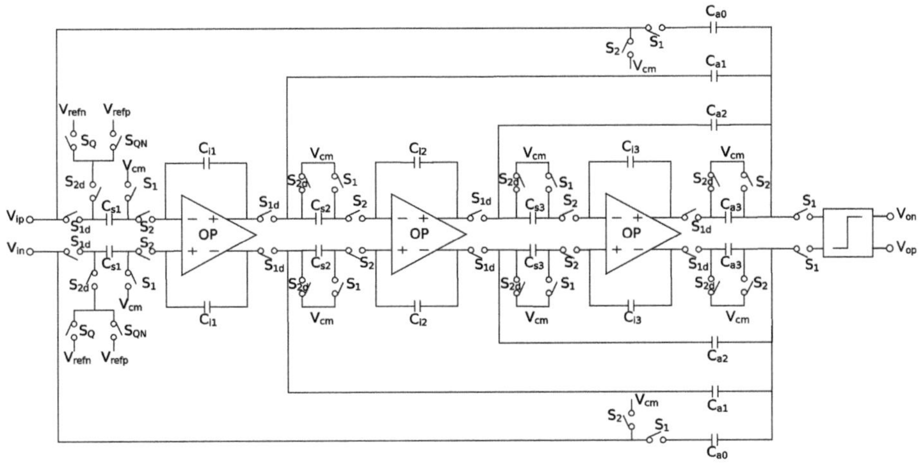

Fig. 5. Modulator Circuit Structure Diagram

Table 1. Optimal modulator coefficients

$a(i)$	$g(i)$	$b(j)$	$c(j)$
$a_1 = 2$	$g_1 = 0$	$b_1 = 0.4$	$c_1 = 0.4$
$a_2 = 1$	–	$b_2 = 0$	$c_2 = 0.5$
$a_3 = 1.5$	–	$b_3 = 0$	$c_3 = 0.2$
–	–	$b_4 = 1$	–

value was selected as the final design parameters. The optimal coefficient combination is summarized in Table 1.

By adjusting the modulator coefficients, the NTF of the modulator can be derived as Eq. (11). Plot the zero-pole diagram of the NTF function as shown in Fig. 6. It can be observed that the function has triple zeros and poles, with all three poles located inside the unit circle, indicating that the system is stable.

$$NTF = \frac{(z-1)^3}{(z-0.7)(z^2-1.47z+0.641)} \tag{11}$$

To verify whether the optimal coefficient combination meets the overload constraints and performance of the modulator, we substitute these coefficient values into the script. We add a Scope module after each integrator in the modulator model to observe whether the integrator is overloaded, and add a module for drawing the power spectral density graph in the script. Then, we run the script. The output of each integrator is shown in Fig. 7, from which it can be observed that the integrator has not been overloaded. The power spectral density is shown in Fig. 8. According to Eq. (12), where N denotes the number of quantization bits and L represents the modulator order, the theoretical maximum SNR of a third-order, single-bit quantized SDM with an OSR of 256 can reach 154.97 dB.

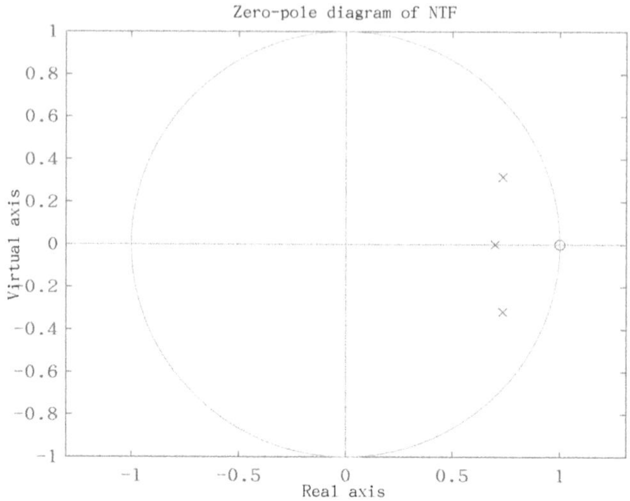

Fig. 6. NTF Zero-Pole Plot

With the optimized coefficient set, simulation results show that the SNR reaches 129.4 dB and the effective number of bits (ENOB) is 21.21 bits.

$$\mathrm{SNR} = \&6.02N + 10(2L+1)\lg(\mathrm{OSR}) + 10\lg\left(\frac{3(2L+1)}{\pi^{2L}}\right) - 3.01 \quad (12)$$

3.2 Modulator Circuit Verification

In the previous section, the rationality of the optimized coefficients was verified at the model level. In this section, these coefficients are mapped onto the actual circuit, completing the full process from system-level modeling to circuit-level validation. The circuit diagram of the modulator is shown in Fig. 5. A fully differential architecture is adopted to reduce harmonic distortion and suppress common-mode interference. Considering thermal noise and the target design accuracy, the sampling capacitor of the first stage is set to 1.6 pF. According to Table 1, the capacitance values of each stage are shown in Table 2.

A fully differential structure is adopted throughout the system to reduce harmonic distortion and common-mode interference on the circuit. The modulator circuit mainly consists of three parts:

- A switched-capacitor-based integrator, which implements high-order noise shaping.
- A single-bit quantizer module, responsible for the nonlinear operation of analog-to-digital conversion.

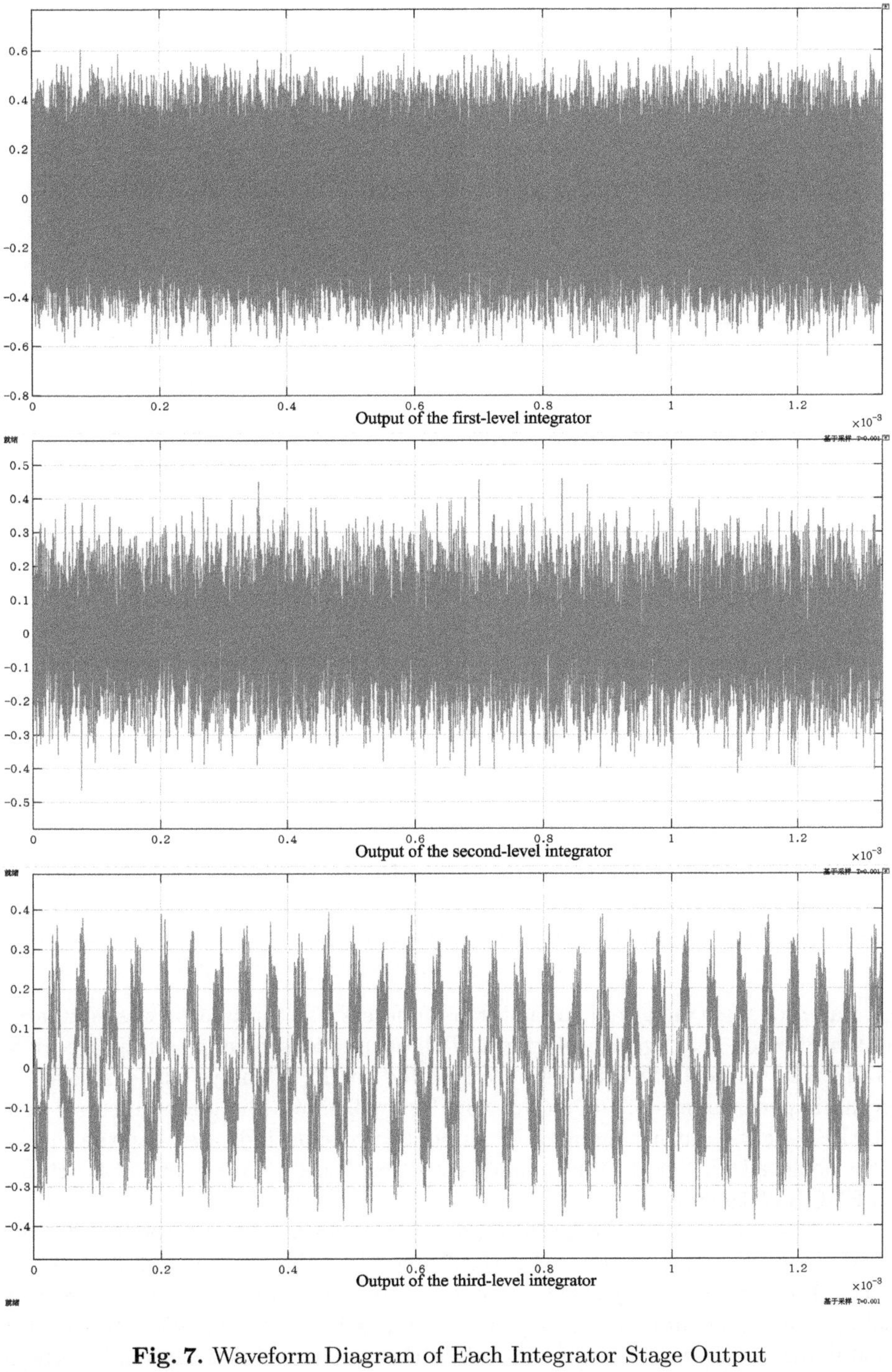

Fig. 7. Waveform Diagram of Each Integrator Stage Output

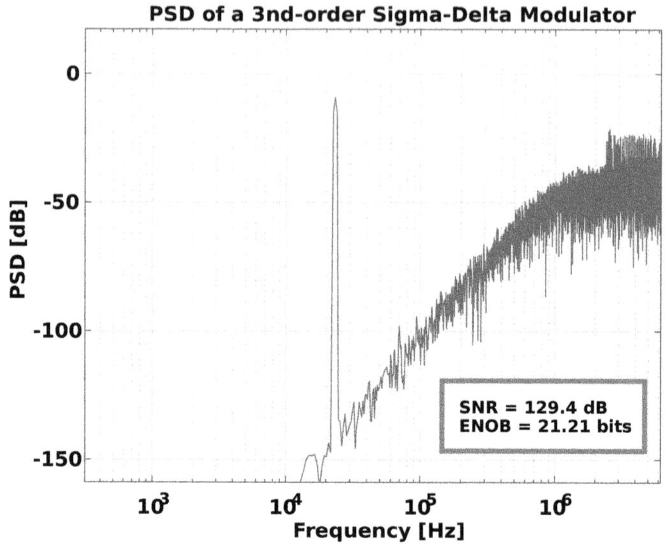

Fig. 8. Power Spectral Density Diagram

Table 2. The specific value of the modulator capacitor

Sampling Capacitor (pF)	Integrating Capacitor (pF)	Feedforward Capacitor (pF)
–	–	$C_{\alpha 0} = 0.18$
$C_{s1} = 1.6$	$C_{i1} = 4$	$C_{\alpha 1} = 0.36$
$C_{s2} = 0.5$	$C_{i2} = 1$	$C_{\alpha 2} = 0.18$
$C_{s3} = 0.5$	$C_{i3} = 2.5$	$C_{\alpha 3} = 0.27$

– A feedforward summation circuit that linearly combines the outputs of multiple integrators in the feedforward path and sends the result to the quantizer, thereby achieving noise shaping and enhancing system stability.

Based on the configured capacitor parameters, the modulator was simulated and verified on the Ngspice platform. The output bitstream was imported into MATLAB, where 16,384 points were selected for FFT analysis to evaluate the dynamic performance of the modulator. Figure 9 shows the power spectral density PSD of the output signal. The simulation results indicate that the modulator achieved an signal-to-noise-and-distortion Ratio (SNDR) of 121.6 dB and an ENOB of 19.90 bits.

Table 3 summarizes the performance comparison between the third-order SDM designed in this work and several recently published related studies. All selected references employ third-order structures, with variations in process technologies and oversampling ratios. The comparison results demonstrate that the modulator design based on the SAC algorithm outperforms traditional methods in terms of SNDR and ENOB.

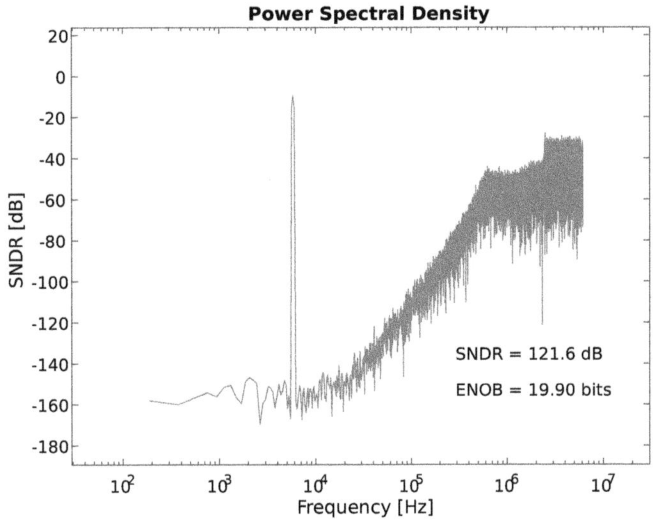

Fig. 9. Modulator Circuit Simulation Results

Table 3. Performance Comparison of Several Published ADCs

	Proposed work	[18]	[19]	[20]
Architecture	3rd-order	3rd-order	3rd-order	3rd-order
Process (nm)	130	90	–	180
OSR	256	256	128	–
SNDR (dB)	121.6	116.7	112.6	104.2
ENOB (bits)	19.90	19.10	18.41	17.02

4 Conclusion

This paper proposes a modeling and design methodology for discrete-time Sigma-Delta modulators based on the SAC reinforcement learning algorithm. By automatically optimizing the feedforward, feedback, coupling, and integrator coefficients, the proposed method achieves a balance between maximizing SNR and maintaining system stability. A third-order, single-bit quantized CIFF-structured modulator is designed and implemented to validate the effectiveness of the approach. Simulation results demonstrate that, compared to conventional methods based on linearized models, the proposed technique achieves significantly improved performance, reduces the dependence on manual experience, and enhances design efficiency, thus offering a novel pathway for system-level optimization in high-precision Sigma-Delta ADC design.

Acknowledgment. This work was supported by JSPS KAKENHIGrant Number JP24K14998.

References

1. Fan, Y., Huijing, Y., Gang, L.: A high performance sigma-delta ADC for audio decoder chip. TELKOMNIKA Indon. J. Electr. Eng. **11**(11), 6570–6576 (2013)
2. Nguyen, M.T., Jabbour, C., Ben Kalaia, K., et al.: A highly flexible passive/active discrete-time delta-sigma receiver. Electronics **13**(7), 1295 (2024)
3. Saatlo, A.N.: Systematic design of stable high-order delta sigma modulators using genetic algorithm. Analog Integr. Circ. Sig. Process **118**(1), 15–24 (2024)
4. An, K.C., Narasimman, N., Kim, T.T.H.: A high-resolution discrete-time second-order $\Sigma\Delta$ ADC with improved tolerance to KT/C noise using low oversampling ratio. Sensors **24**(17), 5755 (2024)
5. Zhao, M., Zhao, Y., Zhang, H., et al.: A 4 μW bandwidth/power scalable delta–sigma modulator based on swing-enhanced floating inverter amplifiers. IEEE J. Solid-State Circ. **57**(3), 709–718 (2021)
6. Schreier, R., Temes, G.C.: Understanding Delta-Sigma Data Converters. IEEE press, Piscataway (2005)
7. Tsenov, G., Mladenov, V., Reiss, J.D.: A design procedure for finding optimal third order Delta-Sigma modulator loopfilters. In: Proceedings of the 13th WSEAS International Conference on Systems, pp. 48–52 (2009)
8. Nowacki, B.: Design of sigma-delta modulators for analog-to-digital conversion intensively using passive circuits. Universidade Nova de Lisboa (2016)
9. Zaky, B.M., Hosny, M.A., Omran, H.A., et al.: A systematic method for scaling coefficients of the continuous-time low-pass $\Sigma\Delta$ modulator using a simulink-based toolbox. Engineering **5**(1), 1–16 (2023)
10. Naskar, S.: Complete design approach of a 3rd order continuous-time sigma-delta ADC with FIR feedback and low-noise low-distortion op-amp achieving 101.8 dB SNDR and –110 dB THD. Integration **91**, 98–106 (2023)
11. Lee, S.C., Chiu, Y.: Digital calibration of capacitor mismatch in sigma-delta modulators. IEEE Trans. Circuits Syst. I Regul. Pap. **58**(4), 690–698 (2010)
12. Pena-Perez, A., Gonzalez-Diaz, V.R., Maloberti, F.: Analog sigma–delta modulation with Op-Amp gain compensation for nanometer technologies. Analog Integr. Circ. Sig. Process **76**, 297–305 (2013)
13. Killat, D., Ulmann, B., Köppel, S.: Hybrid integrators with predictive overload estimation for analog computers and continuous-time $\Delta\Sigma$ modulators. Adv. Radio Sci. **21**(D), 89–100 (2023)
14. Mounika, P., Ahmad, N., Hussain, G., et al.: AI-powered enhancement of sigma delta ADC: the role of artificial neural network-based optimization systems. IEEE Access **12**, 139018–139027 (2024)
15. Gao, P., Yu, T., Wang, F., et al.: Automated design and optimization of distributed filter circuits using reinforcement learning. J. Comput. Des. Eng. **11**(5), 60–76 (2024)
16. Wang, Y., Ni, T.: Meta-sac: Auto-tune the entropy temperature of soft actor-critic via metagradient. arXiv preprint arXiv:2007.01932 (2020)
17. Haarnoja, T., Zhou, A., Abbeel, P., et al.: Soft actor-critic: off-policy maximum entropy deep reinforcement learning with a stochastic actor. In: International Conference on Machine Learning, pp. 1861–1870. PMLR (2018)
18. Sung,, G.M., Zhou, L.L., Jiang, Y.F.: Third-order one-bit switched-capacitor sigma-delta modulator with CIFF structure. In: 2024 International Conference on Consumer Electronics-Taiwan (ICCE-Taiwan), pp. 699–700. IEEE (2024)

19. Li, Y., Liu, M., Zhang, L.: A novel 16-bit ADC based on third-order Σ-Δ modulator with zero optimization. In: 2023 IEEE 15th International Conference on ASIC (ASICON), pp. 1–4. IEEE (2023)
20. Yang, Y.T., Lai, H.J., Wang, L.H., et al.: A delta-sigma ADC design for a wearable ECG application. In: 2019 IEEE International Conference on Consumer Electronics-Taiwan (ICCE-TW), pp. 1–2. IEEE (2019)

Anomaly Detection Method for Tabular Data Based on a Three-Phase Learning Paradigm

Yufei Li, Hongtao Song(✉), and Qilong Han

College of Computer Science and Technology, Harbin Engineering University, Harbin 150001, Heilongjiang, China
{yufeili,songhongtao,hanqilong}@hrbeu.edu.cn

Abstract. Anomaly detection is a crucial step in ensuring data quality. How to accurately and comprehensively identify outliers in data has always been a core challenge in the field of data science. Although existing studies have proposed a variety of anomaly detection methods for tabular data, some methods are often limited to specific types of data and are difficult to play an effective role in general scenarios. While machine learning-based methods can cover multiple types of errors, they are highly dependent on a large amount of high-quality labeled data, resulting in high system costs. The introduction of few-shot learning techniques has alleviated the labeling burden to a certain extent, but the problem of uneven distribution between labeled samples and unlabeled data still significantly restricts the improvement of model performance. To this end, this paper proposes a novel tabular data anomaly detection method (TP-ADM) from the perspective of data selection, adopting a three-stage learning paradigm to solve the above problems. First, a genetic algorithm is used to complete high-quality sample screening and initial label assignment; second, an improved label diffusion algorithm is introduced to alleviate the problem of uneven data distribution; finally, an iterative adaptive generation strategy for pseudo-labels is designed to achieve comprehensive determination of abnormal data. The experimental results on five benchmark datasets show that TP-ADM achieves excellent detection performance without relying on external knowledge bases. In addition, the data selection module proposed in this paper has a plug-and-play architecture feature, which can be integrated into existing anomaly detection frameworks, and its significant role in improving the performance of mainstream models has been verified in experiments.

Keywords: Genetic Algorithm · Anomaly Detection · Tabular Data · Data Cleaning · Data Quality

1 Introduction

As a core technology for data quality assurance, anomaly detection plays a vital role in data-driven decision-making. It aims to identify various types of data

T. Hao et al. (Eds.): BESC 2025, LNCS 16431, pp. 88–106, 2026.
https://doi.org/10.1007/978-981-95-7138-3_7

quality issues, including erroneous values, missing values, duplicate records [20], inconsistencies and other abnormal situations [3]. These data quality problems may stem from various factors such as system failures, human input errors, or defects in data collection processes. If not detected and addressed in a timely manner, they will seriously affect the reliability of downstream applications and the effectiveness of decision-making. Therefore, building an efficient and accurate anomaly detection mechanism has become a key prerequisite for ensuring the successful deployment of data-driven applications.

Traditional anomaly detection methods have many limitations. First, most methods only focus on capturing specific types of anomalies in data, such as numerical anomalies or categorical anomalies, and are difficult to adapt to complex and diverse real-world data environments [5,8,14]. Second, many methods highly rely on the prior knowledge of domain experts and require manual definition of detection rules or setting of threshold parameters, which not only consumes a lot of human and time costs, but also limits the scalability and versatility of the methods [3,32]. In recent years, the rapid development of machine learning, especially deep learning technology, has brought new opportunities for anomaly detection in tabular data. Researchers have proposed various learning-based methods, attempting to reduce the workload of manual intervention by automatically learning data patterns. However, these methods face new challenges: (1) Supervised learning models rely on large amounts of high-quality labeled data, and the cost of obtaining these labels is extremely high; (2) In practical applications, abnormal samples are usually far fewer than normal samples, leading to serious class imbalance problems. For some key fields, such as rare disease diagnosis or financial fraud detection, abnormal data itself is extremely scarce, making model training extremely difficult.

To address the aforementioned challenges, this paper proposes a tabular data anomaly detection method based on a three-phase learning paradigm. The method aims to comprehensively identify various types of data errors under conditions without human intervention. Specifically, it comprises three key phases:

- The first phase introduces a genetic algorithm as a data selector to automatically identify representative samples and assign initial labels through natural selection simulation, eliminating manual intervention and reducing configuration complexity. While genetic algorithms are widely used in optimization, their application to anomaly detection remains unexplored with substantial optimization potential.
- The second phase, serving as a preparatory step before model training, introduces an improved label propagation algorithm to effectively address the issue of label sparsity. By constructing data bags as the basic input units for the model, this phase enhances the model's ability to perceive local data structures.
- The third phase proposes an iterative pseudo-label adaptive generation strategy. Through autoencoder feature reconstruction and Positive-Unlabeled (PU) learning concepts, a confidence-driven training framework enables progressive detection of unlabeled data.

The main contributions of this paper are summarized as follows:

- We innovatively introduce genetic algorithms into the field of tabular data anomaly detection and design a data selection and label assignment method based on an evolutionary mechanism. This method not only enhances the automation level of anomaly detection but also, as an independent module, can be integrated into other advanced detection frameworks to improve data anomaly detection capabilities.
- Aiming at the key problem of unequal distribution between labeled samples and unlabeled data, we propose an improved label diffusion algorithm to alleviate data distribution imbalance and design an iterative adaptive pseudo-label generation strategy to achieve comprehensive determination of multi-class abnormal data, significantly enhancing the model's generalization ability under limited labeling conditions.
- We conduct comprehensive experimental evaluations on five real-world datasets and compare them with nine state-of-the-art anomaly detection methods. The experimental results verify the superiority of the proposed method in terms of automation level and detection performance, providing sufficient empirical evidence for its effectiveness and practicality.

2 Related Work

2.1 Traditional Anomaly Detection Methods

Traditional anomaly detection algorithms only focus on specific types of errors. According to the nature of errors, they can be divided into two categories: quantitative error detection and qualitative error detection. Quantitative data error detection is dedicated to identifying outliers that exceed frequency or distance thresholds [14]. For example, the FAHE [25] framework is specifically designed to detect (pseudo) missing values, while the DBoost [24] integrated framework combines multiple outlier detection strategies to identify data errors. Qualitative data error detection mainly focuses on violations of data integrity or predefined patterns. Methods such as GARF [22], CDC [15], and MLNClean [13] identify non-compliant data by applying integrity constraints. Among them, HoloClean [28], GDR [33], NADEEF [10], and other methods construct rule-based detection methods to solve rule violation errors by enforcing functional dependencies and integrity constraints. However, these methods heavily rely on the expertise of data experts, resulting in complex system configurations, and their effects largely depend on the quality of rules provided by humans. In contrast, the detection method proposed in this study can comprehensively identify different types of data anomalies, significantly expanding the application scope of traditional methods.

2.2 Machine Learning-Based Anomaly Detection Methods

Obviously, the automated strategy through machine learning can reduce the dependence on external corpora and manual intervention, and capture various types of errors. However, this learning method heavily relies on high-quality datasets with uniform distribution. To enable downstream tasks to work properly, there are several data cleaning systems that serve machine learning have been developed [6,16,17]. In some special fields, it is very difficult to obtain training datasets or historical datasets, causing a bottleneck in the learning task. Although SAGED [2] uses an automated strategy to reduce the dependence on external corpora and manual intervention, it requires obtaining a few-shot historical training set for model training. Tools such as ED2 [21], RAHA [18] and ActiveClean [16] simplify the data cleaning process but still require manual input to ensure the feasibility and accuracy of the model. In contrast, the method proposed in this paper learns from its own corpus, does not require users to participate in system rule configuration, and remains unaffected by external knowledge while still demonstrating good performance. Additionally, it maintains strong generality in special application scenarios.

3 Problem Formulation

In this study, the dataset itself is used as the training corpus. Dirty data (containing erroneous data) is taken as the system input, and the detected erroneous cell instances are output after algorithmic processing. For a given dirty dataset D_{dirty}, which has M data tuples $R = \{R_1, R_2, \ldots, R_M\}$ and N data attributes $A = \{A_1, A_2, \ldots, A_N\}$, we establish an anomaly label mapping mechanism for each cell instance $x_{i,j}$ located in the i-th row and j-th column. This mechanism assigns labels to each data instance through the mapping function $G : x \to y \in \{0, 1\}^N$: an anomalous instance is marked as $y = 1$, and a normal instance is marked as $y = 0$. The core objective of the algorithm is to optimize the prediction accuracy of the model, making its output labels highly consistent with the actual anomaly situations, and achieving accurate identification of data quality problems. Specifically, the system can effectively detect and locate multiple error types such as missing values (MV), transcription errors (TP), format anomalies (FI), numerical outliers (OT), and attribute dependency violations (VAD), providing a reliable basis for the subsequent evaluation of the degree of data anomalies.

4 Methodology

This section details the proposed tabular data anomaly detection method based on a three-stage learning paradigm. Figure 1 shows the overall architecture of TP-ADM, comprising three core stages. In the first stage, tuple decomposition is performed on dirty data, a genetic algorithm constructs a selector module for data screening and initial labeling, and encoding is conducted through an embedding layer for basic feature representation. The second stage proposes an improved label propagation algorithm to address sample label conflicts, alleviating label ambiguity and sparsity. Sample data is grouped into packets with different instances and provided with packet-level annotations. The third stage

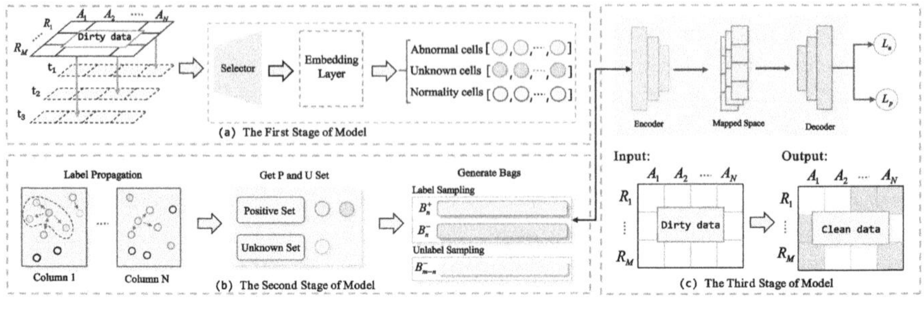

Fig. 1. The overall architecture of TP-ADM.

integrates PU learning and proposes a pseudo-label adaptive generation strategy based on bag-of-learning to train a high-performance anomaly detection model for data quality detection.

4.1 The First Stage of the Model

Genetic Algorithm(GA) is a popular and effective optimization technique that utilizes natural selection and genetic principles for search [4,19]. It starts with a randomly generated set of solutions, which are then evolved towards better ones using the principle of survival of the fittest [30]. In the first stage, it is innovatively applied to the data selection and label assignment process to automatically identify the most representative abnormal and normal samples. As shown in Fig. 2, the selector screens cells with high abnormal features or low abnormal features through an evolutionary mechanism, providing high-quality initial labeled data for subsequent model training.

Data Decomposition. Given the dirty dataset D_{dirty}, first, it is decomposed row-by-row into a set of tuples $T = \{t_1, t_2, \ldots, t_M\}$ with length n, where $t_i = \{x_{i,1}, x_{i,2}, \ldots, x_{i,N}\}$ represents the i-th data tuple. This decomposition method regards each tuple as an independent individual in the genetic algorithm, providing a basis for subsequent evolutionary operations.

Calculation of Fitness Score. This method designs a comprehensive fitness function $F(x_{ij})$ to evaluate the abnormality degree of each cell. This function integrates three key abnormality detection components, including the function dependency violation abnormality score based on the TANE algorithm, the statistical outlier detection score, and the adaptive pattern abnormality detection score. Among them, α, β, and γ are weight coefficients respectively, satisfying $\alpha + \beta + \gamma = 1$.

$$F(x_{ij}) = \alpha S_{\text{TANE}}(x_{ij}) + \beta S_{\text{STAT}}(x_{ij}) + \gamma S_{\text{ADAPT}}(x_{ij}) \tag{1}$$

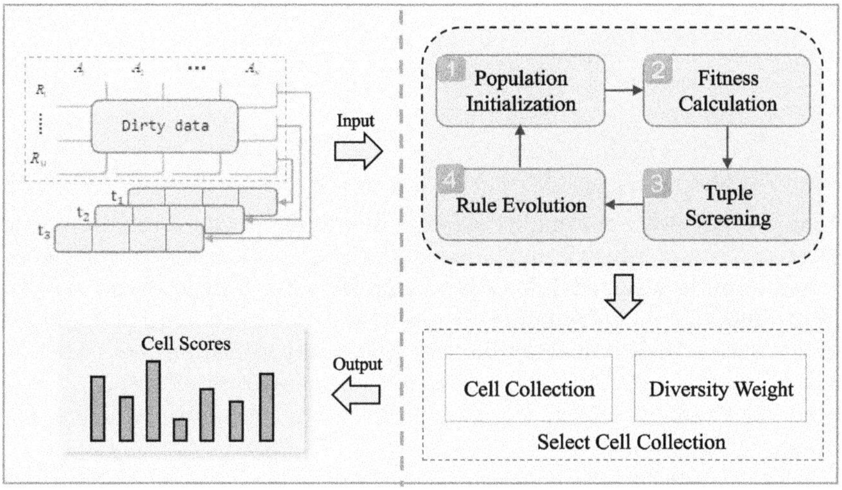

Fig. 2. The method flow of the data selector.

The function dependency violation detection based on the TANE algorithm identifies outliers that violate dependency rules by mining function dependency relationships in the data. This algorithm starts from a single attribute and gradually expands to larger attribute sets. It uses a difference set to efficiently compute the function dependency $X \setminus \{A\} \to A\,(A \in X)$, ensuring that only non-trivial function dependencies are considered. Meanwhile, it excludes attribute combinations that cannot generate new function dependencies through pruning rules.

$$S_{\text{TANE}}(x_{ij}) = \frac{1}{|FD_j|} \sum_{fd \in FD_j} \mathbb{I}(\text{violate}(x_{ij}, fd)) \tag{2}$$

Among them, FD_j is the set of functional dependencies involving the j-th column. $\text{violate}(x_{ij}, fd)$ determines whether a cell violates the dependency function fd, and $\mathbb{I}\{\cdot\}$ is an indicator function. For the rule list extracted by the TANE algorithm, the rules are used to detect cells and generate abnormality scores.

For the statistical outlier detection, inspired by the DBoost method, this model adopts a strategy that combines Gaussian distribution detection and histogram detection to comprehensively capture outliers in the data:

$$S_{\text{STAT}}(x_{ij}) = \omega \cdot S_{\text{HIST}}(x_{ij}) + \omega \cdot S_{\text{GAUSS}}(x_{ij}) \tag{3}$$

The histogram method and the Gaussian method are respectively represented by formulas, where D_j is the value range of the j-th column, and μ_j and σ_j are the mean and standard deviation of the j-th column, respectively.

$$S_{\text{HIST}}(x_{ij}) = 1 - \frac{\text{freq}(x_{ij})}{\max_{v \in D} \text{freq}(v)} \tag{4}$$

$$S_{\text{GAUSS}}(x_{ij}) = 1 - \exp\left(-\frac{(c_{ij} - \mu_j)^2}{2\sigma_j^2}\right) \tag{5}$$

Adaptive pattern abnormality detection: Aiming at the problem of format inconsistency commonly existing in mixed data types, an adaptive pattern detection mechanism is designed. This mechanism automatically analyzes the characteristics of data columns, dynamically generates a set of regular expression rules, and establishes a hierarchical dominant pattern representation. Let the data column A_j contain n cells, and k different pattern categories $\{P_1, P_2, \ldots, P_K\}$ are detected. The theoretical expected frequency when the patterns are randomly distributed is as follows:

$$E_j = \frac{n}{k}, \quad \forall j \in \{1, 2, \ldots, k\} \tag{6}$$

Measure the degree of deviation between the observed distribution and the theoretical distribution, and use the standardized residual to calculate and identify the significant deviation direction of each pattern.

$$z_j = \frac{O_j - E_j}{\sqrt{E_j\left(1 - \frac{1}{k}\right)}} \tag{7}$$

Among them, O_j is the actual observed frequency of pattern P_j. The pattern classification rule is that when $z_j \geq 2$, the pattern at this time is the dominant type of the column, and a corresponding regular rule is generated and marked as a normal value; when $-2 < z_j < 2$, it is the secondary type of the column, the pattern is retained but no detection rule is generated; when $z_j \leq -2$, it is a noise type and marked as an abnormal candidate. Among them, the pattern abnormality score can be derived from different types:

$$S_{\text{ADAPT}}(x_{ij}) = \begin{cases} 1 - \frac{O_j}{n}, & Z_j \leq -2 \\ \frac{1}{1+\exp(-|Z_j|)}, & Z_j \geq 2 \\ 0.1 * \frac{1}{1+O_j}, & \text{other} \end{cases} \tag{8}$$

As shown in Fig. 3, in the adaptive function, the score of $x_{i,j}$ obtained from the function dependency violation detection based on the TANE algorithm is 0.7, and the score from the adaptive pattern abnormality detection is 0.1. Therefore, the adaptive degree score of this cell is 0.8.

Population Initialization and Selection Strategy. First, randomly select a subset composed of k tuples from the tuple set T, denoted as $P = \{t_1, t_2, \ldots, t_k\}$,

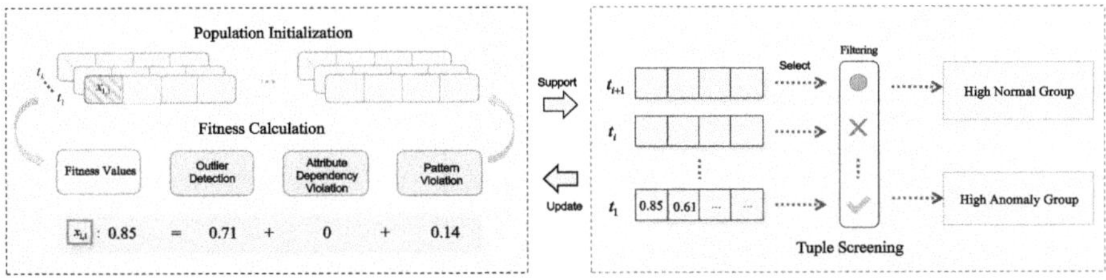

Fig. 3. Specific process of tuple selection by the data selector.

which forms a population, and the total number of populations is T/k. The fitness of each tuple t_i is the weighted sum of the fitnesses of all cells it contains:

$$F(t_i) = \sum_{j=1}^{n} F(x_{ij}) \tag{9}$$

A dual - threshold selection strategy is adopted to respectively select individuals with a high fitness threshold and a low fitness threshold to represent individuals with a high degree of abnormality and a high degree of normality. Among them, the high fitness threshold is $\tau_H = \mu_F + \sigma_F$, and the low fitness threshold is $\tau_L = \mu_F - \sigma_F$. Here, μ_F and σ_F are the mean and standard deviation of the fitness of the current population, respectively.

$$\text{Selected} = \{t \in P : F(t) \geq \tau_H \text{ or } F(t) \geq \tau_L\} \tag{10}$$

Crossover and Mutation Operations. As shown in Fig. 4, the crossover operation is performed on the selected tuple individuals. The paired individuals $t_1 = \{x_{1,1}, x_{1,2}, \ldots, x_{1,N}\}$ and $t_i = \{x_{i,1}, x_{i,2}, \ldots, x_{i,N}\}$ exchange part of their contents according to the difference in fitness. The positions of cells with larger fitness differences are preferentially exchanged to generate new tuples $t_1' = \{x_{1,1}, x_{1,2}', \ldots, x_{1,N}\}$ and $t_i' = \{x_{i,1}, x_{i,2}', \ldots, x_{i,N}\}$. For the mutation operation, a tuple t_k with relatively high fitness is randomly selected, and for the cell $x_{k,j}$ in it, a new value is randomly selected from the candidate cells in the same column for replacement, generating a mutated tuple t_k'. The mutation probability is set to 0.1 times the total number of tuples to be mutated. Through the above-mentioned evolutionary algorithm optimization process, the system can automatically identify the most representative abnormal and normal samples, providing high-quality initial labeled data for subsequent label propagation and model training, effectively reducing the need for manual intervention, and improving the degree of automation in abnormality detection.

Diversity Integrated Selection Strategy. The selection strategy of traditional genetic algorithms often leads to the over - concentration of selection

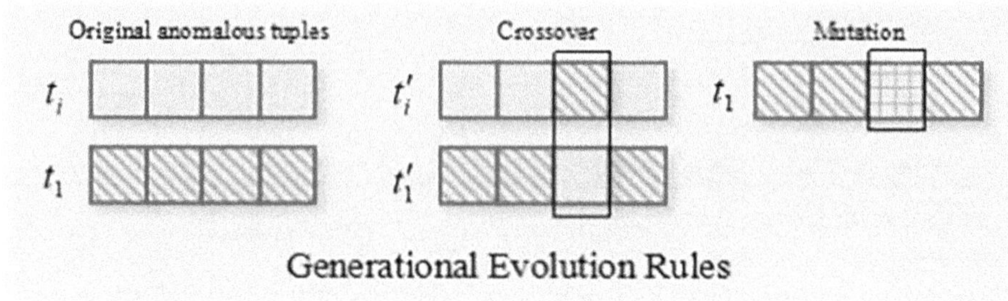

Fig. 4. Generation of evolutionary rules for the data selector.

results on certain specific attribute columns, thus affecting the balance of label distribution and the generalization ability of the model. To solve this problem, this paper proposes a diversity - integrated selection strategy. This strategy analyzes the distribution characteristics of cells in each column within the population and dynamically adjusts the selection weights to ensure the diversity and representativeness of the selection results. For the high - fitness populationP_H, first, calculate the average fitness of all cells in it as the reference value:

$$\overline{F_H} = \frac{1}{|P_H| \times n} \sum_{t_i \in P_H} \sum_{j=1}^{n} F(x_{ij}) \tag{11}$$

Among them, $|P_H|$ represents the scale of the high-fitness population, and n is the dimension of data attributes. Based on this threshold, calculate the proportion of cells in each column j that exceed the average fitness in this population, and take it as the diversity weight of this column:

$$w_j^H = \frac{\left|\{x_{ij} \in P_H : F(x_{ij}) > \overline{F_H}\}\right|}{|P_H|} \tag{12}$$

This weight reflects the degree of concentration of the j-th column in the high-fitness selection. When w_j^H is close to 1, it indicates that most of the cells in this column have high fitness; when w_j^H is small, it indicates that the cells with high fitness in this column are relatively rare. For the low-fitness population P_L, a dual calculation method is adopted to calculate the average fitness of this population:

$$\overline{F_L} = \frac{1}{|P_L| \times n} \sum_{t_i \in P_L} \sum_{j=1}^{n} F(x_{ij}) \tag{13}$$

Then, calculate the proportion of cells in each column that are below the average fitness as the diversity weight:

$$w_j^L = \frac{\left|\{x_{ij} \in P_L : F(x_{ij}) > \overline{F_L}\}\right|}{|P_L|} \tag{14}$$

Integrate the diversity weights into the fitness calculation to obtain the integrated selection degree:

$$S_H(x_{ij}) = F(x_{ij}) \times w_j^H, S_L(x_{ij}) = F(x_{ij}) \times w_j^L \tag{15}$$

This integration mechanism can effectively regulate the selection preference of each column. For high-fitness populations, columns with smaller weights are assigned higher selection priority; for low-fitness populations, columns with smaller weights also receive more attention.

$$\overline{S_j^H} = \frac{1}{|P_H|} \sum_{t_i \in P_H} S_H(x_{ij}), \overline{S_j^L} = \frac{1}{|P_L|} \sum_{t_i \in P_L} S_L(x_{ij}) \tag{16}$$

Among them, C_H contains cells marked as abnormal candidates ($y = 1$), and C_L contains cells marked as normal candidates ($y = 0$).The final selection set is defined as:

$$C_H = \{x_{ij} \in P_H : S_H(x_{ij}) < \overline{S_j^H}\} \tag{17}$$

$$C_L = \{x_{ij} \in P_L : S_L(x_{ij}) < \overline{S_j^L}\} \tag{18}$$

4.2 The Second Stage of the Model

As a preparatory step before model training, after high-quality label samples are screened and initially labeled, it is necessary to further alleviate the problem of label sparsity and enhance the propagation ability of labels in unlabeled samples. This paper introduces a label diffusion algorithm based on a similarity propagation mechanism in the training preparation stage. The core idea of this algorithm is to assign unlabeled cells to the closest known label clusters according to their similarity relationships with labeled samples in the embedding space, thereby achieving effective expansion of labels. Specifically, let the set of known labels be $P = \{x_i, y_i\}$, where $y_i \subset \{0, 1\}$, representing normal or abnormal labels; the set of unlabeled samples is $U = \{x_j\}$, where y_j is to be determined. We first calculate the embedding vector v_i for all samples. This vector is constructed based on the integration of Word2vec encoding, TF-IDF weighting, and a context attention mechanism, and can effectively capture the semantic and context features of data cells. The cosine similarity is used to measure the distance between unlabeled samples and all labeled samples:

$$\text{sim}(x_j, x_i) = \frac{v_j \cdot v_i}{\|v_j\|\|v_i\|} \tag{19}$$

For unlabeled sample $x_j \in U$, select the labeled sample $x_i^* \in P$ with the maximum cosine similarity to it, that is:

$$x_i^* = \arg\max_{x_i \in P} \text{sim}(x_j, x_i) \tag{20}$$

This unlabeled sample is assigned to the label cluster where x_i^* is located, and let $y_j = y_i$. To further enhance the accuracy of the label diffusion results, this paper introduces a neighborhood consistency verification mechanism. Specifically, after completing the initial label diffusion, this mechanism adopts the k - nearest neighbor strategy to perform local consistency verification on each unlabeled sample that has obtained a propagated label. By counting the label distribution of the k nearest neighbors of the target sample, if a significant conflict is found between its current label and the neighborhood labels, the sample is marked as an uncertain sample and removed from the current training set, thus preventing the label pollution phenomenon. It can effectively solve the problem of uneven data distribution and provide reliable label support for the subsequent model training stage.

As the basic unit of model input, rational construction of positive and negative bags is core to this method. In scenarios with few abnormal annotations and abundant unknown data, an instance-level probability estimation mechanism is necessary to effectively evaluate instance abnormality degrees. We regard normal data from one perspective as unknown data from other perspectives, dividing data into two categories: reliable abnormal instances and unlabeled data.

The idea of multi-instance learning is introduced [7,12,35]. k instances are constructed into a bag space, and labels are provided only at the bag level. The setting satisfies that: a positive bag B_i^+ contains at least one instance from $P(\exists \mathbf{x}_{i,k} \in B_i^+, y_x = 1)$, then the label of this bag $Y_B = 1$. All instances in a negative bag B_j^- belong to U, and the label of this bag can be expressed as $Y_B = 0$. By constructing the bag probability function F and the instance probability function f, the model can reasonably assign the abnormal label to each instance and construct a mapping function. When $y = 1$, it indicates that the cell is finally abnormal; when $y = 0$, it indicates that the instance is finally normal, thus solving the problem of incomplete marking.

The positive and negative bag sets are constructed through a dynamic sampling method. Specifically, extract a number of $K \times \theta$ core positive instances from all cells labeled as abnormal in the i-th column, and randomly select $(1-\theta) \times K$ positive samples from the global abnormal cells. Iterate continuously to generate a sufficient number of positive bags B_i^+. For the negative bag B_i^-, it is composed of instances labeled as normal in the i-th column. Using the same method as B_i^+, extract $K \times \theta$ core negative instances from local normal cells, and randomly select $(1 - \theta) \times K$ negative samples from global normal cells to construct the negative bag. Inspired by the MLAD [31] model, by jointly learning the expressive features of the feature vectors to interpret the underlying patterns of the data structure, and using the global dynamic sampling mechanism to ensure the balanced distribution of positive and negative bags, the rational distribution of positive and negative bags is ensured.

4.3 The Third Stage of the Model

This module adopts an autoencoder (AE) as the core anomaly detector, mapping input instances to a lower-dimensional hidden space then back to the original space. Higher reconstruction error indicates greater deviation from normal data and higher anomaly probability. The reconstruction error is $a_\theta(x) =$

$\|x - AE_\theta(x)\|^2$, where $\|\cdot\|$ is the Euclidean norm, $AE_\theta(x)$ is the reconstructed input, and θ represents network parameters. The model uses a dual-component loss function $L = L_u + L_p$ for anomaly detection, where L_u simulates the distribution of seen instances on unlabeled data for effective reconstruction on new data, and L_p learns positive and negative instance labels through provided bag labels. Backpropagation minimizes the loss.

Reconstruction of unlabeled loss L_u: The autoencoder can capture anomalies in any form, and can conform to scenarios with a small number of positive examples in a large amount of unlabeled data, and has good robustness to slightly abnormal data. The reconstruction error for the negative bag can be expressed as $R_\theta(B_i^-) = \frac{1}{k}\sum_{j=1}^{k} a_\theta(x_{i,j})$ and the overall unlabeled part L_u can be expressed as:

$$L_u = \frac{1}{|B^-|} \sum_{B_i^- \in B^-} R_\theta(B_i^-) \tag{21}$$

Calculate the labeled loss L_p: Parameterize the instance probability function f, use Platt scaling to convert the anomaly scores obtained from the autoencoder into probability representations, and jointly calibrate the model accuracy by correlating with bag labels. The calibrated probability after conversion is:

$$f(x) = P(y_x = 1)\hat{} = \frac{1}{1 + \exp(-\alpha a_\theta(x) - \beta)} \tag{22}$$

The calibration parameters $\alpha, \beta \in \mathbb{R}$, and converted instance scores fall within $[0, 1]$. When converting instance probability to bag probability, we adopt a weight redistribution strategy to reflect each instance's contribution to the bag label accurately. This strategy, based on the PUMA [23] model's weight selection method, sorts instances by anomaly scores and assigns corresponding weights w_i. The bag's anomaly probability is determined by the weighted instance values and the highest and lowest anomaly probabilities among them. The final bag anomaly degree is:

$$F(B_i^+) = P(Y_B = 1)\hat{} = 1 - \prod_{x_{i,j} \in B_i^+} (1 - f(x_{i,j}))^{w_{i,j}} \tag{23}$$

For label loss, we perform label correction through instance feature learning to prevent model overfitting on positive instances. We select the most credible negative bag with the lowest anomaly probability for the model's classification task. Based on results updated each round, we continuously adjust the reliable negative bag with lowest anomaly probability to optimize feature learning. The positive-to-negative bag ratio is approximately 1:3 to balance classification performance and improve result credibility. The final classification loss comprises two components: loss for positive bags and loss for the most credible negative bags.

$$L_p = -\log\left(\prod_{B \in B^+} F(B) \prod_{B \in B^-} (1 - F(B))\right) + \lambda(\alpha^2 + \beta^2) \tag{24}$$

Here, λ is the weight parameter balancing the two losses. Network parameters including encoder, decoder, and probability mapping are optimized via backpropagation. The PU multi-instance learning process effectively detects potential anomalies and analyzes features from multiple perspectives, addressing limitations of incomplete and unreliable labels. This model fully utilizes limited label information to tackle label sparsity issues in traditional learning. Through data reconstruction, it comprehensively covers the entire dataset, achieving efficient anomaly detection for heterogeneous tabular data.

5 Experiments

5.1 Experimental Settings

Datasets. To evaluate our proposed approach, We selected six representative real datasets for experiments, covering comprehensive error types such as missing values (MV), typographical errors (TP), format issues (FI), outliers (OT), and violations of attribute dependencies (VAD). These datasets include: Table 1 lists the scale of these datasets and the distribution of error types.

- **Hospital** from the U.S. Department of Health and Human Services, a benchmark adopted by many literatures;
- **Flights** is a real-world dataset that we can obtain from previous research [29]. Due to inconsistent flight times in the data source, we implemented data cleaning procedures to ensure accuracy.
- **Beers** Beers is a real-world dataset that has been collected by scraping the web and has been manually cleaned [18];
- **NASA** is aircraft wing noise data composed of quantitative data. It is an available dataset that covers specific information about multiple types of error data;
- **Breast Cancer** from the UCI Machine Learning Repository, often used to evaluate quantitative models.
- **Soccer** is a synthetic dataset that describes the information of soccer players and their teams [27]. We randomly sampled 20000 tuples for performance evaluation.

Table 1. Dataset Statistics.

Data Set	Rows	Columns	Error Types	Error Rate
Hospital [18]	1000	20	TP, RV, FI	0.03
Flights [18]	2376	7	MV, TP, RV	0.3
Beers [26]	2410	11	MV, RV, TP	0.16
Nasa [2]	1504	6	MV, OT, TP	0.13
Breast Cancer [1]	700	12	MV, TP, OT	0.4
Soccer [34]	20,000	10	MV,FI,RV	0.15

Baselines. We compared TP-ADM with nine independent and advanced detection tools shown in Table 2, including: outlier detector FAHES, integrated method for outlier detection tool dBoost, rule-based data cleaning system Holoclean, CDC and NADEEF, KATARA [9] that uses knowledge base for error detection, the RTClean [11] method which builds an ontology library for detection based on the Holoclean model, the ML-based configuration-free detection RAHA method, and the data cleaning method ActiveClean [16]. The selected baselines cover a series of representative solutions in the fields of error detection and data cleaning, reflecting a variety of technical ideas. To ensure the fairness of experimental comparison, this study uniformly set an annotation budget constraint of 20 samples for all benchmark models that rely on manual annotation and strictly restricted the use of external knowledge bases or additional datasets. For some baseline methods that are difficult to fully reproduce, their performance indicators directly refer to the authoritative results published by the original paper RAHA under the same experimental configuration, ensuring the credibility and comparability of the comparison data.

Table 2. Comparison with error detection baseline.

Method	Hospital			Flights			Beers			Nasa			Breast_Cancer			Soccer		
	P	R	F1	P	R	F1	P	R	F1	P	R	F1	P	R	F1	P	R	F1
FAHES	0.06	0.03	0.04	0.35	0.01	0.03	0.03	0.00	0.00	**1.00**	0.05	0.09	0.11	0.04	0.06	0.03	0.04	0.03
RAHA	**0.94**	0.59	0.72	0.75	0.63	**0.69**	0.76	0.67	0.71	**1.00**	0.33	0.49	0.84	0.10	0.18	0.15	0.68	0.25
DBoost	0.54	0.45	0.49	**0.78**	0.57	0.66	0.54	0.56	0.55	0.98	**0.82**	**0.89**	0.54	**0.99**	0.70	0.21	0.73	0.33
Holoclean	0.02	0.01	0.01	0.56	0.48	0.52	0.07	0.05	0.06	**1.00**	0.00	0.01	**1.00**	0.07	0.14	0.16	0.07	0.10
KATARA	0.06	0.37	0.10	0.07	0.09	0.08	0.08	0.26	0.12	0.00	0.00	0.00	0.00	0.00	0.00	0.03	0.09	0.05
NADEEF	0.05	0.37	0.09	0.30	0.06	0.44	0.13	0.06	0.08	**1.00**	0.72	0.84	0.97	0.67	**0.79**	0.73	0.56	0.63
CDC	0.66	**0.78**	0.71	0.59	0.78	0.67	0.62	0.60	0.61	0.81	0.68	0.73	0.92	0.70	**0.79**	**0.82**	0.66	**0.73**
RTClean	0.09	0.18	0.12	0.57	0.50	0.54	0.19	0.07	0.10	0.75	0.01	0.02	0.50	0.17	0.25	0.23	0.16	0.19
ActivoCloan	0.02	0.14	0.03	0.28	**0.94**	0.44	0.16	**1.00**	0.28	0.03	0.03	0.03	0.00	0.00	0.00	0.26	**0.89**	0.40
TP-ADM	0.73	**0.78**	**0.75**	0.63	0.74	0.68	**0.78**	0.61	**0.68**	0.79	0.63	0.70	0.96	0.62	0.75	0.74	0.69	0.71

5.2 Performance Evaluation

We conducted comprehensive comparative experiments between TP-ADM and nine baseline tools on six datasets. To ensure the validity of the experiments, the average value of three runs was taken as the final result. As shown in Table 2, when other baseline methods require manual provision of rules and labels, TP-ADM outperforms most baseline methods in evaluation indicators such as the F1 score. On qualitative datasets like Hospital, Flights, and Beers, the learning data samples selected by the data detection algorithm based on TANE can show good results. For the quantitative datasets Nasa and Breast Cancer, using detection methods based on statistics can capture most errors. For large - scale comprehensive datasets, our model also shows good results, reflecting its applicability to complex data. In contrast, single - perspective tools such as FAHES and NADEEF are difficult to adapt to datasets containing complex error types in the real world. Moreover, classic learning - based methods, such as Raha, are easily affected by the diversity of data anomalies and the imbalance between positive and negative samples. And tools that require manual annotation, such as ActiveClean, will also encounter certain limitations due to cost constraints.

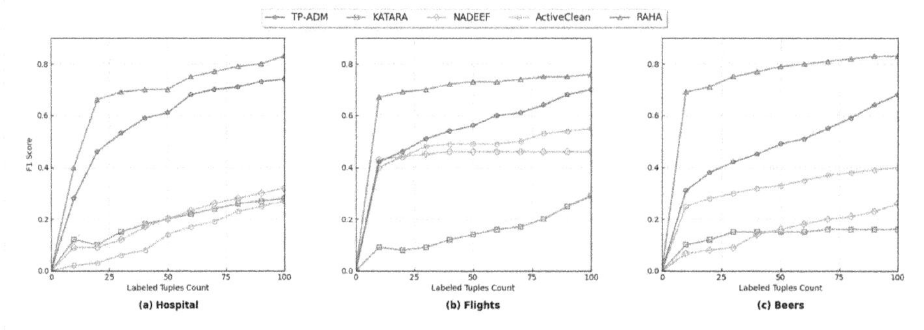

Fig. 5. Effects on model performance under different label budgets.

Performance comparison under different label budgets. In Fig. 5, the x-axis represents the number of labeled samples, ranging from 0 to 100, and the y-axis represents the average F1 score of the corresponding methods. It should be noted that since the method proposed in this paper can be fully implemented without human intervention, the x-axis for TP-ADM refers to the number of samples automatically selected by the selector, rather than the number of labeled samples manually provided by users. As the number of labeled samples increases, the performance of the RAHA method improves, while our method still outperforms most methods without manual labeling, demonstrating significant advantages in automation.

This experiment verifies the effectiveness of the proposed method through a comprehensive performance comparison and analysis between the random sampling method and the evolutionary selector. As shown in Fig. 6, the evolutionary selector strategy demonstrates superior performance over the random sampling method on the two standard datasets, Flights and Nasa. However, the differentiated performance of different selectors on heterogeneous datasets fully illustrates the decisive influence of the intrinsic characteristics of the data on the algorithm performance. In addition, applying the evolutionary selector to the benchmark method can also exhibit more excellent performance.

Appropriately configured bag data can provide ample weakly supervised information; However, an excess number of bags may introduce noise and exacerbate the risk of false positives. Figure 7, Establishing the ratio of positive to

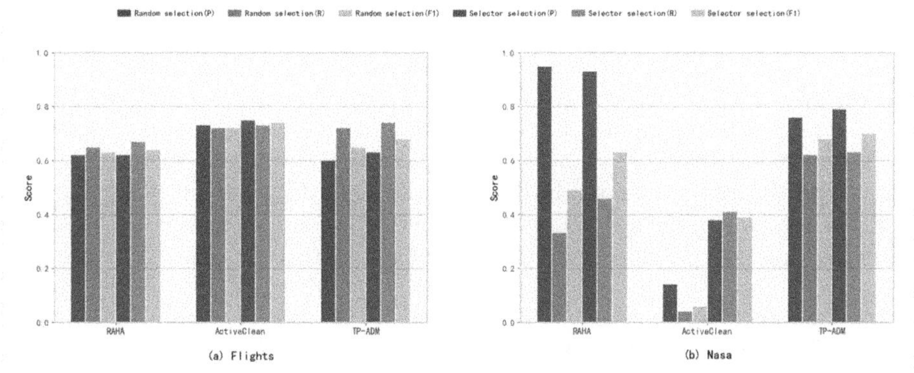

Fig. 6. Comprehensive performance comparison of selection methods.

negative bags between 80:240 and 100:300 can fully leverage the advantages of PU learning. The instances within each bag exhibit slight variations in performance according to the characteristics of different datasets, achieving a balance within the corresponding range that optimizes both performance and efficiency, while also considering detection performance and computational effectiveness.

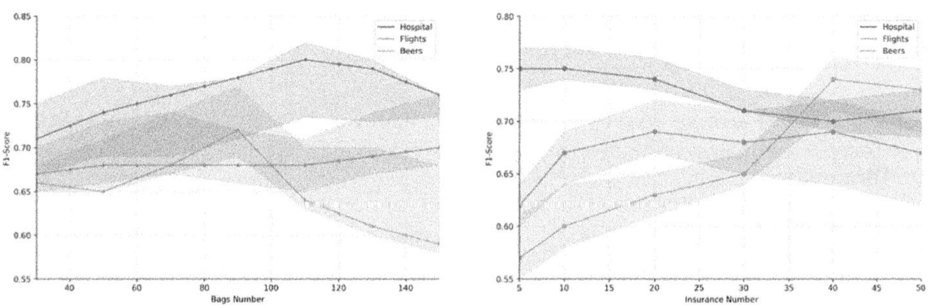

Fig. 7. The influence of package composition and the number of instances on the experiment.

6 Conclusion

This paper studies the problem of anomaly detection in tabular data from the perspective of data selection, i.e., how to learn high-value information without manual labeling costs. We propose integrating genetic algorithms into anomaly detection for tabular data and design a novel method named TP-ADM with a unique three-stage learning paradigm to effectively overcome the challenge of data imbalance. In the first stage, this method optimizes the data selector through an evolutionary mechanism and automatically assigns initial labels; in the second stage, an improved label diffusion module is proposed to address data sparsity and imbalance issues; in the third stage, the model is trained by designing an iterative adaptive generation strategy for pseudo-labels, thus completing the tabular anomaly detection process. Experimental results show that this method performs well without user intervention or external database assistance and can provide effective data selection strategies for other methods.

Acknowledgments. This work was supported by the Heilongjiang Key R&D Program of China under Grant No. GA23A915.

References

1. Abdelaal, M., Koparde, R., Schoening, H.: Autocure: automated tabular data curation technique for ML pipelines. In: Proceedings of the Sixth International Workshop on Exploiting Artificial Intelligence Techniques for Data Management, pp. 1–11 (2023)
2. Abdelaal, M., Ktitarev, T., Städtler, D., Schöning, H.: Saged: few-shot meta learning for tabular data error detection. In: EDBT, pp. 386–398 (2024)
3. Abedjan, Z., et al.: Detecting data errors: where are we and what needs to be done? Proc. VLDB Endow. **9**(12), 993–1004 (2016)
4. Arifovic, J., Gencay, R.: Using genetic algorithms to select architecture of a feedforward artificial neural network. XXPhys. A **289**(3–4), 574–594 (2001)
5. Berti-Equille, L., Dasu, T., Srivastava, D.: Discovery of complex glitch patterns: a novel approach to quantitative data cleaning. In: 2011 IEEE 27th International Conference on Data Engineering, pp. 733–744. IEEE (2011)
6. Biessmann, F., et al.: Datawig: missing value imputation for tables. J. Mach. Learn. Res. **20**(175), 1–6 (2019)
7. Carbonneau, M.A., Cheplygina, V., Granger, E., Gagnon, G.: Multiple instance learning: a survey of problem characteristics and applications. Pattern Recogn. **77**, 329–353 (2018)
8. Chu, X., Ilyas, I.F., Papotti, P.: Discovering denial constraints. Proc. VLDB Endow. **6**(13), 1498–1509 (2013)
9. Chu, X., et al.: Katara: a data cleaning system powered by knowledge bases and crowdsourcing. In: Proceedings of the 2015 ACM SIGMOD International Conference on Management of Data, pp. 1247–1261 (2015)
10. Dallachiesa, M., et al.: Nadeef: a commodity data cleaning system. In: Proceedings of the 2013 ACM SIGMOD International Conference on Management of Data, pp. 541–552 (2013)
11. Del Gaudio, D., Schubert, T., Abdelaal, M.: Rtclean: context-aware tabular data cleaning using real-time OFDS. In: 2023 IEEE International Conference on Pervasive Computing and Communications Workshops and other Affiliated Events (PerCom Workshops), pp. 546–551. IEEE (2023)
12. Dietterich, T.G., Lathrop, R.H., Lozano-Pérez, T.: Solving the multiple instance problem with axis-parallel rectangles. Artif. Intell. **89**(1–2), 31–71 (1997)

13. Ge, C., Gao, Y., Miao, X., Yao, B., Wang, H.: A hybrid data cleaning framework using Markov logic networks. IEEE Trans. Knowl. Data Eng. **34**(5), 2048–2062 (2020)
14. Hellerstein, J.M.: Quantitative data cleaning for large databases (2013)
15. Jäger, S., Biessmann, F.: From data imputation to data cleaning—automated cleaning of tabular data improves downstream predictive performance. In: International Conference on Artificial Intelligence and Statistics, pp. 3394–3402. PMLR (2024)
16. Krishnan, S., Wang, J., Wu, E., Franklin, M.J., Goldberg, K.: Activeclean: interactive data cleaning for statistical modeling. Proc. VLDB Endow. **9**(12), 948–959 (2016)
17. Liu, Z., Zhou, Z., Rekatsinas, T.: Picket: self-supervised data diagnostics for ML pipelines. CoRR (2020)
18. Mahdavi, M., et al.: Raha: a configuration-free error detection system. In: Proceedings of the 2019 International Conference on Management of Data, pp. 865–882 (2019)
19. Mathew, T.V.: Genetic algorithm. Report submitted at IIT Bombay **53**, 18–19 (2012)
20. MESTS, J., Tang, M.: Distributed representations of tuples for entity resolution. Proc. VLDB Endow. **11**(11) (2018)
21. Neutatz, F., Mahdavi, M., Abedjan, Z.: Ed2: a case for active learning in error detection. In: Proceedings of the 28th ACM International Conference on Information and Knowledge Management, pp. 2249–2252 (2019)
22. Peng, J., et al.: Self-supervised and interpretable data cleaning with sequence generative adversarial networks. Proc. VLDB Endow. **16**(3), 433–446 (2022)
23. Perini, L., Vercruyssen, V., Davis, J.: Learning from positive and unlabeled multi-instance bags in anomaly detection. In: Proceedings of the 29th ACM SIGKDD Conference on Knowledge Discovery and Data Mining, pp. 1897–1906 (2023)
24. Pit-Claudel, C., Mariet, Z., Harding, R., Madden, S.: Outlier detection in heterogeneous datasets using automatic tuple expansion (2016)
25. Qahtan, A.A., Elmagarmid, A., Castro Fernandez, R., Ouzzani, M., Tang, N.: Fahes: a robust disguised missing values detector. In: Proceedings of the 24th ACM SIGKDD International Conference on Knowledge Discovery & Data Mining, pp. 2100–2109 (2018)
26. Rahm, E., Do, H.H., et al.: Data cleaning: problems and current approaches. IEEE Data Eng. Bull. **23**(4), 3–13 (2000)
27. Rammelaere, J., Geerts, F.: Explaining repaired data with CFDs. Proc. VLDB Endow. **11**(11), 1387–1399 (2018)
28. Rekatsinas, T., Chu, X., Ilyas, I., Ré, C.H.: Holistic data repairs with probabilistic inference. arxiv 2017. arXiv preprint arXiv:1702.00820
29. Rekatsinas, T., Chu, X., Ilyas, I.F., Ré, C.: Holoclean: holistic data repairs with probabilistic inference. arXiv preprint arXiv:1702.00820 (2017)
30. Rooker, T.: Review of genetic algorithms in search, optimization, and machine learning. AI Mag. **12**(1), 102–102 (1991)
31. Song, H., Li, Y., Han, Q.: Mlad: a two-stage fully automated multi-perspective tabular data anomaly detection framework. In: International Conference on Intelligent Computing, pp. 511–522. Springer (2025)
32. Yakout, M., Berti-Équille, L., Elmagarmid, A.K.: Don't be scared: use scalable automatic repairing with maximal likelihood and bounded changes. In: Proceedings of the 2013 ACM SIGMOD International Conference on Management of Data, pp. 553–564 (2013)

33. Yakout, M., Elmagarmid, A.K., Neville, J., Ouzzani, M., Ilyas, I.F.: Guided data repair. arXiv preprint arXiv:1103.3103 (2011)
34. Zhang, Y., Qin, J., Mao, R., Ji, Y., Wang, Y., Ali, M.A.: Adaptive label cleaning for error detection on tabular data. In: Asia-Pacific Web (APWeb) and Web-Age Information Management (WAIM) Joint International Conference on Web and Big Data, pp. 63–78. Springer (2023)
35. Zhou, Z.H.: Multi-instance learning: a survey. Department of Computer Science & Technology, Nanjing University, Technical Report **1**, 4 (2004)

GADM: Granularity-Aware Diffusion Model for Uncertainty Forecasting in Non-stationary Time Series

Zhuhua Wang, Rui Chen, Hongtao Song(✉), and Qilong Han

Harbin Engineering University, Harbin, China
{S323547035,ruichen,songhongtao,hanqilong}@hrbeu.edu.cn

Abstract. Time series forecasting faces multiple uncertainties in complex dynamic scenarios, such as sudden disturbances and volatile data distributions. Traditional methods typically assume that data exhibits stable regularity, and ignoring such non-stationary characteristics makes it difficult to quantify prediction risks. While existing diffusion models generate probabilistic forecasts, their single-granularity modeling approach results in the loss of non-stationary information. Therefore, this paper proposes a granularity-aware diffusion model that achieves precise modeling of uncertainty through a multi-granularity collaborative learning framework. Firstly, a Dynamic Granularity Decomposition (DGD) is designed, utilizing differentiable probabilistic modeling to determine granularity size. Secondly, the Perturbation Restoration Conditional Encoder (PRCE) reconstructs non-stationary features via Gated Linear Units, incorporating prior knowledge from historical time series. Furthermore, a Multi-granularity Guided Diffusion Generator (MGDG) is designed to align coarse-grained trends with fine-grained fluctuations across different denoising stages, achieving gradual distribution optimization through conditionally constrained Markov chains. Experimental results demonstrate that the proposed framework outperforms existing methods on multi-granularity tasks, particularly exhibiting significant advantages in prediction accuracy and uncertainty forecasting.

Keywords: time series prediction · diffusion model · uncertainty forecasting · granularity guided · perturbation restoration

1 Introduction

Time series forecasting, as the core technology supporting intelligent decision-making, plays a strategic role in energy scheduling [2], traffic control [22,25], financial risk control [7]and other fields [1,17]. With the popularization of Internet of things (IOT) technology, the time series data collected by modern industrial systems show two significant characteristics: (1) multi-scale dynamics, including second-level equipment state fluctuation, hourly load cycle and seasonal trend evolution [20]; (2) Non-stationary uncertainty, affected by emergen-

T. Hao et al. (Eds.): BESC 2025, LNCS 16431, pp. 107–122, 2026.
https://doi.org/10.1007/978-981-95-7138-3_8

cies (such as extreme weather, equipment failure) and external interference (policy regulation, market fluctuations), the data distribution shows time-varying characteristics [9].

The existing methods can roughly be classified into three categories: Traditional statistical methods such as ARIMA [19] and Prophet [3], based on the assumption of stationary, obtain deterministic point estimates through linear modeling or additive decomposition, and are unable to quantitatively predict risks. Although deep learning models such as LSTM [4]and Transformer variants [27,28] improve accuracy through nonlinear mapping, most of them focus on deterministic prediction, and single-granularity modeling is difficult to balance the dynamic dynamics of trends and fluctuations. For example, WaveNet [10] captures long-term dependencies through expanded convolution, but lacks explicit modeling of non-stationary components; FEDformer [28] establishes cross-scale correlations in the frequency domain, but fails to solve the problem of uncertain quantization. In probabilistic generative models [12,14,26], although the diffusion model approximates complex distributions through progressive denoising, the existing methods have significant flaws:

- Most of the models are modeled using diffusion chains with fixed resolution, failing to effectively capture fine-grained features in non-stationary time series, resulting in the loss of unexpected events and fluctuation patterns during the standardization process.
- In the current diffusion models, conditional encoders usually ignore the recovery of non-stationary components, resulting in the inability of the model to fully model the perturbation components when dealing with the dynamic changes in time series data

In order to solve the problem of fixed grain size limitation in traditional methods, we propose a dynamic grain size selection mechanism. Through differentiable probabilistic modeling, the model can adaptively select grain size and better capture multi-level features in time series data. Secondly, a perturbation-aware condition encoder was designed. The lost non-stationary signals were reconstructed based on the GLU gating unit, and a time-varying perturbation factor was introduced in the attention calculation, thereby effectively restoring the non-stationary components in the data and improving the adaptability of the model to dynamic fluctuations. The multi-granularity guided diffusion mechanism builds a conditionally constrained Markov chain and aligns the coarse-grained trend with the fine-grained fluctuation in the reverse denoising stage, ensuring the effective integration of information of different granularities, thereby improving the accuracy and stability of the model in time series prediction. In summary, the main contributions of this paper are as follows:

- Aiming at the problem of the single granularity modeling of the existing diffusion models in time series prediction, a diffusion generation model with multi-granularity feature coupling is proposed. The granularity size selection is achieved through differentiable probability modeling, breaking through the limitation of the fixed granularity in the traditional sliding window. A two-stage diffusion mechanism of "coarse-grained trend alignment - fine-grained

fluctuation correction" is designed. During the reverse denoising process, a Markov chain with multi-granularity conditional constraints is established to achieve the progressive optimization of time-frequency domain features and significantly improve the generation quality of non-stationary time series.
- A perturbation-aware condition encoder module is proposed. By reconstructing the non-stationary components lost during the normalization process through the gated linear unit (GLU), a time-varying perturbation factor is introduced in the attention calculation to effectively retain key signals such as sudden fluctuations.
- By combining multi-granularity data and uncertainty modeling, this method provides a more efficient and accurate prediction solution for time series prediction, especially in dealing with complex time-dependent and uncertainty problems. Through experiments on multiple datasets, the effectiveness of the proposed method has been proved.

2 Related Work

Early studies mainly built prediction models based on stationarity assumption. For example, ARIMA [19] eliminated trend components by difference operation, and Facebook Prophet [3] decomposed seasonal and trend items by additive model. This class of methods performs well in regular periodic data, but it is difficult to capture non-stationary features caused by burst disturbances. With the development of deep learning, machine learning methods such as LSTM [4] improve prediction accuracy through nonlinear mapping, but do not solve the problem of prediction risk quantification.

In recent years, diffusion models [6,8,26] have provided a new paradigm for time-series probabilistic prediction by virtue of their progressive generation ability. Early work such as TimeGrad [12]combined the diffusion model with the autoregressive framework to iteratively generate future sequences through noise, which laid the foundation for the temporal diffusion model. CSDI [21]further proposed a diffusion-based interpolation method, which used the mask mechanism to model the spatio-temporal dependence and transformed the time series prediction into a conditional generation problem. Subsequent improvements such as TimeDiff [18] randomly mix the encoding of historical information with real future data in a certain proportion to form conditional signals. The mixing ratio is controlled by a random mask matrix to alleviate the distribution difference between training and inference. However, these methods are still limited to single-granularity modeling, and it is difficult to coordinate the multi-level dynamic characteristics of trends and fluctuations.

Among the traditional multi-granularity methods, WaveNet [10] extracts features using dilated convolution, but it lacks explicit modeling of non-stationary components. N-BEATS [11] employs hierarchical decomposition to separate the series into trend-seasonal components, but its linear superposition assumption fails to capture complex nonlinear dynamics. Recent Transformer variants, such as Informer [27] and FEDformer [28], enhance multi-scale modeling through frequency domain attention. However, they are still limited to deterministic prediction and struggle to quantify uncertainty.

Traditional probability models such as DeepAR [16] estimate quantiles based on autoregressive likelihood, but are sensitive to sudden fluctuations. VAE-based [5] methods cST-ML [24] and DAC-ML [23] model uncertainty through latent variables, but the prediction interval is conservative due to posterior collapse. Although GP-Copula [15] method introduces nonparametric dependence modeling, it has high computational complexity. The diffusion model gradually optimizes the distribution through the reverse denoising process, and can approach any complex distribution in theory. However, the existing methods such as TMDM[18] weaken the non-stationary signal in the normalization process, resulting in the loss of burst mode.

3 Methodology

This section proposes a multi-granularity collaborative Diffusion non-stationary time series prediction Model GADM. Its core architecture realizes the dynamic analysis and probability generation of non-stationary time series through the organic integration of multi-granularity collaborative modeling and the uncertainty propagation mechanism. As shown in Fig. 1, the model consists of three core components: Dynamic Granularity Decomposition Module (DGD), Perturbation Restoration Conditional Encoder (PRCE) and Multi-granularity Guided Diffusion Generator (MGDG). Each component works collaboratively to form a closed-loop optimization path of "decomposition - encoding - generation".

The DGD realizes the selection of granularity size through differentiable probability modeling. The PRCE embers a bidirectional gated Perturbation recovery mechanism in the standard Transformer architecture. By dynamically reconstructing the joint distribution of non-stationary features and conditional representations, it generates conditional representations. The MGDG takes coarse-grained data as the implicit constraint condition of the intermediate diffusion step and realizes multi-granularity modeling of time series patterns through cross-granularity feature alignment.

3.1 Dynamic Granularity Decomposition

The main task of the dynamic granularity decomposition module is to perform multi-granularity decomposition on the input time series data and divide it into different granularity levels. Through this multi-granularity decomposition, the model is able to extract key information from features of different granularities. Traditional multi-granularity time series generation methods usually rely on preset fixed window sizes for moving average operations. This manually set approach is difficult to adapt to the dynamic characteristics of different datasets. To solve this problem, this paper proposes the adaptive generation of multi-granularity features based on differentiable probability modeling. Specifically, given the candidate window set $S = \{s_1, s_2, \cdots, s_K\}$, where s_K represents the time span of

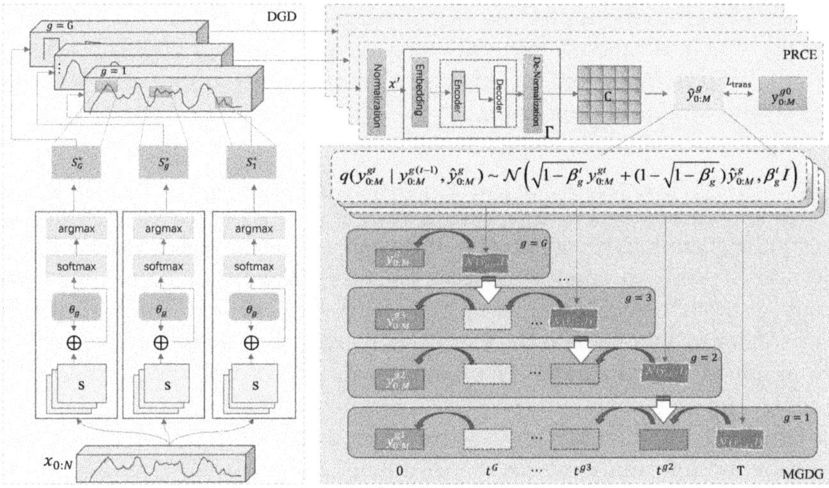

Fig. 1. Overview of the Granularity-Aware Diffusion Model (GADM) model, consisting of three key modules: Dynamic Granularity Decomposition (DGD), Perturbation Restoration Conditional Encoder (PRCE), and Multi-granularity Guided Diffusion Generator (MGDG) for time series forecasting.

the Kth candidate window, covering analysis requirements from fine-grained to coarse-grained. For each granularity level $g \in \{1, \ldots, G\}$ maintain the learnable parameter vector $\theta_g \in \mathbb{R}^K$, and generate the window selection probability distribution through Softmax:

$$p_g^{(k)} = \frac{\exp(\theta_g^{(k)})}{\sum_{i=1}^{K} \exp(\theta_g^{(i)})} \tag{1}$$

where $p_g^{(k)}$ represents the probability of the granularity g choosing the window s_K, and the parameter θ_g is optimized by gradient descent. To achieve differentiable discrete sampling, Gumbel noise is introduced and the temperature annealing strategy is adopted:

$$\tilde{p}_g^{(k)} = \frac{\exp\left(\frac{\log p_g^{(k)} + G_k}{\delta}\right)}{\sum_{i=1}^{K} \exp\left(\frac{\log p_g^{(i)} + G_i}{\delta}\right)} \tag{2}$$

where $G_k \sim \text{Gumbel}(0, 1)$ is independent and identically distributed noise, and δ is the temperature parameter annealed from $\delta_{init} = 1.0$ to $\delta_{final} = 0.01$ according to cosine scheduling. During training, the gradient is calculated through $\tilde{p}_g$, and the maximum probability window is taken during inference.

$$s_g^* = s_{\text{argmax}}(p_g) \tag{3}$$

Based on the selected window s_g, the moving average of the original sequence $\mathbf{X}^{(1)} \in \mathbb{R}^{T \times d}$ is performed to generate a coarse-grained representation. The data of granularity g is replicated s_g times so that the multi-granularity features are aligned in the temporal dimension.

3.2 Perturbation Restoration Conditional Encoder

In the multi-granularity cooperative diffusion model GADM, the PRCE plays a core role. It aims to conduct further feature processing on the time series of different granularities obtained from the DGD, and through the perception and recovery of disturbances, help the model better adapt to the volatility and sudden events in non-stationary data. This module consists of two key parts: stationing processing and perturbation recovery mechanism. They respectively optimize the conditional input of the model from the aspects of stationing control and non-stationary information repair. We adopt an improved Transformer model for feature extraction of multi-granularity time series data.

1) Stationarization Smooth processing in time series prediction, data often have non-stationary, especially on datasets with large fluctuations. Traditional stabilization methods may lose some key signals, especially when facing unexpected events or sharp fluctuations. Therefore, in PRCE, we first perform stabilization processing on the multi-granularity features of the input to reduce the non-stationary of the time series data. Specifically, the input sequence at each granularity level undergoes normalization operations, making the statistical characteristics of the time series more stable and thereby reducing model instability caused by volatility or interference. This process is achieved through the following formula:

$$\begin{cases} \mu_{x^g} &= \dfrac{1}{S}\displaystyle\sum_{i=1}^{s} x_i^g \\ \sigma_{x^g}^2 &= \dfrac{1}{S}\displaystyle\sum_{i=1}^{s} \left(x_i^g - \mu_{x^g}\right)^2 \\ \hat{x}_i^g &= \dfrac{1}{\sigma_{x^p}} \odot \left(x_i^g - \mu_{x^g}\right) \end{cases} \tag{4}$$

$\odot$ is the element-by-element level multiplication. The normalization module reduces the difference in distribution between each input tensors, resulting in a more stable distribution of model inputs.

2) Disturbance-Aware Mechanism In order to effectively extract the non-stationary features in the time series, we designed a perturbation factor generator based on gated linear units (GLU). The core idea of this generator is to utilize one-dimensional convolution operations to learn the dynamic change characteristics of time series and generate perturbation factors through the GLU activation function:

$$\left[\tau^{(g)}, \Delta^{(g)}\right] = \mathrm{GLU}\left(\mathrm{Conv1D}\left(X^{(g)}, e_c\right)\right) \tag{5}$$

Among them, Conv1D(·) represents a one-dimensional convolution operation, which is used to extract local features from the historical sequence. The GLU function is widely used to generate dynamically adjustable activation functions, and its form is:

$$\mathrm{GLU}(a) = a \odot \sigma(W_g a + b_g) \tag{6}$$

where σ is the Sigmoid activation function, and W_g and b_g are learnable parameters in the convolution operation that control the generation of perturbation factors. In this way, we can effectively capture and restore the non-stationary components in the time series, ensuring that the model can better cope with sudden changes in dynamic data.

While generating the perturbation factor, we designed an adaptive attention calculation method based on the perturbation factor to generate appropriate conditional representations at each time step. For each granularity level feature, the model calculates the query (Q), key (K), and value (V) through the following formula:

$$Q' = \tilde{X}^{(g)} W_Q, \quad K' = \tilde{X}^{(g)} W_K \tag{7}$$

where $\tilde{X}^{(g)}$ represents the granularity feature at the gth level, and W_Q and W_K are the weight matrices obtained through learning. Next, the calculation results of queries and keys are adjusted through perturbation factors, thereby enhancing the model's processing ability for non-stationary time series data. We through the following formula to calculate the concentration matrix A_{ij}:

$$A_{ij} = \frac{\tau_i^{(g)} Q_i^{(g)} K_j^{(g)}}{\sqrt{d}} + \Delta_{ij}^{(g)} \tag{8}$$

where $\tau_i^{(g)}$ is for the first g layer granularity characteristics of disturbance factors, Q_i and $K_j^{(g)}$ query and key vector, respectively d for the characteristic dimension. The final self-attention calculation standardizes the attention weights through the Softmax operation.

3.3 Multi-granularity Guided Diffusion Generator

In view of the limitations of single-granularity modeling of traditional diffusion models in non-stationary time series prediction, this section proposes a multi-granularity guided diffusion generator. This module realizes the progressive optimization of multi-level time series features by constructing conditional constrained Markov chains and aligning coarse-grained trends and fine-grained fluctuations respectively at different denoising stages.

Multi-granularity guided diffusion explains how coarser-grained data can be introduced into the diffusion process. The purpose of bootstrapping is to ensure that intermediate steps in the diffusion process are consistent with the coarse-grained data at a particular time step. This approach enables the model to retain high-level features in the data during the learning process, which enhances model stability and guides the model to focus more on key trends in the time series during training.

Coarse-grained bootstrapping: bootstrapping sample generation by ensuring that the intermediate potential space maintains the structure of the time series. Specifically, the diffusion model is bootstrapped at the intermediate diffusion step t^{g^*} by introducing coarse-grained target data. We build the objective function by evaluating the marginal distribution of the coarse-grained data at the diffusion step $t^{g^*} p_\theta(y^g_{0:M})$. By appropriately choosing the diffusion step t^{g^*}, the coarse-grained features recovered from the denoising process can obtain the information from the real coarse-grained samples, and the marginal distributions of the latent variables at the diffusion step t^{g^*} can be represented by $p_\theta(y_{0:M}^{t^{g^*}T})$:

$$p_\theta(y_{0M}^{t^{g^*}}) = \int p(y^T_{0:M}) \prod_{n=N_g+1}^{N} p_\theta(y^{t-1}_{0:M} \mid y^t_{0:M}) dy_{(t^{g^*}+1):T} \tag{9}$$

In this model, the goal of coarse-grained bootstrapping is to allow the coarse-grained data generated by the intermediate state to approximate the true coarse-grained data. At some time step in the diffusion process t^*_g the date $y^g_{0:M}$ generated can be consistent with the distribution of the coarse-grained data, so the goal at this time step is:

$$\log p_\theta(y^g_{0:M}) = \log \int p_\theta(y^{t^{g^*}}_{0:M}, y^{t^{g^*}+1}_{0:M}, ..., y^T_{0:M}) dy_{0:M}^{t^{g^*}+1:T} \tag{10}$$

Multi-granularity bootstrapping: the idea of coarse-grained bootstrapping is extended to a number of different granularities, and after multi-granularity generation and feature extraction, data at G granularity levels are generated $y^{g1}_{0:M}, y^{g2}_{0:M}, ..., y^{G}_{0:M}$ and each level corresponds to different granularity of the time series data, which can be bootstrapped at different steps of the diffusion model. Coarse-grained data will lose more fine-grained features, so they will be closer to the data at the front of the inverse process of the diffusion model, and a larger noise variance coefficient and smaller diffusion step should be predetermined for the coarser-grained data. Thus, for a diffusion process with a particle size of g, $\alpha^t_{\text{g}} = \alpha^t_1$ when $t > t^{g^*}$ and vice versa, $\alpha^t_{\text{g}} = 1$. Based on $x_{0:N}$, using diffusion scheduling $\{\beta^t_g\}^T_{t=1} = \{1 - \alpha^t_g\}^T_{t=1}$, the conditional distribution of the forward process for all other time steps can be defined as:

$$q(y^{gt}_{0:M} \mid y^{g(t-1)}_{0:M}, y^g_{0:M}) \sim \mathcal{N}\left(\sqrt{1-\beta^g_t} y^g_{0:M} + \left(1 - \sqrt{1-\beta^g_t}\right) y^{g(t-1)}_{0:M}, \beta^g_t I\right) \tag{11}$$

The diffusion process can be conceptualized as an interpolation process between the real data $y^g_{0:M}$ and the conditional representation $\hat{y}^g_{0:M}$. The process starts with the real data $y^g_{0:M}$ and gradually transitions to $\hat{y}^g_{0:M}$. This approach effectively utilizes the reliable conditional mean estimation provided by the conditional extraction module. In the corresponding inverse process, initialized to include information about the conditions extracted at different granularities, the generation process is significantly simplified. If the provided conditions are good enough, the model can focus on uncertainty estimation.

3.4 Model Optimization

In this paper, we integrate the transformer conditional feature extraction module with a multi-granularity diffusion model into a unified optimization objective. The conditional generative model combines a transformer structure $\Gamma(\bullet)$ and a network associated with a latent variable C. The model is a multi-granularity denoising model. In the diffusion model component, a multi-granularity denoising model is trained. The GADM optimization objective can be divided into the following parts:

$$\begin{aligned}\mathcal{L}^{g}_{\text{diffusion}} = & \mathbb{E}_q\left[-\log p(y^g_{0:M} \mid y^g_{0:M}, \hat{y}^g_{0:M})\right] \\ & + D_{\text{KL}}\left(q(y^g_{0:M} \mid \hat{y}^g_{0:M}) \| p(y^g_{0:M} \mid \hat{y}^g_{0:M})\right)] \\ & + \sum_{t=2}^{T} D_{\text{KL}}\left(q(y^g_{0:M} \mid \hat{y}^g_{0:M}) \| p(y^g_{0:M} \mid \hat{y}^g_{0:M})\right))\end{aligned} \tag{12}$$

$\mathcal{L}^{\text{g}}_{diffision}$ guide the denoising model predicts uncertainty while fine-tuning the conditional generation model to provide a more appropriate representation of the condition. The multi-granularity guidance process can be represented as

$$\mathcal{L}_{\text{guidance}} = \sum_{g=1}^{G} \omega^{\text{g}} \mathcal{L}^{\text{g}}_{diffiusion}, \omega^{\text{g}} \in (0,1) \tag{13}$$

ω^{g} is a hyperparameter that controls the granularity g bootstrap scale.

To ensure the capability of the conditional feature extraction module, we also introduced $\mathcal{L}_{trans}$ to help guide the conditional generation process during diffusion.

$$\mathcal{L}_{trans} = \mathbb{E}_q(c \mid \Gamma(x^{\text{g}}_{0:N}))\left[-\log p(\hat{y}^{\text{g}}_{0:M} \mid c)\right] + D_{\text{KL}}\left(q(c \mid \Gamma(x^{\text{g}}_{0:N})) \| p(c)\right) \tag{14}$$

the final GADM optimization objective can be expressed as

$$\mathcal{L} = \mathcal{L}_{diffusion} + \lambda \mathcal{L}_{\text{trans}} \tag{15}$$

λ is a hyperparameter that adjusts the relative importance between diffusion losses and conversion losses.

4 Implementation and Evaluation

4.1 Experiment Setup

The datasets used in this thesis are derived from a number of publicly available time-series datasets covering a wide range of domains, including energy consumption, meteorology, transportation, and exchange rates. Table 1 gives specific information about these data.

We conducted experiments on servers equipped with an Intel Xeon Platinum 2.40 GHz CPU, an NVIDIA Quadro RTX 8000 GPU and 754 GB of RAM.

Table 1. Dataset Information

Dataset	Dimension	Freq	Pred
ETTm2	7	15 min	192
Exchange	8	1 day	192
Electricity	321	1 h	192
Weather	21	10 min	192

The diffusion step size was set to T=100. For PICP, 2.5% and 97.5% quantiles were selected. Therefore, the ideal PICP value should be 95%. The experiment used 100 samples to approximately estimate the distribution. All experiments were repeated 10 times, and the mean and standard deviation were recorded. The dataset is divided into the training set, the validation set and the test set. Among them, 70% is used for the training set, 20% for the test set, and 10% for the validation set.

4.2 Baseline

To comprehensively evaluate the method proposed in this paper, this study selects seven baseline models in the field of time series prediction for comparative analysis, covering diffusion-based probability generation, Transformer architecture, and classical generation methods. Among them, the diffusion-based models include: TimeGrad [12] constructs a noise predictor through the GRU network and implements single-granularity conditional guidance in the Markov chain; CSDI [21]is based on the implicit fraction matching theory and uses Fourier neural operators to model the conditional gradient field in the task of filling in missing data. TDT [14]separates temporal features through the unentanglement attention mechanism, but does not explicitly constrain the generation process of multi-granularity components. Transformer-based MAFormer [13]combines mask autoregressive streams with multi-head attention to model non-Gaussian distributions through Jacobian determinant transformations. However, its autoregressive characteristics lead to the accumulation of prediction errors for long sequences. In the generation method class baseline, cST-ML [24] adopts statistical transformation and multi-layer learning strategies to decompose frequency-domain features, and DAC-ML [23] realizes data adaptive collaborative training through the differentiable decomposition module. Both rely on preset rules to handle non-stationary fluctuations. GP-Copula [15] combines the Gaussian process with the Copula function to model the multivariate temporal correlation, but its computational complexity increases cubic with the sequence length.

4.3 Experimental Results and Analysis

Table 2 reports the average PICP and QICE values of 10 independent runs. The results show that our model achieves a high PICP and a low QICE on most datasets, outperforming the baseline model. The improvement of PICP results on the weather dataset is relatively small. This is because the volatility of weather data is greatly affected by climatic factors, but their changes are relatively periodic and will show certain patterns in the long-term trend. Compared with the sudden fluctuations in the energy sector, the fluctuations of weather data are more in line with seasonal changes and belong to relatively stable data, while GADM has more advantages in unstable data.

Table 2. Comparison of PICP and QICE for the model on four real datasets

Dataset	ETTm2		Exchange		Electricity		Weather	
Evaluation	PICP	QICE	PICP	QICE	PICP	QICE	PICP	QICE
MAForm	7.34 ± 0.167	7.89 ± 0.152	7.05 ± 0.167	7.28 ± 0.590	7.31 ± 0.364	7.04 ± 0.080	6.84 ± 0.462	9.07 ± 0.669
cST-ML	6.13 ± 0.164	7.29 ± 0.161	6.65 ± 0.642	7.94 ± 0.786	6.24 ± 0.354	7.99 ± 0.167	6.19 ± 0.624	6.21 ± 0.760
DAC-ML	6.24 ± 0.167	7.60 ± 0.191	6.34 ± 0.116	7.36 ± 0.709	6.62 ± 0.345	7.76 ± 0.153	6.96 ± 0.159	6.91 ± 0.823
GP-Copula	7.19 ± 0.135	6.86 ± 0.180	7.41 ± 0.647	7.71 ± 0.763	6.68 ± 0.354	5.85 ± 0.192	6.89 ± 0.576	8.10 ± 0.545
TimeGrad	7.21 ± 0.167	5.32 ± 0.183	6.57 ± 0.627	5.32 ± 0.826	7.01 ± 0.365	5.34 ± 0.197	7.13 ± 0.349	7.36 ± 0.871
CSDI	7.16 ± 0.164	5.36 ± 0.125	7.06 ± 0.647	5.49 ± 0.606	6.65 ± 0.677	4.74 ± 0.175	6.95 ± 0.169	5.14 ± 0.796
TDT	6.92 ± 0.245	6.34 ± 0.213	6.38 ± 0.574	4.98 ± 0.406	6.62 ± 0.624	4.72 ± 0.065	6.92 ± 0.346	5.78 ± 0.573
GADM	$\mathbf{7.42} \pm 0.139$	$\mathbf{4.32} \pm 0.152$	$\mathbf{7.53} \pm 0.027$	$\mathbf{4.21} \pm 0.192$	$\mathbf{7.38} \pm 0.126$	$\mathbf{3.71} \pm 0.132$	$\mathbf{7.48} \pm 0.204$	$\mathbf{5.08} \pm 0.103$

CSDI [21], TimeGrad [12] and TDT [14] are designed for point-to-point prediction tasks, among which probability prediction is not their main concern. Therefore, their performance on QICE and PICP is not very good, but they still perform well in other aspects. We use two indicators, MSE and MAE, to measure the performance of the model in other aspects. Experiments were conducted on four datasets including Exchange, and the results shown in Fig. 2 were obtained. The comparison results show that the existing methods perform well in the MSE and MAE indicators. In addition to performing well in uncertainty prediction, GADM also has certain improvements in these two indicators, further verifying the effectiveness of the proposed method, especially when facing unstable data. CSDI [21], TimeGrad and TDT, etc. are designed for point-to-point prediction tasks, among which probability prediction is not their main concern. Therefore, their performance on QICE and PICP is not very good, but they still perform well in other aspects.

We use two indicators, MSE and MAE, to measure the performance of the model in other aspects. Experiments were conducted on four datasets including Exchange, and the results shown in Fig. 2 were obtained. The comparison results show that the existing methods perform well in the MSE and MAE indicators. In addition to performing well in uncertainty prediction, GADM also has certain improvements in these two indicators, further verifying the effectiveness of the proposed method, especially when facing unstable data.

4.4 Ablation Experiments

To evaluate the impact of each component in the framework we proposed, we use different models to replace our components. To test the effect of the perturbation-

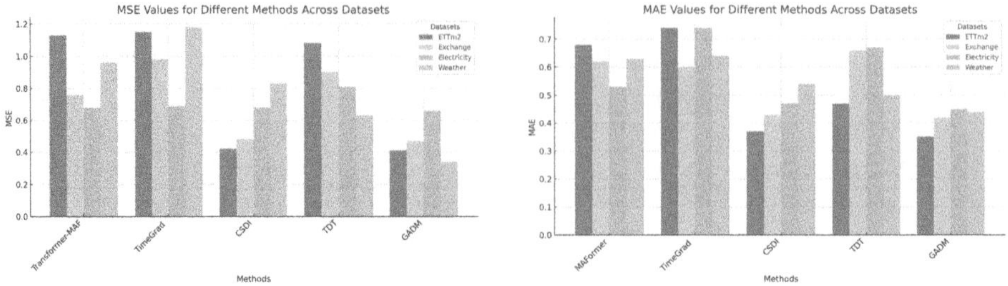

(a) MSE comparison results (b) MAE comparison results

Fig. 2. Comparison of MSE and MAE results.

aware condition encoder, we use RNN for historical condition representation and combine it with our multi-granularity diffusion model. Furthermore, we also tested the effect of the diffusion model using only the finest granularity to verify the effectiveness of multi-granularity diffusion, as well as the situation without prior condition representation and the role of the hybrid optimization we proposed.

Table 3. Comparison of QICE and CRPS for different variants of GADM

Dataset	ETTm2		Exchange		Electricity	
Evaluation	QICE	CRPS	QICE	CRPS	QICE	CRPS
RNN	4.72	0.62	7.62	1.32	6.25	1.73
Fine-granularity	6.63	0.41	5.76	0.65	4.37	0.44
No-prior	6.52	0.39	5.43	0.49	4.55	0.46
No-hybrid	7.76	0.35	4.36	0.46	4.09	0.49
GADM	**4.32**	**0.27**	**4.21**	**0.37**	**3.71**	**0.34**

It can be known from the experimental results in Table 3 that the RNN model performs relatively well on the ETTm2 dataset, but performs poorly on other datasets, with high QICE and CRPS. This indicates that the RNN model may have overfitting or insufficient generalization when dealing with certain datasets, while the improved PRCE module in GADM can solve this problem very well. Compared with the diffusion process that only uses the finest granularity, GADM achieves a reduction of approximately 30% on QICE, indicating the necessity of conducting a multi-granularity diffusion model. Compared with not using the conditional coding module, QICE has decreased by approximately 29% on average, highlighting the advantage of treating conditional information as a prior for both forward and reverse processes. Finally, by comparing the methods that do not use the hybrid optimization, it can be seen that the average value of

QICE decreases by 24%, indicating the effectiveness of the hybrid optimization method.

4.5 Parameter Experiment

To study the influence of coarse granularity on the fine-grained guidance shared rate, we conducted experiments on the Exchange dataset and evaluated the performance of different coarse-grained MGDG using different shared rates. This experiment was conducted in a two-granularity setting, with one coarse-grained one used to guide the learning process of the finest granularity data. As can be seen from Fig. 3 and 4, for each coarse-grained level, the CRPSsum value and NMAEsum initially decrease to their lowest values, and then rise again as the rate increases. Furthermore, we observed that for coarser granularities, this model performed better at a smaller sharing rate. This indicates that when the sharing ratio is selected at the step where the coarse-grained samples are closest to the intermediate state, the model achieves the best performance. Using intermediate granularities such as 4 or 6 h as guidance has greatly improved the performance of the model.

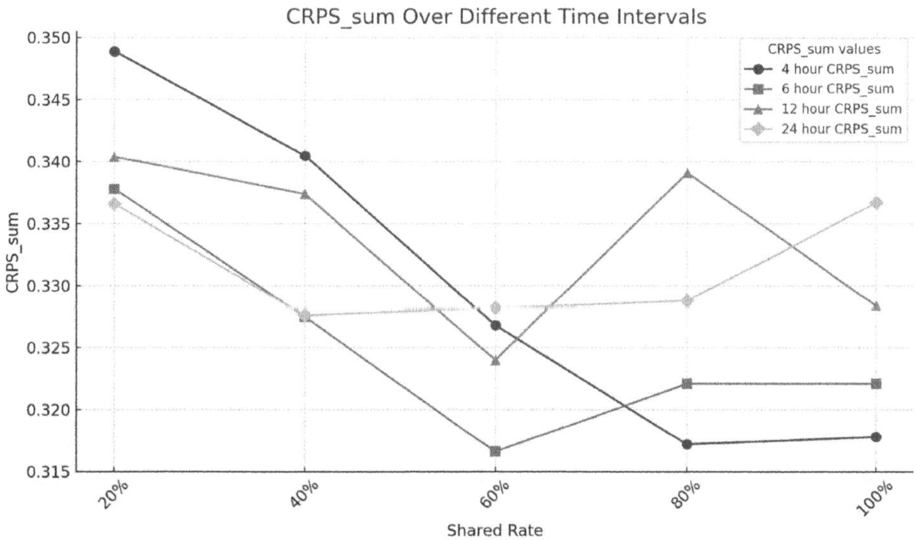

Fig. 3. The CRPSsum results of different granularity sharing ratios on the Exchange dataset.

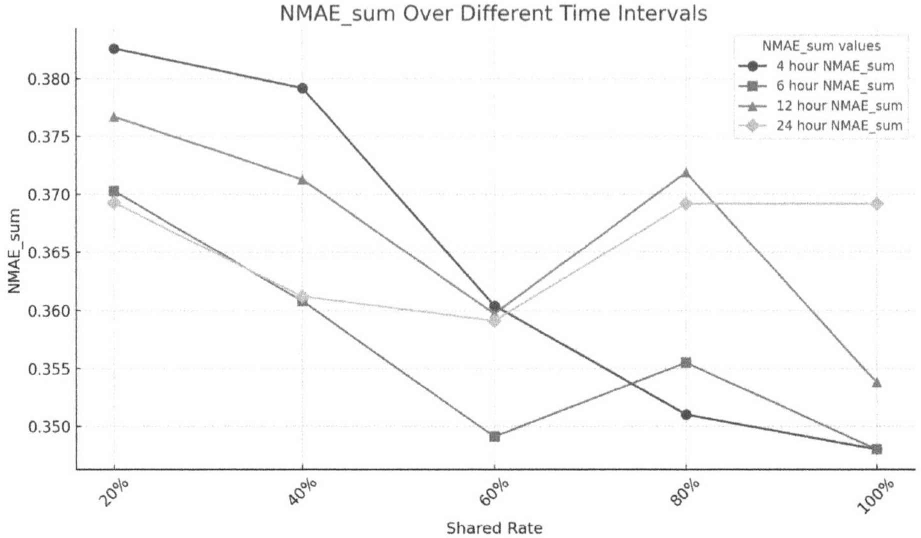

Fig. 4. The NMAEsum results of different granularity sharing ratios on the Exchange dataset.

5 Conclusion

This paper proposes a novel particle-aware diffusion model (GADM), which is specifically designed for time series prediction of uncertainty and volatility problems in non-stationary time series data. Compared with traditional methods, GADM significantly improves the modeling ability of trend and fluctuation characteristics in time series data through the combination of multi-granularity collaborative modeling and uncertainty modeling, especially with high accuracy when dealing with prediction tasks in complex dynamic scenes. By introducing the dynamic granularity decomposition mechanism and the perturbation-aware conditional encoder, GADM can flexibly extract features at different granularity levels and effectively restore non-stationary components during the diffusion process, thereby better quantifying prediction errors and uncertainties. The experimental results show that GADM performs outstandingly on multiple datasets, especially in the aspect of uncertainty prediction. Future research can continue to optimize the GADM model, further explore its applications in other complex fields, such as transportation and energy prediction, and consider how to improve the adaptability and generalization ability of the model through more non-stationary features.

Acknowledgments. This work was supported by the Heilongjiang Key R&D Program of China under Grant No. GA23A915.

References

1. Dai, T., et al.: Periodicity decoupling framework for long-term series forecasting. In: The Twelfth International Conference on Learning Representations (2024)
2. Dong, F., Wang, J., Xu, H., Zhang, X.: A robust real-time energy scheduling strategy of integrated energy system based on multi-step interval prediction of uncertainties. Energy **300**, 131639 (2024)
3. Esfandiari, H., Hajiaghayi, M., Liaghat, V., Monemizadeh, M.: Prophet secretary. SIAM J. Discret. Math. **31**(3), 1685–1701 (2017)
4. Graves, A., Graves, A.: Long short-term memory. Supervised sequence labelling with recurrent neural networks, pp. 37–45 (2012)
5. Higgins, I., et al.: β-VAE: learning basic visual concepts with a constrained variational framework. In: International conference on learning representations (2017)
6. Ho, J., Jain, A., Abbeel, P.: Denoising diffusion probabilistic models. Adv. Neural. Inf. Process. Syst. **33**, 6840–6851 (2020)
7. Huang, H., Chen, M., Qiao, X.: Generative learning for financial time series with irregular and scale-invariant patterns. In: The Twelfth International Conference on Learning Representations (2024)
8. Li, Y., Lu, X., Wang, Y., Dou, D.: Generative time series forecasting with diffusion, denoise, and disentanglement. Adv. Neural. Inf. Process. Syst. **35**, 23009–23022 (2022)
9. Liu, Y., Wu, H., Wang, J., Long, M.: Non-stationary transformers: exploring the stationarity in time series forecasting. Adv. Neural. Inf. Process. Syst. **35**, 9881–9893 (2022)
10. Oord, A.V.D., et al.: Wavenet: a generative model for raw audio. arXiv preprint arXiv:1609.03499 (2016)
11. Oreshkin, B.N., Carpov, D., Chapados, N., Bengio, Y.: N-beats: neural basis expansion analysis for interpretable time series forecasting. arXiv preprint arXiv:1905.10437 (2019)
12. Rasul, K., Seward, C., Schuster, I., Vollgraf, R.: Autoregressive denoising diffusion models for multivariate probabilistic time series forecasting. In: International Conference on Machine Learning, pp. 8857–8868. PMLR (2021)
13. Rasul, K., Sheikh, A.S., Schuster, I., Bergmann, U., Vollgraf, R.: Multivariate probabilistic time series forecasting via conditioned normalizing flows. arXiv preprint arXiv:2002.06103 (2020)
14. Ren, Z., et al.: Physically-guided temporal diffusion transformer for long-term time series forecasting. Knowl.-Based Syst. **304**, 112508 (2024)
15. Salinas, D., Bohlke-Schneider, M., Callot, L., Medico, R., Gasthaus, J.: High-dimensional multivariate forecasting with low-rank gaussian copula processes. Adv. Neural Inf. Process. Syst. **32** (2019)
16. Salinas, D., Flunkert, V., Gasthaus, J., Januschowski, T.: Deepar: probabilistic forecasting with autoregressive recurrent networks. Int. J. Forecast. **36**(3), 1181–1191 (2020)
17. Sapankevych, N.I., Sankar, R.: Time series prediction using support vector machines: a survey. IEEE Comput. Intell. Mag. **4**(2), 24–38 (2009)
18. Shen, L., Kwok, J.: Non-autoregressive conditional diffusion models for time series prediction. In: International Conference on Machine Learning, pp. 31016–31029. PMLR (2023)
19. Shumway, R.H., Stoffer, D.S., Shumway, R.H., Stoffer, D.S.: Arima models. Time series analysis and its applications: with R examples, pp. 75–163 (2017)

20. Sun, S., Yu, R.: Copula conformal prediction for multi-step time series forecasting. arXiv preprint arXiv:2212.03281 (2022)
21. Tashiro, Y., Song, J., Song, Y., Ermon, S.: CSDI: conditional score-based diffusion models for probabilistic time series imputation. Adv. Neural. Inf. Process. Syst. **34**, 24804–24816 (2021)
22. Zhang, W., Zheng, K.: Disentangled traffic forecasting via efficient graph neural network. In: Journal of Physics: Conference Series, vol. 2858, p. 012036. IOP Publishing (2024)
23. Zhang, X., et al.: DAC-ML: domain adaptable continuous meta-learning for urban dynamics prediction. In: 2021 IEEE International Conference on Data Mining (ICDM), pp. 906–915. IEEE (2021)
24. Zhang, Y., Li, Y., Zhou, X., Luo, J.: CST-ML: continuous spatial-temporal meta-learning for traffic dynamics prediction. In: 2020 IEEE International Conference on Data Mining (ICDM), pp. 1418–1423. IEEE (2020)
25. Zhao, L., et al.: T-GCN: a temporal graph convolutional network for traffic prediction. IEEE Trans. Intell. Transp. Syst. **21**(9), 3848–3858 (2019)
26. Zhao, T., Song, G., Li, X., Cui, L., Zhang, C.: Diff-MGR: dynamic causal graph attention and pattern reproduction guided diffusion model for multivariate time series probabilistic forecasting. Inf. Sci. **675**, 120742 (2024)
27. Zhou, H., et al.: Informer: beyond efficient transformer for long sequence time-series forecasting. In: Proceedings of the AAAI Conference on Artificial Intelligence, vol. 35, pp. 11106–11115 (2021)
28. Zhou, T., Ma, Z., Wen, Q., Wang, X., Sun, L., Jin, R.: Fedformer: frequency enhanced decomposed transformer for long-term series forecasting. In: International Conference on Machine Learning, pp. 27268–27286. PMLR (2022)

SpiderGNN: Spatial-Aware Predictive Inference with Dynamic Edge Reasoning for In-building 5G Signal Estimation

Xingyi Gao[1,2](✉), David Hason Rudd[1], Ziang Li[1], Yuming Guo[1], Huan Huo[1], and Guandong Xu[1]

[1] University of Technology Sydney, Sydney 2007, Australia
{david.hasonrudd,huan.huo,guandong.xu}@uts.edu.au,
{ziang.li,yuming.guo}@student.uts.edu.au
[2] AI Research Institute, iFLYTEK Co., Ltd., Hefei 230088, China
xygao19@iflytek.com

Abstract. Indoor wireless coverage has emerged as a persistent constraint in modern 5G deployments, particularly in high-rise urban buildings where signal attenuation, pilot contamination, and architectural obstructions undermine network reliability and user experience. While Unmanned Aerial Vehicles (UAVs) provide a flexible means of acquiring external RF measurements, inferring the interior signal landscape solely from these sparse and non-invasive observations remains an open and pressing challenge.

We propose SpiderGNN (Spatial-aware Predictive Inference with Dynamic Edge Reasoning Graph Neural Network), a topology-adaptive GNN framework for reconstructing indoor 5G signal quality from sparse UAV-based external observations. Unlike conventional distance-based graphs, SpiderGNN builds sparse structures dynamically using attention-derived feature affinity, enabling better modeling of the non-Euclidean nature of signal propagation in complex building environments.

Built upon this learned topology, a residual Graph Attention Network (GAT) encoder propagates multi-hop signal semantics, followed by dual decoding branches tailored to the distinct physical characteristics of RSSI and CQI. To enhance stability and generalization, an ensemble-based fusion layer aggregates predictions across multiple stochastic runs.

Empirical evaluation on a real-world, multi-floor 5G dataset demonstrates that SpiderGNN achieves substantial improvements over state-of-the-art location-aware baselines, reducing RMSE by 76% for RSSI and 89% for CQI, while attaining coefficient of determination (R^2) scores exceeding 0.99 on both metrics.

By uniting sparse UAV sensing, non-Euclidean graph modeling, and spatially contextual inference, SpiderGNN establishes a scalable and non-intrusive paradigm for indoor signal estimation. The framework offers a technically grounded and practically deployable solution to urban-scale wireless planning, bridging the longstanding gap between outdoor sensing and indoor coverage prediction.

X. Gao and D. H. Rudd—These authors contributed equally to this work.

T. Hao et al. (Eds.): BESC 2025, LNCS 16431, pp. 123–140, 2026.
https://doi.org/10.1007/978-981-95-7138-3_9

Keywords: Non-invasive wireless sensing · In-building 5G coverage · Graph neural networks · UAV-based RF sensing · Signal quality prediction · AIoT-enabled smart infrastructure

1 Introduction

With the global deployment of 5G networks and the looming arrival of 6G, the demand for high-reliability, high-capacity indoor wireless coverage has become increasingly acute. It is now well documented that over 80% of mobile data traffic originates from within buildings [1]. Despite this overwhelming demand, in-building coverage (IBC) continues to pose a persistent challenge for cellular communication systems, particularly in densely populated urban areas and high-rise environments [2].

Conventional macro-cell networks are engineered to provide broad horizontal coverage across wide geographical areas, yet they fall short when tasked with delivering consistent vertical penetration into multistorey buildings [3,4]. As a result, upper floors in modern high-rises frequently experience signal degradation, reduced throughput, and intermittent connectivity, all of which contribute to diminished user satisfaction [5].

This problem is further exacerbated by the electromagnetic properties of contemporary building materials [6–8]. Reinforced concrete, metallic insulation, and multilayer glass are commonly used in modern construction and are known to cause severe attenuation, often resulting in signal losses ranging from 20 to 45 dB at operational frequencies [9]. Beyond material-related challenges, systemic issues such as pilot contamination, beam misalignment, and inter-cell interference frequently lead to unstable handovers and inconsistent link quality, especially in elevated indoor spaces [10].

Despite progress in distributed antenna systems (DAS), small-cell deployments, and indoor signal repeaters, existing solutions often suffer from high deployment costs, limited adaptability, and structural rigidity [11–13]. These limitations make them difficult to scale across rapidly evolving urban environments.

In recent years, unmanned aerial vehicles (UAVs) have emerged as a promising platform for radio frequency (RF) sensing and coverage enhancement due to their mobility, flexibility, and cost-effectiveness [14]. Equipped with directional antennas or RF scanning equipment, UAVs can collect signal measurements from diverse vantage points, enabling high-resolution, three-dimensional external observations of building exteriors [15].

When integrated with edge computing and AIoT infrastructures, UAVs offer the potential for adaptive and real-time optimization of indoor coverage [16]. Upon detecting regions of poor signal quality, UAV-mounted base stations can actively direct 5G signals toward target areas, thereby enhancing network coverage with spatial precision [17].

However, a fundamental challenge remains unresolved: UAVs cannot directly access the internal distribution of wireless signals within buildings. Although numerous studies have envisioned UAVs as aerial base stations capable of providing seamless coverage across target areas [18], this assumption overlooks a critical practical constraint. Accurate indoor signal characterization still heavily depends on manual walk-testing—a process that is time-consuming, labor-intensive, and inherently difficult to scale [19].

This gives rise to a central and largely unsolved question:

How can one infer the unobservable indoor signal environment based solely on externally collected UAV measurements?

In recent years, a growing body of research has demonstrated the feasibility of using supervised learning models to predict indoor wireless signal indicators based on external building observations [20–23]. Among these efforts, David et al. (2025) proposed the Location-Aware Deep Neural Network (LA-DNN), which incorporates an attention-based deep learning architecture to capture spatial knowledge of 5G signal distributions [24]. While LA-DNN achieves reasonable accuracy in predicting Received Signal Strength Indicator (RSSI), its performance on Channel Quality Indicator (CQI) prediction remains suboptimal.

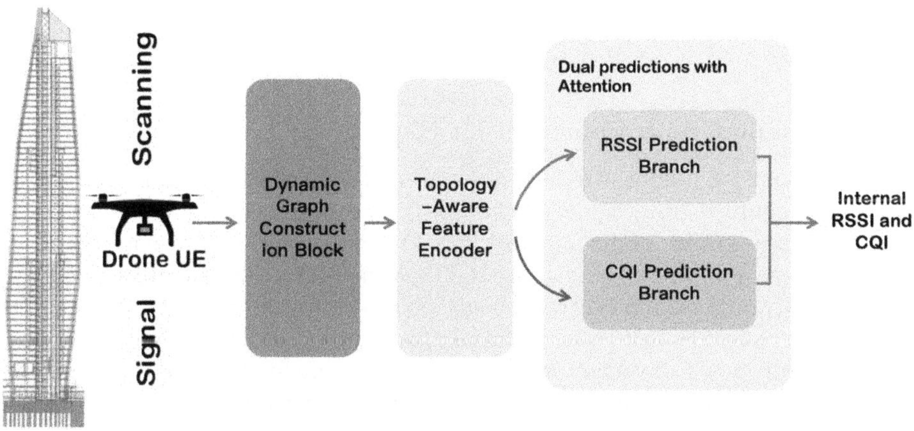

Fig. 1. An overview of the architectural framework.

Meanwhile, studies in the domain of indoor positioning have shown that Graph Neural Networks (GNNs) outperform conventional machine learning models in learning the relationship between spatial locations and signal patterns derived from RSSI measurements [25–28]. Motivated by the success of GNNs in these spatial inference tasks, we explore their application in the more challenging problem of indoor signal field reconstruction based solely on external signal distributions.

Unlike indoor localization, where internal signal parameters are directly observed, our task involves inferring the internal signal environment from external measurements—introducing greater complexity across spatial domains, frequency bands, and interference conditions. This requires the model to generalize across discontinuities, variable building geometries, and propagation anomalies, thereby placing higher demands on spatial reasoning and generalization capacity [29,30].

To address this challenge, we propose SpiderGNN: a Spatial-aware Predictive Inference framework with Dynamic Edge Reasoning based on Graph Neural Networks. An overview of the architectural framework is provided in Fig. 1, while the detailed design and functionality of each module will be presented in the Method section.

2 Method

This section outlines the architectural design and core functional components of SpiderGNN, along with its associated training strategy. The model consists of three principal modules: a Dynamic Graph Construction Block, which infers signal-aware topologies from input features; a Topology-Aware Feature Encoder, which captures spatially contextualized representations; and a Prediction Head, responsible for estimating wireless quality indicators. Each module is tailored to address key challenges in modeling signal propagation across heterogeneous indoor and outdoor environments. To promote robust learning and improve generalization, SpiderGNN is trained within an ensemble learning framework that unifies structural inference and signal prediction in a cohesive optimization pipeline.

2.1 Dynamic Graph Construction Block

In the context of indoor wireless environments, spatial proximity frequently becomes decoupled from signal consistency. The presence of architectural elements, including walls, floors and structural voids, gives rise to discontinuities in signal propagation, thereby violating the fundamental assumptions of Euclidean geometry [31]. Consequently, two sensing points captured by UAVs may be separated by a mere few metres in physical space, yet experience entirely different wireless conditions. Conversely, spatially distant points may exhibit strong correlation due to shared propagation paths shaped by structural layouts and material properties.

In such conditions, graph construction methods based on k-nearest neighbours or geometric heuristics inherently encode a flawed prior, as they represent spatial adjacency rather than the underlying characteristics of wireless propagation. Conversely, the exterior airspace surrounding buildings is relatively open, with minimal obstructions. Fully connected Graph Attention Networks (GATs) applied to such environments have been observed to overfit, as the learned attention weights have been found to reflect superficial spatial patterns rather than meaningful signal interactions. This compromises the generalisability of the model when applied to complex indoor contexts.

In order to address this challenge, SpiderGNN introduces a sparse, attention-based graph construction mechanism that accounts for both the variability of signal propagation and the need for structural efficiency. The fundamental principle of this design is predicated upon the utilisation of a Dynamic Graph Construction Block, the function of which is to infer the graph topology directly from the input features, as illustrated in Fig. 2. This approach, driven by data, eliminates the need for manually defined connectivity. It allows the model to recover a signal interaction structure that reflects actual propagation behaviour rather than physical proximity. In doing so, the model aligns its representation with wireless communication dynamics across both indoor and outdoor domains.

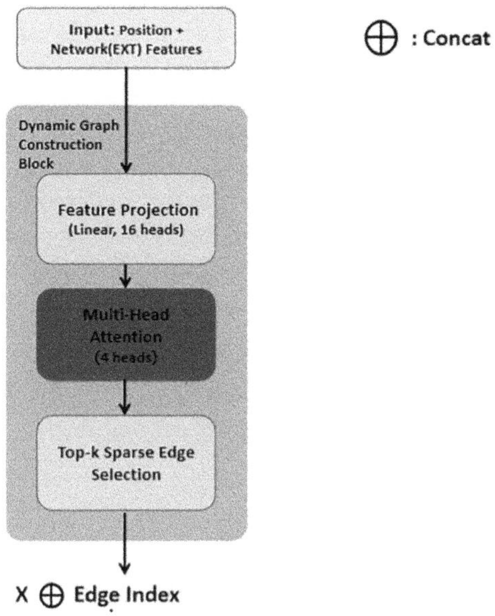

Fig. 2. Dynamic Graph Construction Block.

Each UAV-sensed point is initially represented by a vector $\mathbf{x}_i \in \mathbb{R}^d$, embedding both geometric descriptors (e.g., latitude, longitude, altitude) and signal parameters (e.g., $RSSI_{\text{ext}}$, $RSPP_{\text{ext}}$, SNR_{ext}, Timing Advance, and building-relative metrics such as core distance or penetration depth). These vectors are passed through a shared linear projection $\mathbf{W} \in \mathbb{R}^{d \times d'}$ to map them into a latent attention space, yielding projected embeddings $\mathbf{q}_i = \mathbf{x}_i\mathbf{W}$.

We then compute attention scores between every pair of nodes, defining the affinity from $node_i$ to $node_j$ as:

$$\alpha_{ij} = \frac{\mathbf{q}_i \cdot \mathbf{q}_j^\top}{\sqrt{d'}}$$

This interaction is symmetric in formulation but asymmetric in usage: we only retain, for each $node_i$, its top-k neighbors j with the highest scores α_{ij}, forming a sparse directed graph $G = (\mathcal{V}, \varepsilon)$. In this way, the edge set $\varepsilon \subseteq \mathcal{V} \times \mathcal{V}$ reflects learned propagation relevance, not spatial adjacency.

$$\mathcal{N}_i = \text{TopK}_{j \neq i}(\alpha_{ij}), \quad \varepsilon = \bigcup_i \{(i, j) | j \in \mathcal{N}_i\}$$

The output of this module is an edge index structure ε, dynamically recomputed per batch, and passed downstream to the graph encoder. The node features themselves are untouched; only their connective context is altered. This design decision preserves the original semantic fidelity of the input, while aligning the message-passing topology with observed signal behavior.

This module aligns the learning mechanism with the physics of indoor signal propagation. By letting the model learn what connectivity means, we enable it to discover long-range, non-obvious interactions induced by architectural structure. Unlike geometric heuristics, this graph is informed by feature similarity in the signal domain, offering an inductive bias more faithful to the task. Moreover, the dynamic construction is performed per forward pass, allowing the model to adapt to different input distributions and capture scenario-specific topologies.

This dynamic construction process is not a convenience—it is a necessity. In scenarios where architectural structure trumps geometry, and propagation paths bend around walls or traverse voids, it is only through such learned topology that graph models can remain truthful to the domain. The result is not merely a better graph; it is a more honest one.

2.2 Topology-Aware Feature Encoder

If the dynamic graph construction stage determines how signals should propagate, then the feature encoder defines what is actually propagated and how it transforms. In the context of indoor signal prediction, raw measurements are sparse, noisy, and entangled with structural constraints. It is therefore not sufficient to model node-level properties in isolation; what matters is how signal characteristics diffuse across the inferred graph and how structural priors shape semantic flow.

To address this, we adopt a residual topology-aware feature encoder, built upon the Graph Attention Network (GAT) paradigm, and designed to respect both multi-hop dependencies and representational stability, as illustrated in Fig. 3. The encoder receives as input the raw node features $\mathbf{X} \in \mathbb{R}^{n \times d}$ and a dynamically generated sparse graph ε.Its goal is to produce a deep embedding $\mathcal{H}^{(3)} \in \mathbb{R}^{n \times h}$ for each UAV-sensed point, where each embedding integrates local propagation context with higher-order signal structure.

The encoder is composed of three stacked GATConv layers, with residual connections introduced after the second and third layers to mitigate over-smoothing and facilitate gradient flow. Let us denote the hidden representation at layer l as $\mathcal{H}^{(l)}$, with the initial condition $\mathcal{H}^{(0)} = \mathbf{X}$. The update rules are defined as:

$$\mathcal{H}^{(1)} = \text{ReLU}\left(\text{BN}_1\left(\text{GAT}_1^{16\to256}(\mathcal{H}^{(0)}, \varepsilon)\right)\right)$$

$$\mathcal{H}^{(2)} = \text{ReLU}\left(\text{BN}_2\left(\text{GAT}_2^{256\to256}(\mathcal{H}^{(1)}, \varepsilon) + \mathcal{H}^{(1)}\right)\right)$$

$$\mathcal{H}^{(3)} = \text{ReLU}\left(\text{BN}_3\left(\text{GAT}_3^{256\to256}(\mathcal{H}^{(2)}, \varepsilon) + \mathcal{H}^{(2)}\right)\right)$$

Here, each residual term $+\mathcal{H}^{(l)}$ adds the previous activation before nonlinearity, preserving the semantic integrity of mid-level features while allowing higher layers to refine and deepen the representation. Importantly, no skip connection jumps across layers – a design that encourages hierarchical feature growth rather than shortcut-based overfitting.

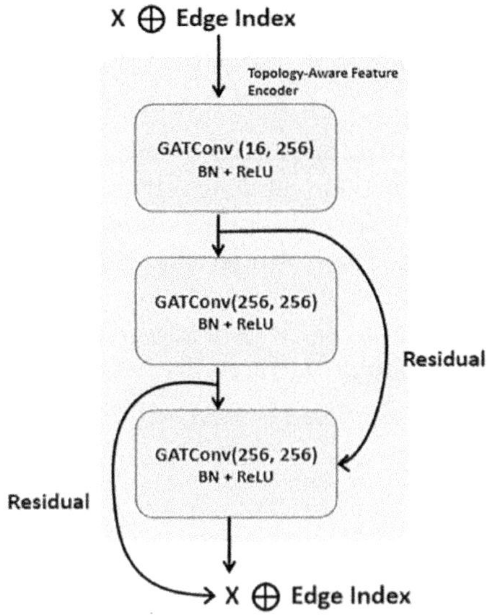

Fig. 3. Topology-Aware Feature Encoder.

Each GAT layer performs masked self-attention over the sparse edge index, which was dynamically constructed in the previous module. This attention allows the model to weigh neighbor contributions adaptively, learning which signal relationships matter and which do not, even when the neighbors are irregular or sparse.

The inclusion of batch normalization and dropout after each layer ensures numerical stability and improves generalization. The encoder thus transforms a geometry-oblivious point cloud into a semantically structured signal field, where each node embedding encodes not just local information, but its contextual relevance across the learned topology.

The output $\mathcal{H}^{(3)} \in \mathbb{R}^{n \times 256}$ serves as a task-agnostic latent embedding. It captures propagation-aware signal structure, suitable for downstream estimation tasks such as RSSI and CQI prediction.

2.3 Dual Predictions with Attention

To decode wireless signal behavior from structural representations, SpiderGNN employs a bifurcated prediction head composed of two parallel branches: one for RSSI (Received Signal Strength Indicator) and one for CQI (Channel Quality Indicator). Although both branches operate on the same encoded topology-aware features, they are designed to capture distinct physical regimes of wireless communication. RSSI corresponds to large-scale power attenuation and varies smoothly over space; CQI, by contrast, encapsulates a fine-grained view of link capacity shaped by interference, modulation, and multi-path effects. Modeling these two phenomena in a unified architecture without task entanglement requires structural independence, tailored representation, and specialized decoding pathways. Below we detail each branch.

RSSI Prediction Branch

Received Signal Strength Indicator (RSSI) reflects the physical-layer power of a wireless signal measured at a point in space. It is governed primarily by large-scale path loss—attenuation due to distance and structural obstruction—and typically varies smoothly over space. Unlike channel quality metrics that respond sharply to interference, multipath, or scheduling decisions, RSSI evolves gradually with geometry. In this sense, it is a low-frequency function over spatial topology, and its modeling should favor robustness over complexity (Fig. 4).

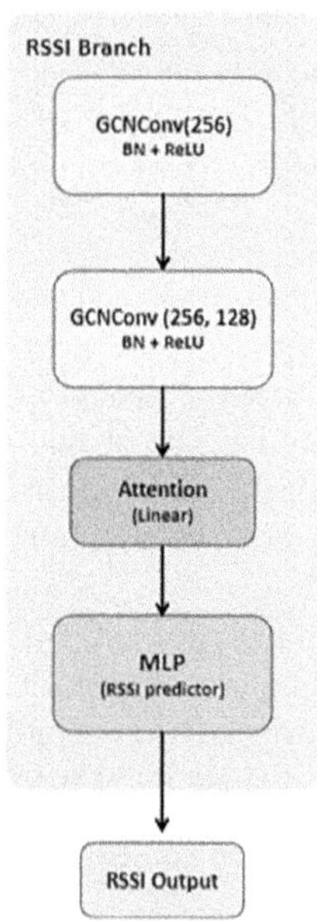

Fig. 4. RSSI Prediction Branch.

In SpiderGNN, we separate RSSI prediction into its own branch, following the shared topology-aware encoder. This design serves two purposes. First, it preserves inductive purity: by decoupling signal power from quality, we allow each branch to align with its respective physical mechanism. Second, it allows each task to optimize its own structural filters, learning what neighborhood information is essential without interference from orthogonal tasks.

The RSSI branch begins by accepting the output from the topology encoder – denoted $\mathbf{H}^{(3)} \in \mathbb{R}^{n\times 256}$ – which encodes multi-hop signal structure shaped by the data-driven graph. Over this, we apply two graph convolution layers (GCN), each with batch normalization and ReLU activation.

The first maintains channel width; the second reduces dimensionality to 128, compressing the signal into a more tractable subspace. Letting $\mathbf{z}^{(1)}$ and $\mathbf{z}^{(2)}$ denote these layers' outputs:

$$\mathbf{Z}^{(1)} = \mathrm{ReLU}\left(\mathrm{BN}_1\left(\mathrm{GCN}_{256\to 256}(\mathbf{H}^{(3)}, \varepsilon)\right)\right)$$

$$\mathbf{Z}^{(2)} = \mathrm{ReLU}\left(\mathrm{BN}_2\left(\mathrm{GCN}_{256\to 128}(\mathbf{Z}^{(1)}, \varepsilon)\right)\right)$$

To stabilize prediction across diverse building geometries, we apply a scalar weighting to each node output. For each $node_i$, a linear attention layer produces a soft gate $\alpha_i \in [0, 1]$, which modulates the predicted contribution of that location:

$$\tilde{\mathbf{z}}_i = \alpha_i \cdot \mathbf{z}_i^{(2)}, \quad \alpha_i = \sigma(\mathbf{w}^\top \mathbf{z}_i^{(2)} + b)$$

Here, the attention is not learned from graph structure, but from local feature relevance—it acts as a self-regulator, allowing the model to suppress predictions in structurally ambiguous zones (e.g., vertical shafts, wall boundaries) and highlight those with clearer path characteristics.

Finally, the gated features $\tilde{\mathbf{z}}_i$ are passed to a multi-layer perceptron, yielding the scalar RSSI estimate $\hat{y}_i^{\mathrm{RSSI}}$. This prediction is optimized under mean-squared error loss against normalized empirical values.

This branch is deliberately shallow. It relies on the topology encoder to resolve non-local structure, and focuses only on low-dimensional, locally coherent transformations. It is, in effect, a projection layer over a structural base, designed not to interpret signal behavior in full, but to recover signal amplitude from its spatial imprint.

CQI Prediction Branch

Whereas RSSI captures large-scale signal attenuation, the Channel Quality Indicator (CQI) reflects a far more nuanced quantity: the instantaneous capacity of the wireless link, conditioned on interference, multipath fading, scheduling, and modulation-coding schemes. Unlike RSSI, CQI is non-monotonic in distance, irregular across time, and discontinuous across space. It is a high-frequency response function over the propagation topology – sensitive to both spatial microstructure and channel-specific fluctuations.

For this reason, SpiderGNN treats CQI as a distinct modeling target, assigned to a dedicated prediction branch whose architecture mirrors its complexity. Building atop the shared feature encoder, the CQI branch is designed to isolate, enhance, and fuse multi-dimensional information patterns relevant to link-level behavior.

As illustrated in Fig. 5, after receiving the output $\mathrm{H}^{(3)} \in \mathbb{R}^{n\times 256}$ from the topology-aware feature encoder, the CQI prediction branch shares the same two GCN layers as the RSSI branch. Therefore, the network output corresponds to the representation $\mathrm{Z}^{(2)}$ as defined in 2)RSSI Prediction Branch.

To decompose signal behavior, we introduce a dual-attention decoding block. The first path – channel-wise attention – analyzes inter-feature correlations. Each feature vector $\mathrm{z}_i^{(2)} \in \mathbb{R}^{128}$ is passed through a learnable gating function that selectively emphasizes the most informative signal dimensions:

$$\alpha_i^{\mathrm{chan}} = \sigma(\mathrm{MLP}^{\mathrm{chan}}(\mathrm{z}_i^{(2)})), \quad \mathrm{z}_i^{\mathrm{chan}} = \alpha_i^{\mathrm{chan}} \bigodot \mathrm{z}_i^{(2)}$$

The second path – spatial attention – acts orthogonally: it evaluates each node's context relevance across the graph, encoding the spatial saliency of the node under varying geometry. Again, a nonlinear projection and gating are applied:

$$\alpha_i^{\mathrm{spat}} = \sigma(\mathrm{MLP}^{\mathrm{spat}}(\mathrm{z}_i^{(2)})), \quad \mathrm{z}_i^{\mathrm{spat}} = \alpha_i^{\mathrm{spat}} \cdot \mathrm{z}_i^{(2)}$$

The two outputs are concatenated and passed through a fusion MLP, designed to merge local feature relevance and broader spatial sensitivity. To maintain gradient flow and preserve input integrity, a residual connection is introduced from $\mathrm{z}_i^{(2)}$:

$$\mathrm{z}_i^{\mathrm{fused}} = \mathrm{MLP}^{\mathrm{fusion}}\left(\left[\mathrm{z}_i^{\mathrm{chan}} \parallel \mathrm{z}_i^{\mathrm{spat}}\right]\right) + \mathrm{z}_i^{(2)}$$

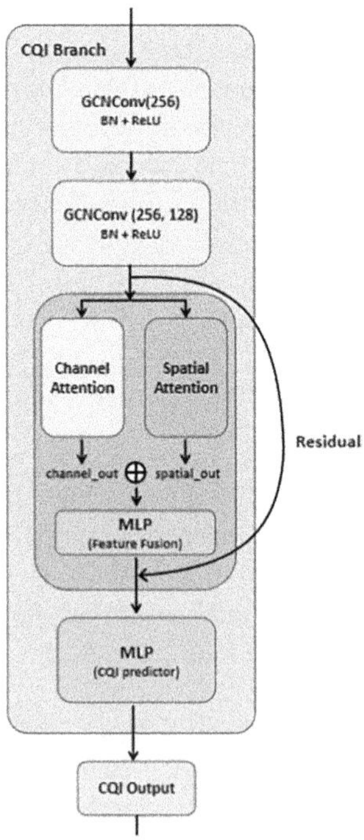

Fig. 5. CQI Prediction Branch.

Finally, the fused feature is fed into a prediction MLP that outputs the scalar CQI estimate $\hat{y}_i^{\text{CQI}}$, trained via MSE against ground truth CQI values.

This decoding structure serves a dual purpose. Architecturally, it extends the representational capacity of the model in directions that matter: across signal dimension (channels) and spatial layout (nodes). This architectural choice is grounded in the physical characteristics of wireless channels, where the observed signal quality depends not only on the transmitted information but also on the spatial context of reception. Such interactions are not adequately captured by shallow models or standard regression approaches.

Together with the RSSI branch, this component completes the inference head of SpiderGNN. Both heads are independently optimized, but jointly benefit from the shared dynamic topology and residual graph encoding, forming a coherent yet specialized signal modeling pipeline.

2.4 Meta-ensemble Prediction Fusion

The outputs of learning-based models can vary due to random initialization, training data selection, or convergence path. This sensitivity, while often negligible in toy scenarios, becomes non-trivial in field-deployed systems where signal environments vary across buildings, floors, and materials.

To suppress this output-level variance, we introduce a simple but effective model fusion stage. Several SpiderGNN models are trained independently using identical architecture but different training seeds or batch sequences. Each model produces its own prediction for RSSI and CQI (Fig. 6).

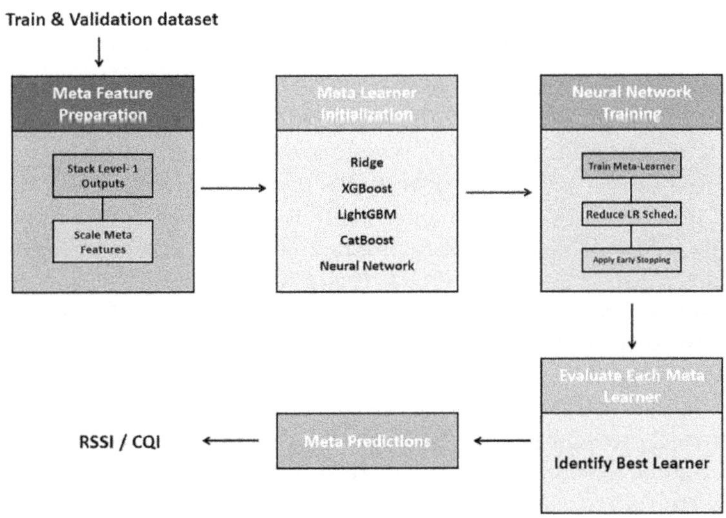

Fig. 6. Ensemble Learning Pipeline.

At inference time, we collect the predictions from all models and treat them as inputs to a secondary regression process. This regression is trained on a held-out validation set and selects the best combination of these inputs to approximate the true values. For this purpose, we test a small set of low-complexity regressors: ridge regression, boosted trees, and a small fully-connected model with fixed capacity. The regressor with the lowest validation error is used as the fusion rule.

This approach does not modify the core model or training process. It is added only at the prediction layer and can be adapted to any number of base models. In practice, it improves the stability of outputs across environments without increasing the complexity of deployment.

We apply this method independently for RSSI and CQI, ensuring that the fused prediction reflects both the structure learned by SpiderGNN and the observed behavior of the base model ensemble.

This fusion procedure consists of four practical steps. First, we collect the outputs of all base models on the validation dataset and concatenate them as aligned prediction vectors. These vectors are scaled to remove bias across models, and serve as the input features for the fusion layer. Second, we initialize a set of candidate regressors, including regularized linear models, tree-based estimators, and a shallow neural predictor. Each candidate is trained on the validation features to approximate the true signal values. Third, we evaluate their performance on a held-out validation fold, selecting the model with the lowest prediction error as the final combiner. Fourth, this selected fusion model is then used to aggregate the predictions of the base SpiderGNNs at test time.

3 Experiment and Results

3.1 Field Measurement Dataset and LA-DNN Baseline

The dataset used in this study was obtained through field measurements conducted by the UTS In-Building Coverage (IBC) team. A rotary-wing drone was equipped with two off-the-shelf RF scanning tools: TEMS Pocket^{TM} from Infovista and G-MoN, a network performance monitoring application. The drone was flown around the perimeter of a multi-storey building in central Sydney, maintaining a lateral distance of approximately one meter from the building's outer facade.

The flight was conducted at a constant horizontal speed of 4 km/h. RF measurements were recorded every 3 s, resulting in 83 discrete observation points for each floor level. The scanning time per level was approximately 4.5 min. The measured data includes multiple downlink signal indicators such as Received Signal Strength Indicator (RSSI), Reference Signal Received Power (RSRP), Reference Signal Received Quality (RSRQ), Channel Quality Indicator (CQI), and Signal-to-Noise Ratio (SNR).

To provide a comparative benchmark, we reference a baseline model developed in prior work by the UTS IBC team, known as the Location-Aware Deep Neural Network (LA-DNN) [24], which was specifically designed to predict in-building wireless metrics based on external observations.

3.2 Dynamic Graph Ablation Study

To further examine the role of graph topology design in SpiderGNN, we introduce two additional ablation variants that replace the dynamic edge construction mechanism with fixed graph structures based on alternative heuristics.

In the **Ablation-1**, a static graph is constructed using a k-nearest neighbors (k-NN) algorithm based on Euclidean distances between observation points. The connectivity pattern is determined once at the beginning of training and remains unchanged thereafter. Although message passing still operates through attention layers, the edge set is fixed and reflects only geometric proximity. No consideration is given to signal features or environmental context, and the model assumes that physical closeness implies interaction relevance.

In the **Ablation-2**, we employ a fully connected graph structure using Graph Attention Network (GAT) layers, in which every node exchanges information with all others. The attention weights are learned during training, but the connectivity pattern itself is not subject to adaptation or pruning. This configuration assumes a dense interaction field where signal relationships are globally distributed and not subject to sparsity or spatial constraints.

These variants allow us to examine how different assumptions about graph structure – static geometric proximity and uniform full connectivity – compare to the data-driven edge construction in SpiderGNN. All architectural components and training hyperparameters are held constant across experiments to ensure that any observed performance differences can be attributed to the nature of the graph topology.

3.3 Results

To comprehensively evaluate model performance, we compare the proposed SpiderGNN with the baseline LA-DNN model and the two ablation variants introduced earlier. All models are evaluated on the same dataset and tested on two indoor wireless signal prediction tasks: RSSI and CQI.

The evaluation is conducted using five metrics: Root Mean Square Error (RMSE), Mean Absolute Error (MAE), R-squared (R^2), Total Squared Error, and Pearson Correlation Coefficient. These metrics collectively assess the accuracy, deviation, and correlation between predicted values and ground truth. The quantitative results are summarized in Table 1.

In addition to standard regression metrics, we visualize the distribution of predicted and ground truth values using histograms. This allows us to assess whether the model's performance is uniformly distributed across the full range of signal indicators, or whether accuracy is disproportionately concentrated in high-density intervals. Such visualization is crucial for identifying potential biases in model behavior, particularly in underrepresented regions of the signal space where elevated errors may be concealed by aggregate metrics like RMSE. Specifically, Fig. 7 presents the histogram and scatter plot comparisons for all four models:

Figure 7(a) illustrates the baseline LA-DNN results, including the predicted distributions of RSSI and CQI, as well as the corresponding scatter plots against ground truth.

Figure 7(b) shows the results for Ablation Variant 1, in which the graph structure is constructed using static geometric proximity.

Figure 7(c) presents the results for Ablation Variant 2, which employs a fully connected GAT without structural sparsity.

Figure 7(d) depicts the performance of the proposed SpiderGNN, demonstrating a closer alignment between predicted and actual signal distributions across both metrics.

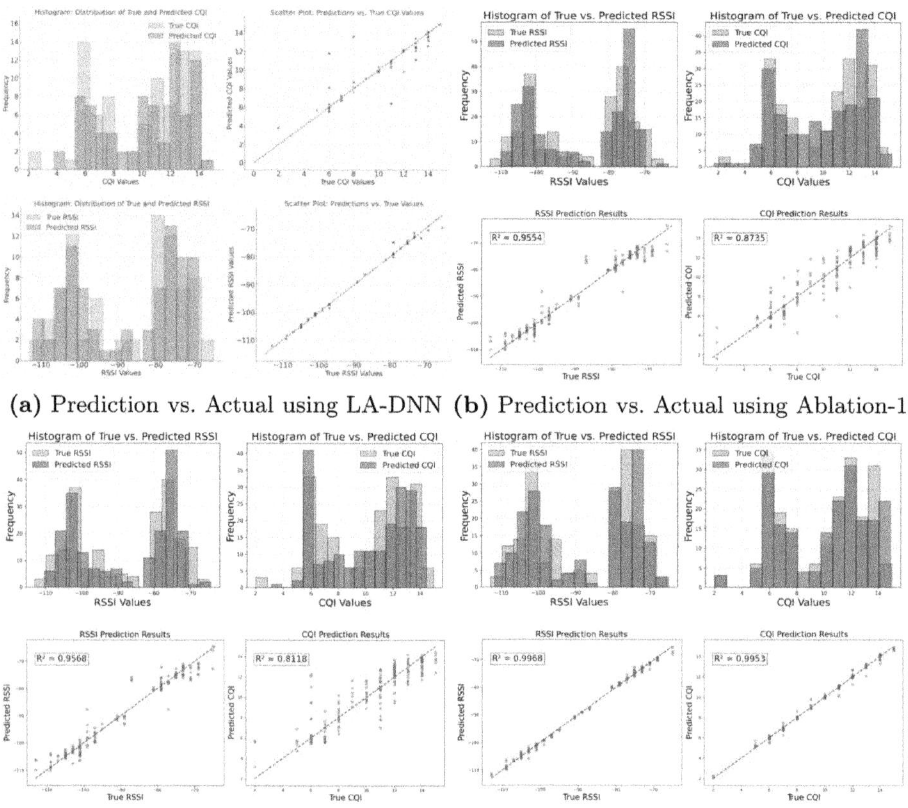

(a) Prediction vs. Actual using LA-DNN (b) Prediction vs. Actual using Ablation-1

(c) Prediction vs. Actual using Ablation-2 (d) Prediction vs. Actual using Our Model

Fig. 7. Visual and quantitative comparison of different model predictions for RSSI and CQI.

The results in Table 1 and Fig. 7 jointly highlight the superiority of SpiderGNN over both the baseline and ablation variants across all evaluated metrics and both prediction tasks.

In terms of RSSI prediction, SpiderGNN achieves the lowest RMSE of 0.7893, significantly outperforming LA-DNN (3.335), Ablation-1 (2.7551), and Ablation-2 (2.6941). Similarly, the MAE is reduced to 0.5808, compared to 2.263 for LA-DNN and over 1.7 for both ablations. The R-squared score reaches 0.9967, indicating an almost perfect fit, while the Pearson correlation coefficient is 0.9984, further confirming strong alignment between predicted and ground truth values. This is also visually evident in Fig. 7(d), where the RSSI prediction scatter plot tightly follows the identity line, with minimal dispersion.

Table 1. Prediction results and performance comparison across models.

Error Metrics	LA-DNN		Ablation 1		Ablation 2		SpiderGNN	
	RSSI	CQI	RSSI	CQI	RSSI	CQI	RSSI	CQI
RMSE	3.335	1.975	2.7551	1.0249	2.6941	1.1805	**0.7893**	**0.2270**
MAE	2.263	1.465	1.7835	0.7340	1.7345	0.8464	**0.5808**	**0.1390**
R-squared	0.939	0.608	0.9601	0.8964	0.9619	0.8625	**0.9967**	**0.9949**
Squared Error	16.459	12.485	7.5904	1.0503	7.2580	1.3936	**0.6229**	**0.0515**
Correlation	0.959	0.213	0.9799	0.9472	0.9808	0.9345	**0.9984**	**0.9975**

For CQI prediction, SpiderGNN again achieves the best performance, with an RMSE of 0.2270, a substantial improvement over LA-DNN (1.975), Ablation-1 (1.0249), and Ablation-2 (1.1805). The MAE is reduced to 0.1390, and the R-squared rises to 0.9949, compared to 0.608 for LA-DNN and around 0.86–0.89 for the ablations. Figure 7(d) clearly shows that the predicted CQI values align closely with the ground truth across the entire range, whereas Fig. 7(a-c) reveal increased variance, underestimation in low-CQI regions, and overestimation in mid-range CQI values.

Furthermore, the histograms provide additional insight into each model's ability to approximate the full distribution of RSSI and CQI. LA-DNN in Fig. 7(a) demonstrates substantial misalignment in both signal distributions, especially underrepresenting low CQI values and overestimating RSSI in the −90 to −70 dBm range. Ablation-1 and Ablation-2 (Figs. 7(b, c)) partially improve alignment, but still suffer from over-smoothing and visible mismatch in extreme intervals. In contrast, SpiderGNN captures both central and edge distributions with high fidelity, maintaining consistent performance across the full value range.

These results confirm that the adaptive, feature-driven graph construction in SpiderGNN significantly enhances signal prediction accuracy and robustness, particularly in regions where traditional spatial heuristics or fixed full connectivity assumptions fail to capture the underlying propagation dynamics.

4 Conclusions

This work introduces SpiderGNN, a Spatial-aware Predictive Inference framework with Dynamic Edge Reasoning based on Graph Neural Networks, designed for inferring indoor 5G signal coverage using sparse, exterior RF observations collected by UAVs. By moving beyond static, distance-based graph construction, SpiderGNN leverages dynamic edge reasoning based on learned feature affinity, allowing the model to better capture the complex, non-Euclidean relationships governing signal propagation in urban high-rise environments. The integration of a residual attention-based encoder and dual-task decoding branches enables precise modeling of both signal strength and quality, while ensemble fusion mitigates prediction instability across training runs. Experimental results on a real-world, multi-floor dataset demonstrate significant improvements over conventional baselines, achieving high fidelity in both RSSI and CQI predictions—with RMSE reductions of 76% and 89%, respectively, and R^2 scores exceeding 0.99 for both tasks. The reconstructed 3D signal maps further provide interpretable visualizations aligned with building geometry, offering practical utility for wireless network planning.

Future work will focus on enhancing the generality and decision-making capacity of SpiderGNN. First, incorporating support for multiple frequency bands – including millimeter wave (mmWave) – and integrating additional quality-of-service indicators such as latency, throughput, RSRP, RSRQ, and SNR, will broaden the model's applicability to heterogeneous 5G and beyond-5G environments. Second, a unified end-to-end system is envisioned, wherein the UAV is not merely a passive data collector but an active agent. By estimating the information gain associated with prospective sampling points, the UAV can autonomously determine high-value exterior positions that most effectively inform internal signal distribution inference. This would enable adaptive flight path planning and efficient data acquisition, minimizing redundancy and further reducing reliance on intrusive in-building measurements.

We believe this framework opens promising avenues for scalable, non-intrusive indoor coverage modeling in future urban wireless systems.

Acknowledgment. This work is partially supported by the Australian Research Council under grant number: DP22010371, LE220100078, DP200101374 and LP170100891.

The authors would also like to thank Xianzhi Wang, Md Rafiqul Islam, Cesar Sanin, Koh Ming En, and Mehedi Hasan for their valuable support and contributions.

References

1. Chandra, K., Prasad, R.V., Quang, B., Niemegeers, I.: Cogcell: cognitive interplay between 60 ghz picocells and 2.4/5 ghz hotspots in the 5G era. IEEE Commun. Mag. **53**(7), 118–125 (2015)
2. Wang, C.X., et al.: Cellular architecture and key technologies for 5G wireless communication networks. IEEE Commun. Mag. **52**(2), 122–130 (2014)
3. Shakya, D., Chizhik, D., Du, J., Valenzuela, R.A., Rappaport, T.S.: Dense urban outdoor-indoor coverage from 3.5 to 28 ghz. In: ICC 2022-IEEE International Conference on Communications, pp. 932–937. IEEE (2022)

4. Karner, W., Paier, A., Rupp, M.: Indoor coverage prediction and optimization for UMTS macro cells. In: 2006 3rd International Symposium on Wireless Communication Systems, pp. 625–630. IEEE (2006)
5. Promise, E., Otasowie, P.: Investigation of GSM signal loss in multi-story building. In: International Conference and Exhibition on ICT Telecommunication, p. 65 (2016)
6. Ng, J.P.S., Sum, Y.L., Soong, B.H., Maier, M., Monteiro, P.J.: Electromagnetic wave propagation through composite building materials in urban environments at mid-band 5G frequencies. IET Microwaves Antennas Propag. **16**(10), 627–638 (2022)
7. Ayeni, A.A., Yusuf, A.A., Onidare, S.O.: Correlation between the electromagnetic properties of building materials and wireless signal penetration loss. IEEE Trans. Antennas Propag. **70**(12), 12040–12048 (2022)
8. Pavlík, M., Bereš, M., Beňa, L.: The influence of various commonly used building materials on the shielding effectiveness, reflection and absorption of the electromagnetic wave. Appl. Sci. **14**(6), 2521 (2024)
9. Asp, A., Sydorov, Y., Valkama, M., Niemelä, J.: Radio signal propagation and attenuation measurements for modern residential buildings. In: 2012 IEEE Globecom Workshops, pp. 580–584. IEEE (2012)
10. Ghanem, K., Alradwan, H., Motermawy, A., Ahmad, A.: Reducing ping-pong handover effects in intra eutra networks. In: 2012 8th International Symposium on Communication Systems, Networks & Digital Signal Processing (CSNDSP), pp. 1–5. IEEE (2012)
11. Ma, C., Yang, X., Wang, J., Yang, G., Zhang, W., Ma, S.: Reconfigurable distributed antennas and reflecting surface: a new architecture for wireless communications. IEEE Trans. Commun. (2024)
12. Jafari, A.H., López-Pérez, D., Song, H., Claussen, H., Ho, L., Zhang, J.: Small cell backhaul: challenges and prospective solutions. EURASIP J. Wirel. Commun. Netw. **2015**(1), 1–18 (2015). https://doi.org/10.1186/s13638-015-0426-y
13. Paulo, R.R., Velez, F.J., Khan, B.: Study of indoor small cell deployments. J. Mob. Multimedia 329–344 (2021)
14. Fotouhi, A., et al.: Survey on UAV cellular communications: practical aspects, standardization advancements, regulation, and security challenges. IEEE Commun. Surv. Tutor. **21**(4), 3417–3442 (2019)
15. Martian, A., Paleacu, C., Marcu, I.M., Vladeanu, C.: Direction-finding for unmanned aerial vehicles using radio frequency methods. Measurement **235**, 114883 (2024)
16. Ficili, I., Giacobbe, M., Tricomi, G., Puliafito, A.: From sensors to data intelligence: leveraging IoT, cloud, and edge computing with ai. Sensors **25**(6), 1763 (2025)
17. Cicek, C.T., Gultekin, H., Tavli, B., Yanikomeroglu, H.: UAV base station location optimization for next generation wireless networks: Overview and future research directions. In: 2019 1st International Conference on Unmanned Vehicle Systems-Oman (UVS), pp. 1–6. IEEE (2019)
18. Cui, J., Hu, B., Chen, S.: A decision-making scheme for UAV maximizes coverage of emergency indoor and outdoor users. Ad Hoc Netw. **112**, 102391 (2021)
19. Rocha, L., Ferreira, S., Vivaldini, K.C.T., Araújo, J., Batalha, I.: Ziwi: indoor and outdoor planning network–framework to collection, modeling and network structure based on computational optimization and measurements. Soft. Comput. **27**(10), 6761–6781 (2023)
20. Kurner, T., Meier, A.: Prediction of outdoor and outdoor-to-indoor coverage in urban areas at 1.8 ghz. IEEE J. Sel. Areas Commun. **20**(3), 496–506 (2002)

21. Maduraga, M., Abeysekara, R.: Comparison of supervised learning-based indoor localization techniques for smart building applications. In: 2021 International Research Conference on Smart Computing and Systems Engineering (SCSE), vol. 4, pp. 145–148. IEEE (2021)
22. Raj, N.: Indoor RSSI prediction using machine learning for wireless networks. In: 2021 International Conference on Communication Systems & Networks (COMSNETS), pp. 372–374. IEEE (2021)
23. Konak, A., Delattre, S., Bartolacci, M.: Wireless signal prediction using deep learning models for wifi positioning and security concerns (2024)
24. Hason Rudd, D., et al.: Drone-based machine learning for 5G indoor building 3D coverage prediction in high-rise urban environments
25. Zhang, M., Fan, Z., Shibasaki, R., Song, X.: Domain adversarial graph convolutional network based on RSSI and crowdsensing for indoor localization. IEEE Internet Things J. **10**(15), 13662–13672 (2023)
26. Lezama, F., González, G.G., Larroca, F., Capdehourat, G.: Indoor localization using graph neural networks. In: 2021 IEEE URUCON, pp. 51–54. IEEE (2021)
27. Lezama, F., Larroca, F., Capdehourat, G.: On the application of graph neural networks for indoor positioning systems. In: Machine Learning for Indoor Localization and Navigation, pp. 239–256. Springer (2023)
28. Vishwakarma, R., Joshi, R.B., Mishra, S.: Indoorgnn: a graph neural network based approach for indoor localization using wifi RSSI. In: International Conference on Big Data Analytics, pp. 150–165. Springer (2023)
29. Torun, M., Cai, H., Mostofi, Y.: Spatial prediction of channel signal strength map using deep fully convolutional neural network. In: 2022 56th Asilomar Conference on Signals, Systems, and Computers, pp. 553–558. IEEE (2022)
30. Tarhuni, N., Al Saadi, I., Asif, H.M., Mesbah, M., Eldirdiry, O., Hossen, A.: Machine-learning-based ground-level mobile network coverage prediction using UAV measurements. J. Sens. Actuator Netw. **12**(3), 44 (2023)
31. Yarkony, N., Blaunstein, N.: Prediction of propagation characteristics in indoor radio communication environments. In: 2nd European Conference on Antennas and Propagation (EuCAP 2007). IET (2007)

Contrastive Representation Learning of Floor Plan Images Using Human Annotated Attributed Graphs

Ibuki Uda[1(✉)] and Tomonobu Ozaki[2]

[1] Graduate School of Integrated Basic Sciences, Nihon University, 3-25-40 Sakurajosui, Setagaya, Tokyo 156-8550, Japan
uda.ibuki@nihon-u.ac.jp

[2] Department of Information Science, Nihon University, 3-25-40 Sakurajosui, Setagaya, Tokyo 156-8550, Japan
ozaki.tomonobu@nihon-u.ac.jp

Abstract. In recent years, increasingly diverse customer values and lifestyles in housing selection have underscored the need for flexible floor plan retrieval systems that reflect subjective perspectives such as storage sufficiency, circulation efficiency, and spatial connectivity. However, conventional retrieval approaches based on labeled graphs struggle to represent fine-grained spatial structures and room attributes, leading to limited accuracy and flexibility. To address these limitations, we model each floor plan as an attributed graph that encodes both inter-room connections and room-specific attributes, and we define twelve customer-oriented conditions as the presence or absence of characteristic subgraphs. We then propose a vectorization framework that combines ResNet-18 image features with these condition vectors in a contrastive-learning paradigm. The resulting embedding space places floor plans with similar conditions in close proximity. Experiments show superior classification performance on several conditions, confirming the effectiveness of the proposed approach.

Keywords: floor plan · attributed graph · contrastive learning · vectorization

1 Introduction

Floor plans are indispensable for visually conveying a building's internal structure in the real-estate and construction industries. Consequently, there is a growing need for technologies that enable efficient retrieval of floor plans tailored to individual needs—whether in the context of architectural design by professionals or property selection by potential buyers or renters.

In particular, customer needs reflect diverse personal values and lifestyles, extending beyond room size to include factors such as storage layout, circulation flow, and natural lighting. These requirements are often ambiguous and cannot

T. Hao et al. (Eds.): BESC 2025, LNCS 16431, pp. 141–154, 2026.
https://doi.org/10.1007/978-981-95-7138-3_10

always be explicitly defined as concrete conditions. Therefore, there is a need for technologies that not only represent the structural and functional characteristics of floor plans in a formal and quantitative manner, but also accommodate such ambiguity to enable accurate and flexible retrieval.

Previous studies have attempted to bridge customer needs and floor plans by quantifying the domain knowledge of professional architects [1]. Specifically, based on interviews with multiple architects, several key perspectives—such as ease of household chores, ample storage, productivity in work, and enjoyment of hobbies—have been identified. For each perspective, representative features such as the presence of an indoor drying area, a high storage-to-area ratio, the existence of three or more Western-style rooms, and the inclusion of a courtyard or patio have been extracted and quantitatively evaluated. Furthermore, by mapping each representative feature to a specific substructure of the floor plan, prior studies have demonstrated the feasibility of floor plan retrieval based on customers' subjective preferences.

On the other hand, a widely adopted formal representation of floor plans is based on labeled graphs, in which rooms are represented as nodes and their connections as edges. While labeled graph representations are sufficient for capturing room types and their connections, they are not necessarily adequate for expressing finer-grained details—such as room size, spatial location, or the presence and extent of storage—which are often directly linked to customer preferences. Manual annotation of these finer-grained details in floor plans is costly and difficult to scale. Furthermore, even recently developed deep learning models do not necessarily achieve sufficient accuracy in annotation, especially when considering fine-grained details such as room size, spatial location, and storage features.

Motivated by these challenges, this study takes a first step toward realizing flexible floor plan retrieval that accounts for customer perspectives by proposing a vectorization method for floor plan images based on fine-grained attributed subgraph features. Specifically, we propose representing floor plan images as attributed graphs and applying contrastive learning that leverages the presence or absence of subgraphs corresponding to customer perspectives, aiming to construct a general encoder for floor plan images. The overall structure of the proposed method is shown in Fig. 1.

In the proposed method, each floor plan image used for training is first manually converted into an attributed graph. At the same time, feature vectors are extracted from the images using ResNet-18 [11], and these representations are used to construct a dataset for training the vector encoder. Subsequently, the vector encoder is trained using a contrastive learning framework based on triplet loss [10]. This approach is expected to enable the construction of a generalizable vectorization model for floor plan images that effectively captures graph-based features.

The remainder of this paper is organized as follows. Section 2 reviews related work. Section 3 describes the dataset and its annotation process. Section 4 explains the training of the embedding model using the annotated dataset.

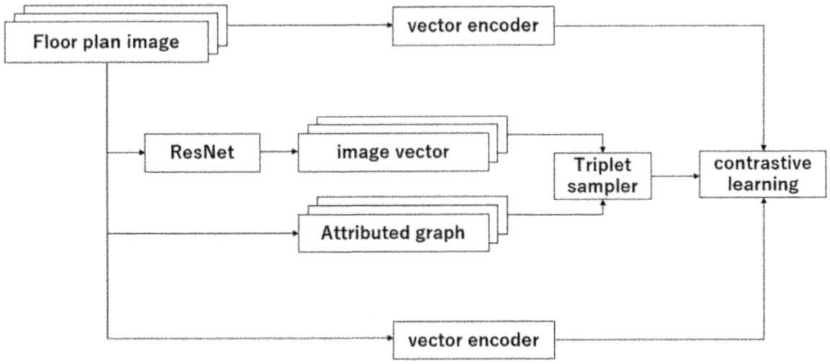

Fig. 1. The overall structure of the proposed method

Section 5 reports the results of the evaluation experiments. Finally, Sect. 6 concludes the paper and discusses future work.

2 Related Work

Numerous studies have been conducted on floor plan retrieval and analysis using graph-based representations [2–7].

For example, [2] automatically extracts an access graph from a floor plan and utlizes a Graph Convolutional Network (GCN) to quantitatively evaluate the influence of spatial configurations on rental prices. Similarly, [3] proposes a method for directly extracting graphs from CAD data and identifying door positions using a Graph Neural Network (GNN). Beyond analysis, [4] proposes a method that represents existing floor plans as graph structures and employs graph matching techniques to automatically generate new floor plans, thereby aiming to improve work efficiency during the early stages of architectural design. In [5], a system is proposed that converts floor plans into graph structures consisting of room nodes and connection edges, and retrieves similar floor plans using graph matching. Additionally, [6] presents a method that represents building floor plans as undirected graphs and uses a graph neural network (GNN) to classify the category of each room. Furthermore, [1] analyzes the relationship between customer perspectives and floor plan structures based on interviews with architects.

Regarding the vectorization of floor plan images, [8] conducts research that aimsed at significantly improving work efficiency in the construction and real estate industries through the automatic vectorization of raster images. Additionally, [9] proposes a method that converts floor plans with design information and behavioral features into attributed graphs, which are then vectorized using an LSTM-VAE. This approach enables a variety of applications such as similarity search and generation.

Building on these previous studies and challenges, this study aims to develop a vectorization method that appropriately accounts for the structural features of floor plans.

Table 1. Room labels and their frequencies in the dataset

Label	Frequency	Label	Frequency
wash	1,035	veranda	134
bath	1,036	terrace	13
Japanese	891	corridor	1,009
Western	2,235	wc	1,037
entrance	1,036	cl	4,029
K	250	WCL	94
DK	16	door	15,296
LD	250	garden	5
LDK	766	window	2,549
balcony	1,144	others	31

Table 2. Statistics of the Number of Vertices and Edges

	Number of Vertices	Number of Edges
Mean	10.5	21.5
Standard Deviation	0.8	2.5
Minimum	8.0	12.0
First Quartile	10.0	20.0
Median	10.0	22.0
Third Quartile	11.0	22.0
Maximum	14.0	34.0

3 Dataset and Annotation

In this study, 1,036 single-story houses located in the Tokyo area were extracted from the LIFULL HOME'S dataset [12] and utilized as target data.

The extracted floor plan images were annotated using an the AnyLabeling system[1]. The room labels employed in this study were primarily based on the proposal in [7]. We included additional labels such as "walk-in closet" and "garden", while excluding unnecessary elements such as "walls" and "stairs". In addition, as room properties, we collect and assign the room area, the centroid coordinates of the room, the number of windows, and the storage area. On the other hand, for room adjacency, edge information is annotated with one attribute:connection distance. As a result, the entire floor plan image is represented as an attributed graph with attributes assigned to both vertices and edges.

The room labels and their frequencies in the dataset are shown in Table 1. The statistics of the obtained graphs are shown in Table 2, and examples are presented in Fig. 2. As shown in Table 1, it can be observed that there is a

[1] https://github.com/vietanhdev/anylabeling.

significant imbalance in the label distribution. Additionally, according to Table 2, the standard deviations of both the number of vertices and the number of edges are not particularly large, suggesting that the graphs are relatively uniform in terms of size and density.

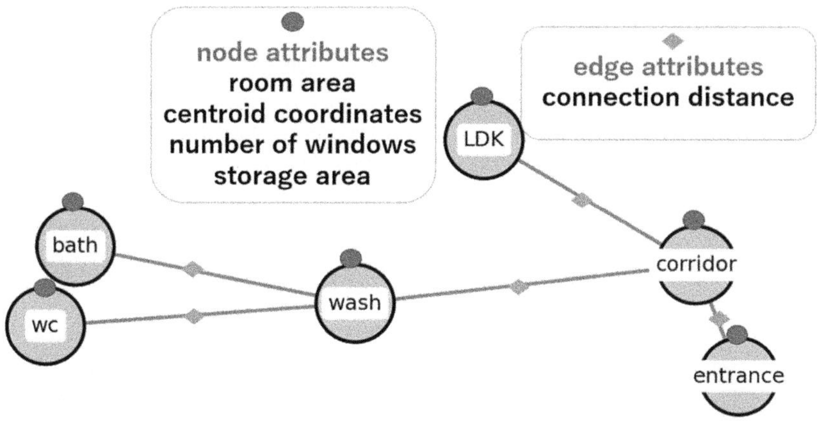

Fig. 2. An example of the generated graph

4 Training of the Vector Encoder

In this study, we propose a framework for training the vector encoder (Fig. 1) through contrastive learning based on triplet sampling, utilizing both image features and graph-based features of floor plans.

4.1 Perspectives on Floor Plans and Subgraphs

In [1], an attempt was made to associate floor plan features with various perspectives, such as "ease of household chores," based on interviews with architects.

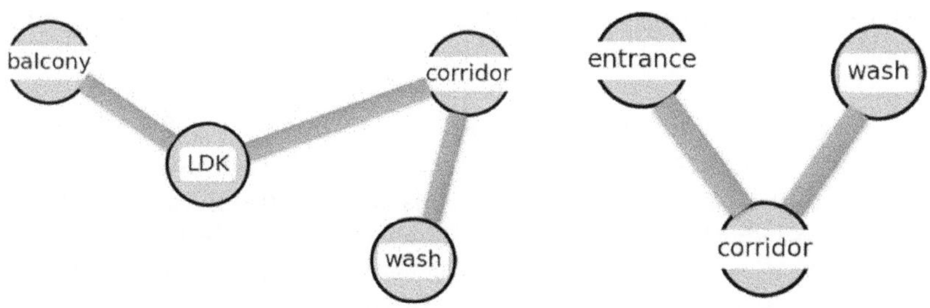

Good laundry flow hygiene flow

Fig. 3. Examples of attributed subgraphs used to evaluate the conditions

Table 3. Perspectives on Floor Plans and Their Condition Definitions

No.	Condition	Definition
1	Presence of a laundry room	Presence of a washroom with an area above a predefined threshold
2	Good laundry flow	Short path from washroom to balcony to living room
3	Efficient wet area flow	Short path from washroom to kitchen
4	Availability of large-capacity storage	Presence of a walk-in closet, storage room, or storage area above a predefined threshold
5	High storage ratio	Ratio of total storage area to total floor area exceeds a predefined threshold
6	Presence of an open living area	Presence of a living room directly connected to a balcony
7	Sufficient balcony space	Presence of two or more balconies
8	Excellent ventilation	Ratio of total windows to number of rooms exceeds a predefined threshold
9	Circulation efficiency	Short path from entrance to living room
10	High connectivity with shared spaces	Presence of two or more rooms directly connected to the living room
11	High privacy	Private rooms (Western/Japanese) are separated by at least a predefined distance
12	Good hygiene flow	Short path from entrance to washroom

Building on these findings, our study expresses 12 perspectives on floor plans—such as circulation efficiency, storage sufficiency, and room connectivity—as conditions that can be computed from attributed subgraphs. These conditions are then used for triplet sampling in the training process. The adopted conditions are shown in Table 3. For example, in the table, the condition "Good laundry flow" assumes a path exists from the laundry room, through the balcony, and to the living room. The validity of this condition is determined by whether the shortest path length is below a specified threshold, which can be evaluated based on the corresponding attributed subgraph, as illustrated in Fig. 3 (left). Specifically, in this subgraph, the shortest path is measured from the washroom to the LDK via the corridor and balcony. Another example is the condition "Good hygiene flow", which evaluates whether the washroom is easily accessible from the entrance. As shown in Fig. 3 (right), this condition is evaluated by measuring the shortest path from the entrance to the washroom. In the illustrated subgraph, the path passes through the corridor, capturing a typical circulation route within the floor plan.

4.2 Triplet Data Extraction Based on Image and Graph Features

We define D as the set comprising all floor plan images employed in this study. For each floor plan image $d \in D$, we denote a binary condition vector as v_d. The vector v_d is a multi-dimensional vector whose elements are binary values representing the presence or absence of the corresponding conditions listed in Table 3. Specifically, $v_d[i] = 1$ indicates that the floor plan d satisfies the i-th condition. On the other hand, we denote the image embedding of d, which is obtained using a pre-trained ResNet-18 [11], as V_d. We define the Jaccard similarity between two condition vectors v_{d_1} and v_{d_2} as $J(v_{d_1}, v_{d_2})$. Likewise, the cosine similarity between two image embeddings V_{d_1} and V_{d_2} is defined as $\cos(V_{d_1}, V_{d_2})$.

In this study, both the Jaccard similarity of the condition vectors and the cosine similarity of the image embeddings are effectively utilized to construct the triplet data. Specifically, following the concept of hard negatives introduced in [10], positive data are selected as pairs that exhibit high Jaccard similarity in their condition vectors but low cosine similarity in their image embeddings. Conversely, negative data are selected as pairs with low Jaccard similarity in their condition vectors but high cosine similarity in their image embeddings.

In this context, for a given anchor image $a \in D$, the positive candidate set $P(a)$ and the negative candidate set $N(a)$ are derived respectively as follows:

$$\begin{aligned} P(a) &= \{p \in D \mid J(v_a, v_p) \geq \tau_{\text{high}} \wedge \cos(V_a, V_p) \leq \sigma_{\text{low}}\}, \\ N(a) &= \{n \in D \mid J(v_a, v_n) \leq \tau_{\text{low}} \wedge \cos(V_a, V_n) \geq \sigma_{\text{high}}\} \end{aligned} \tag{1}$$

where τ_{high} and τ_{low} are thresholds for the Jaccard similarity, and σ_{high} and σ_{low} are thresholds for the cosine similarity of the image embeddings.

If the number of candidates is insufficient, additional candidates are supplemented in descending order based on the Jaccard similarity or the cosine similarity score.

Finally, for each anchor a, a positive data point p and a negative data point n are selected, and the triplet dataset is constructed as

$$T(D) = \{\langle a, p, n \rangle \mid a \in D,\, p \in P(a),\, n \in N(a)\}. \tag{2}$$

To suppress data imbalance, we set M as the maximum number of times the same image can be used as positive or negative candidates.

Next, using the constructed dataset $T(D)$, the vector encoder f is trained to minimize the triplet loss

$$L = \max\left(0,\, \|f(a) - f(p)\|^2 - \|f(a) - f(n)\|^2 + \alpha\right) \tag{3}$$

where α is the margin parameter.

This approach is expected to construct an embedding space in which data with similar condition vectors are mapped close to each other, while data with different conditions are mapped farther apart. Specifically, the model is optimized so that floor plan images (a, p) with a high Jaccard similarity between their condition vectors are transformed into similar vectors, representing data that both satisfy the same conditions. Conversely, floor plan images (a, n) with a low Jaccard similarity are transformed into dissimilar vectors, representing data with different conditions.

This is expected to enable the model to estimate the degree to which a new floor plan satisfies specific conditions based on its relative position in the embedding space.

5 Evaluation Experiments

5.1 Experimental Setup

In the evaluation experiments, we used 1,036 floor plan images of single-story houses in the Tokyo area, as described in Sect. 3. The dataset was split into 80% for training, 10% for validation, and 10% for testing. Each floor plan image was resized to 224×224 pixels, and RGB channel normalization was applied. For the vector encoder, we used a ResNet-18 model pre-trained on ImageNet [11], with its final layer modified to output a 256-dimensional vector. During training, the batch size was set to 32, the learning rate to 1×10^{-4}, and the number of epochs to 20. L2 normalization was applied to unify the scale of the output vectors. To comprehensively evaluate the effectiveness of the proposed method, we compared eight models based on the following three axes.

The first axis concerns the method of constructing triplet data, as described in Sect. 4. In the hard triplet approach, triplets are constructed by selecting positive examples with high Jaccard similarity of condition vectors but low cosine similarity of image embeddings, and negative examples with low Jaccard similarity but high cosine similarity. In contrast, the random triplet approach randomly selects positive and negative examples based on the binary labels of each condition. This comparison aims to clarify the effectiveness of learning with hard triplets.

The second axis concerns the architecture of the vector encoder. We compared a shared model, which learns a common representation across all conditions, with individual models, in which separate vector encoders are independently trained for each condition. Specifically, for the training of vector encoder on the i-th condition in the individual setting, we empoly an image $a \in D$ such that $v_a[i] = 1$ as an anchor, and prepare positive and negative candidate set as $P_i(a) = \{p \in P(a) \mid v_p[i] = 1\}$ and $N_i(a) = \{n \in N(a) \mid v_n[i] = 0\}$, respectively.

The third axis is the classification method applied after embedding. We prepare two approaches. One approach is the k-nearest neighbors (k-NN) method, where the embedding vectors obtained from the trained model are compared with those of the training set stored as a retrieval memory. The similarity metric employed is the Euclidean distance. In this method, the predicted label $\hat{y}_i$ for condition i of a test image d is defined as

$$\hat{y}_i = \begin{cases} 1 & \text{if } \frac{1}{k} \sum_{x \in nn(d,k)} v_x[i] \geq \tau, \\ 0 & \text{otherwise,} \end{cases} \tag{4}$$

where $nn(d, k)$ denotes the set of k-nearest neighbors of d. The parameters k and τ were determined via grid search to maximize the F1 score on the validation set.

The other approach is prototype-based classification. In this method, the prototype for i-th condition is defined as the mean of the embedding vectors of the training samples that satisfy the i-th condition, denoted as the set $D_i = \{d \in D \mid v_d[i] = 1\}$. A test image d is considered to satisfy the i-th condition if the distance between its embedding and the prototype is less than or equal to a threshold θ. Formally, the predicted label $\hat{y}_i(d)$ is defined as

$$\hat{y}_i(d) = \begin{cases} 1 & \text{if } \left\| f(d) - \frac{1}{|D_i|} \sum_{p \in D_i} f(p) \right\|_2 \leq \theta, \\ 0 & \text{otherwise,} \end{cases} \tag{5}$$

where f denotes the shared vector encoder used for all conditions. In the individual-encoder experiment, we simply replace f with condition-specific encoders f_i. The threshold θ is tuned to maximize the F1 score on the validation set.

For each of the eight model configurations described above, we compared the precision, recall, and F1 scores for every condition label. These metrics were used to quantitatively compare the proposed method and assess the effectiveness of each individual component.

5.2 Results and Discussion

Table 4 present the precision, recall, and F1 scores for the 12 condition labels across the eight model configurations.

First, we focus on the average F1 scores of the configurations using k-NN. When the setting of hard triplet was employed, the classification performance consistently outperformed that of random triplet. Specifically, in the shared model setting, the F1 score rises from 0.71 to 0.73 (+0.02). In the individual model setting, it improves from 0.69 to 0.70 (+0.01). Thus, every k-NN configuration shows a measurable performance gain.

In analyzing the source of these gains, we observe different trends across configurations. In the shared model setting, the hard triplet led to an increase in precision from 0.65 to 0.67 and in recall from 0.79 to 0.81. These results suggest that both metrics improved in a balanced manner. Thus, we interpret that training in the shared model setting was stably facilitated by the introduction of hard triplet. In the individual model, recall rises sharply from 0.66 to 0.86 (+0.20), whereas precision declines markedly from 0.72 to 0.58 (−0.14), indicating a clear trade-off. This result suggests that the encoders trained independently for each condition become more sensitive to true positives under the hard triplet setting, but simultaneously generate a larger number of false positives. Thus, whereas the shared model achieves consistent improvements in both precision and recall, the

Table 4. Experimental Results

Condition	Shared model with k-NN inference						Shared model with prototype inference					
	Random Triplet			Hard Triplet			Random Triplet			Hard Triplet		
	P	R	F1	P	R	F1	P	R	F1	P	R	F1
01	0.42	0.57	0.48	0.41	0.52	0.46	0.30	0.71	0.42	0.32	0.51	0.40
02	0.73	0.84	0.78	0.78	0.87	0.82	0.84	0.74	0.79	0.75	0.77	0.76
03	0.76	0.85	0.81	0.82	0.86	0.84	0.74	0.93	0.82	0.71	0.92	0.80
04	0.46	0.72	0.56	0.47	0.67	0.55	0.29	0.94	0.45	0.33	0.94	0.49
05	0.65	0.76	0.70	0.57	0.78	0.66	0.53	0.86	0.66	0.49	0.97	0.65
06	0.84	0.94	0.89	0.86	0.97	0.91	0.80	0.84	0.82	0.82	0.93	0.87
07	0.40	0.76	0.52	0.46	0.75	0.57	0.60	0.24	0.34	0.44	0.48	0.46
08	0.64	0.85	0.73	0.68	0.79	0.73	0.62	0.69	0.66	0.60	0.71	0.65
09	0.79	0.77	0.78	0.82	0.89	0.85	0.70	0.87	0.78	0.68	0.99	0.80
10	0.73	0.82	0.77	0.77	0.90	0.83	0.59	0.73	0.65	0.57	0.87	0.68
11	0.72	0.81	0.76	0.73	0.86	0.79	0.68	0.73	0.71	0.61	0.80	0.69
12	0.61	0.84	0.70	0.65	0.90	0.75	0.61	0.84	0.71	0.58	0.85	0.69
Mean	0.65	0.79	0.71	0.67	0.81	0.73	0.61	0.74	0.64	0.57	0.79	0.65

Condition	Individual model with k-NN inference						Individual model with prototype inference					
	Random Triplet			Hard Triplet			Random Triplet			Hard Triplet		
	P	R	F1	P	R	F1	P	R	F1	P	R	F1
01	0.41	0.23	0.29	0.28	0.87	0.43	0.56	0.16	0.25	0.42	0.32	0.36
02	0.76	0.73	0.75	0.63	0.88	0.73	0.72	0.75	0.74	0.84	0.66	0.74
03	0.81	0.77	0.79	0.73	0.97	0.83	0.71	0.95	0.81	0.73	0.88	0.80
04	0.67	0.31	0.43	0.33	0.53	0.41	0.55	0.34	0.42	0.88	0.22	0.35
05	0.71	0.58	0.64	0.55	0.93	0.69	0.55	0.98	0.71	0.53	0.97	0.68
06	0.83	0.97	0.89	0.81	1.00	0.89	0.82	0.99	0.90	0.84	1.00	0.91
07	0.83	0.43	0.57	0.50	0.65	0.57	0.60	0.65	0.63	0.65	0.65	0.65
08	0.85	0.65	0.74	0.62	0.83	0.71	0.69	0.85	0.76	0.72	0.79	0.75
09	0.80	0.80	0.80	0.66	0.96	0.78	0.73	0.81	0.77	0.71	0.94	0.81
10	0.82	0.79	0.80	0.64	0.87	0.74	0.68	0.87	0.77	0.60	0.94	0.73
11	0.73	0.83	0.78	0.69	0.92	0.79	0.73	0.85	0.78	0.71	0.82	0.76
12	0.74	0.80	0.77	0.58	0.95	0.72	0.68	0.88	0.77	0.72	0.79	0.75
Mean	0.72	0.66	0.69	0.58	0.86	0.70	0.66	0.74	0.69	0.67	0.73	0.70

individual model exhibits an excessive rise in recall coupled with a pronounced drop in precision, indicating that it may be exhibiting overfitting behavior.

Focusing on the inference methods, k-NN achieves higher F1 scores than prototype classification in every configuration. In particular, the combination of hard triplet training with the shared model attains the best mean F1 score of 0.73, underscoring the clear advantage of k-NN. This superiority is likely due to k-NN's ability to flexibly exploit the local structure of the embedding space, enabling it to adapt well to nonlinear decision boundaries.

Examining the results by condition, the conditions 6 (open living area), 9 (circulation efficiency), and 10 (connectivity with shared spaces) achieve the F1 scores above 0.80 across all configurations, demonstrating that the proposed method captures spatially driven conditions with high accuracy. These conditions are defined by the connectivity and spatial arrangement of multiple rooms—such as living areas, corridors, and balconies—so graph structure and spatial relationships are strongly reflected in their labels. As a result, global structural features extracted from the floor plan images contribute directly to the decision and remain well separated in the embedding space. In particular, for conditions 06 and 10, cues such as balcony connectivity and overall room openness are prominently expressed in the layout, which likely accounts for their high discriminability.

By contrast, for the conditions 1 (presence of a laundry room), 4 (presence of large-capacity storage), and 7 (sufficient balcony space), even the best-performing configuration yields F1 scores no higher than 0.57, indicating that these categories remain challenging to classify. These conditions depend on localized, quantitative attributes—such as the presence or size of specific rooms—that are difficult to capture through the abstract structural features derived from the entire image. For example, a laundry room may appear only as a small section of a washroom, and subtle variations in floor area or storage availability are seldom preserved in the embedding space. As similar, balcony space availability relies on quantitative aspects such as size or count; unless these factors are explicitly extracted, mere structural connectivity is insufficient, which may lead to false positives.

From these results, we conclude that while the proposed method is effective for conditions governed by structural attributes, its current embedding representation clearly limits its performance for conditions hinging on non-structural or highly localized features.

6 Summary

In this study, we proposed a flexible floor plan retrieval method that reflects customers' subjective preferences by vectorising floor plan images as attributed subgraphs and constructing an embedding space through contrastive learning. In the model training with a triplet loss, both of image features extracted with ResNet-18 and a 12-dimensional condition vector—covering subjective criteria—are effectively utilized.

The configuration that combines a shared model, hard triplet, and k-NN inference achieved the average F1 score of 0.73, outperforming the random triplet baseline by 0.02. This improvement indicates that hard triplet effectively draws floor plans with similar condition vectors closer together in the embedding space. Furthermore, the hard triplet setting improved both precision and recall in the shared model. In contrast, for individual models, it markedly increased recall at the expense of precision, revealing a trade-off associated with higher false-positive rates. In addition, k-NN inference consistently outperformed the prototype-based approach in every configuration, underscoring the advantage of exploiting local neighbourhood structures in the embedding space.

At the condition level, the model achieved an F1 score of approximately 0.80 for structurally driven criteria—such as open living areas, circulation efficiency, and spatial connectivity—demonstrating strong discriminative capability. In contrast, for more local and quantitative conditions, including the presence of a laundry room, the presence of large-capacity storage, and sufficient balcony space, the F1 score remained at only 0.57, revealing that the current embedding fails to capture non-structural or highly localized features adequately.

To address this limitation, it is necessary to incorporate not only the global structural features extracted from the entire image but also fine-grained and quantitative information at the room level—such as floor area, the number of storage units, and the number of windows—into the embedding representation. In particular, features such as the presence of a laundry room, the amount of storage space, and the size of the balcony tend to appear only in localized regions of a floor plan and are often difficult to infer solely from overall spatial structure or room connectivity. These elements are also visually inconspicuous and, therefore, are not easily captured within a contrastive learning framework that relies on holistic image-based representations. In practice, these conditions exhibited lower F1 scores compared to structurally defined conditions, indicating limitations in the current embedding approach.

As such, localized and small-scale features tend to be overshadowed in embedding representations learned through global image-based feature extraction and contrast with condition vectors. To mitigate this, it is essential to move beyond representing the entire image with a single vector and instead introduce mechanisms that explicitly extract and preserve features at the room level. For example, methods that segment the floor plan by room and extract visual and attribute-based features from each region, or approaches that incorporate spatial attention mechanisms to allow the model to focus on relevant local areas, can be effective. Furthermore, directly incorporating node-level attributes such as room area and the number of facilities, and integrating them with visual features, is expected to improve classification performance for non-structural conditions.

In addition, all floor plan annotations in this study were manually created, which required considerable effort and posed limitations on data scalability. To overcome this, it is important to incorporate technologies that can automatically or semi-automatically extract room boundaries, types, connectivity, and attribute values from floor plan images and generate attributed graphs. Such automation would enable the efficient collection of a larger volume of training data and improve the generalization capability of the model, particularly in handling a diverse range of conditions involving localized features.

Furthermore, integrating non-visual information—such as room names, annotations, orientation, and floor area written on the drawings, as well as metadata related to building type and structure—with visual features can be effective in resolving ambiguous elements and improving classification accuracy. Designing models capable of leveraging such multimodal information remains an important direction for future research and development.

In summary, advancing floor plan retrieval systems requires the development of representation methods that can more accurately capture non-structural and localized conditions, the expansion of training data through automated annotation, and the integration of diverse information sources. These efforts are essential for achieving more flexible and accurate retrieval systems that reflect subjective user preferences.

Acknowledgment. In this study, we used the LIFULL HOME'S dataset provided by LIFULL Co., Ltd. through the IDR Dataset Provision Service of the National Institute of Informatics. This work was partially supported by JSPS KAKENHI Grant Number 22K12173.

References

1. Kohno, Y., Kajiyama, T.: Quantification of architectural experts' knowledge using floor plans of detached houses. J. Japan Soc. Kansei Eng. **23**(4), 275–283 (2024). (in Japanese)
2. Takizawa, A.: Extracting real estate values of rental apartment floor plans using graph convolutional networks, arXiv preprint arXiv:2303.13568 (2023)
3. Simonsen, C.P., Thiesson, F.M., Philipsen, M.P., Moeslund, T.B.: Generalizing floor plans using graph neural networks. In: Proceedings of IEEE International Conference on Image Processing (ICIP), pp. 654–658 (2021)
4. Wang, X.-Y., Yang, Y., Zhang, K.: Customization and generation of floor plans based on graph transformations. Autom. Constr. **94**, 405–416 (2018)
5. Sabri, Q.U., Bayer, J., Ayzenshtadt, V., Bukhari, S.S., Althoff, K.-D., Dengel, A.: Semantic pattern-based retrieval of architectural floor plans with case-based and graph-based searching techniques and their evaluation and visualization. In: Proceedings of 6th International Conference on Pattern Recognition Applications and Methods (ICPRAM), pp. 50–60 (2017)
6. Paudel, A., Dhakal, R., Bhattarai, S.: Room classification on floor plan graphs using graph neural networks, arXiv preprint arXiv:2108.05947 (2021)
7. Yamada, M., Ting, X., Yamazaki, T., Aizawa, K.: Graph-based representation of real estate floor plans using deep learning and its application to property retrieval. In: Proceedings of 33rd Annual Conference of the Japanese Society for Artificial Intelligence (JSAI), 3N4-J-10-03 (2019). (in Japanese)
8. Song, W., Abyaneh, M.M., Shabani, M.A., Furukawa, Y.: Vectorizing building blueprints. In: Proceedings of Asian Conference on Computer Vision (ACCV), pp. 1044–1059 (2022)
9. Azizi, V., Usman, M., Zhou, H., Faloutsos, P., Kapadia, M.: Graph-based generative representation learning of semantically and behaviorally augmented floor plans, arXiv preprint arXiv:2012.04735 (2020)
10. Xuan, H., Stylianou, A., Liu, X., Pless, R.: Hard negative examples are hard, but useful. In: Proceedings of European Conference on Computer Vision (ECCV), pp. 126–142 (2020)

11. He, K., Zhang, X., Ren, S., Sun, J.: Deep residual learning for image recognition. In: Proceedings of the IEEE Conference on Computer Vision and Pattern Recognition (CVPR), pp. 770–778 (2016)
12. LIFULL Co., Ltd.: LIFULL HOME'S dataset, provided via the IDR Dataset Provision Service, National Institute of Informatics, Japan (2015). https://doi.org/10.32130/idr.6.0

AgentLesson: LLM-Based Multi-agent System for Educational Lesson Plan Generation

Yakun Chen, Yu Yang, and Guandong Xu(✉)

Centre for Learning, Teaching and Technology, The Education University of Hong Kong, Hong Kong SAR, China
{cyakun,yangyy,gdxu}@eduhk.hk

Abstract. Recent advancements in Large Language Models (LLMs) have demonstrated their potential in automating pedagogical content generation. However, the design and evaluation of high-quality lesson plans still require iterative refinement and pedagogical alignment. In this paper, we propose **AgentLesson**, a multi-agent framework that simulates human-like collaboration between a Writer Agent and an Evaluator Agent to iteratively generate and improve lesson plans. Given a subject, grade, and topic, the Writer Agent creates an initial plan based on Gagné's Nine Events of Instruction, while the Evaluator Agent provides rubric-based feedback across five dimensions: Clarity, Integrity, Depth, Practicality, and Pertinence. This feedback is used to guide the Writer Agent in multiple rounds of refinement. We conduct extensive experiments across multiple subjects and topics, and quantitatively evaluate plan quality under single-agent, one-round, and multi-round agent settings. Our results show that multi-agent collaboration significantly enhances lesson quality, with notable improvements in Depth and Pertinence. This work highlights the promise of LLM-based agent collaboration in educational content creation and opens new directions for teacher-assistive technologies.

Keywords: Large Language Models (LLMs) · Multiple Agents · Lesson Plan Generation · Pedagogy-Driven System

1 Introduction

Lesson planning is a fundamental yet time-intensive task in education. High-quality lesson plans provide pedagogical structure, align with curriculum standards, and facilitate effective teaching and learning experiences. As education systems increasingly adopt technology to support teachers, Large Language Models (LLMs) have emerged as promising tools for automating lesson planning [4,20]. Their ability to generate context-aware instructional content opens new possibilities for supporting both novice and experienced educators. Recent studies have explored various strategies to improve the alignment between LLM outputs and instructional frameworks. For example, Jia et al. [7] demonstrated

T. Hao et al. (Eds.): BESC 2025, LNCS 16431, pp. 155–170, 2026.
https://doi.org/10.1007/978-981-95-7138-3_11

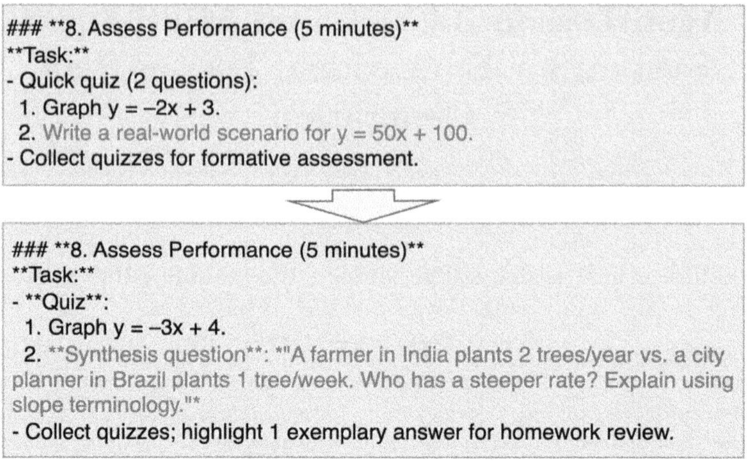

Fig. 1. A side-by-side comparison of the assessment design in Part 8 of two lesson plans on Graphing Linear Functions in Slope-Intercept Form for Grade 8 Mathematics. The top segment shows the initial single-agent output with a basic quiz and a generic open-ended question. The bottom segment illustrates the improved multi-agent version, which introduces a higher-order synthesis question grounded in a realistic context and integrates terminology use and comparative reasoning.

that incorporating Gagné's Nine Events of Instruction [5] into prompt engineering and fine-tuning significantly enhances the pedagogical quality of generated plans. Similarly, Ye et al. [17] proposed logical chain prompting and fine-tuned EDU-GPT to produce more granular and structured outputs. These works validate the feasibility of using LLMs for lesson generation and highlight the importance of domain-specific prompting and instructional scaffolding.

Despite these advancements, most existing approaches follow a single-shot generation paradigm, where an LLM produces a lesson plan based on a prompt without further revision or structured feedback. This limits the system's ability to improve over time or incorporate external pedagogical judgments. Although some systems incorporate refinement mechanisms—such as self-critique [20] or post-editing by teachers—these are often static or rely on the same model for both generation and evaluation, which can lead to mode collapse or lack of critical reflection. Moreover, few studies explore how multiple specialized agents can collaborate iteratively to improve the quality of educational content in a structured, explainable manner. To concretely illustrate this gap, Fig. 1 presents a comparison between lesson plans produced by a single agent and those refined through multi-agent collaboration. Both excerpts correspond to the "Assess Performance" stage of an 8th-grade mathematics lesson on graphing linear functions. While the single-agent plan includes a basic quiz with a generic prompt, the multi-agent version introduces a higher-order synthesis question that contextualizes the problem, prompts comparative reasoning, and uses domain-specific terminology. This qualitative contrast highlights the limitations of single-shot generation and motivates our exploration of interactive multi-agent strategies that support pedagogical depth, iterative refinement, and domain-relevant cognitive challenge.

This gap motivates our study. We aim to explore whether multi-agent collaboration—specifically between a writer and an evaluator agent—can support a more dynamic and pedagogically sound lesson planning process. Our goal is to simulate human-like iterative improvement by allowing the writer agent to generate lesson plans and the evaluator agent to provide structured feedback based on a fine-grained rubric. Inspired by the multi-agent strategy used in EduPlanner [19], our framework, **AgentLesson**, adopts a modular architecture where generation and evaluation are disentangled but closely integrated through multiple rounds of interaction. Each agent leverages a different LLM and prompt design to ensure role diversity and mitigate redundancy. In summary, our contribution can be summarized as follows:

- We propose a novel LLM-based multi-agent framework, AgentLesson, that leverages collaboration between a writer agent and an evaluator agent to iteratively co-generate and refine lesson plans.
- We introduce an in-depth analysis of the multi-round optimization dynamics. Our empirical results show that most tasks converge within three interaction rounds, with minimal fluctuation, suggesting the practicality of the framework for real-world deployment.
- We conduct a fine-grained rubric-based analysis to identify which aspects of lesson plan quality benefit most from optimization.

2 Related Work

2.1 LLM-Based Multi-agent Systems

The application of large language models (LLMs) in multi-agent systems has emerged as a key paradigm for decomposing complex tasks into collaborative subtasks, particularly in domains requiring iteration, critique, and modular decision-making. Zhang et al. [19] introduced *EduPlanner*, a multi-agent instructional system combining evaluator, optimizer, and question-analyst roles in a feedback loop. While effective in tailoring content via a skill-tree model and a CIDDP rubric, EduPlanner lacks a decoupled evaluation loop and focuses more on math-domain skill alignment than pedagogical quality.

Beyond this, recent frameworks have explored more generalized collaborative strategies. In the general domain, frameworks like AutoGen [16], MetaGPT [6], and CAMEL [10] have demonstrated how multiple, role-playing agents can converse to solve complex problems. These works highlight the power of role specialization and structured communication, principles that are increasingly being adapted into the educational domain. For example, Wang et al. [13] proposed *GenMentor*, a hierarchical tutoring system that schedules different agents for explanation and feedback. Similarly, Li et al. [11] introduced *ARCHED*, a human-centered framework with specialized agents like a 'verifier' and 'rationale builder' to support transparent and explainable educational AI. While ARCHED is conceptually robust, its evaluation is limited to small-scale tasks without sustained refinement cycles.

Our work builds on these trends by introducing *AgentLesson*, a focused two-agent system where a Writer Agent and Evaluator Agent interact iteratively over multiple rounds, each instantiated with distinct LLMs and prompt specializations. This separation allows for deeper critique, rubric-aware feedback, and dynamic stopping criteria based on convergence. Unlike most prior works that either entangle evaluation within generation or rely on static prompts, AgentLesson emphasizes process transparency, role distinction, and convergence-aware optimization for pedagogy.

2.2 LLMs for Education and Lesson Planning

The use of LLMs in lesson plan generation has seen rapid development, especially through prompt engineering and instructional alignment. Fan et al. [4] proposed *LessonPlanner*, which embeds Gagné's Nine Events of Instruction into prompts to guide novice teachers. Their user study indicated that such structuring improves plan completeness and user confidence. Jia et al. [8] went further by comparing Chain-of-Thought (CoT) prompting [14] with LoRA-based fine-tuning, targeting math lessons aligned with Gagné's model. Their results showed that prompt-only approaches struggle with consistency, while lightweight fine-tuning better captures structural fidelity.

Complementary to this, Ye et al. [18] designed *EDU-GPT*, a planning model that integrates logical chains and domain knowledge bases. Their multi-step prompting method yielded lesson plans with richer conceptual scaffolding and more nuanced progression. Moreover, Zheng et al. [20] advanced a self-critique pipeline using Retrieval-Augmented Generation (RAG), a technique that builds on broader research into the self-correction capabilities of LLMs [12]. Although effective, such pipelines typically employ the same model for generation and critique, limiting perspective diversity. These specific advancements in lesson planning tools are part of a broader academic discussion on the opportunities and challenges that large language models bring to the entire educational landscape [9].

A key gap in these studies is the reliance on single-shot or two-stage generation models, which may overlook the iterative nature of pedagogical refinement. Additionally, human evaluations are often limited in scale or separated from the generation loop. Our work complements these efforts by embedding evaluation within the agentic process itself—allowing an evaluator agent to apply multi-dimensional rubric-based feedback over rounds, resulting in more controlled and explainable improvements.

2.3 Instructional Frameworks and Rubric-Based Evaluation

The theoretical foundation for much of this work lies in classical instructional design theory, notably Gagné's Nine Events [5]. This model has been repeatedly

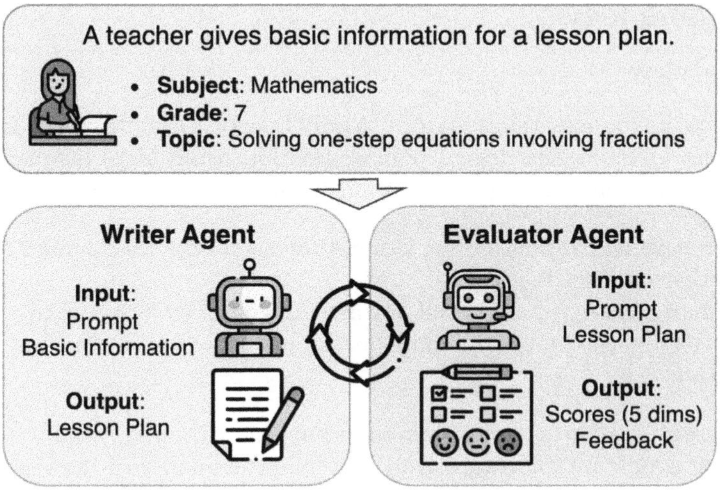

Fig. 2. AgentLesson framework: a teacher provides a lesson topic, and two LLM-based agents collaborate to iteratively generate and evaluate lesson plans. The Writer Agent produces plans based on instructional prompts, while the Evaluator Agent scores them along five dimensions and returns improvement feedback to refine the next round.

shown to support effective knowledge acquisition when used as a structural guide in educational content. Niu et al. [2] further provide a practitioner's guide that shows how the Nine Events can be aligned with digital learning experiences, reinforcing its relevance in AI-driven lesson planning. This model has been repeatedly shown to support effective knowledge acquisition... reinforcing its relevance in AI-driven lesson planning. In addition to Gagné's framework, other pedagogical taxonomies like Bloom's Taxonomy have also been explored to structure and elevate the cognitive complexity of LLM-generated educational content [1,3]. For example, researchers have used Bloom's levels to prompt LLMs for generating questions of varying difficulty. Our work focuses on Gagné's model for its process-oriented structure, but acknowledges the importance of these cognitive frameworks in educational AI design.

Assessment of pedagogical quality is another key dimension. Zhao et al. [19] demonstrated that a CIDDP-style rubric (Clarity, Integrity, Depth, Practicality, Pertinence) enables reliable, multi-dimensional assessment of lesson quality, particularly when applied iteratively. Such rubric-guided evaluation is central to our system, which not only scores along these dimensions but uses the same dimensions as inputs for evaluator feedback and stopping conditions. In doing so, our system turns the evaluation rubric into an actionable scaffold for agent interaction, rather than merely a post-hoc judgment.

3 Methodology

3.1 Overview

This section introduces the design of **AgentLesson**, a multi-agent framework that enables collaborative lesson plan generation using large language models (LLMs). As illustrated in Fig. 2, the framework consists of two core agents:

- **Writer Agent:** Responsible for generating or revising lesson plans given task instructions and feedback.
- **Evaluator Agent:** Responsible for assessing a given lesson plan along multiple pedagogical dimensions and providing rubric scores and improvement suggestions.

The system supports both single-round and multi-round collaborative planning, where agents interact iteratively to refine the quality of the lesson plan.

3.2 Prompt Design for Agents

We carefully design dedicated prompts for different stages of the system:

- **Plan Generation Prompt (Fig.** 3**):** Used by the Writer Agent to produce the first draft of a lesson plan based on curriculum, subject, and topic.
- **Plan Improvement Prompt (Fig.** 4**):** Injects Evaluator Agent's feedback into Writer Agent's prompt to drive plan revisions.
- **Evaluation Prompt (Fig.** 5**):** Guides the Evaluator Agent to assess the plan across rubric dimensions such as clarity, integrity, depth, practicality, and pertinence.

This prompt design ensures that each agent receives contextualized and role-specific instructions, enabling effective collaboration and feedback incorporation.

To ensure pedagogical rigor and consistency, the Writer Agent is guided by Gagné's Nine Events of Instruction [5], a well-established instructional design framework. Each generated lesson plan is structured to explicitly address the following sequential events: (1) Gain Attention, (2) Inform Learners of Objectives, (3) Stimulate Recall of Prior Knowledge, (4) Present the Content, (5) Provide Learning Guidance, (6) Elicit Performance, (7) Provide Feedback, (8) Assess Performance, and (9) Enhance Retention and Transfer. This structure not only scaffolds the generation process but also aligns the lesson output with cognitive learning processes, thereby increasing its practical applicability in classroom settings. This structure is embedded into the Writer Agent's prompt template to guide the model in producing well-formed, instructionally grounded lesson plans.

Lesson Plan Generation Prompt for Writer Agent

You are an experienced curriculum designer. Create a detailed lesson plan based on the following information:
- Subject: {subject}
- Grade Level: {grade}
- Topic: {topic}

The lesson must rigorously follow **Gagné's Nine Events of Instruction**, including:
1. Gain Attention
2. Inform Learners of Objectives
3. Stimulate Recall of Prior Knowledge
4. Present the Content
5. Provide Learning Guidance
6. Elicit Performance
7. Provide Feedback
8. Assess Performance
9. Enhance Retention and Transfer

Each step must be clearly labeled and include:
- Time estimates (e.g., "5 minutes")
- Specific learning tasks or questions
- Materials or visuals required
- Strategies to address various learning styles (visual, auditory, kinesthetic)
- Interaction opportunities (group work, pair discussion, individual reflection)
- Cognitive challenge or higher-order thinking elements

Additionally, include the following sections at the end:
- **Materials Needed**
- **Differentiation Strategies** (for both struggling and advanced learners)
- **Assessment Tools** (formative and summative)
- **Follow-Up Suggestions**

Maintain professional tone, precise structure, and markdown-style formatting. The output should be immediately usable in a classroom.

Fig. 3. Plan Generation Prompt.

Lesson Plan Improvement Prompt for Writer Agent

You are an expert instructional designer.

--- Context ---
This is Round {round_num} of iterative refinement. The goal is to continuously improve the lesson plan based on evaluation feedback, especially targeting instructional weaknesses identified in prior reviews.
--- Evaluation Feedback (from Round {prev_round}) ---
{evaluation}
--- Previous Lesson Plan (v{prev_round}) ---
{plan}

--- Your Task ---
Revise the lesson plan to:
- Explicitly address all weaknesses mentioned in the evaluation
- Implement concrete improvements (e.g., clearer instructions, stronger scaffolding, more interaction, better feedback)
- For each instructional event that received a score in the 0–6 range, implement targeted improvements designed to elevate it into the next scoring band (e.g., from "problematic" to "average", or from "average" to "solid")
- Focus on improvements in alignment, sequencing, clarity, higher-order thinking, or inclusiveness based on the evaluation comment
- For each such revision, add a short `> Justification:` note explaining the rationale for the change
- Preserve the existing section headers, instructional flow, markdown formatting, and age appropriateness
- Do not alter instructional events that received a score of 7 or above unless necessary for flow or coherence

--- Reference (for High Scoring Criteria) ---
Instructional events scoring 7–8 demonstrate:
- Clear goals aligned with authentic assessments
- Strong sequencing and concept-to-practice integrity
- Higher-order thinking tasks (e.g., synthesis, perspective-taking, real-world transfer)
- Culturally responsive and inclusive design
- Realistic pacing and differentiated support

Scores of 9–10 are rare and reserved for flawless, innovative designs with no pedagogical weakness.

--- Output Format ---
Only output the **revised lesson plan (v{round_num})** in markdown. Do not include any explanation or summary outside the lesson content.

Fig. 4. Plan Improvement Prompt.

Lesson Plan Evaluation Prompt for Evaluator Agent

You are a professional instructional design auditor. Your task is not to confirm quality but to challenge it. Your default stance is skepticism. You must identify weaknesses that would hinder learning, equity, or classroom implementation. You are expected to critically scrutinize even well-intended plans.

You are not reviewing this plan to find what is good, but what is *missing, fragile, unscaffolded, or misaligned*.

Evaluation Criteria (score each from 0 to 10):
1. **Clarity**: Is every part of the structure coherent, transitions logical, labels non-redundant, and timing realistic? Any ambiguity, overlap, jargon, or skipped logic drops the score.
2. **Integrity**: Does the plan fully integrate concept explanation with practice? Does each activity build on the prior? Are assessments authentic and aligned with goals? Missing scaffolding, weak sequencing, or disconnected assessments are penalized.
3. **Depth**: Are tasks designed for *synthesis*, *perspective-taking*, or *transfer*, not just activity completion? Is there support for higher-order thinking? Tasks that remain at summary-level or ask students to "list" or "describe" do *not* deserve high scores.
4. **Practicality**: Can the plan be realistically implemented *in a diverse, time-limited classroom*? Does it consider prep time, cognitive load, material access, and differentiation labor? If timing is tight or materials are vague, the plan is impractical.
5. **Pertinence**: Does the lesson engage students from varied cultural backgrounds, abilities, and perspectives? Are voices beyond the dominant narrative integrated—not just mentioned? Any tokenism or "extension-only" diversity lowers the score.

Scoring Rubric (Strict Threshold):
- **9–10**: Rare. Reserved only for truly *flawless* and innovative work with complete alignment and no pedagogical weakness.
- **7–8**: Solid, but must still include clear strengths in structure, scaffolding, and responsiveness. Use sparingly.
- **4–6**: Average. This is the **default** range for most lesson plans. They are functional but pedagogically limited.
- **0–3**: Problematic. Serious pedagogical, cultural, or logistical flaws.

Important Instructions:
- Be as critical as a curriculum auditor evaluating for national adoption.
- Always assume that if something isn't clearly described, it is missing.
- Penalize for vagueness, assumptions of prior knowledge, under-specified differentiation, and time mismanagement.

Output Format: Return a pure JSON array with 5 items. Each item includes:
- `event`: one of ["Clarity", "Integrity", "Depth", "Practicality", "Pertinence"]
- `score`: integer 0–10
- `reason`: a short, critical explanation (1–2 sentences)

Return *only* the JSON array.

Fig. 5. Evaluation Prompt.

3.3 Formalization of Multi-round Optimization

Let x denote the initial task input (e.g., subject, grade, topic), and $P^{(0)}$ be the initial lesson plan generated by the Writer Agent given prompt $\mathcal{G}(x)$:

$$P^{(0)} = \text{WriterAgent}(\mathcal{G}(x)). \tag{1}$$

For each iteration $t \in \{1, 2, \ldots, T\}$, the Evaluator Agent assigns a set of rubric scores $\{s_i^{(t)}\}_{i=1}^{K}$ to the plan $P^{(t-1)}$, where K is the number of rubric dimensions (e.g., $K = 5$). We define the total score at round t as:

$$S^{(t)} = \sum_{i=1}^{K} s_i^{(t)}. \tag{2}$$

The Evaluator Agent also returns a textual feedback $F^{(t)}$, which is used to construct the next revision prompt $\mathcal{R}(x, P^{(t-1)}, F^{(t)})$:

$$P^{(t)} = \text{WriterAgent}(\mathcal{R}(x, P^{(t-1)}, F^{(t)})). \tag{3}$$

The optimization process continues until either of the following stopping criteria is met:

- **Convergence:** $|S^{(t)} - S^{(t-1)}| < \epsilon$;
- **Maximum rounds:** $t = T_{\max}$.

We denote the final output after convergence as P^*, and its associated score vector as $\mathbf{s}^* = [s_1^*, \ldots, s_K^*]$. This formulation enables us to analyze learning trajectories, convergence behavior, and per-rubric improvements across rounds.

3.4 Scoring and Evaluation Mechanism

Given a plan P, the Evaluator Agent computes rubric scores s_i as:

$$s_i = \text{EvaluatorAgent}(\mathcal{E}(P))[i], \quad i = 1, \ldots, K, \tag{4}$$

where $\mathcal{E}(P)$ is the evaluation prompt shown in Fig. 5. The output includes both numerical scores and qualitative feedback, enabling gradient-free plan refinement through multi-agent dialogue.

4 Experiments

In this section, we evaluate our AgentLesson framework through a series of experiments designed to answer the following research questions:

- **RQ1**: Does multi-agent collaboration lead to better lesson plan quality compared to a single agent?
- **RQ2**: How does one-round multi-agent interaction compare to multi-round optimization?
- **RQ3**: How stable and efficient is the multi-round optimization process?
- **RQ4**: What specific aspects improve during optimization?

4.1 Experiment Setup

We choose Qwen-32B as the backbone for the writer agent and GPT-4o for the evaluator agent. The temperatures for the writer and evaluator are 0.7 and 0.3. The maximum round is set to 10, and the patience is set to 3.

To evaluate the generality and robustness of our multi-agent lesson planning framework, we selected 10 representative tasks across five major school subjects (Mathematics, Science, English Language Arts, Social Studies, and Digital Technology), covering Grades 5 to 10. Each task includes a specific topic aligned with typical curriculum standards. Table 1 summarizes the tasks used in our evaluation.

4.2 Evaluation Metrics

Inspired by [19], we applied a 5-D evaluation system comprising **C**larity, **I**ntegrity, **D**epth, **P**racticality, and **P**ertinence (CIDPP) for the evaluator agent. We provide a detailed description in the prompt to enable the agent to gain a thorough understanding of the evaluation criteria. To have a critical evaluator agent, we also give some instructions to avoid very high scores for the lesson plan generated by the writer agent (Table 2).

Table 1. List of Evaluation Tasks Used in Experiments

ID	Subject	Grade	Topic
1	Mathematics	7	Solving one-step equations involving fractions
2	Science	8	Constructing an electric circuit to test conductivity
3	English Language Arts	5	Writing a persuasive letter to the school principal
4	Social Studies	9	Analyzing the Treaty of Versailles from multiple perspectives
5	Mathematics	10	Factoring quadratic trinomials using the box method
6	Science	7	Investigating the effect of pH on enzyme activity
7	Digital Technology	9	Designing a survey and visualizing data in spreadsheets
8	English Language Arts	10	Evaluating rhetorical devices in "I Have a Dream" speech
9	Social Studies	7	Simulating a UN debate on climate migration
10	Mathematics	8	Graphing linear functions in slope-intercept form

Table 2. A 5-D evaluation system.

Metrics	Description
Clarity	structure coherent, transitions logical, labels non-redundant, and timing realistic
Integrity	integrate concept explanation with practice; each activity builds on the prior; assessments are authentic and aligned with goals
Depth	tasks designed for synthesis, perspective-taking, or transfer, not just activity completion; support for higher-order thinking
Practicality	The plan is realistically implemented in a diverse, time-limited classroom; consider prep time, cognitive load, material access, and differentiation labor
Pertinence	the lesson engage students from varied cultural backgrounds, abilities, and perspectives; voices beyond the dominant narrative are integrated, not just mentioned

4.3 Baselines

We define the following baselines for comparison:

- **Single Agent**: The initial plan generated by the writer without evaluation.
- **Multi-Agent w/ Single Round**: The updated plan after one round of evaluation-feedback-update.

To make a fair comparison, we use the same LLM backbones for the writer agent in our baselines, thereby avoiding score differences due to the LLM's capabilities.

4.4 Overall Performance (RQ1 and RQ2)

Table 3 reports the average rubric scores and standard deviations for three methods: *Single Agent*, *Multi-Agent w/ Single Round*, and the proposed full method

Table 3. Overall performance. STD denotes standard deviation.

Methods	Mean ↑	STD ↓
Single Agent	19.1	**1.1**
Multi-Agent w/ Single Round	20.7	2.5
AgentLesson	**23.5**	1.4

AgentLesson (i.e., Multi-Agent with Multi-Round Optimization). The results indicate a consistent improvement in lesson plan quality as the system becomes more collaborative and iterative. Specifically, the baseline **Single Agent** configuration achieves an average score of 19.1 with low variance (std = 1.1), indicating stable but limited performance. Introducing an evaluator agent in a one-round setting (**Multi-Agent w/ Single Round**) increases the average score to 20.7, reflecting a gain of +1.6 points, albeit with a higher variance (std = 2.5). This suggests that even a single round of feedback from a dedicated evaluation agent can lead to noticeable improvements, though the stability may vary depending on the task. The full **AgentLesson** configuration, which incorporates multi-round interactions between planner and evaluator agents, achieves the best performance with an average score of 23.5 and a moderate variance (std = 1.4). Compared to the **Single Agent** baseline, this corresponds to a significant gain of +4.4 points, demonstrating the efficacy of iterative multi-agent collaboration in optimizing lesson plan quality. These findings support the conclusion that multi-agent feedback—especially when extended across multiple rounds—is a key contributor to the generation of higher-quality instructional plans.

4.5 Stability and Efficiency Analysis (RQ3)

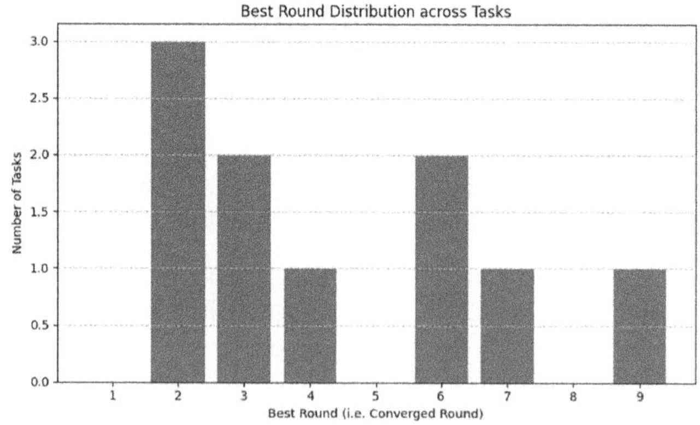

Fig. 6. Convergence analysis.

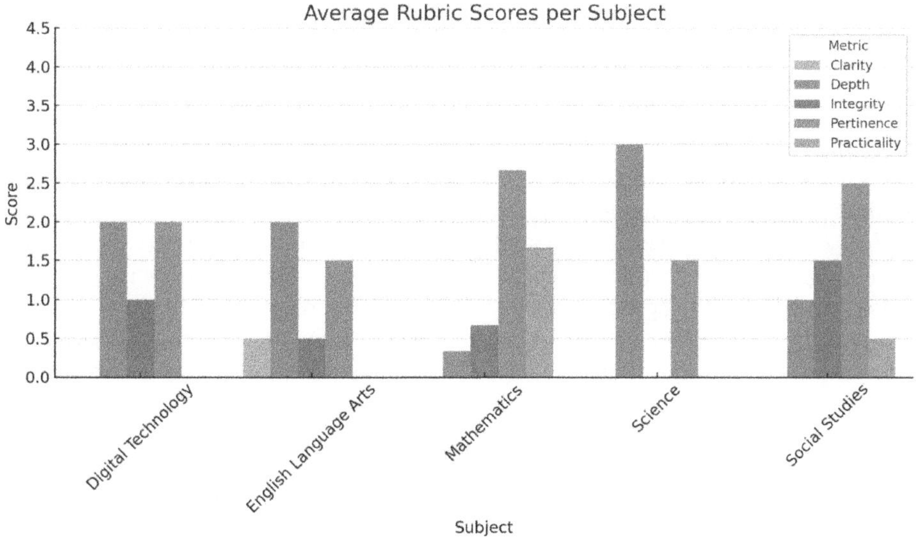

Fig. 7. Average rubric scores per subject.

To evaluate the stability and efficiency of the multi-round optimization process, we analyze at which round each task achieves its best score and whether this convergence occurs within an acceptable number of rounds. Figure 6 shows the distribution of the best round across all tasks.

Half of the tasks (5/10) converge to their best score within 3 rounds, indicating that the multi-round optimization is generally efficient. Furthermore, only 2 out of 10 tasks exhibit score fluctuation patterns, suggesting that the optimization trajectory is relatively stable. These findings support the feasibility of using early stopping strategies and indicate that the system maintains robustness during iterative collaboration.

4.6 Specific Aspects Analysis (RQ4)

To better understand how the quality of lesson plans varies across different subjects and rubric dimensions, we performed an averaged dimension-wise analysis. Specifically, we calculated the mean scores of five evaluation dimensions—*Clarity*, *Depth*, *Integrity*, *Pertinence*, and *Practicality*—for each subject category based on the best-performing lesson plan produced via multi-agent interaction.

As shown in Fig. 7, *Pertinence* emerges as the most consistently high-performing dimension across nearly all subjects. This indicates that the multi-agent optimization process is particularly effective at aligning lesson content with task requirements and educational standards. The collaborative evaluation-feedback loops likely enable agents to refine topical focus iteratively, leading to clearer alignment with learning goals and grade-level expectations.

Depth also exhibits strong improvements, especially in content-heavy subjects such as Science and English Language Arts. This suggests that the inclusion of an evaluator agent, combined with multiple rounds of revision, contributes to richer pedagogical strategies and better elaboration of conceptual content. In contrast, subjects like Mathematics and Digital Technology show relatively lower *Depth* scores, possibly due to the operational nature of tasks in these domains that emphasize procedural fluency over conceptual narrative.

Integrity and *Practicality* present moderate and domain-sensitive patterns. For example, Social Studies tasks tended to achieve higher scores in *Integrity*, indicating that multi-agent plans in these domains were more likely to include complete instructional components (e.g., clear objectives, assessment steps, and differentiation strategies). Conversely, *Practicality* was more variable: while some subjects like Science demonstrated practical, hands-on designs, others remained abstract, revealing a potential limitation of LLMs in simulating realistic classroom constraints or resource limitations.

Interestingly, *Clarity* remains the lowest-scoring dimension across most subjects, and also displays minimal variation. This may suggest two things: either initial plans were already sufficiently clear due to the base LLM's linguistic strengths, or that the multi-agent revision process prioritizes structural and substantive feedback over surface-level language optimization. This opens avenues for future work, where a dedicated "clarity critic" agent could be introduced to improve stylistic precision and audience appropriateness, particularly in domains with technical language demands.

In summary, this analysis not only reveals which aspects of lesson plans benefit most from multi-agent optimization but also highlights subject-specific challenges and opportunities. These insights can inform the design of more adaptive agent configurations and prompting strategies, tailored to the pedagogical nuances of each discipline.

5 Conclusion

This paper introduces AgentLesson, a novel multi-agent framework for lesson plan generation that leverages large language models (LLMs) in a collaborative loop between a Writer Agent and an Evaluator Agent. Through systematic experiments, we demonstrate that multi-agent interaction substantially improves the quality of generated lesson plans compared to single-agent baselines. Specifically, multi-round optimization not only outperforms single-round collaboration but also exhibits stable and consistent improvements across five key pedagogical dimensions: clarity, integrity, depth, practicality, and pertinence. Our analysis further reveals that certain aspects, such as depth and pertinence, benefit more significantly from iterative refinement, highlighting the value of structured feedback in educational content generation. By integrating rubric-based evaluation into the generation loop, AgentLesson offers a scalable approach to producing high-quality, pedagogically grounded materials.

Looking forward, we envision several extensions of this work. First, the framework can be generalized beyond lesson plans to support broader educational tasks such as formative assessment design, adaptive tutoring strategies, or curriculum sequencing. Second, future work may incorporate human-in-the-loop mechanisms [15] to guide or override agent decisions, thereby enhancing trustworthiness and pedagogical alignment. Third, expanding the rubric dimensions and grounding the evaluation in empirical classroom outcomes will further validate the system's real-world applicability. Finally, extending the agent roles to include a content reviewer or curriculum planner opens up new directions for orchestrated multi-agent educational design. By bridging LLM capabilities with instructional design principles, AgentLesson represents a step toward more intelligent, adaptive, and collaborative AI tutors in education.

Acknowledgements. This work was supported by the EdUHK project under Grant No. RG 67/2024-2025R.

References

1. Bloom, B.S., Engelhart, M.D., Furst, E.J., Hill, W.H., Krathwohl, D.R.: Taxonomy of educational objectives: the classification of educational goals. David McKay Company (1956)
2. Citl, N.I.U.: Gagné's nine events of instruction: a structured guide for teaching. Teaching Resources Guide (2021)
3. Faker, P., Abdel-Salam, M.: Unlocking the potential of chatgpt: a comprehensive exploration of its applications and limitations in modern education. J. Future Gener. Comput. Syst. 1–24 (2023). https://ssrn.com/abstract=4507022
4. Fan, H., Chen, G., Wang, X., Peng, Z.: LessonPlanner: assisting novice teachers to prepare pedagogy-driven lesson plans with large language models. In: Proceedings of the 37th Annual ACM Symposium on User Interface Software and Technology, pp. 1–20. ACM, Pittsburgh PA USA (2024)
5. Gagné, R.M.: The Conditions of Learning and Theory of Instruction. Holt, Rinehart and Winston (1985)
6. Hong, S., et al.: Metagpt: meta programming for multi-agent collaborative framework. In: Proceedings of the 29th ACM SIGKDD Conference on Knowledge Discovery and Data Mining, pp. 5057–5067 (2023). https://arxiv.org/abs/2308.00352
7. Jia, L., Qi, C., Wei, Y., Sun, H., Yang, X.: Fine-tuning large language models for educational support: leveraging gagne's nine events of instruction for lesson planning. In: 28th Global Chinese Conference on Computers in Education (GCCCE 2024). arXiv (2025). https://doi.org/10.48550/arXiv.2503.09276
8. Jia, L., Qi, C., Wei, Y., Sun, H., Yang, X.: Fine-tuning large language models for educational support: leveraging gagne's nine events of instruction for lesson planning. arXiv preprint arXiv:2503.09276 (2025)
9. Kasneci, E., et al.: Chatgpt for good? On opportunities and challenges of large language models for education. Learn. Individ. Differ. **103**, 102274 (2023)
10. Li, G., et al.: Camel: communicative agents for "mind" exploration of large language model. In: Thirty-Seventh Conference on Neural Information Processing Systems (2023). https://arxiv.org/abs/2303.17760
11. Li, H., et al.: Arched: a human-centered framework for transparent, responsible, and collaborative ai-assisted instructional design. arXiv preprint arXiv:2503.08931 (2025)

12. Madaan, A., et al.: Self-refine: iterative refinement with self-feedback. In: Advances in Neural Information Processing Systems, vol. 36 (2023). https://arxiv.org/abs/2303.17651
13. Wang, T., et al.: LLM-powered multi-agent framework for goal-oriented learning in intelligent tutoring system. In: Companion Proceedings of the ACM on Web Conference 2025, pp. 510–519 (2025)
14. Wei, J., et al.: Chain-of-thought prompting elicits reasoning in large language models. In: Advances in Neural Information Processing Systems, vol. 35, pp. 24824–24837 (2022). https://proceedings.neurips.cc/paper_files/paper/2022/hash/9d5609613524ecf4f15af0f7b31bcb4d-Abstract-Conference.html
15. Wu, M., Zhang, Y., Yu, Z., Li, D., Luo, Y.: A survey on human-in-the-loop for machine learning. Futur. Gener. Comput. Syst. **137**, 41–59 (2022)
16. Wu, Q., et al.: Autogen: enabling next-gen LLM applications via multi-agent conversation. In: Thirty-Seventh Conference on Neural Information Processing Systems (2023). https://arxiv.org/abs/2308.08155
17. Ye, F., Cui, H., Ke, C., Zhong, W., Zhang, S., Zhang, L.: An automatic model for lesson plans generation based on logical chains and prompt tuning. In: Hao, T., et al. (eds.) SETE, vol. 15589, pp. 250–264. Springer, Singapore (2025)
18. Ye, F., Cui, H., Ke, C., Zhong, W., Zhang, S., Zhang, L.: An automatic model for lesson plans generation based on logical chains and prompt tuning. In: Lecture Notes in Computer Science (SETE) (2025)
19. Zhang, X., Zhang, C., Sun, J., Xiao, J., Yang, Y., Luo, Y.: EduPlanner: LLM-based multiagent systems for customized and intelligent instructional design. IEEE Trans. Learn. Technol. **18**, 416–427 (2025). https://doi.org/10.1109/TLT.2025.3561332
20. Zheng, Y., et al.: Automatic lesson plan generation via large language models with self-critique prompting. In: International Conference on Artificial Intelligence in Education, pp. 163–178. Springer (2024)

Bridging Dependency Enhanced Counterfactual Supporting for Multi-hop Question Generation

Kaixi Hu[1], Lin Li[2](✉), Haohan Zhang[2], Jianwei Zhang[3], and Xiaohui Tao[4]

[1] Wuhan Textile University, Wuhan, China
kxhu@wtu.edu.cn
[2] Wuhan University of Technology, Wuhan, China
{cathylilin,283013}@whut.edu.cn
[3] Iwate University, Iwate, Japan
zhang@iwate-u.ac.jp
[4] University of Southern Queensland, Toowoomba, Australia
Xiaohui.Tao@unisq.edu.au

Abstract. Multi-hop Question Generation (MQG) aims to create questions that require synthesizing multiple, dispersed pieces of supporting evidence from different passages. The fundamental challenge lies in the dependence among different reasoning steps where each step relies on the preceding one. Traditional approaches generally rely on learning observed dependency during the training process, which limits their adaptability to value-changed instances in the reasoning chains. To this end, we propose a model-agnostic method, termed *CS2MQG*, that employs Counterfactual Supporting with bridging dependency prototype invariance for Multi-hop Question Generation. Specifically, we focus on key bridging nodes with high centrality or rich contextual information. And then, the counterfactuals are systematically generated by keeping the node type while modifying its value. Through the reassignment of these nodes, new causal relationships will be introduced into models, ensuring the generated questions are accurately centered around these nodes. Experiments conducted on the widely used HotpotQA and MuSiQue datasets demonstrate that CS2MQG consistently improves the performance of five state-of-the-art MQG models in terms of BLEU, METEOR, and ROUGE scores. And, our counterfactuals also enhance the performance of zero-shot MQG.

Keywords: Multi-hop question generation · counterfactual supporting · Model-agnostic · Bridging node

1 Introduction

Question generation (QG) refers to the task of automatically creating questions based on a given context [21]. It plays a crucial role in a variety of applica-

T. Hao et al. (Eds.): BESC 2025, LNCS 16431, pp. 171–187, 2026.
https://doi.org/10.1007/978-981-95-7138-3_12

Paragraph A: Kiss and Tell (1945 film)
Kiss and Tell is a 1945 American comedy film starring then 17-year-old Shirley Temple as Corliss Archer.In the film, two teenage girls cause their respective parents much concern when they start to become interested in boys.
Paragraph B: Shirley Temple
Shirley Temple Black (April 23, 1928 – February 10, 2014) was an American actress, singer, dancer, businesswoman, and diplomat who was Hollywood's number one box-office draw as a child actress from 1935 to 1938. As an adult, she was named United States ambassador to Ghana and to Czechoslovakia and also served as Chief of Protocol of the United States.
Answer: Chief of Protocol

Single-hop Question:
What government position was held by Shirley Temple?
Multi-hop Question:
What government position was held by the woman who portrayed Corliss Archer in the film Kiss and Tell?

Fig. 1. A comparison of a multi-hop problem and a single-hop problem in Hot–pot. The complexity of MQG arises from the dependency of each reasoning step on the previous one, making it crucial to accurately handle these dependencies.

tions, including question-answering systems [28], dialogue systems [20], educational platforms [1], and legal systems [3]. Most previous research has primarily focused on shallow, fact-based questions—commonly referred to as single-hop questions—which are generated from the sentence containing the answer or from nearby sentences within the same paragraph [6,12,37].

Recent studies have increasingly focused on generating more complex multi-hop questions [18,22,23,25,32]. These questions require synthesizing multiple, scattered pieces of evidence from different passages and reasoning over them to produce factually coherent questions related to a given answer. Compared to single-hop questions, multi-hop questions present two primary challenges [33]: *Firstly,* generating such questions requires a model to understand the relationships between disjoint pieces of information distributed across multiple documents [22]. *Secondly,* the complexity of multi-hop question generation lies in the intricate entity connections that form the reasoning chain. If the chain is too simple, the task degenerates into a single-hop problem [18].

In Fig. 1, given that the answer is "*Chief of Protocol*" a single-hop question might directly ask, "*What position does Shirley Temple hold in the government?*". In contrast, a multi-hop question could ask, "*What government position was held by the woman who portrayed Corliss Archer in the film Kiss and Tell*". This requires a bridging reasoning process where the model identifies that the actress playing Corliss Archer (A) is Shirley Temple (B) who holds the position of Chief of Protocol (C), thus requiring reasoning over $A \rightarrow B \rightarrow C$. Previous work on QG has primarily focused on single-hop questions using neural network-based methods and sequence-to-sequence (Seq2Seq) frameworks, with different encoder-decoder architectures designed to combine answer and context information for single-hop reasoning [17,36]. Recent research on multi-hop QG has mainly sought to advanced model structures to generate questions with complex reasoning chains, thereby ensuring their complexity [6,24]. Usually a reason chain includes nodes with their corresponding value and type, and inter-node connections. However, existing methods often learn the dependency patterns present during training, limiting their adaptability to unseen dependencies instances in reasoning chains. Especially the assigned value with a node may be different in different chains, which leads to unsatisfied performance across different supporting facts.

To address this issue, we propose a model-agnostic method, so called *CS2MQG* that employs Counterfactual Supporting with bridging dependency invariance for Multi-hop Question Generation. Our method specifically targets key bridging nodes within causal chains. Considering the nodes with high centrality or rich contextual information, our CS2MQG systematically generates synthetic counterfactuals by keeping the specific type of a node type and modifying its assigned value. These nodes, due to their central position in the information flow, play a crucial role in bridging different pieces of evidence or reasoning steps. By reconstructing these high-centrality nodes, we introduce variations in the causal chain that compel the model to reassess its reasoning process. It is observed that the bridge nodes not only connect disparate pieces of information but also serve as crucial links in maintaining the coherence and complexity of multi-hop reasoning tasks. Consequently, adjusting these bridging nodes forces the model to handle a broader range of dependencies, thereby enhancing its adaptability and performance across different supporting facts and question types.

Overall, our method works to handle complex reasoning among multi-hop question generation. Its main contributions are summarized as follows:

- We introduce a model-agnostic yet effective method that take advantages of counterfactual supportings to enhance multi-hop question generation. Notably, it is a pioneering work in incorporating counterfactuals into the multi-hop question generation process.
- Through bridging dependency prototype invariance to generate counterfactual supportings, our CS2MQG is compelled to reassess and adjust to new causal relationships, thereby enhancing its generalization to broader dependencies.
- The experimental results indicate that our method significantly enhances the performance of five MQG models on the widely used Hotpot-QA dataset, with an improvement of approximately 2.3% to 4.5%. What's more, our method even achieves by 10.8% over the zero-shot of the LLaMA3.1 70b, while on the Musique dataset, our improvement is 4.6%, and in the OOD experiments on Musique, the improvement is approximately 5.1%.

2 Related Work

Early works on QG [8,9,16] manily focus on the rule-based approaches that rely on heuristic rules or handcrafted templates, with low scalability. Recent works adopt the attention-based sequence-to-sequence neural model for QG tasks, taking sentences with the answer as input and outputting the question [4], which works better than the rule-based.

Nowadays, there has been an increasing interest in MQG, to capture the complex information among different input documents, RefNet [18] and MulQG [25] employed the GNN-based encoder in semantic graph and entity graph respectively, and the strong transformer-based graph model is used in [22]. CQG [5] introduced controllable generation to ensure the complexity of the generation problem. QA4QG [24] and MultiFactor [30] presented a multi-hop QA module to identify bridging nodes to constrain the generated questions. Those approaches learn dependency patterns during training without considering the complicated entity connections.

Multi-hop question generation also has been explored using large language models (LLM) combined with prompt-based approaches, which have demonstrated effectiveness in few-shot settings [15]. Those leverages prompts to guide LLM in generating multi-hop questions by understanding type-aware semantics. In contrast, we apply our method on LLM in zero-shot settings and also achieve promising results, demonstrating its effectiveness.

3 Our Method CS2MQG

This section will give a detailed illustration of the proposed method. The overview is illustrated in Fig. 2. We start by generating counterfactual supportings that modify key bridge nodes. The originals and counterfactual Supportings are then processed through a dual-encoder structure, with contrastive learning applied to enhance the model adaption to different dependencies.

3.1 Problem Description

The input for the Multi-hop Question Generation (MQG) task consists of a set of context documents $C = \{d_1, d_2..., d_k\}$, where k represents the number of documents, and an answer $A = [a_1, a_2..., a_m]$, with m denoting the length of the answer. These documents can be lengthy and contain multiple sentences, represented as $d_i = [s_1, s_2..., s_n]$, where each sentence $s_j = [w_{j1}, w_{j2}..., w_{jt}]$ is a sequence of tokens. Here, n and t indicate the number of sentences and the length of each sentence, respectively. The primary objective of MQG is to generate a question $y = [y_1, y_2..., y_m]$ based on the given context and answer.

Successfully addressing this question requires reasoning across multiple context documents. Question characterized by multiple dependencies exemplifies a multi-hop question. A dependency refers to a logical or causal link between two

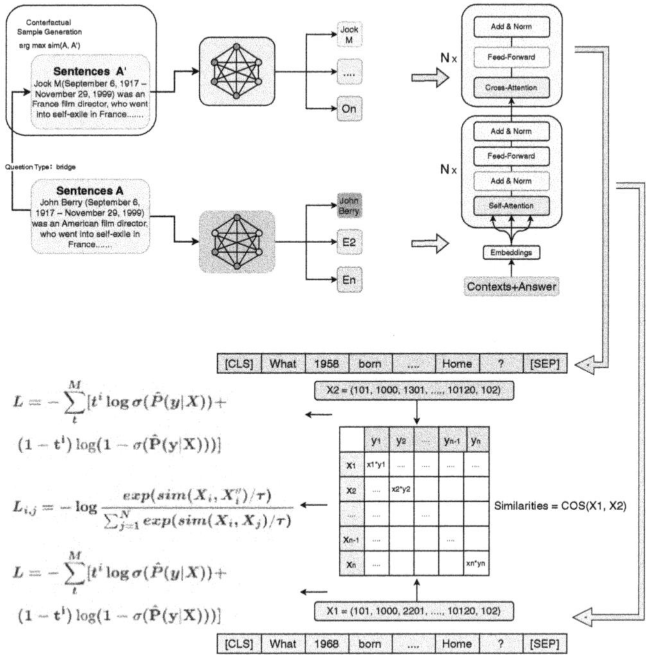

Fig. 2. The overview of Our CS2MQG.

or more entities or variables within a reasoning chain. The dependency type outlines a structural relationship, while a dependency instance represents a specific implementation or value within that structure. While the type remains consistent across various instances, the instance itself can change, allowing the specific values involved in the relationship to vary. For instance, a dependency type might define a relationship like "date of birth" (type), whereas an instance could be "born in 1958" or "born in 1968" (value).

3.2 Counterfactual Supporting Generation

The definition of counterfactual reasoning is given by [7]. Counterfactuals have some key requirements when generating them. First, many factors may affect the final result. However, counterfactuals must apply the smallest possible changes to achieve this goal. Second, counterfactuals must be feasible and reasonable. The heuristic counterfactual generation is classic [27], defined as follows:

$$L(x, x', y, y') = \lambda \hat{f}(x' - y')^2 + d(x, x'), \tag{1}$$

where x denotes the target instance. x' is counterfactual. y' represents the desired outcome. y is the term used to balance two distances, reflecting the tolerance for the distance.

Algorithm 1. Counterfactual Supporting Generation(CSG)

Input:
original training sample:
Original Sentence Set X — a set of sentences from multiple paragraphs;
question y
Output:
Counterfactual supporting X' — a set of modified sentences with altered dependency structures.
1: GAT = Graph Attention Network
Use GAT to model the relationships between sentences
2: Key Bridge Node B = GAT(X)
The Key bridge nodes represent nodes that connect the most information
3: **if** type(y) == Bridge **then**
4: $X' = \text{change}(X, B)$
5: optimize $L(X, X', y, \lambda)$ $\quad with \quad X'$
counterfactuals must apply as small as possible changes to achieve such a goal
6: **while** $|\hat{f}(X') - y| > \theta$ **do**
7: increase λ by step-size α
8: optimize $L(X, X', y, \lambda)$ with new X'
9: **end while**
10: **return** X'
11: **end if**

The above equation is the objective function of the heuristic counterfactual generation algorithm. It maximizes the distances in predictions and minimizes the distance between the original instance y and the counterfactual y'. Our counterfactual supporting generation only changes the key bridging nodes in the reasoning chain. Furthermore, in Eq. 1, we know that the designed counterfactual supporting should be changed as *little* as possible. In MQG, the nodes with high centrality or rich contextual information will affect reasoning results. Therefore, we only change such key bridging nodes in the reasoning chain.

As shown in Algorithm 1, our method contains the following steps: firstly, the key bridging nodes are identified in Line 1 to Line 2. Secondly, the type of the original question is determined in Line 3. Thirdly, counterfactual supporting is generated in Line 4; Finally, we fine-tune the generated counterfactual supporting in Line 5 to Line 8. The details are as follows:

Identifying Key Bridging Nodes. The first step in our method involves identifying key bridging nodes within the causal chains of multi-hop questions. These nodes are distinguished by their high in-degree and out-degree, signifying their role as crucial hubs for information flow and connection between various pieces of evidence. We identify the node with the highest combined in-degree and out-degree as the bridge node. The reasoning paths are analyzed within our experimental dataset via manual checking, as they are most likely to influence the reasoning steps necessary to arrive at the correct answer. For example, in a question reasoning across multiple documents, a bridging node might be a shared entity or concept that connects otherwise unrelated facts.

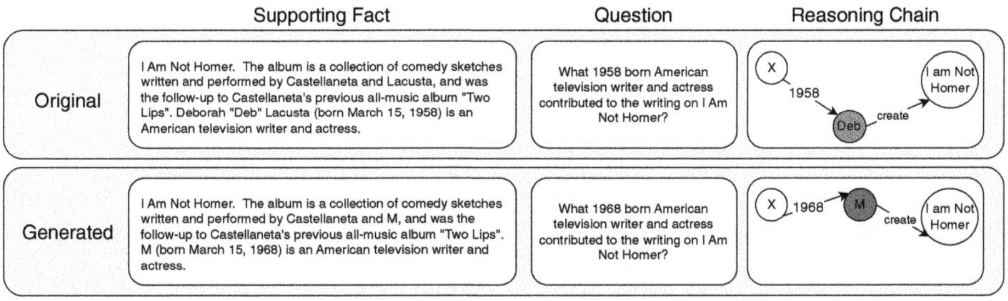

Fig. 3. An example of a counterfactual explanation. We modify key node(s) and their corresponding attribute values to generate counterfactual supporting.

Generating Counterfactual Supporting. Once a key bridging node is identified, a new instance is generated while keeping same type as that node. These homogeneous instances preserve the underlying dependency types, which enables the generation of counterfactual examples with unchanged bridging dependencies. As depicted in Fig. 3, our counterfactual generation process follows the key requirements of counterfactual reasoning.

Different Instances with the Same Attributes. First, we identify a key bridging node, such as "Jeck", and generate a different instance, like "Jock", which retains the same set of attributes. Both nodes share identical properties, ensuring that the underlying dependency type remains unchanged. For example, "Jeck" and "Jock" represent different actor, maintaining the actor-related attributes.

Modifying the Instance Attributes. Once the new instance "Jock" is created, we proceed to modify its attributes using Algorithm 1. This involves fine-tuning specific values, such as changing the birth year from 1958 to 1968, while keeping the bridging dependency type intact. This adjustment generates counterfactual supporting with the bridging dependency invariance, offering varied but logically consistent instances for the model to process.

3.3 Training Loss

To further benefit from the counterfactual supporting generation, our model training consists of a cross-entropy training loss and a contrastive training loss.

Cross-Entropy Training. Following state-of-the-art MQG models, binary cross-entropy loss is used as training objective function, as follows:

$$L = -\sum_{t}^{M}[t^i log\sigma(\hat{P}(y|X)) + \quad (1-t^i)log(1-\sigma(\hat{P}(y|X))], \tag{2}$$

where σ denotes the sigmoid activation function, and it is the soft target score of i-th ground-truth question.

Contrastive Training. The counterfactual mechanism is adopted to generate supportings. After that, contrastive learning is adopted between the original sample and the generated supporting. In this paper, we follow a simple and widely-used contrastive learning schema to conduct it, i.e., ArcCon [35]. Traditional contrastive learning methods face limitations in learning sentence representations, particularly when relying solely on Euclidean space to define similarity or dissimilarity. We leverages contrastive learning in angular space to more effectively capture subtle differences between sentences. Our training comprises Angle Contrast and Triple Contrast.

- *Angle Contrast*: this component focuses on learning the angular relationships between sentences by maximizing the cosine similarity of supporting while minimizing that of counterfactual supporting.
- *Triple Contrast*: by introducing a triple contrast loss function, we transform the angular relationships among triplet samples into a problem of cosine similarity comparison within the feature space.

Finally, the training loss is defined as Eq. 3:

$$l_{i,j} = -\log \frac{exp(sim(X_i, X_i')/\tau)}{\sum_{j=1}^{N} exp(sim(X_i, X_j)/\tau)}, \tag{3}$$

where $sim(X_i, X_j)$ is the cosine similarity, τ is the temperature hyper parameter, and n is the number of sentences in batch size.

4 Experiments

In the experiment, we aim to answer the following four research questions:

RQ1: How effective is our CS2MQG method in enhancing the overall performance of multi-hop question generation?

RQ2: How is our counterfactual supporting when compared with popular adversarial learning?

RQ3: How does our CS2MQG method perform when key bridging nodes are not selected for counterfactual supporting generation?

RQ4: How does our CS2MQG method perform when evaluated on large language models (LLM) under different experimental conditions?

4.1 Data and Evaluation

To fully demonstrate the performances of the proposed method, experiments are conducted on the widely used Hotpot-QA dataset [31], which comprises approximately 100,000 crowd-sourced questions necessitating reasoning across individual Wikipedia articles. Each question is accompanied by two supporting documents that provide the essential evidence for inferring the answer.

Table 1. Hotpot-QA Dataset Statistics

Name	Description	# Samples
train-easy	single-hop	18089
train-medium	multi-hop	56814
train-hard	hard multi-hop	15661
dev	hard multi-hop	7405
test-distractor	hard multi-hop	7405
test-fullwiki	hard multi-hop	7405
Total		112779

To further evaluate the proposed method, zero-shot testing was performed on Musique [26], utilizing large language models (LLM), which contains about 25K 2-hop questions, using seed questions from 5 existing one-hop datasets.

Although there is another commonly used dataset, like SQuAD [21] (The Stanford Question Answering Dataset) with a collection of over 100,000 question-answer pairs based on Wikipedia articles, it is not suitable for MQG. The reason is that each question is answered using a text segment from the corresponding paragraph. Most questions are non-conversational and do not involve multi-round dialogue or context-related queries, limiting its ability to handle complex questions. Additionally, answers are typically short phrases, which restricts the dataset's capacity to manage longer or more complex responses.

Following previous studies [31], the supporting facts and answers are utilized as input to generate multi-hop questions, which includes 90,447 examples for training and 7,405 for development. Since the test set is not public, we set the original development set as the test set and divide the original training set into training set and validation set. In general, the splitting is that 89,947/500/7405 samples are used as training set, validation set and test set respectively. The specific data distribution is shown in Table 1.

BLEU [19], ROUGE-L [2] and METEOR [13] are utilized as evaluation metricss. BLEU measures the average ngram overlap on a set of reference sentences. Both METEOR and ROUGE-L specialize BLEU's ngram overlap idea for machine translation and text summarization evaluation, respectively.

All MQG models are run on three NVIDIA Titan Xp GPUs, each equipped with 12 GB of memory. For the hyper parameters specific to each model, we adhered strictly to the configurations outlined in its original paper. This approach ensured consistency and reproducibility in our experiments, allowing us to accurately assess the performance and capabilities of the models under study.

4.2 Baselines

Our CS2MQG is integrated into five state-of-art models by applying the proposed counterfactual supporting with bridging dependency invariance. RefNet [17] employs a refinement network to iteratively enhance the quality of generated questions by refining initial drafts through feedback loops, improving relevance and clarity. MulQG [25], a Multi-faceted Question Generation Framework, generates diverse and contextually rich questions by leveraging multiple perspectives within the input data, capturing various dimensions of the source material for comprehensive and varied questions. CQG [5], a Simple and Effective Controlled Generation Framework for Multi-hop Question Generation, uses a control mechanism to guide the generation process, capturing intricate relationships between multiple pieces of information and ensuring coherence and contextual relevance. QA4QG [24], a Question Answering Framework for Question Generation, leverages a dual-purpose architecture to enhance question quality by integrating a question answering module to inform and refine the generation process, ensuring accuracy and contextual appropriateness. MultiFactor [30], a Multi-factor Attention Framework for Automatic Question Generation, employs a multi-layered attention architecture to improve question quality by integrating multiple attention mechanisms to guide and refine the generation process, ensuring precision and contextual relevance.

Table 2. The Improvement of CS2MQG Over Five MQG Models

Model	Venue	BLEU-1	BLEU-2	BLEU-3	BLEU-4	ROUGE-L
RefNet [17]	EMNLP'19	29.79	19.58	14.41	10.56	36.88
+CS2MQG (Ours)	—	30.82	20.03	14.88	**11.14**	**38.04**
MulQG [25]	EMNLP'20	40.08	26.58	19.61	14.78	34.81
+CS2MQG (Ours)	—	41.05	27.14	20.16	**15.31**	**35.49**
CQG [5]	ACL'22	49.71	37.04	29.93	24.28	41.18
+CS2MQG (Ours)	—	50.76	37.97	30.75	**25.39**	**42.44**
QA4QG [24]	ICASSP'22	48.55	36.83	29.49	24.82	45.46
+CS2MQG (Ours)	—	50.07	37.73	30.95	**25.89**	**46.38**
MultiFactor [30]	EMNLP'23	53.17	40.25	32.34	27.31	43.04
+CS2MQG (Ours)	—	54.28	41.03	33.18	**27.93**	**44.12**

4.3 RQ1: Overall Performance

In order to run a fair comparison, the experimental results we obtained are run by original models under the same parameters reported in their papers. Table 2 presents the experimental results obtained from the HotpotQA dataset, highlighting the effectiveness of our method. When evaluated using BLEU-4, which is the primary metric for assessing text generation quality, our generated counterfactual supporting demonstrates a substantial enhancement in model performance. Specifically, our method performance improvements ranging from 2.3% to 4.5% in terms of BLEU-4 scores. This improvement underscores the robustness of our data generation process. Furthermore, our method not only excels in BLEU-4 but also achieves superior results across a majority of the evaluation metrics. These significant improvements across various metrics illustrate

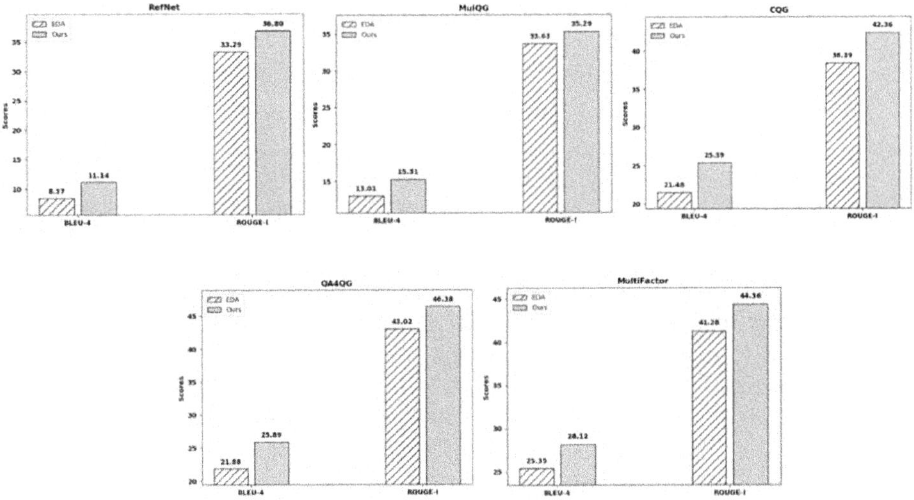

Fig. 4. Adversarial learning vs our approach on five models.

the comprehensive effectiveness and adaptability of our method in enhancing MQG performance.

4.4 RQ2: The Effect of Counterfactual Supporting Generation

In natural language processing, a straightforward data generation is to leverage adversarial learning to generate new training examples by challenging the model to predict the presence of certain words or phrases in the original text [29]. We has implemented this method involves two primary steps:

- Pre-training: this step closely resembles standard NLP tasks. Typically, a large corpus, such as Wikipedia, is used to train a pre-trained model, which will be instrumental in the subsequent data augmentation phase.
- Generating: in this phase, the pre-trained model generates new text samples by randomly selecting certain words or phrases. These augmented texts are then used as input for training the model using the Next Sentence Prediction (NSP) task.

Figure 4 presents a comparison of the performance of our proposed method with traditional adversarial learning across various baseline models. The results indicate that adversarial learning does not enhance the model's ability to handle multi-hop question generation tasks. Even due to the introduction of noisy data, the model cannot learn the reasoning chain hidden in supporting very well, resulting in a significant decline in the performance of the model.

There are several reasons for this observation:

- **Lack of context sensitivity in adversarial learning:** Traditional adversarial learning, primarily relies on basic text manipulation methods like synonym replacement, random insertion, deletion, or swapping. While these

Table 3. The ablation study on CQG

Model	BLEU-1	BLEU-2	BLEU-3	BLEU-4	ROUGE-L
CQG	49.71	37.04	29.93	24.28	41.18
Ours(-)	48.49	36.41	29.56	24.13	41.26
Ours(+)	**50.76**	**37.97**	**30.75**	**25.39**	**42.44**

methods can generate a variety of text samples, they do not effectively capture the complex dependencies and reasoning chains required for multi-hop questions. As a result, these generated supports fail to provide the MCG models with the necessary context and logical bridges that are critical for multi-hop reasoning, leading to suboptimal training and potential performance degradation.

- **Inefficiency in modeling dependency structures:** Unlike our counterfactual approach that strategically modifies key bridging nodes in the causal chain, traditional methods do not focus on altering the dependency structure. Our method targets the most informative nodes—those with the highest in-degree and out-degree, forcing the model to adapt to varied and more complex reasoning paths. In contrast, adversarial learning based methods may inadvertently generate samples that do not contribute to learning these dependencies, thereby reducing overall performance.

Additionally, the reproduced results of baselines, did not exactly match those reported in their published articles, even following their parameter settings. This discrepancy highlights that parameter sensitivity and implementation details may significantly impact model performance, further underscoring the need for counterfactual supporting generation.

4.5 RQ3: Ablation Study and Analysis

To further evaluate and investigate the role of key bridging nodes in our model-agnostic method, we perform ablation studies on the CQG model and show the results in Table 3. Ours (-) indicates that we do not modify the key bridge node but instead randomly select a node for processing. As seen in Table 3, our method exhibits a 4.18% improvement, highlighting the significance of key bridge nodes to our method. The following key advantages are offered:

Enhanced Diversity and Robustness: Our method ensures the generation of counterfactual supporting that exhibit a wide range of dependency patterns. It is reached by altering key bridging nodes with high centrality and rich contextual information that carry the most significant amount of information in a causal chain. This diversity enables the model to learn a broader spectrum of reasoning paths, which is crucial for handling unseen dependencies in different supporting.

Improved Generalization: Our experimental results show that models trained with counterfactual data augmentation significantly outperform those using tra-

Table 4. Performance Comparison Across Datasets and Models

Model	BLEU-1	BLEU-2	BLEU-3	BLEU-4	ROUGE-L
HotpotQA (test 7K)					
Ours(-)	34.88	22.13	15.61	11.01	**25.16**
Ours(+)	**37.24**	**23.50**	**16.47**	**11.52**	25.05
Musique (test 2K)					
Ours(-)	23.51	12.45	7.65	4.71	32.24
Ours(+)	**26.47**	**13.67**	**8.39**	**5.22**	**32.56**

ditional methods on datasets like HotpotQA. The augmented training data effectively reduces the model's tendency to overfit to specific observed patterns, thereby enhancing its capacity to generalize across diverse domains and supporting. This improvement is particularly evident when the model is exposed to new or more complex reasoning chains, where our method achieves higher BLEU scores and accuracy compared to baseline models.

Sensitivity to Complex Reasoning Chains: The introduction of counterfactual supporting with bridging dependency invariance that reconstruct key causal nodes compels the model to reassess and adapt to new relationships within the data. This process heightens the model's sensitivity to variations in dependency structures, leading to better performance in generating questions that require multiple, interconnected reasoning steps. As a result, our approach not only maintains but also enhances the complexity of multi-hop questions, ensuring their factual coherence and relevance to the answer.

4.6 RQ4: The Performance on LLM

As shown in Table 4, to evaluate the performance of our method on large language models (LLM), we have selected LLaMA 3.1 70B as a zero-shot model due to its strong performance and wide applicable scenarios. On the HotpotQA dataset, directly generating multi-hop questions resulted in a BLEU-4 score of 11.01%. By designing prompts based on our generated supporting, the BLEU-4 score is improved to 11.52%, achieving a relative improvement of 4.63%. Similarly, on the Musique dataset, the BLEU-4 score for directly generating multi-hop questions is 4.71%, which increased to 5.22% when using prompts designed with our method, resulting in a relative improvement of 10.83%. These results highlight the effectiveness of our method using counterfactual to enhancing multi-hop question generation performance on LLM.

4.7 Visualization of Embedding Distribution

KL divergence is computed between the training and testing distributions for both the baseline and our proposed method. The results indicate that introducing the CS2MQG method significantly increases the KL divergence between

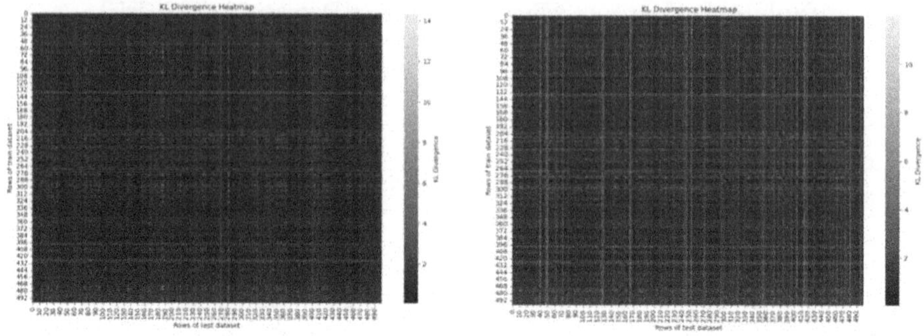

(a) Original data (b) CS2MQG data

Fig. 5. KL divergence comparison.

Table 5. Transferring to Musique Dataset when Trained on HotpotQA

Model	BLEU-1	BLEU-2	BLEU-3	BLEU-4	ROUGE-L
CQG	27.89	14.35	8.36	4.92	21.95
Ours	**29.82**	**14.82**	**8.73**	**5.17**	**23.02**

the training and testing distributions, as shown in Fig. 5. This suggests that our method alters the embedding distributions, leading to a more distinct separation between training and testing data.

As shown in Table 5, we further validate the above observation through a transfer experiment. Both the baseline CQG model and our proposed CS2MQG-enhanced model are first trained on the HotpotQA dataset, and then evaluated on the MuSiQue test set. Our method achieves an improvement of approximately 5.1% over the baseline. These results demonstrate that CS2MQG not only outperforms the baseline but also exhibits stronger transferability and better adaptability to new data distributions.

5 Conclusions and Future Work

In this paper, we introduce a model-agnostic method for generating counterfactual support by leveraging bridging dependency invariance. Unlike traditional data augmentation techniques such as synonym replacement and random deletion, our method targets counterfactual changes in key bridging nodes with rich information. Our experiments show that this method significantly enhances the model's ability to handle complex dependencies and improves the performance of existing MQG models in generating and supporting facts. Future research can explore more effective methods, such as utilizing generative adversarial networks (GANs) or reinforcement learning (RL), to generate representative counterfactuals with bridging dependency more rapidly. We will also exploit multi-modal information [34] and delve into advanced modal alignment techniques in other domains [10,11,14].

Acknowledgments. This work was supported in part by the National Natural Science Foundation of China (No. 62276196) and Wuhan Textile University (No. 2025254).

References

1. Bulathwela, S., Muse, H., Yilmaz, E.: Scalable educational question generation with pre-trained language models. In: AIED. Lecture Notes in Computer Science, vol. 13916, pp. 327–339. Springer, Cham (2023)
2. Chin-Yew, L.: Rouge: a package for automatic evaluation of summaries. In: Proceedings of the Workshop on Text Summarization Branches Out (2004)
3. Deng, Y., Zhang, W., Lam, W.: Multi-hop inference for question-driven summarization. In: EMNLP, vol. 1, pp. 6734–6744. Association for Computational Linguistics (2020)
4. Du, X., Shao, J., Cardie, C.: Learning to ask: Neural question generation for reading comprehension. In: ACL, vol. 1, pp. 1342–1352. Association for Computational Linguistics (2017)
5. Fei, Z., et al.: CQG: a simple and effective controlled generation framework for multi-hop question generation. In: ACL, vol. 1, pp. 6896–6906. Association for Computational Linguistics (2022)
6. Fei, Z., Zhang, Q., Zhou, Y.: Iterative GNN-based decoder for question generation. In: EMNLP, pp. 2573–2582. Association for Computational Linguistics (2021)
7. Goldberg, L.R.: The book of why: The new science of cause and effect: by judea pearl and dana mackenzie, basic books (2018). isbn: 978-0465097609. (2019)
8. Heilman, M.: Automatic Factual Question Generation from Text. Carnegie Mellon University (2011)
9. Heilman, M., Smith, N.A.: Good question! statistical ranking for question generation. In: HLT-NAACL, pp. 609–617. The Association for Computational Linguistics (2010)
10. Hu, K., Li, L., Liu, J., Sun, D.: Duronet: a dual-robust enhanced spatial-temporal learning network for urban crime prediction. ACM Trans. Internet Technol. **21**(1), 24:1–24:24 (2021)
11. Hu, K., Li, L., Xie, Q., Liu, J., Tao, X., Xu, G.: Decoupled progressive distillation for sequential prediction with interaction dynamics. ACM Trans. Inf. Syst. **42**(3), 72:1–72:35 (2024)
12. Kim, Y., Lee, H., Shin, J., Jung, K.: Improving neural question generation using answer separation. In: AAAI, pp. 6602–6609. AAAI Press (2019)
13. Lavie, A., Agarwal, A.: METEOR: an automatic metric for MT evaluation with high levels of correlation with human judgments. In: WMT@ACL, pp. 228–231. Association for Computational Linguistics (2007)
14. Li, L., Hu, K., Zheng, Y., Liu, J., Lee, K.A.: Coopnet: multi-modal cooperative gender prediction in social media user profiling. In: ICASSP, pp. 4310–4314. IEEE (2021)
15. Lin, Z., Chen, W., Song, Y., Zhang, Y.: Prompting few-shot multi-hop question generation via comprehending type-aware semantics. In: NAACL-HLT (Findings), pp. 3730–3740. Association for Computational Linguistics (2024)

16. Mostow, J., Chen, W.: Generating instruction automatically for the reading strategy of self-questioning. In: AIED. Frontiers in Artificial Intelligence and Applications, vol. 200, pp. 465–472. IOS Press (2009)
17. Nema, P., Mohankumar, A.K., Khapra, M.M., Srinivasan, B.V., Ravindran, B.: Let's ask again: refine network for automatic question generation. In: EMNLP/IJCNLP, vol. 1, pp. 3312–3321. Association for Computational Linguistics (2019)
18. Pan, L., Xie, Y., Feng, Y., Chua, T., Kan, M.: Semantic graphs for generating deep questions. In: ACL, pp. 1463–1475. Association for Computational Linguistics (2020)
19. Papineni, K., Roukos, S., Ward, T., Zhu, W.: Bleu: a method for automatic evaluation of machine translation. In: ACL, pp. 311–318. ACL (2002)
20. Puri, R., Spring, R., Shoeybi, M., Patwary, M., Catanzaro, B.: Training question answering models from synthetic data. In: EMNLP, pp. 5811–5826. Association for Computational Linguistics (2020)
21. Rajpurkar, P., Zhang, J., Lopyrev, K., Liang, P.: Squad: 100, 000+ questions for machine comprehension of text. In: EMNLP, pp. 2383–2392. The Association for Computational Linguistics (2016)
22. Sachan, D.S., Wu, L., Sachan, M., Hamilton, W.L.: Stronger transformers for neural multi-hop question generation. CoRR **abs/2010.11374** (2020)
23. Shi, Z., et al.: Generate-then-ground in retrieval-augmented generation for multi-hop question answering. In: ACL, vol. 1, pp. 7339–7353. Association for Computational Linguistics (2024)
24. Su, D., Xu, P., Fung, P.: QA4QG: using question answering to constrain multi-hop question generation. In: ICASSP, pp. 8232–8236. IEEE (2022)
25. Su, D., Xu, Y., Dai, W., Ji, Z., Yu, T., Fung, P.: Multi-hop question generation with graph convolutional network. In: EMNLP (Findings), pp. 4636–4647. Findings of ACL, Association for Computational Linguistics (2020)
26. Trivedi, H., Balasubramanian, N., Khot, T., Sabharwal, A.: Musique: multihop questions via single-hop question composition. Trans. Assoc. Comput. Linguist. **10**, 539–554 (2022)
27. Wachter, S., Mittelstadt, B.D., Russell, C.: Counterfactual explanations without opening the black box: automated decisions and the GDPR. CoRR **abs/1711.00399** (2017)
28. Wang, L., Xu, Z., Lin, Z., Zheng, H., Shen, Y.: Answer-driven deep question generation based on reinforcement learning. In: COLING, pp. 5159–5170. International Committee on Computational Linguistics (2020)
29. Wei, J.W., Zou, K.: EDA: easy data augmentation techniques for boosting performance on text classification tasks. In: EMNLP/IJCNLP, pp. 6381–6387. Association for Computational Linguistics (2019)
30. Xia, Z., et al.: Improving question generation with multi-level content planning. In: EMNLP (Findings), pp. 800–814. Association for Computational Linguistics (2023)
31. Yang, Z., et al.: Hotpotqa: a dataset for diverse, explainable multi-hop question answering. In: EMNLP, pp. 2369–2380. Association for Computational Linguistics (2018)
32. Yu, J., Quan, X., Su, Q., Yin, J.: Generating multi-hop reasoning questions to improve machine reading comprehension. In: WWW, pp. 281–291. ACM / IW3C2 (2020)
33. Yu, J., Su, Q., Quan, X., Yin, J.: Multi-hop reasoning question generation and its application. IEEE Trans. Knowl. Data Eng. **35**(1), 725–740 (2023)

34. Zhang, Q., et al.: An entailment tree generation approach for multimodal multi-hop question answering with mixture-of-experts and iterative feedback mechanism. In: ACM Multimedia, pp. 4814–4822. ACM (2024)
35. Zhang, Y., Zhu, H., Wang, Y., Xu, N., Li, X., Zhao, B.: A contrastive framework for learning sentence representations from pairwise and triple-wise perspective in angular space. In: ACL, pp. 4892–4903. Association for Computational Linguistics (2022)
36. Zhao, Y., Ni, X., Ding, Y., Ke, Q.: Paragraph-level neural question generation with maxout pointer and gated self-attention networks. In: EMNLP, pp. 3901–3910. Association for Computational Linguistics (2018)
37. Zhou, Q., Yang, N., Wei, F., Tan, C., Bao, H., Zhou, M.: Neural question generation from text: a preliminary study. In: Huang, X., Jiang, J., Zhao, D., Feng, Y., Hong, Yu. (eds.) NLPCC 2017. LNCS (LNAI), vol. 10619, pp. 662–671. Springer, Cham (2018). https://doi.org/10.1007/978-3-319-73618-1_56

NLCC: Noisy Label Correction with CLIP for Robust Few-Shot Learning

Bowen Han[1], Shizhuo Deng[1,2](✉), Jiaqi Chen[1], Zehua Gan[1], Dongyue Chen[1], and Yue Zhu[1]

[1] College of Information Science and Engineering, Northeastern University, Shenyang, Liaoning, China
{2370719,2270691,2370888}@stu.neu.edu.cn, chendongyue@ise.neu.edu.cn
[2] Foshan Graduate School of Innovation, Northeastern University, Foshan, Guangdong, China
dengshizhuo@mail.neu.edu.cn

Abstract. In social media crowdsourced annotation, image-text multimodal data grows rapidly, but user-generated labels often contain noise (e.g., mislabeling a wolf as a husky). This issue is particularly prominent during the cold start phase of new users, where few-shot data with noisy labels exerts a more significant influence due to the limited data for robust learning. To address this, we propose a multimodal approach for correcting noisy labels. First, we leverage the image-text matching capability of the pre-trained CLIP model to filter mismatched multimodal data and correct erroneous labels via similarity metrics. However, since CLIP's correction results are not entirely accurate, we introduce a multi-label mechanism that incorporates the top-k labels filtered by CLIP with weighted integration into training, forming a plug-and-play multimodal noisy label correction method. This provides a solution to the cold start problem with noisy behaviors. We embedded our method in 11 datasets and two classic methods, and experimental results validate its effectiveness.

Keywords: noisy label · multimodal · social computing

1 Introduction

Social networks are experiencing a rapid growth of multimodal information, such as images, text, and videos, enriching the diversity of content and interactions. However, a significant portion of image data relies on crowdsourced labels contributed by users, which frequently contain inaccuracies. This leads to substantial label noise. For instance, on Instagram, a photo of a tiger cat might be mislabeled as a "tiger" due to visual similarities. This issue becomes particularly critical during the cold-start phase for new users, where limited training data in few-shot scenarios amplifies the adverse effects of noisy annotations. The

T. Hao et al. (Eds.): BESC 2025, LNCS 16431, pp. 188–203, 2026.
https://doi.org/10.1007/978-981-95-7138-3_13

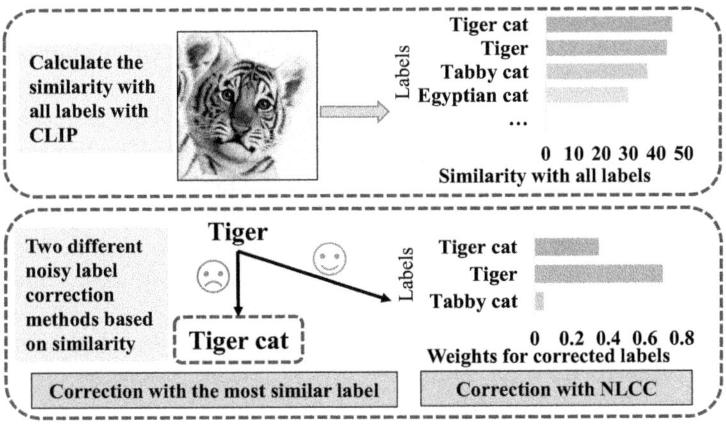

Fig. 1. Comparison of two correction methods.

early-stage label errors could bias personalized recommendations, resulting the reliability and utility of social media platforms.

To enhance the learning capabilities of models with limited data, few-shot learning (FSL) has emerged, which focuses on extracting knowledge from a small amount of data. FSL is highly sensitive to partially correct labels, which is defined as noisy labels. Most labels are obtained through manual annotation or web collection, where noisy labels are inevitable, making the correction of noisy labels highly valuable. Therefore, learning from noisy labels is becoming a practical and urgent problem in robust few-shot learning.

Many noisy label correction methods in few-shot learning rely on single-modal information. They typically process noisy labels based on the distribution of image features in the feature space, enhancing the robustness of the prototypes [1,2], or assigning smaller weights to labels identified as incorrect [3]. The relationships between image-text pairs are rarely leveraged in research addressing few-shot robust learning with noisy labels.

Recently, a more intuitive method with multi-modal information to deal with noisy labels has been widely researched [4–6]. Huang first proposes the noisy correspondence problem, utilizing the difference in similarity between correctly matched and incorrectly matched image-text pairs to fit two distributions, thereby identifying noisy labels. However, aligning image-text features to calculate similarity requires more training data. Fitting distributions based on similarity also demands more data, making this approach unsuitable for few-shot learning. CLIP [7] is a cross-modal model pre-trained on 400 million image-text pairs, enabling the model to achieve a powerful ability to obtain the similarity between text descriptions and images. CLIP allows for the identification of low-corresponding noisy labels and replacing them with high-similarity correct labels with few-shot datasets.

However, CLIP-based methods encounter the problem of wrong correction when handling noisy labels in few-shot learning. Specifically, when calculating the similarity between an image and all labels, there may be mismatched label that result in the highest similarity. As shown in Fig. 1, we compute the similarity between the image labeled as "tiger" and all labels by CLIP. The top three highest similarities are "tiger cat", "tiger" and "tabby cat". The original label ranks second in the similarity list, which creates a perplexing situation. Depending on whether the original label is correct, this situation can be attributed to two different causes. **(1)** The original label is correct, but due to the imperfect matching by CLIP, it only achieves the second-highest similarity. **(2)** The most similar label calculated by CLIP is correct, while the original incorrect label coincidentally ranks second due to its high similarity to the image. Since the original labels are noisy, it is difficult to distinguish between these two scenarios. Therefore, improving the accuracy of CLIP and achieving a tradeoff between the original label and the most similar label is a significant challenge. There are two problems to be considered.

Q1: How to make the CLIP generalize well on noisy few-shot data? Although CLIP has aligned the feature spaces of images and text well, there is still significant room for accuracy improvement in specific tasks. And according to the theory proposed in [8,9], deep learning models tend to prioritize fitting clean labels. So, it is meaningful and feasible to fine-tune CLIP using a few-shot dataset with noisy labels to reduce the probability of wrong matching with CLIP.

Q2: How to avoid the negative effect of the mismatching between feature pairs caused by CLIP? As is discussed in Fig. 1, hard correction with the most similar label "tiger cat" calculated by CLIP would lead to mistakes. Meanwhile, soft correction, which considers multimodal information to incorporate the top three most similar labels, addresses the issue of hard correction.

To address the above issues, we propose a plug-and-play **N**oisy **L**abel **C**orrection method with **C**LIP for robust few-shot learning called NLCC, aiming to improve the effectiveness of few-shot learning by enhancing data quality with two steps. First, we fine-tune CLIP on a noisy few-shot dataset to improve its matching accuracy. Second, we use the *top-k* most similar labels for label correction, assigning weights based on similarity, achieving a more robust correction.

The main contributions of our method are as follows:

- A novel solution called NLCC is designed to correct noisy labels in few-shot learning with CLIP. To the best of our knowledge, CLIP-based correction for noisy labels is rarely researched in recent few-shot work but has great practical value.
- We propose a multi-label weighting module that integrates CLIP's prior knowledge with original label information, achieving more robust noisy label correction compared to directly using CLIP.
- Our method is plug-and-play, and the corrected labels can be widely applied to other few-shot learning methods with CLIP.
- We conduct extensive experiments on different public datasets with different noise types to validate the performance and the effectiveness of NLCC.

2 Related Works

Few-Shot Learning with Noisy Labels. The scarcity of data in few-shot learning constrains the detection of noisy labels, thereby limiting research in this area. These methods address the issue by constructing more robust prototypes, assigning weights to labels based on their reliability, or leveraging meta-learning. RNNP [2] generates mixed prototypes through linear interpolation of samples in the support set, enhancing the robustness of prototypes. TraNSF [1] addresses the limitations of few-shot models in handling noisy labels by replacing the mean operator used in ProtoNet [10] with a more robust aggregation method. To calculate label weights based on reliability, RapNet [3] introduces a parametric attention module composed of a learnable bidirectional long short-term memory network [11] and a fully connected network [12], which generates attention weights to effectively handle noisy labels in few-shot learning scenarios. DCML [13] utilizes meta-learning with class-level sampling and example-level sampling to dynamically adjust during training, minimizing the impact of noisy labels and enhancing model robustness.

Few-Shot Learning with CLIP. Fine-tuned CLIP [7], which better captures image-text relationships through cosine similarity with few-shot datasets, is divided into three methods. **(1) Prompt tuning.** CoOp [14] and CoCoOp [15] enhance few-shot learning by transforming CLIP's text descriptions ("a photo of [class]") into learnable vectors, optimizing performance through prompt tuning. While these methods achieve promising results, they require more computational resources and training time. **(2) Adapter tuning.** CLIP-Adapter [16] offers a lightweight fine-tuning approach by adding two linear layers directly after the image encoder, preserving CLIP's capabilities with residual connections to prevent forgetting CLIP's zero-shot capabilities. **(3) Cache tuning.** Tip-Adapter [17] constructs a cache model using image features and labels from the training set, presenting a training-free CLIP fine-tuning method to better leverage few-shot datasets. Tip-Adapter-F further enhances adaptation by unfreezing the cache model with adapter method. CaFo [18] combines these methods by using GPT-3 [19] for text prompts and DALL-E [20] for image generation, leveraging a cache model to combine the textual and visual prior knowledge of CLIP and DINO [21] to achieve better few-shot learning results.

Emerging CLIP-based few-shot learning methods [22–24] continue to evolve, yet these approaches have not considered the potential negative impact of fine-tuning on noisy datasets. Leveraging CLIP's robust performance to address noisy labels in few-shot learning remains an unexplored area.

3 Method

3.1 Overview

To address fault corrections caused by imperfect CLIP [7] matching, we propose NLCC, a **N**oisy **L**abel **C**orrection method with **C**LIP for robust few-shot learning. As shown in Fig. 2, there are two components, Fine-Tuned CLIP and Multi-Label Weighting Module in NLCC. Fine-tuned CLIP improves the matching accuracy of CLIP in few-shot learning tasks. In the Multi-Label Weighting Module, the single label matching mechanism in original CLIP is expanded to *top-k* most similar labels with different weights, which aims to cover the right labels and improve the robustness of label correction.

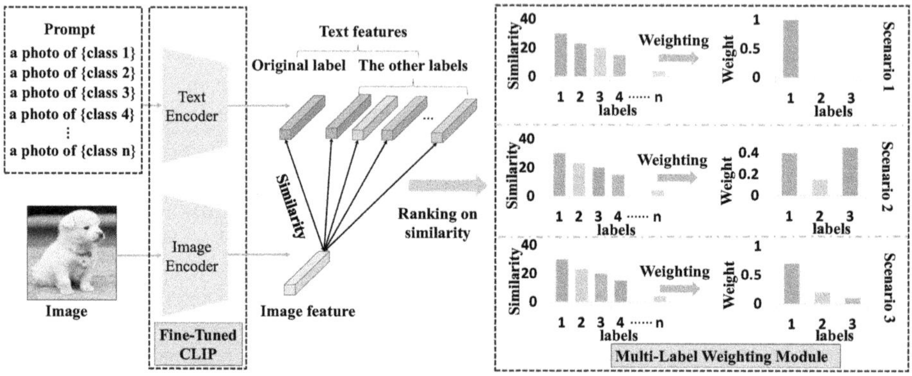

Fig. 2. Overview of NLCC. Red cylindrical represents the similarity score of the original label. Scenario 1 indicates the original label is the most similar label. Scenario 2 indicates that the original label is not the most similar but among the *top-k* (Color figure online) labels. Scenario 3 indicates that the original label is not among the *top-k* labels.

3.2 Fine-Tuned CLIP

To improve CLIP's accuracy in detecting noisy labels, we use the adapter-based method CLIP-Adapter [16] to fine-tune CLIP. Its structural diagram is shown in Fig. 3. The CLIP text encoder $f_t()$ and CLIP image encoder $f_i()$ can map labels and images into an aligned feature space. Specifically, the input class names are converted into class label descriptions $L = \{l_1, l_2, \ldots, l_n\}$ in the style of "a photo of {class}", where n represents the number of categories. The corresponding text features $T = \{t_1, t_2, \ldots, t_n\} = \{f_t(l_1), f_t(l_2), \ldots, f_t(l_n)\}$ could be calculate through $f_t()$.

The image is input to the $f_i()$ to calculate the image feature X. The image feature is fine-tuned through an adapter network consisting of two linear layers. In order not to forget the powerful capabilities of the original CLIP, the image feature is adjusted using residual structure. The fine-tuned image feature can be calculated by

$$\begin{aligned} X^* &= (1-\lambda)X + \lambda adapter(X) \\ &= (1-\lambda)X + \lambda(ReLU(XW_1)W_2), \end{aligned} \tag{1}$$

where W_1 and W_2 represent the learnable parameters of the two linear layers.

The similarity score $S = \{s_1, s_2, \ldots, s_n\}$ and the probability of belonging to each category $P = \{p_1, p_2, \ldots, p_n\}$ can be calculated using the fine-tuned image feature and all label features by

$$s_i = \exp\left(\cos(X^*, t_i)/\tau\right), \tag{2}$$

$$p_i = \frac{s_i}{\sum_{j=1}^{N} s_j} = \frac{\exp\left(\cos(X^*, t_i)/\tau\right)}{\sum_{j=1}^{N} \exp\left(\cos(X^*, t_j)/\tau\right)}, \tag{3}$$

where cos() denotes cosine similarity and τ is a temperature parameter for softmax.

During fine-tuning, the two linear layers can be optimized using the cross entropy loss as

$$L(\theta) = -\frac{1}{M} \sum_{m=1}^{M} \sum_{i=1}^{n} y_i^{(m)} \log \hat{y}_i^{(m)}, \tag{4}$$

where M is the total number of training samples. $y_i = 1$ if i equals the ground-truth category label $\hat{i}$, otherwise $y_i = 0$. $\hat{y}_i = p_i$ is the predicted probability for class i. $\theta = \{W_1, W_2\}$ represents all learnable parameters.

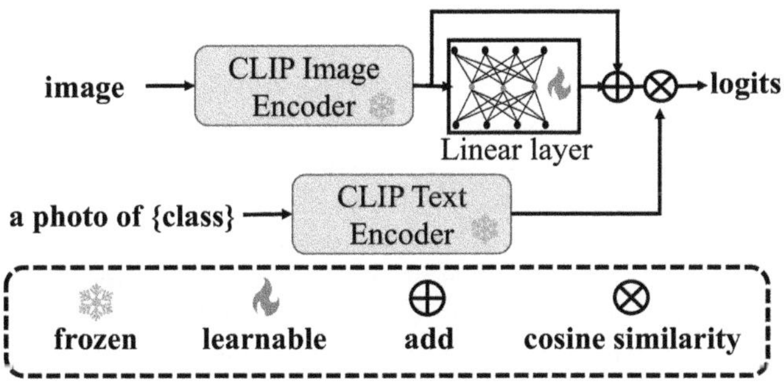

Fig. 3. Structure of CLIP-Adapter.

3.3 Multi-label Weighting Module

To avoid missing the correct label, we introduce the *top-k* highest similar labels as multi-labels into the training phase. Multi-labels make it more possible to cover the right matching patterns.

With Fine-Tuned CLIP, the similarity between the image feature X^* and the semantic features $T = \{t_1, t_2, \ldots, t_n\}$ of all classes can be calculated using Eq. 2. These similarities are sorted in descending order in $S^* = \{s_1^*, s_2^*, s_3^*, \ldots, s_n^*\}$. In particular, We denote the similarity between the original label feature and the image feature as s_r^* ($s_r^* \in S^*$), where r represents the rank of s_r^* in S^* and $1 \leq r \leq n$.

Top-k most similar labels are denoted as $S_k^* = \{s_1^*, s_2^*, s_3^*, \ldots, s_k^*\}$. We calculate the weights $w = \{w_1, w_2, w_3, \ldots, w_k\}$ of these multi-labels on three scenarios according to the relationship between r and k , where w_i represents the weight of the label ranked i in similarity. The label with higher probabilities is assigned larger weights.

(1) scenario 1: $r = 1$.

At this point, the original label is treated as the correct label. The weight of the original label is 1, and the weights of the remaining $k - 1$ labels are set to 0. The weight w can be calculated by

$$w_i = \begin{cases} 1 \ \textit{if} \ i = 1, \\ 0 \ \textit{otherwise}. \end{cases} \tag{5}$$

(2) Scenario 2: $1 < r \leq k$.

In this situation, it is caused by incorrectly annotated noisy labels or imperfect CLIP matches, so both the original label and the most similar label are considered useful labels. We use α to balance between the original label and the most similar label, where α represents the loyalty to the original label and $1 > \alpha > 0$. Empirically, as the rank r increases, its corresponding weight should be smaller. Therefore, the original label's weight is $\alpha \cdot \gamma^{r-2}$, where $1 > \gamma > 0$.

The remaining weight, $1 - \alpha \cdot \gamma^{h-2}$, is allocated among the remaining $k - 1$ labels. Naturally, the label with the highest similarity should receive a larger weight, but assigning excessive weight may reduce the significance of correct information from the remaining $k - 2$ labels. Therefore, we introduce another hyperparameter β to balance this situation. β represents the importance of the label with the highest similarity in multi-labels other than the original label and $1 > \beta > 0$. At this stage, the weight assigned to the label with the highest similarity is $\beta \cdot (1 - \alpha \cdot \gamma^{h-2})$, while the weights of the remaining $k - 2$ labels are allocated based on their distances from the label with the highest similarity, denoted as $s_1^* - s_i^*$. The weight w can be calculated by

$$w_i = \begin{cases} (1 - \alpha \cdot \gamma^{r-2}) \cdot \beta & \textit{if} \ i = 1, \\ \alpha \cdot \gamma^{r-2} & \textit{if} \ i = r, \\ (1 - \alpha \cdot \gamma^{r-2}) \cdot (1 - \beta) & \\ \cdot \dfrac{s_1^* - s_i^*}{\sum\limits_{j=2 \wedge j \neq r}^{k} (s_1^* - s_j^*)} & \textit{otherwise}. \end{cases} \tag{6}$$

(3) Scenario 3: $k < r \leq n$.

At this point, the original label is considered an incorrect label and is discarded. We then correct it using the *top-k* labels, balancing the weight of the most similar label and others with hyperparameter β. The weights of the remaining $k-1$ labels are allocated based on their distances from the most similar label.

The weight w can be calculated by

$$w_i = \begin{cases} \beta & if\, i = 1, \\ (1-\beta) \cdot \dfrac{s_1^* - s_i^*}{\sum_{j=2}^{k}(s_1^* - s_j^*)} & otherwise. \end{cases} \tag{7}$$

After obtaining the weights $\mathbf{w}$ corresponding to the *top-k* labels, in order to introduce the similarity relationship between image-text pairs, we multiply the corresponding elements of $\mathbf{S_k^*}$ and $\mathbf{w}$, and then divide by the sum of all elements to obtain the normalized weight vector $\mathbf{w}^* = \{w_1^*, w_2^*, w_3^*, \ldots, w_k^*\}$ with the following equation:

$$w_i^* = \frac{s_i^* . w_i}{\sum_{j=1}^{k} s_j^* . w_j}. \tag{8}$$

3.4 Overall Objective

After obtaining the corrected multi-labels and their corresponding weights for each image, we modify the original loss function to adapt it to our plug-and-play method by

$$L^* = \frac{1}{M}\sum_{m=1}^{M}\sum_{k=1}^{K} L_o^{(mk)} . w^{*(mk)}, \tag{9}$$

where $L_o^{(mk)}$ represents the loss value of the *m-th* sample for the *k-th* corrected label on the original loss function, which belongs to the base model. $w^{*(mk)}$ represents the weight represented by the *k-th* corrected label of the *m-th* image, which can be calculated using Eq. 5, 6, 7.

4 Experiments

4.1 Experimental Settings

Datasets. We conduct primary experiments on the general object recognition dataset *Caltech101* [25] and the action recognition dataset *UCF101* [26]. Both datasets contain 101 classes and are widely used in public researches. Additionally, we conduct experiments on the other seven datasets to verify the genelization of the NLCC. These datasets include: *ImageNet* [27] for generic object recognition; *OxfordPets* [28], *StanfordCars* [29], *Flowers102* [30], and *Food101* [31] for fine-grained image recognition; *SUN397* [32] for scene recognition; *DTD* [33] for texture classification. The diversity of the evaluation dataset ensures a solid evaluation of our method across various types of image recognition tasks.

Noisy Label Settings. We evaluate our method using symmetric noise and asymmetric noise. Symmetric noise [34] randomly replaces a proportion of labels with other labels according to noise rate δ. Asymmetric noise [35] deliberately replaces the labels of each class with incorrect labels in the same class, thus increasing the noise intensity. For each class of the aforementioned datasets, we simulate few-shot setting by limiting the number of samples per class and set the δ to 0, 0.2, 0.4, 0.6, and 0.8, representing the proportion of incorrect labels in each class.

Baselines and Evaluation. To demonstrate the plug-and-play ability of our method, we select two typical CLIP-based few-shot learning baselines: the adapter-based method CLIP-Adapter [16] and the cache-based method Tip-Adapter-F [17]. These two baselines are classic works in CLIP-based few-shot learning and have inspired various subsequent studies. We train them on few-shot datasets with noisy labels before and after applying our correction method NLCC, and evaluate the performance on the metric of accuracy. We conduct experiments using 5-shot and 10-shot few-shot settings without limiting the number of categories to increase the classification difficulty.

Implementation Details. For CLIP, we utilize ResNet-50 [36] as the backbone for image feature extraction and a transformer architecture [37] for text encoding. During fine-tuning, the residual parameter λ is set to 0.2, the same as in CLIP-Adapter [16]. We adopt the AdamW optimization algorithm [38] with a learning rate of 0.001 and a cosine scheduler. The batch size is set to 64 for *ImageNet* and set to 8 for the other datasets. The number of training epochs is set to 20–100. To ensure a fair comparison, epochs for each dataset remains consistent before and after applying NLCC. As the δ increases, the reliability of the original labels decreases. Therefore, α is 0.9 when δ is 0.0, and α is 0.8 for δ is 0.2, 0.4, and 0.6 respectively. $\alpha = 0.6$ for $\delta = 0.8$. β and γ are set to 0.8 and 0.9 respectively, and the number of multi-labels k is set to 3. The experiment is conducted on an NVIDIA RTX 3090 GPU (24 GB), Windows 10 OS, and PyTorch 1.12.1. The random seed for constructing the noisy few-shot dataset and training is set to 1.

Table 1. Accuracy (%) on symmetric noise on *Caltech101*

methods	5-shot					10-shot				
	0	0.2	0.4	0.6	0.8	0	0.2	0.4	0.6	0.8
CLIP-Adapter	91.81	90.26	89.05	87.22	82.39	90.91	88.56	87.38	84.1	79.03
+NLCC	91.52$^{\downarrow}$	90.43$^{\uparrow}$	89.21$^{\uparrow}$	88.4$^{\uparrow}$	85.23$^{\uparrow}$	90.95$^{\uparrow}$	89.57$^{\uparrow}$	88.8$^{\uparrow}$	87.71$^{\uparrow}$	84.26$^{\uparrow}$
Tip-Adapter	91.4	88.15	86.33	79.68	63.08	92.41	88.11	84.18	76.75	58.9
+NLCC	91.28$^{\downarrow}$	88.32$^{\uparrow}$	88.72$^{\uparrow}$	83.94$^{\uparrow}$	80.04$^{\uparrow}$	92.37$^{\downarrow}$	89.61$^{\uparrow}$	87.02$^{\uparrow}$	85.6$^{\uparrow}$	80.97$^{\uparrow}$

Table 2. Accuracy (%) on symmetric noise on *UCF101*

methods	5-shot					10-shot				
	0	0.2	0.4	0.6	0.8	0	0.2	0.4	0.6	0.8
CLIP-Adapter	72.96	67.43	63.89	59.87	51.28	75.07	68.38	64.18	62.33	53.24
+NLCC	72.06$^{\downarrow}$	67.94$^{\uparrow}$	66.09$^{\uparrow}$	61.41$^{\uparrow}$	54.85$^{\uparrow}$	75.81$^{\uparrow}$	71.45$^{\uparrow}$	67.72$^{\uparrow}$	63.68$^{\uparrow}$	56.86$^{\uparrow}$
Tip-Adapter	73.22	69.55	65.27	59.95	50.65	75.5	67.49	63.76	58.37	45.6
+NLCC	73.35$^{\uparrow}$	68.83$^{\downarrow}$	65.72$^{\uparrow}$	60.24$^{\uparrow}$	49.91$^{\downarrow}$	75.36$^{\downarrow}$	70.68$^{\uparrow}$	67.75$^{\uparrow}$	60.4$^{\uparrow}$	52.37$^{\uparrow}$

4.2 Experimental Results

(1) Results on Symmetric Noise. To validate the effectiveness of the NLCC in correcting noisy labels, we compare the performance of CLIP-Adapter, Tip-Adapter-F and these two methods by applying NLCC, (CLIP-Adapter)+NLCC and (Tip-Adapter-F)+NLCC respectively. As shown in Table 1 and Table 2, upward arrow indicates an improvement with NLCC, while downward arrow indicates the opposite.

On *Caltech101*, correction performance for the noise improves as the δ increases. It's expected that accuracy may slightly decrease when there is no noise. In clean datasets, using the NLCC inevitably introduces a small number of incorrect labels, resulting in a minor drop in classification accuracy. However, as the δ increases beyond 0, the benefits of our method become increasingly evident.

From the comparison of 5-shot and 10-shot, it can be seen that the increment in the number of shots will increase the number of incorrect labels, thereby having a greater impact. For instance, using CLIP-Adapter at a 0.8 noise rate, the accuracies for 5-shot and 10-shot are 82.39% and 79.03% respectively, with a decrease of 3.36%. However, after applying NLCC, the accuracies for 5-shot and 10-shot are 85.23% and 84.26%, with only a 0.97% decrease, indicating that our method effectively mitigates the severe impact of increased incorrect labels.

Tip-Adapter-F initializes the model using a cache constructed from the dataset. Therefore, its performance is superior to CLIP-Adapter when the δ is 0. In the 10-shot setting, the accuracy of Tip-Adapter-F is improved from 90.91% to 92.41% compared to CLIP-Adapter. After applying NLCC, the accuracy improves from 90.95% to 92.37%, indicating that NLCC does not affect the performance of the original method but rather serves as a plug-and-play module. However, since Tip-Adapter-F utilizes a cache constructed from the dataset, it is more affected by noise. At a δ of 0.8 in 10-shot, the accuracies of Tip-Adapter-F and CLIP-Adapter are 58.9% and 79.03% respectively, suffering a catastrophic impact. After applying NLCC, the accuracy of (Tip-Adapter-F)+NLCC improves to 80.97%, higher than that of CLIP-Adapter without NLCC, indicating that although the constructed cache is severely affected, the NLCC significantly mitigate this impact.

For the action recognition dataset *UCF101* on video, The high similarity for data of each action and complex backgrounds make it harder in few-shot scenario.

As seen from the Table 1 and Table 2, in most cases, there is an improvement by both methods with NLCC. However, in the 5-shot experiments conducted with Tip-Adapter-F, the accuracy fluctuates within 1% on the original basis. This is because the categories in the UCF dataset are easily confused, and with 5-shot data, only few features can be learned, affecting the multi-label correction process. Additionally, noisy cache in Tip-Adapter-F also has a negative impact, thus limiting the effectiveness of NLCC in this setting.

(2) Results on Asymmetric Noise. To further evaluate the performance of NLCC, we conduct 10-shot experiments under more extreme noise condition, as shown in Table 3. It can be seen that under asymmetric noise, (CLIP-Adapter)+NLCC and (Tip-Adapter)+NLCC show an improvement. For (CLIP-Adater)+NLCC, the improvement initially increases and then decreases. For example, for Caltech101, the improvements after using NLCC at δ values of 0.2, 0.4, 0.6, and 0.8 are 0.16%, 2.64%, 3.86%, and 1.18%, respectively. This is because asymmetric noise tends to assign incorrect labels to the same class. When the δ exceeds 0.5, the majority of incorrect labels belong to the same class, significantly impacting the fine-tuning process and influencing NLCC's performance. For (Tip-Adapter)+NLCC, the improvement increases significantly with δ. This is because using asymmetric noise to construct the cache has a larger impact, leading to a noticeable decrease in accuracy at high noise rates. When $\delta = 0.8$, the accuracy of Tip-Adapter-F is only 25.72% on *Caltech101* and 17.1% on *UCF101*, which means the model has learned very little knowledge. However, NLCC significantly mitigates this impact, resulting in accuracy improvements of 48.48% and 33.15% on *Caltech101* and *UCF101*, respectively.

Table 3. Accuracy (%) on asymmetric noise

methods	*Caltech101*					*UCF101*				
	0.0	0.2	0.4	0.6	0.8	0.0	0.2	0.4	0.6	0.8
CLIP-Adapter	91.81	89.7	87.38	83.85	76.06	75.07	70.47	65.58	60.56	52.29
+NLCC	91.52$^{\downarrow}$	89.86$^{\uparrow}$	90.02$^{\uparrow}$	87.71$^{\uparrow}$	77.24$^{\uparrow}$	75.81$^{\uparrow}$	72.59$^{\uparrow}$	66.67$^{\uparrow}$	61.49$^{\uparrow}$	52.5$^{\uparrow}$
Tip-Adapter-F	92.41	89.49	80.73	57.85	25.72	75.5	68.15	59.45	40.97	17.1
+NLCC	92.37$^{\downarrow}$	89.25$^{\downarrow}$	88.24$^{\uparrow}$	83.29$^{\uparrow}$	74.2$^{\uparrow}$	75.36$^{\downarrow}$	70.63$^{\uparrow}$	66.53$^{\uparrow}$	58.52$^{\uparrow}$	50.25$^{\uparrow}$

4.3 Ablation Study

We conduct ablation experiments on the *UCF101* dataset to evaluate the fine-tuning process and the multi-label weighting module of NLCC. The single-label represents training with the label that has the highest similarity score. As shown in the Table 4, the use of the multi-label weighting module improves performance

Table 4. Accuracy (%) in Ablation Study

Method	5-shot	10-shot
CLIP + Single-Label	61.67	61.43
CLIP + Multi-Label	65.61	65.58
CLIP + Fine-tuning + Single-Label	63.94	66.38
CLIP + Fine-tuning + Multi-Label	**66.09**	**67.72**

by 3.94% and 4.15% in the 5-shot and 10-shot tasks, respectively, and the fine-tuning module improves performance by 2.27% and 4.95%. It can be observed that the performance of the fine-tuning module is affected by the number of samples, while the multi-label weighting module is barely impacted. When both modules are applied, the performance improves by 4.42% and 6.29%, respectively, indicating that the two modules power each other.

4.4 Hyper-parameter Analysis

This section discusses the roles of α, β and the number of epochs in the training process on *UCF101*. We conduct experiments using a 10-shot dataset with symmetric noise in CLIP-Adapter when $\delta = 0.6$.

Loyalty to Original Label α. The results with different α are shown in Table 5. It can be seen that as α increases, the accuracy has two peaks at 0.5 and 0.8 respectively, and the maximum accuracy 63.68% is reached when α is 0.8. The reason is that both the original label and the label with the highest similarity are playing a role, as α increases, the importance of the original label becomes larger, and the importance of the label with the highest similarity becomes smaller. Therefore, the two peaks represent the primary role of the corrected label and the primary role of the original label in the correction process. This also proves that our setting of parameter α is reasonable, and greater weight should be assigned to the original labels to achieve optimal balance.

Table 5. Accuracy (%) in different α

α	0.4	0.5	0.6	0.7	0.8	0.9
Acc	62.94	**63.28**	62.44	63.31	**63.68**	63.55

Confidence in the most similar label β. The results with different β are shown in Table 6. When β is 0.8, the accuracy is the highest, and as β increases or decreases, the accuracy shows a decreasing trend. This means that when allocating multi-label weights, the label with the highest similarity should be given a larger weight, but the remaining labels may also contain the correct label, which proves the necessity of β parameter.

Table 6. Accuracy (%) in different β

β	0	0.2	0.4	0.6	0.8	1.0
Acc	60.32	61.14	61.12	62.86	**63.68**	63.2

Performance on Different Epochs. To verify the performance of the NLCC across different epochs, we set different noise rates and record the performance at different epochs before and after using NLCC. The results are illustrated in Fig. 4. It can be seen that corrected data not only achieves higher accuracy but also has two additional advantages. First, when the accuracy of the original data starts to decline due to overfitting to noise, the accuracy of the NLCC continues to increase, indicating that our method delays the impact of noise and extends the effective training time. Second, after the accuracy stabilizes, the decline from the max value represents the influence of noisy label on the model. Using NLCC, the accuracy drops by 0.1%, 0.45%, 1.3%, and 4.4% at noise rates of 0.2, 0.4, 0.6, and 0.8, respectively. In contrast, with noisy data, the accuracy drops by 7.88%, 12.76%, 21.73%, and 26.41%, respectively. This demonstrates that NLCC significantly reduces the impact of noise on the original model.

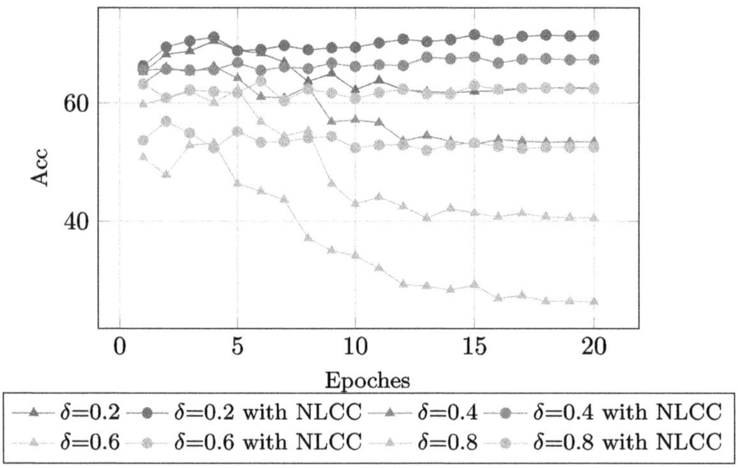

Fig. 4. Accuracy (%) during training with different δ.

4.5 Genelization on Other Datasets

We further conduct experiments using CLIP-Adapter on seven other datasets in 5-shot and 10-shot with different symmetric noise rates to verify the generality of NLCC. As shown in Fig. 5, NLCC improves classification accuracy on noisy datasets, and the improvement becomes more obvious as the δ increases. For the *ImageNet* dataset, although the performance is improved with NLCC, the improvement is minimal, resulting in an overall performance lower than the average level. This is because the zero-shot accuracy of CLIP on *ImageNet* reaches 60.32%, and only increases to 67.72% after fine-tuning with CLIP-Adapter on the clean 10-shot dataset. This indicates that CLIP is already highly sensitive to *ImageNet*, and fine-tuning with few-shot dataset has less impact, resulting in slight increase for the corrected data.

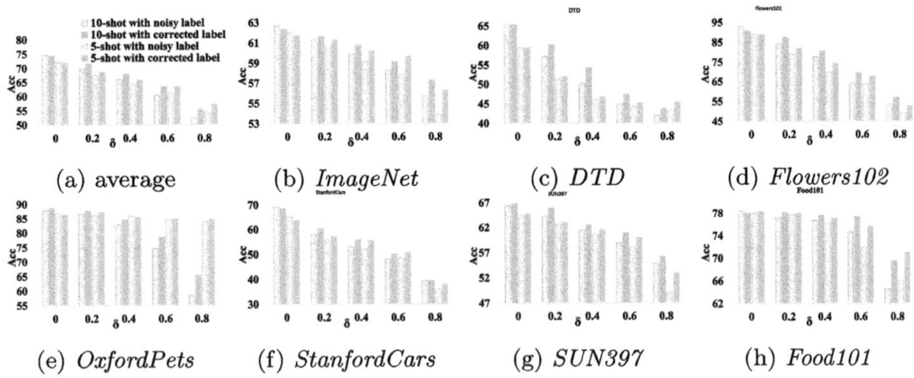

(a) average (b) *ImageNet* (c) *DTD* (d) *Flowers102*

(e) *OxfordPets* (f) *StanfordCars* (g) *SUN397* (h) *Food101*

Fig. 5. Accuracy (%) on other datasets

5 Conclusion

In this paper, we investigate the problem of noisy labels stemming from crowdsourcing in social networks, especially targeting few-shot data in cold-start scenarios. We propose a plug-and-play method based on CLIP, which can be applied directly to other few-shot learning methods. To address the issue of introducing incorrect labels when directly using CLIP for noisy label correction, we incorporate potentially correct labels as multi-labels into the training process. The multi-labels are weighted by combining CLIP prior knowledge with the original label information. Through comprehensive experiments, we demonstrate the performance of our method from multiple perspectives and validate the effectiveness of our design. In future work, we will apply NLCC to prototype networks [10], building more robust prototypes using multi-labels and corresponding weights.

Acknowledgments. This work was supported by the National Key R&D Program of China (2024YFB4710900); Guangdong Basic and Applied Basic Research Foundation (2024A1515010244); National Natural Science Foundation of China (62202087, 62173083, 62206043 and U22A2063); Fundamental Research Funds for the Central Universities (N2404008, N2404011); 111Project (B16009).

Disclosure of Interests. The authors have no competing interests to declare.

References

1. Liang, K.J., Rangrej, S.B., Petrovic, V., Hassner, T.: Few-shot learning with noisy labels. In: CVPR, pp. 9089–9098 (2022)
2. Mazumder, P., Singh, P., Namboodiri, V.P.: RNNP: a robust few-shot learning approach. In: WACV, pp. 2664–2673 (2021)
3. Lu, J., Jin, S., Liang, J., Zhang, C.: Robust few-shot learning for user-provided data. IEEE Trans. Neural Netw. Learn. Syst. **32**(4), 1433–1447 (2021). https://doi.org/10.1109/TNNLS.2020.2984710
4. Huang, Z., et al.: Learning with noisy correspondence for cross-modal matching. In: Ranzato, M., Beygelzimer, A., Dauphin, Y., Liang, P.S., Wortman Vaughan, J., (eds.) NeurIPS, vol. 34, pp. 29406–29419. Curran Associates, Inc. (2021)
5. Han, H., Miao, K., Zheng, Q., Luo, M.: Noisy correspondence learning with meta similarity correction. In: CVPR, pp. 7517–7526 (2023)
6. Yang, Y., Wang, L., Yang, E., Deng, C.: Robust noisy correspondence learning with equivariant similarity consistency. In: CVPR, pp. 17700–17709 (2024)
7. Radford, A., et al.: Learning transferable visual models from natural language supervision. In: ICML, pp. 8748–8763 (2021)
8. Arpit, D., et al.: A closer look at memorization in deep networks. In: ICML, pp. 233–242 (2017)
9. Xia, X., Liu, T., Han, B., Gong, C., Wang, N., Ge, Z., Chang, Y.: Robust early-learning: hindering the memorization of noisy labels. In: ICLR (2020)
10. Snell, J., Swersky, K., Zemel, R.: Prototypical networks for few-shot learning. In: NeurIPS, vol. 30 (2017)
11. Hochreiter, S., Schmidhuber, J.: Long short-term memory. Neural Comput. **9**(8), 1735–1780 (1997). https://doi.org/10.1162/neco.1997.9.8.1735
12. Long, J., Shelhamer, E., Darrell, T.: Fully convolutional networks for semantic segmentation. In: CVPR, pp. 3431–3440 (2015)
13. Que, X., Yu, Q.: Dual-level curriculum meta-learning for noisy few-shot learning tasks. In: Proceedings of the AAAI Conference on Artificial Intelligence, vol. 38, no. 13, pp. 14740–14748 (2024)
14. Zhou, K., Yang, J., Loy, C.C., Liu, Z.: Learning to prompt for vision-language models. Int. J. Comput. Vis. (2022)
15. Zhou, K., Yang, J., Loy, C.C., Liu, Z.: Conditional prompt learning for vision-language models. In: CVPR, pp. 16816–16825 (2022)
16. Gao, P., et al.: Clip-adapter: better vision-language models with feature adapters. Int. J. Comput. Vis. **132**(2), 581–595 (2024)
17. Zhang, R., et al.: Tip-adapter: training-free adaption of clip for few-shot classification. In: ECCV, pp. 493–510, Springer, Cham (2022)
18. Zhang, R., et al.: Prompt, generate, then cache: cascade of foundation models makes strong few-shot learners. In: CVPR, pp. 15211–15222 (2023)
19. Brown, T., et al.: Language models are few-shot learners. In: Larochelle, H., Ranzato, M., Hadsell, R., Balcan, M.F., Lin, H., (eds.) Advances in Neural Information Processing Systems, vol. 33, pp. 1877–1901. Curran Associates, Inc. (2020)
20. Ramesh, A., et al.: Zero-shot text-to-image generation. In: Meila, M., Zhang, T., (eds). ICML, vol. 139, pp. 8821–8831. PMLR (2021)
21. Caron, M., Touvron, H., Misra, I., Jégou, H., Mairal, J., Bojanowski, P., Joulin, A.: Emerging properties in self-supervised vision transformers. In: ICCV, pp. 9650–9660 (2021)

22. Tang, Y., Lin, Z., Wang, Q., Zhu, P., Hu, Q.: AMU-tuning: effective logit bias for CLIP-based few-shot learning. In: CVPR, pp. 23323–23333 (2024)
23. Silva-Rodríguez, J., Hajimiri, S., Ben Ayed, I., Dolz, J.: A closer look at the few-shot adaptation of large vision-language models. In: CVPR, pp. 23681–23690 (2024)
24. Huang, Y., Shakeri, F., Dolz, J., Boudiaf, M., Bahig, H., Ben Ayed, I.: LP++: a surprisingly strong linear probe for few-shot CLIP. In: CVPR, pp. 23773–23782 (2024)
25. Fei-Fei, L., Fergus, R., Perona, P.: Learning generative visual models from few training examples: an incremental bayesian approach tested on 101 object categories. In: CVPR Workshop, pp. 178–178 (2004). https://doi.org/10.1109/CVPR.2004.383
26. Soomro, K., Zamir, A.R., Shah, M.: UCF101: a dataset of 101 human actions classes from videos in the wild (2012). arXiv:1212.0402. https://arxiv.org/abs/1212.0402
27. Deng, J., Dong, W., Socher, R., Li, L.-J., Li, K., Fei-Fei, L.: ImageNet: a large-scale hierarchical image database. In: CVPR, pp. 248–255 (2009). https://doi.org/10.1109/CVPR.2009.5206848
28. Parkhi, O.M., Vedaldi, A., Zisserman, A., Jawahar, C.V.: Cats and dogs. In: CVPR, pp. 3498–3505 (2012). https://doi.org/10.1109/CVPR.2012.6248092
29. Krause, J., Stark, M., Deng, J., Fei-Fei, L.: 3D object representations for fine-grained categorization. In: ICCV Workshops, pp. 554–561 (2013)
30. Nilsback, M.-E., Zisserman, A.: Automated flower classification over a large number of classes. In: ICVGIP, pp. 722–729 (2008). https://doi.org/10.1109/ICVGIP.2008.47
31. Bossard, L., Guillaumin, M., Van Gool, L.: Food-101 – mining discriminative components with random forests. In: Fleet, D., Pajdla, T., Schiele, B., Tuytelaars, T. (eds.) ECCV 2014. LNCS, vol. 8694, pp. 446–461. Springer, Cham (2014). https://doi.org/10.1007/978-3-319-10599-4_29
32. Xiao, J., Hays, J., Ehinger, K.A., Oliva, A., Torralba, A.: SUN database: large-scale scene recognition from abbey to zoo. In: CVPR, pp. 3485–3492 (2010). https://doi.org/10.1109/CVPR.2010.5539970
33. Cimpoi, M., Maji, S., Kokkinos, I., Mohamed, S., Vedaldi, A.: Describing textures in the wild. In: CVPR, pp. 3606–3613 (2014)
34. Ren, M., Zeng, W., Yang, B., Urtasun, R.: Learning to reweight examples for robust deep learning. In: ICML, pp. 4334–4343. PMLR (2018)
35. Li, J., Socher, R., Hoi, S.C.H.: DivideMix: learning with noisy labels as semi-supervised learning. In: ICLR (2020). https://openreview.net/forum?id=HJgExaVtwr
36. He, K., Zhang, X., Ren, S., Sun, J.: Deep residual learning for image recognition. In: CVPR, pp. 770–778 (2016)
37. Vaswani, A., et al.: Attention is all you need. In: NeurIPS, vol. 30 (2017)
38. Kingma, D.P., Ba, J.: Adam: a method for stochastic optimization (2017). arXiv:1412.6980. https://arxiv.org/abs/1412.6980

Quantifying Off-Ball Attacking Contribution in Football: A GCN-LSTM Approach Supervised by Expert Assessments

Daiki Yoshikawa[1(✉)] and Tomonobu Ozaki[2]

[1] Graduate School of Integrated Basic Sciences, Nihon University, 3-25-40 Sakurajosui, Setagaya, Tokyo 156-8550, Japan
chda25018@g.nihon-u.ac.jp

[2] Department of Information Science, Nihon University, 3-25-40 Sakurajosui, Setagaya, Tokyo 156-8550, Japan
ozaki.tomonobu@nihon-u.ac.jp

Abstract. Accurate evaluation of off-ball player contributions in soccer remains a critical challenge, as players spend the majority of match time without possession. While existing performance models focus predominantly on on-ball actions, they often overlook the subtle, context-dependent movements that influence team success. This study presents a machine learning framework for evaluating off-ball player contributions during attacking sequences, grounded in expert annotations. We construct a graph-based dataset from tracking and event data of J. League matches, and train a model combining Graph Convolutional Networks (GCN) and Long Short-Term Memory (LSTM) networks to capture both spatial and temporal aspects of play. To improve model robustness under limited and imbalanced data, we additionally applied data augmentation techniques such as mirroring, time shifting, and controlled noise addition. Evaluation experiments show that the model not only aligns well with expert judgments but also effectively identifies high-quality plays when trained under strategically filtered conditions. These findings suggest that our method offers interpretable, context-aware evaluations of off-ball player behavior, contributing to more comprehensive soccer analytics.

Keywords: soccer analytics · off-ball evaluation · player performance · tracking data · expert annotation · sports data mining

1 Introduction

Quantitative evaluation of player performance in soccer is essential for improving decision-making in areas such as tactical planning, player development, and recruitment strategies. Although various performance metrics have been proposed in recent years due to advancements in data collection technologies, several important challenges remain.

T. Hao et al. (Eds.): BESC 2025, LNCS 16431, pp. 204–218, 2026.
https://doi.org/10.1007/978-981-95-7138-3_14

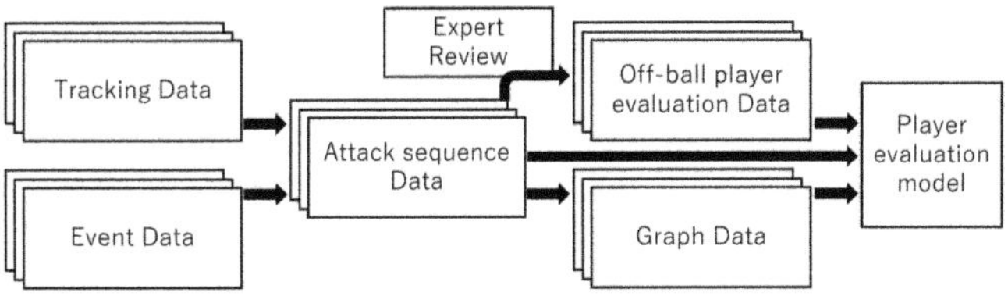

Fig. 1. Overall framework of this study

First, most existing studies focus on on-ball actions like shooting and passing, while research evaluating off-ball contributions is still limited. However, players typically possess the ball for only about 2 to 3 min per match [1], meaning the vast majority of game time is spent off-ball. During this period, players perform various actions that directly influence the flow of the game, including creating space, positioning appropriately, and preparing defensively. Therefore, to accurately understand the success and build-up of attacks, it is crucial to quantitatively assess players' off-ball contributions.

Second, conventional evaluation models are often biased toward mathematical formulas and statistical methods. While these approaches offer objectivity, they may differ from the nuanced judgments made by experienced analysts and coaches, who take into account the overall flow of play and players' intentions. Thus, achieving more human-like evaluation requires a novel approach that directly incorporates expert knowledge into the model. However, such attempts have not been sufficiently explored.

Given these backgrounds, this study aims to comprehensively evaluate players' off-ball contributions to attacking phases by considering human judgment processes. Figure 1 illustrates the overall framework of this study. To this end, we construct an evaluation dataset and develop a machine learning model specifically designed for this purpose. Specifically, we build the evaluation dataset by combining graph-structured sequence data derived from tracking data—including player and ball positions—and expert evaluation data based on event data recording actions such as passes and shots. Using this dataset as a training signal, we develop a player evaluation model based on an architecture that integrates Graph Convolutional Networks (GCN) and Long Short-Term Memory (LSTM) networks, enabling simultaneous capture of player interactions and temporal changes in play. Additionally, by varying input features and evaluation conditions, we analyze the model's behavior in detail to verify its validity.

This approach offers a new perspective focused on off-ball player contributions, which have been insufficiently evaluated so far, aiming to realize highly interpretable player evaluations by considering the context of play. Moreover, the dataset consists of actual match plays by professional players in the J. League in Japan, where the overall quality of play is high and occurrences of clearly "Negative" plays are rare. Therefore, this study places particular emphasis on accurately evaluating and detecting "good" plays.

The structure of this paper is as follows. Section 2 discusses related work. Section 3 explains the construction method of the off-ball player evaluation dataset. Section 4 describes the development of the machine learning model for player evaluation, and Sect. 5 presents the evaluation experiments. Finally, Sect. 6 summarizes the study and discusses future challenges.

2 Related Work

In the field of player evaluation in soccer, numerous approaches have focused primarily on actions performed while in possession of the ball (on-ball actions). A representative example is the Expected Goals (xG) model [2], which is widely used as a framework to quantify a player's contribution to scoring based on the estimated probability of a shot resulting in a goal. Approaches that further advance the evaluation of on-ball actions include VAEP (Valuing Actions by Estimating Probabilities) [3], deep reinforcement learning-based methods that learn action value functions [4], and models that quantify the risk and return of passes [5,6]. These methods utilize event data or tracking data to analyze how a player's decisions contribute to the creation of scoring opportunities. They have also been applied in practice through visualization of evaluation results and the generation of player rankings [7,8].

On the other hand, efforts to quantify off-ball contributions—those made while not in possession of the ball—have also advanced in recent years. Off-ball movements, such as securing passing lanes, creating space, or covering defensively, are closely tied to tactical contexts, yet traditional metrics have struggled to visualize such contributions. For instance, indirect contributions that are not captured by models like expected goals have been highlighted as critical [9]. In response, several methods have been proposed, including trajectory prediction approaches to evaluate a player's positioning and its impact on creating scoring opportunities [10], models that quantify player availability based on pass feasibility [11], and statistical models focusing on space creation [1].

Furthermore, integrated evaluation methods that consider both on-ball and off-ball contributions have emerged. For example, the Regularized Adjusted Plus-Minus (RAPM) model [12] estimates a player's overall impact—regardless of ball possession—by analyzing how their presence influences the team's goal difference. Approaches using Multi-Agent Deep Reinforcement Learning have also been proposed [13], where the entire match state is used as input to dynamically learn the action value of all players. Similarly, causality-based methods [14] offer a framework to quantify the causal effect of specific players or actions on team performance by comparing actual and counterfactual outcomes, enabling comprehensive contribution analysis across both on-ball and off-ball contexts. In addition, practical tools such as Action-Evaluator [7], which visualizes and compares the impact of player actions, and machine learning-based evaluation models like PlayeRank [8], designed for generating player rankings, are actively being developed with real-world application in mind.

These studies have contributed to enabling objective assessments of player performance by quantitatively measuring individual contributions. However, in actual match settings, subjective impressions and tactical contexts significantly influence player evaluations by coaches and analysts. Current models have yet to be sufficiently validated in terms of how well they align with such human cognition and expert judgment.

In light of this context, the present study aims to construct an evaluation model capable of quantitatively estimating off-ball player contributions in a manner consistent with expert subjective assessments. Leveraging positional and movement data obtained from tracking systems, we design predictive models from both regression and classification perspectives and verify their effectiveness.

3 Construction of the Off-Ball Player Evaluation Dataset

In this study, we utilize tracking data and event data from the 2023 Meiji Yasuda J1 League season provided by Data Stadium Inc. These data consist of time-series recorded at a sampling rate of 25 Hz. The tracking data includes the coordinate information of the players on the field and the ball, while the event data records actions such as passes and shots. It is possible to align these two datasets frame by frame.

3.1 Creation of Attack Sequences

In this study, we create attack sequences, which are then converted into graph sequences to form the input data for player evaluation. The procedure for creating attack sequences is described below.

Successful pass events are extracted from the event data, and the position data within the preceding 8 s are obtained from the tracking data to define a single attack sequence. During this process, the data are downsampled to 5 Hz, converting each attack sequence into a time series of 40 frames (8 s $\times$ 5 Hz).

3.2 Graph Representation of Attack Sequences

In this study, we propose representing the match situation in each frame of an attack sequence as a graph, where the nodes correspond to the ball or players, and the edges represent relationships between the ball and players or between players themselves.

Each node includes the following seven attributes:

1. x: the x-coordinate value,
2. y: the y-coordinate value,
3. v_x: velocity component in the x-direction,
4. v_y: velocity component in the y-direction,
5. speed: movement speed,
6. id: an id indicating the attacking team, defending team, or the ball,
7. zoneid: an id representing the area in which the player is located (ranging from 0 to 29).

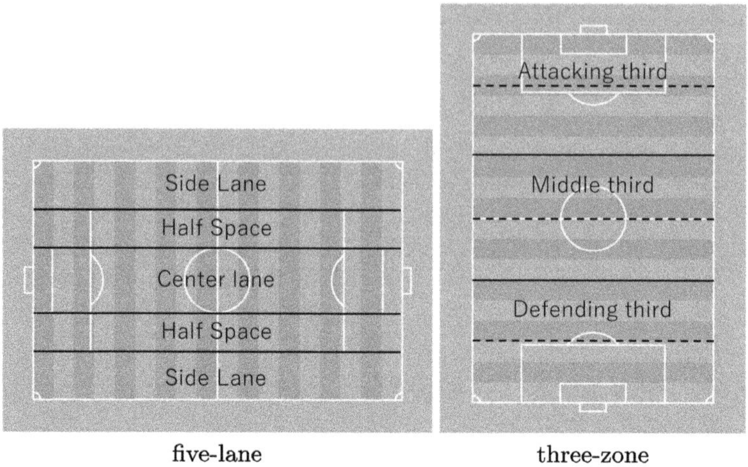

Fig. 2. Overview of zoneid

The zoneid feature is introduced to provide the model with the tactical context of a player's absolute position on the field. Specifically, the field is divided into 30 discrete areas based on the commonly used "five-lane" and "three-zone" principles in soccer tactics, as illustrated in Fig. 2. This division is achieved by further splitting each of the three horizontal zones defined by the three-zone principle into two subzones, resulting in a 5×6 grid. Each area is assigned a unique ID from 0 to 29, which is used as the player's zoneid. Since this ID represents categorical information, it is encoded as a 30-dimensional one-hot vector when used as input to the model.

Regarding edges, the following three types are defined:

Ball – On-ball Player:
Connects the ball node with the player currently in possession of the ball.

Attacking Player – Attacking Player:
Edges are constructed between attacking players based on pass availability. Specifically, assuming each attacking player has the ball, edges are added to all other attacking players who could receive a pass from them. This expresses the relationships and coordination among attacking players.

Attacking Player – Defending Player:
Edges are constructed between attacking and defending players based on defensive pressure. Using a pressure model [15], edges are added from each defending player to all attacking players estimated to be under non-zero pressure. This represents the influence exerted by defenders.

By converting each frame into a graph in this manner, the entire attack sequence is transformed into a sequence of graphs.

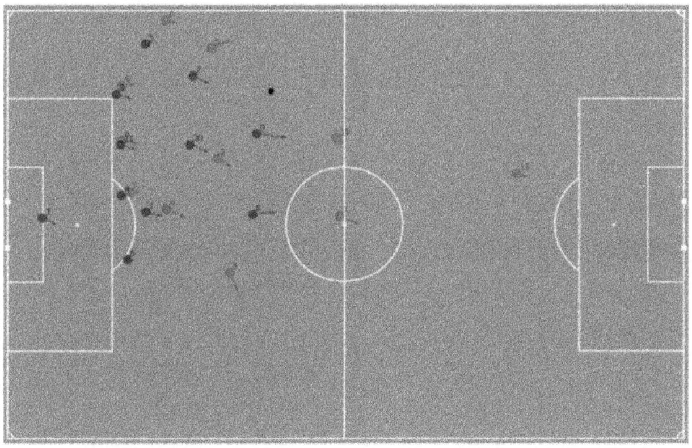

Fig. 3. Screenshot of the visualization tool

Table 1. Distribution of evaluation scores

Evaluation Score	Percentage
Positive (+1)	14.53%
Neutral (0)	80.90%
Negative (−1)	4.50%

3.3 Construction of the Player Evaluation Dataset

In this study, each attack sequence was presented to an expert, who annotated the quality of off-ball movements of all 11 attacking players throughout the sequence. The evaluation was conducted on a three-level scale: "Positive (+1)", "Neutral (0)", and "Negative (−1)".

For presenting the attack sequences, a simple visualization tool shown in Fig. 3 was developed. In the figure, the black dot represents the ball, red and blue dots represent players, and arrows indicate the direction and speed of player movement.

Following this procedure, annotations were conducted by one expert on 872 attack sequences from three matches, resulting in the construction of the dataset. The distribution of evaluation scores is shown in Table 1.

"Neutral (0)" category accounts for approximately 81% of the data, indicating a significant class imbalance. In particular, the "Negative (−1)" category accounts for only 4.5%, which is likely due to the fact that the dataset consists of professional players in the J1 League whose quality of play is maintained at a certain level. The "Positive (+1)" category also accounts for only 14.5%, and such an imbalanced distribution can adversely affect the accuracy of machine learning models in identifying "Positive" plays. Therefore, learning strategies that emphasize samples containing "Positive" plays are necessary.

Table 2. Reliability of Annotation Data

	Cohen's Kappa	Accuracy	Recall	Precision
Evaluator 1				
Overall	0.45	0.87	0.66	0.69
Positive (+1)	0.43	0.89	0.55	0.44
Neutral (0)	0.43	0.87	0.91	0.94
Negative (−1)	0.59	0.98	0.60	0.60
Evaluator 2				
Overall	0.53	0.87	0.61	0.75
Positive (+1)	0.58	0.91	0.77	0.53
Neutral (0)	0.52	0.87	0.89	0.96
Negative (−1)	0.41	0.96	0.60	0.33

3.4 Quantitative Evaluation of the Player Evaluation Dataset

To assess the reliability of the dataset, two soccer coaches, different from the expert who performed the original annotation, annotated 20 attack sequences using the same evaluation criteria. Cohen's Kappa coefficient, accuracy, recall, and precision were calculated. The results are shown in Table 2.

Compared with Evaluator 1, a moderate agreement was obtained with a Cohen's Kappa of 0.45, and accuracy was also high at 0.87. Particularly for the "Neutral (0)" category, recall and precision were very high at 0.91 and 0.94, respectively. On the other hand, for the "Positive (+1)" category, both recall and precision were somewhat lower.

Compared with Evaluator 2, the Cohen's Kappa was higher at 0.53, indicating better agreement than with Evaluator 1. The "Neutral (0)" category consistently showed high accuracy with recall of 0.89 and precision of 0.96. Conversely, the "Negative (−1)" category showed low precision of 0.33, and for the "Positive (+1)" category, recall was 0.77 while precision remained limited at 0.53.

These results suggest that the constructed dataset shows moderate agreement on basic evaluations among experts, while also reflecting variability due to subjective factors such as individual tactical perspectives and expectations of players.

3.5 Dataset Augmentation

The performance of deep learning models heavily depends on the quantity and diversity of the training data. However, creating annotated data by experts incurs high costs, which limits the amount of available data. Training models with limited data risks overfitting to specific patterns, resulting in degraded performance on unseen data.

Therefore, in this study, aiming to improve the model's generalization ability and build a more robust evaluation model, we introduce the following three data augmentation techniques:

Mirroring (horizontal flipping):
Since a soccer pitch is horizontally symmetrical, a certain play pattern can be considered tactically equivalent to its horizontally flipped counterpart. Utilizing this property, we generate horizontally symmetric data by flipping the sign of all players' y coordinates and v_y (velocity component in the y direction). This enables the model to learn that attacks from either side are essentially the same pattern.

Time shifting:
Attack sequences are generated from high-frequency time-series data by downsampling. Time shifting is a method that produces slightly different sequences by shifting the start frame of the sampling. Specifically, by shifting the sampling start position by two frames forward or backward, different versions of the same play are created.

Adding noise:
To enhance model robustness, noise is added to player coordinates. However, to minimize the impact on play evaluation, noise is only added to players who are at least 20 m away from the ball, and random noise of up to 50 cm is added to their x and y coordinates. By restricting both the distance of players and the magnitude of noise, this approach balances data diversity and label consistency.

An example of the graph representation of a frame within an attack sequence, along with its three augmentations, is shown in Fig. 4.

4 Construction of a Machine Learning-Based Evaluation Model

Expert evaluations of players are considered to be based on player positions during attacking sequences, interactions with the ball and other players, and the temporal evolution of these factors. In this study, we construct a machine learning model to estimate each player's contribution to the attack, using the graph sequence data defined in the previous section. Specifically, we employ a Graph Convolutional Network (GCN) to capture spatial relationships, a Long Short-Term Memory (LSTM) network to capture temporal dynamics, and a Multi-Layer Perceptron (MLP) to estimate the contribution scores of the 11 attacking players. The overall model architecture is illustrated in Fig. 5.

At each time step t, the model takes as input the graph-structured data $G_t = (V_t, E_t)$, and applies a GCN using the node feature matrix $X_t \in \mathbb{R}^{N \times F}$ and adjacency matrix $A_t \in \mathbb{R}^{N \times N}$ as follows:

$$H_t = \mathrm{GCN}(X_t, A_t) \tag{1}$$

Here, $N = 23$ denotes the number of nodes (22 players and the ball), F is the input feature dimension, and $H_t \in \mathbb{R}^{N \times D}$ represents the spatial feature matrix output by the GCN, with D being the output feature dimension. The GCN

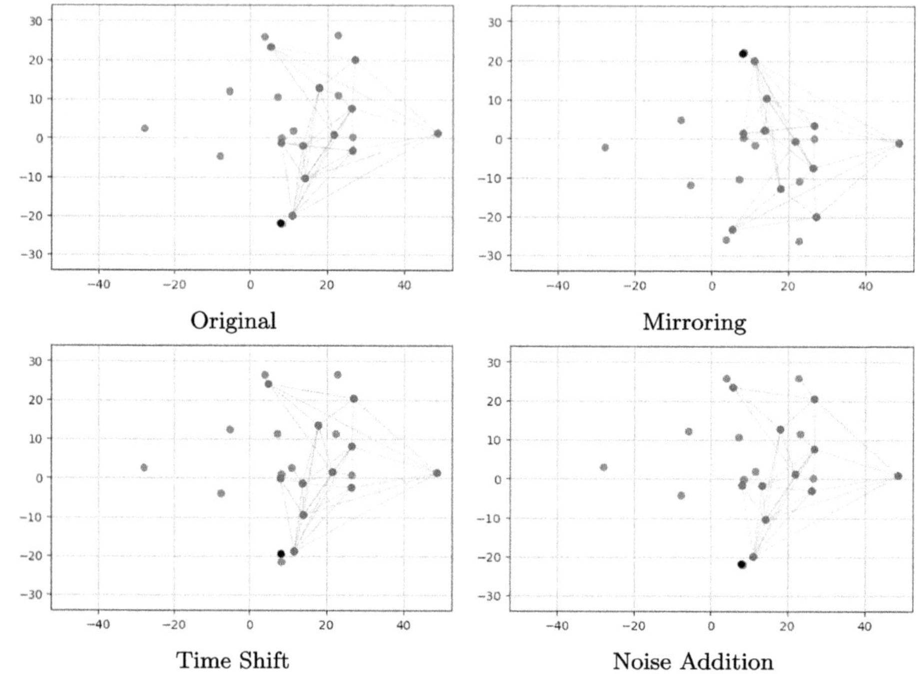

Fig. 4. Graph representation of an attack scene and its augmentations

consists of two layers, each followed by a ReLU activation function, and uses a normalized adjacency matrix with self-loops $\tilde{A}_t = A_t + I$. We set F to either 6 or 36, and D to 64.

From H_t, we extract and concatenate the feature vectors of the 11 attacking players to form a time-series representation of the attacking unit, denoted by $Z_{1:T}$:

$$Z_t = \text{Concat}(H_t^{(1)}, H_t^{(2)}, \dots, H_t^{(11)}) \in \mathbb{R}^{11D} \quad (2)$$

The sequence $Z_{1:T}$ is then input to a single-layer, unidirectional LSTM to model the temporal dynamics of the attacking sequence. The LSTM hidden state dimension is set to 128, and the hidden state at the final time step T, denoted

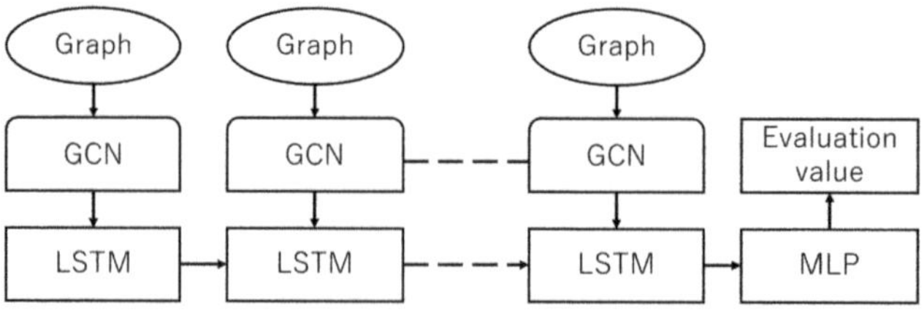

Fig. 5. Overview of the player evaluation model

$h_T \in \mathbb{R}^{128}$, is used as the overall representation of the attacking action:

$$h_T = \mathrm{LSTM}(Z_{1:T}) \tag{3}$$

Finally, the feature vector h_T is passed through an MLP to estimate the evaluation scores $y \in \mathbb{R}^{11}$ for the 11 attacking players:

$$y = \mathrm{MLP}(h_T) \tag{4}$$

The MLP first compresses the input to 64 dimensions using a ReLU activation function, and then applies a Tanh activation in the final layer to normalize the outputs to the range $[-1, 1]$. This normalization enables comparison of relative contribution scores across different attacking sequences.

5 Evaluation Experiments

5.1 Experimental Setup

To verify the extent to which the proposed evaluation score estimation model can reflect subjective aspects such as on-field judgments and human cognition regarding off-ball player evaluation, computational experiments were conducted. In the experiments, the expert-annotated evaluation scores were used as ground truth labels, and model performance was assessed based on consistency with these labels. The dataset was split into 70% training data, 15% validation data, and 15% test data. The model was trained using mean squared error (MSE) as the loss function, with a batch size of 16 and for 20 epochs.

The evaluation scores used in this study are on a three-level scale: "Positive (+1)", "Neutral (0)", and "Negative (−1)". However, the actual evaluation data exhibit an imbalanced distribution, with the majority of samples labeled as "Neutral (0)" and very few labeled as "Negative (−1)". In particular, since this study uses play data from professional J. League players, "Negative (−1)" plays are rare, and the occurrence of "Positive (+1)" plays is also limited. This imbalance may cause the model to be biased toward predicting "Neutral (0)" for most cases.

Therefore, this study focuses on improving the identification accuracy of "Positive (+1)" plays by introducing conditional training that limits the dataset to attack sequences containing at least one or two players with an evaluation score of 1. Specifically, three types of training conditions were established, and comparative experiments of the models were conducted under each condition:

Normal: Use all data.
Condition 1: Use only data containing at least one player with an evaluation score of 1.
Condition 2: Use only data containing at least two players with an evaluation score of 1.

Furthermore, to examine the impact of the spatial feature zoneid on performance, model training and evaluation were conducted under each condition both including and excluding the zoneid feature.

Table 3. Evaluation as a regression model

	MSE	MAE	R^2
with zoneid			
Normal	0.07	0.18	0.63
Condition 1	0.08	0.19	0.60
Condition 2	0.07	0.18	0.68
without zoneid			
Normal	0.08	0.19	0.59
Condition 1	0.07	0.17	0.68
Condition 2	0.07	0.17	0.69

5.2 Results and Discussion

The performance of the proposed model was evaluated by comparing the model outputs on the test data with expert evaluations. The evaluation was conducted in two ways: first, as a regression model producing continuous values; second, as a classification model by discretizing the outputs into three categories (Positive, Neutral, and Negative). Additionally, the impact of the imbalanced data distribution and the presence or absence of the zoneid spatial feature on performance were also examined and compared.

Evaluation as a Regression Model. The evaluation results as a regression model are shown in Table 3. The evaluation metrics used were Mean Squared Error (MSE), Mean Absolute Error (MAE), and the coefficient of determination (R^2).

Overall, the MSE and MAE values were relatively low, confirming that the model outputs continuous values close to the expert evaluations. The R^2 values ranged from 0.59 to 0.69, indicating that the proposed model can explain approximately 60âĂŞ70% of the variance in the expert evaluation scores.

When comparing the results by training conditions, the model trained under the "two or more players with a score of 1" condition achieved the highest R^2 of 0.69 in the case with zoneid included. This is considered to be because focusing the training on data containing multiple high-quality plays enabled the model to more accurately capture evaluation trends. Moreover, adding zoneid significantly improved the R^2 especially under the "one or more players with a score of 1" and "two or more players with a score of 1" conditions. This suggests that the positional information of players is an effective feature for identifying high-value plays.

Evaluation as a Classification Model. Next, the model outputs were discretized into three classes (1: Positive, 0: Neutral, −1: Negative), and the performance was evaluated as a classification task. Precision, Recall, and F1-score

Table 4. Evaluation as a Classification Model (overall)

	Precision	Recall	F1-score
with zoneid			
Normal	0.88	0.85	0.86
Condition 1	0.88	0.82	0.84
Condition 2	0.91	0.86	0.88
without zoneid			
Normal	0.83	0.84	0.84
Condition 1	0.88	0.86	0.87
Condition 2	0.89	0.87	0.88

Table 5. Evaluation as a Classification Model (Positive)

	Precision	Recall	F1-score
with zoneid			
Normal	0.86	0.84	0.85
Condition 1	0.85	0.84	0.85
Condition 2	0.89	0.86	0.88
without zoneid			
Normal	0.85	0.84	0.84
Condition 1	0.87	0.89	0.88
Condition 2	0.88	0.89	0.88

Table 6. Evaluation as a Classification Model (Neutral)

	Precision	Recall	F1-score
with zoneid			
Normal	0.96	0.97	0.96
Condition 1	0.95	0.96	0.95
Condition 2	0.95	0.96	0.95
without zoneid			
Normal	0.96	0.95	0.96
Condition 1	0.96	0.96	0.96
Condition 2	0.95	0.96	0.96

Table 7. Evaluation as a Classification Model (Negative)

	Precision	Recall	F1-score
with zoneid			
Normal	0.82	0.73	0.77
Condition 1	0.85	0.64	0.73
Condition 2	0.89	0.74	0.81
without zoneid			
Normal	0.69	0.74	0.72
Condition 1	0.82	0.72	0.76
Condition 2	0.85	0.76	0.80

were used as evaluation metrics. The results are presented for the overall data in Table 4 as well as for each class separately in Table 5, 6 and 7.

The overall F1 scores ranged from 0.84 to 0.88, confirming that the proposed model performs effectively in the classification task as well. In particular, under the condition of "two or more players with a score of 1", the highest F1 score of 0.88 was recorded regardless of the presence or absence of zoneid.

For the "Neutral" class (Table 6), the F1 scores were very high at 0.95 to 0.96, indicating stable identification of the majority class. For the "Positive" class (Table 5), F1 scores were also favorable, ranging from 0.84 to 0.88, and cases were observed where the precision improved up to 0.89 by adding zoneid. This suggests that spatial information serves as an effective cue for distinguishing "Positive" plays.

On the other hand, for the "Negative" class (Table 7), the F1 scores ranged from 0.72 to 0.81, which were lower compared to other classes. This is considered to be due to the imbalance caused by the extremely small amount of data labeled as −1. Notably, the F1 score improved when the model was trained under the condition of "two or more players with a score of 1". This suggests that by learning the characteristics of "Positive" plays, the differences from "Negative" plays became clearer, leading to improved discrimination accuracy.

However, cases were observed where adding zoneid led to a decrease in precision, indicating that the effect of zoneid on identifying "Negative" plays may be limited.

From the above results, it was demonstrated that the proposed model can accurately reproduce expert evaluations in both regression and classification tasks. In particular, training focused on data containing high-value plays, such as those with "two or more players rated 1", was shown to be effective in improving predictive performance. Furthermore, while the inclusion of zoneid proved useful for identifying "Positive" plays, its effect on recognizing "Negative" plays was limited.

Future work should aim to mitigate the impact of data imbalance by introducing modifications to the loss function and implementing balancing techniques, thereby enhancing the discrimination accuracy for "Negative" plays.

6 Conclusion

In this study, we constructed a model to quantitatively evaluate the offensive contributions of off-ball players using tracking and event data of professional players from the J. League. By representing offensive sequences as graph series along the time axis and designing an architecture that integrates Graph Convolutional Networks with Long Short-Term Memory, we proposed a method that simultaneously captures both spatial and temporal features.

The evaluation data was constructed based on expert annotations; however, a significant imbalance in label distribution was observed, with "Neutral (0)" accounting for approximately 81% of the data, "Positive (+1)" for 14%, and "Negative (−1)" for only about 4.5%. This skew is believed to stem from the high level of play characteristic of professional players in the J1 League.

To address this imbalance, conditional learning was introduced, limiting training data to attacking sequences containing at least one or two players with a "Positive (+1)" evaluation. The model's performance was then evaluated on both classification and regression tasks. Results confirmed that training under these conditions improved the prediction accuracy of the model. Additionally, incorporating spatial features such as zoneid was found to particularly enhance the model's ability to identify "Positive (+1)" plays. Conversely, due to the scarcity of "Negative (−1)" plays, the identification accuracy for this class was relatively low, and the effect of including zoneid was limited.

Future challenges include the incorporation of play data from a wider range of skill levels, strengthening the annotation system to improve the reliability of evaluation labels, and the introduction of loss functions and data augmentation techniques capable of handling imbalanced data. Through these efforts, it is expected that a player evaluation model with greater reliability and generalizability can be realized.

Acknowledgment. This research utilized J. League tracking data and event data provided by Data Stadium Co., Ltd. This work was partially supported by JSPS KAKENHI Grant Number 22K12173.

References

1. Fernández, J., Bornn, L.: Wide open spaces: a statistical technique for measuring space creation in professional soccer. In: Proceedings of 12th MIT Sloan Sports Analytics Conference, pp. 1–19 (2018)
2. Robberechts, P., Davis, J.: How data availability affects the ability to learn good XG models. In: Proceedings of 7th International Workshop on Machine Learning Data Mining Sports Analytics, Ghent, Belgium, pp. 17–27 (2020)
3. Decroos, T., Bransen, L., Van Haaren, J., Davis, J.: Actions speak louder than goals: valuing player actions in soccer. In: Proceedings of 25th ACM SIGKDD International Conference on Knowledge Discovery Data Mining, pp. 1851–1861 (2019)
4. Liu, G., Luo, Y., Schulte, O., Kharrat, T.: Deep soccer analytics: learning an action-value function for evaluating soccer players. Data Min. Knowl. Discov. **34**(5), 1531–1559 (2020)
5. Goes, F.R., Kempe, M., Meerhoff, L.A., Lemmink, K.A.P.M.: Not every pass can be an assist: a data-driven model to measure pass effectiveness in professional soccer matches. Big Data **7**(1), 57–70 (2019)
6. Power, P., Ruiz, H., Wei, X., Lucey, P.: Not all passes are created equal: objectively measuring the risk and reward of passes in soccer from tracking data. In: Proceedings of 23rd ACM SIGKDD International Conference on Knowledge Discovery Data Mining, pp. 1605–1613. Halifax, Canada (2017)
7. Cao, A., Xie, X., Zhou, M., Zhang, H., Xu, M., Wu, Y.: ActionEvaluator: a visualization approach for player action evaluation in soccer. IEEE Trans. Vis. Comput. Graph. **30**(1), 880–890 (2024)
8. Pappalardo, L., Cintia, P., Ferragina, P., Massucco, E., Pedreschi, D., Giannotti, F.: PlayeRank: data-driven performance evaluation and player ranking in soccer via a machine learning approach. ACM Trans. Intell. Syst. Technol. **10**(5), 1–27 (2019)
9. Spearman, W.: Beyond expected goals. In: Proceedings of 12th MIT Sloan Sports Analutics Conference, pp. 1–17 (2018)
10. Teranishi, M., Tsutsui, K., Takeda, K., Fujii, K.: Evaluation of creating scoring opportunities for teammates in soccer via trajectory prediction. In: Proceedings of International Workshop Machine Learning Data Mining Sports Analytics, pp.. 53–73. Springer, Cham (2022)
11. Dick, U., Link, D., Brefeld, U.: Who can receive the pass? A computational model for quantifying availability in soccer. Data Min. Knowl. Discov. **36**(3), 987–1014 (2022)
12. Bajons, R., Hornik, K.: Regularized adjusted plus-minus models for evaluating and scouting football (soccer) players using possession sequences. arXiv preprint arXiv:2407.17832 (2024)
13. Nakahara, H., Tsutsui, K., Takeda, K., Fujii, K.: Action valuation of on- and off-ball soccer players based on multi-agent deep reinforcement learning. IEEE Access **11**, 131237–131244 (2023)

14. Cecchin, A.: A new performance metric for player evaluation based on causality. In: Proceedings of StatsBomb Conference (2022)
15. Herold, M., et al.: Off-ball behavior in association football: a data-driven model to measure changes in individual defensive pressure. J. Sports Sci. **40**(12), 1412–1425 (2022)

Optimizing Urban Commercial Landscapes with POI Strategic Group Analysis: A Meta-learning Hypergraph Approach

Jiaqi Jiang[1], Xin Lin[1], Jiahui Jin[1(✉)], Siyuan Huang[2], Haoyu Chen[1], and Xigang Sun[1]

[1] School of Computer Science and Engineering, Southeast University, Nanjing 211189, China
{xin_l,jjin,xigangsun}@seu.edu.cn

[2] College of Software Engineering, Southeast University, Nanjing 211189, China
siyuanhuang@seu.edu.cn

Abstract. The rapid growth of urban data presents significant opportunities for optimizing resource allocation and economic strategies, yet traditional strategic group analysis overlooks location-specific factors crucial for urban planning. We focus on POI-level strategic group analysis, leveraging semantic and spatial information. However, modeling multi-dimensional strategic relationships is challenging and is further hindered by the limited availability of labeled data. To address these issues, we propose a novel framework, the Hypergraph Conditional Neural Process (HCNP). We represent POI relationships using a heterogeneous urban hypergraph, where strategic group interactions are formulated as hyperedges connecting similar POIs. Additionally, we enhance the meta-learning process with auxiliary tasks to improve performance in sparse data settings. Experiments on three city-wide datasets validate the effectiveness of our approach, offering valuable insights for urban planning and sustainable economic growth.

Keywords: Point of interest (POI) relationship mining · Hypergraph conditional neural processes · Meta-learning

1 Introduction

Recently, the surge in urban data has created new opportunities for more efficient resource allocation and the optimization of regional economic development strategies, all in an effort to reach the goals of sustainable urban development. Based on the in-depth exploration of urban data, strategic group analysis plays a significant role in both urban planning and economic development. As illustrated in Fig. 1, a strategic group comprises entities sharing similar market positioning, target customers, and value propositions, as exemplified by fast-food brands that can be clustered into distinct competitive groups based on multiple dimensions including customer preferences, geographic distribution, and price range. By

T. Hao et al. (Eds.): BESC 2025, LNCS 16431, pp. 219–235, 2026.
https://doi.org/10.1007/978-981-95-7138-3_15

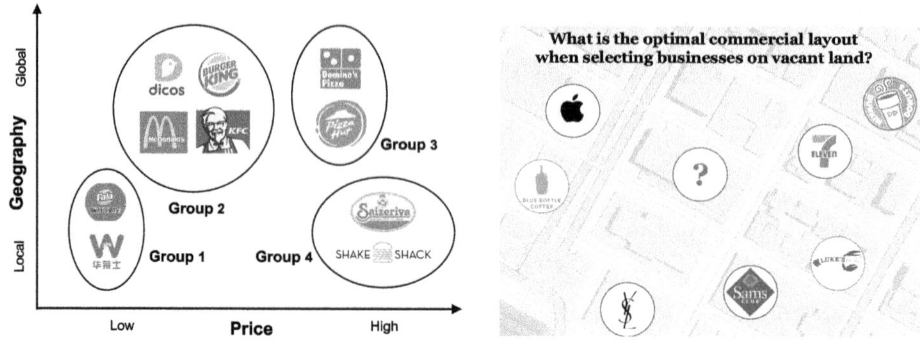

Fig. 1. Example of brand strategic groups (left), and the application of POI strategic group analysis in urban planning (right).

analyzing the strategic groups, planners can determine the areas where certain types of businesses are concentrated and the resources they require, avoiding resource wastage or incompatible land use clustering. For example, as shown in Fig. 1, when selecting businesses for development on vacant land, analyzing strategic groups nearby can provide insights into more optimal commercial layouts, thereby fostering the sustainable development of regional economies.

Conventional strategic group analysis has primarily focused on brand-level interactions, yet these methods often fall short in providing practical guidance for real-world scenarios, such as business selection for vacant land, due to their limited consideration of location and surrounding contexts. The growing collection of Point of Interest (POI) data provides detailed insights into a brand's semantic characteristics and target customers at specific locations, offering a more refined understanding of business strategy. It allows for a more detailed analysis of strategic groups at the POI level, offering tailored solutions for regional planning.

Despite this potential, two key challenges are yet to be addressed in POI strategic group analysis. Firstly, modeling multi-dimensional strategic group relationships across geographic space is considerately complex, requiring the integration of diverse factors such as spatial distribution, customer behavior, and business characteristics. We can see from Fig. 1 that while competition exists in all fast-food establishments, the nature and intensity of strategic group relationships vary significantly across different groups. The modeling of POI groups through multiple dimensions and their varied strategic nature poses substantial challenges. While existing studies have investigated POI relationship inference, their focus has largely been limited to pairwise competition [3,12,13], failing to adequately capture group-level strategic dynamics. Second, the scarcity of labeled training data poses obstacles to learn the inherent patterns between the strategic groups. This limitation is due to two main factors, including the high cost of manpower in data collection and the limited availability of data from local brands operating at smaller scales.

To address the above challenges, we model the multi-relational POI structure in a heterogeneous urban hypergraph and represent strategic group relationships as hyperedges connecting POIs that share similarities across multiple dimensions. Subsequently, the POI competitive strategic group discovery problem is formulated as a hyperedge prediction task. To capture the complex multi-dimensional relationships between POIs in data-sparse scenarios, we propose a novel meta-learning model based on **H**ypergraph **C**onditional **N**eural **P**rocess (HCNP) for discovering POI competitive strategic groups. Our model learns competitive strategic group distributions from limited labeled data using a neural network conditioned on existing observations, while the meta-training process with auxiliary tasks captures shared knowledge to improve few-shot performance.

Overall, the key contributions of our work are summarized as follows:

- A novel formulation of POI-level competitive strategic group discovery using hypergraphs to model higher-order relationships.
- A meta-learning-based HCNP framework that automatically discovers competitive relationships within hypergraph neighborhoods, addressing the challenge of sparse labeling through auxiliary tasks.
- Comprehensive validation on three real-world city-wide datasets, demonstrating the effectiveness of our HCNP in practical few-shot scenarios.

2 Related Work

2.1 POI Relationship Prediction

As noted by [3,12,13,23], previous studies focus on pairwise POI relationship prediction using attribute similarity in a graph, suggesting that more similar POIs are likely competitors. DeepR [13] uses a heterogeneous POI network with spatially adaptive graph convolution, while PRIM [3] employs a weighted GNN and spatial context extractor for multi-type POI relationships. SEENET [12] introduces a spatially evolving GNN to study dynamic location relationships, integrating temporal and geographic factors. However, these methods rely on pairwise POI construction, which is computationally expensive and unsuitable for POI competitive group discovery.

Additionally, recent studies [10] have started to explore competitive relationships among groups of POIs, employing hypergraphs to model higher-order relationships between POIs [21]. [10] introduced a query-driven multi-hop attention hypergraph learning framework, namely EAGLE, which demonstrated higher efficiency in POI competitive group discovery compared to previous models. Nevertheless, EAGLE struggles with sparse competitive group labels, leading to a significant decline in accuracy in few-shot scenarios.

2.2 Few-Shot Graph Learning

Recent works [2,11,15,17–19,24] leverage GNNs for tasks like node and graph classification, utilizing message passing to classify unseen graph data. In few-shot learning, GNNs can be integrated with meta-learning [8,16,20,22] to swiftly

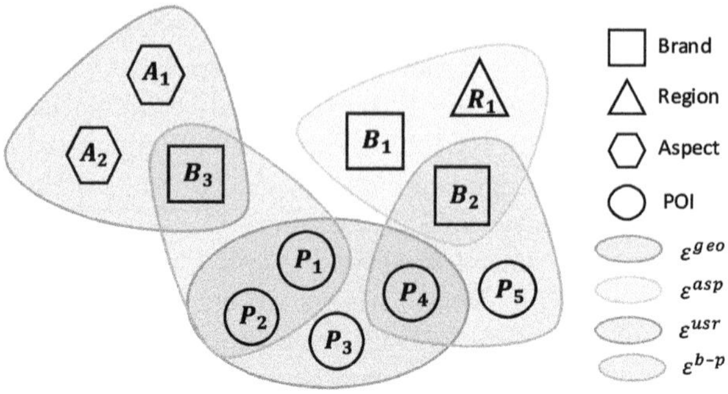

Fig. 2. Urban hypergraph schema.

adapt models by learning shared prior knowledge across tasks, thereby enhancing the model's generalization performance on new tasks.

Meta-learning approaches are mainly categorized as optimization-based and metric-based. Optimization-based methods like MAML [8], optimize model parameters during meta-learning to enable rapid adaptation to new tasks. Metric-based methods, such as GPN [5], calculate prototypes for each class by averaging the representations of the support set and predict based on query-prototype distances. Nonetheless, they require high-quality samples and balanced positive and negative instances. Besides, research [6] applies conditional neural process (CNP) to graph data, leveraging implicit kernel functions and distance functions to learn the probability distribution of graph generation, addressing the few-shot problem in graph-level community search.

In summary, existing works mainly adopt meta-learning approaches for few-shot graph tasks, which are often scenario-specific and lack a fully end-to-end paradigm for the scenario in this paper.

3 Preliminaries

Definition 1 (Urban Data). The set of POIs in an urban is denoted as $\mathcal{P}=\{p_1,\ldots,p_{|\mathcal{P}|}\}$, where each POI is associated with a geo-coordinates $loc=(lon, lat)$ which belongs to a region $r \in \mathcal{R}, \mathcal{R}=\{r_1,\ldots,r_{|\mathcal{R}|}\}$. The regions are defined as enclosed spaces within the city. Besides, each POI has multiple attributes, such as its category $\mathcal{C}=\{c_1,\ldots,c_{|\mathcal{C}|}\}$, the brand $\mathcal{B}=\{b_1,\ldots,b_{|\mathcal{B}|}\}$ it belongs to, and the products/services $\mathcal{A}=\{a_1,\ldots,a_{|\mathcal{A}|}\}$ offered by the brand.

Definition 2 (Brand Strategic Groups). A brand strategic group $\mathcal{S}$ is a subset of brands with similar business strategies, i.e. $\mathcal{S} \subseteq \mathcal{B}$. Since a brand can provide multiple products or services, it may belong to several different strategic groups from various business strategy perspectives. For instances, $\{\mathcal{S}_1,\ldots,\mathcal{S}_m\}$ all include brand b.

Brand strategic groups are typically based on commercial reports considering factors like foot traffic, location, and pricing. However, these reports are often

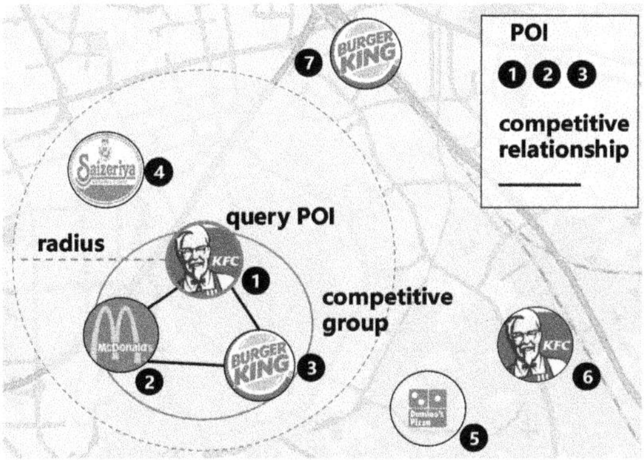

Fig. 3. Illustration of strategic group discovery issues.

incomplete for accurately identifying POI strategic groups. To overcome this, we propose a machine learning approach that uses hypergraphs to model higher-order relationships among POIs, capturing both brand and user similarities. This transforms the identification of strategic groups into a hyperedge prediction problem. Definitions are provided below.

An urban hypergraph is defined as $\mathcal{G}=(\mathcal{V},\mathcal{E})$, where the node set $\mathcal{V}$ contains entity nodes or attribute nodes such as region $\mathcal{R}$, POI $\mathcal{P}$, brand $\mathcal{B}$, and product service $\mathcal{A}$ in the city, i.e. $\mathcal{V} = \mathcal{R} \cup \mathcal{P} \cup \mathcal{B} \cup \mathcal{A}$. As shown in Fig. 2, the set of hyperedges $\mathcal{E}$ includes four types of hyperedges: co-region hyperedges $\mathcal{E}^{geo}$, co-visit hyperedges $\mathcal{E}^{usr}$, brand-affiliation hyperedges $\mathcal{E}^{b\text{-}p}$, along with co-service hyperedges $\mathcal{E}^{asp}$, which correspond to four dimensions of higher-order relationships, i.e., $\mathcal{E} = \mathcal{E}^{geo} \bigcup \mathcal{E}^{usr} \bigcup \mathcal{E}^{b\text{-}p} \bigcup \mathcal{E}^{asp}$.

Specifically, each hyperedge connects nodes that satisfy specific constraints. As shown in Fig. 2, two brands, B_1 and B_2, located in the same region R, form a co-region hyperedge $\mathcal{E}^{geo}$. Similarly, brands B_2 and B_3 offering products A_1 and A_2 create a co-service hyperedge $\mathcal{E}^{asp}$, while brand B_3 and its affiliated POIs P_3 and P_4 form a brand-affiliation hyperedge $\mathcal{E}^{b\text{-}p}$. Additionally, POIs P_1 and P_2 visited by the same user group form a co-visit hyperedge $\mathcal{E}^{usr}$.

Problem Statement (POI Strategic Group Discovery): Given an urban hypergraph $\mathcal{G}$ and a query POI $q \in \mathcal{P}$, within the perception radius ra of q, and based on the POI type, a candidate set of POIs $\mathcal{K}_q$ can be determined, as shown in Fig. 3. Thus, strategic group discovery of POIs aims to identify the set of POIs $C_q \in \mathcal{K}_q$, that belong to the same strategic group as query q, ensuring that the brands corresponding to the POIs within this set are in the same strategic group as query q. This process involves learning a scoring function $f_{\mathcal{G}}(\boldsymbol{l}_q|q,\mathcal{K}_q) \rightarrow \{0,1\}^{|\mathcal{K}_q|}$, where $\boldsymbol{l}_q \in \{0,1\}^{|\mathcal{K}_q|}$ is the ground truth vector for query q. Each entry in this vector indicates whether the corresponding candidate POI in $\mathcal{K}_q$ belongs to the true strategic group of q.

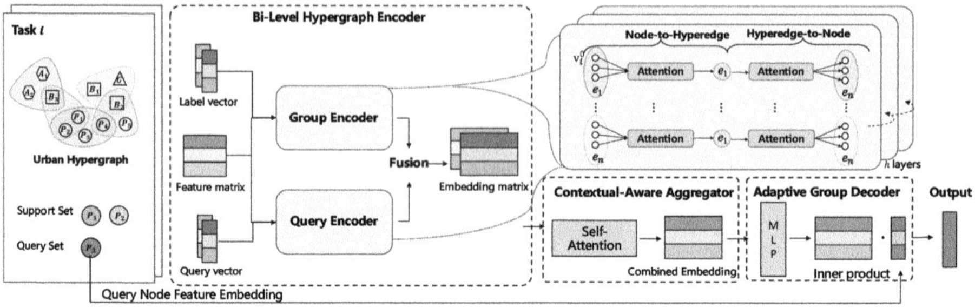

Fig. 4. The Architecture of HCNP.

4 Methodology

4.1 Overview

To address the challenge of few-shot strategic group discovery in urban hypergraphs, we propose the HCNP model, a meta-learning framework with an encoder-decoder architecture. HCNP is designed to capture the distribution of strategic groups across diverse tasks by leveraging shared prior knowledge, thereby enhancing generalization to new tasks. The HCNP model consists of three components: a Bi-Level Hypergraph Encoder ϕ_θ, a Contextual-Aware Aggregator $\bigoplus$, and an Adaptive Group Decoder ψ_θ. The overall architecture of HCNP is illustrated in Fig. 4.

For a POI strategic group discovery task $\mathcal{T} = (\mathcal{Q}, \mathcal{K}, \mathcal{L})$, a meta-model $\mathcal{M}$ directly models the probability prediction distribution $y(\hat{\boldsymbol{l}}_{q^*}|q^*, \mathcal{T})$ for a new query POI $q^* \in \mathcal{P}\backslash\mathcal{Q}$, where $\hat{\boldsymbol{l}}_{q^*} \in \{0,1\}^{|\mathcal{K}_{q^*}|}$ represents the binary classification predictions of the new query q^* for all candidate POIs in $\mathcal{K}_{q^*}$. In this work, we design an bi-level encoder ϕ_θ, which is an h-layer hypergraph attention network, to encode each combination of query q and its ground truth $\boldsymbol{l}_q$ in task $\mathcal{T}$, resulting in $|\mathcal{Q}|$ query-specific group feature matrices $\{\boldsymbol{H}_q\}_{q\in\mathcal{Q}}$. Then, we use operation $\bigoplus$ to aggregate features $\{\boldsymbol{H}_q\}_{q\in\mathcal{Q}}$ from each query POI, generating the group feature matrix $\boldsymbol{H}$ of task $\mathcal{T}$. Finally, combining the newly observed query q^* with the group feature $\boldsymbol{H}$, the decoder ψ_θ is used to generate the classification prediction $\hat{\boldsymbol{l}}_{q^*}$ for q^*. The overall process is as follows:

$$f(\hat{\boldsymbol{l}}_{q^*}|q^*, \mathcal{T}) = \psi_\theta\left(q^*, \bigoplus_{(q,\boldsymbol{l}_q)\in(\mathcal{Q},\mathcal{L})} \phi_\theta(q, \boldsymbol{l}_q)\right) \tag{1}$$

Meta-tasks Construction. We design the meta-model $\mathcal{M}$ to handle strategic group queries in an urban hypergraph $\mathcal{G}$, trained on a set of meta-tasks $\mathcal{D} = \{\mathcal{T}_i\}_{i=1}^N$, including strategic group discovery tasks and auxiliary tasks.

The discovery of strategic groups for each type of POI is viewed as a task $\mathcal{T} = (\mathcal{Q}, \mathcal{K}, \mathcal{L})$, where $\mathcal{Q} = \{q_1, \cdots, q_j | q_j \in \mathcal{P}\}$ denotes represents a set of j query POIs within $\mathcal{G}$. Since POIs that are too far apart are not influential, the search focuses on local candidate sets instead of the entire graph. $\mathcal{K}=\{\mathcal{K}_{q_1},\cdots,\mathcal{K}_{q_j}|\mathcal{K}_{q_j}\in\mathcal{P}\}$ denotes candidate sets of nearby POIs for each query POI based on geographic proximity. $\mathcal{L}=\{\boldsymbol{l}_{q_1},\cdots,\boldsymbol{l}_{q_j}\}$ is the ground truth of j query POIs, respectively.

Due to the scarcity of ground truth data for strategic groups, we construct an auxiliary task $\mathcal{T}^a$ with sufficient samples by treating a set of POIs with similar attribute features as an attribute group, thus assisting the model learning. The attribute group auxiliary task is represented as a triplet $\mathcal{T}^a=(\mathcal{Q},\mathcal{K}^a,\mathcal{L}^a)$, with methods for constructing the candidate attribute POI set $\mathcal{K}^a$ and attribute group groud-truth $\mathcal{L}^a$ detailed in Sect. 4.5.

4.2 Bi-level Hypergraph Encoder

To effectively capture the strategic group features of POIs in urban hypergraphs, we propose a bi-level hypergraph encoder that maps hypergraph nodes to embedding representations. This encoder operates at two levels: the group level and the query level, facilitating a unified embedding space for accurate group distribution prediction. Specifically, the bi-level encoder $\phi_\theta(q,\mathcal{G})$ comprises two components: the group encoder $\phi_\theta^G(q,\mathcal{G})$ for group-level feature extraction, and the query encoder $\phi_\theta^Q(q,\mathcal{G})$ for query-specific feature extraction.

Both components are implemented as h-layer hypergraph attention networks. Inspired by the two-stage message propagation mechanism in [10], our method incorporates a hypergraph attention network with a node-to-hyperedge attention mechanism and a hyperedge-to-node attention mechanism. Attention parameters $\boldsymbol{\alpha}_k^V$ and $\boldsymbol{\alpha}_r^E$ are assigned to k-type nodes and r-type hyperedges, respectively, ensuring that node and hyperedge types are distinctively weighted during propagation. The entire hypergraph feature extraction process is defined as:

$$\text{Hyper}(\boldsymbol{X}) = \text{EdgeToNode}(\text{NodeToEdge}(\boldsymbol{X},\boldsymbol{\alpha}_r^E),\boldsymbol{\alpha}_k^V), \tag{2}$$

where $\boldsymbol{X}\in\mathbb{R}^{|\mathcal{V}|\times d}$ is the input feature matrix, and d is the feature dimension. After message propagation, the output matrix Hyper($\boldsymbol{X}$) retains the same shape as the input, ensuring compatibility for subsequent tasks.

Both encoders propagate information within the neighborhood of node q in the urban hypergraph. Using $\mathcal{N}_q$ as defined in Eq. (3) to represent the K-hop neighbors of q and integrate various node types, including brands, regions, and labels, we initialize their feature vectors as $\boldsymbol{N}_q^p,\boldsymbol{N}_q^b,\boldsymbol{N}_q^l,\boldsymbol{N}_q^a$. Concatenate them row-wise to form the neighborhood feature matrix $\boldsymbol{N}_q=[\boldsymbol{N}_q^p,\boldsymbol{N}_q^b,\boldsymbol{N}_q^l,\boldsymbol{N}_q^a]\in\mathbb{R}^{|\mathcal{N}_q|\times d}$, with d as the unified feature dimension.

$$\mathcal{N}_q = \bigcup_{q\in\mathcal{K}_q} \mathcal{N}^K(q) \tag{3}$$

Group Encoder. The group encoder $\phi_\theta^G(q,\mathcal{G})$ takes the neighborhood feature matrix and the ground truth $\boldsymbol{l}_q$ of the target POI as inputs to the network, aiming to obtain a node feature matrix $\widetilde{\boldsymbol{N}}_q \in \mathbb{R}^{|\mathcal{N}_q| \times d}$ in the hypergraph space. Meanwhile, to model the distribution between inputs and outputs based on observational data, it is necessary to encode the target POI along with its ground truth during encoding. Hence, the output neighboring matrix of the group encoder is:

$$\widetilde{\boldsymbol{N}}_q^G = \text{Hyper}([\boldsymbol{l}_q \quad \boldsymbol{N}_q]) \tag{4}$$

Query Encoder. The query encoder $\phi_\theta^Q(q, \mathcal{G})$ indicates the query POI node in the urban hypergraph. Therefore, it is necessary to integrate information related to the query POI q into the neighborhood feature matrix $\boldsymbol{N}_q$. To better utilized the query-specific information, the query POI q is converted into a one-hot indicator vector $\boldsymbol{v}_q = \{0, 1\}^{|\mathcal{N}_q|}$. For each node $v_i \in \mathcal{N}_q$, if v_i shares common hyperedges with the query POI q, the corresponding element is set to 1; otherwise, it is set to 0, as defined in Eq. (5).

$$\boldsymbol{v}_{q,i} = \begin{cases} 1, & v_i \in \{b_q\} \cup \{r_q\} \cup \{a_q\} \\ 0, & \text{else} \end{cases} \tag{5}$$

Each element of $\boldsymbol{v}_q$ is concatenated to the beginning of the corresponding row of $\boldsymbol{N}_q$, forming the query feature matrix with fused information about the query POI. This matrix is then input into the urban hypergraph attention network to generate the target neighborhood matrix as follows:

$$\widetilde{\boldsymbol{N}}_q^Q = \text{Hyper}([\boldsymbol{v}_q \quad \boldsymbol{N}_q]) \tag{6}$$

Query-Specific Group Feature Fusion. Subsequently, two parts of the features are fused to obtain a neighborhood feature matrix $\widetilde{\mathcal{N}}_q$ of the urban hypergraph specific to the target POI q. Then, update feature matrix $\boldsymbol{X}$ of all nodes in the urban hypergraph utilizing $\widetilde{\mathcal{N}}_q$, resulting in the query-specific group feature matrix $\boldsymbol{H}_q$ from the view of the query POI q.

$$\widetilde{\boldsymbol{N}}_q = \text{Fusion}(\widetilde{\boldsymbol{N}}_q^G, \widetilde{\boldsymbol{N}}_q^Q), \quad \boldsymbol{H}_q = \text{Update}(\widetilde{\boldsymbol{N}}_q, \boldsymbol{X}) \tag{7}$$

4.3 Contextual-Aware Aggregator

To effectively adapt to new tasks, it is essential to leverage knowledge from previous tasks while integrating the unique contextual features of each query. This paper introduces a contextual-aware aggregation mechanism to construct a task-specific strategic group feature representation $\boldsymbol{H}$, serving as shared knowledge to enable robust distribution learning.

The aggregation process employs a self-attention mechanism to integrate query-specific features $\boldsymbol{H}_q$ from all queries in $\mathcal{Q}$, leveraging the structural context of the urban hypergraph $\mathcal{G}$. Each feature $\boldsymbol{H}_q$ is weighted by learnable attention weights w_q, producing the combined strategic group feature representation:

$$\boldsymbol{H} = \sum_{q \in \mathcal{Q}} w_q \boldsymbol{H}_q,$$

where $\{w_q\}_{q\in\mathcal{Q}} \in \mathbb{R}^{|\mathcal{Q}|}$ is shared across all node types in $\mathcal{G}$.

To compute w_q, the feature vectors $\boldsymbol{H}_q[v]$ of each node $v \in \mathcal{V}$ are extracted and concatenated across all query-specific matrices $\{\boldsymbol{H}_q\}_{q\in\mathcal{Q}}$:

$$\boldsymbol{H}_v = \{\boldsymbol{H}_q[v]\}_{q\in\mathcal{Q}} \in \mathbb{R}^{|\mathcal{Q}|\times d}.$$

Two learnable weight matrices, $\boldsymbol{W}_q, \boldsymbol{W}_k \in \mathbb{R}^{d_h\times d'}$, linearly transform $\boldsymbol{H}_v$, and the attention scores are computed as:

$$\{w_q\}_{q\in\mathcal{Q}} = \text{softmax}\left(\boldsymbol{H}_v\boldsymbol{W}_q(\boldsymbol{H}_v\boldsymbol{W}_k)^\top\right).$$

This attention-based mechanism ensures the aggregated features $\boldsymbol{H}$ capture both the contextual relationships among queries and hypergraph structural properties, making the representation highly task-specific and adaptable.

4.4 Adaptive Group Decoder

The objective of the decoder is to predict task-specific strategic group results from a shared strategic group distribution. Specifically, it generates the predicted probability distribution vector $y(\hat{\boldsymbol{l}}_{q^*}|q^*, \boldsymbol{H})$ for the candidate POI corresponding to the new query q^*.

To efficiently adapt to various meta-task focuses, we utilize a Multilayer Perceptron (MLP) as the decoder, enhancing adaptability by integrating additional transformations into the merged features $\boldsymbol{H}$. Initially, the decoder applies these transformations to $\boldsymbol{H}$, followed by feeding the transformed features into the inner-product operator. Compared to a naive inner-product encoder, this design introduces extra parameterization, improving the encoder's ability to model complex group relationships. The decoder is formulated as follows:

$$\hat{\boldsymbol{l}}_{q^*} = \text{MLP}(\boldsymbol{H}) = \text{softmax}(\boldsymbol{H}\boldsymbol{W} + \boldsymbol{b}) \tag{8}$$

4.5 Meta-training

In the following, we present detailed information to construct training samples for strategic group discovery tasks and auxiliary tasks. For strategic group tasks, positive samples are obtained from dataset. A negative sample is formed by replacing several POIs in positive ones with POIs from other groups, based on a predefined positive-to-negative sample ratio.

To construct auxiliary tasks, each POI is represented by an attribute vector $\mathcal{Z}=\{z_1, \cdots, z_j\}$ of equal length, and clustering divides the POI set into attribute clusters $\mathcal{P}(\mathcal{Z})$, serving as the ground truth for attribute groups. For a query POI q in cluster $\mathcal{C}_j$, we define a candidate set $\mathcal{K}_q$ centered on q with a radius ra, and the ground truth $\boldsymbol{l}_q$ is inferred from $\mathcal{C}_j$. This process generates a training instance $(q, \mathcal{K}_q, \boldsymbol{l}_q)$, which collectively define the auxiliary task $\mathcal{T}^a$:

$$\mathcal{T}^a = \bigcup_{\mathcal{C}_j\in\mathcal{P}(\mathcal{Z}),\ q\in\mathcal{C}_j} (q, \mathcal{K}_q, \boldsymbol{l}_q) = (\mathcal{Q}, \mathcal{K}^a, \mathcal{L}^a) \tag{9}$$

Table 1. Statistics of the datasets.

Data	NYC	HOU	LA
$\|\mathcal{P}\|$	73469	61942	59801
$\|\mathcal{B}\|$	4281	3724	2773
$\|\mathcal{R}\|$	645	799	412
$\|\mathcal{A}\|$	502	552	448
$\|\mathcal{E}^{geo}\|$	15243	13180	12998
$\|\mathcal{E}^{usr}\|$	19201	21674	19555
$\|\mathcal{E}^{asp}\|$	3345	2887	2832
$\|\mathcal{E}^{b\text{-}p}\|$	4274	3714	3740
GS	564	412	423
AS	8.13	9.23	11.28

Similar to MAML [8], for one training task $\mathcal{T}_i$, we divide the training dataset $\mathcal{Q}_i = \{q_j\}_{j=1}^{J}$ and $\mathcal{L}_i = \{\boldsymbol{l}_{q_j}\}_{j=1}^{J}$, into the support set $S_i' = \{(q_j, \boldsymbol{l}_{q_j})\}_{j=1}^{J'}$ and the query set $\mathcal{Q}_i' = \{(q_j, \boldsymbol{l}_{q_j})\}_{j=J'+1}^{J}$. Here, the superscript on the query set $\mathcal{Q}_i'$ is used primarily to distinguish it from the task's POI set $\mathcal{Q}_i$. The learning objective of meta-model $\mathcal{M}$ is to minimize the negative log-likelihood loss over the query set $\mathcal{Q}_i'$ conditioned on the support set S_i' across all tasks in $\mathcal{D}$:

$$\mathcal{L} = -\sum_{\mathcal{T}_i \in \mathcal{D}} \sum_{(q, \boldsymbol{l}_q) \in \mathcal{Q}'} \log f(\boldsymbol{l}_q | q, S_i') \tag{10}$$

5 Experiments

5.1 Experiment Settings

Datasets. Experiments are conducted on three real-world citywide datasets from New York City (NYC), Houston (HOU), and Los Angeles (LA). Detailed dataset information is provided in Table 1, where GS denotes the number of POI competitive strategic groups and AS represents the average POI group size. Each dataset consists of two components:

1) **Competitive POI Group Data**: Sourced from industry reports by IBISWorld https://www.ibisworld.com/ and brand-level market data from Statista https://www.statista.com/. This data maps competitive brand groups within a specified region to identify competitive POI groups.
2) **Spatial POI Perception Data**: Provided by SafeGraph https://www.safegraph.com/, this dataset includes POI attributes (brand, type, business district, product/service), passenger flow, and demographic information.

Baselines. To verify the effectiveness of the proposed model in POI strategic group discovery scenario with small samples, we compare it against three types of baseline methods:

Table 2. Experiment results on three cities.

Framework	Model	NYC				HOU				LA			
		1-shot		5-shot		1-shot		5-shot		1-shot		5-shot	
		F1	ΔF1	F1	ΔF1	F1	ΔF1	F1	ΔF1	F1	ΔF1	F1	ΔF1
MAML	DeepR	0.322	4.59%	0.328	6.31%	0.303	9.69%	0.307	11.10%	0.317	11.18%	0.321	12.60%
	PRIM	0.350	13.28%	0.342	10.63%	0.312	6.08%	0.311	5.86%	0.286	1.40%	0.283	0.26%
	SEENet	0.348	5.83%	0.352	6.91%	0.352	9.05%	0.355	10.06%	0.317	3.57%	0.324	5.72%
	HGNN	0.395	4.22%	0.399	5.40%	0.372	−2.06%	0.374	−1.53%	0.360	7.70%	0.373	11.67%
	HyperGAT	0.463	13.94%	0.475	16.78%	0.425	9.26%	0.431	10.91%	0.336	−2.98%	0.358	3.60%
	HHGNN	0.435	−0.38%	0.442	1.20%	0.442	5.72%	0.454	8.52%	0.432	12.86%	0.442	15.48%
	EAGLE	0.526	10.17%	0.553	15.87%	0.468	5.09%	0.479	7.74%	0.469	13.41%	0.474	14.52%
GPN	DeepR	0.392	27.02%	0.385	24.97%	0.336	21.71%	0.341	23.29%	0.355	24.68%	0.364	27.54%
	PRIM	0.390	26.08%	0.388	25.56%	0.363	23.39%	0.361	23.03%	0.346	22.55%	0.358	26.92%
	SEENet	0.413	25.44%	0.413	25.44%	0.378	17.08%	0.387	19.95%	0.382	24.69%	0.384	25.46%
	HGNN	0.478	26.11%	0.485	27.89%	0.472	24.28%	0.468	23.25%	0.421	26.07%	0.427	27.88%
	HyperGAT	0.502	23.58%	0.517	27.26%	0.468	20.28%	0.498	28.06%	0.425	22.76%	0.437	26.20%
	HHGNN	0.534	22.33%	0.527	20.83%	0.515	23.06%	0.500	19.62%	0.465	21.37%	0.487	27.27%
	EAGLE	0.568	19.08%	0.571	19.67%	0.544	22.22%	0.558	25.36%	0.476	15.19%	0.506	22.40%
HCNP	**HCNP**	**0.673**	-	**0.677**	-	**0.631**	-	**0.627**	-	**0.551**	-	**0.566**	-

1) **POI Relationship Prediction Methods: DeepR** [13], **PRIM** [3] and **SEENet** [12]. These methods predict relationships between pairwise POIs by constructing a heterogeneous graph centered on the POIs and extracting features. We keep their representation module and replace the downstream tasks with our task.
2) **Hypergraph-based Methods: HyperGAT** [4], **HHGNN** [14], and **HGNN** [7]. These methods use hypergraphs to model higher-order relationships among POIs. HGNN extends GNN with a two-stage information propagation process. HGAT adds an attention mechanism to HGNN. HHGNN further extends it to heterogeneous hypergraphs, capturing the importance of different nodes and hyperedges, improving downstream task performance. In the experiment, these models act as encoders, with extracted features fed into a decoder for result calculation.
3) **POI relationship group discovery: EAGLE** [10] also uses hypergraph to model the high-order POI relationships, but does not address the sparse label issue of strategic groups.

To ensure the fairness of the comparison, we adapt two classic few-shot learning methods for the above comparison methods: MAML and GPN, to prove the effectiveness of HCNP. These two methods are independent of the internal representation model, making them applicable to the models discussed above. In these experiments, we carry out 1-shot and 5-shot tests across the NYC, HOU, and LA datasets with a positive-to-negative sample ratio of 1:3 and a classification threshold of 0.5. The shot number refers to the number of labeled samples available when facing new tasks.

Evaluation Metrics. We adopt F1 value as the evaluation metric for a single meta-task, and Macro-F1 as well as Micro-F1 for multiple meta-tasks. F1 value comprehensively evaluates the accuracy and recall rate of the model, with higher

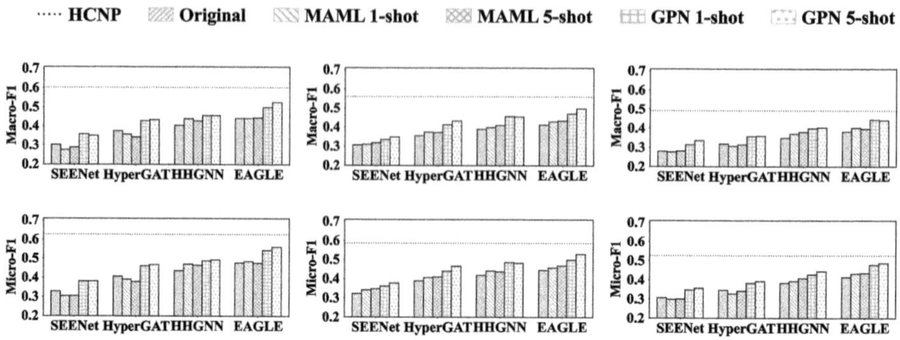

(a) NYC (b) HOU (c) LA

Fig. 5. Overall performance

values indicating better model performance. Macro-F1 and Micro-F1 calculation in multi-task evaluation share similar rules with F1 where the total True Positives in multi-task scenarios is defined as: $TP(\mathcal{D})=\sum_{\mathcal{T}\in\mathcal{D}}\sum_{q\in\mathcal{T}.\mathcal{Q}} TP_q$ while False Positives $FP(\mathcal{D})$ and False Negatives $FN(\mathcal{D})$ can be obtained. The formulas for Macro-F1 and Micro-F1 are as follows.

$$\text{Micro-F1} = \frac{2 \cdot TP(\mathcal{D})}{2 \cdot TP(\mathcal{D}) + FN(\mathcal{D}) + FP(\mathcal{D})} \tag{11}$$

$$\text{Macro-F1} = \frac{1}{|\mathcal{D}|} \cdot \sum_{\mathcal{T}\in\mathcal{D}} \text{F1}(\mathcal{T}) \tag{12}$$

5.2 Overall Performance

In our experiment, two few-shot learning frameworks are applied to the base POI representation models for fair comparison. Table 2 shows the performance of the comparison methods for a single catering type and we use ΔF1 to measure the performance change after applying the few-shot framework.

First, even with existing few-shot learning methods, the representation models do not outperform the proposed HCNP model. The best baseline, GPN on EAGLE, trails HCNP by 6% on the LA dataset in the 5-shot setting, while the worst baseline, MAML on DeepR, shows a 24% performance gap. These results underscore that current few-shot methods fall short in competitive POI group discovery, highlighting the superior effectiveness of HCNP. Second, MAML occasionally degrades performance due to its unstable two-stage optimization process, which heavily relies on task similarity. The quality of the auxiliary task during meta-training significantly impacts performance. Third, GPN outperforms the optimization-based MAML by 20% to 25% in terms of both performance and stability, with less training overhead. Finally, while GPN achieves comparable results to HCNP in some cases, it has limitations. GPN struggles when no real

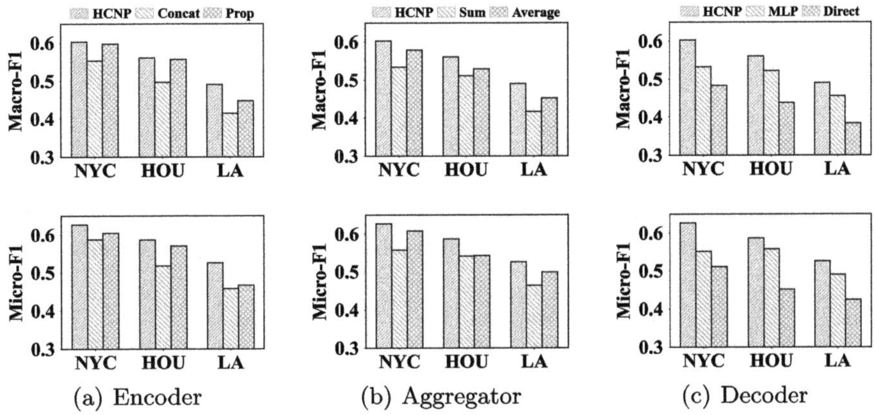

Fig. 6. Effectiveness of Each Component.

labels are available, as the prototype calculation relies on labeled data. In such cases, users must provide a small number of positive and negative samples for prototype computation.

To evaluate HCNP's performance across various competitive POI strategic group discovery tasks, Fig. 5 compares HCNP with the top four methods. The results show consistent trends in both single-type and multi-type analyses. In single-type tasks, MAML-based methods exhibit instability, leading to performance degradation. GPN models outperform MAML by 9% to 15%, while even few-shot learning frameworks still lag behind HCNP by 8% to 12%, further confirming HCNP's superiority in complex POI group discovery.

5.3 Effectiveness of Each Component

To verify the effectiveness of each component in HCNP, we replace the encoders, aggregators, and decoders. The experiment results are shown in Fig. 6.

Effectiveness of Query Encoder. To demonstrate the effectiveness of the proposed attention-based bi-level hypergraph encoder, we compare it with two alternative encoders: "Concat" and "Pro", as shown in Fig. 6(a). Supported by [1, 9], Prop outperforms Concat by 5% to 17% across two metrics. Building on Prop, our local structure-based method further enhances performance by 6% to 12%.

Effectiveness of Aggregator. We replace the existing aggregator with sum aggregation (Sum) and mean aggregation (Average) for comparison. As seen in Fig. 6(b), Average generally performs better than Sum, while our proposed self-attention-based aggregator further improves performance by approximately 3% to 12%. This is because the self-attention aggregator can adaptively assign importance to different observed data and is more flexible than Sum and Average.

Effectiveness of Decoder. The decoder converts feature vectors from upstream methods into scores indicating whether candidates belong to the target

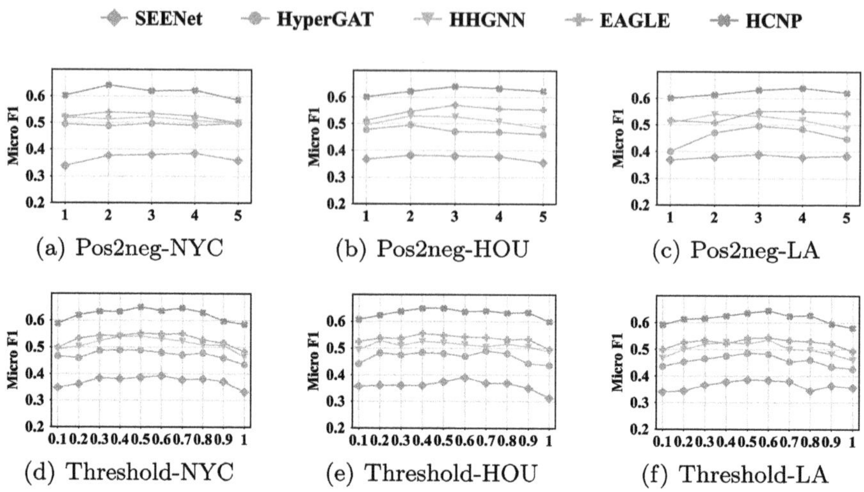

(a) Pos2neg-NYC (b) Pos2neg-HOU (c) Pos2neg-LA

(d) Threshold-NYC (e) Threshold-HOU (f) Threshold-LA

Fig. 7. Hyper-parameters sensitivity studies of HCNP.

strategic group. We use "MLP" and "Direct" to indicate if features pass through an MLP before the activation function. As shown in Fig. 6(c), both comparison methods have a 20% performance drop on two metrics. This is because strategic group discovery aims to bring POIs within the same group closer in feature space. The MLP-based decoder achieves this, while the others underperform due to inadequate metric learning.

5.4 Hyper-parameters Sensitivity

To analyze the model's sensitivity to hyperparameters, we conduct experiments on the positive-to-negative sample ratio and classification threshold across two metrics in three cities. The results are demonstrated in Fig. 7.

Positive-to-negative Sample Ratio (Pos2neg). POI strategic group discovery is framed as a binary classification problem, where the positive-to-negative sample ratio is crucial for generalization. We compared model performance across different ratios, as shown in Figs. 7(a)–7(c). where the x-axis represents the ratio. Most models improve initially but decline as the ratio increases, indicating that the traditional 1:1 ratio is insufficient. A 3:1 ratio (negative to positive samples) improves the model's ability to distinguish irrelevant POIs.

Classification Threshold. The classification threshold is a key hyper-parameter for decoder performance. Experiments in Figs. 7(d)–7(f) indicate all models perform poorly when the threshold > 0.8 or < 0.2, while threshold within 0.3–0.7 stabilize HCNP's performance, unlike other methods that fluctuate. This suggests that extreme thresholds disrupt the precision-recall balance, significantly lowering both Macro-F1 and Micro-F1 scores. With an optimal threshold, our model effectively separates competitive from non-competitive POIs, scoring

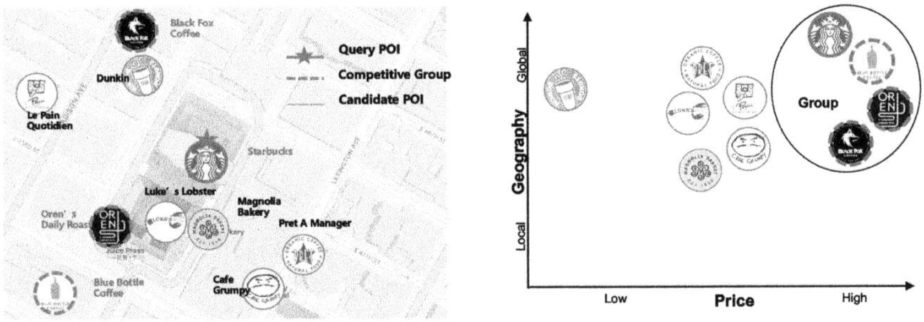

Fig. 8. Case study of coffee strategic group.

non-competitive POIs lower and competitive ones closer to 1, whereas other methods yield unstable predictions, scoring between 0.3 and 0.7.

5.5 Case Study

To demonstrate the practical applicability of HCNP, we conducted a case study in NYC to identify POI strategic groups in the catering sector. Using a Starbucks near Grand Central Terminal as the query POI within a 500 m radius, we found a strategic group highlighted by the red dashed circle in Fig. 8. This group includes three nearby stores offering similar products, such as light meals and coffee, and sharing overlapping customer bases due to their proximity to the station. However, stores like Dunkin', which focuses on donuts, and Le Pain Quotidien and Magnolia Bakery, which specialize in bread, are not considered direct competitors to Starbucks, despite some potential customer overlap. This demonstrates HCNP's ability to effectively identify strategic groups in few-shot scenarios, capturing subtle differences in product offerings.

6 Conclusion

This paper introduces the HCNP model, a meta-learning approach for discovering competitive POI groups. To capture the multi-dimensional, higher-order relationships among POIs, we first construct a heterogeneous urban hypergraph. The HCNP model then uses neural networks to model the competitive group distributions of POIs. By incorporating auxiliary tasks during meta-training, HCNP learns shared prior knowledge across different POI groups, addressing the challenge of sparse ground truth data. We validate HCNP's effectiveness through experiments on three real-world datasets, demonstrating its ability to identify competitive POI groups in few-shot settings.

Acknowledgments. This work is supported by the National Key R&D Program for the 14th-Five-Year Plan of China (2023YFC3804104 in 2023YFC3804100).

References

1. Behrouz, A., Hashemi, F.: Cs-mlgcn: multiplex graph convolutional networks for community search in multiplex networks. In: Proceedings of the 31st ACM International Conference on Information & Knowledge Management, pp. 3828–3832 (2022)
2. Chen, J., et al.: A review of few-shot and zero-shot learning for node classification in social networks. IEEE Trans. Comput. Soc. Syst. (2024)
3. Chen, Y., et al.: Points-of-interest relationship inference with spatial-enriched graph neural networks. arXiv preprint arXiv:2202.13686 (2022)
4. Ding, K., Wang, J., Li, J., Li, D., Liu, H.: Be more with less: hypergraph attention networks for inductive text classification. arXiv preprint arXiv:2011.00387 (2020)
5. Ding, K., Wang, J., Li, J., Shu, K., Liu, C., Liu, H.: Graph prototypical networks for few-shot learning on attributed networks. In: Proceedings of the 29th ACM International Conference on Information & Knowledge Management, pp. 295–304 (2020)
6. Fang, S., Zhao, K., Li, G., Yu, J.X.: Community search: a meta-learning approach. In: 2023 IEEE 39th International Conference on Data Engineering (ICDE), pp. 2358–2371. IEEE (2023)
7. Feng, Y., You, H., Zhang, Z., Ji, R., Gao, Y.: Hypergraph neural networks. In: Proceedings of the AAAI Conference on Artificial Intelligence, vol. 33, pp. 3558–3565 (2019)
8. Finn, C., Abbeel, P., Levine, S.: Model-agnostic meta-learning for fast adaptation of deep networks. In: International Conference on Machine Learning, pp. 1126–1135. PMLR (2017)
9. Jiang, Y., Rong, Y., Cheng, H., Huang, X., Zhao, K., Huang, J.: Query driven-graph neural networks for community search: from non-attributed, attributed, to interactive attributed. arXiv preprint arXiv:2104.03583 (2021)
10. Jin, J., Zhang, H., Bai, W., Lin, X., Zhang, J.: Inferring point-of-interest relationship for strategic group discovery guided by user demands. IEEE Trans. Consum. Electron. (2024)
11. Lai, Y., Su, Y., Wei, L., Wang, T., Zha, D., Wang, X.: Adaptive spatial-temporal hypergraph fusion learning for next poi recommendation. In: ICASSP 2024 - 2024 IEEE International Conference on Acoustics, Speech and Signal Processing (ICASSP), pp. 7320–7324 (2024)
12. Li, S., Zhou, J., Liu, J., Xu, T., Chen, E., Xiong, H.: Multi-temporal relationship inference in urban areas. In: Proceedings of the 29th ACM SIGKDD Conference on Knowledge Discovery and Data Mining, pp. 1316–1327 (2023)
13. Li, S., Zhou, J., Xu, T., Liu, H., Lu, X., Xiong, H.: Competitive analysis for points of interest. In: Proceedings of the 26th ACM SIGKDD International Conference on Knowledge Discovery & Data Mining, pp. 1265–1274 (2020)
14. Li, Y., et al.: Heterogeneous hypergraph neural network for friend recommendation with human mobility. In: Proceedings of the 31st ACM International Conference on Information & Knowledge Management, pp. 4209–4213 (2022)
15. Liu, Z., et al.: KDRank: knowledge-driven user-aware poi recommendation. Knowl.-Based Syst. **278**, 110884 (2023)
16. Song, Y., Wang, T., Cai, P., Mondal, S.K., Sahoo, J.P.: A comprehensive survey of few-shot learning: evolution, applications, challenges, and opportunities. ACM Comput. Surv. **55**(13s), 1–40 (2023)

17. Wang, N., Luo, M., Ding, K., Zhang, L., Li, J., Zheng, Q.: Graph few-shot learning with attribute matching. In: Proceedings of the 29th ACM International Conference on Information & Knowledge Management, pp. 1545–1554 (2020)
18. Wang, S., Chen, C., Li, J.: Graph few-shot learning with task-specific structures. Adv. Neural. Inf. Process. Syst. **35**, 38925–38936 (2022)
19. Wang, X., Fukumoto, F., Cui, J., Suzuki, Y., Li, J., Yu, D.: EEDN: enhanced encoder-decoder network with local and global context learning for poi recommendation. In: Proceedings of the 46th International ACM SIGIR Conference on Research and Development in Information Retrieval, pp. 383–392 (2023)
20. Wen, Z., Fang, Y., Liu, Z.: Meta-inductive node classification across graphs. In: Proceedings of the 44th International ACM SIGIR Conference on Research and Development in Information Retrieval, pp. 1219–1228 (2021)
21. Yan, X., et al.: Spatio-temporal hypergraph learning for next poi recommendation. In: Proceedings of the 46th International ACM SIGIR Conference on Research and Development in Information Retrieval, pp. 403–412 (2023)
22. Yao, H., et al.: Graph few-shot learning via knowledge transfer. In: Proceedings of the AAAI Conference on Artificial Intelligence, vol. 34, pp. 6656–6663 (2020)
23. Zhou, J., et al.: Competitive relationship prediction for points of interest: a neural graphlet based approach. IEEE Trans. Knowl. Data Eng. **34**(12), 5681–5692 (2021)
24. Zhou, Y., Zhou, L., Wang, J., Wang, L., Kong, B.: Spatial-aware community search over heterogeneous information networks. In: International Conference on Spatial Data and Intelligence, pp. 103–114. Springer (2023)

DCSN: Dynamic Calibration and Contrastive Sharpening for MultiModal Recommendation

Jicheng Sun[1], Shuai Xu[1,2](✉), and Yicong Li[1]

[1] Nanjing University of Aeronautics and Astronautics, Nanjing, China
{sunjicheng,xushuai7,liyicong}@nuaa.edu.cn
[2] Key Laboratory of Social Computing and Cognitive Intelligence, Dalian University of Technology, Ministry of Education, Dalian, China

Abstract. Multimodal Recommender Systems (MMRS) alleviate data sparsity and enhance item understanding by integrating auxiliary information, such as images and text, making them a prominent research direction. However, they face two limitations. Traditional models typically statically concatenate an item's modal and behavioral features, restricting the effective utilization of its key physical attributes for improving recommendation accuracy. Additionally, graph propagation can induce representation over-smoothing; after several rounds of information aggregation, the representations of modally-similar items homogenize. This process masks critical personalized features that attract specific users, thereby diminishing the discriminative power necessary for precise recommendations. To address these limitations, we propose a novel framework for multimodal recommendation, the Dual Calibration and Sharpening Network (DCSN). This framework operates on a two-stage calibration-sharpening paradigm to optimize feature fusion and representation quality. For calibration, DCSN employs a collaborative interaction gating module where an item's physical attributes serve as dynamic contexts to reshape its core behavioral representation, thus overcoming static fusion limitations. To counteract representation over-smoothing, the sharpening stage introduces a Decoupled Modal Contrastive Control (DMCC) module. This module utilizes a combined contrastive and reconstruction loss to refine the modal representations, maximizing their discriminative power while enhancing robustness. Extensive experiments conducted on two public datasets validate the effectiveness of our method.

Keywords: Multi-modal Recommendation · Graph Neural Networks · Contrastive Learning

1 Introduction

The rapid growth of the internet has exacerbated information overload. Recommender systems [16] have emerged as a key technology to mitigate this problem

T. Hao et al. (Eds.): BESC 2025, LNCS 16431, pp. 236–251, 2026.
https://doi.org/10.1007/978-981-95-7138-3_16

by predicting users' potential interests from their historical interactions. However, traditional systems that rely solely on user-item interactions [2] suffer from inherent data sparsity, which significantly impairs recommendation accuracy and scope [22]. Consequently, integrating multimodal information, such as images and text, has become an effective solution, as user preferences are naturally influenced by such content. A common approach [8] involves using pre-trained neural networks to extract multimodal features. These are subsequently fused with user behavioral data to construct a user-item bipartite graph [21], upon which Graph Convolutional Networks (GCNs) learn enhanced user and item representations. This integration allows the model to capture stronger collaborative signals, improving performance in data-sparse scenarios.

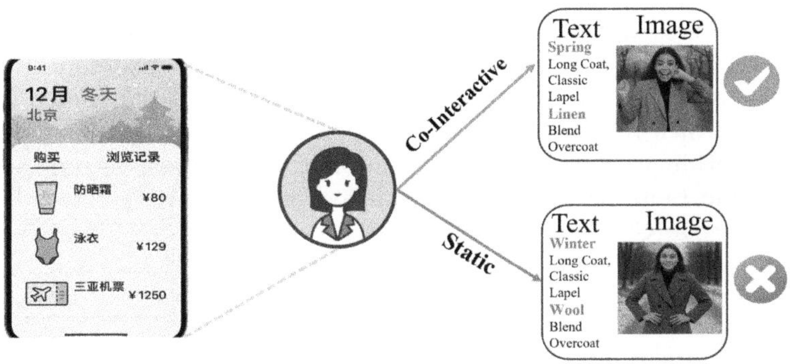

Fig. 1. An illustration of leveraging synergistic context to resolve recommendation ambiguity.

Early works began to incorporate multimodal content into recommender systems. For instance, VBPR [5] enhanced item representations by integrating ID embeddings with visual features, while CKE [27] extended matrix factorization (MF) with visual information. With the advent of Graph Neural Networks (GNNs), a new paradigm has become mainstream: modeling user-item relationships on bipartite graphs and leveraging GCNs to capture higher-order semantics. Following this direction, MMGCN [21] constructs modality-specific user-item graphs and propagates information via GCNs to capture distinct user preferences within each modality, thereby improving micro-video recommendation. To capture deeper latent relationships, models like LATTICE [28] and FREEDOM [31] introduce inter-item semantic graphs. Similarly, MGCN [26] employs a behavior purifier to mitigate modality noise and performs its final prediction by combining multi-view propagation with feature fusion. Collectively, these GCN-based methods have demonstrated significant performance gains.

However, existing models [5,26] often employ static strategies, like weighted summation, to integrate multimodal information. This approach fails to account for the dynamic and context-dependent nature of user preferences for an item's physical attributes. For instance, when a user's explicit context (e.g., being in

Beijing in winter) conflicts with their implicit intent revealed by purchase behavior (e.g., preparing for a vacation), static fusion strategies that rely on simple concatenation or addition are likely to be misled by superficial signals, as they are incapable of capturing such a complex synergistic context, leading to inappropriate recommendations (as shown in Fig. 1). Furthermore, GNN-based models [9,26] are susceptible to over-smoothing when aggregating information on separate modality-specific graphs. While propagation enhances shared features, it concurrently dilutes the unique characteristics of individual items. This leads to homogenized representations across modalities, diminishing the discriminative power for fine-grained recommendations and ultimately capping the model's performance.

To tackle these challenges, this paper proposes the DCSN, a framework designed to counteract static fusion and representation over-smoothing. To address static fusion, DCSN employs a collaborative interaction gating module that leverages user interaction behavior as dynamic context to calibrate and reshape raw modal features. These calibrated features are subsequently propagated through their respective item-item modality similarity graphs. To mitigate the over-smoothing risk from this propagation, the framework introduces a novel DMCC module. Optimized via a compound loss of contrastive and reconstruction objectives, the DMCC module actively sharpens the aggregated representations, yielding more discriminative and robust final representations for both users and items. The main contributions of this paper are summarized as follows:

- We propose a Co-Interactive Gate that achieves dynamic contextual calibration of item representations by fusing user behavior and situation.
- We design a DMCC task that counteracts GNN-induced over-smoothing by sharpening post-propagation representations via a composite contrastive and reconstruction loss.
- We conducted extensive experiments on two real-world datasets. The experimental results demonstrate the effectiveness of DCSN.

2 Related Work

2.1 Multimodal Recommendation

To address data sparsity, numerous studies integrate multimodal information, often using pre-trained models like VGG-16 [17] (vision) and Sentence Transformer [14] (text) for feature extraction. The seminal VBPR [5], for example, incorporated visual content to enhance personalized ranking and mitigate the cold-start problem, while subsequent works [1,11] fused visual and textual data for more holistic embeddings.

GNNs have since become the mainstream paradigm for modeling the bipartite user-item graph. Early models like MMGCN [21] used GCNs to capture high-order collaborative signals. To enrich semantic modeling, later works explored diverse graph structures, including homogeneous item-item (LATTICE [28],

FREEDOM [31]) and user-user graphs (DualGNN [20]), external multimodal knowledge graphs (MKGAT [18]), and hybrid graphs (DRAGON [29]).

Other research has focused on information quality and representation depth. This includes mitigating information noise (FREEDOM [31], MGCN [26]), capturing multi-level user interests (LGMRec [3]), and incorporating novel architectures like diffusion models (DiffMM [7]). Despite these advances, existing methods primarily concentrate on the fusion of multi-source information, largely overlooking a core issue: how an item's physical attributes should dynamically and non-linearly influence its behavioral popularity within user groups.

2.2 Contrastive Learning

GNNs are a pivotal technology in modern recommender systems, achieving state-of-the-art performance in areas like sequential [13] and social recommendation [24]. To address the issue of data sparsity in the recommendation, Contrastive Learning (CL) has been widely integrated into GNN-based frameworks [10]. CL operates by maximizing agreement between augmented data views, typically generated via structural or noise-based perturbations. Structural perturbation, exemplified by SGL, creates views through methods like node and edge dropping to derive self-supervised signals. A more recent trend is noise-based augmentation. SimGCL [25] pioneered this by adding uniform noise directly to the embedding space, forgoing complex graph alterations. Building on this, XSimGCL [24] refined control over representation uniformity, while GUME [9] and Mentor [23] inject noise at different stages (into historical data or GNN layers, respectively) to enhance robustness. Distinct from these perturbation-focused approaches, another line of research concentrates on the amount of shared information between views, the method [4] aim to control similarity directly, for instance, by using a reconstruction loss to prevent views from becoming overly similar. However, these input perturbation methods neglect a critical issue in GNNs: representation over-smoothing. This phenomenon homogenizes neighbor information, obscuring personalized features and diminishing discriminative power.

3 Preliminaries

Let $U = \{u_1, \ldots, u_M\}$ and $I = \{i_1, \ldots, i_N\}$ be the sets of M users and N items, respectively. The user-item interaction matrix is denoted by $Y \in \mathbb{R}^{M \times N}$, where $y_{ui} = 1$ indicates an observed interaction between user u and item i, and $y_{ui} = 0$ otherwise.

Each user and item is represented by a d-dimensional identity (ID) embedding, collectively forming an embedding matrix $E_{id} \in \mathbb{R}^{d \times (|U|+|I|)}$. Each item i is also associated with features from a set of modalities $\mathcal{M}$. The feature vector for item i in modality $m \in \mathcal{M}$ is denoted as $e_i^m \in \mathbb{R}^{d_m}$. In this work, we focus on visual and textual modalities ($\mathcal{M} = \{v, t\}$), though our method is readily extensible to others.

Given the user-item interaction matrix $\mathbf{Y}$ and the multimodal features of items, the goal is to predict user preferences (i.e., the interaction probability $\hat{y}_{ui}$) and recommend the top-k most relevant items to each user. These items should be ranked according to their predicted preference scores, ensuring that the items of greatest interest to the user are displayed first.

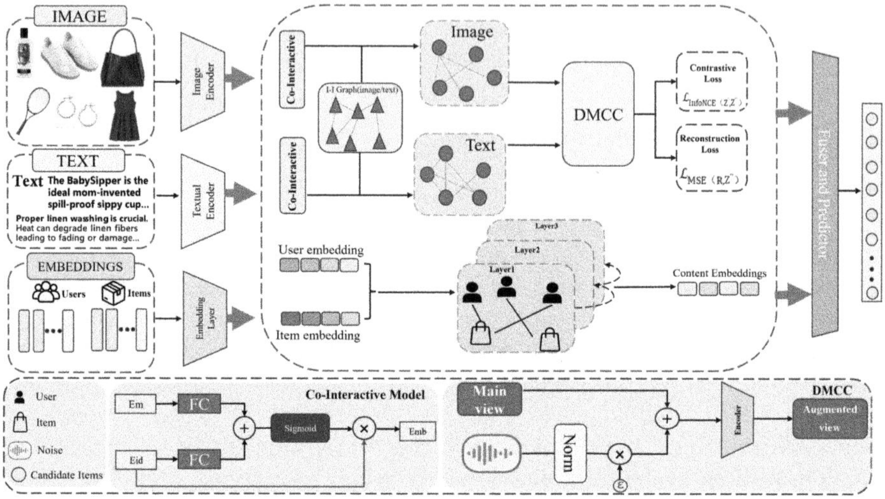

Fig. 2. The overall architecture of the proposed DCSN.

4 Our Approach

Figure 2. illustrates the overall architecture of our proposed DCSN. The framework simultaneously learns collaborative signals and modal features, while employing a two-stage pathway for modal information enhancement. We employ the classic LightGCN as our collaborative filtering backbone to learn fundamental behavioral representations from the user-item interaction graph. Concurrently, the modal pathway begins with a collaborative interaction gating module that performs context-aware calibration, using behavioral signals as dynamic contexts to reshape raw modal features. After these features are aggregated on a modality similarity graph, our DMCC module then sharpens the resulting representations. The DMCC is optimized by a compound loss function that combines both contrastive and reconstruction objectives. This optimization is designed to mitigate over-smoothing while enhancing the discriminative power of the final modal embeddings.

4.1 Co-interactive Gating Model

Modal information provides rich semantic descriptions for items, but the raw modalities lack awareness of the collaborative behavior context. To address this issue, we design a novel Co-Interactive Gating mechanism to achieve dynamic calibration of representations.

Specifically, we first project the raw modal features of items, denoted as E_m (where $m \in \{v, t\}$ represent visual and textual modalities, respectively), through a learnable linear layer to obtain higher-order modal features $\hat{E}_m$ that are aligned with the dimensionality of the behavioral representations:

$$\hat{E}_m = W_{trs,m} E_m + b_{trs,m} \tag{1}$$

where $W_{trs,m}$ and $b_{trs,m}$ are a trainable transformation matrix and bias vector, respectively.

Then, departing from traditional methods, our gating signal is generated through a joint negotiation between the modal features and the behavioral features (ID embeddings E_{id}). We feed the higher-order modal features $\hat{E}_m$ and the behavioral features E_{id} into separate linear layers to produce their respective intermediate signal vectors, s_m and s_{id}:

$$s_m = W_{gate,m} \hat{E}_m + b_{gate,m} \tag{2}$$

$$s_{id} = W_{gate,id} E_{id} + b_{gate,id} \tag{3}$$

These two vectors are then summed and passed through a Sigmoid activation function to yield the final dynamic gating vector g_m:

$$g_m = \sigma(s_m + s_{id}) \tag{4}$$

where all W and b terms are learnable parameters, and σ is the Sigmoid non-linear function.

Finally, we apply this context-rich gating vector g_m to the core behavioral features E_{id} via the Hadamard product ($\odot$) to obtain the calibrated and modality-aware representation $\tilde{E}_m$, which is then used for subsequent graph propagation:

$$\tilde{E}_m = E_{id} \odot g_m \tag{5}$$

4.2 User-Item View

To effectively capture the high-order collaborative relations between users and items, we construct a graph convolutional network module to propagate information on the user-item interaction graph.

Specifically, we concatenate the user ID embeddings $E_U \in \mathbb{R}^{N_u \times d}$ and the item ID embeddings $E_I \in \mathbb{R}^{N_i \times d}$ to form the initial node representations $E^{(0)} \in \mathbb{R}^{(N_u+N_i) \times d}$ for the graph convolutional network.

Following [6], we adopt a simplified graph convolution method to aggregate neighborhood information. The information propagation at the l-th layer can be formulated as:

$$E^{(l)} = \tilde{A} E^{(l-1)} \tag{6}$$

where $E^{(l)}$ represents the enhanced user and item representations after the l-th convolution layer. $\tilde{A}$ is the symmetrically normalized adjacency matrix we construct from the user-item interaction matrix R, formulated as $\tilde{A} = D^{-\frac{1}{2}}AD^{-\frac{1}{2}}$, where A is the adjacency matrix that includes R and R^T. This simplified propagation method preserves the core collaborative filtering capability of the model while avoiding the additional training difficulty that can be introduced by non-linear transformations and feature transformation matrices.

After L_{ui} layers of propagation, we retain the embedding results from each layer. To integrate neighborhood information of different orders, we aggregate the representations from all layers (from layer 0 to layer L_{ui}) by taking their average to obtain the final collaborative behavior representation E_{beh}:

$$E_{beh} = \frac{1}{L_{ui}+1}\sum_{l=0}^{L_{ui}} E^{(l)} \tag{7}$$

4.3 Item-Item View

Following [26], to capture the deep semantic correlations of items within a specific modality, we construct a separate Item-Item similarity graph for each modality and enrich the item's modal representations through graph convolution operations.

Constructing a fully-connected similarity graph is computationally expensive and prone to noise from low-relevance edges. To address this, we employ a K-Nearest Neighbors (KNN) based graph sparsification strategy. Specifically, we first compute pairwise cosine similarities between items using their raw modal features. For each item, we then retain only the edges to its top-K most similar neighbors. This procedure yields a sparse modal graph that more effectively captures core semantic associations.

To maintain numerical stability and prevent gradient issues during graph convolution, we apply symmetric normalization to this sparse adjacency matrix $\mathcal{A}_m$, yielding the final modal graph adjacency matrix $\tilde{\mathcal{A}}_m$ used for propagation:

$$\tilde{\mathcal{A}}_m = D_m^{-\frac{1}{2}}\mathcal{A}_m D_m^{-\frac{1}{2}} \tag{8}$$

where D_m is the degree matrix of $\mathcal{A}_m$.

Subsequently, we take the calibrated modal representations $\tilde{E}_m$ (the output of Eq. (5)) from the preceding "Co-Interactive Gating" module as the initial input, $\tilde{E}_m^{(0)}$, for this graph convolutional network. We then perform L_m layers of propagation on this modal graph to aggregate multi-order semantic information from neighbors:

$$\tilde{E}_m^{(l)} = \tilde{\mathcal{A}}_m \tilde{E}_m^{(l-1)} \tag{9}$$

After L_m layers of propagation, we similarly employ a layer-aggregation strategy, averaging the outputs from all layers to obtain the final enhanced item modal representation $\bar{E}_m$.

Finally, after completing the modal information propagation on the item side, we further aggregate the enhanced item modal representations to the user side via the user-item interaction matrix R. This generates a specific modal preference representation, $\bar{E}_{u,m}$, for each user:

$$\bar{E}_{u,m} = R \cdot \bar{E}_m \tag{10}$$

Through the steps described above, we generate information-rich and neighborhood-enhanced user and item representations for each modality.

4.4 Decoupled Modal Contrastive Control

Although item representations have aggregated rich neighborhood information after propagation on the modal graph, this also introduces the risk of over-smoothing, which can lead to the loss of key discriminative features. We design a DMCC module. This module intervenes after graph propagation and aims to perform a final sharpening and enhancement of the representations through a carefully designed self-supervised task.

The core of DMCC lies in constructing three different views for each modality $m \in \{v, t\}$, starting from an item's enhanced modal representation $\bar{E}_m$:

Main View (Z_m): We directly use the item modal representation $\bar{E}_m$, which has undergone graph propagation and layer aggregation, as the main view Z_m for contrastive learning. It represents the highest-quality representation we currently possess, rich in neighborhood context.

$$Z_m = \bar{E}_m \tag{11}$$

Intermediate View (R_m): We generate the intermediate view R_m by adding random noise Δ_m, sampled from a uniform distribution, to the main view Z_m. The magnitude of this noise is controlled by a hyperparameter ϵ. This view simulates minor perturbations that features might encounter in the real world.

$$R_m = Z_m + \epsilon \cdot \frac{\Delta_m}{||\Delta_m||_2} \tag{12}$$

Augmented View (Z''_m): We feed the noise-infused intermediate view R_m into a learnable linear encoder $f_{\text{enc},m}(\cdot)$ to generate the final augmented view Z''_m. To stabilize training, the weights of this encoder are initialized as an identity matrix.

$$Z''_m = f_{\text{enc},m}(R_m) \tag{13}$$

To achieve the dual objectives of "sharpening" and "stabilizing" the representations, we design a composite loss function comprising a contrastive loss and a reconstruction loss:

Contrastive Loss ($\mathcal{L}_{\text{CL},m}$): This loss employs the InfoNCE loss function. It sharpens the representations by maximizing the agreement between the main view Z_m and the augmented view Z''_m, thereby preserving core discriminative information. It is formulated as:

$$\mathcal{L}_{\text{CL},m} = -\log \frac{\exp(\text{sim}(Z_m, Z''_m)/\tau)}{\sum_{Z'_m \in \{Z''_m\} \cup \mathcal{N}} \exp(\text{sim}(Z_m, Z'_m)/\tau)} \tag{14}$$

where τ is the temperature hyperparameter and $\mathcal{N}$ is the set of negative samples.

Reconstruction Loss ($\mathcal{L}_{\text{recon},m}$): This loss uses the Mean Squared Error (MSE). It requires the augmented view Z''_m to be able to reconstruct the noisy intermediate view R_m. This constraint acts as a regularization to prevent the encoder from learning a trivial solution and ensures the robustness of the final representation.

$$\mathcal{L}_{\text{recon},m} = ||R_m - Z''_m||_2^2 \tag{15}$$

Finally, the total loss of DMCC, $\mathcal{L}_{\text{DMCC}}$, is obtained by a weighted sum of these two loss terms, covering all modalities:

$$\mathcal{L}_{\text{DMCC}} = \lambda_1 \sum_{m \in \{v,t\}} \mathcal{L}_{\text{CL},m} + \lambda_2 \sum_{m \in \{v,t\}} \mathcal{L}_{\text{recon},m} \tag{16}$$

where λ_1 and λ_2 are hyperparameters that control the weight of each loss term. By jointly optimizing these two objectives, DMCC can produce final modal representations that are both highly discriminative and robust.

4.5 Multimodal Fusion Module

After learning high-quality collaborative behavioral representations (E_{beh}) and multimodal representations ($\bar{E}_m$), we move into the final feature fusion stage. Here, following [26], the fusion module aims to flexibly weight and fuse information from different modalities based on the modal preferences extracted from user behavior. Specifically, the fusion module first uses a shared attention mechanism to automatically identify and extract the modality-shared features (E_s) from the representations of each modality ($\bar{E}_v$, $\bar{E}_t$). Subsequently, by subtracting the shared features from the complete representation of each modality, we obtain the exclusive features ($\tilde{E}_m$) for each modality.

To achieve personalized fusion, we further learn a preference gating (P_m) for each modality from the user's collaborative behavioral representation (E_{beh}), and use it to weight the exclusive features ($\tilde{E}_m$) of each modality. Finally, we aggregate the preference-weighted exclusive features with the modality-shared features to obtain the fused multimodal representation (E_{mul}). This process can be summarized as:

$$E_{\text{mul}} = E_s + \text{Aggregate}\left(\left\{\tilde{E}_m \odot P_m\right\}_{m \in \{v,t\}}\right) \tag{17}$$

4.6 Prediction and Optimization

By capitalizing on the enhanced ID representations and the fused multimodal representations, we first acquire the final representations for user u and item i:

$$e_u = \hat{e}_{u,id} + \hat{e}_{u,mul} \quad , \quad e_i = \hat{e}_{i,id} + \hat{e}_{i,mul} \tag{18}$$

The estimated preference score is then computed as the dot product of their representations: $\hat{y}_{ui} = e_u^T e_i$.

For model optimization, we employ the pairwise Bayesian Personalized Ranking (BPR) loss [15], which prioritizes higher scores for observed items over unobserved ones:

$$\mathcal{L}_{BPR} = \sum_{(u,i,j)\in\mathcal{O}} -\ln \sigma(\hat{y}_{ui} - \hat{y}_{uj}) \tag{19}$$

Here, $\mathcal{O}$ represents the set of training triplets, where (u, i) is an observed interaction and (u, j) is an unobserved one, and σ denotes the sigmoid function. We then perform joint optimization in conjunction with our proposed Disentangled Modality Contrastive Control (DMCC) task and an auxiliary contrastive learning task. Thus, the overall loss function is given by:

$$\mathcal{L} = \mathcal{L}_{BPR} + \mathcal{L}_{DMCC} + \lambda_{cl}\mathcal{L}_{CL} + \lambda_{reg}||\Theta||_2^2 \tag{20}$$

where λ_{cl} and λ_{reg} are hyperparameters that regulate the influence of the auxiliary contrastive task and the L2 regularization term on the model parameters Θ, respectively.

5 Experiment

In this section, we conduct experiments to validate the effectiveness of our proposed DCSN model and aim to answer the following questions:

- **RQ1:** How does DCSN perform in the multimodal recommendation task compared with the baseline methods?
- **RQ2:** How do different components in DCSN contribute to the performance?

Table 1. Statistics of the experimental datasets.

Dataset	#User	#Item	#Behavior	Density
Baby	19445	7050	160792	0.117%
Sports	35598	18357	296337	0.045%

5.1 Datasets

Our experiments are conducted on two multimodal datasets from the Amazon product collection [12], Baby and Sports, to assess the efficacy of our DCSN model. These datasets feature both visual and textual information for every item. We adhere to a common preprocessing protocol [32] by filtering the datasets to a 5-core setting. The items are represented by 4096-dimensional pre-extracted visual features and 384-dimensional textual features generated by a pre-trained sentence transformer [30]. A statistical overview of the datasets is provided in Table 1.

5.2 Experimental Settings

5.2.1 Evaluation Metrics: To ensure a rigorous and comparable evaluation, we employ two standard metrics for top-K recommendation: Recall@K (R@K) and Normalized Discounted Cumulative Gain@K(NDCG@K). Following common practice, we adopt an 8:1:1 ratio to randomly split the data into training, validation, and test sets [31]. For every user in the test set, we compute both metrics and report the average scores. The evaluation is conducted for $K \in \{10, 20\}$, which are typical cut-off values in recent literature.

5.2.2 Baselines: We consider the following baselines:

General Recommenders: We select the following models for comparison: a matrix factorization (MF) model, BPR [15], and a graph-based model, LightGCN [6].

Multi-modal Recommenders: For a comprehensive evaluation, we compare our proposed model against several representative multimodal recommender systems. These baselines include the matrix factorization (MF) model VBPR [5] and a suite of graph-based models:MMGCN [21], SLMRec [19], MGCN [26], BM3 [32], FREEDOM [31], DiffMM [7], and LGMRec [3].

5.2.3 Hyperparameter Settings: We set the user and item embedding size to 64 for all models. The batch size is set to 2048, and we train each model for up to 1000 epochs, employing an early stopping strategy with a patience of 20 epochs. For the number of GCN layers, we use 3 for the Baby dataset and 2 for the Sports dataset. All models are optimized using Adam, with an initial learning rate of 1×10^{-4} and parameters initialized by the Xavier method.

The key hyperparameters for our model are set as follows: the temperature for contrastive learning τ is 0.5, the weight coefficient for the contrastive loss λ_{cl} is 0.1, and the coefficient for the reconstruction loss λ_{rec} is 1.5.

5.3 Overall Performance (RQ1)

The primary results are reported in Table 2, from which we draw the following observations:

Table 2. Performance comparison of different recommendation models in terms of Recall@K (R@K) and NDCG@K (N@K).

Model	Baby				Sports			
	R@10	R@20	N@10	N@20	R@10	R@20	N@10	N@20
BPR	0.0382	0.0595	0.0207	0.0263	0.0417	0.0633	0.0232	0.0288
LightGCN	0.0479	0.0754	0.0257	0.0328	0.0569	0.0864	0.0311	0.0387
VBPR	0.0423	0.0663	0.0223	0.0284	0.0558	0.0856	0.0307	0.0384
MMGCN	0.0424	0.0668	0.0223	0.0286	0.0386	0.0627	0.0204	0.0266
SLMRec	0.0545	0.0831	0.0296	0.0371	0.0676	0.1017	0.0374	0.0462
BM3	0.0564	0.0883	0.0301	0.0383	0.0656	0.0980	0.0355	0.0438
MGCN	0.0620	0.0964	0.0339	0.0427	<u>0.0729</u>	<u>0.1106</u>	<u>0.0397</u>	<u>0.0496</u>
FREEDOM	0.0627	0.0992	0.0330	0.0424	0.0724	0.1089	0.0390	0.0481
DiffMM	0.0625	0.0971	0.0306	0.0401	0.0715	0.1043	0.0350	0.0431
LGMRec	<u>0.0644</u>	<u>0.1002</u>	<u>0.0349</u>	<u>0.0440</u>	0.0720	0.1068	0.0385	0.0480
DCSN	**0.0676**	**0.1020**	**0.0360**	**0.0448**	**0.0753**	**0.1149**	**0.0412**	**0.0514**

Our proposed DCSN model demonstrates notable performance, outperforming all baselines on both datasets. For instance, on the Sports dataset, DCSN achieves a 3.63% improvement in NDCG@20 relative to the top-performing baseline, MGCN. Furthermore, on the Baby dataset, it surpasses the strongest baseline, LGMRec, by 1.82% on the same metric. These findings underscore the effectiveness of our framework.

The model's success corroborates the efficacy of our proposed paradigm: A Dual-Stage Paradigm of Early Representation Calibration and Late Contrastive Refinement. The Co-Interactive Gating module enriches initial inputs by dynamically calibrating modal features with behavioral context. Subsequently, to counteract potential over-smoothing from GNNs, our DMCC module intervenes after propagation. It employs a self-supervised task, guided by a composite of contrastive and reconstruction objectives, to re-sharpen the representations and recover critical personalized features.

5.4 Ablation Study (RQ2)

To evaluate the contributions of different components in our model, we perform an ablation study by analyzing two variants of DCSN:

- **w/o-CI:**We remove the Co-Interactive Gating Model of DCSN.
- **w/o-DMCC:**We remove the DMCC module of DCSN.

Our ablation study (Table 3) validates the effectiveness of each core component, as removing either leads to a notable performance degradation. Without Co-Interactive Gating (w/o CI), the model loses the ability to dynamically calibrate modal representations using behavioral context. In contrast, lacking the

Table 3. Ablation Study on Two Datasets.

Variants	Metrics	Datasets	
		Baby	Sports
DCSN	R@20	0.1020	0.1149
	N@20	0.0448	0.0514
w/o CI	R@20	0.0495	0.0577
	N@20	0.0211	0.0261
w/o DMCC	R@20	0.0958	0.1125
	N@20	0.0435	0.0504

DMCC module, it cannot perform the contrastive sharpening needed to counteract GNN-induced over-smoothing, thereby losing critical discriminative power. These results confirm the necessity of both components in addressing their targeted problems.

6 Conclusion

This paper addresses two prevalent challenges in multi-modal recommendation, namely static fusion and representation over-smoothing, by proposing the DCSN framework.

The framework addresses these challenges through a two-stage process. It begins by employing a Co-Interactive Gating mechanism to dynamically calibrate modal features with the behavioral profile as context. This is complemented by the DMCC module, which sharpens the post-propagation representations using a composite contrastive and reconstruction loss to alleviate over-smoothing and enhance discriminative power.

Experimental results on two public datasets demonstrate that our proposed DCSN achieves effective performance improvements on key recommendation metrics compared to several baseline models.

Acknowledgments. This work is supported by the Natural Science Foundation of China under Grant No. 62302213, the Key Laboratory of Social Computing and Cognitive Intelligence (Dalian University of Technology), Ministry of Education, China.

Disclosure of Interests. The authors have no competing interests to declare that are relevant to the content of this article.

References

1. Chen, X., et al.: Personalized fashion recommendation with visual explanations based on multimodal attention network: towards visually explainable recommendation. In: Proceedings of the 42nd International ACM SIGIR Conference on Research and Development in Information Retrieval, pp. 765–774. SIGIR'19, Association for Computing Machinery, New York (2019). https://doi.org/10.1145/3331184.3331254
2. Chen, Z., Xu, J., Hu, H.: Don't lose yourself: boosting multimodal recommendation via reducing node-neighbor discrepancy in graph convolutional network (2024). https://arxiv.org/abs/2412.18962
3. Guo, Z., Li, J., Li, G., Wang, C., Shi, S., Ruan, B.: Lgmrec: local and global graph learning for multimodal recommendation (2024). https://arxiv.org/abs/2312.16400
4. Guo, Z., et al.: Information-controllable graph contrastive learning for recommendation. In: Proceedings of the 18th ACM Conference on Recommender Systems, pp. 528–537. RecSys 2024, Association for Computing Machinery, New York (2024). https://doi.org/10.1145/3640457.3688122
5. He, R., McAuley, J.: Vbpr: visual bayesian personalized ranking from implicit feedback (2015). https://arxiv.org/abs/1510.01784
6. He, X., Deng, K., Wang, X., Li, Y., Zhang, Y., Wang, M.: Lightgcn: simplifying and powering graph convolution network for recommendation (2020). https://arxiv.org/abs/2002.02126
7. Jiang, Y., Xia, L., Wei, W., Luo, D., Lin, K., Huang, C.: Diffmm: multi-modal diffusion model for recommendation (2024). https://arxiv.org/abs/2406.11781
8. Lei, F., Cao, Z., Yang, Y., Ding, Y., Zhang, C.: Learning the user's deeper preferences for multi-modal recommendation systems. ACM Trans. Multimedia Comput. Commun. Appl. **19**(3s) (2023). https://doi.org/10.1145/3573010
9. Lin, G., Meng, Z., Wang, D., Long, Q., Zhou, Y., Xiao, M.: Gume: graphs and user modalities enhancement for long-tail multimodal recommendation (2024). https://arxiv.org/abs/2407.12338
10. Lin, Z., Tian, C., Hou, Y., Zhao, W.X.: Improving graph collaborative filtering with neighborhood-enriched contrastive learning. In: Proceedings of the ACM Web Conference 2022, pp. 2320–2329. ACM (2022). https://doi.org/10.1145/3485447.3512104
11. Liu, S., Chen, Z., Liu, H., Hu, X.: User-video co-attention network for personalized micro-video recommendation. In: The World Wide Web Conference, pp. 3020–3026. WWW '19, Association for Computing Machinery, New York (2019). https://doi.org/10.1145/3308558.3313513
12. McAuley, J., Targett, C., Shi, Q., van den Hengel, A.: Image-based recommendations on styles and substitutes (2015). https://arxiv.org/abs/1506.04757
13. Quadrana, M., Cremonesi, P., Jannach, D.: Sequence-aware recommender systems (2018). https://arxiv.org/abs/1802.08452
14. Reimers, N., Gurevych, I.: Sentence-bert: sentence embeddings using siamese bert-networks (2019). https://arxiv.org/abs/1908.10084
15. Rendle, S., Freudenthaler, C., Gantner, Z., Schmidt-Thieme, L.: BPR: Bayesian personalized ranking from implicit feedback (2012). https://arxiv.org/abs/1205.2618

16. Sarwar, B., Karypis, G., Konstan, J., Riedl, J.: Item-based collaborative filtering recommendation algorithms. In: Proceedings of the 10th International Conference on World Wide Web, pp. 285–295. WWW 2001, Association for Computing Machinery, New York (2001). https://doi.org/10.1145/371920.372071
17. Simonyan, K., Zisserman, A.: Very deep convolutional networks for large-scale image recognition (2015). https://arxiv.org/abs/1409.1556
18. Sun, R., et al.: Multi-modal knowledge graphs for recommender systems. In: Proceedings of the 29th ACM International Conference on Information & Knowledge Management, pp. 1405–1414. CIKM 2020, Association for Computing Machinery, New York (2020). https://doi.org/10.1145/3340531.3411947
19. Tao, Z., et al.: Self-supervised learning for multimedia recommendation. IEEE Trans. Multimedia **25**, 5107–5116 (2023). https://doi.org/10.1109/TMM.2022.3187556
20. Wang, Q., Wei, Y., Yin, J., Wu, J., Song, X., Nie, L.: Dualgnn: dual graph neural network for multimedia recommendation. IEEE Trans. Multimedia **25**, 1074–1084 (2023). https://doi.org/10.1109/TMM.2021.3138298
21. Wei, Y., Wang, X., Nie, L., He, X., Hong, R., Chua, T.S.: Mmgcn: multi-modal graph convolution network for personalized recommendation of micro-video. In: Proceedings of the 27th ACM International Conference on Multimedia, pp. 1437–1445. MM '19, Association for Computing Machinery, New York (2019). https://doi.org/10.1145/3343031.3351034
22. Wu, L.: Advances in collaborative filtering and ranking (2020). https://arxiv.org/abs/2002.12312
23. Xu, J., Chen, Z., Yang, S., Li, J., Wang, H., Ngai, E.C.H.: Mentor: multi-level self-supervised learning for multimodal recommendation (2024). https://arxiv.org/abs/2402.19407
24. Yu, J., Xia, X., Chen, T., Cui, L., Hung, N.Q.V., Yin, H.: Xsimgcl: towards extremely simple graph contrastive learning for recommendation (2023). https://arxiv.org/abs/2209.02544
25. Yu, J., Yin, H., Xia, X., Chen, T., Cui, L., Nguyen, Q.V.H.: Are graph augmentations necessary? Simple graph contrastive learning for recommendation (2022). https://arxiv.org/abs/2112.08679
26. Yu, P., Tan, Z., Lu, G., Bao, B.K.: Multi-view graph convolutional network for multimedia recommendation. In: Proceedings of the 31st ACM International Conference on Multimedia, pp. 6576–6585. ACM (2023). https://doi.org/10.1145/3581783.3613915
27. Zhang, F., Yuan, N.J., Lian, D., Xie, X., Ma, W.Y.: Collaborative knowledge base embedding for recommender systems. In: Proceedings of the 22nd ACM SIGKDD International Conference on Knowledge Discovery and Data Mining, pp. 353–362. KDD 2016, Association for Computing Machinery, New York (2016). https://doi.org/10.1145/2939672.2939673
28. Zhang, J., Zhu, Y., Liu, Q., Wu, S., Wang, S., Wang, L.: Mining latent structures for multimedia recommendation. In: Proceedings of the 29th ACM International Conference on Multimedia, pp. 3872–3880. ACM (2021). https://doi.org/10.1145/3474085.3475259
29. Zhou, H., Zhou, X., Zhang, L., Shen, Z.: Enhancing dyadic relations with homogeneous graphs for multimodal recommendation (2023). https://arxiv.org/abs/2301.12097
30. Zhou, X.: Mmrec: simplifying multimodal recommendation. In: Proceedings of the 5th ACM International Conference on Multimedia in Asia Workshops. MMAsia '23

Workshops, Association for Computing Machinery, New York, NY, USA (2023). https://doi.org/10.1145/3611380.3628561
31. Zhou, X., Shen, Z.: A tale of two graphs: freezing and denoising graph structures for multimodal recommendation. In: Proceedings of the 31st ACM International Conference on Multimedia, pp. 935–943. ACM (2023). https://doi.org/10.1145/3581783.3611943
32. Zhou, X., et al.: Bootstrap latent representations for multi-modal recommendation. In: Proceedings of the ACM Web Conference 2023, pp. 845–854. ACM (2023). https://doi.org/10.1145/3543507.3583251

Echoes or Adversaries? Asymmetric Polarization in Elite Digital Communication

Meng-Jie Wang[1(✉)], Xiao-Cui Zhang[2], and Lin Qiu[1]

[1] The Chinese University of Hong Kong, Sha Tin 999077, Hong Kong SAR, China
mengjiewang@cuhk.edu.hk

[2] Television New Zealand, Auckland 1010, New Zealand

Abstract. While numerous studies have examined affective polarization, much of that work has centered on public opinion or voter engagement within traditional media contexts at a single point, leaving it unclear how these dynamics unfold in peer-level interactions among political elites in digital spaces. Moving beyond conventional approaches, here we leverage social network and sentiment analysis on Twitter/X corpora spanning both the 2018 and 2022 U.S. Senate elections, exploring: a) how Senate candidates engage with partisan allies versus ideological rivals online, and b) to what extent the emotional tenor of both intra-party and cross-party discourse shifts over time. While tightly knit networks formed on both political fronts, where connections within consistently surpassed those beyond, the results reveal a notable divergence across electoral cycles, with Democrats increasingly extending their outreach – frequently marked by negative tones – whereas Republicans significantly concentrated on reinforcing their bonds, characterized by substantial positive messaging. Given the enduring role of elite messaging in shaping political norms, these findings illuminate the dynamics of asymmetric ideological division, shedding light on the evolving trajectories through which political figures forge alliances or confront adversaries via social media networks from the Trump to Biden era.

Keywords: Affective Polarization · Social Network · Sentiment Analysis · Digital Political Communication · Trump-Biden Era

1 Introduction

"*Our politics has become less about what we believe and more about who we hate*", as political scientist Lilliana Mason incisively observes [1]. Such candid appraisals underscore the profound transformation sweeping through the American political arena – a terrain long shaped by its entrenched two-party system, which has consistently served as a battleground for impassioned debates over pivotal national concerns. From the intricate efforts surrounding healthcare reform and the fervent discourse concerning gun control, to the pressing challenges of climate change and immigration policies [2–4], these discussions often reflect divergent perspectives and entrenched ideological divides. Especially during electoral cycles, such underlying tensions tend to be amplified, with candidates strategically sharpening contrasts to sway public sentiment and mobilize their base [5].

T. Hao et al. (Eds.): BESC 2025, LNCS 16431, pp. 252–266, 2026.
https://doi.org/10.1007/978-981-95-7138-3_17

Against this backdrop, a troubling tide of negativity has permeated much of the electoral climate. An emerging body of work has identified an accelerating trend in partisan allegiance and deepening hostility toward opposing factions [6]. During the 2016 and 2020 U.S. campaigns, for instance, elite actors were frequently observed prioritizing denunciation of opponents over advocacy for their own platforms [7, 8], with some even emphasizing the threats posed by their adversaries more than the virtues of their own agendas. This intensifying animosity culminates in what Finkel et al. [9] describe as affective polarization – a uniquely corrosive dynamic wherein in-group favoritism continues to grow, and animosity deepens across party lines.

Within this intensifying climate, the rise of Donald Trump to the presidency marked an inflection point that brought many latent tensions to the surface [10]. As noted by Gross and Johnson [6], the partisan chasm during this era deepened considerably, with public discourse – traditionally a space for competing ideas – undergoing a notable transformation. Figures across the ideological spectrum – particularly those aligned with or reacting against the Trump administration – increasingly deployed divisive narratives and rhetorical attacks, using them not merely for communication but as strategic instruments to activate partisan identities. This combative style, undergirded by a growing distrust in democratic institutions, contributed to a broader environment in which affective polarization tends to be normalized – and, in some contexts, arguably incentivized.

While the Biden administration arrived with calls for national healing and bipartisan unity [11], questions remain as to whether such appeals have meaningfully reshaped the tone of elite discourse – or if combative patterns cemented during the Trump era have endured. Though there have been extensive bodies of literature examining affective polarization [1, 9], much of this work has centered on public opinion or voter engagement within traditional media contexts at a single point, leaving it unclear how such dynamics manifest in peer-directed interactions among political candidates in the digital realm over time. In particular, to what extent do candidates engage partisan allies versus ideological opponents? And how do their emotional tones – whether marked by hostility or civility – vary over time? These dynamics, especially as they unfold across contrasting leadership eras, have yet to be thoroughly understood, forming the core focus of our study here.

Despite the escalating tide of affective polarization appearing pervasive, its manifestation may not be entirely symmetrical across the political spectrum. According to Grossmann and Hopkins [12], Democrats and Republicans may adopt divergent communicative and engagement strategies that reflect deeper asymmetries in partisan behavior. The Democratic Party, specifically, as a coalition of diverse interest groups, tends to prioritize policy deliberation and cross-cutting dialogue, whereas the Republican Party – more ideologically homogeneous and identity-driven – often emphasizes cohesion over compromise. Given these theoretical distinctions regarding asymmetric polarization, how such partisan differences manifest in peer-level digital exchanges among candidates – particularly during high-stakes campaigns – remains largely unknown.

Moving beyond conventional approaches – often confined to single electoral cycles or narrow temporal scopes [13] – here we seek to address this gap through an examination of Twitter/X corpora spanning both the 2018 and 2022 U.S. elections. Specifically, leveraging social network and sentiment analysis, the study probes a) how Senate candidates engage with partisan allies versus ideological rivals online, and b) to what extent the emotional tenor of both intra-party and cross-party discourse shifts across contrasting presidential administrations. By illuminating the evolving trajectories of such interactions, the present work may offer a unique glimpse, shedding light on the ways in which elite-level affective polarization unfolds dynamically within digital political arenas.

2 Method

2.1 Dataset

Leveraging the Twitter API via the Tweepy Python library [14], the study extracted interactive tweets published by Senate candidates over nine weeks surrounding the 2018 (October 09 – December 04, with election date November 6) and 2022 (October 11 – December 06, with election date November 8) U.S. midterm elections – comprising four weeks prior, four weeks following, and one week during the election period – a timeframe most likely to capture electorally salient communication activity.

Focusing on the two leading candidates in each race – those who advanced to the final election phase – we specifically captured tweets from Senate candidates that either included user mentions ("@username") or were explicitly marked as retweets ("RT"). Such tweets often serve as critical mechanisms for message dissemination – whether signaling endorsement or opposition – and as key indicators of user engagement [15–17], offering a valuable lens through which to explore how candidates mobilize supporters, challenge adversaries, or shape discursive boundaries within partisan networks online.

To ensure data integrity and analytical rigor, we implemented a filtering procedure to verify user (candidate) accounts:

- **Direct Party Affiliation**: Each account was confirmed to be directly affiliated with a major-party candidate (i.e., Democratic or Republican), excluding those associated with third-party contenders (e.g., Independents).
- **Authentic Candidacy Verification**: Each account either displayed an official verification badge or was manually validated through cross-referencing with official campaign websites, public candidate lists, or formal declarations, ensuring a confirmed and credible association with the respective candidacy.

2.2 Social Network Analysis

To examine candidates' interactive patterns, social network analysis (SNA) was utilized to assess intra- (within the same party alignment) and inter-group (across opposing affiliations) engagement on Twitter/X. Specifically, for each election cycle, distinct networks were constructed for Democratic and Republican candidates, alongside overarching cross-party interactions.

Within these networks, each candidate is represented as a node [18], with the 2018 cycle comprising 62 nodes (Democrats = 32; Republicans = 30), while the 2022 cycle involved 63 nodes (Democrats = 31; Republicans = 32). Given that candidates may engage with either in-group allies or out-group opponents, edges within these networks denote directional relationships. For instance, a directed edge is established when a candidate mentions or retweets another, signaling an information flow or exchange from the initiator to the recipient. In total, 2,453 connections (Democrats = 1,029; Republicans = 1,424) and 1,791 connections (Democrats = 871; Republicans = 920) were recorded across the 2018 and 2022 elections, respectively.

Leveraging Python's NetworkX library, network density was computed for partisan networks [19]. Specifically, this metric quantifies the proportion of observed edges relative to the maximum number of possible directed edges within a given network, as follows:

$$Network\ Density = \frac{E}{N(N-1)} \tag{1}$$

where E denotes the number of unique directed edges and N represents the number of nodes. For intra-group analysis, where self-mentions are included, the maximum number of possible directed edges is defined as $N \times N$.

According to Qu et al. [20], a high network density may signify a closely knit community characterized by frequent interactions, often implying strong cohesion or unified messaging. Conversely, a low network density may suggest sporadic interactions or network fragmentation, potentially reflecting divisions or a diminished level of cohesion among those candidates. By utilizing this metric, we may provide a critical lens for identifying intra- and inter-party interactions across political divides, providing insight into the evolving dynamics of partisan engagement among U.S. Senate candidates over the election cycles online.

2.3 Sentiment Analysis

Expanding beyond social network analysis, we further incorporated the Linguistic Inquiry and Word Count 2022 (LIWC-22) – a widely validated tool for psycholinguistic analysis – to examine the potential shifts in candidates' tone across intra- and inter-group messaging over time [21].

Developed by James Pennebaker and colleagues in the early 1990s, LIWC is a dictionary-based method that analyzes text by mapping words to a structured lexicon of psychologically meaningful categories [22]. Each category – such as sentiment tones, cognitive processes, or social dynamics – is composed of carefully curated lexical items, enabling the quantification of linguistic features as proportions of total word count, yielding a transparent and replicable measure of a text's underlying psychological content. Refined through several iterations, LIWC-22 represents one of the most advanced tools for computational text analysis to date. Given its robust psychometric foundation, high reliability, and methodological transparency, this tool has been widely adopted across diverse fields including psychology, communication, computer science, and public health (see [23] for reviews).

Table 1. Sample tweets processed by LIWC-22

Date	Poster		Interacted User		Positive Tone	Negative Tone
	Senate Candidate	Party Affiliation	Senate Candidate	Party Affiliation		
21/10/18	G. Diehl	Republican	E. Warren	Democratic	2.38	14.29
	"#ElizabethWarren used violent imagery to describe what she would do to political opponents, attacks our police officers as "racists," and puts illegal immigrants ahead of our Angel Moms whose children were killed. We are not safe with @SenWarren in the Senate. #WGBYDebate"					
02/11/18	T. Smith	Democratic	T. Smith	Democratic	33.33	0.00
	"RT @carlymelin: Proud to support @TinaSmithMN!"					
07/11/18	T. Smith	Democratic	A. Klobuchar	Democratic	17.39	0.00
	"Congratulations to my friend and colleague Senator @amyklobuchar on her decisive win tonight. Thank you for always being a strong voice for Minnesotans."					
02/11/22	A. Laxalt	Republican	C. Masto	Democratic	0.00	11.90
	"Families in this country are hurting. Nevadans are hurting. Biden his rubber stamp, @CortezMasto, are to blame. I'm running for US Senate because we need to change course. I will fight back on the failed liberal policies, fight for ALL Nevadans. https://t.co/AtjLjvLTUP"					
06/11/22	M. Mullin	Republican	M. Oz	Republican	0.00	0.00
	"Overflow crowd in Bettendorf Scott County is pumped up to elect @GrassleyWorks @KimReynoldsIA @millermeeks @AdamGreggIA @BrennaBird @MikeNaigIA @PateforIowa @RobySmithIA #iaSen https://t.co/yjAwIfkTxW"					

Note: The poster refers to the candidate who authored the tweet, while connected user(s) denotes individuals who were mentioned or referenced within the tweet. Candidate names are abbreviated herein to facilitate concise data representation, in alignment with principles of ethical data handling and reporting consistency

As shown in Table 1, leveraging the positive (tone_pos) and negative tone (tone_neg) of LIWC-22, here we quantified the sentimental valence of each tweet, with outputs represented as the proportion of words in a given message that fall into each category. For example, consider the tweet:

"RT @carlymelin: Proud to support @TinaSmithMN!"

the analysis yielded a positive tone of 33.33 and a negative tone of 0.00, suggesting a predominantly affirmative tone, potentially indicating endorsement, approval, or commendation of the candidate or their actions. In contrast, consider the tweet:

"Families in this country are hurting. Nevadans are hurting. Biden his rubber stamp, @CortezMasto, are to blame. I'm running for US Senate because we need

to change course. I will fight back on the failed liberal policies, fight for ALL Nevadans. https://t.co/AtjLjvLTUP"

the analysis produced a negative tone of 11.90 and a positive tone of 0.00, indicating a message primarily characterized by criticism or opposition, potentially reflecting disapproval, blame attribution, or adversarial positioning within the political discourse.

Tweets lacking a discernible valence – typically comprising objective statements or neutral inquiries – were classified as neutral, with both positive and negative tones at 0.00. To ensure a comprehensive assessment of communicative intent, our analysis here was conducted on entire tweets rather than isolated sentences, capturing the full sentiment valence conveyed through intra- and inter-party communication across Democratic and Republican networks over time.

3 Results

3.1 Messaging Distribution

Overall, from 2018 to 2022, U.S. Senate candidates exhibited a contraction in elite-to-elite interactions on Twitter/X. As depicted in Table 2, the total volume of messaging exchanges – including both mentions and retweets – declined by nearly 27%, dropping from 2,453 in 2018 to 1,791 in 2022. Notably, such a downward trajectory was particularly pronounced among Republican candidates, whose messaging decreased by approximately 35%, from 1,424 to 920, compared to a modest 15% reduction among their Democratic counterparts, from 1,029 to 871.

Table 2. Distribution of intra-and inter-group messaging by democratic and republican candidates

Year	Party Affiliation	Intra-group n (%)	Inter-group n (%)	Total
2018	Democrats	839 (82%)	190 (18%)	1,029
	Republicans	795 (56%)	629 (44%)	1,424
	Total	1,634 (67%)	819 (33%)	2,453
2022	Democrats	690 (79%)	181 (21%)	871
	Republicans	612 (66%)	308 (34%)	920
	Total	1,302 (73%)	489 (27%)	1,791

Note: n denotes the total number of tweets, while the percentage (%) indicates the proportion of these tweets relative to the total volume of messages produced by each party during the corresponding election cycle

Despite this overall decline in messaging exchanges, candidate interactions tended to be increasingly polarized, with their intra-party connections (i.e., messaging directed at same-party candidates) consistently exceeding inter-party outreach (i.e., messaging towards the opposing side). The proportion of in-group tweets, for instance, rose from 67% (n = 1,634) in 2018 to 73% (n = 1,302) in 2022 – marking a nearly 6% increase overall. Their out-group exchanges, conversely, declined from 33% (n = 819) to 27% (n = 489) across this period, potentially underscoring an erosion of bipartisan engagement within campaign discourse on such sites.

Democratic candidates, specifically, maintained a strong intra-party orientation. Roughly 80% of their connections were directed toward their co-partisans (2018: n = 839, 82%; 2022: n = 690, 79%). Though this internal alignment remained relatively stable, a slight uptick in cross-party messaging exchanges emerged – from 18% (n = 190) in 2018 to 21% (n = 181) in 2022 – potentially revealing a growing propensity to engage Republican counterparts, either to delineate contrasting policy positions or to amplify partisan distinctions throughout the election cycles.

Republican candidates, however, evinced an even more pronounced recalibration manifesting in the opposite direction. In 2018, for instance, an elevated level of inter-party focus was identified, with 44% of messages (n = 629) directed at their counterparts – nearly triple the out-group exchange rate observed among Democrats that year. In 2022, by contrast, such communication became substantially more inward facing. The proportion of their out-group messaging declined by approximately 10% to 34% (n = 308), while their in-group connections rose by the same margin, from 56% (n = 795) to 66% (n = 612). Such a shift may suggest an accelerating trend toward reinforcing base solidarity while diminishing broader discursive engagement with the opposing side on the digital sphere.

3.2 Network Structure and Patterns of Connectivity

To rigorously investigate the evolving patterns of candidate interactions on Twitter/X, Social Network Analysis (SNA) was employed to ascertain network density, thereby evaluating the cohesion and potential fragmentation both within and across partisan lines online. Key metrics of this analysis were:

- **Intra-Group Density**, which quantifies the degree to which candidates within the same party interact with one another – offering a measure of internal cohesion or fragmentation.
- **Inter-Group Density**, which reflects the degree of connectivity between opposing parties – serving as an indicator of bipartisan communication.

Additionally, to provide further insight into candidate interactions within and beyond party lines, we also assessed the average degree – the average number of unique connections or edges (i.e., mentions or retweets) initiated by candidates, directed either towards their co-partisans or opposing counterparts, across the election cycles. Such a metric, which quantifies how many different individuals a candidate engages with, may capture the number of distinct relationships formed, shedding light on the breadth of a candidate's outreach or the diversity of their communication network.

As depicted in Table 3, distinct structural patterns emerged in 2018 partisan communication. Democratic candidates, for instance, cultivated a dense network of intra-party interactions, with a group density of 0.077. On average, each Democratic candidate established 2.54 unique connections with their fellows, in contrast to just 1.00 such connection directed toward their counterparts. Republican candidates across the 2018 cycle, however, exhibited a less cohesive pattern of intra-party interaction, reflected by a group density of only 0.044. On average, each Republican candidate initiated 1.53 unique edges toward fellow party members – a figure considerably lower than that observed among Democrats. Their cross-party outreach, however, tended to be more active, with an average of 1.11 unique connections directed toward the opposition – slightly higher than the Democratic average during the same period (for a visual overview of interaction trends, see Figs. 1–2).

Overall, their inter-group density in 2018, which quantifies how densely connected the two opposing parties are to each other, was notably low at 0.033, with each candidate, on average, establishing just 0.51 unique interconnections, regardless of direction (i.e., from Democrats to Republicans or vice versa).

Table 3. Intra- and inter-group network density and average degree of messaging by democratic and republican candidates

Year	Party Affiliation	Intra-group Density (Average Degree)	Inter-group Density (Average Degree)
2018	Democrats	0.077 (2.54, 1.00)	0.033 (0.51)
	Republicans	0.044 (1.53, 1.11)	
2022	Democrats	0.084 (2.70, 1.18)	0.036 (0.57)
	Republicans	0.086 (2.83, 1.06)	

Note: Intra-group density indicates average unique connections to same-party members, while inter group density reflects the overall average unique cross party connections initiated by candidates, regardless of sender or direction

In 2022, the Democratic party's network remained robust, with its group density slightly increasing to 0.084. On average, each Democratic candidate established 2.70 unique internal connections and 1.18 cross-party ties – both marginally higher than those observed in 2018, potentially signaling a renewed impetus to broaden external engagement while maintaining strong internal cohesion throughout.

Republicans, notably, exhibited a more pronounced increase in cohesion within their own ranks, with group density significantly rising to 0.086 in 2022. Each Republican candidate, on average, forged 2.83 unique internal connections – slightly surpassing that of Democrats in the same period. Their cross-party connectivity, however, declined to a level even lower than that of Democrats, averaging 1.06, potentially underscoring increased communicative siloing throughout the election cycles.

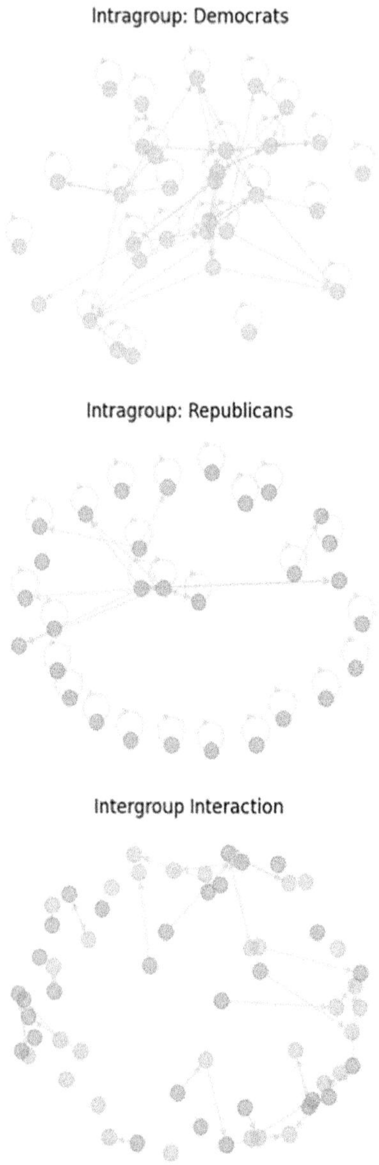

Fig. 1. Candidate Interaction Networks During the 2018 U.S. Midterm Elections

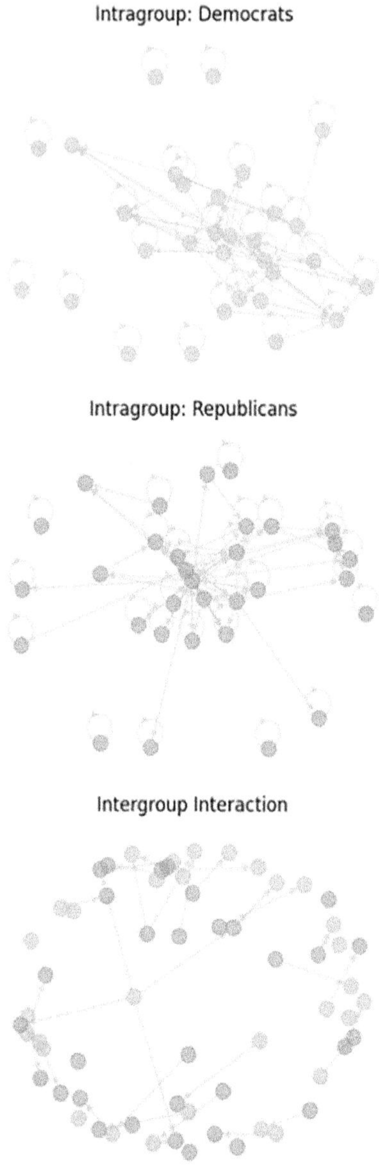

Fig. 2. Candidate Interaction Networks During the 2022 U.S. Midterm Elections

Overall, the inter-group density remained constrained at 0.036 in 2022, accompanied by an average degree of 0.57. Such consistently low inter-party connectivity may illustrate the limited nature of bipartisan interaction on Twitter/X. Both parties consistently prioritized intra- over inter-group communications, yet their messaging emphasis diverged across the period, with Democrats maintaining strong internal cohesion while showing a slight inclination towards expanding external engagement, and Republicans significantly intensifying their focus on reinforcing internal bonds while reducing their outward-facing outreach from 2018 to 2022.

3.3 Partisan Sentiments and Affective Boundaries

While prior results identify that candidates increasingly engaged within their own co-partisan circles while diverging across party lines, the emotional contours of these interactions – how tone evolves across political divides – remain unclear. Leveraging LIWC-22, we further examined the sentiments of candidates' tweets to quantify the prevalence of positive and negative tone in intra- and inter-party communications during the 2018 and 2022 U.S. elections. To contextualize the potential shifts in such messaging tone, we also assessed thematic patterns, derived from the most frequently occurring terms within group discourse, providing deeper insights into the emotional dynamics online.

As evinced in Table 4, a pervasive pattern of affective polarization emerged, with candidates, regardless of affiliation, consistently showing pronounced in-group favoritism and out-group hostility in messaging. Within their own partisan circles, for instance, candidates employed significantly more positive than negative language, with intra-party positivity rising markedly from a mean of 3.80 (SE = 0.11) in 2018 to 4.92 (SE = 0.15) in 2022, while negative tone simultaneously declined from 1.05 (SE = 0.06) to 0.92 (SE = 0.06). The inter-party communications, by contrast, presented a starkly contrasting emotional landscape, where those candidates often deployed heightened negativity when addressing the opposition, with overall mean negative tones remaining elevated at 2.06 (SE = 0.10) in 2018 and 2.07 (SE = 0.15) in 2022, while positive tones stayed comparatively subdued at 1.91 (SE = 0.09) and 1.73 (SE = 0.12) during the same period.

Their inter-group messaging, however, often conveyed a high level of negativity, with mean negative tone holding steady from 1.96 (SE = 0.20) to 1.98 (SE = 0.27), consistently higher than the corresponding positive tone at 1.71 (SE = 0.18) and 1.75 (SE = 0.19). Such persistent negativity was coupled with thematic shifts, from addressing issues – such as healthcare or pre-existing conditions in 2018 – to embracing more confrontational themes in 2022, including exerting power, endorsing enforcement measures, emphasizing voter choice, directly opposing former President Trump, and intensifying efforts to mobilize support for their agendas – a potential pivot to engage and challenge opposing factions with heightened assertiveness throughout the elections.

Though Republican candidates exhibited a similar trend in intra-group messaging, with mean positive tone rising from 3.70 (SE = 0.16) to 4.85 (SE = 0.21) while mean negative tone dropped from 1.16 (SE = 0.10) to 1.07 (SE = 0.09), the thematic content embedded in such messaging varied across successive campaigns. As illustrated in Figs. 3b-4b, their 2018 tweets directed at allies often invoked appreciation or pride, rallying support by emphasizing shared values and collective achievements. By 2022, however, this narrative evolved into urgent calls to action, highlighting a fight for the future and the preservation of the American dream, while strengthening internal bonds through intensified efforts to mobilize voters and defend conservative principles – with galvanizing rhetoric aimed at consolidating unity and energizing their voter base.

The tone embedded in their inter-group discourse, by contrast, maintained a consistently high level of negativity, with mean negative tone reaching 2.09 (SE = 0.11) in

Table 4. Intra- and inter-group sentiment by democratic and republican candidates

Year	Party Affiliation	Intra-group Sentiment		Inter-group Sentiment	
		M Pos (SE)	M Neg (SE)	M Pos (SE)	M Neg (SE)
2018	Democrats	3.89 (0.16)	0.96 (0.08)	1.71 (0.18)	1.96 (0.20)
	Republicans	3.70 (0.16)	1.16 (0.10)	1.96 (0.10)	2.09 (0.11)
	Total	3.80 (0.11)	1.05 (0.06)	1.91 (0.09)	2.06 (0.10)
2022	Democrats	4.99 (0.21)	0.79 (0.07)	1.75 (0.19)	1.98 (0.27)
	Republicans	4.85 (0.21)	1.07 (0.09)	1.71 (0.15)	2.13 (0.17)
	Total	4.92 (0.15)	0.92 (0.06)	1.73 (0.12)	2.07 (0.15)

Note: M Pos and M Neg represent the average percentage of words within tweets identified by LIWC-22 as positive or negative language, respectively, with higher values indicating greater emotional intensity in the corresponding direction. SE = standard error of the mean

2018 and 2.13 (SE = 0.17) in 2022, alongside a comparatively low level of positive tone at around 1.96 (SE = 0.10) and 1.71 (SE = 0.15). Such messaging, notably, often manifested as criticisms directed at key opposition figures or Democrats in general, casting them as antagonists and potentially delineating clear in-group vs. out-group boundaries, irrespective of the election cycle.

Overall, despite the consistent exhibition of in-group favoritism and out-group hostility across both factions' messaging, a discernible affective divergence emerged – Democratic candidates typically cultivated a more positive stance toward both co-partisans and rivals, while Republican counterparts evinced greater negativity, especially in their external communications.

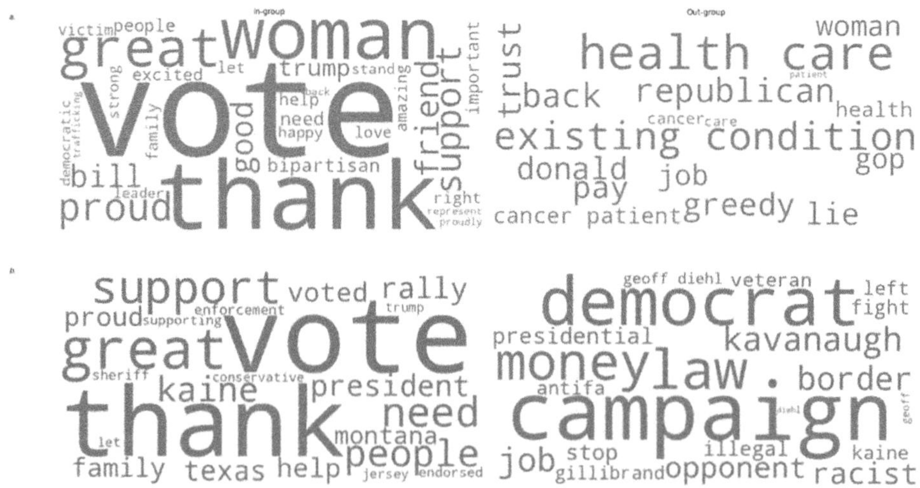

Fig. 3. Most frequently tweeted words and phrases by a) Democratic and b) Republican candidates during the 2018 campaign, with word size corresponding to relative frequency

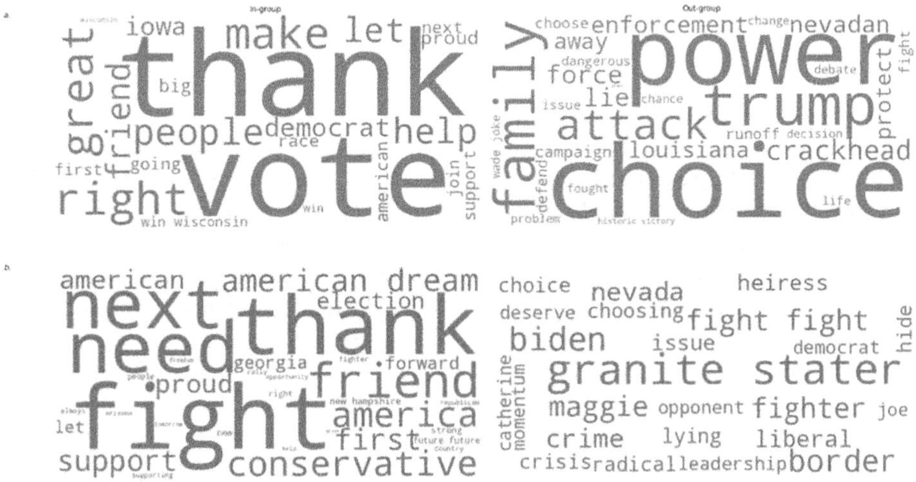

Fig. 4. Most frequently tweeted words and phrases by a) Democratic and b) Republican candidates during the 2022 campaign, with word size corresponding to relative frequency

4 Discussion

While existing literature has extensively charted the rise of affective polarization in political discourse, much of this work has primarily focused on public opinion or voter engagement within traditional media contexts, leaving a critical gap in understanding how these dynamics unfold among political elites – particularly through their direct, peer-level interactions in digital spaces. Moving beyond conventional approaches – often limited to single election cycles or narrow temporal scopes – the current research addresses this gap through a cross-sectional examination of Twitter/X corpora spanning both the 2018 and 2022 U.S. elections. Specifically, leveraging social network and sentiment analysis, we probe a) how Senate candidates engage with partisan allies versus ideological rivals online, and b) to what extent the emotional tenor of both intra-party and cross-party discourse shifts across contrasting presidential administrations, shedding light on the dynamics of elite-level engagement in a polarized digital environment.

Both parties across election cycles exhibited tightly knit communities characterized by significantly stronger intra- over inter-group connections, consistently employing positive tones toward their allies, which contrasted sharply with negative rhetoric directed against the opposition. Such patterns resonate with recent findings pinpointing the increasingly toxic dynamic in U.S. political discourse, marked by "affective polarization", wherein in-group favoritism continues to grow and animosity deepens across party lines [9]. According to Dagnes [24], such tactics – driven by the imperative to consolidate support – may sharply intensify the "us vs. them" divide, fostering insular communities that further entrench ideological fragmentation over time. Particularly during high-stakes campaigns, candidates may strategically foreground criticism of political adversaries [7], at times prioritizing perceived external threats over substantive promotion of their own platforms [25]. The recurring deployment of hostile narratives to galvanize support – as observed across our samples here – may serve to rally electoral bases around shared grievances or identities, even as it risks further alienating those across the aisle [16].

Beyond the general patterns of affective polarization, strikingly, our cross-temporal analysis further identifies a troubling intensification of these dynamics over time. From 2018 to 2022, both parties exhibited intensified intra-group density, increasingly surrounding themselves with ideologically like-minded allies while maintaining consistently low levels of cross-party engagement. This growing insularity was further accompanied by a discernible rise in positive tones within party lines, juxtaposed against a slight uptick in negativity toward the opposition. As noted by Woods et al. [26], the deepening rift observed during Trump's presidency may not have been a temporary disruption but rather signify the emergence of a new norm – one that could persist and evolve, challenging the mechanisms that have historically ensured stability in U.S. politics. Despite renewed calls for bipartisan cooperation under the Biden administration [11], these efforts may have fallen short, as deep-seated polarization appears to have endured or even worsened. Now, with Donald Trump's return to the political stage, the U.S. once again may stand at a precipice [27]. Whether this resurgence will reinforce – or rupture – existing patterns of elite polarization remains a pressing question, necessitating future research to continue examining how these evolving partisan dynamics continue to reshape the norms of political discourse over time.

While our findings broadly confirm the deepening of affective polarization in elite digital discourse, a more granular examination reveals a marked asymmetry in the communicative strategies adopted by Democratic and Republican candidates across electoral cycles. Drawing on theories of asymmetric polarization – which posit that partisan groups may not polarize to the same extent or in the same manner [12] – our analysis highlights distinct trajectories in how political elites interact with partisan allies and ideological adversaries over time. Democratic candidates, for instance, consistently maintained a cohesive intra-party orientation, while displaying a modest yet sustained pattern of engagement across party lines, even if negatively. In contrast, Republican candidates underwent a more pronounced recalibration in their engagement strategy – exhibiting a high volume of oppositional outreach in 2018, often marked by a negative tone; followed by a significant turn inward toward intra-group consolidation by 2022.

This observed asymmetry – wherein one party, such as the Republicans in this case, retreated further into a partisan echo chamber and reduced cross-party visibility in the public sphere – may offer compelling support for Grossmann and Hopkins [12]'s framework, underscoring how party-specific strategic shifts and identity-driven incentives may shape polarized engagement in elite digital discourse. While speculative, such dynamics risk further entrenching political gridlock, weakening prospects for bipartisan cooperation, and fueling public disillusionment with democratic institutions and actors. Given the enduring role of elite messaging in shaping political norms, further research could continue to explore the evolving mechanisms that drive partisan interaction – and to examine their manifestation within digital arenas over extended timeframes.

5 Limitations and Future Directions

While this study offers dynamic insights into the evolving contours of elite-level polarization within digital political discourse, several limitations merit reflection. The platform transformation from Twitter to X under Elon Musk's ownership introduces a new and largely uncharted dynamic [28]. The notable decline in candidate messaging observed between 2018 and 2022 raises important questions about how shifting platform governance and user norms may reshape the visibility and tenor of elite communication, which warrants further research. In addition, although our focus on retweets and mentions captures meaningful dimensions of candidate interaction, these indicators reflect only a fragment of the increasingly multimodal and cross-platform nature of political expression. With digital campaigning now extending beyond text-based formats to include short-form videos and influencer-driven outreach, future work should broaden its analytical lens across platforms and political tiers to capture a fuller picture of strategic elite communication. Finally, while network and sentiment analyses illuminate patterns of interaction, they offer limited access to the underlying psychological motivations driving these behaviors. Integrating complementary methodologies – such as surveys or experimental designs – could enrich our understanding of the affective and strategic logics animating elite discourse in a deeply polarized digital age.

Acknowledgments. In accordance with Twitter/X's data-sharing policy, the original dataset remains proprietary. All associated code and sampling procedures are available via OSF.

References

1. Mason, L.: I disrespectfully agree": the differential effects of partisan sorting on social and issue polarization. Amer. J. Polit. Sci. **59**(1), 128–145 (2015)
2. Gordon, C.: Dead on Arrival: The Politics of Health Care in Twentieth-Century America. Princeton University Press, Princeton (2009)
3. Spitzer, R.J.: Gun accessories and the second amendment: assault weapons, magazines, and silencer. Law Contemp. Probl. **83**(2), 231 (2020)
4. Antonio, R.J., Brulle, R.J.: The unbearable lightness of politics: climate change denial and political polarization. Sociol. Quart. **52**(2), 195–202 (2011). https://doi.org/10.1111/j.1533-8525.2011.01199.x
5. Frymer, P.: Uneasy Alliances: Race and Party Competition in America. Princeton University Press, Princeton (2011)
6. Gross, J.H., Johnson, K.T.: Twitter taunts and tirades: negative campaigning in the age of Trump. Polit. Sci. Polit. **49**(4), 748–754 (2016). https://doi.org/10.1017/S1049096516001700
7. Bankert, A.: Negative partisanship among independents in the 2020 U.S. presidential elections. Electoral Stud. **78**, 102490 (2022). https://doi.org/10.1016/j.electstud.2022.102490
8. Brady, W.J., Wills, J.A., Jost, J.T., Tucker, J.A., Van Bavel, J.J.: Emotion shapes the diffusion of moralized content in social networks. Proc. Nat. Acad. Sci. USA **114**(28), 7313–7318 (2017). https://doi.org/10.1073/pnas.1618923114
9. Finkel, E.J., et al.: Political sectarianism in America. Science **370**(6516), 533–536 (2020). https://doi.org/10.1126/science.abe1715

10. Nai, A., Maier, J.: Dark necessities? Candidates' aversive personality traits and negative campaigning in the 2018 American midterms. Electoral Stud. **68**, 102233 (2020). https://doi.org/10.1016/j.electstud.2020.102233
11. Moncayo, A.: Why a presidential call for unity can never be enough. AmeriQuests **17**(1) (2022)
12. Grossmann, M., Hopkins, D.A.: Asymmetric Politics: Ideological Republicans and Group Interest Democrats. Oxford University Press, Oxford (2016)
13. Eisenstein, J., O'Connor, B., Smith, N.A., et al.: Diffusion of lexical change in social media. PLoS ONE **9**(11), e113114 (2014). https://doi.org/10.1371/journal.pone.0113114
14. Tweepy.: Tweepy documentation (2009). http://docs.tweepy.org/en/v3.5.0/. Accessed 12 June 2023
15. Wang, M.J., Yogeeswaran, K., Sivaram, S., Nash, K.: Examining spread of emotional political content among Democratic and Republican candidates during the 2018 US mid-term elections. Humanit. Soc. Sci. Commun. **8**(1), 1–12 (2021)
16. Wang, M.J., Yogeeswaran, K., Nash, K., Sivaram, S.: Morality and partisan social media engagement: a natural language examination of moral political messaging and engagement during the 2018 US midterm elections. J. Comput. Social Sci. **7**(2), 1699–1726 (2024)
17. Wang, M.J.: Tweeting from left to right: tracing the dynamics of emotional messaging and public engagement during the 2018 vs. 2022 US campaigns. In: Proceedings of the 2023 IEEE International Conference on Parallel & Distributed Processing with Applications, Big Data & Cloud Computing, Sustainable Computing & Communications, Social Computing & Networking (ISPA/BDCloud/SocialCom/SustainCom), pp. 961–971 (2023)
18. Oliveira, M., Gama, J.: An overview of social network analysis. Wiley Interdiscip. Rev. Data Min. Knowl. Discov. **2**(2), 99–115 (2012). https://doi.org/10.1002/widm.1048
19. Platt, E.L.: Network Science with Python and NetworkX Quick Start Guide: Explore and Visualize Network Data Effectively. Packt Publishing Ltd., Birmingham (2019)
20. Qu, Y., Saffer, A.J., Riffe, D.: The social network antecedents to consumer engagement: revealing how consumers' conversations influence online engagement behaviors. Corp. Commun. Int. J. **27**(2), 226–244 (2022). https://doi.org/10.1108/CCIJ-04-2021-0046
21. Boyd, R.L., Ashokkumar, A., Seraj, S., Pennebaker, J.W.: The Development and Psychometric Properties of LIWC-22. University of Texas at Austin, Austin (2022)
22. Pennebaker, J.W., Mehl, M.R., Niederhoffer, K.G.: Psychological aspects of natural language use: our words, our selves. Annu. Rev. Psychol. **54**(1), 547–577 (2003)
23. Eichstaedt, J.C., et al.: Closed-and open-vocabulary approaches to text analysis: a review, quantitative comparison, and recommendations. Psychol. Methods **26**(4), 398 (2021)
24. Dagnes, A.: Us vs. Them: Political Polarization and the Politicization of Everything. Super Mad at Everything All the Time: Political Media and Our National Anger, pp. 119–165 (2019)
25. Garzia, D., Ferreira, S.F.: The electoral consequences of affective polarization? Negative voting in the 2020 US presidential election. Am. Polit. Res. **50**(3), 303–311 (2022). https://doi.org/10.1177/1532673X221074633
26. Woods, E.T., Fortier-Chouinard, A., Closen, M., et al.: The battle for the soul of the nation: nationalist polarization in the 2020 American presidential election and the threat to democracy. Polit. Commun. **41**(2), 173–198 (2024). https://doi.org/10.1080/10584609.2023.2291150
27. Sivin, D.D.: Trump: a disaster for health, safety, and environment. New Solutions: J. Environ. Occupat. Health Policy **34**(4), 248–252 (2025)
28. Bisbee, J., Munger, K.: The vibes are off: did Elon musk push academics off twitter? PS: Polit Sci. Polit. **58**(1), 139–146 (2025)

Student Learning Engagement Recognition Method Based on Video Transformer

Wenhao Liao[1], Yuanyuan Wang[1(✉)], Xinwei Zhai[1], Sineng Yan[1], Kai Zhong[1], and Eugene Yujun Fu[2]

[1] Shenzhen University, Shenzhen, China
yywang@szu.edu.cn
[2] The Education University of Hong Kong, Ting Kok, Hong Kong S.A.R., China
eugenefu@eduhk.hk

Abstract. The widespread adoption of online learning has made traditional engagement evaluation methods, which rely on teachers' subjective judgments, no longer practical. It is essential to develop an accurate and automatic evaluation method. However, most existing methods for assessing student learning engagement rely on CNNs, whose limited receptive fields restrict their capacity to model long-range dependencies in video data. Additionally, the scarcity of low-engagement students compared to highly engaged ones in real classrooms introduces model bias, resulting in the misclassification of low-engagement (rare) instances as high-engagement (common) classes. They lead to limited accuracy in engagement recognition methods. This paper investigates approaches to enhance recognition accuracy by optimizing video representation and addressing data imbalance. Specifically, we introduce a dual-stream pre-trained video transformer framework into student engagement recognition, which jointly learns spatial representations and temporal dynamics to generate more discriminative video representations. Furthermore, we improve model performance on rare categories by calibrating prediction scores to achieve better inter-class balance. We conducted extensive experiments on the challenging DAiSEE benchmark, with our method achieving promising results. Comparative experiments show that our method achieves a 9.02% improvement in accuracy compared to Vision Transformer, which also employs transformer, and outperforms all CNN-based methods.

Keywords: Learning engagement · Engagement recognition · Online learning · Video Transformer · Deep learning

1 Introduction

The paradigm shift in pedagogical approaches from teacher-centered to learner-centered models has placed a spotlight on students' learning engagement in the classroom. Active learning engagement not only stimulates intrinsic motivation and improves academic performance, but it also piques interest in learning and

T. Hao et al. (Eds.): BESC 2025, LNCS 16431, pp. 267–281, 2026.
https://doi.org/10.1007/978-981-95-7138-3_18

cultivates positive learning attitudes. Consequently, learning engagement serves as a critical indicator for both learning outcomes and teaching quality, enabling educators to implement evidence-based instructional adjustments.

The significance of online learning has increased dramatically after the COVID-19 outbreak, as it has become the new normal for education [32]. On the one hand, this educational model provides cross-spatiotemporal learning convenience and cost-effective access to educational resources. On the other hand, the physical separation across time and space makes students prone to insufficient learning engagement, while instructors struggle to promptly identify students facing learning difficulties. Instructors often have to rely on limited interaction data (such as attendance rates and assignment submissions) for delayed assessments, which further constrains the potential of online education.

Conventional approaches to assessing learning engagement primarily depend on instructors' subjective evaluations, which are inherently limited by individual teaching experiences and career backgrounds. The shift to online education has further exacerbated these limitations, as educators can no longer effectively monitor all students' classroom performance simultaneously [29]. Consequently, accurate manual assessment of learning engagement has become progressively more challenging, highlighting the critical need for developing objective, precise, and automated recognition methods.

Recent advances in automated assessment of student behavior [25], cognitive state [36], and attention levels [23] have introduced novel approaches to address the limitations of conventional engagement evaluation methods. Nevertheless, existing engagement recognition systems still confront two fundamental challenges: (1) effective video representation modeling and (2) class imbalance in training data, both of which significantly limit recognition accuracy.

1.1 Video Representation Modeling

The recognition of learning engagement is typically based on video understanding, which evaluates student engagement by analyzing their behavioral patterns [2], postural cues [35], and other visual indicators during instructional activities [5,18]. Unlike static images, videos encapsulate temporal dynamics of object movements and interactions, introducing additional complexity for representation learning. For video representation modeling, two predominant strategies exist: (1) combining CNNs for spatial feature extraction with sequential models (e.g., LSTM [14]) for temporal analysis, and (2) processing decomposed video frames independently. While CNNs demonstrate strong performance in image processing tasks, their constrained receptive fields limit their ability to model long-range dependencies crucial for classroom behavior analysis. Furthermore, frame-independent processing inherently neglects essential temporal relationships, consequently compromising engagement recognition performance.

In contrast, numerous studies [6,10,34] have demonstrated the capability of transformer as universal vision architectures, achieving state-of-the-art performance across diverse computer vision tasks. Beyond static image applications, emerging research [3,22] has demonstrated the potential of transformer in video understanding. The self-attention mechanism inherent in transformers enables simultaneous processing of sequence elements, facilitating accurate modeling of long-range dependencies in student behavior patterns, addressing the constrained receptive fields limitation of CNNs. Furthermore, transformers dynamically weigh relationships across all time steps, capturing both spatial and temporal interactions, which accommodates students' shifting gaze or intermittent gestures, and resolves the issue of missing essential temporal relationships caused by frame-independent processing. Therefore, conducting in-depth research on Transformer-based learning engagement recognition methods, as well as addressing its limitations, is of great theoretical and practical significance for advancing this field. We select Video Swin Transformer [22] due to its computationally efficient architectures, which achieves competitive performance while maintaining moderate computational requirements.

In [30], it was demonstrated that different video samples (dynamic or relatively static) exhibit different preferences for spatial and temporal clues. We argue that videos of active and quiet students in real classrooms present analogous challenges for instructional video analysis. Specifically, the frequent body movements of active students tend to rely more on temporal cues to capture behavioral features, whereas quiet students require more demanding spatial cues to extract subtle information (e.g., facial expressions). Furthermore, we employ BEVT [30], a Video Swin Transformer model incorporating BERT-style pre-training for comprehensive video representation learning.

1.2 Data Imbalance

Data imbalance presents a fundamental challenge in learning engagement recognition. To be clear, the number of students with low engagement is extremely limited compared to students with high engagement in large-scale datasets. This imbalance may create bias in model, favoring predictions of high-engagement patterns while compromising detection accuracy for low-engagement cases. Such biased predictions risk generating unreliable educational interventions, particularly problematic since identifying low-engagement students is precisely where accurate recognition matters most for effective pedagogical support.

To mitigate this imbalance, we implement Margin Calibration (MARC) [31], a method that calibrates classification boundaries to produce more equitable prediction scores across engagement levels. For authentic evaluation, we select the DAiSEE dataset [15], which has a significant imbalance between high- and low-engagement samples, thereby accurately reflecting real-world classroom distribution challenges.

1.3 Contributions

To sum up, our contributions are as follows:

- While CNN-based methods currently dominate engagement recognition research, we explore the performance of transformer-based approaches by using Video Swin Transformer [22], which shows excellent performance in video tasks, as the backbone.
- Our framework incorporates BEVT [30], a dual stream image-video pre-training approach, for engagement recognition, which offers insights for future research on improving the performance of learning engagement recognition through deep learning methods.
- In the field of engagement recognition, existing research on handling imbalanced data primarily focuses on data resampling and optimizing the loss function. We take a different approach by focusing on class margins and achieve a promising result.

2 Related Works

Before the application of artificial intelligence in the field of education, researchers had been devoted to studying how to assess students' learning engagement using artificial methods. [33] summarized common evaluation methods for learning engagement, including self-report, rating scales, and observation checklists. These methods and their combinations can effectively assess learning engagement, but they have some issues such as subjectivity, complexity, and the need for significant effort. The growth of online education has exacerbated these challenges by reducing teacher-student interaction, rendering traditional assessment approaches increasingly impractical. This paradigm shift has motivated growing scholarly interest in automated engagement recognition method.

However, most of the datasets in the field of learning engagement recognition are self-built or small datasets, making it difficult to compare different models and methods, which limits the development of this field. [15] advanced the field by introducing DAiSEE, which is the first large-scale public dataset of student online learning videos. Benchmark evaluations using InceptionNet [27], C3D [28], and LRCN [9] established baseline accuracies of 46.4%, 56.1%, and 57.9% respectively across the four engagement levels (very low to very high).

Recent advances in DAiSEE benchmark research demonstrate progressive improvements in engagement recognition. [13] used the C3D model to classify video data into four levels of engagement and introduced focal loss [20] to improve the loss function and address the class imbalance in DAiSEE, achieving an accuracy of 56.2%. [19] proposed Deep Facial Spatio-Temporal Network (DFSTN), which used pre-trained SE-ResNet-50 to extract spatial features and LSTM networks to extract temporal features, achieving an accuracy of 58.84%. [1] improved the model's performance in learning engagement recognition by integrating ResNet with TCN and implementing a customized sampling strategy to address the class imbalance, achieving an accuracy of 63.9%. Some researchers have explored the application of lightweight models in student engagement recognition. [26] proposed using EfficientNet B7 with TCN, LSTM, and Bi-LSTM to extract spatiotemporal information, achieving an accuracy of 67.48%. [17] used ShuffleNet v2 with SENet attention, obtaining an accuracy of 63.9%.

Apart from CNN-based methods, due to the success of Transformers in the field of computer vision, some researchers have attempted to apply Transformers to the evaluation of learning engagement. [24] utilized the Vision Transformer (ViT) [11] to automatically estimate learning engagement by learning end-to-end features from facial images. They also studied the impact of different loss functions in addressing class imbalance, achieving an accuracy of 55.18% in DAiSEE. However, this model was trained only on video frames without modeling temporal information, ignoring the continuity of behavior, and thus unable to accurately evaluate engagement. Therefore, our research will further explore the application of Transformer in evaluating learning engagement.

3 Methodology

3.1 Dataset

We employ the DAiSEE dataset [15], a benchmark multi-label video classification dataset for affective state recognition. Comprising 9068 videos from 112 participants during online learning, each video is annotated with four affective dimensions (boredom, confusion, engagement, frustration) at four intensity levels (0: very low to 3: very high). Our study specifically analyzes engagement levels, treating this as a 4-class classification task.

Figure 1 illustrates representative frames across engagement levels. All videos share consistent technical specifications: 10-second duration, 30 fps frame rate, and 640×480 resolution. TData collection spanned six diverse environments (including dorm rooms, crowded labs, and libraries) under three lighting conditions (light, dark, neutral), ensuring data diversity. As Table 1 demonstrates, the dataset exhibits significant class imbalance across the train, validation, and test sets.

Table 1. The distribution of samples on DAiSEE.

Level of Engagement	Training	Validation	Test	Total
0	34	23	4	61
1	213	143	84	440
2	2617	813	882	4312
3	2494	450	814	3758
Total	5358	1429	1784	8571

Fig. 1. Examples of video frames with different levels of engagement.

3.2 Video Swin Transformer

Building upon the Swin Transformer architecture [21], the Video Swin Transformer [22] was subsequently developed to incorporate temporal modeling capabilities for video sequence analysis.

Figure 2 illustrates the four-stage architecture. The input video consists of T frames, with each frame containing H×W×3 (Height * Width * color channels) values. Before Stage 1, the input video data undergoes the 3D Patch Partition layer, which divides the input into individual patches of size 2×4×4. Consequently, after processing with the 3D Patch Partition layer, we obtain T/2×H/4×W/4 3D patches, each with 96 channels.

In Stage 1, the patches are first projected into an arbitrary dimension represented by C using the Linear Embedding layer, resulting in an image size of T/2×H/4×W/4×C. The processed patches then go through several Video Swin Transformer Blocks. Since Transformer do not alter the image size, the final output of Stage 1 remains T/2×H/4×W/4×C.

Stage 2 employs a Patch Merging layer that spatially downsamples features by 2×, yielding T/2×H/8×W/8×4C dimensional representations. To maintain consistency with CNNs, a 1×1 convolution is then applied for dimension reduction, resulting in an image size of T/2×H/8×W/8×2C. The processed image continues to be handled by several Video Swin Transformer Blocks. The structures of Stage 3 and Stage 4 are similar to Stage 2, with the only difference being the number of Video Swin Transformer Blocks used.

The Video Swin Transformer architecture offers multiple configurations that primarily vary in two aspects: (1) the channel dimension C of the Stage 1 Linear Embedding output, and (2) the quantity of Transformer blocks per stage. Table 2 systematically compares these architectural variants.

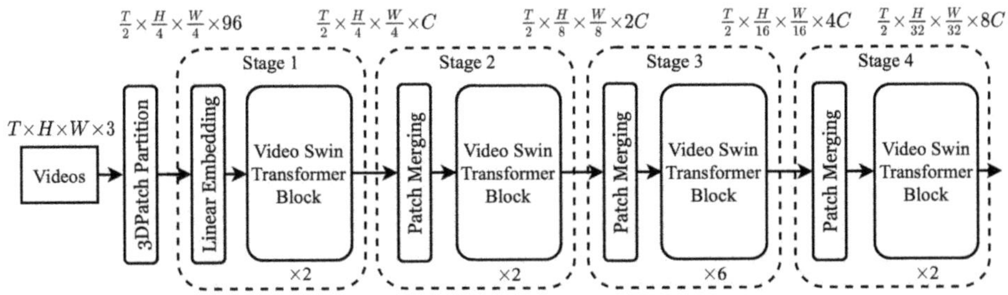

Fig. 2. The architecture of a Video Swin Transformer [22].

Table 2. Parameters of different versions of Video Swin Transformer.

Name	C	Stage 1	Stage 2	Stage 3	Stage 4
Swin-Tiny	96	2	2	6	2
Swin-Small	96	2	2	18	2
Swin-Base	128	2	2	18	2
Swin-Large	192	5	2	18	2

3.3 BERT Pretraining of Video Transformer

The remarkable effectiveness of transformers in NLP stems largely from BERT's pretraining framework [8]. Building on this success, BEVT [30] implements a novel dual-stream (image and video) self-supervised pretraining approach. This architecture enhances the Video Swin Transformer [22] by combining its computational advantages with BERT-inspired pretraining, thereby optimizing spatiotemporal feature learning for video understanding tasks.

As illustrated in Fig. 3, BEVT addresses the computational inefficiency of training video transformers from scratch through a two-phase approach: (1) self-supervised pretraining of the image stream on ImageNet to acquire robust spatial representations, followed by (2) video stream initialization using these image-derived weights with shared parameters for joint optimization. The framework employs complementary objectives: masked image modeling preserves spatial feature learning, while masked video modeling facilitates temporal dynamics extraction.

Figure 4 illustrates the decoder architecture designed to align transformer-extracted features with ground truth token dimensions. The video stream decoder first uses a deconvolutional layer to perform spatial oversampling on the feature map output by Video Swin Transformer Stage 4, and then splices it with the feature map output by Stage 3 in the feature dimension. Next, another deconvolutional layer is used for temporal oversampling to restore the feature map to an appropriate size. Finally, a linear classifier is used to output the predictions of discrete visual tokens at each location. The design of the image stream decoder is similar, but does not include a temporal oversampling module.

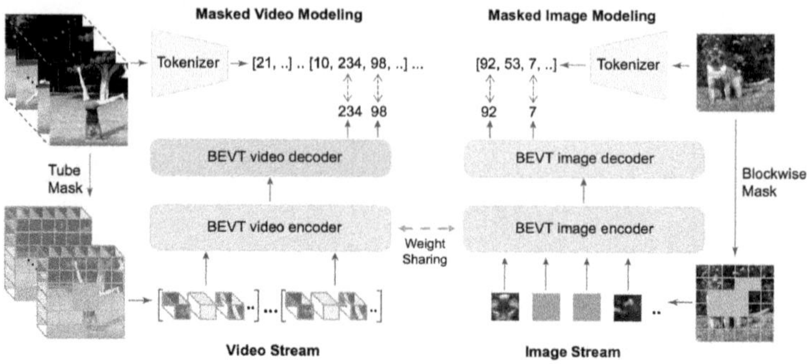

Fig. 3. An overview of BEVT [30].

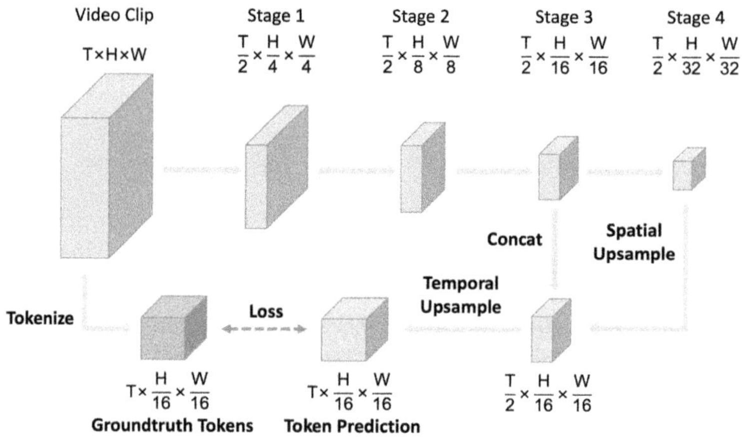

Fig. 4. BEVT encoder and decoder for masked video modeling [30].

3.4 Margin Calibration

The Margin Calibration (MARC) [31] method addresses the issue of class-specific imbalance by training a margin calibration model tailored to each class. This model incorporates two learnable parameters for class j, ω_j and β_j, which are used to calibrate the original margin d_j. The calibrated margin $\hat{d_j}$ is computed using the following equation:

$$\hat{d_j} = \omega_j \cdot d_j + \beta_j \tag{1}$$

Here, the original margin d_j is calculated by dividing the predicted score (logit) by the L2 norm of the linear classifier's weight $\|\mathbf{W}_j\|$. The predicted score (logit) is typically obtained through the dot product of the linear classifier's weight $\mathbf{W}_j$ and the input feature $\mathbf{z}_1$ in the feature space, plus a bias term $\mathbf{b}_j$.

$$d_j = \frac{\mathbf{W}_j \cdot \mathbf{z}_i + \mathbf{b}_j}{\|\mathbf{W}_j\|} \tag{2}$$

The calibrated predicted score $\hat{s_j}$ is then calculated by multiplying the calibrated margin $\hat{d_j}$ by the norm of the classifier's weight $\|\mathbf{W}_j\|$.

$$\hat{s_j} = \hat{d_j} \cdot \|\mathbf{W}_j\| \tag{3}$$

This process fine-tunes the margin for each class, improving the handling of class imbalance and enhancing classification performance across different classes.

4 Experiment

4.1 Dataset Processing

We incorporate samples from categories 0 (very low) and 1 (low) in the validation set into the training set and then evaluate on the test set. A custom sampling strategy is implemented to ensure that each batch contains samples from all four categories. We observed that using too many input video frames (300 frames/video) leads to overfitting. Consequently, we remove the beginning and end of each video, splitting the middle portion into two samples, each sample containing 128 frames.

4.2 Set Up

To maintain experimental consistency, all experiments are conducted under the same conditions. We conducted experiments using MMAction2 [7], which is a video understanding framework. All experiments were trained and evaluated using PyTorch on a server equipped with Intel(R) Xeon(R) E5-2680 v3 CPU and NVIDIA GeForce RTX 4090 GPU.

For comparative experiments, the hyperparameters follow the optimal hyperparameters proposed by the authors in the original paper. For Video Swin Transformer-Base (Swin), we fine-tuned it using pre-trained weights from ImageNet-1K (Im1K) for 25 epochs with a batch size of 4 and a learning rate of 0.001. For BEVT, Video Swin Transformer-Base is chosen as the backbone. In the pretraining stage, the image stream of BEVT is first pretrained on ImageNet-1K. Subsequently, both streams are pretrained on ImageNet-1K and Kinetics-400, initialized from Video Swin Transformer pretrained using the image stream. We utilized the pretrained model provided by the original authors. The pretrained model will be transferred to the DAiSEE dataset for fine-tuning. we train the model for 30 epochs with a batch size of 4. During data preprocessing, the input video sample was extracted into 128 frames. These frames were then resized, normalized, and structured into the NCTHW format (batch size, channels, time, height, width), with both the height and width set to 224. For the optimization process, we utilized the AdamW optimizer with an initial learning rate of 10^{-4} and a weight decay of 0.002 to prevent overfitting. To stabilize the learning rate in the early stages of training, a linear warmup schedule [16] was employed over the first 3 epochs. Following the warmup, the learning rate was adjusted using a Cosine Annealing policy, which begins with a maximum learning rate and gradually decreases it following a cosine curve as training progresses. The minimum learning rate was set to 0.

4.3 Effectiveness Validation of BEVT

To evaluate the effectiveness of BEVT, we compare its performance against several state-of-the-art methods on the benchmark DAiSEE. As shown in Table 3, BEVT achieves a top accuracy of 64.96%, outperforming all baseline and competing approaches. Compared to Swin-Im1K, BEVT shows a 4.13% increase in accuracy, indicating the impact of incorporating joint pre-training with video streams.

Table 3. Accuracy of different methods on DAiSEE.

Baseline	
Video-level InceptionNet [15]	46.40%
Frame-level InceptionNet [15]	47.10%
C3D [15]	48.60%
C3D FineTuning [15]	56.10%
LRCN [15]	57.90%
Comparison	
ResNet+TCN [1]	62.61%
ResNet+LSTM [1]	60.20%
EfficientNet B7+LSTM [26]	63.85%
ShuffleNet v2 [17]	61.15%
ViT [24]	55.94%
Swin-Im1K	60.83%
BEVT	64.96%

Furthermore, to examine the model's performance on each individual category, the confusion matrix is presented in Fig. 5. All methods are significantly impacted by class imbalance in categories 0 (very low) and 1 (low). Specifically, the accuracy for all methods in category 0 is 0, while accuracy in category 1 varies from 0 (ViT) to 14.3% (BEVT). It can be observed that category 2 achieves the highest number of correctly classified samples, which may be attributed to its larger representation in the training dataset.

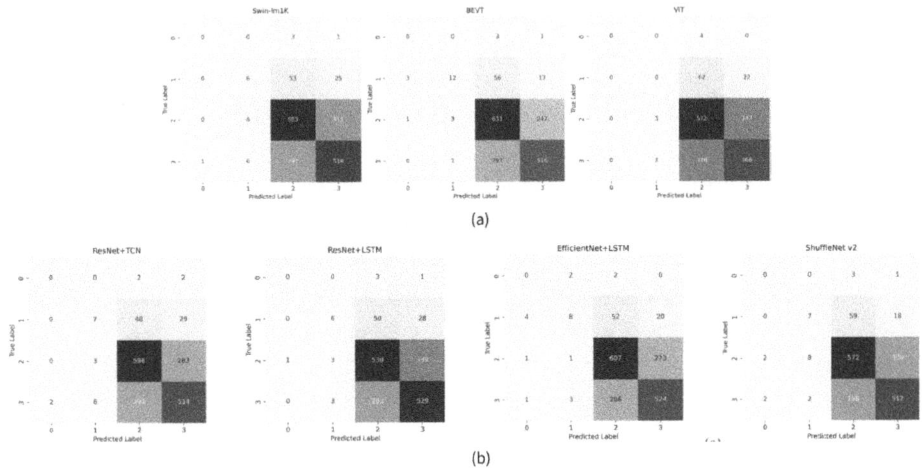

Fig. 5. Confusion matrices of different methods, (a) transformer-based methods, (b) CNN-based methods.

4.4 Effectiveness Validation of MARC

To address the class imbalance, we implement MARC across various approaches, while comparing representative approaches from two other strategy categories: data resampling and loss function adjustment. The accuracy is depicted in Table 4. MARC achieves comparable performance to LDAM [4] on ShuffleNet v2 while demonstrating superior results on all other models, with the best performance reaching 66.82% (BEVT+MARC), which clearly shows the effectiveness of MARC. Contrary to expectations, Class Balanced Sampling (CBS) underperforms standard training across all evaluated models, suggesting potential limitations in its application for this task. We hypothesize this may be caused by underfitting on the head class and overfitting on the tail class, leading to worse data representations compared to standard training, as noted in existing research [4,12].

The F1 score metric is chosen to provide a more comprehensive reflection of model performance on imbalanced categories. The F1 score is depicted in Table 5. Following the application of MARC, all methods demonstrate improvements in the F1 score for category 1, with BEVT achieving the highest increase of 0.149. For category 0, the maximum improvement is 0.222, observed with Swin-Im1K. BEVT+MARC achieves the best performance with an average F1 score of 0.456. For transformer-based methods, performance in category 2 declines after applying MARC, with the most significant drop being 0.086 in the F1 score for BEVT, although it also shows the greatest improvement in the imbalanced categories.

Table 4. Accuracy of different class imbalance strategies.

Method	MARC	(CBS)	LDAM
ResNet+TCN	64.01%	59.14%	63.06%
ResNet+LSTM	61.43%	54.82%	59.14%
EfficientNet B7+LSTM	64.97%	59.75%	63.23%
ShuffleNet v2	62.11%	57.90%	62.28%
ViT	56.11%	53.08%	56.73%
Swin-Im1K	62.33%	54.26%	61.49%
BEVT	66.82%	59.64%	65.75%

Table 5. F1 scores of different methods for different categories on DAiSEE.

Method	0	1	2	3	Average
ResNet+TCN	0.000	0.140	0.655	0.626	0.355
ResNet+LSTM	0.000	0.124	0.614	0.619	0.339
EfficientNet B7+LSTM	0.000	0.163	0.664	0.642	0.367
ShuffleNet v2	0.000	0.138	0.631	0.622	0.348
ViT	0.000	0.000	0.583	0.565	0.287
Swin-Im1K	0.000	0.122	0.628	0.619	0.342
BEVT	0.000	0.241	0.675	0.647	0.391
(ResNet+TCN)+MARC	0.200	0.173	0.659	0.652	0.421
(ResNet+LSTM)+MARC	0.000	0.133	0.614	0.618	0.341
(EfficientNet B7+LSTM)+MARC	0.000	0.218	0.665	0.663	0.387
ShuffleNet v2+MARC	0.000	0.189	0.634	0.639	0.366
ViT+MARC	0.000	0.065	0.578	0.573	0.304
Swin-Im1K+MARC	0.222	0.176	0.604	0.619	0.405
BEVT+MARC	0.168	**0.390**	0.589	**0.676**	**0.456**
(ResNet+TCN)+CBS	0.00	0.079	0.623	0.591	0.323
(ResNet+LSTM)+CBS	0.000	0.041	0.564	0.563	0.292
(EfficientNet B7+LSTM)+CBS	0.000	0.102	0.623	0.603	0.332
ShuffleNet v2+CBS	0.000	0.020	0.599	0.592	0.298
ViT+CBS	0.000	0.000	0.554	0.535	0.272
Swin-Im1K+CBS	0.000	0.038	0.562	0.582	0.296
BEVT+CBS	0.000	0.145	0.626	0.593	0.341
(ResNet+TCN)+LDAM	**0.286**	0.102	0.66	0.631	0.42
(ResNet+LSTM)+LDAM	0.000	0.084	0.606	0.606	0.324
(EfficientNet B7+LSTM)+LDAM	0.000	0.086	0.662	0.634	0.346
ShuffleNet v2+LDAM	0.000	0.189	0.634	0.639	0.366
ViT+LDAM	0.000	0.106	0.589	0.572	0.317
Swin-Im1K+LDAM	0.000	0.13	0.637	0.625	0.348
BEVT+LDAM	0.000	0.253	**0.682**	0.660	0.399

5 Conclusion

We introduce the Video Transformer into the recognition of student learning engagement. Specifically, we select the Video Swin Transformer to explore its potential applications and competitiveness in this context. Furthermore, we use the Video Swin Transformer as the backbone, employing an image-video dual-stream joint pre-training approach to enhance its feature extraction capabilities. Additionally, a method for calibrating category margins is applied to improve its performance on imbalanced categories. Overall, we have identified common challenges in student learning engagement recognition, including the difficulty of image-pretrained models in effectively handling both dynamic and relatively static videos, as well as issues related to class imbalance, and we propose corresponding improvements to address these challenges.

By enhancing the accuracy and achieving better performance on imbalanced categories, this research will facilitate practical implementations in educational settings. We hope this work will provide valuable insights for improving learning engagement recognition methods and inspire further applications of Video Transformer in this field.

Acknowledgments. This research was supported in part by the Shenzhen Education Sciences Planning Project under Grant RGZN23004, and by the Education University of Hong Kong under Grant RG 73/2024-2025R.

Disclosure of Interests. The authors declare they have no financial interests related to this work.

References

1. Abedi, A., Khan, S.S.: Improving state-of-the-art in detecting student engagement with resnet and TCN hybrid network. In: 2021 18th Conference on Robots and Vision (CRV), pp. 151–157. IEEE (2021)
2. Altuwairqi, K., Jarraya, S.K., Allinjawi, A., Hammami, M.: Student behavior analysis to measure engagement levels in online learning environments. SIViP **15**(7), 1387–1395 (2021). https://doi.org/10.1007/s11760-021-01869-7
3. Arnab, A., Dehghani, M., Heigold, G., Sun, C., Lučić, M., Schmid, C.: Vivit: a video vision transformer. In: Proceedings of the IEEE/CVF International Conference on Computer Vision, pp. 6836–6846 (2021)
4. Cao, K., Wei, C., Gaidon, A., Arechiga, N., Ma, T.: Learning imbalanced datasets with label-distribution-aware margin loss. In: Advances in Neural Information Processing Systems, vol. 32 (2019)
5. Chen, Y., Zhou, J., Gao, Q., Gao, J., Zhang, W.: MDNN: predicting student engagement via gaze direction and facial expression in collaborative learning. Comput. Model. Eng. Sci. (CMES) **136**(1) (2023)
6. Chen, Y., et al.: Mobile-former: bridging mobilenet and transformer. In: Proceedings of the IEEE/CVF Conference on Computer Vision and Pattern Recognition, pp. 5270–5279 (2022)

7. Contributors, M.: Openmmlab's next generation video understanding toolbox and benchmark (2020). https://github.com/open-mmlab/mmaction2
8. Devlin, J., Chang, M.W., Lee, K., Toutanova, K.: Bert: pre-training of deep bidirectional transformers for language understanding. arXiv preprint arXiv:1810.04805 (2018)
9. Donahue, J., et al.: Long-term recurrent convolutional networks for visual recognition and description. In: Proceedings of the IEEE Conference on Computer Vision and Pattern Recognition, pp. 2625–2634 (2015)
10. Dong, X., et al.: Cswin transformer: a general vision transformer backbone with cross-shaped windows. In: Proceedings of the IEEE/CVF Conference on Computer Vision and Pattern Recognition, pp. 12124–12134 (2022)
11. Dosovitskiy, A., et al.: An image is worth 16 × 16 words: transformers for image recognition at scale. arXiv preprint arXiv:2010.11929 (2020)
12. Ganganwar, V.: An overview of classification algorithms for imbalanced datasets. Int. J. Emerg. Technol. Adv. Eng. **2**(4), 42–47 (2012)
13. Geng, L., Xu, M., Wei, Z., Zhou, X.: Learning deep spatiotemporal feature for engagement recognition of online courses. In: 2019 IEEE Symposium Series on Computational Intelligence (SSCI), pp. 442–447. IEEE (2019)
14. Graves, A., Graves, A.: Long short-term memory. Supervised sequence labelling with recurrent neural networks, pp. 37–45 (2012)
15. Gupta, A., D'Cunha, A., Awasthi, K., Balasubramanian, V.: Daisee: towards user engagement recognition in the wild. arXiv preprint arXiv:1609.01885 (2016)
16. Hu, J., Shen, L., Sun, G.: Squeeze-and-excitation networks. In: Proceedings of the IEEE Conference on Computer Vision and Pattern Recognition, pp. 7132–7141 (2018)
17. Hu, Y., Jiang, Z., Zhu, K.: An optimized CNN model for engagement recognition in an e-learning environment. Appl. Sci. **12**(16), 8007 (2022)
18. Li, C., Weng, X., Li, Y., Zhang, T.: Multimodal learning engagement assessment system: an innovative approach to optimizing learning engagement. Int. J. Hum.-Comput. Interact. **41**(5), 3474–3490 (2025)
19. Liao, J., Liang, Y., Pan, J.: Deep facial spatiotemporal network for engagement prediction in online learning. Appl. Intell. **51**(10), 6609–6621 (2021). https://doi.org/10.1007/s10489-020-02139-8
20. Lin, T.Y., Goyal, P., Girshick, R., He, K., Dollár, P.: Focal loss for dense object detection. In: Proceedings of the IEEE International Conference on Computer Vision, pp. 2980–2988 (2017)
21. Liu, Z., et al.: Swin transformer: hierarchical vision transformer using shifted windows. In: Proceedings of the IEEE/CVF International Conference on Computer Vision, pp. 10012–10022 (2021)
22. Liu, Z., et al.: Video swin transformer. In: Proceedings of the IEEE/CVF Conference on Computer Vision and Pattern Recognition, pp. 3202–3211 (2022)
23. Mallibhat, K.: Student attention detection using multimodal data fusion. In: 2024 IEEE International Conference on Advanced Learning Technologies (ICALT), pp. 295–297. IEEE (2024)
24. Mandia, S., Singh, K., Mitharwal, R.: Vision transformer for automatic student engagement estimation. In: 2022 IEEE 5th International Conference on Image Processing Applications and Systems (IPAS), pp. 1–6. IEEE (2022)
25. Pabba, C., Bhardwaj, V., Kumar, P.: A visual intelligent system for students' behavior classification using body pose and facial features in a smart classroom. Multimed. Tools Appl. **83**(12), 36975–37005 (2024)

26. Selim, T., Elkabani, I., Abdou, M.A.: Students engagement level detection in online e-learning using hybrid efficientnetb7 together with TCN, LSTM, and Bi-LSTM. IEEE Access **10**, 99573–99583 (2022). https://doi.org/10.1109/ACCESS.2022.3206779
27. Szegedy, C., et al.: Going deeper with convolutions. In: Proceedings of the IEEE Conference on Computer Vision and Pattern Recognition, pp. 1–9 (2015)
28. Tran, D., Bourdev, L., Fergus, R., Torresani, L., Paluri, M.: Learning spatiotemporal features with 3D convolutional networks. In: Proceedings of the IEEE International Conference on Computer Vision, pp. 4489–4497 (2015)
29. Venton, B.J., Pompano, R.R.: Strategies for enhancing remote student engagement through active learning (2021)
30. Wang, R., et al.: BEVT: BERT pretraining of video transformers. In: Proceedings of the IEEE/CVF Conference on Computer Vision and Pattern Recognition, pp. 14733–14743 (2022)
31. Wang, Y., Zhang, B., Hou, W., Wu, Z., Wang, J., Shinozaki, T.: Margin calibration for long-tailed visual recognition. In: Asian Conference on Machine Learning, pp. 1101–1116. PMLR (2023)
32. Wang, Y.: Probing into the boredom of online instruction among Chinese English language teachers during the covid-19 pandemic. Curr. Psychol. **43**(13), 12144–12158 (2024)
33. Whitehill, J., Serpell, Z., Lin, Y.C., Foster, A., Movellan, J.R.: The faces of engagement: automatic recognition of student engagementfrom facial expressions. IEEE Trans. Affect. Comput. **5**(1), 86–98 (2014)
34. Wu, H., et al.: CVT: introducing convolutions to vision transformers. In: Proceedings of the IEEE/CVF International Conference on Computer Vision, pp. 22–31 (2021)
35. Xie, N., Liu, Z., Li, Z., Pang, W., Lu, B.: Student engagement detection in online environment using computer vision and multi-dimensional feature fusion. Multimed. Syst. **29**(6), 3559–3577 (2023)
36. Xinhan, N.: Intelligent analysis of classroom student state based on neural network algorithm and emotional feature recognition. J. Intell. Fuzzy Syst. **40**(4), 7171–7182 (2021)

Interpretable and Transparent Experimentation on Policy Ideas in a Social Simulation Environment

Nikitas M. Sgouros(✉)

Department of Digital Systems, University of Piraeus, 18534 Piraeus, Greece
sgouros@unipi.gr
https://www.ds.unipi.gr/en/faculty/sgouros-en/

Abstract. A main motivation for using social simulation lies in its ability to offer a risk-free experimentation environment for the conceptual design of future policies. To this end, we develop a prototype for an agent-based social simulation environment that can support policy researchers in the design, interpretation, and documentation of their policy ideas. Our system accepts as input a policy model in its modeling language and automatically generates a first pass of online documentation for the structure and function of the model via a semantic and qualitative analysis of its code. This can be further edited by the designer. Furthermore, our app generates an editable first-pass for the documentation and explanation of alternative instantiations of the model along with the automatic evaluation of their simulation results and ranking with respect to their intended effects. Finally, it supports the formation and verification of hypotheses related to qualitative trends between policy parameters in the simulated alternatives. Consequently, the system provides an interpretable, transparent, and verifiable online account of the policy model and the experimentation of its designer with different alternatives. Our prototype is available online for testing and evaluation.

Keywords: Agent-based Modeling · Social Computing · Social Simulation

1 Introduction

A main motivation for using social simulation in policy design is that it can offer a risk-free experimentation environment for the formation and analysis of ideas for future policies. This stems from the frequent lack of data to guide the design and analysis of future policies [1]. In many cases, our knowledge of the effects of alternative policies comes from data only for the ones that have been applied to the target population in the past and not for others that were never actually applied to this population. In this case, simulation offers a promising solution to the analysis of such unobserved policies. However, the highly technical nature of social simulations can reduce their adoption for policy design due to the

T. Hao et al. (Eds.): BESC 2025, LNCS 16431, pp. 282–301, 2026.
https://doi.org/10.1007/978-981-95-7138-3_19

complexity of documenting and explaining their content and results. Therefore, it is important to enrich these environments in order to facilitate the creation of online records that succinctly explain complex policy models and results at various levels of detail and describe the experimentation of the designer with various policy ideas stemming from alternative instantiations of her models. This becomes especially important in action research approaches to the design of social policies [22,23], where the purpose of the social simulation model and its results is to mediate the communication between participants to solve relevant problems in a given context.

To this end, we develop languages and methods for the creation, interpretation, and simulation of policy models that reflect complex social environments. We achieve this through the definition of a special-purpose rule-based modeling language and through the simulation of the parallel operation of multiple agent networks in the same population. In addition, we develop automatic methods for the semantic analysis of the model code that extract a set of qualitative relations between the parameters of the model in terms of their behavior, their dependencies, influences, and operating context. Based on the results of such an analysis, we automatically generate natural language descriptions and dataflow diagrams that provide a first pass in interpreting the rules that implement model dynamics. Furthermore, we enable the formation and explanation in natural language of qualitative hypotheses related to the comparative performance of parameters between model variants and develop automatic methods for the verification of such hypotheses. All these natural language descriptions can be further edited by the designer. We support all this functionality with a web GUI with components related directly to answering questions about the workings and outcomes of simulation experiments. Our prototype is available online for testing and evaluation purposes [8]. It is implemented using the Phoenix web framework[1] that interacts with our policy simulator built in Elixir[2]. As a motivating example that can be accessed online, we explore policy ideas to counteract radicalization in a social group [8].

2 Description of the Modeling Environment

In order to capture the interplay of multiple processes in a social group, we support the existence of multiple models of agent networks operating in parallel in a population of multiply connected agents. For example, we allow kinship and friendship networks to co-exist in the same population. Figure 1 describes the structure of each such network model that consists of the following components:

A list of individual attributes and their initial values. These describe the characteristics of each individual agent in the particular network. For example, in our radicalization-related policy scenario, these can include the individual's current radicalization status or its education/income level.

[1] https://www.phoenixframework.org/.
[2] https://elixir-lang.org/.

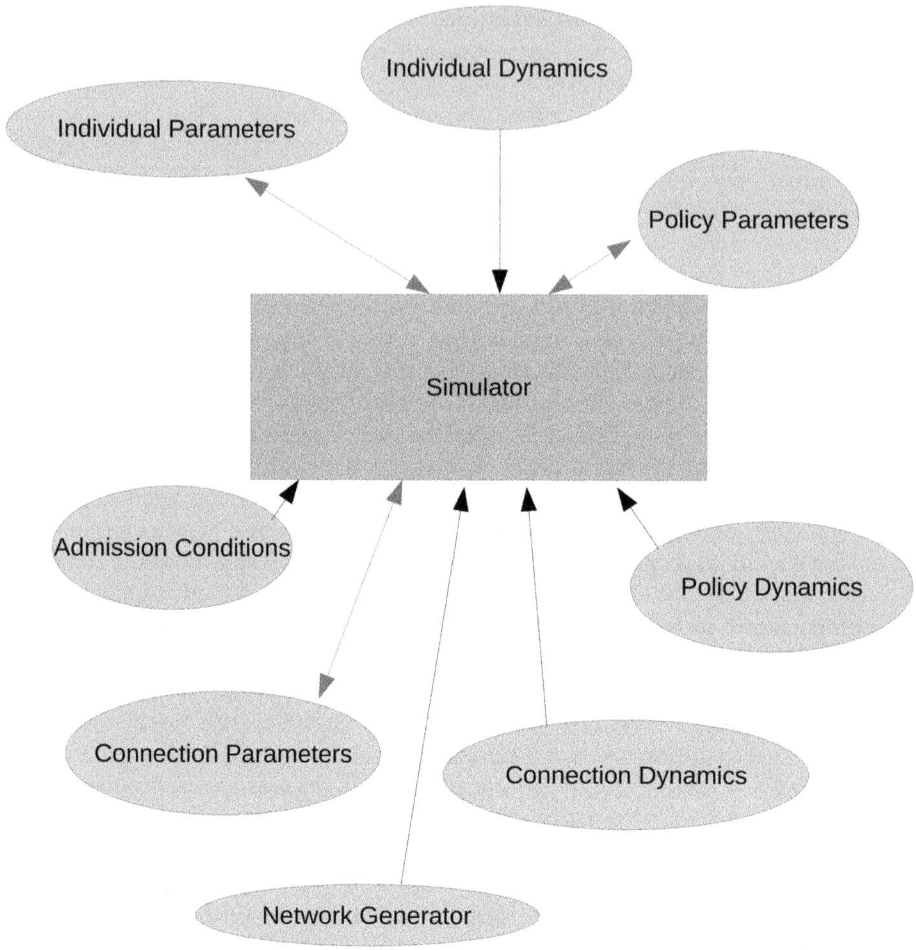

Fig. 1. Structure of a network model. Bidirectional red arrows indicate data sources which the simulator can read and/or update. Unidirectional black arrows indicate user-defined data sources which the simulator can only read. (Color figure online)

A list of connection attributes and their initial values. These describe the attributes of connections between individuals in the population. Each such connection is represented as an edge with attributes between two individuals in a graph. Each edge contains a set of attributes that characterize this connection, and their values may change during simulation. For example, in a friendship network, such an attribute can represent the strength of the social link from one individual to another. Each individual can be connected to multiple other individuals. Each connection is unidirectional. During each simulation cycle, the simulator updates the attributes of all the connections for each individual in the population.

The state of an individual consists of its individual attributes along with the connection attributes for all edges that originate from it.

A list of policy attributes and their initial values. These include parameters relevant to a policy that characterize a network population. For example, the percentage of radicals in such an agent network and the current cost of applying a specific policy in it are examples of such attributes.

The modeling language used by the system represents individual, connection, or policy attributes as keyword/value strings as in:

```
radicals: 15, policy_cost: 85
```

As the example indicates, strings ending in ':' are names for attributes, while the rest are the parameter values.

A set of rules for individual dynamics. These describe how the attributes for each individual are updated during the simulation. Some of the attributes of each individual can be influenced by various functions (e.g. sum, min, max) of the attributes of its incoming edges in order to capture the social input it receives from other individuals.

A set of rules for connection dynamics. These describe how both connections and their attributes change during the simulation. Such dynamics depend on the attributes of the nodes at both ends of the connections and on the policy-relevant attributes.

A set of rules for policy dynamics. These rules specify how the policy attributes change during the simulation. The current prototype assumes that the values of policy attributes are computed on the basis of aggregation of individual attributes in a network via built-in system functions (e.g. average, max/min).

A set of admission conditions. These determine the preconditions under which an individual can become a member of a particular network. For example, a high income level can be one of the preconditions for participating in an economic elite network.

The specifications of a network generator component. These are used whenever the user wants to simulate policy effects on a synthetic population generated from a known network model such as a random graph or various power-law networks. The features of such a model are provided as a set of key-value pairs. For example, the following are instructions to the network generator to create a population where each individual has at least one and at most five outgoing unidirectional edges and where the specific number of edges is randomly selected from a uniform distribution between these extreme values.

```
max_edges: 5, min_edges: 1, directed?: false,
degree_distribution: :homogeneous
```

In the rest of the paper, all examples are taken from our modeling of policy ideas on reducing radicalization in a social group that are described in detail in [7].

2.1 Model Compilation

During each simulation cycle, the simulator spawns a set of concurrent processes, one for each individual, that run the individual and connection dynamics rules for it and update its state. The simulation proceeds in a sequence of rounds with a number of cycles per round. All types of dynamics (policy, individual or connection) are specified as lists of IF..DO rules of the form

```
IF < IF-part of rule > DO < DO-part of rule >
```

For example, such a rule in our anti-radicalization example has the following form:

```
if :isolated == 0 and
   :radicalization > global(:restriction_threshold)
do :isolated = 1 end
```

where the names starting with ':' correspond to attributes, = is the assignment operator and the *global* operator signifies that *restriction_ threshold* is a policy attribute for the agent network in which this rule is executed. The particular rule indicates that a previously unrestricted individual (one for which its *:isolated* attribute equals to 0) with a *:radicalization* estimate greater than the *:restriction_ threshold* becomes restricted (its *:isolated* attribute becomes equal to 1).

The simulator compiles the rules into Elixir functions. In the case of individual dynamics rules, these functions have, in pseudocode, the general form:

```
function (this, networks, cycle) {
  if <IF-part of rule> then
    updated_this = <DO-part of rule>
    return updated_this
  else
    return this }
```

where `this` and `updated_this` refer to the current state of the individual executing this rule and the one resulting from executing the do-part of the rule, respectively. In addition, `networks` refers to the values of the attributes of all networks operating in the population and `cycle` is the current simulation cycle number. In order to avoid data races and indeterminate updating of agent states in a concurrent rule execution environment, each individual dynamics rule can only update the attributes of the individual executing the rule. The rest of the attributes are read-only for such a rule.

Conceptually, individual dynamics rules utilize:

- attribute values for the individual involved for all of the networks that she belongs
- macroscopic connection data (e.g., number of incoming/outgoing connections for the individual) for the current network
- existence, filtering and/or comparison of certain connection attribute values in incoming connections for the current network

- results of aggregated function evaluations on attributes of incoming connections (e.g. sum, threshold, mean, min/max) for the current network.
- current values of policy attributes for all networks

Connection dynamics rules, are compiled into functions that have the following form:

```
function (this, networks, cycle, edge, distal) {
  if <IF-part of rule> then
    updated_edge = <DO-part of rule>
    return updated_edge
  else
    return edge }
```

Compared to the previous case, such functions have two additional arguments/variables: `edge` and `updated_edge` that refer to the current attributes and their updates, respectively, of the specific connection that executes the rule. In addition, `distal` refers to the attributes of the individual at the receiving end of the connection. Conceptually, connection dynamics rules can read the attributes of individuals at both ends of the connection, the policy attributes for all networks along with the attributes of the specific connection. For safe concurrency, they can only update the attributes of that connection.

Finally, policy dynamics rules are compiled similar to the individual dynamics rules as:

```
function (this, networks, cycle) {
  if <IF-part of rule> then
    updated_this = <DO-part of rule>
    return updated_this
  else
    return this }
```

where `this` refers to the policy attributes of the particular network that executes this rule. Conceptually, policy dynamics rules can read current values of policy attributes for all networks while also computing aggregated population attributes based on the attributes of individuals in the current network. They can only update the policy parameters of the specific network they belong.

Each cycle sequentially executes for each network and for each individual in it its connection, and individual dynamics rules in this order. At the end of each cycle, it executes the policy dynamics rules for all networks.

3 Semantic Analysis

The goal of semantic analysis is to extract the dependencies between the model attributes in terms of behavior, influence, and context during the computation of the model dynamics. As we explain below, its results are used to support the generation of automatic explanations for the model code and the proposed alternative policy instantiations.

Semantic analysis of the model code starts with computing, for each rule, its abstract syntax tree (AST) representation. The AST is a sequence of tuples and lists where the head of each tuple is an operator (e.g., +:, =:) or a statement (if:, do:) with its arguments given as lists. For its computation, we take advantage of the metaprogramming capabilities in Elixir by transforming each rule statement to an Elixir expression and using the Elixir interpreter to compute and return its AST for us. For example, the AST for the example rule in the previous Sect. 2 has the following form:

```
{if:
 [{and:
   [{==: [{attr: [:isolated]}, {constant: [0]}]},
    {>: [{attr: [:radicalization]},
         {global:
           [{attr: [:restriction_threshold]}]}]}]},
 {do: [{=: [{attr: [:isolated]},
                   {constant: [1]}]}]}]}
```

where the *attr* operator denotes that its argument is an attribute, while the *constant* operator denotes that its argument is a numerical constant.

The analysis continues with determining the dependencies among the attributes contained in the AST. More specifically, we consider an attribute to be *independent* if it does not appear as the first argument in an assignment operation in any dynamics rule, otherwise it is considered to be *dependent*. Given that the only way for an attribute to change its initial value in the simulator is through the execution of a dynamics rule, this means that independent attributes essentially behave as constants throughout the simulation.

The dependency of an attribute is a complex concept, since it can refer to either the arguments of the function (and their dependencies in turn) by which the attribute updates its value (*functional dependency*) and/or to the contextual conditions under which such an update takes place (*contextual dependency*). In order to compute the dependencies between the attributes involved in a rule, we simplify its initial AST further by omitting single-successor nodes that correspond to the methods for accessing the value or type of each attribute during rule execution (e.g., omitting the *global*, *attr* or *constant* operands, which are irrelevant for computing dependencies). For example, simplification of the AST of our example rule produces the following tree structure:

```
{if:
  [{and:
    [{==: [:isolated, 0]},
    {>: [:radicalization,
         :restriction_threshold]}]},
   {do:  [{=: [:isolated, 1]}]}]}
```

where all value and type operands are omitted. Then we flatten the simplified AST structure in order to associate for each attribute the operand path in the tree that leads to it.

In our example, the flattened AST for the if-part of our example rule has the following form:

```
{0 => ".and.equal", :isolated => ".and.equal",
 :radicalization => ".and.greater",
 :restriction_threshold => ".and.greater"}
```

indicating that the *:radicalization* and *:restriction_threshold* attributes are arguments of a *greater* operand that is embedded in an *and* operator higher up in a tree, while *:isolated* and *0* are arguments of an *equal* operand that is also embedded in an *and* operation.

Similarly, the do-part of this rule becomes:

```
{1 => ".assign", :isolated => ".assign"}
```

indicating that the *:isolated* attribute and *1* are involved in an assignment operation. Further analysis of the assignment operator and the context of the rule as defined by its if-part indicates that the *:isolated attribute* behaves as follows:

- there is no functional dependency of its new value on some other attribute as its new value is determined by a numerical constant
- there are contextual dependencies for the *:isolated* attribute on itself, on the *:radicalization* individual attribute and on the *:restriction_threshold* global attribute based on the if-part of the rule (:radicalization > :restriction_threshold).

4 Interpreting Model Dynamics and Goals

We explore the automatic generation of interpretations of model dynamics at the rule level, where we provide natural language descriptions of the workings of each dynamics rule. More specifically, for each rule, we traverse its AST and generate parameterized text descriptions for each operand in the tree. For example, Fig. 2 depicts the interpretation generated automatically by the system for the rule in Sect. 2. Furthermore, using the simplified AST tree as input, we automatically create a dataflow graph for each rule that provides a visual description of its workings. Figure 3 depicts this diagram for our example rule.

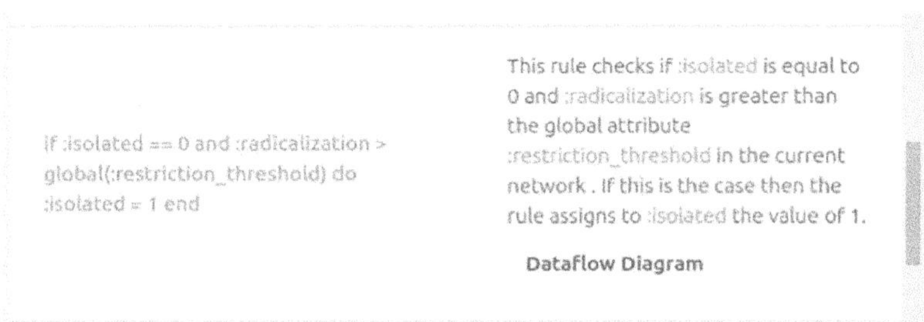

Fig. 2. Automatically-generated interpretation for the example rule.

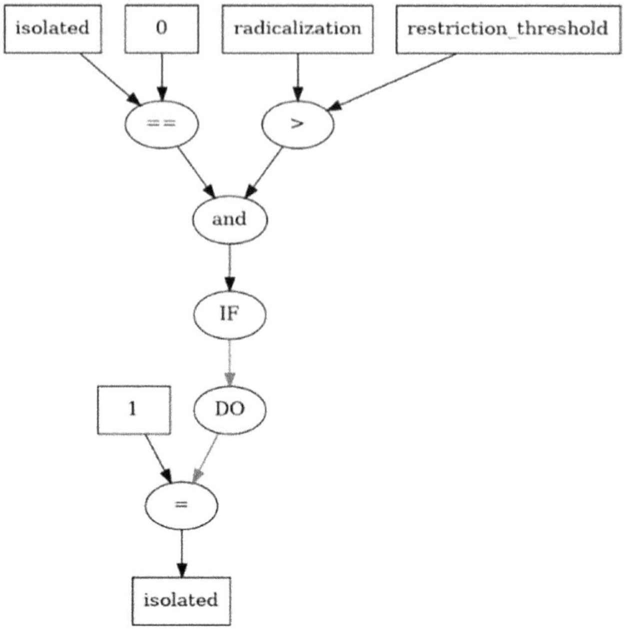

Fig. 3. Dataflow graph for the example rule. Boxes denote attributes while circles denote operands in the rule. The attributes involved as arguments in each operand appear in the order specified in each rule. Red arrows connect operands with executional semantics (e.g. :if, :do, =). (Color figure online)

Our app allows the designer to specify a set of policy goals. Each goal is coded as a condition that involves policy variables from all networks. The system checks whether and where these conditions are satisfied in the simulation results of each policy alternative. In order to provide a first pass in interpreting a policy goal, the system generates a natural language description for it, based on the computation of the AST tree of its conditions as in the case of the model dynamics rules. For example, Fig. 4 shows how the designer coded and the system interpreted a goal to check whether an alternative is successful in eliminating radicalization in the population.

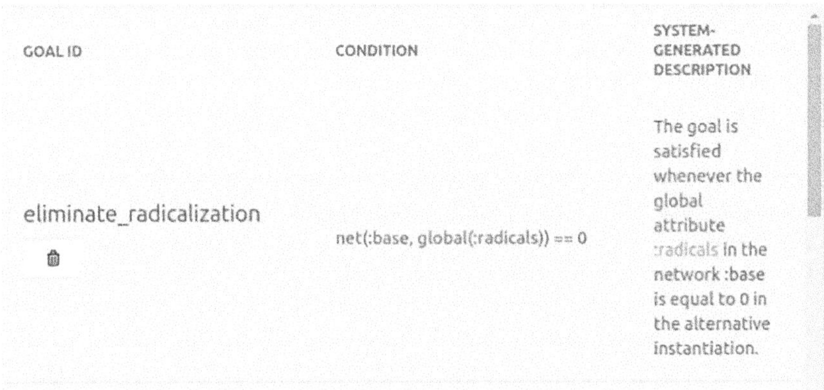

Fig. 4. Automatically-generated explanation for a model goal for eliminating radicalization.

5 Explanation of Model Variants

We assume that independent global attributes refer to modeling assumptions. We also assume that there is a *baseline* model variant that corresponds to the status quo in the population. We define an *alternative* variant as a set of values for the independent policy attributes of a model that are different from the ones in the *baseline* model. Each alternative is implemented as a set of attribute-value pairs, indexed under the agent network they belong.

For example, we define an alternative titled "p 0.1 3 0.5" as:

```
{"p 0.1 3 0.5" => {base: {restriction_threshold: 0.5}}}
```

indicating that it differs from the *baseline* only in the value for the *:restriction_threshold* attribute in the *:base* agent network.

Our focus on independent policy attributes stems from our interest in analyzing the comparative effects of different choices in a model. To this end, we follow the pathways through which these attributes influence simulation outcomes in terms of both functional and contextual dependencies. In our example rule, *:restriction_threshold* participates in defining the context under which a non isolated individual becomes isolated under an anti-radicalization policy. Therefore, differences in the values of this attribute between alternatives are important, as they can delineate different population segments in which various policy dynamics are applied through the contextual dependencies that they create.

Furthermore, we assume that the role of each type of attribute and dynamics in the model is different. In particular, individual and connection attributes and dynamics correspond to fundamental characteristics and processes acting on the population, independent of the particular alternative applied on it. For example, the general computation of social influence in a group is assumed to be independent of any radicalization containment policy in our example. Consequently, such dynamics should remain unchanged, in order to make the comparative evaluation of alternatives valid. This is why we do not allow an alternative to define different dynamics from the ones in the *baseline*.

The large number of independent policy parameters frequently associated with complex agent networks (currently our example model has 18 such attributes) can lead to a significant number of possible alternatives. In order to help the user make sense out of such a potentially large set, for each attribute (e.g., X) mentioned in an alternative (e.g., A), we discover automatically the pathways through which X affects other attributes and describe possible effects that differences in X's value between A and *baseline* can have. This computation is based on transforming the flattened representation of the AST of a rule into a pathway structure denoting the influence from each independent attribute to a dependent attribute in this rule.

For example, in rule:

```
if :radicalization == 2 do:
radicalization = toss(global(:radicalization_prob), 0, 1, -1, 0) end
```

such a structure has the following form:

```
{radicalization_prob: {
 explanation:
 "The :radicalization_prob attribute influences the computation of the
 :radicalization attribute via rule if :radicalization == 2 do:
radicalization = toss(global(:radicalization_prob), 0, 1, -1, 0) end.
This happens if :radicalization is equal to 2. ",
pathways: {radicalization: ".toss"}}}
```

The *pathways* field in this structure indicates that the *:radicalization_prob* policy attribute affects the *:radicalization* attribute through the *toss* operand in the dynamics rule. Toss denotes a system function generating a random value that can take a range of values R_1 ([0, 1] in this example) with a given probability p (p is *:radicalization_prob* in our example rule) and another range of values R_2 ([-1, 0] in this example) with probability 1-p. The contents of the *explanation* field are generated automatically using the method in Sect. 4 and provide a natural language description of the particular pathway implemented through a rule. As Fig. 5 indicates, a description of the actual differences in the value of X between A and *baseline* precedes the pathway description.

Furthermore, if the qualitative effects of the differences between A and *baseline* on some of the policy attributes are unambiguous, then the system highlights these effects. These include cases in which X appears in a function f that assigns a value to attribute Y (Y = f(X, ...)) and either:

- f is linear on X, i.e., $\partial f/\partial X = c$, where c is the same constant for A and *base*. If this is the case, then any qualitative change (increase or decrease) in the value of X in A compared to the *baseline* can lead to a change in Y consistent with the type of monotonicity (increasing or decreasing) of f on X, assuming that everything else remains the same.

- X changes to/from zero in A and X is part of a product expression in f (e.g. Y = X*Z). In this case the pathway description indicates that Y will stop/begin to be influenced, respectively, by this expression.
- f is a function with clear qualitative effects on Y (e.g. toss).

Currently, the algorithm describing such qualitative effects proceeds as follows. For each dependent attribute Y appearing in the do-part of a rule, we pair it with each independent attribute X that appears on the right-hand side of the assignment expression for Y. If X satisfies one of the unambiguous qualitative effects described above, the system instantiates a template in natural language with the names of the attributes involved and appends it to the explanation. For example, based on the pathway structure identified above, Fig. 5 describes at the end of the Pathways column the qualitative effects generated by the system for the detected difference between A and *baseline* in the value of *radicalization_prob*.

6 Discovering Qualitative Trends

In order to help users understand the joint behavior of model attributes in the simulated alternatives, we enable them to form and validate hypotheses related to their qualitative trends. Such a hypothesis states that between two alternatives in which a specified set of attributes C remain the same, another set of attributes V changes in the same or opposite directions. The syntax for forming such hypotheses is similar to the one for rules. In the if-part of a hypothesis the user lists the attributes that are assumed to remain constant between pairs of alternatives. The do-part of the hypothesis investigates whether a specific trend between the attributes in V exists in each pair of alternatives under the constancy assumptions for the attributes in C. Currently, we check for the existence of two trends between the average values in all simulation rounds of attributes X and Y:

- qplus(X, Y), the values of X and Y change in the same direction between a pair of alternatives, i.e. when the value of X increases/decreases between alternatives so does the value of Y.
- qminus(X, Y), the values of X and Y change in the opposite direction between a pair of alternatives, i.e., when the value of X increases/decreases between alternatives the value of Y decreases/increases.

radicalization_prob	0.5	~~0.1~~	Pathways. The alternative uses a higher value for :radicalization_prob than the baseline. The :radicalization_prob attribute influences the computation of the :radicalization attribute via rule if :radicalization == 2 do:radicalization = toss(global(:radicalization_prob), 0, 1, -1, 0) end . This happens if :radicalization is equal to 2. In this case, an increase in the value of :radicalization_prob makes it more possible for :radicalization to assume a value between 0 and 1 .

Fig. 5. Automatically-generated description of the influence pathways and their qualitative effects related to the difference between an alternative (e.g. A) and *baseline* in the value of the *radicalization_ prob* attribute (see the Pathways column). The figure indicates in its second and third column that A uses a value (0.5) for *radicalization_ prob* that is different from the one in the *baseline* (0.1).

QUESTION	HYPOTHESIS	CODE
Is there an inverse trend between dangerous and restriction_threshold?	For pairs of alternatives for which the values of the attributes :min_edges , :max_edges , :radicalization_prob are the same, check whether the value for :dangerous changes inversely to the value for :restriction_threshold .	if constant([:min_edges, :max_edges, :radicalization_prob]) do qminus(:dangerous, :restriction_threshold) end

Fig. 6. Description of a trend hypothesis created by the designer. The description includes three columns: (i) the question it seeks to answer, (ii) a natural language description of the constancy assumptions and the nature of the trend that will be examined, and, (iii) the actual code for implementing the hypothesis.

For example, Fig. 6 describes a user-specified hypothesis that the value for the *:dangerous* attribute changes inversely (qminus) to the value for the *:restriction_ threshold* attribute, assuming that in each pair of alternatives that are compared, the respective values for each of the attributes *:min_ edges*, *:max_ edges* and *radicalization_ prob* do not change. The natural language description of this hypothesis in the second column is generated automatically by the AST description of the hypothesis code in the third column.

Given such a hypothesis, the app selects from all possible pairs of simulated alternatives, the ones that satisfy the constancy assumptions. It then checks whether the differences in the values of the attributes in V between the elements of each such pair are consistent with the hypothesis. Figure 7 shows the results for the verification of the example hypothesis that are shown to the user.

7 User Interaction

We organize user interaction along components focused directly on empowering exploration activities related to policy ideas. Figure 8 depicts the main page of the app that is organized in six action components:

1. Examine: Examine the contents of the model code for all agent networks in the *baseline* model. Examination includes viewing the actual model code and explaining its behavior through natural language descriptions and workflow diagrams.
2. Explore: Create and examine alternative instantiations of the model and specify a set of goals and ranking methods to evaluate them. For each alternative instantiation, the system seeks to explain the effects of its differences with the *baseline* model by describing the pathways through which different behavior can be generated.
3. Simulate: Simulate the *baseline* model and its alternative instantiations. Manage the simulation parameters (population size, number of rounds and number of cycles for each round) that will be used in all simulations so that all comparisons can be based on the same execution scheme.
4. Inspect: Inspect data tables and charts generated automatically by the system with the results of the simulation. The user can inspect tables and charts with the values of all model attributes at the end of each simulation round.
5. Compare: Compare and rank the alternative instantiations of the model according to the achievement of the goals in each round and the performance of the global attributes. For each dependent global attribute, the user is provided with charts that show its average value in each simulated alternative along with the ranking position and the ranking dynamics of this alternative based on the ranking method set by the user in the Explore component.
6. Experiment: Form and test hypotheses over qualitative trends related to the comparative performance of global attributes between simulated alternatives. For each hypothesis and pair of alternatives that satisfy its constancy assumptions the system describes whether it satisfies this hypothesis and displays the actual values of all the attributes involved.

The app automatically generates the GUI from a text description of the *baseline* model components that is supplied by the designer. These include the subject of the specific model exploration environment that will be created, the main questions it seeks to answer, the code for the *baseline* model, the explanation of the model attributes, and the specification of their types and input ranges. The

Fig. 7. Verification results for the example hypothesis in the app. For each pair of alternatives, a result table is displayed that shows in its first column the names of the attributes in V that were compared and in its second and third columns the values for these attributes per alternative in the pair. The third row indicates with a tick or x whether the specific pair satisfies or not the hypothesis, respectively. The final row contains the attributes and their values that were constant for the specific pair of simulated alternatives.

input for generating the current exploration environment for containing radicalization is given in [6]. As we have already mentioned, the first pass for all the explanations for the model dynamics and the pathways relevant to each alternative instantiation are generated automatically by the system. The environment is completely transparent as both the model code and the functionality of the system in terms of simulations, alternatives, comparisons and hypothesis testing is open to all users. We provide a video showcasing our app in action [9].

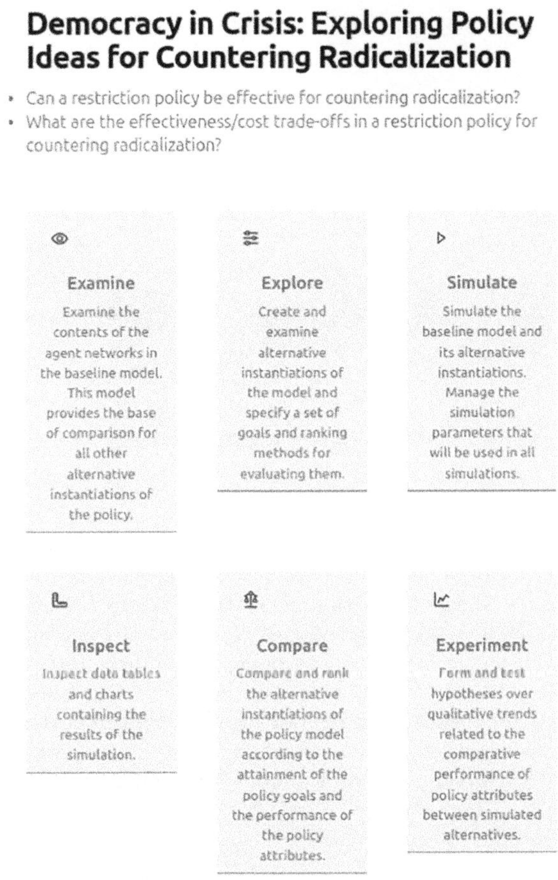

Fig. 8. Main Page for the web app. The subject of the current model exploration and the questions at the top of the page are supplied by the modeler.

8 Indicative Visualizations

In order to facilitate the interpretation of various policy alternatives, the app supports the creation of charts for the comparative evaluation of their performance with regards to policy attributes chosen by the user, their overall ranking in terms of such attributes and the attainment of policy goals in them. Figure 9 provides a flavor of these capabilities.

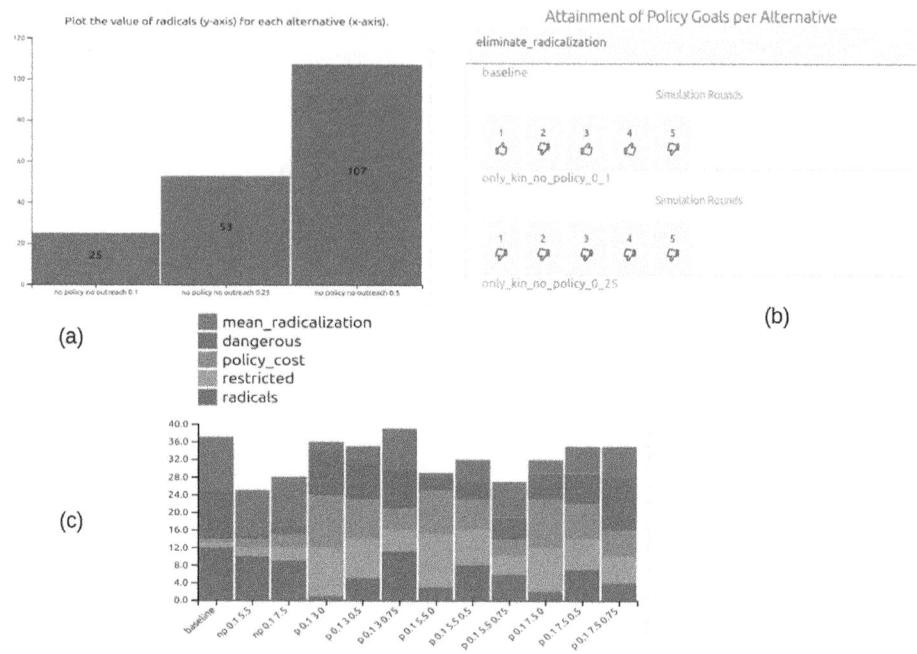

Fig. 9. Indicative visualizations of simulation results. Image (a) shows the average number of radicals (a policy attribute) for three policy alternatives at the end of all simulation rounds, (b) shows the attainment (thumbs up) or not (thumbs down) of various policy goals for two such alternatives (c) shows the average ranking of twelve alternatives for a chosen set of dependent policy attributes. In (a) and (c) the x-axis shows the titles of all the alternatives that were currently simulated. In (c) the scale of the y-axis helps us to determine the height of each box that indicates its ranking among the alternatives with respect to a dependent policy attribute. For each alternative we indicate its ranking with respect to all the policy attributes as a stack of boxes.

9 Discussion and Related Work

Most of the current agent-based modeling (ABM) systems [18] offer either an Application Programming Interface over a general-purpose programming language (e.g. NetLogo [19] using a dialect of Logo, Repast HPC [3] using C++) or a special-purpose modeling language (e.g. Gama[4] using Gaml). We have opted for the second approach and designed a simple rule-based language for ABM,

[3] https://repast.github.io.
[4] https://gama-platform.github.io/.

while providing an efficient execution environment that hides algorithmic and implementation complexity of preparing and executing a simulation from the designer. Although simple by design, the language is able to express models of endogenous social dynamics arising from local interactions, interactions between multiple agent networks running in parallel, exogenous dynamics arising from global policy interventions on various networks, or combinations of all of the above. Furthermore, it allows the generation of simple AST structures that can guide automatic methods to document and interpret the model code.

Our approach in providing qualitative explanations and critical analysis of model alternatives is inspired by work on qualitative representations that seek to formalize our intuitive knowledge and methods of reasoning about continuous phenomena and systems [2]. We contextualize this research in the field of agent-based simulation and extend its ontology and capabilities for comparative analysis in model exploration. We achieve this through the development of a methodology for forming and validating hypotheses on qualitative trends in models and for the automated extraction and description of influence pathways from multiple agent networks operating in parallel in ABMs. In this respect our approach for explanation is similar to the one adopted in [4] and focuses on the establishment of possible causal pathways from a set-up to its consequences in terms of the mechanisms in a simulation.

With regard to modeling policy alternatives, there is always an ad hoc character in their creation since policy analysis and design is essentially a political process, and, as such, it reflects political opinions in framing and solving problems [11]. Computational policy models are not immune from similar criticisms that focus on the possible use of unreasonable assumptions, over-simplification and under-estimation of model limitations [12]. Furthermore, consensus building in policy design is quite challenging because it needs to reconcile objective knowledge coming from observational data and/or simulations with its subjective interpretation, as is often the case in the social domain [17]. We seek to address such problems by making the experimentation of policy designers with different models transparent and interpretable through an openly accessible online environment. However, the effectiveness of our app depends on a redesign of the policy design practice around the use of such open and transparent tools that may require brave political decisions.

There has been a significant interest in the use of new technologies for policy making [14]. With regard to simulation, this has led to the development of methodological proposals [10,16], case studies in ABM [5,13,20,21] or the use of modeling and decision support tools from other disciplines, such as operational research [15]. We extend this research by offering a general, online environment that seeks to simultaneously cover modeling and simulation of policy alternatives and their documentation, reasoning about their outcomes, and comparative explanation of policy alternatives.

The growing interest in agent-based models as a computational framework for simulating complex systems has led to an increased interest in improving their communication potential [24]. Recently, efforts have been made to develop protocols, such as ODD, that provide guidelines for producing a standardized document form for a logical and readable account of the structure and dynamics of ABMs [3]. However, there is a lack of tools that can automatically generate and communicate such descriptions from the model code and the simulation results. We seek to address this problem by offering automated methods for interpreting the workings of the model code while integrating such interpretations into an interactive simulation framework for policy exploration.

10 Conclusions and Future Work

We have described a novel social simulation environment for the exploration of policy models with built-in methods to interpret their structure and content at various levels of detail. Our prototype enables researchers to document, explain, and critically analyze their experimentation with policy ideas through the simulation and comparison of alternative model variants and through the exploration of possible qualitative trends between model attributes. Future work will focus on testing our prototype with actual policymakers, on extending our qualitative reasoning methods on model content, and on experimenting with LLMs to enhance our explanation capabilities. Furthermore, we intend to allow designers to describe in natural language the mechanics of their simulation models and enable our system to code them automatically. Finally, we will investigate the development of automatic methods for the comparative interpretation and evaluation of models with different dynamics and structure and pursue the effective integration of our system in action research methodologies for policy design.

Acknowledgements. The presentation of this work was partially supported by the University of Piraeus Research Center.

References

1. Manski, C.F.: Public Policy in an Uncertain World: Analysis and Decisions. Harvard University Press (2013)
2. Forbus, K.D.: Qualitative Representations: How People Reason and Learn about the Continuous World. MIT Press (2019)
3. Grimm, V., et al.: The ODD protocol for describing agent-based and other simulation models: a second update to improve clarity, replication, and structural realism. J. Artif. Soc. Soc. Simul. **23**(2), 7 (2020). https://doi.org/10.18564/jasss.4259. http://jasss.soc.surrey.ac.uk/23/2/7.html
4. Edmonds, B., et al.: Different modelling purposes. J. Artif. Soc. Soc. Simul. **22**(3), 6 (2019). https://doi.org/10.18564/jasss.3993
5. Sgouros, N.M.: Politika: implementing a novel meta-simulation methodology for public policy design on the web. Digital Government: Research and Practice. ACM (2022). https://doi.org/10.1145/3568167
6. Sgouros, N.M.: Example of Model Input to the System (2025). https://drive.google.com/file/d/1W1tDIW4HCKyafu2eqmlBCkr0kB0T7RNg/view?usp=sharing

7. Sgouros, N.M.: Democracy in crisis: using social simulation to explore policies for countering radicalization. In: Advances in Social Simulation: Proceedings of the 19th Social Simulation Conference, Crakow, Poland, 16–20 September 2024. Springer Proceedings in Complexity (2025)
8. http://sgouros2.ted.unipi.gr:4000/users/log_in
9. https://youtu.be/9lCy0dDSg_4
10. Clapham, W.B., Jr., Pestel, R.F., Arnaszus, H.: On the scenario approach to simulation modeling for complex policy assessment and design. Policy Sci. **11** (1979). https://doi.org/10.1007/BF00139827
11. Cairney, P.: The Politics of Policy Analysis. Palgrave Macmillan (2021)
12. Aodha, L., Edmonds, B.: Some pitfalls to beware when applying models to issues of policy relevance. In: Edmonds, B., Meyer, R. (ed.) Simulating Social Complexity – A Handbook, 2nd edn. Springer, Cham (2017)
13. Ruiz, M., Zabaleta, N., Elorza, U.: Decision making through simulation in public policy management field. In: 10th International Technology, Education and Development Conference, IATED 2016 (2016)
14. Janssen, M., Helbig, N.: Innovating and changing the policy-cycle: policy-makers be prepared! Gov. Inf. Q. **35** (2018)
15. Larsson, A., Ibrahim, O.: Modeling for policy formulation: causal mapping, scenario generation, and decision evaluation. In: Tambouris, E., et al. (eds.) ePart 2015. LNCS, vol. 9249, pp. 135–146. Springer, Cham (2015). https://doi.org/10.1007/978-3-319-22500-5_11
16. Charalabidis, Y., Gionis, G., Ferro, E., Loukis, E.: Towards a systematic exploitation of web 2.0 and simulation modeling tools in public policy process. In: Tambouris, E., Macintosh, A., Glassey, O. (eds.) ePart 2010. LNCS, vol. 6229, pp. 1–12. Springer, Heidelberg (2010). https://doi.org/10.1007/978-3-642-15158-3_1
17. Martini, C.: Seeking consensus in the social sciences. In: Martini, C., Boumans, M. (eds.) Experts and Consensus in Social Science. Springer, Cham (n.d.)
18. Abar, S., Theodoropoulos, G.K., Lemarinier, P., O'Hare, G.M.: Agent based modelling and simulation tools: a review of the state-of-art software. Comput. Sci. Rev. **24**, 13–33 (2017)
19. Railsback, S.F., Grimm, V.: Agent-Based and Individual-Based Modeling: A Practical Introduction, 2nd edn. Princeton University Press (2019)
20. Atkinson, J.-A., Page, A., Wells, R., Milat, A., Wilson, A.: A modelling tool for policy analysis to support the design of efficient and effective policy responses for complex public health problems. Implement. Sci. **10**, 26 (2015)
21. Zellner, M.L.: Embracing complexity and uncertainty: the potential of agent-based modeling for environmental planning and policy. Plann. Theory Pract. **9**, Article no. 4 (2008)
22. Reason, P., Bradbury, H. (eds.): Handbook of Action Research. Participative Inquiry and Practice, 2nd edn. Sage, London (2008)
23. Saam, N.J.: The users' judgements—the stakeholder approach to simulation validation. In: Beisbart, C., Saam, N.J. (eds.) Computer Simulation Validation. SFMA, pp. 405–431. Springer, Cham (2019). https://doi.org/10.1007/978-3-319-70766-2_17
24. Arnejo, Z., Gaudou, B., Saqalli, M., Bantayan, N.: Communicating agent-based models to stakeholders: a scoping review. J. Artif. Soc. Soc. Simul. **28**(2) (2025). https://doi.org/10.18564/jasss.5623. http://jasss.soc.surrey.ac.uk/28/2/2.html

Do You Tolerate System Failures? An Experimental Study on the Influence of Providing Prior Statements on Human Evaluation of System Failures

Masahide Yuasa(✉)

Shonan Institute of Technology, Fujisawa, Japan
yuasa@info.shonan-it.ac.jp

Abstract. While the number of services using information technology has increased, artificial intelligence (AI) systems and services are not perfect for certain intelligent tasks, like humans are not perfect sometimes. Mistakes in technology services are frustrating and lead to service cancellations. Additionally, it would be beneficial for system developers to have an effective way for users to tolerate system failures. Therefore, in this paper, we argue that prior information can influence users' tolerance of such failures. Our hypothesis is that when people are made aware of potential weaknesses in an artificial intelligence system, they are more likely to tolerate an incorrect response if it can be attributed to those known limitations. To verify this hypothesis, we conducted an experiment using a hypothetical webpage. The webpage displayed the "feelings" (emotional responses) that many users would normally describe having when looking at an image. In the experiment, the webpage simulated image recognition of user-uploaded images, while the accuracy of the responses was strictly controlled. Three ways of providing prior information were prepared: Type 1: No explanation; Type 2: The system is not yet perfect; and Type 3: The system does not perfectly identify hidden objects. The results demonstrated a different distribution between the users' evaluations for Type 3 from Types 1 and 2, which exhibited a typical distribution. Additionally, providing detailed information about the system's limitations was shown to mitigate system failure. The proposed approach may be an effective way for imperfect systems to induce certain attributions and avoid system evaluation reduction.

Keywords: Human Behavior · Human Interface · Attribution Theory · Prior Information · Information System Success

1 Introduction

The number of services and artificial intelligence (AI) systems that utilize information technology is increasing. By contrast, services and systems are not perfect for certain intelligent tasks because humans are sometimes imperfect and do not have accurate answers. It is expected that the number of cases in which services and systems are

T. Hao et al. (Eds.): BESC 2025, LNCS 16431, pp. 302–313, 2026.
https://doi.org/10.1007/978-981-95-7138-3_20

incapable of handling situations insufficiently will increase. Generally, mistakes in technology services frustrate people and lead them to stop using these services and systems [1–3]. Therefore, it would be beneficial for system developers to develop an effective method for users to tolerate system failures.

Accordingly, this study examines a method for compensating for system failures by providing users with prior information about how the system may cause a failure. We hypothesize that if users are aware of a specific weakness in an artificial intelligence system, and the system's response is incorrect due to that weakness, negative responses to the failure can be avoided. This concept is based on a previous study [4] that investigated the influences of different statements on a user's mental model and outcome. Studies on 'attribution theory,' which may be attributed to the failure of several factors, are also based on [5].

To confirm our hypothesis, we developed a hypothetical webpage that displayed the "feelings" (emotional responses) that people would normally describe having when looking at an image. The webpage pretended to recognize and evaluate images when the users loaded them. Controlled images and incorrect responses were used.

In our experiment, we prepared different types of prior information, although the failure patterns were identical. We examined the change in the failure evaluation distribution using different types of prior information. The method using prior information would be useful for service developers to avoid reducing the evaluations of difficult tasks.

2 Related Works

2.1 Studies Regarding Prior Information

In the robotic research field, similar studies have investigated how first impressions influence impressions and decision-making [6, 7]. Most studies focused on the different appearances of robots and the consequences (success or failure) of certain tasks that significantly influence feelings or decisions. However, the target of these studies was the influence of first impressions, which were not prior statements.

Previous studies have also investigated the 'primacy effect,' which examines the influence of prior information. Primacy effects have been studied in various domains, such as music competitions [8, 9], sales presentations [10], and elections [11]. Most studies considered varying the order of the same stimuli to conduct experiments under uniform conditions. Here, we examine the influence of the existence or absence of prior information, which differs from previous studies.

Studies on prior information have also investigated the priming effect [12], which indicates how the priming stimulus influence the processing of the second stimulus that appeared shortly after the presented stimulus. Most early studies on the priming effect have targeted visual or auditory stimuli, short words, and voices. These studies focused on the cognitive process during the short time between priming and the second stimulus. By contrast, Pataramitaporn et al. [4] focused on different priming statements and studied how prior statements influenced users' mental models of conversational AI. As they investigated the influences on user's behaviors and outcomes for different prior statements, it is possible that the prior information in our study also influenced the users' evaluation of the system failure.

Snead et al. [5] studied the 'attribution theory' for an information system that responded success or failure. Although they focused on whether success and failure were attributable to external or internal factors, attributing the causes of system failure to prior information has not been well studied. Therefore, our aim was to attribute system failure to prior information when the system responded incorrectly. The presence of prior information and its attribution may render users able to tolerate failure.

2.2 Hypothesis

Based on the above considerations, we formulated the following hypothesis and developed a web system to confirm it:

Hypothesis: If users are informed about a potential weakness in an artificial system, and the system's response is incorrect due to that weakness, they will evaluate the system more sensibly based on the identified weakness.

3 Experimental Design

3.1 Control of Experiment

To confirm our hypothesis, the experiment in this study required a stable system, one in which external factors (for example, individual differences, subjective evaluation) remained consistent, with only the prior information varying. Therefore, we chose to use a hypothetical web-page system that generated comments (feeling) based on images loaded by participants. This approach was simpler (requiring less time and fewer steps) and allowed the experiments to be conducted under uniform conditions, as opposed to tasks such as voice recognition, object detection, or image generation, which involve longer procedures and are more susceptible to external disturbances.

To strictly control the experimental conditions, we developed a simulated web page system that mimicked image recognition. The system produced the same comments for all participants based on predefined rules, without relying on any algorithms.

In addition, we considered what specific system weakness the participants should be made aware of. The initial candidates for weaknesses included: images containing many identical objects; tilted or non-horizontal images; upside-down images; and images in which the target object is obscured. Ultimately, we selected the last option, images in which the target is hidden, as the designated weakness. This was because even actual AI systems struggle with such cases. Furthermore, this condition allowed users to clearly see whether the system could recognize the target or not, which made them to attributing incorrect responses to the system's known weakness easy.

3.2 Preparation of Images and Responses

Based on our preliminary testing, we selected images in which the target was clearly hidden by another object. We excluded images where understanding whether the target was hidden was difficult, in order to prevent situations where users could not determine the reason for the system's incorrect responses.

Similarly, we prepared response outputs that were clearly identifiable as either correct or incorrect. Ambiguous responses were avoided. Additionally, before the experiment began, participants were informed that the system would display "feelings" that many people would typically express when viewing the image. This explanation helped participants generally judge whether a system response was appropriate or not.

3.3 Order of Correct and Incorrect Responses

We also considered the number of images and the number of incorrect responses. Taking into account cognitive load (i.e., the "magical number" [13]), short experiment duration, and the convenience of scoring based on a scale of 100, we decided to use five images, with two of them producing incorrect responses.

Furthermore, we accounted for potential order effects (primacy and recency effects) [14–17]. We chose a pattern in which only the second and fourth images were those with hidden targets and associated incorrect responses (e.g., "a lot" and "spicy" for a cat). This arrangement reduced order effects because incorrect responses were not arranged with any bias.

Thus, in the experiment, all participants were shown the same five images, with the same incorrect responses, presented in the same order.

3.4 Development of Experimental Web Page

We developed the hypothetical web page that displayed the "feelings", as described above. As shown in Fig. 1, we prepared images above the frame of the system. When a user drags and drops the image from the top to the frame below and press the judgment button, the feelings (e.g. "cute", "fluffy") are displayed.

We prepared five images in the experiment. Participants in our experiments were required to drag and drop the five images into the frame of the system in order of 1–5. A different order will result in an error and participants have to try again. When the participant drops the image and pushes the judgement button, a loading animation which indicated the system was progressing with the task was shown (the second image in Fig. 1), and then the feeling was displayed.

3.5 Types of Explanation

A participant in the experiment experienced the web page only once, and previous explanations were different. The first type did not have an explanation regarding system limitations (Type 1: No explanation). The second type provided the information that the system was still experimental and incomplete (Type 2: The system is not yet perfect). The third type informed participants that the system was not good at evaluating images in which the subject was hidden behind something (Type 3: The system does not perfectly identify hidden objects). Figure 2 shows the differences in the explanations of Type 1–3.

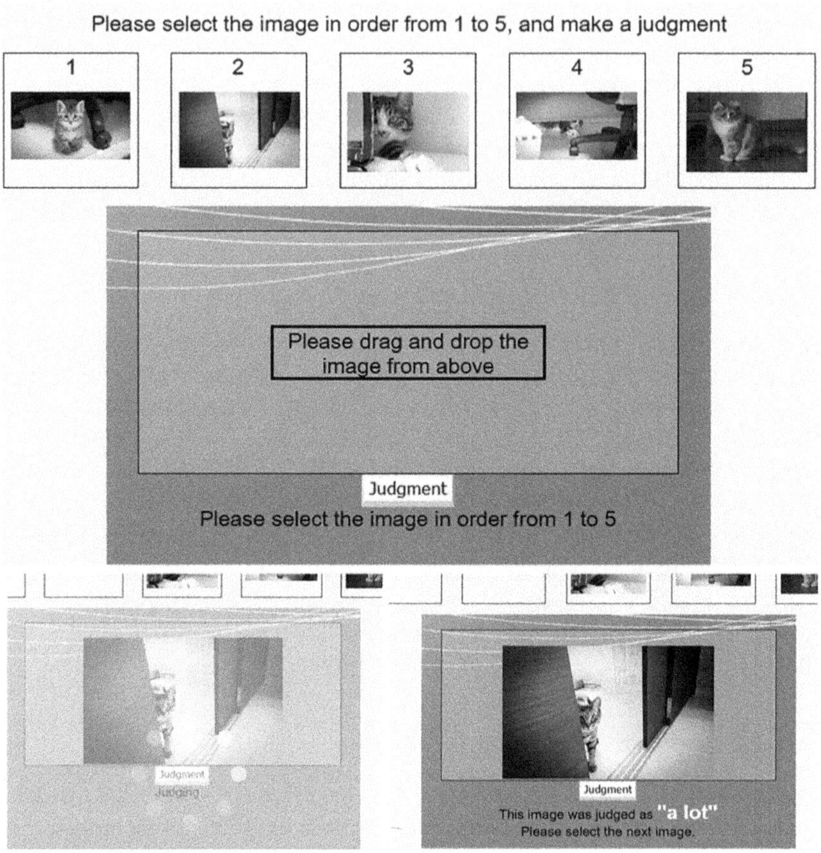

Fig. 1. The hypothetical web page that displayed the feelings.

3.6 Participants and Experiment Procedure

The participants were recruited through Amazon Mechanical Turk (a crowdsourcing platform). An informed consent procedure, approved by our institution, was followed. Only individuals who provided consent participated in the experiment. Participants received points that could be redeemed on shopping websites.

In addition, participants were informed in advance that the system's accuracy and recognition performance might be intentionally manipulated, and that some errors could occur deliberately as part of the experimental design.

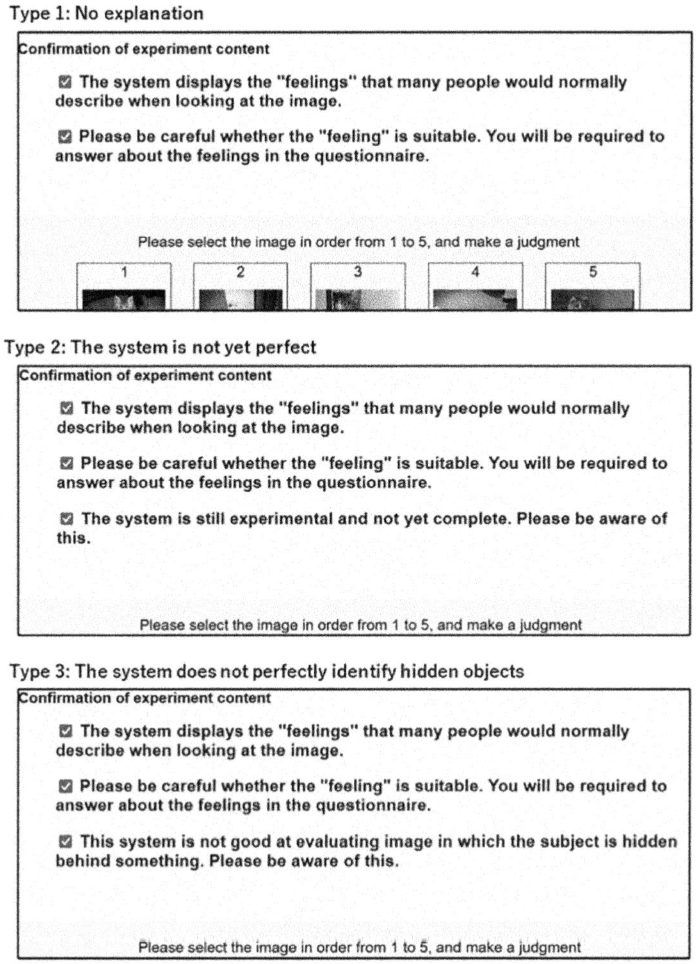

Fig. 2. Differences in explanations for Type 1–3. After reading the instructions and checking the checkboxes, the participant can proceed with the experiment.

Participants were randomly assigned to one of three groups. When a participant opened the web page, a specific condition (type) was automatically selected, and the participant experienced that condition once.

Furthermore, to prevent the participants from skipping the explanation, the experiment did not proceed until they checked the confirmation checkbox (see Fig. 2). The participants were also required to read and check other confirmations (two confirmations for Type 1 and three for Types 2 and 3; Fig. 2). The first two confirmations were common instructions for all the conditions.

In the preliminary test, we noticed that some participants did not understand the outcomes of our system and were not careful about whether the sensation was suitable. Therefore, they were required to check these statements.

After completing the task with five images and receiving the system's responses, participants were asked to complete a questionnaire. First, they were required to report the number of incorrect responses, which served as a check to ensure they were engaged with the task ("How many times did the system make mistakes?"). The second question was regarding the point of the system, which might vary according to different information ("At the present moment, out of 100 points, what is the completeness of this system?").

The participants were also required to answer how to grade the point (e.g., 'Evaluated by adding points for each correct answer, starting from zero points,' 'Evaluated by subtracting points for each incorrect answer, starting from 100 points'). Additionally, other questions asked the participants how to grade their points in detail (e.g., 'I did not give it as harsh a score since it was unavoidable, when an image that seemed to be difficult to judge was given an incorrect answer'). The importance of the scoring was also assessed.

4 Results

4.1 Statistical Analysis

The experiment involved over three hundred participants[1]. As explained above, each task included two incorrect responses; however, several participants did not correctly report the number of mistakes (e.g., did not answer "2" for the question "How many times did the system make mistakes?"). Responses that included an incorrect count of mistakes, as well as other inappropriate responses (e.g., invalid entries in the free-description field), were excluded.

After removing inappropriate responses, the number of valid responses was 49 for Type 1, 74 for Type 2, and 51 for Type 3. The age distribution of participants was as follows: 18–20 (2%), 21–30 (30%), 31–40 (37%), 41–50 (20%), and 51 and above (10%). In terms of nationality, 75% of participants were from the U.S., 6% from the U.K., 6% from India, and 13% from other countries.

Figure 3 shows the score distributions for Type 1–3. A bimodal distribution is estimated in Type 1 and 2. Conversely, a trimodal distribution is projected in Type 3. We conducted the Silverman test [18, 19]. The test is conducted to determine the number of modes in a distribution. When the expected number of peaks is k, the test examines whether the population from which the data are drawn has more than k modes (histogram peaks). Therefore, the null hypothesis is "the population has at most k modes," and the alternative hypothesis is "the population has more than k modes." The procedure begins by testing the *p*-value with k set to 1. Subsequently, k is incremented by 1, and the *p*-value is tested again for each value of k. The estimated number of modes corresponds to the first k for which the *p*-value exceeds the significance level. In our analysis, the test was performed using the statistical software R and the package silvermantest available at [20].

Table 1 lists the results of the mode estimation using the Silverman test. For our analysis, the significance level was set to $p < .10$. A bimodal distribution for Type 1 and

[1] We used participants with a specified qualification of "HIT Approval Rate greater than 90%" and "Number of HITs Approved greater than 50".

2, and a trimodal distribution for Type 3, were indicated, as listed in Table 1. Figure 4 displays the kernel density estimations and local maxima corresponding to modes 2 and 3 for Type 1–3.

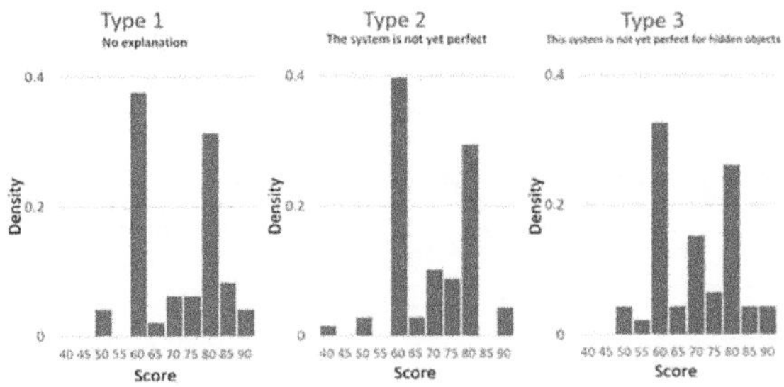

Fig. 3. Distributions of scores in Type 1–3.

Table 1. Estimations of the number of modes using the Silverman test for Type 1–3.

Type 1. No explanation			
Number of modes	1	2	-
Null hypothesis	Unimodal	**Bimodal**	-
Bandwidth	8.743	3.016	-
p-value	0.002	0.190	-
Result of test (Significance level p < .10)	Reject	Fail to reject	-
Type 2. The system is not yet perfect			
Number of modes	1	2	-
Null hypothesis	Unimodal	**Bimodal**	-
Bandwidth	7.458	3.802	-
p-value	0.004	0.312	-
Result of test (Significance level p < .10)	Reject	Fail to reject	-
Type 3. The system does not perfectly identify hidden objects			
Number of modes	1	2	3
Null hypothesis	Unimodal	Bimodal	**Trimodal**
Bandwidth	7.096	3.738	2.74
p-value	0.011	0.092	0.125
Result of test (Significance level p < .10)	Reject	Reject	Fail to reject

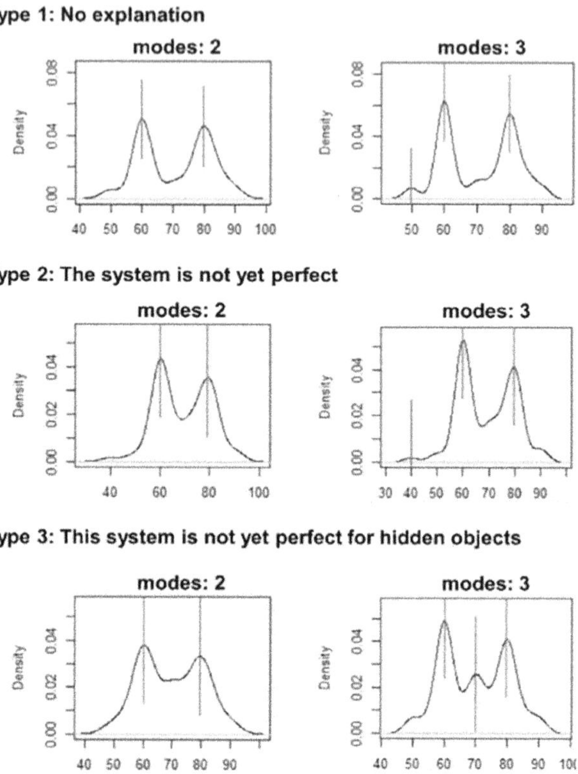

Fig. 4. Kernel density estimation and local maxima for mode 2 and 3 of Type 1–3.

4.2 Results of the Questionnaire

Regarding the responses to questions about 'Evaluated by adding points for each correct answer, starting from zero points' and 'Evaluated by subtracting points for each incorrect answer, starting from 100 points,' 37.9% of participants selected the first item and 63.2% selected the second item (multiple responses allowed). The number of participants who used the subtraction method was higher than the number of participants who used the point-adding method. 37.4% of participants selected 'I did not give it as harsh a score since it was unavoidable, when an image that seemed to be difficult to judge was given an incorrect answer.' By contrast, 23.6% of participants answered 'I gave it a harsh score since it was against expectations, when an image that seemed to be easy to judge was given an incorrect answer.' The number of participants who mitigated incorrect answers for images that seemed difficult to judge was larger than that for the others.

Regarding the questions 'Please select the item(s) that is the important for scoring' (multiple answers allowed), the participants who focused on 'Number of correct and incorrect answers' was 81.6%, the largest among other items, such as 'How fun the system was,' 'Whether UI was easy to see,' and 'Utility of the system.' The second-largest number of responses was for "Future potential of the system" at 36.8%. In our research, including our previous experiments, a large proportion of participants focused on the number of system failures. Thus, the number of failures is significantly associated with the system evaluation.

5 Discussion

5.1 Confirmation of the Hypothesis

The results showed that there were mainly two peaks at around 60 and around 80 in the scores of Type 1–3. It is believed that the score of 60 was based on a three-out-of-five evaluation, because three of the five responses were correct (3/5 = 60/100. Several participants wrote the similar comments in optional comment field, such as, 'The system misjudged 2 images out of 5 so I provided a percentage for completeness which is 60 out of 100.') Regarding the score of 80, it is estimated that participants evaluated the system by subtracting points for incorrect responses from a perfect score of 100. This trend appears to be common in the evaluation of our system and similar systems, as the two peaks appeared across all types. The trend was represented by the results of our questionnaire. The results showed that there was a certain percentage of participants answered that they evaluated by subtracting points for incorrect answers.

In contrast, although Type 1 and 2 exhibited bimodal distributions, a trimodal distribution was observed in Type 3. We conducted the Silverman test and confirmed that Type 1 and 2 had bimodal distributions, whereas Type 3 had a trimodal distribution. Although the only difference between the types was the inclusion or exclusion of an explanation, some participants in Type 3 assigned higher scores. Thus, our hypothesis was supported.

It is also notable that the density of the score around 60 in Type 3 was lower than in Type 1 and 2. It is strongly estimated that some participants who would have given a score of 60 instead gave a score of 70, due to the influence of the prior explanation.

Furthermore, this may be associated with the results of the questionnaire, as a certain proportion of participants answered that they did not provide a severe score because it was unavoidable. Using prior information, participants were induced to make certain attributions (the failure was unavoidable), and they might partly tolerate the system failure.

Therefore, by conveying prior information that may cause a failure to the participants, users may attribute the failure to the information and mitigate the failure when the system responds incorrectly. This method is considered to be an effective way for imperfect systems to induce attribution and avoid reducing the system evaluation.

5.2 Limitation

In our experiment, the number of incorrect responses was fixed at two. The results may vary with a different number of incorrect answers. Moreover, the total number of responses, which was five in our experiment, would also influence the outcomes. Future experiments should explore varying both the number of incorrect responses and the total number of responses. Furthermore, experiments should also examine whether the severity of incorrect responses—serious or minor—affects evaluations, because we used only clearly disambiguated images. The degree of error may influence participants' evaluations.

It is also possible that the order of presentation (primacy/recency effects [15–17]) could impact evaluations. In our experiment, we used a pattern in which the effects of order were assumed to be minimal (i.e., the second and fourth images contained the incorrect responses). Future studies should consider alternative presentation orders.

Further surveys using questionnaires are needed because the detailed process by which the participants added points was not clear. Although we prepared more appropriate questions (e.g., asking for adding or subtracting points for correct or incorrect answers) in our preliminary experiments to investigate this detailed process, the questions should be improved to investigate the deep process. Additionally, we plan to increase the number of participants in future experiments and investigate the scoring process for system failure.

In addition, further experiments are needed to examine cultural and age group differences, as the countries and age groups of participants in our study were limited.

6 Conclusions

We hypothesized that people's evaluations of an artificial system would change when prior information was provided. To test this, we developed a hypothetical system on a web page. Controlled images and incorrect responses were used in the experiment. The results showed that detailed information about the system's limitations led to higher evaluations.

Further experiments will investigate different numbers of incorrect responses and different presentation orders. Moreover, it is necessary to explore other types of systems, as our current study used a system that generated emotional responses based on images. It is also important to examine differences across other groups (e.g., age groups, cultural backgrounds).

Acknowledgments. We are grateful to Yuika Matsuo (Shonan Institute of Technology) for their assistance with the experiments and to all participants who took part in this study. We thank to the site providing the images which were used in our experiment and we appreciate to response that there was no problem with using the images in an academic paper.

Disclosure of Interests. The authors have no competing interests to declare that are relevant to the content of this article.

References

1. Komatsu, T., Yamada, S.: How does the agents' appearance affect users' interpretation of the agents' attitudes – experimental investigation on expressing the same artificial sounds from agents with different appearances. Int. J. Hum.-Comput. Interact. **27**(3), 260–279 (2011). https://doi.org/10.1080/10447318.2011.537209
2. Sung, J., Christensen, H.I., Grinter, R.E.: Robots in the wild: understanding long-term use. In: Proceedings of the 4th ACM/IEEE International Conference on Human Robot Interaction (HRI 2009), pp. 45–52 (2009). https://doi.org/10.1145/1514095.1514106

3. Lohse, M.: Bridging the gap between users' expectations and system evaluations. In: Proceedings of 2011 IEEE International Workshop on Robot and Human Communication (ROMAN 2011) (2011). https://doi.org/10.1109/ROMAN.2011.6005252
4. Pataranutaporn, P., Liu, R., Finn, E., Maes, P.: Influencing human–AI interaction by priming beliefs about AI can increase perceived trustworthiness, empathy and effectiveness. Nat. Mach. Intell. **5**, 1076–1086 (2023). https://doi.org/10.1038/s42256-023-00720-7
5. Snead, K.C., Jr., Magal, S.R., Christensen, L.F., Ndede-Amadi, A.A.: Attribution theory: a theoretical framework for understanding information systems success. Syst. Pract. Action Res. **28**(3), 273–288 (2015). https://doi.org/10.1007/s11213-014-9328-x
6. Xu, J., Howard, A.: The impact of first impressions on human-robot trust during problem-solving scenarios. In: 27th IEEE International Symposium on Robot and Human Interactive Communication (RO-MAN), Nanjing, China, pp. 435–441 (2018). https://doi.org/10.1109/ROMAN.2018.8525669
7. Reeves, B., Hancock, J., Liu, X.: Social robots are like real people: first impressions, attributes, and stereotyping of social robots. Technol. Mind Behav. **1**(1) (2020). https://doi.org/10.1037/tmb0000018
8. Flores, R.G., Ginsburgh, V.A.: The Queen Elisabeth musical competition: how fair is the final ranking? Statistician **45**, 97–104 (1996). https://doi.org/10.2307/2348415
9. Glejser, H., Heyndels, B.: Efficiency and inefficiency in the ranking in competitions: the case of the Queen Elisabeth Music Contest. J. Cult. Econ. **25**, 109–129 (2011). https://doi.org/10.1023/A:1007659804416
10. Wagner, J.A., Klein, N.M.: Who wants to go first? Order effects within a series of competitive sales presentations. J. Pers. Selling Sales Manage. **27**(3), 259–276 (2007). https://doi.org/10.2753/PSS0885-3134270305
11. Miller, J.M., Krosnick, J.A.: The impact of candidate name order on election outcomes. Public Opin. Q. **62**(3), 291–330 (1998). https://doi.org/10.1086/297848
12. Kidder, C.K., White, K.R., Hinojos, M.R., Sandoval, M., Crites, S.L., Jr.: Sequential stereotype priming: a meta-analysis. Pers. Soc. Psychol. Rev. **22**(3), 199–227 (2018). https://doi.org/10.1177/1088868317723532. Epub 2017 Aug 24. PMID: 28836887
13. Miller, G.A.: The magical number seven, plus or minus two: some limits on our capacity for processing information. Psychol. Rev. **63**(2), 81–97 (1956), https://doi.org/10.1037/h0043158
14. Yuasa, M.: Do you forgive past mistakes of animated agents? A study of instances of assistance by animated agents. J. Adv. Comput. Intell. Intell. Inform. **24**(3), 404–412 (2020). https://doi.org/10.20965/jaciii.2020.p0404
15. Asch, S.E.: Forming impressions of personality. J. Abnormal Soc. Psychol. **41**(3), 258–290 (1946). https://doi.org/10.1037/h0055756
16. Luchins, A.S.: Definitiveness of impression and primacy-recency in communications. J. Soc. Psychol. **48**, 275–290 (1958). https://doi.org/10.1080/00224545.1958.9919292
17. Mayo, C.W., Crockett, W.H.: Cognitive complexity and primacy-recency effects in impression formation. J. Abnormal Soc. Psychol. **68**(3), 335–338 (1964). https://doi.org/10.1037/h0041716
18. Silverman, B.W.: Some properties of a test for multimodality based on kernel density estimates. In: Kingman, J.F.C., Reuter, G.E.H. (eds.) Probability, Statistics and Analysis, pp. 248–259. Cambridge University Press, Cambridge (1983)
19. Silverman, B.W.: Density Estimation for Statistics and Data Analysis. Chapman and Hall, London (1986)
20. Silvermantest. https://github.com/jenzopr/silvermantest. Accessed 11 July 2025

Classroom-Free Educational Experimentation: A Stochastic Learning-Design Simulation Framework with LLM Optimization

Da Gong(✉)

The Education University of Hong Kong, Ting Kok, Hong Kong SAR, China
ericgongda@gmail.com
https://www.eduhk.hk

Abstract. Empirical evaluation of instructional innovations traditionally relies on time-consuming and resource-intensive classroom trials, limiting the pace and breadth of design exploration. This research introduces a "classroom-free" simulation framework that models learner self-drive and instructional barriers via closed-form stochastic operators and integrates gradient-based optimisation with a large-language-model (LLM) feedback loop. Our contributions are threefold. First, we derive a mathematically grounded simulator whose self-drive component admits analytic gradients and whose barrier operator captures dynamic disruptions with Gaussian noise. Second, we embed an LLM-in-the-loop optimiser that generates interpretable micro-tweaks to instructional design parameters, enabling human–AI co-design. Third, we validate the simulator against a real-world dataset of 45 Grade-8 students' pre–/post-test gains, demonstrating that our model predicts the direction of learning gains (Wilcoxon $W = 173.5$, $p<0.001$). Ablation studies reveal that single-shot LLM feedback accelerates early optimisation but plateaus without continuous prompting. We discuss limitations—Gaussian noise assumptions, learner homogeneity, and ceiling effects—and outline future work on heteroskedastic noise, hierarchical priors, and dynamic LLM prompting. Our results suggest that computational proxies can triage instructional designs rapidly and at scale, offering a practical virtual wind tunnel for educational research and policymaking.

Keywords: Computational social science · Instructional design · Simulation · Large language models · Stochastic optimisation

1 Introduction

1.1 Motivation: High Cost and Time of In-Class Experiments

Empirical evaluation of instructional innovations has historically relied on experimental classroom trials [1,11]. Such studies require months of coordination,

T. Hao et al. (Eds.): BESC 2025, LNCS 16431, pp. 314–330, 2026.
https://doi.org/10.1007/978-981-95-7138-3_21

recruitments of teachers and learners, and ethically sensitive data collection [12]. These may slow the feedback loop between theory and practice and limit the breadth of designs that can be tested. A computational alternative that approximates learning outcomes *ex-ante* would therefore provide immense leverage for both researchers and practitioners.

Existing educational research often struggles with issues of scalability, cost, and reliability of empirical data [2,3]. Traditional methods of assessment in classrooms may be limited by small sample sizes, biases in selection, and external factors that are difficult to control [4,5]. Additionally, large-scale studies can be resource-intensive and challenging to implement effectively [6]. To address these issues, some have proposed the use of simulations to model the complex dynamics of teaching and learning [7,8]. However, many existing approaches remain limited in their ability to accurately simulate the stochastic nature of learning and the nuances of instructional interventions [9,10].

1.2 Research Questions and Objectives

This study addresses three research questions (RQs):

RQ1 Can a stochastic simulation model, incorporating learner self-drive and instructional barriers, approximate observed learning gains without recourse to live classroom deployment?

RQ2 Does embedding a large-language-model (LLM) optimiser in the simulation loop yield lesson-plan refinements that improve predicted outcomes?

RQ3 To what extent do the simulator's predicted instructional gains correspond to the empirical pre–/post-test outcomes observed in real classrooms?

To answer these questions we (i) formally derive the model, (ii) implement a prototype, and (iii) empirically validate predictions against a 45-participant dataset.

1.3 Contributions to Computational Social Science

Our work makes three key contributions:

1. **Theoretical**: We create a new model with a Gaussian-noise barrier operator and closed-form gradient, enabling efficient optimisation.
2. **Methodological**: We introduce an LLM-in-the-loop procedure that generates incremental, explainable plan tweaks during optimisation—opening a novel human–AI co-design avenue for social-science simulations.
3. **Empirical**: Using real classroom data we demonstrate that the simulator's predictions track observed learning gains, establishing external validity and paving the way for wider classroom-free experimentation.

2 Related Work

The following studies collectively offer a coherent and comprehensive foundation for conceptualizing schooling as a complex system and exploring AI-driven enhancements.

Early efforts to treat schooling as a *complex system* have relied on multi-level agent-based models (ABMs) [17,19]. Vulic *et al.* simulate teacher–student interactions across socio-cognitive strata, revealing emergent patterns of learning inequality, yet their framework may omit large-language-model (LLM) support and may not include a formal optimisation routine to refine design parameters [7]. Ingram's doctoral work likewise employs ABMs to reproduce classroom lesson flows but may stop short of linking simulation outputs to analytic gradients or automated design search [15].

The advent of generative AI has prompted attempts to *embed* LLMs inside virtual classrooms. Zhang *et al.* orchestrate LLM-empowered agents to mimic student discourse, demonstrating richer behavioural realism; however, the study remains descriptive, as it may lack the mathematical stochasticity, closed-form gradients, and convergence guarantees required for systematic design optimisation [13]. Kinder *et al.* and Lopez-Gazpio each probe LLM feasibility from a pedagogical lens—adaptive feedback in teacher education and inclusive access, respectively—but these analyses may be restricted to case studies or conceptual discussion, with no generalisable simulator or cost–benefit model [14,16].

Compared with the above, our work contributes a **mathematically grounded stochastic simulator that (i) admits closed-form gradients, (ii) couples those gradients with an LLM *optimizer* that proposes interpretable micro-tweaks, and (iii) validates predictions against real pre–/post-test gains.**

3 Mathematical Foundations

This section formalises the stochastic learning-design model underlying our simulator. We first define the state space and parameters, followed by precise formulations of the self-drive operator A, the stochastic barrier operator B, and the resulting performance index J. For clarity we treat the continuous-time case; discrete-time simulations follow by straightforward Euler discretisation [18].

3.1 State Space and Parameter Definitions

Let $\mathbf{s}(t) \in \mathbb{R}^n$ denote the latent learner–classroom state at time $t \in [0, T]$, where each dimension encodes a construct such as cognitive mastery, motivation, or engagement. The simulator does not evolve $\mathbf{s}(t)$ dynamically—instead we integrate its quadratic form (Sect. 3.4) to obtain expected learning gains.

We group controllable or measurable inputs into three vectors:

- **Knowledge difficulty** $\boldsymbol{\kappa} = (\kappa_1, \ldots, \kappa_m)^\top$, $\kappa_k \in [0, 1]$, normalised from domain experts' ratings.
- **LLM strength** $\boldsymbol{\lambda} = (\lambda_1, \ldots, \lambda_p)^\top$, $\lambda_j \in [0, 1]$, representing calibrated prompt or system parameters that modulate LLM assistance.
- **Instructional-design knobs** $\boldsymbol{\delta} = (\delta_1, \ldots, \delta_q)^\top$, $\delta_i \in [0, 1]$, derived from the proportion or intensity of activities (e.g., quiz duration, peer-instruction cycles).

In this paper, $\boldsymbol{\delta}$ is defined as an abstract parameter representing the proportion or intensity of instructional design features. The specific dimensions are left to the user to define according to their research goals and context. For instance, in a classroom setting, δ may correspond to quiz duration, peer-instruction frequency, or AI hint density. Our framework does not rely on any fixed mapping, thereby ensuring generality.

Associated deterministic feature weights $E_j^{(\mathrm{LLM})}$, $E_i^{(\mathrm{ID,int})}$, $F_k^{(\mathrm{KD})}$, and $F_i^{(\mathrm{ID,bar})}$ are fixed scalars absorbed into summations below; without loss of generality we set them to 1 for this exposition.

3.2 Self-Drive Operator A(Logistic / ReLU)

We posit that learner self-drive arises from a linear combination of LLM support and interactive design effort:

$$A_{\mathrm{lin}} = \sum_{j=1}^{p} \lambda_j E_j^{(\mathrm{LLM})} + \sum_{i=1}^{q} \delta_i E_i^{(\mathrm{ID,int})}. \tag{1}$$

Two activation choices capture saturation or threshold effects:

$$A_{\mathrm{log}}(\boldsymbol{\lambda}, \boldsymbol{\delta}) = \sigma(A_{\mathrm{lin}}) = \frac{1}{1 + e^{-A_{\mathrm{lin}}}}, \tag{2}$$

$$A_{\mathrm{relu}}(\boldsymbol{\lambda}, \boldsymbol{\delta}) = \max\{0, A_{\mathrm{lin}} - b_0\}, \tag{3}$$

where $b_0 \geq 0$ is a tunable threshold. Their partial derivatives, needed for gradient descent, are

$$\frac{\partial A_{\mathrm{log}}}{\partial A_{\mathrm{lin}}} = \sigma(A_{\mathrm{lin}})\left[1 - \sigma(A_{\mathrm{lin}})\right] \tag{4}$$

$$\frac{\partial A_{\mathrm{relu}}}{\partial A_{\mathrm{lin}}} = \mathbb{I}\{A_{\mathrm{lin}} > b_0\} \tag{5}$$

Because $E_i^{(\mathrm{ID,int})} = 1$, the gradient with respect to each design knob simplifies to $\partial A / \partial \delta_i = \partial A / \partial A_{\mathrm{lin}}$.

3.3 Stochastic Barrier Operator $B$with Gaussian Noise

Learning rarely proceeds unhindered: interruptions, cognitive overload, or technology glitches form dynamic barriers. We encode these effects via

$$B_{\mathrm{det}} = \sum_{k=1}^{m} \kappa_k F_k^{(\mathrm{KD})} + \sum_{i=1}^{q} \delta_i F_i^{(\mathrm{ID,bar})}, \tag{6}$$

augmented by an additive Gaussian noise term: [20]

$$B(t) = B_{\mathrm{det}} + \sigma\, \xi(t), \qquad \xi(t) \sim \mathcal{N}(0, 1), \tag{7}$$

where $\sigma > 0$ modulates stochastic intensity. It follows that $\mathbb{E}[B(t)] = B_{\mathrm{det}}$ and $\mathrm{Var}[B(t)] = \sigma^2$. In practice we draw ξ once per simulation step to mirror shock-like classroom disruptions.

3.4 Performance Index $J$and Optimisation Objective

Instantaneous learning "energy" is measured by the gap between barrier and self-drive:

$$J(t) = B(t) - A(\boldsymbol{\lambda}, \boldsymbol{\delta}). \tag{8}$$

Lower values are desirable. We integrate the quadratic form of J against the latent state to obtain a scalar objective:

$$\mathcal{J}(\boldsymbol{\delta}) = \mathbb{E}\left[\int_0^T \mathbf{s}(t)^\top J(t)\,\mathbf{s}(t)\,\mathrm{d}t\right], \tag{9}$$

where the expectation is taken over the Gaussian noise ξ. Because $\mathbb{E}[\xi] = 0$, the noise contributes only a constant variance term independent of $\boldsymbol{\delta}$ and thus does not bias gradient estimates.

Since the Gaussian perturbation has zero mean, it does not affect the optimisation path in expectation. Its role is instead to shape individual simulation runs, generating variability and capturing the shock-like disruptions characteristic of classroom practice.

Closed-Form Gradient. Substituting (8) and noting $\frac{\partial B}{\partial \delta_i} = F_i^{(\mathrm{ID,bar})} = 1$, we derive

$$\frac{\partial \mathcal{J}}{\partial \delta_i} = \int_0^T \mathbf{s}(t)^\top \left(1 - \frac{\partial A}{\partial \delta_i}\right) \mathbf{s}(t)\,\mathrm{d}t. \tag{10}$$

Under the assumption $\|\mathbf{s}(t)\|_2 = 1$ (normalised latent energy), the gradient reduces to

$$\frac{\partial \mathcal{J}}{\partial \delta_i} = 1 - \frac{\partial A}{\partial \delta_i}. \tag{11}$$

Hence the simulation updates $\boldsymbol{\delta}$ via fixed-step descent:

$$\boldsymbol{\delta}^{(k+1)} = \boldsymbol{\delta}^{(k)} - \eta\big(\mathbf{1} - \nabla_{\boldsymbol{\delta}} A\big), \tag{12}$$

followed by clipping to $[0,1]^q$ to maintain interpretability. When the logistic activation is used, $\nabla_{\boldsymbol{\delta}} A = \sigma(A_{\mathrm{lin}})\big[1 - \sigma(A_{\mathrm{lin}})\big]\mathbf{1}_q$; for ReLU, it is the indicator vector $\mathbb{I}\{A_{\mathrm{lin}} > b_0\}$. These closed-form expressions eliminate the need for finite-difference estimation and enable *deterministic* gradients despite the stochastic barrier.

Interpretation as Energy Minimisation. Minimising $\mathcal{J}$ can be viewed as steering the system to a low-energy manifold where intrinsic drive exceeds extrinsic obstacles. Unlike typical ABMs that update each agent state, we instead optimise design-level parameters—a macro-policy knob more aligned with instructional design practice [21,22].

Extension to Discrete-Time Implementation. For simulation we partition $[0,T]$ into N equal steps of size Δt. Setting $\sigma_{\text{disc}} = \sigma\sqrt{\Delta t}$ keeps variance consistent. Equations (7) and (9) then translate into

$$\mathcal{J}_{\text{disc}} = \sum_{n=1}^{N} \mathbf{s}_n^{\top} (B_n - A)\, \mathbf{s}_n\, \Delta t. \tag{13}$$

4 Corollary: The Impact of Instructional Design on Other Factors

In this section, we expand upon the mathematical derivations from Sect. 3 to explore how instructional design parameters affect other factors, particularly student agency and knowledge barriers. These corollaries allow for a better understanding of the role different instructional designs play in student learning acceptance and provide theoretical support for optimizing instructional design.

4.1 Impact of Student Agency

First, we analyze the effect of student agency (self-driven factors) on instructional design. According to the derivations in Sect. 3, student agency is calculated through the activation function $A(\boldsymbol{\lambda}, \boldsymbol{\delta})$, which is determined by the linear combination $A_{\text{lin}} = \sum_{j=1}^{p} \lambda_j + \sum_{i=1}^{q} \delta_i$, representing the student's self-driven factors.

When the knowledge difficulty $\boldsymbol{\kappa}$ and LLM strength $\boldsymbol{\lambda}$ remain unchanged, modifying the instructional design parameters $\boldsymbol{\delta}$ directly impacts the student agency $A(\boldsymbol{\lambda}, \boldsymbol{\delta})$, i.e.,

$$A_{\text{lin}} = \sum_{i=1}^{q} \delta_i \quad \Rightarrow \quad A_\sigma = \sigma(A_{\text{lin}}) \tag{14}$$

The student agency A_σ increases with larger $\boldsymbol{\delta}$, especially when the logistic activation function is used. In this case, A_σ will increase rapidly at first but eventually saturate. This suggests that increasing interactive and engaging elements in instructional design (e.g., interactive quizzes, AI simulations) can effectively enhance student agency.

4.2 Impact of Knowledge Barriers

The impact of knowledge barriers, controlled by $\boldsymbol{\kappa}$, on instructional design is reflected in how it limits the student's ability to learn. When the student's self-driven factors and instructional design parameters are fixed, changes in knowledge difficulty will affect the learning outcome. According to the derivations in Sect. 3, the barrier operator $B(\boldsymbol{\kappa}, \boldsymbol{\delta}, t)$ contains a noise term, and its deterministic (expected) part is given by

$$\mathbb{E}[\,B(\boldsymbol{\kappa},\boldsymbol{\delta},t)\mid\boldsymbol{\kappa},\boldsymbol{\delta}\,] = B_{\mathrm{det}}(\boldsymbol{\kappa},\boldsymbol{\delta}) = \sum_{k=1}^{m}\kappa_k + \sum_{i=1}^{q}\delta_i. \tag{15}$$

If the instructional design is kept constant, increasing the knowledge difficulty $\boldsymbol{\kappa}$ will directly increase the deterministic barrier operator B_{det}, thereby increasing the learning difficulty. In this case, knowledge difficulty $\boldsymbol{\kappa}$ acts as a barrier to learning, requiring higher levels of student agency or instructional design to overcome the increased challenge. By manipulating $\boldsymbol{\kappa}$, we can assess the impact of knowledge difficulty on student performance, while keeping the effects of self-driven factors and instructional design constant.

The overall workflow of the research is illustrated in Fig. 1.

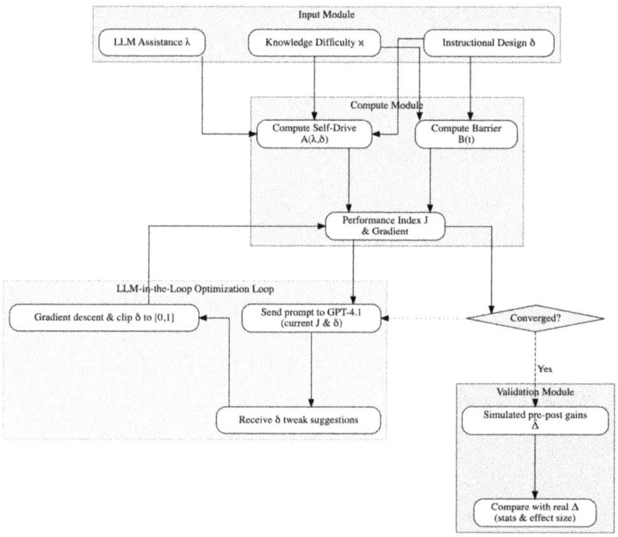

Fig. 1. Workflow of the research.

4.3 Implications for Optimizing and Comparing Instructional Designs

The insights from the previous two sections provide valuable tools for optimizing instructional designs. If we change the student's self-driven factor while keeping $\boldsymbol{\kappa}$ and $\boldsymbol{\delta}$ constant, we can evaluate the student's acceptance of a particular instructional design. Similarly, by adjusting knowledge barriers $\boldsymbol{\kappa}$ while holding the other factors constant, we can understand the impact of the inherent difficulty of knowledge on the student's learning process.

For example, by testing the student's agency within different knowledge difficulty scenarios, we can determine whether a specific design fosters greater engagement or whether a more challenging subject matter requires different types of interventions. Furthermore, the ability to manipulate these parameters separately allows for more precise comparison between traditional and innovative instructional designs. Such comparisons are critical in identifying which teaching methods or strategies are best suited for various student populations or educational contexts.

Through these corollaries, we gain not only a deeper understanding of how instructional designs interact with student and knowledge factors but also the means to optimize and refine these designs based on specific learning goals or constraints.

5 Algorithmic Implementation

The core of the optimization process is implemented in a python script. This script combines traditional mathematical optimization techniques with a large language model (LLM) for dynamic adjustments of instructional designs. The architecture of the script involves accepting input parameters, including knowledge difficulty ($\boldsymbol{\kappa}$), LLM strength ($\boldsymbol{\lambda}$), and instructional design parameters ($\boldsymbol{\delta}$), all of which are normalized into the range [0,1]. The script uses these parameters in mathematical models to simulate learning outcomes and calculate performance scores.

At each iteration, the LLM is called to suggest minor adjustments to the instructional design based on the current performance score. These suggestions are incorporated into the optimization process, with design parameters being updated using gradient descent based on the gradients of the performance index $J(\boldsymbol{\delta})$. The gradients are derived analytically and used to minimize the performance index by adjusting the instructional design parameters.

The LLM optimization loop is integrated into the algorithm by generating prompts that include the current performance score and design parameters. The LLM provides suggestions for improving the design, which are logged for transparency. The entire optimization process is repeated iteratively until convergence.

6 Simulation Study

6.1 Simulation Without LLM

In this section, we present the results of the simulation study that addresses the first research question (RQ1): Can a computational simulation estimate the effectiveness of instructional designs? We conduct two variations of the study—one using LLM feedback and one without LLM feedback. The first design follows traditional methods, while the second design incorporates digital tools, allowing AI to act as an expert to score the instructional design and difficulty (κ, λ, and δ).

The three parameters (κ, λ, and δ) were set to a value of 1 each to measure the indicators. The simulation was run for 300 iterations, and the results of the training loss (MSE) are shown in the figure below.

To avoid an arbitrary iteration count, we adopted an adaptive stopping rule: the run terminates once either the gradient norm or the 25-step moving-average improvement falls below a fixed threshold, with A safety cap of $N_{\max} = 1000$. In practice, learning curves typically plateau well before 300 iterations. We therefore display results up to 300 steps only as a visual upper bound to show the full transient-to-plateau trajectory, rather than as an optimal or unique iteration number.

Figure 2 compares the training curves of the traditional and new designs, highlighting their different optimization behaviors.

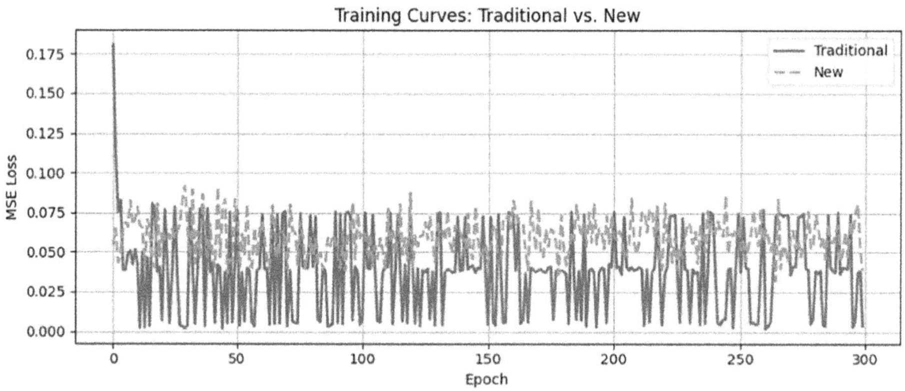

Fig. 2. Training curves: traditional vs. new.

From the figure, it can be observed that although the "New" design (which integrates digital tools and LLM feedback) shows a smaller loss early in the simulation, the curve quickly flattens. After initial improvement, the loss fluctuates within a narrow range, suggesting that the model neither converges nor diverges fully but instead oscillates. This implies that the "New" design experiences diminishing returns after the early stages of optimization.

In contrast, the "Traditional" design shows a steadier but slower decrease in loss. While the traditional design does not experience the rapid initial improvement of the new design, it demonstrates more consistent optimization over time.

Conclusion for RQ1: While it is possible to roughly estimate the quality of an instructional design using a computational model, the LLM feedback was only involved in the initial stage of the optimization process. The model did not receive ongoing feedback during the middle iterations, which likely hindered its further optimization. This lack of continuous LLM involvement leads to a less effective "New" design, as evidenced by its fluctuating loss curve. Therefore, the optimization method that does not incorporate LLM feedback consistently performs better over time in this particular simulation.

This result highlights the importance of continuous refinement in the optimization process. The lack of ongoing LLM feedback, after the initial intervention, shows a limitation in using LLMs in instructional design optimization. It suggests that, for optimal performance, an iterative and continuous LLM feedback loop is necessary. Although LLM can help in providing initial recommendations, without further interactions, the design's potential remains under-utilized.

Thus, we conclude that the integration of continuous LLM feedback is essential for achieving a better learning outcome from the simulated instructional design, while the traditional approach without LLM involvement appears to be more stable and consistent in this case.

6.2 Simulation with LLM: GPT-4.1 Optimization

In this part of the study, we present the results of the simulation with the integration of LLM, specifically using GPT-4.1for 20 iterations. For the LLM-assisted setting we report results over 20 optimisation iterations, which is sufficient to capture the early-phase convergence behaviour; beyond this point the learning curves plateau and additional iterations do not materially change the outcomes.

The performance of the two instructional designs, "Traditional" and "New", is evaluated by monitoring the values of A, B, and J throughout the iterations. The results are summarized below:

Changes in A values:

- **Traditional Design:** The A value starts at 0.9873 and gradually decreases to 0.9352, showing a steady decline. This suggests that the traditional design stabilizes over time as it undergoes optimization.
- **New Design:** The A value starts at 0.9918 and drops to 0.9352. Like the traditional design, the value decreases over time, but the decline is more rapid in the early iterations (especially between the 1st and 4th iterations). This indicates that the new design's performance improves more significantly in the early optimization stages.

Changes in B values:

- **Traditional Design:** The B value begins at 3.3748 and decreases to 1.6971, showing a consistent downward trend, suggesting that the barrier to learning is reduced as the design is optimized.
- **New Design:** The B value starts at 3.7668 and decreases to 1.5994. While the new design's B value also decreases, it starts higher than the traditional design and has a slower rate of decline.

Changes in J values:

- **Traditional Design:** The J value starts at 2.3876 and drops to 0.7619, indicating that the performance improves gradually, as the decreasing J value signals an approach toward the optimal solution.
- **New Design:** The J value starts at 2.7751 and decreases to 0.6642. While the J value drops more quickly than the traditional design, it follows a similar

overall trend, eventually reaching a lower value. This suggests that the new design also performs well after optimization.

Conclusion:

While the traditional design demonstrates a smoother optimization process, with a relatively steady decline in A, B, and J, the new design exhibits a more rapid initial improvement, particularly in the early iterations. Despite this faster initial optimization, the new design eventually reaches a comparable or even slightly lower J value, suggesting that the new design, with its interactive elements and digital tools, may offer a performance that is competitive with, if not superior to, the traditional design after sufficient adjustments.

The faster improvement of the new design in the early stages indicates that its interactive components (e.g., digital tools and AI simulations) contribute more significantly in the initial phases of learning, while the traditional design tends to stabilize more gradually.

The optimization dynamics with LLM assistance are shown in Fig. 3, while Fig. 4 illustrates the relationships among the A, B, and J metrics in a 3D surface plot.

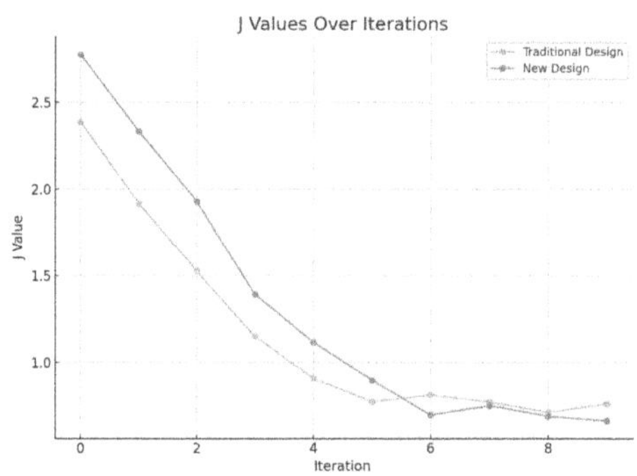

Fig. 3. Training curves with LLM: traditional vs. new.

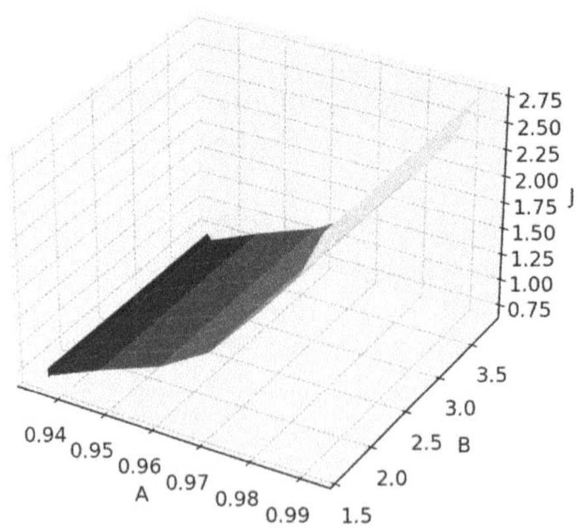

Fig. 4. 3D surface plot of A, B, and J metrics.

Answer to RQ2:

The integration of the LLM significantly influenced the optimization process of the new design. The results demonstrate that LLM can be used to refine instructional designs by providing initial feedback, but continuous LLM involvement is likely necessary for maintaining long-term improvements. The conclusion drawn from this is that LLM feedback plays a vital role in the early optimization stages, and its continuous involvement could yield even better results. The comparison shows that while both designs ultimately performed well, the new design's initial boost, provided by the LLM, led to a slightly better final outcome in terms of the performance index J.

7 Empirical Validation with Real Classroom Data

7.1 Dataset Description

The simulator is benchmark-tested against the open-access *Geometric Optics Conceptual Understanding Test* (GOCUT) corpus hosted on Mendeley Data[1][23, 24]. The corpus provides *paired* pre-/post-test scores from 45 Grade-8 students; one of the originally uploaded 46 records was excluded owing to a missing post-test score.

Following the GOCUT dataset, the "Traditional" design refers to a teacher-centred lesson without digital augmentation, whereas the "New" design integrates PhET simulations and YouTube videos as interactive tools to foster active learning of geometric optics.

7.2 Analytical Pipeline

Validation proceeds through three consecutive stages:

1. **Descriptive indices.** For each learner we compute the raw gain $\Delta_i = \text{post}_i - \text{pre}_i$ and its normalised form $g_i = \Delta_i/(20 - \text{pre}_i)$; sample location and dispersion statistics are recorded.
2. **Within-group significance (real data).** The distribution $\{\Delta_i\}$ is first subjected to a Shapiro–Wilk normality check [25], followed by a paired t test and the Wilcoxon signed-rank test [26].
3. **Model–data comparison.** For every simulation seed we form the analogue $\widehat{\Delta}_j$ and contrast $\{\Delta_i\}$ with $\{\widehat{\Delta}_j\}$ using Welch's unequal-variance t test [28] and the Mann–Whitney U test [27], complemented by error-based diagnostics.

7.3 Results

Within-Group Validity. Table 1 verifies that both empirical and simulated gain distributions are approximately normal. Table 2 shows that the real classroom intervention produces a significant post-test improvement (paired t and Wilcoxon both $p < 0.001$), while the simulator also registers a statistically significant uplift.

[1] https://data.mendeley.com/datasets/mmtpw5nvg3/1.

Table 1. Normality assessment of gain distributions.

Test	W	p
Real gain Δ	0.9635	0.1662
Simulated gain $\widehat{\Delta}$	0.9587	0.1092

Table 2. Within-group pre–post comparisons.

Test	Statistic	p
Real paired t	$t_{44} = 4.1779$	0.000137
Real Wilcoxon W	173.5	0.000473
Simulated paired t	$t_{44} = 57.9684$	3.40×10^{-43}
Simulated Wilcoxon W	0	≈ 0.0000

Model–Data Comparison. The two-sample statistics in Table 3 reveal that, although the simulator captures the *direction* of learning gains, it systematically *underestimates their magnitude*— a conclusion corroborated by both parametric and non-parametric tests.

7.4 Discussion and Limitations

The stochastic framework satisfactorily forecasts a positive shift in conceptual understanding, thereby offering preliminary external validity. Nevertheless, its attenuation of absolute effect size points to three plausible causes: (i) a homoskedastic Gaussian noise assumption that neglects heavy-tailed classroom variability; (ii) treating simulated learners as independent and identically distributed, in contrast to the heterogeneous real cohort; and (iii) the absence of a ceiling mechanism that limits further gains by high pre-test scorers.

Future work will incorporate heteroskedastic noise, hierarchical learner priors and logistic growth ceilings. These refinements aim to retain the model's correct *directional* predictions while bringing the scale of simulated gains into closer alignment with classroom observations.

8 General Discussion

8.1 Theoretical Significance for Computational Social Science

Our findings advance the argument that *computational proxies can stand in for costly, low-throughput classroom trials* when the goal is rapid, design-space

Table 3. Empirical vs. simulated gain comparison.

Test	Statistic	p
Welch two-sample t	3.7078	0.000582
Mann–Whitney U	320.0	0.0383

exploration. By marrying a closed-form stochastic learner model with gradient-based control and a lightweight LLM optimiser, we demonstrate that *learning gain is—at least to first order—a computable function of instructional design.* This result adds a quantitative plank to recent calls for a "model-first" paradigm in computational social science, where simulated counterfactuals precede—and inform—the allocation of empirical testing resources.

8.2 Practical Implications for Designers and Policymakers

For instructional designers, our framework operates as a **virtual wind tunnel**: dozens of lesson variants can be stress-tested overnight, highlighting the few configurations worth piloting with real learners. School systems facing tight budgets may thus allocate observation time to only the most promising interventions. Policymakers, in turn, can rehearse scenario analyses—for example, varying class sizes, device availability, or teacher workload—before legislating large-scale programmes. The LLM-in-the-loop feature is especially attractive in regions with limited instructional design capacity: it supplies on-demand micro-tweaks that expert human designers would otherwise have to craft manually.

8.3 Limitations

Data Scope. The empirical benchmark comprises a single cohort of Grade-8 students learning geometric optics. Generality to other ages, subjects, and cultural contexts remains untested.

Model Assumptions. (i) Barrier noise is Gaussian and homoskedastic; real disruptions may follow heavy-tailed or state-dependent processes. (ii) Learner self-drive is modelled as a linear function of design knobs, which ignores potential synergies (e.g. peer discussion *and* AI feedback producing supra-linear motivation). (iii) Ceiling constraints on post-test scores are absent, causing the simulator to under-predict high achievers.

LLM Feedback Cadence. Our ablation shows that a single, front-loaded LLM suggestion accelerates early optimisation but plateaus thereafter. Continuous or adaptive prompting schedules were not explored.

8.4 Future Work

1. **Richer noise processes.** Incorporate heteroskedastic and heavy-tailed shocks, as well as non-Gaussian, event-driven interruptions.
2. **Hierarchical learner priors.** Embed latent ability and motivation distributions, allowing seed–student alignment and mixed-effects inference.
3. **Dynamic LLM prompting.** Replace static, one-shot prompting with a reinforcement-learning loop that schedules LLM calls based on marginal information gain.

4. **Cross-domain validation.** Replicate the study on multiple datasets (languages, STEM fields, socio-economic strata) to probe external validity and calibrate effect-size scaling factors.

8.5 Synthesis

Taken together, the simulation and empirical evidence suggest a pragmatic workflow: *simulate broadly, pilot selectively, measure deeply.* Our classroom-free framework does not seek to replace empirical evaluation but to *triage* it, ensuring that scarce instructional time is spent on high-leverage designs. The broader vision is a virtuous cycle in which simulated insights guide policy pilots, whose data in turn refine the simulation—steadily tightening the feedback loop between theory and practice in computational social science.

9 Conclusion

This study provides a novel approach for simulating instructional designs and evaluating their effectiveness without the need for in-class experimentation. The simulation model, which incorporates learner self-drive, instructional barriers, and instructional design parameters, was validated against real-world data and shown to effectively predict learning outcomes for traditional teaching designs. The incorporation of LLM feedback during the optimization process further enhanced the model's ability to generate optimized instructional designs.

The answers to the research questions highlight the potential of computational simulations in educational research. For RQ1, we demonstrated that a stochastic simulation model can estimate learning gains without live classroom deployment. For RQ2, we showed that embedding an LLM optimizer into the simulation loop can refine instructional designs, though continuous feedback is necessary for optimal performance. Finally, for RQ3, we found that the simulator's predicted instructional gains were broadly consistent with the empirical pre–/post-test outcomes, providing preliminary support for its validity.

This work offers a "classroom-free" approach to educational experimentation, with the potential to accelerate the design and testing of instructional methods while reducing costs and logistical barriers. As future research refines the model and incorporates more diverse data, this computational approach could become an essential tool for both researchers and educators, helping to optimize learning outcomes in a more scalable and efficient manner.

References

1. Angrist, J.D.: Randomized trials and quasi-experiments in education research. NBER Reporter Online, pp. 11–14 (2003). https://www.nber.org/reporter/summer-2003/randomized-trials-and-quasi-experiments-education-research

2. Bhatt, M.P., Guryan, J., Khan, S.A., LaForest-Tucker, M., Mishra, B.: Can Technology Facilitate Scale? Evidence from a Randomized Evaluation of High Dosage Tutoring. National Bureau of Economic Research, Working Paper 32510 (2024). https://doi.org/10.3386/w32510
3. Dillenbourg, P.: The challenges of scaling-up findings from education research. Brookings Institution (2017). https://www.brookings.edu/articles/the-challenges-of-scaling-up-findings-from-education-research/
4. Shavelson, R.J., et al.: Problems with the use of student test scores to evaluate teachers. Economic Policy Institute, Briefing Paper #278 (2010). https://www.epi.org/publication/bp278/
5. Burke, P., Lehane, P.: Weaving the Literature on Integration, Pedagogy and Assessment: Insights for Curriculum and Classrooms. National Council for Curriculum and Assessment, Report 2 (2023). https://ncca.ie/media/6371/weaving-the-literature-on-integration-pedagogy-and-assessment.pdf
6. Shoemaker DeMio, P.: Scaling Up High-Dosage Tutoring is Crucial to Students' Academic Success. Center for American Progress (2024). https://www.americanprogress.org/article/scaling-up-high-dosage-tutoring-is-crucial-to-students-academic-success/
7. Vulic, J., Jacobson, M.J., Levin, J.A.: Exploring education as a complex system: computational educational research with multi-level agent-based modeling. Educ. Sci. **14**(5), 551 (2024). https://doi.org/10.3390/educsci14050551
8. Stančić, H., Seljan, S., Cetinić, A., Sanković, D.: Simulation models in education. In: INFuture2007: Digital Information and Heritage, Zagreb, Croatia, p. 470 (2007)
9. Davis, E., Marcus, G.: The scope and limits of simulation in cognitive models. arXiv preprint arXiv:1506.04956 (2015)
10. Manzo, G., Matthews, T.: The potential and limitations of agent-based simulation: an introduction. Rev. Fr. Sociol. **55**(4), 653–688 (2014). https://doi.org/10.3917/rfs.554.0653
11. Campbell, D.T., Stanley, J.C.: Experimental and Quasi-Experimental Designs for Research. Rand McNally & Company, Chicago (1963)
12. Taber, K.S.: Experimental research into teaching innovations: responding to methodological and ethical challenges. Stud. Sci. Educ. **55**(1), 69–119 (2020). https://doi.org/10.1080/03057267.2019.1658058
13. Zhang, Z., et al.: Simulating classroom education with LLM-empowered agents. arXiv preprint arXiv:2406.19226 (2024)
14. Kinder, A., et al.: Effects of adaptive feedback generated by a large language model: a case study in teacher education. Comput. Educ.: Artif. Intell. **8**, 100349 (2025). https://doi.org/10.1016/j.caeai.2024.100349
15. Ingram, F.J.: An agent-based classroom lessons model and simulation. Ph.D. thesis, Lancaster University (2020). https://www.researchgate.net/publication/354625019
16. Lopez-Gazpio, I.: Integrating large language models into accessible and inclusive education. Information **16**(6), 473 (2025). https://doi.org/10.3390/info16060473
17. Carmichael, T., Hadzikadic, M., Blink, M.J., Stamper, J.C.: A multi-level complex adaptive system approach for modeling of schools. In: Trausan-Matu, S., Boyer, K.E., Crosby, M., Panourgia, K. (eds.) ITS 2014. LNCS, vol. 8474, pp. 623–624. Springer, Cham (2014). https://doi.org/10.1007/978-3-319-07221-0_83
18. Butcher, J.C.: Numerical Methods for Ordinary Differential Equations, 2nd edn. Wiley, Chichester (2008)

19. Gibson, D.: SimSchool: a complex systems framework for simulating teaching and learning. In: de Freitas, S., Maharg, P. (eds.) Digital Games and Learning, pp. 63–76. Continuum International Publishing, New York (2011)
20. Øksendal, B.: Stochastic Differential Equations: An Introduction with Applications, 6th edn. Universitext. Springer, Heidelberg (2003). https://doi.org/10.1007/978-3-642-14394-6
21. Bonabeau, E.: Agent-based modeling: methods and techniques for simulating human systems. PNAS **99**(Suppl 3), 7280–7287 (2002). https://doi.org/10.1073/pnas.082080899
22. Furtado, B.A., Andreão, G.O.: Machine Learning Simulates Agent-Based Model Towards Optimal Policy: A Surrogate Model for Public Policy Assessment. Institute for Applied Economic Research (IPEA), Discussion Paper 273 (2023). https://doi.org/10.38116/dp273
23. Ndihokubwayo, K., Uwamahoro, J., Ndayambaje, I.: Pre-Post-Test GOCUT Data: Senior 4 Rwandan physics students. Mendeley Data, v1 (2021). https://doi.org/10.17632/mmtpw5nvg3.1
24. Ndihokubwayo, K., Uwamahoro, J., Ndayambaje, I.: Effectiveness of PhET simulations and youtube videos to improve the learning of optics in rwandan secondary schools. Afr. J. Res. Math. Sci. Technol. Educ. **24**(2), 253–265 (2020). https://doi.org/10.1080/18117295.2020.1818042
25. Shapiro, S.S., Wilk, M.B.: An analysis of variance test for normality (complete samples). Biometrika **52**(3–4), 591–611 (1965). https://doi.org/10.1093/biomet/52.3-4.591
26. Wilcoxon, F.: Individual comparisons by ranking methods. Biometrics Bull. **1**(6), 80–83 (1945)
27. Mann, H.B., Whitney, D.R.: On a test of whether one of two random variables is stochastically larger than the other. Ann. Math. Stat. **18**(1), 50–60 (1947). https://doi.org/10.1214/aoms/1177730491
28. Welch, B.L.: The generalization of 'Student's' problem when several different population variances are involved. Biometrika **34**(1–2), 28–35 (1947). https://doi.org/10.1093/biomet/34.1-2.28

An Examination of Methods for Resolving Reviewer Dissatisfaction in Hotel Recommendation Systems

Yujiro Hayashi[1](✉), Jianwei Zhang[2], Yukiko Kawai[3], and Shinsuke Nakajima[1]

[1] Kyoto Sangyo University, Kyoto, Japan
{i2486183,nakajima}@cc.kyoto-su.ac.jp
[2] Iwate University, Morioka, Iwate, Japan
zhang@iwate-u.ac.jp
[3] Kansai University, Suita, Osaka, Japan

Abstract. The review text in hotel search systems is beneficial for the general public searching for hotels. However, the benefits of posting reviews for reviewers themselves are limited, and the number of users posting reviews is not large. Therefore, we thought that we could increase the number of users posting reviews by developing a system that provides useful information for reviewers. Based on the six evaluation items commonly found on conventional hotel reservation sites, we created 19 new evaluation items aimed at eliminating user dissatisfaction. For each of these evaluation items, we constructed a model that classifies reviews into positive, negative, and unmentionable reviews using word embedding technology. This model allows us to analyze which evaluation items the reviewers express dissatisfaction with and which they express satisfaction with. It then predicts a score for each evaluation item that indicates the likelihood of eliminating the reviewer's dissatisfaction, and recommends hotels that exceed the predicted score. This paper proposes several methods for calculating reviewer dissatisfaction resolution scores and examines dissatisfaction resolution methods through evaluation experiments. We also examine ranking methods for presenting recommended hotels to users.

Keywords: Hotel Recommendation · BERT

1 Introduction

In recent years, numerous hotel booking websites such as Rakuten Travel [1] and Jalan [2] have been operated, where users can view reviews and scores for various evaluation criteria of accommodations. When deciding on a hotel to stay at, general users often refer to reviews posted by others, and such review information is highly useful for collecting information about hotels they have never experienced. However, only a small portion of users who stay at hotels

T. Hao et al. (Eds.): BESC 2025, LNCS 16431, pp. 331–345, 2026.
https://doi.org/10.1007/978-981-95-7138-3_22

actually post reviews, and compared to an ideal scenario where all users post reviews, valuable information is lost, and there is a possibility of bias due to reliance on a limited subset of users' opinions (Fig. 1). We believe that the current situation, where only a few users' reviews are shared, is not desirable.

One of the reasons why users refrain from posting reviews is that posting a review merely benefits other users without providing any substantial incentive for the reviewer themselves. In some cases, point rewards are offered to increase the number of reviews, but this approach may lead users to post reviews solely for the purpose of receiving points, resulting in a trend where the quantity of reviews increases regardless of their quality.

Therefore, this study proposes a system that can provide useful information to reviewers themselves, based on the idea that if posting reviews offers benefits to users, the number of reviewers will increase. Currently, hotel booking sites such as Rakuten Travel and Jalan use six evaluation criteria. However, many of these criteria encompass broad aspects, such as rooms and meals, which may not sufficiently address users' specific dissatisfactions. To solve this issue, we introduced 19 new evaluation criteria. For each of these 19 criteria, we constructed a model that determines whether the posted review contains positive feedback, negative feedback, or no mention. This model enables the analysis of which evaluation criteria the user was dissatisfied with or satisfied with in their review. Subsequently, we predict the scores that are likely to leave the user satisfied for each evaluation criterion. Hotels that have scores exceeding the predicted scores in all criteria are then recommended to the reviewers. This paper proposes methods for calculating scores to address user dissatisfaction and ranking techniques for presenting recommendations. To address dissatisfaction, we propose multiple methods for updating scores for each evaluation criterion, and through evaluation experiments, determined the optimal method. The ranking method presented to participants orders hotels based on the weighted sum of price, average score, and scores for the criteria corresponding to dissatisfactions, sorted in descending order. An ideal hotel ranking was created through participant experiments, and we explored the weighting that brings the ranking closer to participants' ideal ranking to determine the weights used for recommendations.

Our contributions are as follows:

- A hotel recommendation system was proposed to reviewers that analyzes posted reviews and eliminates complaints.
- We proposed a method to resolve reviewer dissatisfaction and confirmed its effectiveness through evaluation experiments.

2 Related Work

A well-known hotel booking site is Rakuten Travel. Rakuten Travel features many accommodation facilities, such as hotels and inns, along with their reviews, allowing users to compare ratings and consider different hotels. The widespread

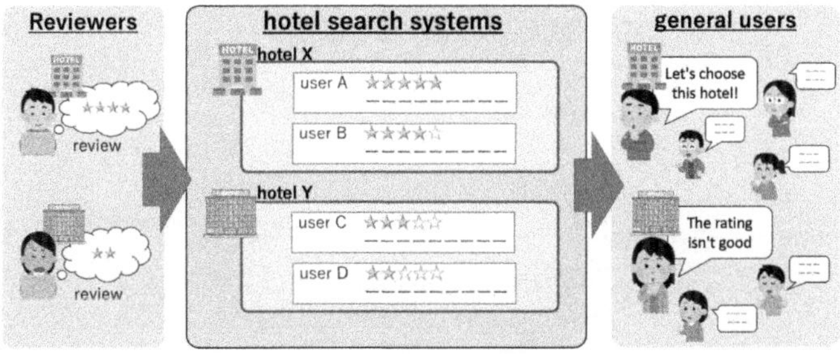

Fig. 1. General Review Submission Process

use of review-based sites like Rakuten Travel has led to numerous studies focusing on the analysis of reviews.

Abe et al. have proposed a method for creating a detailed evaluation expression dictionary for hotel evaluation items and performing automatic scoring [4,5].

Aoyagi et al. have proposed a method for extracting complaints from review texts on accommodation booking sites, performing content analysis, and identifying issues [6].

Hayashibe et al. have proposed a method for extracting linguistic knowledge, such as "positive facts" and "recommended items", from hotel reviews [7].

Takuma et al. propose a method for recommending hotels based on the hotel evaluation items ranked by users. They count the number of nouns for each evaluation items from the submitted reviews, rank the evaluation items in order of number, and recommend reviews with high user similarity. [8].

Wada et al. have proposed a method for extracting gap sentences described in reviews on accommodation booking sites and presenting them for each evaluation items [9].

Md. Shafiul Alam Forhad et al. have proposed a hotel recommendation system considering both hotel reviews and nearby facilities. They categorize and score surrounding facilities, analyze and score reviews, and recommend hotels based on a combined overall score derived from the scores of nearby facilities and reviews [10].

Y. Pramudya et al. used BERT and RoBERTa to build a personalized review-based recommendation system. They recommended hotels with high similarity to reviews, with RoBERTa showing better results [11].

H. Adiningtyas et al. conducted a customer satisfaction analysis of five-star hotel reviews based on sentiment analysis. Tangible and intangible attributes were set and sentiment analysis was conducted for each. The percentage of positives and negatives for each attribute differed from hotel to hotel, allowing the analysis of the characteristics of each hotel [12].

As mentioned, there are numerous studies analyzing user-posted reviews, feature vectors, rankings, and more to provide information recommendations. These studies are beneficial for general users planning to make hotel reservations.

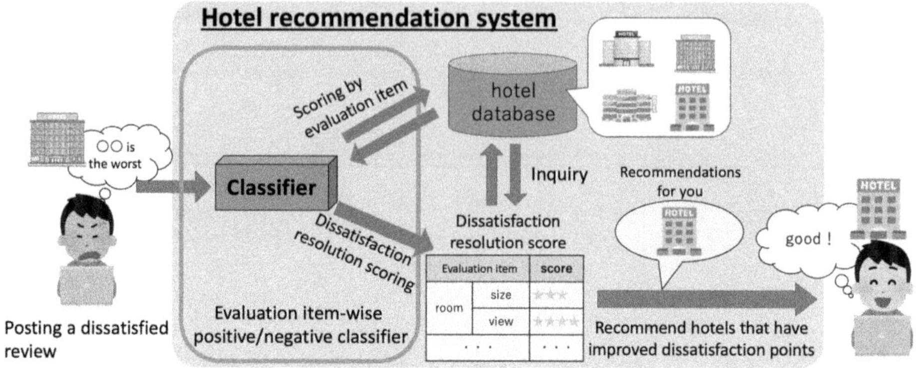

Fig. 2. Schematic diagram of the hotel recommendation system to resolve reviewer dissatisfaction

However, there is a lack of research focused on providing benefits specifically to review contributors.

3 Hotel Recommendation System to Resolve Reviewer Dissatisfaction

3.1 Overview

The overview of the proposed system is depicted in Fig. 2. Users post reviews after staying at a hotel. Using a classifier, submitted dissatisfaction reviews are used to generate user ratings for the hotel where they stayed. Similarly, a classifier is employed to create a hotel score. A dissatisfaction resolution score is then computed based on the user rating and hotel score to address dissatisfaction points. Subsequently, hotels that align well with the dissatisfaction resolution score are searched and recommended to the review contributors.

3.2 Hotel Database

In this section, we describe the hotel review database where past review data is stored. The hotel review database stores data from users who have conducted reviews in a structure similar to Fig. 3. Using data stored in this database, recommendations are generated. The management of this database employs the MySQL database management system. Each column includes: "username" for user identification, "hotelname" for the hotel's name, "review-text" for the review content, and other columns such as "location", "room", "food", "bath", "service", "facility", and "total" which represent ratings for respective aspects. As sample data for creating this database, approximately 2.5 million reviews from Rakuten Travel were used [3].

user_name	hotel_name	location	room	food	bath	service	facility	total	review_text
[illegible]	[illegible]	4	3	0	3	3	3	4	とても清潔な部屋でした。周辺は
[illegible]	[illegible]	5	5	4	5	5	5	4	貸切風呂がとても良かったです。
[illegible]	[illegible]	5	5	0	4	5	5	5	ダブルでの利用は初めてでした。
[illegible]	[illegible]	4	4	0	3	4	4	4	フロントの方の対応も感じ良く
[illegible]	[illegible]	2	5	4	4	3	4	4	部屋は広く、ベランダもあったので
[illegible]	[illegible]	5	5	2	5	5	3	5	ホテルの外観も内装もとっても素敵
[illegible]	[illegible]	3	4	2	4	3	3	4	とにかく安いプランがあって部屋は
[illegible]	[illegible]	5	3	3	4	3	2	3	ビジネスホテルのユニットバスでは
[illegible]	[illegible]	5	5	3	4	5	4	4	この度は両親子供と四人でお世話に
[illegible]	[illegible]	4	4	3	3	4	4	4	駅から近くとても便利で良かったで
[illegible]	[illegible]	5	5	5	4	4	5	5	いつも利用させて頂いています。今
[illegible]	[illegible]	4	4	4	3	5	2	4	深夜に予約・チェックインしました

Fig. 3. Example of data in database

3.3 Valuation Expression Dictionary

How to Create an Evaluation Expression Dictionary. In this section, we describe the method used in prior research to create a hotel-specific evaluation expression dictionary. Users post reviews about hotels from various perspectives. To construct an item-specific evaluation expression dictionary, actual expressions used in reviews were registered into the dictionary. Hotel review data from Rakuten Travel, a hotel reservation site, was employed for constructing this dictionary. Specifically, the construction of the dictionary involved parsing evaluation expressions found in past review texts into keywords, features, and degrees, categorizing them by evaluation items, and registering them into the dictionary.

19 New Evaluation Items. Table 1 presents a list of conventional evaluation items and 19 detailed evaluation items proposed in prior research. Scores are assigned to the evaluation expressions for these detailed evaluation items and registered into the evaluation expression dictionary. The scoring of evaluation expressions was determined by conducting a survey with five men and women in their twenties, who rated the expressions on a scale of 0 to 5. The final scores were calculated as the average of these ratings, supplemented by data from Rakuten Travel.

3.4 Scoring Method Based on Evaluation Expression Dictionary

In this section, we outline the procedure for automatically scoring unknown review data, as conducted in prior research. To assign scores to detailed evaluation items, we perform morphological analysis on review texts using the MeCab morphological analysis engine. We search for combinations of segmented keywords, features, and degrees in the evaluation expression dictionary. If an evaluation expression from the dictionary matches, we assign the predetermined score

Table 1. Conventional and proposed detailed evaluation items

Conventional evaluation items	Detailed evaluation items
location	Access to convenience stores and supermarkets
	Nearby restaurants
	Access to Sightseeing Spots
	Access to the hotel
meal	splendor
	variety
	amount
	taste
room	size
	view
	cleanliness
	quietness
bath	hot spring
	view
Service	staff
	seeing off and meeting on return
Facilities and Amenities	amenity
	Internet environment
	machinery and tools

to that evaluation criterion. Figure 4 illustrates the actual scoring process. In this review, evaluations are written regarding the view from the room and the size of the room. After analyzing the review, we match expressions in the evaluation expression dictionary and assign scores accordingly to "view" and "room size".

The method for calculating user ratings using the evaluation expression dictionary involves scoring only the reviews posted by users using the evaluation expression dictionary. As a result, items scoring 2.0 or below are considered dissatisfactory, while items scoring 4.0 or above are considered satisfactory. Items without mentions where scoring is not possible are categorized as not mentioned. The method for calculating hotel scores involves scoring all reviews of a particular hotel using the evaluation expression dictionary. Subsequently, the average value is computed for each evaluation items, and that value serves as the hotel score.

3.5 Constructed Classifier Analyzing the Frequency of Mentions of Product Features in Review Videos

In this study, we constructed two classifiers for each evaluation items of the room: one using fastText and another using BERT, to classify positive and negative

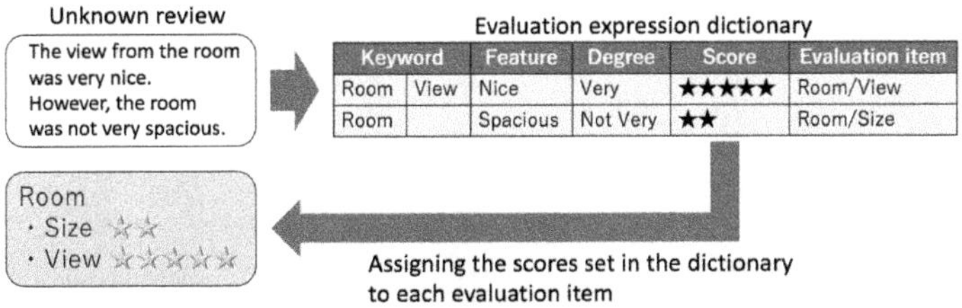

Fig. 4. Example of item-specific scoring using an evaluation expression dictionary

elements. All classifiers perform binary classification. Training data consisted of 10,000 positive and 10,000 negative samples extracted from approximately 1.5 million reviews from Rakuten Travel. Figures 5 and 6 depict the accuracy and F1 scores of the models constructed. The subscript P and N after each evaluation items denote the positive and negative models, respectively. Except for the negative model for "view", the models constructed with fastText demonstrate superior accuracy and F1 scores compared to other models. The negative model for "view" shows lower accuracy and F1 scores compared to other models, indicating a need for improvement through enhancements in training data and other factors.

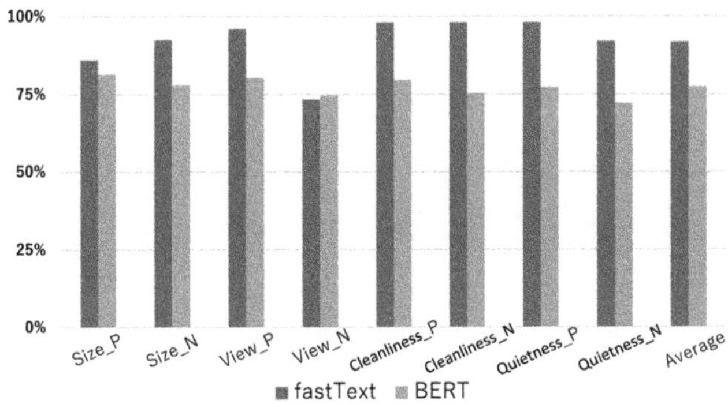

Fig. 5. Percentage of Accuracy for each model

3.6 Review Classification Methods Using Classifiers

In this section, we explain the scoring method using classifiers. Firstly, classifiers are used to classify the presence or absence of mentions in unknown reviews for each evaluation items. In this study, we employ two binary classifiers for each evaluation items: a positive classifier and a negative classifier, combining them comprehensively. Figure 7 illustrates an example of classification using the criterion of "room size". If the classifier for "spacious" classifies as positive and the

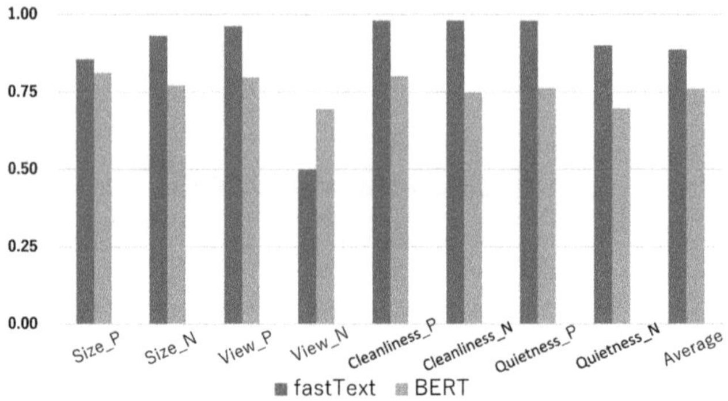

Fig. 6. Percentage of F1 score for each model

classifier for "small" as negative, the review is classified as "spacious". Conversely, if the "spacious" classifier is negative and the "small" classifier is positive, the review is classified as "small". If both classifiers classify as negative, the review is categorized as "not mentioned". If both classifiers classify as positive, indicating a potential error, the classifier with the higher probability is selected.

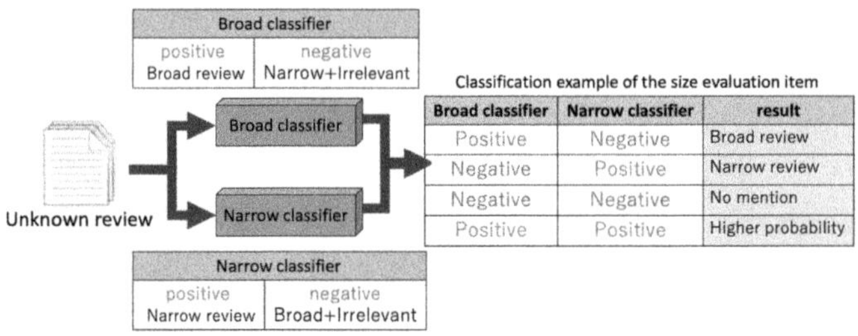

Fig. 7. How to classify unknown reviews

Creating Regression Models. This section describes the regression model used to predict the scores. For this regression model, subjects were asked to read the reviews and respond with a score of 1–5 for the hotel. The reviews presented to the subjects are pre-labeled positive-negative. The mean of the subjects' responses is the objective variable. Multiple regression analysis was performed using the percentage of positive and negative reviews among the presented reviews as explanatory variables, and equations were calculated for each evaluation item.Here are the regression model equations for the four evaluation items related to room features. Each letter subscript represents a specific evaluation items: 1 = Room Size, 2 = View, 3 = Cleanliness, 4 = Quietness.S is the hotel score, which is adjusted to 1 if the calculated result is 1 or lower, and to 5 if the result is 5 or higher. P represents the proportion of positive reviews, where if positive reviews constitute 10%, it is converted to 0.1 and calculated as a decimal. Similarly, N represents the proportion of negative reviews, also converted to a decimal for calculation, following the same principles as P.

$$S_1 = 2.91 + 7.64 * P_1 - 8.38 * N_1 \tag{1}$$

$$S_2 = 3.01 + 11.5 * P_2 - 13.1 * N_2 \tag{2}$$

$$S_3 = 3.30 + 3.62 * P_3 - 5.46 * N_3 \tag{3}$$

$$S_4 = 2.45 + 16.9 * P_4 - 2.77 * N_4 \tag{4}$$

Scoring Accuracy. This section describes the accuracy of the review scoring methods. In our prior research, we compared the scoring performance of four approaches: fastText, BERT, a sentiment expression dictionary, and a baseline method.

The goal of our scoring method is to approximate the score that a human would intuitively assign after reading a review. To evaluate this, we conducted a user study in which participants were shown multiple reviews and asked to assign scores to each. The average of these scores was used as the Ground Truth.

We then calculated the Mean Squared Error (MSE) between the scores generated by each method and the Ground Truth, in order to evaluate scoring accuracy. As a baseline, we used the review scores published on hotel booking websites.

The results are shown in Fig. 8. The method using fastText achieved the highest accuracy with an average MSE of 0.434. This was followed by the BERT-based method with an average MSE of 0.728, demonstrating the effectiveness of machine learning-based approaches for review scoring.

Calculation Method of Hotel Score. In this section, I will explain the method of calculating hotel scores using classifiers. We classify all reviews for a particular hotel into positive reviews, negative reviews, and reviews without any specific mention for each evaluation items using classifiers. Then, we determine the percentage of positive reviews and negative reviews for each criterion. This method allows us to systematically assess and predict hotel scores based on the sentiment and content of reviews categorized by evaluation items.

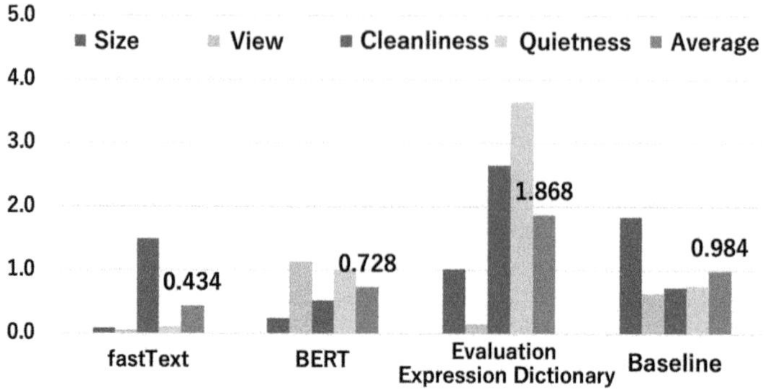

Fig. 8. MSE for each method

Calculation Method of User Evaluation. In this section, we will describe the method for calculating user evaluations of a hotel based on reviews they have submitted. Using a classifier, each evaluation items in the submitted reviews is categorized into positive, negative, or neutral. Evaluation items classified as positive indicate satisfaction, those classified as negative indicate dissatisfaction, and those classified as neutral indicate no specific mention.

3.7 Dissatisfaction Resolution Score

This section describes the dissatisfaction resolution score used when recommending hotels to users. In this study, we define the dissatisfaction-resolution score as the minimum score required to resolve a user's dissatisfaction. The score is calculated based on the hotel scores and user evaluations obtained in Sects. 3.6 and 3.6. We consider hotels that meet or exceed the dissatisfaction resolution score in all evaluation criteria as candidates for recommendation. Although user budgets for hotels may vary depending on the purpose or region, we assume that they are generally similar. Moreover, hotels with higher total hotel scores tend to have higher accommodation costs. Based on these assumptions, we adopt the following policy for updating scores. Evaluation items for dissatisfaction: increase the hotel score. Evaluation items for satisfaction or no mention: decrease the hotel score. This adjustment aims to recommend hotels within the same price range by maintaining a consistent total score. Regarding the update methods for the dissatisfaction-resolution score, we examined four approaches in our prior research. The methods are composed as follows. Methods for dissatisfied evaluation items: Method X and Method Y. Methods for satisfied or no mentioned evaluation items: Method A and Method B. These were combined to form four variations (X-A, X-B, Y-A, Y-B), which were compared with a baseline method.

For dissatisfied criteria, the score is increased by either 50% (Method X) or 75% (Method Y) of the difference between the maximum value and the current score. For example, if the current hotel score is 2.0,

$$MethodX : 2.0 + (5.0 - 2.0) * 0.5 = 3.5 \tag{5}$$

The difference between Method X and Method Y lies in how much emphasis is placed on resolving dissatisfaction.

To maintain a consistent total score, the increased value for dissatisfied criteria is offset by reducing the scores of satisfied or unmentioned criteria. Methods A and B differ in how this reduction is distributed.

As a baseline method, hotels are ranked based on the "room" score on hotel booking websites in descending order.

We conducted recommendations based on the four methods and the baseline, and carried out a five-point Likert scale survey to evaluate whether the users' dissatisfactions were resolved. The results, shown in Fig. 9, indicate that significant differences were observed only between the baseline and Y-A/Y-B methods.

Based on these results, we adopted Method Y, which places greater emphasis on resolving dissatisfaction, as the most effective approach in this study.

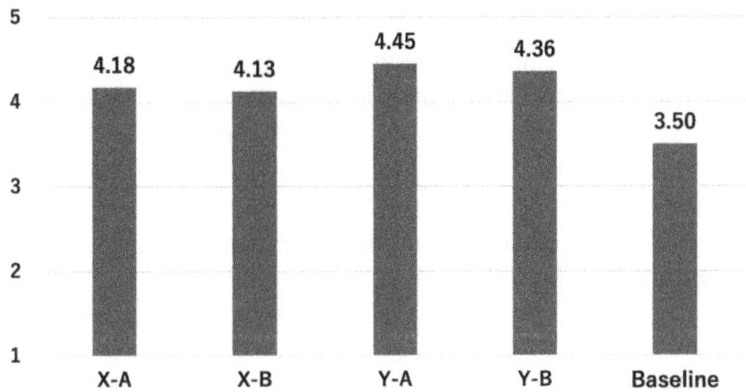

Fig. 9. Average of the five-point evaluation for each method

Hotel Recommendation Using Dissatisfaction Score. This section describes the hotel ranking method. Using the dissatisfaction resolution scores calculated in Sect. 3.7, we determine the set of hotels to be recommended. The goal is to resolve user dissatisfaction using the dissatisfaction resolution score and improve the satisfaction of recommendations through the proposed ranking method. In the ranking process, the following three elements are considered: price (Price), the total hotel score (S_t), and the dissatisfaction evaluation items score (S_d). These three elements are multiplied by their respective weights and summed, and hotels are ranked in descending order of the total score, as shown in Eq. 6, and then recommended to users.

$$Score = \alpha * Price + \beta * S_t + \gamma * S_d (\alpha + \beta + \gamma = 1.0) \tag{6}$$

However, the extent to which each user values the three elements differs. Therefore, it is considered most effective for improving satisfaction to assign different weights to each user. Nevertheless, assigning different weights to each user requires information collection through questionnaires at the time of recommendation, which may impose a burden on users. Thus, this study proposes the following three weighting methods: a method of assigning different weights to each user; a method of grouping users based on which element they prioritize and assigning weights to each group; and a method of assigning the same weights to all users. Through evaluation experiments, we determine the optimal weights that improve recommendation satisfaction without imposing a burden on the users.

4 Evaluation Experiment

4.1 Experiment Overview

In order to evaluate the effectiveness of the ranking methods used for hotel recommendations to users, we conducted an experiment. In the procedure of the experiment, participants were asked to assume that they had stayed at a particular hotel, and were presented with both information about the hotel and a dissatisfaction-based review. The hotel information was obtained from Rakuten Travel [1], a major hotel booking website. As for the dissatisfaction-based review, a review containing descriptions related to "the room" was generated in this study and shown to the participants.

Subsequently, five candidate hotels were presented to each participant as recommendation options. The participants were then asked to rank these five hotels in the order in which they would prefer to stay. The ranking created by each participant was defined as their ideal ranking. The experiment was conducted in four regions: Kyoto, Osaka, Nagoya, and Tokyo, with a total of ten university student participants (both male and female).

As proposed methods, we considered three weighting approaches: assigning different weights to each user based on Eq. 6; grouping users according to the elements they prioritize and assigning weights to each group; and assigning the same weights to all users. For the baseline, we asked participants to rate the importance of each of the following three factors—price, total hotel score, and the score of dissatisfaction-related evaluation items—on a scale of 1.0 to 5.0, and calculated weights based on the ratio of the responses. For the application of these weights, we prepared three methods: using individual weights for each participant; using the average response value within each group as the weight; and using the overall average of all participants' responses as a common weight.

In addition, we compared the results with methods that simply ranked hotels by ascending price for participants who prioritized cost, or ranked by the factor they selected as most important. For the comparison, we used nDCG@5 as the evaluation metric. We calculated and compared the nDCG between the ideal rankings created by the participants and the rankings generated using the weights derived by each method.

4.2 Experiment Result

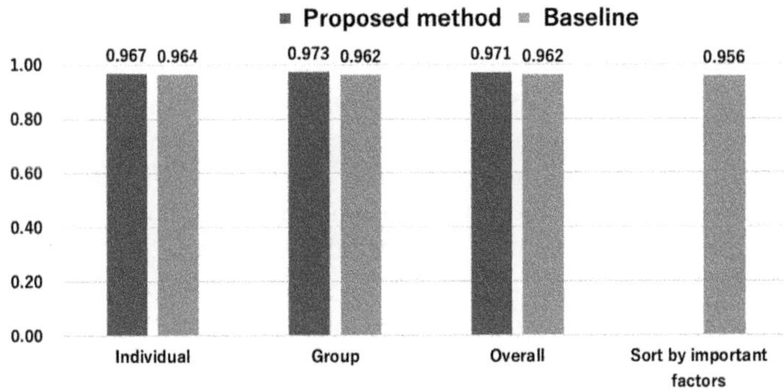

Fig. 10. nDCG for each method

Figure 10 shows the nDCG results for each method. The horizontal axis represents the proposed and baseline methods applied to the individual, group, and overall settings, as well as the sorting method based on the element that each user prioritizes. As a result, the sorting-based method showed the lowest nDCG among all methods. This suggests that the proposed method is more effective in increasing user satisfaction with the recommendations than simple ranking approaches such as sorting by price, total score, or dissatisfaction-related item scores.

Moreover, in all three settings—individual, group, and overall—the proposed method outperformed the baseline in terms of nDCG. In particular, the method that assigns weights at the group level achieved the highest nDCG among all methods. A statistical significance test revealed a significant difference only between the group-based proposed method and the sorting-based method.

Initially, it was hypothesized that assigning weights individually would be the most effective, as user preferences are inherently diverse. However, assigning weights on an individual basis requires users to create their own ideal rankings, which imposes a considerable burden on them. In contrast, the group-based weighting method only requires users to select which of the three elements—price, total score, or dissatisfaction-related score—they value most, thereby reducing the burden.

Considering both the user burden and the nDCG results, this study adopts the method of assigning weights at the group level as the most practical and effective approach.

5 Conclusion

In this study, we proposed a hotel recommendation system designed to increase the incentive for users to post reviews by providing them with valuable feedback. Existing hotel booking websites often aggregate broad aspects such as rooms and meals into a single evaluation, making it difficult to accurately identify and address user dissatisfaction. To address this issue, we defined 19 more granular evaluation categories and developed a model that classifies each user review by category into satisfied, dissatisfied, or not mentioned. Based on this, we calculated the minimum required score (dissatisfaction resolution score) needed to resolve the user's dissatisfaction and proposed a ranking method to recommend hotels that meet or exceed this score, thereby improving user satisfaction. Through a user study, we demonstrated that our proposed method enables more preference-aligned recommendations compared to conventional ranking methods, and that weighting by user groups is particularly effective.

In future work, we plan to implement the proposed recommendation method into an actual system and conduct large-scale user studies to evaluate its generalizability and practical utility. Furthermore, we aim to enhance the system's accuracy and multidimensionality by incorporating additional data such as location information and travel purposes.

Acknowledgment. This work was supported by JSPS KAKENHI research grants (23K24955). It is also a product of research activities of the Institute of Advanced Technology and the Center for Human Informatics(M2301), which were financially supported by the Kyoto Sangyo University Research Grants. In this paper, we used"Rakuten Dataset" (https://rit.rakuten.com/data_release/) provided by Rakuten Group, Inc. via IDR Dataset Service of the National Institute of Informatics.

References

1. Rakuten Travel. https://travel.rakuten.co.jp
2. Jalan net. https://www.jalan.net
3. Rakuten Group, Inc.: Rakuten Dataset. Informatics Research Data Repository, National Institute of Informatics (2014)
4. Abe, K., Nakajima, F.: Hotel recommendation system based on automatic review scoring system. In: DEIM Forum 2020, pp. 1–28 (2020)
5. Abe, K., Sakai, S., Matsunami, Y., Nakajima, F.: Proposal of a hotel recommendation method using scores by review evaluation items. In: DEIM Forum 2019, pp. 1–134 (2019)
6. Aoyagi, N., Hasuike, T.: Extraction of complaints in user reviews of accommodation reservation sites and identification of issues through content analysis. FIT2021, CE-002 (2021)
7. Hayashibe, Y.: Extracting positive facts and objectives of recommendation from lodging reviews. In: The 25th Annual Meeting of the Association for Natural Language Processing, pp. 554–557 (2019)
8. Taguma, K., Hukuhara, K., Kamei, K., Fujita, S.: A hotel recommendation method based on extracting preferences using word of mouth. In: 78th National Convention of Information Processing Society of Japan, 5K-01 (2016)
9. Wada, T., Toyoda, T., Ohara, K.: Analysis of accommodation reviews focusing on the gap between expectations and reality and its application to search. Inf. Process. Soc. Jpn. **2018-IFAT-129**(6) (2018)

10. Forhad, M.S., Arefin, M., Kayes, A.S.M., Mohammad, K., Chowdhury, J., Kumara, I.: An effective hotel recommendation system through processing heterogeneous data. In: The 5th International Conference on Advanced Computing and Intelligent Engineering (ICACIE) (2020)
11. Pramudya, Y., Alamsyah, A.: Hotel reviews classification and review-based recommendation model construction using BERT and RoBERTa. In: 2023 6th International Conference on Information and Communications Technology (ICOIACT) (2023). https://doi.org/10.1109/ICOIACT59844.2023.10455890
12. Adiningtyas, H., Millanyani, H.: Analysis of customer satisfaction levels based on online customer reviews. In: 2024 2nd International Conference on Software Engineering and Information Technology (ICoSEIT) (2024). https://doi.org/10.1109/ICoSEIT60086.2024.10497518

Developing a Novel Tag Cloud System for Optimized Visualization and Behavioural Analytics in Cosmetic Review Platforms

Shizuku Kitamura[1], Asaka Cheng Lan[1(✉)], Fumiya Yamaguchi[1], Mayumi Ueda[2,3], and Shinsuke Nakajima[1]

[1] Kyoto Sangyo University, Kyoto, Japan
{g2253424,a007532,yamaguchi.fumiya,nakajima}@cc.kyoto-su.ac.jp
[2] Otemon Gakuin University, Osaka, Japan
may-ueda@otemon.ac.jp
[3] Osaka University, Osaka, Japan

Abstract. In the competitive landscape of e-commerce—especially in the cosmetics sector—user reviews significantly influence consumer decision-making. However, the overwhelming volume of reviews often leads to information overload, making it difficult for users to extract meaningful insights. This study introduces a novel tag cloud-based feature visualization method that summarizes consumer sentiments (positive and negative) extracted from textual reviews. Through a counterbalanced within-subjects experiment, we demonstrate that our interactive visualization system improves decision-making efficiency and user satisfaction compared to traditional text-based reviews. Methodologically, this approach offers a scalable and interpretable framework for integrating sentiment analysis with visual analytics, bridging the gap between qualitative user-generated content and quantitative decision support systems. Our findings indicate that the proposed method not only enhances consumers'ability to identify products aligned with their preferences but also reinforces the connection between visual behavioral analytics and consumer belief in brands (CBB). Consequently, it contributes to a deeper understanding of the cognitive mechanisms underlying consumer purchase decisions (CPD) and offers practical insights for enhancing brand competitiveness in digital marketplaces, while also illuminating how visual information processing influences consumer behavior and strategic brand positioning.

Keywords: Consumer Review Analytics · Feature Visualization · Decision Making Process · Tag Cloud

1 Introduction

In recent years, a multitude of e-commerce platforms that furnish detailed information about products or retail outlets have augmented their offerings to include

T. Hao et al. (Eds.): BESC 2025, LNCS 16431, pp. 346–361, 2026.
https://doi.org/10.1007/978-981-95-7138-3_23

not only visual descriptions but also consumer feedback. With the rapid evolution of e-commerce enterprises, online review systems have become crucial in helping consumers navigate through a vast array of offerings, playing a decisive role in consumers' purchase decision behaviors, and emerging as instrumental strategic tools for getting competitive advantages [3,8,16,20,29,33]. Notably, platforms like @cosme are extensively utilized within the cosmetics sector, with a significant portion of consumers consulting review data prior to making purchases. each product typically accumulates a vast number of reviews, requiring considerable time and effort to fully understand the comprehensive characteristics of each item. The integration of review information on digital platforms, such as Amazon.com and Rakuten Ichiba, which feature reviews across a broad spectrum of products, as well as specialized platforms like Tabelog and Jalan.net focused on sectors such as food and travel, demonstrates the widespread use of review data. Within the beauty industry, platforms like Hot Pepper Beauty and @cosme are particularly noteworthy. As of June 2024, @cosme reported over 400,000 registered products, 20.8 million cumulative reviews, and 17.8 million active monthly users, highlighting significant user engagement [18].

Although design features and visualization in online review systems hold significant potential to enhance information search and processing, their utilization and effectiveness vary significantly and are not yet fully optimized. For instance, Information overload is believed to confuse individual consumers, leading to less effective problem-solving and poor decisions [9,14,15,17,34]. Moreover, as illustrated in Fig. 1, conventional cosmetic e-commerce sites often fail to facilitate the identification of nuanced differences between top-rated products based on specific evaluative criteria, such as "long-lasting color", even when employing filters aimed at isolating specific attributes. Hence, the development of a system capable of visualizing the attributes of cosmetic items as delineated in consumer reviews would substantially facilitate users in effortlessly understanding these characteristics.

Prior studies have not only underscored the significance of exploring the tech-driven review system design [2,4], but have also contributed extensively to our understanding of how technical elements within online review systems influence user experience, such as the effect of prominent top reviews on information provision efficiency [24,25,29], designing online review systems that support information search [6,19], and establishment of user experience quantification model from online user reviews [10,22]. Given our previous research [31,32], we developed a system that visualizes the distinctions between cosmetic items by scoring their attributes, significantly assisting users in comprehending the characteristics of each item and selecting products that align with their preferences. While this system is highly effective in differentiating between a user's habitual cosmetic items and alternative options, its efficacy in distinguishing among top-ranked cosmetic items remains limited. Consequently, there has been relatively less exploration into the interplay and cumulative effects of various design features when combined.

Building on current research achievements, this study proposes a novel method to visualize both positive and negative review content for each cosmetic item. This is based on the textual analysis of these reviews, thereby optimizing the process of understanding characteristic differences among various cosmetic products. We intend to utilize tag clouds approach to visually represent characteristic terms. The categories for this visualization draw from twelve aspects, namely, Pearl/Shimmer, Moisturizing/Penetration, Whitening/UV Care, Natural/Tinted, Fit/Adherence, Long-lasting Color, Low Irritation, Color Payoff, Anti-aging Care, Cost Performance, Glossy Finish, and Matte Finish. This approach aims to enhance the digital user experience by providing a streamlined and more accessible means of assessing product features directly from consumer feedback, thus supporting more informed purchasing decisions in the cosmetics sector. In this paper, we strive to advance a notable integration of an interactive component within the tag cloud to enhance the utility of the visual summaries provided. This feature allows users to engage directly with the data by selecting specific attributes within the tag cloud to access in-depth reviews related to these features. Such an interaction not only bridges the research gap between quantitative summarization and qualitative insights but also significantly enriches the user's decision-making process.

The main contributions of this paper are summarized as follows:

- We implemented a tag cloud-based visualization method that summarizes and highlights key features from digital cosmetic reviews, enabling users to quickly grasp the overall sentiment (both positive and negative).
- We integrated an interactive component that allows users to click on elements within the tag cloud to access in-depth reviews related to specific features. This objective aims to bridge the gap between quantitative data representation and qualitative information, enhancing user engagement through interactive exploration.
- We conducted a comprehensive evaluation experiment to assess how different methods of information presentation, specifically tag clouds versus traditional text reviews, affect decision-making processes in terms of efficiency (response time) and satisfaction in cosmetic item selection.

While this study presents a novel approach to review visualization, we acknowledge that it serves as a Pioneering exploration rather than a large-scale deployment. Our primary objective is to evaluate the feasibility and usability of tag cloud-based summarization in consumer-computer interfaces, with future work aimed at scaling this method using automated sentiment analysis and broader user testing.

2 Related Works

Recent studies highlight the critical role of online review visualization systems and contextual strategies in shaping consumer information-seeking behaviors, a pivotal consideration as technologies advance in the digital era [12,13,30,35]. A

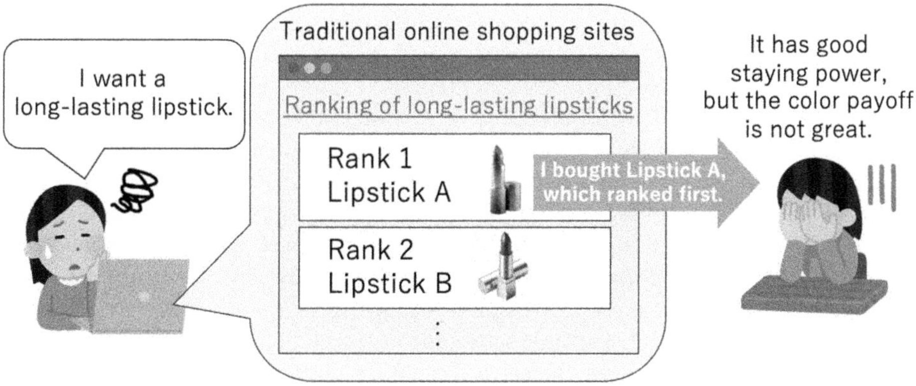

Fig. 1. Example of conventional cosmetic website usage

substantial body of research, including the use of sentiment analysis, has been dedicated to categorizing online user reviews into positive, negative, or neutral categories. Notably, advanced machine learning techniques have been employed for aspect-based sentiment analysis across diverse contexts, which not only evaluates a product's market position relative to its competitors but also integrates online ratings with content analysis. This integration facilitates the identification of causal relationships between user experiences and consumer satisfaction [5,23]. Such methodologies align with the Information Processing Theory of Consumer Choice, which underscores the significant impact of context and task structure on consumer information acquisition strategies [28].

The proliferation of review-based platforms has catalyzed a significant amount of research into review analytics. While traditional visualization systems for online reviews have primarily concentrated on quantitative measures like customer ratings and price levels to depict product attributes, recent studies indicate that these metrics do not fully capture the breadth of consumer feedback [26,30]. It has been demonstrated that many product or service characteristics are inadequately represented by numerical data alone, underscoring the importance of a more comprehensive analysis of the textual content in reviews to facilitate informed consumer decision-making.

In a specific application within the cosmetics industry, Abe et al. designed a recommendation system that tailors reviews to user preferences, considering factors such as skin type, age, and brand, utilizing data from @cosme [1]. This approach achieved noteworthy accuracy and highlighted the potential for personalizing reviews based on user characteristics. However, it also revealed significant challenges, such as data imbalance and the limited exploration of textual content, which can restrict the effectiveness of such systems. Further explorations in review visualization have been conducted to analyze movie reviews related to infectious diseases and natural disasters. Their research utilized text mining to track shifts in public sentiment over time, providing insights into how societal changes influence media perceptions [7]. Additionally, Ogawa et al. applied Self

Organizing Maps to uncover trends in product reviews, identifying pivotal temporal events and user demographics through cluster analysis [27]. In the realm of cosmetics, Fukumoto et al. investigated how different makeup patterns are perceived, using visualization techniques to show how varying feature words in visual representations can reflect temporal trends in makeup preferences [11].

Despite these advancements, research that specifically focuses on the visualization of cosmetic reviews, particularly employing tag clouds, remains scant. This study seeks to fill this void by introducing a novel visualization methodology tailored for cosmetic reviews, aiming to enhance user comprehension of product differences. This new approach leverages and expands on previous methods, thereby making a substantial contribution to the field of consumer research. These developments highlight the critical need for platform providers to thoughtfully integrate features into their review systems, as evidenced by the substantial impact these features can have on user engagement and understanding.

3 Method

We have developed a structured, three-stage methodology to visualize and analyze feature quantities in cosmetic reviews, utilizing advanced tech-driven methods to improve consumer decision-making behavior in the cosmetics market.

3.1 Stage 1: Visualization Approach Framework

In conventional online review platforms, consumers often face information overload, a problem exacerbated by context-dependent variables such as the vast volume of reviews and the uncertain origin and quality of these reviews. To address this, our proposed system, illustrated in Fig. 2, employs tag clouds to display positive and negative review content for each cosmetic product. This approach allows users to quickly discern key product features, facilitating a comparative analysis of top-ranking cosmetics based on desired attributes. For instance, as shown in Fig. 3, a user interested in "long-lasting color" can use negative tag clouds to avoid products with "poor pigmentation". Alternatively, they might consider products with less critical issues, such as "causes dryness", if these issues are more tolerable. This visual representation enhances users' ability to rapidly identify significant characteristics, leading to more informed and efficient purchasing decisions.

3.2 Stage 2: Methodology for Feature Visualization

This stage outlines the technical process for feature visualization in cosmetic reviews. As depicted in Fig. 3, the methodology begins with the segmentation of reviews into individual sentences, which are manually categorized as positive or negative. These categorized sentences are then used to generate corresponding tag clouds: sentences with positive sentiments contribute to the positive tag cloud, while those with negative sentiments form the negative tag cloud. This approach simplifies the visualization of complex review data and assists users in discerning nuanced product differences.

3.3 Stage 3: Novel Technique for Presenting Feature-Specific Reviews

The final stage introduces a novel technique for displaying reviews based on feature-specific tag clouds, as demonstrated in Fig. 4. When a user selects a feature from the tag cloud on the left side of the figure, the system presents related reviews on the right side. This functionality allows users to explore in-depth specific features of a cosmetic item, such as "glitter", providing not just the presence but also detailing the intensity and prevalence as described in the reviews. This feature-specific presentation method offers users detailed insights into cosmetic items, significantly enhancing their decision-making process by providing precise, feature-related information.

For this exploratory study, sentiment classification was conducted manually to ensure high labeling accuracy and contextual relevance. While this approach limits scalability, it provides a reliable foundation for evaluating the effectiveness of the visualization interface. In future iterations, we plan to replace manual annotation with automated sentiment classification models to improve efficiency and generalizability.

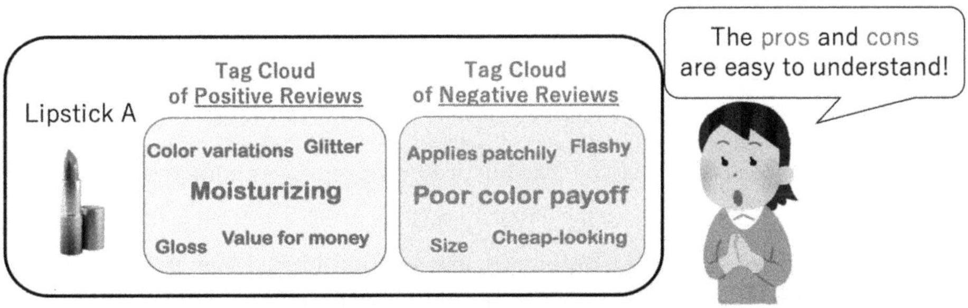

Fig. 2. System proposed in this study

4 Experiments

In this section, we conduct experiments to evaluate the effectiveness of our proposed method. Our experiments intend to answer the following research questions. The principal aim of this study was to empirically assess the efficacy of tag clouds for visualizing feature quantities within the context of cosmetic reviews. While tag clouds have been utilized across various informational contexts, their specific utility in enhancing decision-making efficacy in consumer behavior has not been comprehensively studied. This experiment was designed to contrast the effects of tag clouds against traditional text-based review presentations, with the goal of determining their impact on consumer decision-making processes in the cosmetic industry. In this vein, the aim of this study is to address the following research questions (RQs),

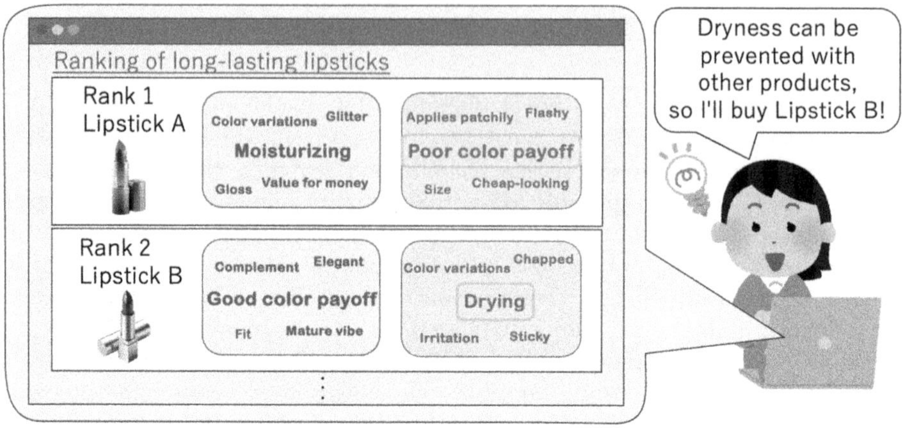

Fig. 3. Feature visualization method

Fig. 4. Presenting reviews of cosmetics based on their characteristics

- RQ1: How does the novel online review evaluation system perform in the evaluation task compared with the baseline methods?
- RQ2: How does the tag cloud visualization of feature quantities influence decision-making efficiency in cosmetic item selection?
- RQ3: In what kind of mechanism does the interactive functionality of the tag cloud enhance user engagement and depth of information understanding?

4.1 Experimental Design

The experimental design adhered to a counterbalanced within-subjects framework to ensure that the effects of the order of presentation were evenly distributed across participants. This design is particularly advantageous in behavioral studies where the order can influence responses due to learning or fatigue effects [21]. By having participants experience both conditions (tag cloud UI as the proposed method and traditional review UI as a baseline method), we could directly compare their effects within the same subjects, enhancing the internal validity of the findings. Our study utilized a counterbalanced within-subjects design to control for order effects and maximize the reliability of the results by allowing each participant to experience both conditions of the experiment:

traditional review texts and tag cloud visualizations. This approach not only mitigates biases associated with presentation sequence but also enhances the comparative analysis between different information presentation methods.

4.2 Participants and Procedures

The experiment engaged a total of ten female participants, carefully selected to include both younger and older adults to investigate age-related differences in processing digital information. Eight participants were in their twenties, representing a technologically adept cohort with a propensity for frequent cosmetic usage. Two participants were over fifty, providing insights into the usability and effectiveness of the visualization methods for older adults, who may have different cognitive and perceptual capabilities. This age diversity helps in examining the generalizability of the findings across a broader age spectrum. These participants were randomly divided into two groups to facilitate a counterbalanced methodological approach, ensuring robustness in testing the effects of information presentation order. Although the sample size is limited to ten participants, the experiment was designed to serve as a controlled usability test rather than a statistically generalizable study. The demographic skew toward younger users reflects the primary user base of cosmetic review platforms, but future studies will include more diverse and larger cohorts to improve external validity.

4.3 Task

Participants were exposed to detailed descriptions of five distinct lip products via two different methods: the conventional review texts (Review UI) and the proposed tag cloud visualization (Tag cloud UI). The experiment was structured around two specific decision-making tasks:

- Task 1: Choosing a lip product for a casual social outing.
- Task 2: Selecting a lip product for a formal occasion, such as a wedding.

For Task 1, participants selected one item from five options labeled Lip A to Lip E, while for Task 2, they selected from a different set of five options labeled Lip F to Lip J. In each task, participants interacted first with one presentation method, followed by the other, with Group 1 beginning with Reviews UI and Group 2 starting with Tag cloud UI. Key metrics collected included decision time, decision satisfaction, and cognitive load.

4.4 Measurement Instruments

To address the effectiveness of the novel online visualization system, we conduct the experimental study by examining these two measurement instruments:

- Decision Time: This was recorded as the interval from the presentation of product information to the completion of the product selection.

- Post-Interaction Questionnaire: This instrument was designed to capture data on perceived information adequacy, utility, stress level, and the preference for the method of information presentation. It included both five-point Likert-scale items and open-ended questions to provide a comprehensive understanding of participant experiences.

5 Results and Analysis

To rigorously evaluate the impact of different user interfaces on decision-making behavior, this section presents the empirical findings derived from the experimental tasks. Figure 5 shows the average response times for each task according to two types of UIs (Tag cloud UI and Reviews UI), and Fig. 6 shows the cosmetic items selected by participants for each task. This section presents the results of item selection, illustrated using pie charts. For Task 1, the selected lip products are represented by distinct colors: pink for Lip A, blue for Lip B, orange for Lip C, green for Lip D, and yellow for Lip E. A similar color-coding scheme is applied to Task 2 to facilitate comparison. The results indicate that, in both Task 1 and Task 2, a considerable number of participants selected different items depending on whether the tag cloud UI or the review UI was provided. These results include aggregated data from both Group 1 and Group 2. The average response time was shorter for the tag cloud UI than for the review UI in both Task 1 and Task 2. The selection results also showed that many participants chose different cosmetics depending on whether the information was provided in a review UI or a tag cloud UI. However, since the goal of this experiment was for participants to choose a lip product they personally found satisfactory, this difference in selection results is not considered problematic.

Figure 7, Fig. 8, Fig. 9, and Fig. 10 show the results of the questionnaire responses to Questions 1 through 4, respectively. These also include aggregated results from Group 1 and Group 2. For Question 1, the average rating for the tag cloud UI was 4.1, while the review UI received an average of 3.9, indicating a higher perceived usefulness for tag cloud. For Question 2, the average rating for the tag cloud UI was 3.0, while the review UI received an average of 4.7, suggesting that reviews were perceived to provide more sufficient information. For Question 3, the average rating for tag cloud UI was 2.2, whereas the review UI received an average of 4.3. This indicates that participants felt less stress when using tag clouds. For Question 4, 60% of participants stated they would prefer to use tag clouds again, while 40% preferred reviews, meaning that more than half of the participants favored the tag cloud method. The qualitative data gleaned from the post-experiment questionnaires provided nuanced insights into the participants' perceptions and experiences, which are summarized below:

- **Perceived Helpfulness:** Participants predominantly favored the tag cloud UI for its ability to succinctly highlight key features and sentiments. This visualization strategy was noted for its efficiency in streamlining the decision-making process by allowing quicker and more focused evaluations of the products.

- **Perceived Information Sufficiency:** Although tag cloud UI provided less detail compared to the comprehensive traditional reviews UI, many participants appreciated the concise format. This aspect was particularly valued for its role in reducing cognitive overload, thereby simplifying the decision-making process.
- **Experienced Stress Levels:** A correlation was observed between the reduced decision time and lower stress levels reported by participants using the tag cloud UI. This finding suggests that the streamlined presentation method effectively diminishes cognitive strain, enhancing the overall user experience.
- **Future Preference:** While a significant majority of participants expressed a preference for the tag cloud UI due to its efficiency and reduced cognitive load, there was also notable support for a hybrid approach. This preference indicates a desire for combining the rapid, feature-focused benefits of tag cloud UI with the depth and detail offered by traditional review UI, suggesting an optimal balance that could cater to varying user needs and contexts.

	Task1	Task2	Average
Tag cloud UI	126.9 s	86.1 s	106.5 s
Review UI	284.5 s	296.1 s	290.3 s

Fig. 5. Average Response Time by Visualization Method for Each Task

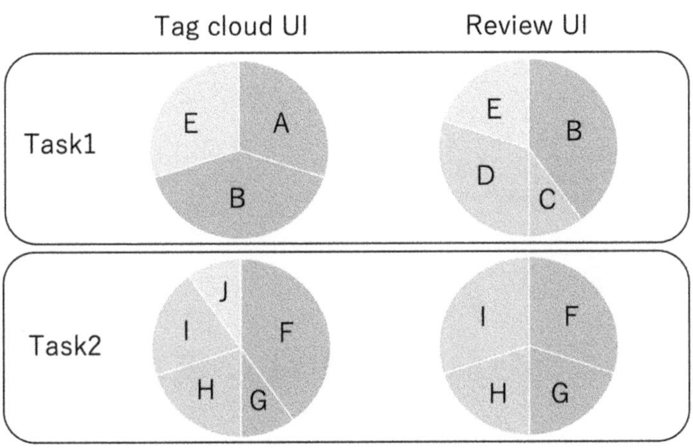

Fig. 6. Cosmetic Item Selection Results

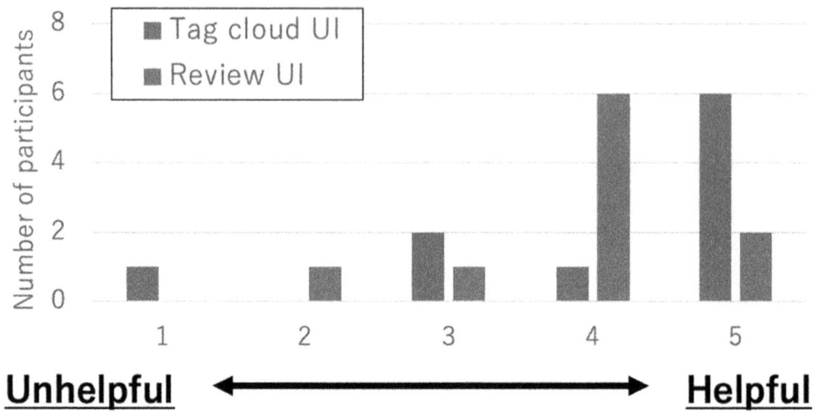

Fig. 7. Responses for Question 1

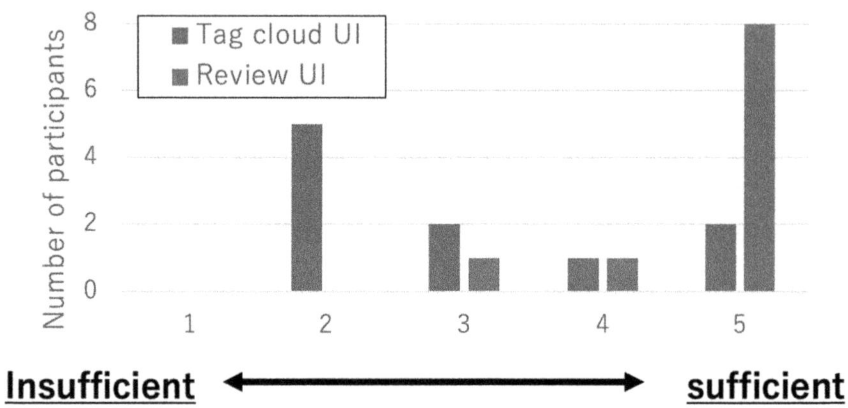

Fig. 8. Responses for Question 2

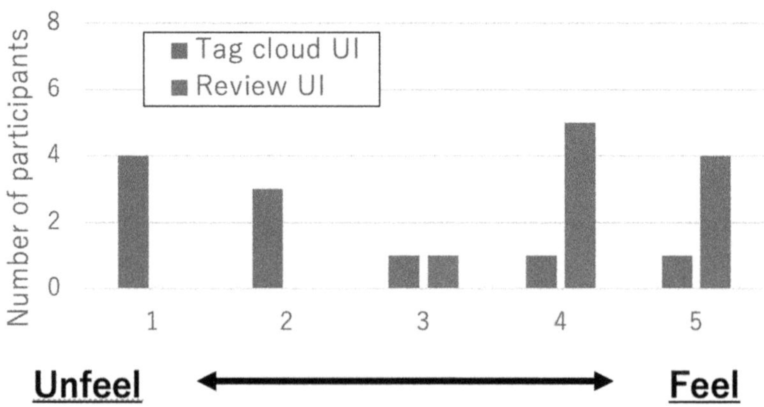

Fig. 9. Responses for Question 3

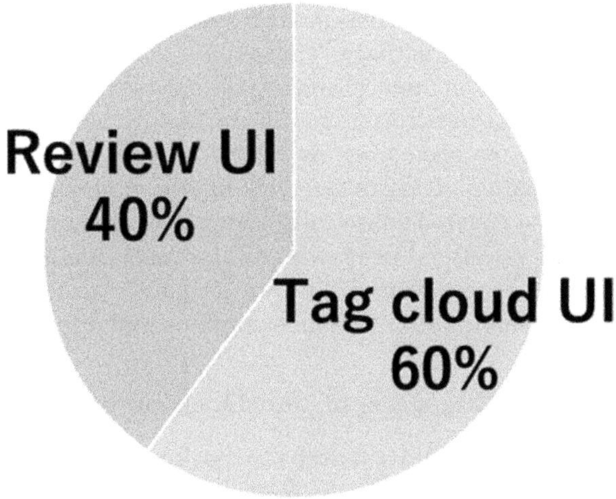

Fig. 10. Responses for Question 4

6 Conclusion and Implication

We have developed a novel feature visualization system employing machine learning technologies with the following three main research contributions. This innovation is designed to mitigate information overload, enhance visual analytics, and optimize the consumer decision-making process.

6.1 Methodological Innovation in Visualization

In this study, we developed and implemented an innovative method for the visualization of feature quantities in cosmetic reviews. Our approach specifically entailed the generation of tag clouds that encapsulate the frequency and sentiment of mentions—both positive and negative—pertaining to each cosmetic item within user-generated content. This visualization technique not only provides a high-level summary of consumer sentiments but also serves as an interactive tool, enabling users to delve deeper into specific attributes by selecting elements within the tag cloud. The feature terms used in the tag cloud were extracted using frequency analysis combined with manual curation to ensure semantic relevance across cosmetic-specific attributes. While this approach is effective for domain-specific prototyping, future work will explore the use of automated keyword extraction algorithms—such as TF-IDF, RAKE, or topic modeling—to enhance the objectivity and scalability of the process.

6.2 Integration of Interactive Review Access in Tag Cloud Visualization

A significant enhancement introduced in this research is the interactive component embedded within the tag cloud technology. This feature is innovatively designed to allow users to access detailed reviews pertinent to specific features of interest directly. Such interactivity represents a crucial advancement in data visualization, particularly in how it merges quantitative summarization with qualitative analysis. This integration significantly enriches the user experience by facilitating a more nuanced and informed decision-making process. Upon interacting with the tag cloud, users can click on any highlighted feature, which triggers the display of a curated subset of reviews that discuss this feature extensively. This capability is critical as it extends the functionality of the tag cloud from a mere graphical representation of data frequency to a dynamic interface that offers in-depth insights into consumer opinions and experiences.

6.3 Impact on User Engagement and Decision-Making

The interactive tag clouds facilitate a deeper engagement with the content, allowing users to transition seamlessly from observing general trends in the data to exploring specific attributes in detail. This process not only aids users in making more informed decisions but also enhances their understanding of the product through a direct examination of the experiences of others. By providing this depth of context, the tag cloud becomes more than just a visual summary; it transforms into an interactive tool that empowers users to explore data in a personalized and meaningful way.

This rigorous examination and discussion not only strengthen the academic rigor of our findings but also lay a foundational framework for future studies aiming to enhance user interaction and satisfaction in digital commerce environments. In future developments, we aim to augment the clustered layout word cloud by integrating advanced analytics features such as time-series analysis of cosmetics reviews and sentiment analysis of textual data. Furthermore, we plan to deploy sophisticated machine learning algorithms to optimize the processing of review content. To better serve business intelligence needs, we also intend to enhance the tag cloud's capabilities by incorporating features for semantic search and data mining, improving the precision and utility of keyword discovery and trend analysis.

Although this study benchmarks the proposed system against a traditional review interface, future research strives to incorporate additional baselines, such as aspect-based summaries or sentiment visualization tools, to more comprehensively assess the relative effectiveness of different review presentation modalities. The interactive and visually engaging nature of the tag cloud interface may have introduced evaluation bias, particularly due to the well-documented novelty effect in human-computer interaction research. Participants may have favored the tag cloud UI not solely because of its functional advantages, but due to its perceived innovativeness. To mitigate this bias, future studies aims to adopt a longitudinal evaluation design, allowing participants to engage with both interfaces over an extended period. This approach would yield more accurate insights into sustained user preferences and long-term usability.

The integration of statistical and qualitative findings provides a comprehensive understanding of the advantages and limitations associated with each information presentation method. Our research findings also highlight an opportunity for future research and development in digital interfaces, where combining the immediacy of tag clouds with the detailed insights from traditional reviews could lead to more sophisticated, user-centered decision support systems in e-commerce and beyond.

Acknowledgments. This work was supported by JSPS KAKENHI research grants (22K12281), and a Kyoto Sangyo University Grant from the Institute of Advanced Technology and the Center for Human Informatics (M2301). We would like to express our gratitude to istyle Inc. who provided the review data of cosmetic items.

Disclosure of Interests. The authors declare that there is no conflict of interest.

References

1. Abe, S., Kobayashi, I.: Development of a review recommendation system using cosmetic product review data. Tech. Rep. Database Syst. (DBS) **2015**(7), 1–7 (2015)
2. Benlian, A., Titah, R., Hess, T.: Differential effects of provider recommendations and consumer reviews in e-commerce transactions: an experimental study. J. Manage. Inf. Syst. **29**(1), 237–272 (2012). https://doi.org/10.2753/MIS0742-1222290107
3. Bhattacharyya, S., Banerjee, S., Bose, I.: One size does not fit all: rethinking recognition system design for behaviorally heterogeneous online communities. Inf. Manage. **57**(7), 103245 (2020). https://doi.org/10.1016/j.im.2019.103245
4. Bolton, G., Greiner, B., Ockenfels, A.: Dispute resolution or escalation? The strategic gaming of feedback withdrawal options in online markets. Manage. Sci. **64**(9), 4009–4031 (2018). https://doi.org/10.1287/mnsc.2017.2802
5. Brar, G.S., Sharma, A.: Sentiment analysis of movie review using supervised machine learning techniques. Int. J. Appl. Eng. Res. **13**(16), 12788–12791 (2018)
6. Büschken, J., Allenby, G.M.: Sentence-based text analysis for customer reviews. Mark. Sci. **35**(6), 953–975 (2016). https://doi.org/10.1287/mksc.2016.0993
7. Cen, T., Watanabe, H.: Visualization of movie reviews over time using word clouds: a case study of the infectious disease themed film contagion. J. Digit. Arch. Soc. **5**(s1), s47–s50 (2021)
8. Chen, P.Y., Hong, Y., Liu, Y.: The value of multidimensional rating systems: evidence from a natural experiment and randomized experiments. Manage. Sci. **64**(10) (2017)
9. Chen, W., Gu, B., Ye, Q., Zhu, K.X.: Measuring and managing the externality of managerial responses to online customer reviews. Inf. Syst. Res. (30(1)), 81–96 (2019). https://doi.org/10.1287/isre.2018.0781
10. Dai, W.D., Jin, G., Lee, J., Luca, M.: Aggregation of consumer ratings: an application to yelp.com. Quantit. Mark. Econ. (QME) **16**(3), 289–339 (2018). https://doi.org/10.1007/s11129-017-9194-9
11. Fukumoto, M., Ushiama, T., Sumiya, K.: Visualization and time-series analysis of makeup pattern characteristics using cosmetic reviews. In: IEICE Conferences Archives. The Institute of Electronics, Information and Communication Engineers (2023)

12. Gutt, D., Neumann, J., Zimmermann, S., Kundisch, D., Chen, J.: Design of review systems – a strategic instrument to shape online reviewing behavior and economic outcomes. J. Strateg. Inf. Syst. **28**(2), 104–117 (2019). https://doi.org/10.1016/j.jsis.2019.01.004
13. Heo, H., Lee, S.: Consumer information-seeking and cross-media campaigns: an interactive marketing perspective on multi-platform strategies and attitudes toward innovative products. J. Theor. Appl. Electron. Commer. Res. **20**(2) (2025). https://doi.org/10.3390/jtaer20020068
14. Fen Hu, H., Krishen, A.S.: When is enough, enough? investigating product reviews and information overload from a consumer empowerment perspective. J. Bus. Res. **100**, 27–37 (2019). https://doi.org/10.1016/j.jbusres.2019.03.011
15. Huang, L., Tan, C.H., Ke, W., Wei, K.K.: Do we order product review information display? How? Inf. Manage. **51**(7), 883–894 (2014). https://doi.org/10.1016/j.im.2014.05.002
16. Hussain, J., Azhar, Z., Ahmad, H.F., Afzal, M., Raza, M., Lee, S.: User experience quantification model from online user reviews. Appl. Sci. **12**(13) (2022). https://doi.org/10.3390/app12136700
17. Hussain, J., et al.: A multimodal deep log-based user experience (UX) platform for UX evaluation. Sensors **18**(5) (2018). https://doi.org/10.3390/s18051622
18. istyle Inc.: @cosme, surpasses 10 million members on its 25th anniversary!. https://prtimes.jp/main/html/rd/p/000000381.000005126.html
19. Jabr, W., Rahman, M.: Online reviews and information overload: the role of selective, parsimonious, and concordant top reviews1. MIS Q.: Manage. Inf. Syst. **46**(3), 1517–1550 (2022).https://doi.org/10.25300/MISQ/2022/16169
20. Janina, S., Kristin, K., Maren, S., Dennis, K., Ralf, K.: "Sorry, too much information" - designing online review systems that support information search and processing. Electron. Mark. **33**, 47 (2023). https://doi.org/10.1007/s12525-023-00664-1
21. Keren, G.: Between-or within-subjects design: a methodological dilemma. In: A Handbook for Data Analysis in the Behaviorial Sciences 1, p. 257–272. Psychology Press (2014)
22. Kim, Y., Krishnan, R.: On product-level uncertainty and online purchase behavior: an empirical analysis. Manage. Sci. **61**(10), 2449–2467 (2015). https://doi.org/10.1287/mnsc.2014.2063
23. Kuriyozov, E., Matlatipov, S., Alonso Pardo, M., Gómez-Rodríguez, C.: Deep learning vs. classic models on a new Uzbek sentiment analysis dataset. In: Human Language Technologies as a Challenge for Computer Science and Linguistics, pp. 258–262 (2019)
24. Kwark, Y., Chen, J., Raghunathan, S.: User-generated content and competing firms' product design. Manage. Sci. **64**(10), 4608–4628 (2018). https://doi.org/10.1287/mnsc.2017.2839
25. Kwon, B.C., Kim, S.H., Duket, T., Catalán, A., Yi, J.S.: Do people really experience information overload while reading online reviews? Int. J. Hum.-Comput. Interact. **31**(12), 959–973 (2015). https://doi.org/10.1080/10447318.2015.1072785
26. Mousavi, R., Hazarika, B., Chen, K., Razi, M.: The effect of online Q&AS and product reviews on product performance metrics: Amazon.com as a case study. J. Inf. Knowl. Manage. **20**(01), 2150005 (2021). https://doi.org/10.1142/S0219649221500052
27. Ogawa, K., Tamura, T., Hayami, S.: Cluster analysis and visualization focusing on time-series information in product reviews, p. 1F55. The Japanese Society for Artificial Intelligence (2016)

28. Ross, I.: Reviewed work: an information processing theory of consumer choice James R. Bettman. J. Mark. **43**(3), 124–126 (1979)
29. Shams, R., Chatterjee, S., Chaudhuri, R.: Developing brand identity and sales strategy in the digital era: moderating role of consumer belief in brand. J. Bus. Res. **179**, 114689 (2024). https://doi.org/10.1016/j.jbusres.2024.114689
30. Srivastava, V., Kalro, A.D.: Enhancing the helpfulness of online consumer reviews: the role of latent (content) factors. J. Interact. Mark. **48**(1), 33–50 (2019). https://doi.org/10.1016/j.intmar.2018.12.003
31. Ueda, M., Nakajima, S.: Cooking recipe recommendation method focusing on the relationship between user preference and ingredient quantity. In: Yang, G.-C., Ao, S.-I., Huang, X., Castillo, O. (eds.) Transactions on Engineering Technologies, pp. 385–395. Springer, Dordrecht (2015). https://doi.org/10.1007/978-94-017-9588-3_29
32. Ueda, M., Takata, N., Morishita, Y., Nakajima, S.: Utilizing various user moods for automatic recipe-metadata generation. In: Ao, S.-I., Kim, H.K., Huang, X., Castillo, O. (eds.) IMECS 2016, pp. 115–129. Springer, Singapore (2017). https://doi.org/10.1007/978-981-10-3950-8_9
33. Ueda, M., Taniguchi, Y., Matsunami, Y., Okuda, A., Nakajima, S.: Analyzing the tendency of review expressions for the automatic construction of cosmetic evaluation dictionaries. In: IAENG Transactions on Engineering Sciences, Special Issue for the International Association of Engineers Conferences 2019, pp. 81–95. World Scientific Publishing Co. Pte. Ltd (2020)
34. Vermeeren, A., Law, L.C., Roto, V., Obrist, M., Hoonhout, J., Väänänen, K.: User experience evaluation methods: current state and development needs. In: NordiCHI 2010: Extending Boundaries - Proceedings of the 6th Nordic Conference on Human-Computer Interaction, pp. 521–530 (2010). https://doi.org/10.1145/1868914.1868973
35. Zinko, R., Stolk, P., Furner, Z., Almond, B.: A picture is worth a thousand words: how images influence information quality and information load in online reviews. Electron. Mark. **30**(4), 775–789 (2020). https://doi.org/10.1007/s12525-019-00345-y

Leveraging Comment Data for Enhanced Content Discovery Through Time Series Analysis of Impressive Scenes in Videos

Akito Sasahara[1(✉)], Asaka Cheng Lan[1], Da Li[1], Fumiya Yamaguchi[1], Mayumi Ueda[2,3], Shinsuke Nakajima[1]

[1] Kyoto Sangyo University, Kyoto, Japan
{i2486093,a007532,lida,yamaguchi.fumiya,nakajima}@cc.kyoto-su.ac.jp
[2] Otemon Gakuin University, Osaka, Japan
may-ueda@otemon.ac.jp
[3] Osaka University, Osaka, Japan

Abstract. In the dynamically evolving domain of digital media, users of platforms like YouTube and Niconico face significant challenges in discovering content that aligns with their emotional and thematic preferences. Traditional video selection methods, largely dependent on titles and thumbnails, often result in viewer dissatisfaction due to mismatches between expected and actual content. To address this challenge, we developed an intuitive video recommender system that employs a novel set of evaluation criteria designed to capture nuanced viewer impressions. By scoring videos based on these criteria, the system enables users to more accurately assess potential satisfaction prior to engagement. To enhance the precision of our recommender system, we integrated the 'Niconico Classifier', developed using the advanced capabilities of the BERT model. This strategic enhancement significantly improves the identification of relevant video segments, or 'impression scenes', by analyzing timestamped comments. Our evaluation experiments demonstrated a notable reduction in the time users spend searching for content, with substantial improvements in accuracy and efficiency across various impression metrics. The findings from this study not only highlight the practical utility of our system but also establish a scalable framework that advances personalized, context-aware strategies for media consumption. This approach underscores the transformative potential of adaptive technologies in digital media, paving the way for future research into personalized content curation and optimization of user interactions.

Keywords: Video Recommendation Systems · Time Series Analysis · BERT · User Engagement · Content Personalization

T. Hao et al. (Eds.): BESC 2025, LNCS 16431, pp. 362–378, 2026.
https://doi.org/10.1007/978-981-95-7138-3_24

1 Introduction

A colossal amount of video content is being uploaded to video-sharing platforms such as YouTube[1] and Niconico[2] every day. For instance, approximately 720 h of video content are being uploaded to YouTube every minute in 2024 [10]. On these platforms, users often search for videos that interest them using keywords and decide whether a video meets their expectations based on the video title and thumbnail. However, traditional keyword-based search methods have limitations in finding videos that users may intuitively want to watch. For example, if someone searches for videos with the keyword 'エモい' ('Emo') (a Japanese word meaning 'emotional' or 'touching'), the search will return videos that contain the word in the video title or description. In reality, these videos might not actually create an 'Emo' impression on the user when being watched. Similarly, many videos that users would consider 'Emo' may not actually use that keyword in their title or description, leading to missed results. To address this problem, we suggested an emotionally intuitive video recommendation system which allows users to search for videos based on their feelings, using category-specific evaluation scores. The system created classifier models for eight impression-related categories and displays emotional features of the video to users through radar charts. This approach enables effective retrieval of videos that do not explicitly include impression-based keywords such as 'Emo' in their titles or descriptions. In this paper, we refer to terms such as 'Emo' or 'きゅん' ('Kyun') (a Japanese word meaning a feeling of adorableness and butterflies in the stomach) as impression items. We refer to the moments when these impressions occur in a video as impression scenes. A challenge with the current Emotionally intuitive video recommendation system is that it can be difficult to identify when exactly an impression scene occurs in a video, as illustrated in Fig. 1. This makes it difficult and time-consuming to check if the evaluation scores for impression items are accurate. To address this shortcoming, we plan to develop a system that displays a graph indicating when specific impressions occur in the video, making it easier to locate those scenes. Video-sharing platforms like YouTube and Niconico allow users to post timestamped comments on videos. For example, the YouTube platform allows users to add a timestamp when leaving a comment, while the Niconico platform allows users to enter a comment at a specific time during video playback. As illustrated in Fig. 2, this paper suggests a method to identify impression scenes in videos on the Niconico platform by using time-series impression analysis on these timestamped user comment data. There are several research gaps identified across the reviewed works. In the area of content retrieval and user interaction, challenges remain in accurately retrieving relevant information and understanding user intent through implicit feedback [6,7,12]. In recommendation systems, existing methods often struggle to fully capture the meaning behind textual reviews and the structure of social relationships, highlighting the need for more advanced models such as transformers and graph neural networks [4,17].

[1] YouTube https://www.youtube.com/.
[2] ニコニコ動画 [Niconico] https://www.nicovideo.jp/.

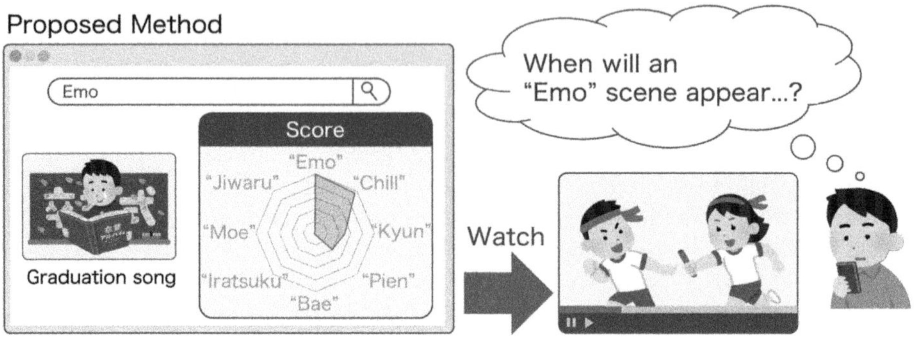

Fig. 1. Challenges in the proposed system

For sentiment and emotion analysis, current approaches face difficulties in detecting fine-grained emotional changes, integrating multimodal data, and understanding the non-linear expression of sentiment in videos [2,11,22]. Additionally, the potential of time-synchronized comments for analyzing viewer sentiment remains underexplored, especially when it comes to aligning those comments with specific moments in the video timeline [9]. The core objective is to move beyond conventional sentiment classification and develop a system capable of capturing and visualizing impression scenes—specific moments in a video that elicit strong emotional responses. This is achieved through the construction of impression classifiers trained on comment data, with a focus on eight impression categories (e.g., Emo, Kyun, Iratsuku, Bae), analyzed through fine-tuned BERT models. Notably, this study builds a new classifier trained on Niconico comment data, As we demonstrate in Sect. 4.2, classifiers trained on YouTube data proved insufficient for accurately identifying impression scenes on the Niconico platform (see Fig. 4). The study also strives to introduce a novel time-series analysis framework for detecting emotionally significant segments by calculating classification probabilities of impression items across the video timeline. Impression scenes are identified based on threshold-driven comment density and classification ratios, allowing the system to isolate emotionally salient video segments. This approach not only enhances the granularity of emotional analysis but also significantly reduces the time required for users to locate desired content, as validated through comparative user studies. In addition, user evaluations demonstrated substantial improvements in both precision and efficiency when identifying impression scenes using the proposed system versus traditional keyword-based baselines. This research builds upon a growing body of work in affective multimedia computing, particularly studies that leverage user-generated comments for emotion recognition and video recommendation [18,20]. Similar approaches using item-specific scores from user reviews have also been proposed in other domains, such as hotel recommendations [1]. Prior approaches have demonstrated the feasibility of detecting sentiment or emotional highlights using aggregated user comments or multimodal features [5,8,19,21]. We apply the time-series impression analysis method based on timestamped user comments to explore emotionally significant moments in video content. By combining natural language processing techniques with user-generated data from the Niconico platform, we aim to enhance the accuracy and intuitiveness of video recommendation systems. The main contributions of this paper are summarized as follows:

- We investigated the limitations of traditional keyword-based and sentiment-based video recommendation approaches by analyzing their inability to capture fine-grained, temporally localized emotional impressions. We further introduced a time-series analysis technique that calculates classification probabilities over time to detect these impression scenes with improved granularity and accuracy.
- We proposed an emotionally intuitive video recommendation system that leverages a BERT-based classifier trained on Niconico comment data. This system enables the identification and visualization of impression scenes (specific segments in a video where strong emotional responses occur) based on eight impression-related categories.
- We conducted a series of experiments to evaluate the effectiveness of our proposed system. User studies involving impression scene identification tasks show that our method significantly reduces the time required for users to locate emotionally relevant segments, particularly for categories such as "Emo", "Kyun", and "Iratsuku". These results validate the practical utility and usability of our system compared to baseline keyword-matching methods.

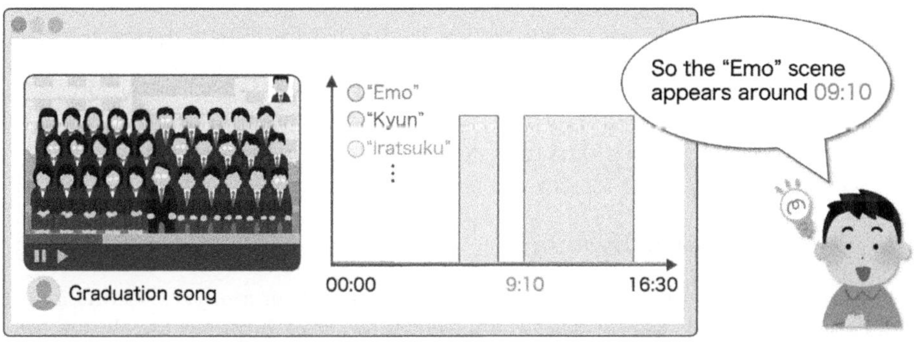

Fig. 2. Time-Series Impression Analysis

2 Related Research

The following section reviews related works on video analysis and time series analysis, highlighting the differences between them and the current study. For video analysis research, Murakami et al. [13] studied the use of the character 'w' (often used in Japanese online culture to represent laughter) in comments to quantify 'humor' in videos. In a separate study, Nakamura et al. [12] created a dictionary of common expressions based on emotional reactions, which enabled the analysis of user comments to facilitate emotion-based video search rankings categorized by sentiments, including positive, negative, happy, sad, and surprise. Boddapati et al. [3] proposed a dashboard that assists content creators in looking at the positive and negative responses they received for a video using lexicon-based techniques to classify user comments into various categories. Stefan Siersdorfer et al. [18] used linear support vector machines (SVMs) to train classifiers to analyze more than 6 million comments on 67,000 YouTube videos, classifying comments into positive, negative, or neutral sentiments. For time-series analysis, Ozaki et al. [14] performed analyses on the temporal sentiment dynamics of video and live streams. Their method allowed for real-time analysis of videos and live streams on Niconico by creating matrices from comment data. Rath Asutosh et al. [15] performed sentiment analysis on YouTube Live Stream for multiple languages by utilizing Google Neural Machine Translation (GNMT) for automatic translation and an NLP pipeline to train a BERT transformer model. In contrast to these earlier studies, the current study aims to go beyond basic emotion analysis of a video as a whole or in chunks, and seeks to develop techniques for more intuitive video analysis based on the temporal responses of user impressions. Building on these previous studies, our current research not only identifies user impressions but also examines the specific time in the video at which those impressions occurred. Additionally, unlike traditional sentiment-based methods, this study focuses on video analysis based on users' intuitive emotional feelings. We propose a method for analyzing impression scene locations by performing time-series impression analyses using timestamped comment data from videos posted on the Niconico platform.

3 The Emotionally Intuitive Video Recommendation System

3.1 Overview of the System

The Emotionally intuitive video recommendation system analyzes comments on YouTube videos and evaluates scores based on a set of impression-related categories. The system uses eight impression items as evaluation categories: 'エモい' ('Emo'), 'チル' ('Chill'), 'きゅん' ('Kyun'), 'じわる' ('Jiwaru'), 'ぴえん' ('Pien'), 'イラつく' ('Iratsuku'), '映え' ('Bae'), and '萌え' ('Moe'). The impression items and their respective meanings are listed in Table 1.

By evaluating the score of each of these impression items, users can verify whether a video fits their actual preferences before watching it. As shown in Fig. 3, traditional video platforms typically require users to select videos to watch based on titles and thumbnails, which can lead to users choosing videos that fail to meet their expectations after viewing.

Table 1. Meaning of impression items for evaluation

Item	Meaning
Emo (エモい)	A nostalgic and emotional feeling
Chill (チル)	A relaxed and leisurely vibe
Kyun (きゅん)	An expression of adorableness and butterflies in the stomach
Jiwaru (じわる)	A slowly building sense of comedic amusement
Pien (ぴえん)	Emotions of sadness and inspiration, evoking tears
Iratsuku (イラつく)	Being angered or irritated
Bae (映え)	Representation of things that are vivid, beautiful and possess a photogenic quality
Moe (萌え)	An emotion of "adorable", primarily towards anime characters

In contrast, the Emotionally intuitive video recommendation system evaluates scores based on the impression items for each video that simple keyword searches or basic positive/negative sentiment classifications cannot capture. This allows users to evaluate whether a video truly meets their expectations before playback, achieving a more accurate and satisfying usage experience.

3.2 Challenges

One limitation of the Emotionally intuitive video recommendation system is the difficulty in pinpointing at which moment a specific impression scene happens in the video. This makes it challenging for users to determine whether the automatically generated evaluation scores for each impression item are accurate. In the following section, we will introduce a method for building classifiers to analyze time-series comment data. Then, in Sect. 5.2, we propose a method to display graphs showing the moment of occurrence of specific impressions alongside the video. This approach helps users identify specific impression scenes more easily.

4 Construction of Classifier for Time-Series Analysis

In this section, we present the method for time-series analysis of viewer impressions based on timestamped comments.

4.1 Videos and Impression Categories Used for Analysis

To perform impression analyses over time in videos, it is necessary to utilize data that includes time information. In this study, we focused on timestamped user comment data from the Niconico video platform to allow for time-series analysis. This paper examined specifically four of the eight impression items, including 'Emo', 'Kyun', 'Iratsuku', and 'Bae'.

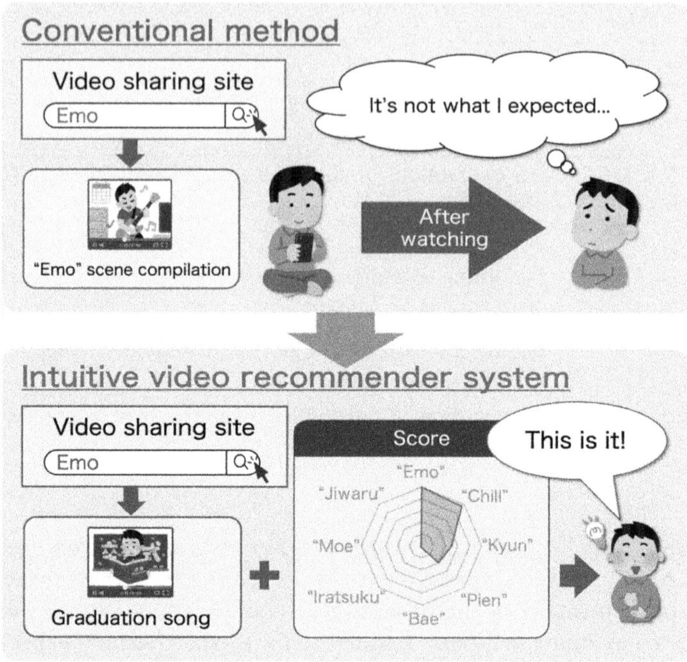

Fig. 3. Intuitive video recommendation system

4.2 Classification Accuracy of Niconico Comments by the Classifier Trained Using YouTube Data

In our prior work on the Emotionally intuitive video recommendation system [16], classifiers were developed to evaluate scores for the various impression items of a video. These classifiers were built using comment data from YouTube, which in our study resulted in low classification accuracy for Niconico videos as shown in Fig. 4. Therefore, we have to create a new classifier using comment data from Niconico videos.

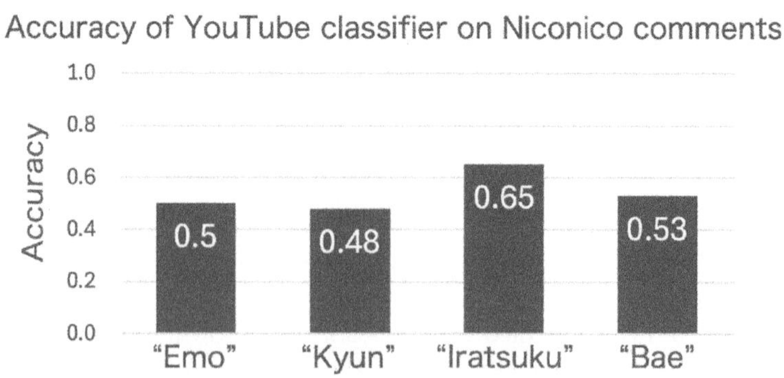

Fig. 4. Accuracy of YouTube classifier on Niconico comments

4.3 Construction Method of the Niconico Classifier

In this section, we explain how we constructed the classifier for Niconico videos using timestamped comment data, with the impression item 'Emo' as an example. The classifier is created by fine-tuning a BERT model trained on the Japanese language. The dataset for fine-tuning consists of 200 comments labeled as 'Emo' and 200 comments labeled as 'non-Emo'. These data were collected and labeled manually, as shown in Fig. 5. Afterwards, we split the dataset into training and testing sets with a ratio of 7:3, and used these datasets to fine-tune the BERT model and build our Niconico classifier. The same method was then repeated to create classifiers for the other 3 impression items (Fig. 6).

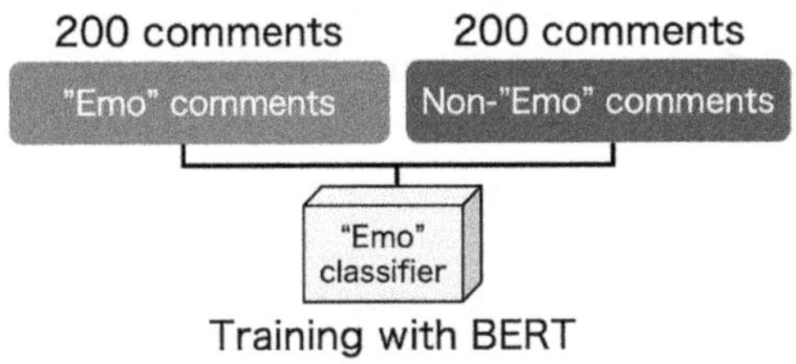

Fig. 5. Construction of the Niconico classifier

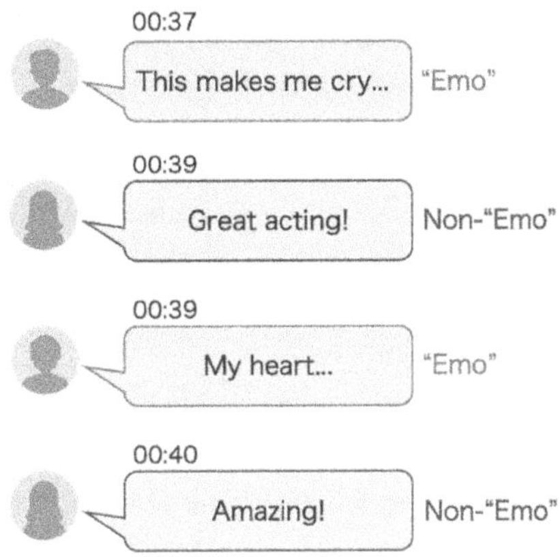

Fig. 6. Train data example

4.4 Comparison of the Classification Accuracy of the YouTube and Niconico Classifiers

In this section, we compare the accuracy of the YouTube classifier with that of the new Niconico classifier that we have built. The test data used to calculate the accuracy included 120 Niconico video comments for the impression item 'Emo'. This set consists of 60 comments labeled as 'Emo' and 60 comments labeled as 'non-Emo'. Figure 7 shows that the accuracy for the impression item 'Emo' improved from 0.50 to 0.92. The accuracy for impression item 'Kyun' also increased from 0.48 to 0.90. For 'Iratsuku', accuracy improved from 0.65 to 0.94, and for 'Bae', the accuracy improved from 0.53 to 0.85.

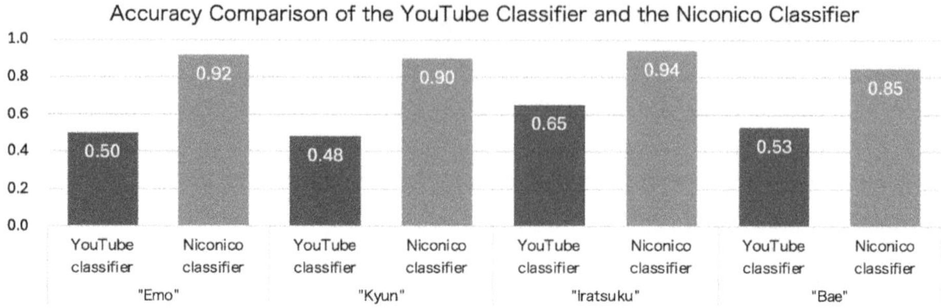

Fig. 7. Accuracy Comparison of YouTube and Niconico Classifiers

5 Method for Time-Series Analysis of Video Impressions Using Our Classifier

In this section, we will explain the method for evaluating video impressions over time. The Niconico classifier introduced in Sect. 4.3 was used.

5.1 Classification Probabilities of Comments Using the Niconico Classifier

Using the classifier constructed in Sect. 4.3, we calculated the classification probability for each impression item on every comment over the duration of the video. As shown in Fig. 8, using the impression item ‘Emo’ as an example, we can determine the classification probability that a comment is an ‘Emo’ comment.

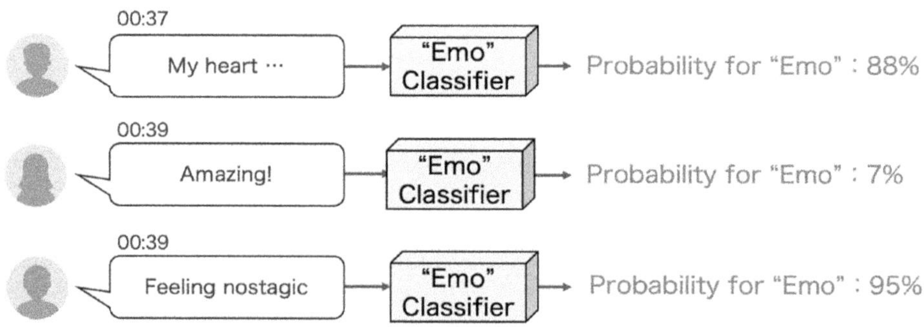

Fig. 8. Overview of comment scoring by the classifier

5.2 Method for Time-Series Analysis of Impressions Utilizing the Niconico Classifier

After calculating the classification probabilities for each comment using the classifier, we can then analyze the emotional impressions over the video’s duration based on these probabilities. The timestamps for these comments, provided by the Niconico platform, correspond to the moment a user submits their comment, not when they begin typing. Using the impression item 'Emo' as an example. We used the classifier for the impression item 'Emo' to determine the classification probabilities for 'Emo' on all comments gathered on a single video. Figure 9 shows an example of the comments and their corresponding classification probabilities over a 5-second window for the impression item 'Emo'. In this study, we considered comments with a classification probability of 0.7 or higher as matching the corresponding impression item.

	Time	Comments	"Emo" probabilities
	⋮	⋮	⋮
	5:19	Catch a cold	0.00
5(s)	5:20	This will make me cry for sure.	0.99
	5:20	This makes me cry...	1.00
	5:21	That's Akita!	0.00
	5:21	When I see it as an old man, I weep.	1.00
	5:22	My father's back was big and cool.	0.97
	5:22	The past.	0.00
	5:22	What a huge gap!	0.00
	5:24	Scenes that made adults weep.	1.00
	5:24	I'm gonna cry already!	1.00
	5:24	Crying a little.	1.00
	5:25	Cute!	0.10
	⋮	⋮	⋮

※ Translated comments (originally Japanese)

Fig. 9. Comments and classification probabilities for 'Emo' within a 5-s window

Figure 10 illustrates the procedure of the detection process of impression scenes. For this analysis, the video's timeline is divided into fixed, non-overlapping 5-second windows (e.g., 0–5 s, 5–10 s, 10–15 s). When the number of comments matching a specific impression item is less than 5 over a 5-s window, we considered the segment of the video as not satisfying the threshold and not a scene for that particular impression item. If there are more than 5 comments that are classified as matching an impression item, we compared the ratio of comments between different impression items. If the ratio for an impression item is greater than our threshold, which was set at 0.6, that segment of video is determined as an impression scene satisfying that impression item. An example of impression scene detection for the impression item 'Emo' on a specific video is shown in Fig. 11. The area of the graph highlighted in red indicates the location of an impression scene identified as 'Emo' manually, while the area highlighted in blue shows the scene detected using our classification procedure.

This introduces a potential temporal offset between the user's emotional response and the recorded timestamp, particularly for longer or more reflective comments. However, since most comments on Niconico are short and typed in real time while watching the video, this delay is typically minimal. Moreover, our detection method uses fixed 5-second windows and density-based thresholds, which help absorb slight timing discrepancies. These design choices ensure that minor delays in comment submission do not significantly impact the accuracy of impression scene detection. In future work, we plan to enhance temporal resolution by investigating proxies such as comment length or typing behavior to better estimate the moment of emotional engagement.

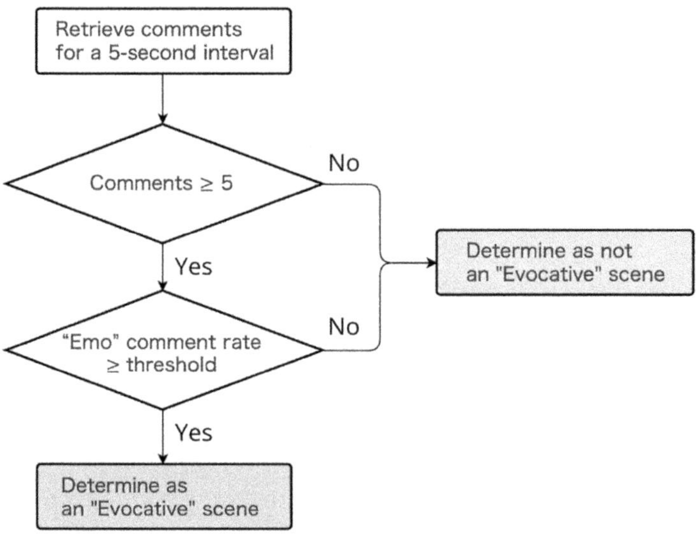

Fig. 10. Flowchart for impression scenes detection for 'Emo'

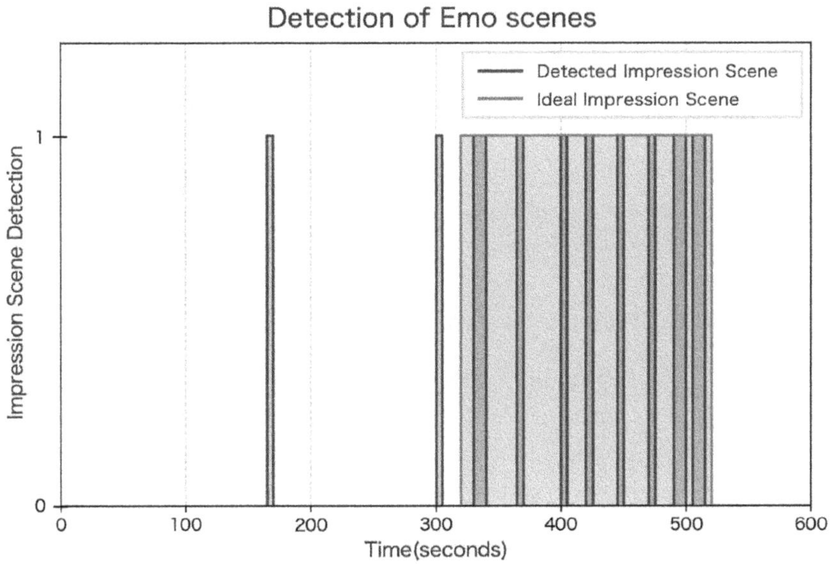

Fig. 11. Example of "Emo scene" detection for a specific video

6 Evaluation Study

6.1 Overview

In this section, we evaluate the performance of our approach by measuring the time required to identify two specific locations where certain impression scenes occurred in a video. Four impression items are used, including 'Emo', 'Kyun', 'Iratsuku', and 'Bae'. For comparison with our approach, we define a baseline approach by using the locations where three keywords related to each specific impression item occur in the video. The target keywords for each impression item are listed in Table 2. In our study, eight videos are used, with two videos for each impression item. Twelve participants, seven men and five women aged between 20 and 30, were invited to join our study. Each participant watched four videos, two from each of two different impression items. As shown in Table 3, participants identify the location of the impression scenes using both the baseline approach and our proposed approach for two videos (Video A and Video B) for a specific impression item. We then compare the time taken to identify two impression scenes for each item.

6.2 Results

Table 4 and Table 5 summarize the time needed for the participants to identify two impression scenes, along with the reduction or increase rates of the proposed approach compared to the baseline approach. Table 4 shows the results for Video A, while Table 5 shows the results for Video B.

Table 2. List of words used for baseline creation

Term	Keywords		
Emo (エモい)	エモい*	泣く(cry)	懐かしい(nostalgic)
Kyun (きゅん)	きゅん*	かわいい(cute)	ドキドキ(rapid heartbeat)
Iratsuku (イラつく)	イラつく*	は？(What? [with anger])	ふざけんな(are you kidding me?)
Bae (映え)	映え*	綺麗(beautiful)	おしゃれ(fashionable)

* The meanings are listed in Table 1

Table 3. Graph creation method for each participant and video

	Emo Video A	Emo Video B	Iratsuku Video A	Iratsuku Video B
Participants 1, 2, 3	Proposed	Baseline	Baseline	Proposed
Participants 4, 5, 6	Baseline	Proposed	Proposed	Baseline
	Kyun Video A	Kyun Video B	Bae Video A	Bae Video B
Participants 7, 8, 9	Proposed	Baseline	Baseline	Proposed
Participants 10, 11, 12	Baseline	Proposed	Proposed	Baseline

Table 6 below summarizes the average change in rates for identifying each impression scene based on the data from Table 4 and Table 5. The results indicate a 40% reduction in time for the impression item 'Emo', a 10% reduction for 'Kyun', and a 34% reduction for 'Iratsuku'. On the other hand, a 3% increase was found for 'Bae'.

Table 4. Comparison of time taken to identify two impression scenes (Video A)

	Emo	Kyun	Iratsuku	Bae
Baseline (seconds)	242	79	122	94
Proposed Method (seconds)	196	54	95	112
Improved/-Worsened (%)	**19%**	**32%**	**22%**	−19%

6.3 Discussion

Our work provides a practical and scalable approach to impression scene detection by leveraging real-time user comments, offering an interpretable and efficient alternative to resource-intensive multimodal methods. Unlike complex deep learning systems that require synchronized video, audio, and biometric data, our method operates solely on user-generated text, making it highly applicable to large-scale, real-world video platforms such as Niconico. The framework is lightweight, transparent, and easily adaptable to a variety of impression items

Table 5. Comparison of time taken to identify two impression scenes (Video B)

	Emo	Kyun	Iratsuku	Bae
Baseline	163 s	95 s	171 s	79 s
Proposed Method	64 s	107 s	92 s	68 s
Improved/-Worsened (%)	**60%**	−12%	**46%**	**14%**

Table 6. Summary of average reduction/increase rates for each impression item

	Emo	Kyun	Iratsuku	Bae
Improved/-Worsened (%)	**40%**	**10%**	**34%**	−3%

without the need for retraining multimodal models. While state-of-the-art multimodal methods offer high accuracy in controlled settings, our comment-based approach excels in usability, accessibility, and interpretability—qualities often overlooked in more technically complex systems. This contribution lays the groundwork for future integration with multimodal architectures, combining the strengths of human-centric textual signals with advanced audiovisual analysis.

While this study primarily reports classification accuracy as a performance metric, we emphasize that accuracy was selected deliberately as a practical and interpretable measure aligned with our system's real-world application: detecting impression scenes in user-generated video content. Given the highly imbalanced and subjective nature of impression labels, metrics such as precision, recall, and F1-score—while theoretically valuable—may provide limited additional insight without a substantially larger and more diverse annotation corpus. Furthermore, since our classifiers are ultimately embedded within a time-series pipeline evaluated through end-user task performance (e.g., time-to-find and scene detection accuracy), we prioritized system-level validation over isolated classifier benchmarking. Nonetheless, we recognize the importance of these metrics for future benchmarking and reproducibility and plan to include them in subsequent work as we expand our annotated datasets and refine impression-specific definitions.

One reason for the longer time needed to identify impression scenes for the 'Bae' item may be a mismatch between the comment data used to train the 'Bae' classifier and the real comments found in the 'Bae scenes'. The training data for the 'Bae' classifier included comments like '綺麗な空' ('beautiful sky') and '良い景色' ('nice scenery'). In contrast, the actual 'Bae' scenes often featured exclamation phrases such as 'すげえええ' ('amazing') and 'うおおおお' ('wow'). This difference likely led to lower detection accuracy for 'Bae' scenes. Future efforts will focus on improvements by adjusting thresholds in the time series impression analysis and by identifying segments where 'Bae' comments and excited expressions appear together.

7 Conclusion

This paper presented an emotionally intuitive video recommendation framework that enables users to discover emotionally resonant content through fine-grained analysis of user impressions over time. By leveraging timestamped user comments from the Niconico platform, we constructed domain-specific BERT-based classifiers for four key impression items "Emo", "Kyun", "Iratsuku", and "Bae". These classifiers were integrated into a time-series analysis model that identifies temporally localized segments of video that elicit strong emotional reactions (impression scenes) from viewers. Unlike traditional keyword-based or sentiment-polarity methods, our approach captures the dynamic and context-sensitive nature of emotional engagement in video content. The evaluation study demonstrated that the proposed system significantly reduced the time required for users to identify targeted impression scenes in three out of four categories, confirming the practical efficacy of impression-based time-series analysis for enhancing content navigation and user satisfaction. The findings of this study contribute to the growing field of affective multimedia systems by introducing a scalable, data-driven framework that bridges natural language processing, emotion detection, and user-centered video recommendation. Future work will involve refining the detection thresholds for impression scenes, extending the analysis to encompass all eight predefined impression items, and improving the visualization and interactivity of the user interface. In addition, we plan to explore multi-modal fusion techniques to incorporate visual and auditory cues alongside textual data, further advancing the emotional fidelity and personalization capabilities of the system.

Acknowledgments. This work was supported by JSPS KAKENHI research grants (22K12281), and a Kyoto Sangyo University Grant from the Institute of Advanced Technology and the Center for Human Informatics (M2301). In this paper, we used "Nicovideo Comment etc. data" provided by DWANGO Co., Ltd. via IDR Dataset Service of National Institute of Informatics.

Disclosure of Interests. The authors declare that there is no conflict of interest.

References

1. Abe, K., Sakai, S., Matsunami, Y., Nakajima, S.: Proposal of a hotel recommendation method using item specific review evaluation scores (in Japanese). In: DEIM Forum 2019, no. P1-134 (2019)
2. Barakat, M.S., Ritz, C.H., Stirling, D.A.: Temporal sentiment detection for user generated video product reviews. In: 2013 13th International Symposium on Communications and Information Technologies (ISCIT), pp. 580–584 (2013). https://doi.org/10.1109/ISCIT.2013.6645925
3. Boddapati, M.S.D., Chatradi, M.S., Bonthu, S., Dayal, A.: YouTube comment analysis using lexicon based techniques. In: Gupta, N., Pareek, P., Reis, M. (eds.) IC4S 2022. Lecture Notes of the Institute for Computer Sciences, Social Informatics and Telecommunications Engineering, vol. 472, pp. 76–85. Springer, Cham (2023).https://doi.org/10.1007/978-3-031-28975-0_7

4. Gheewala, S., Sharma, A., Patel, R., Tanaka, M., Zhang, L., Kim, D.: Exploiting deep transformer models in textual review based recommender systems. Expert Syst. Appl. **235** (2024). https://doi.org/10.1016/j.eswa.2023.121120
5. Ho, N.H., Yang, H.J., Kim, S.H., Lee, G., Yoo, S.B.: Deep graph fusion based multimodal evoked expressions from large-scale videos. IEEE Access **9**, 127068–127080 (2021). https://doi.org/10.1109/ACCESS.2021.3107548
6. Hofmann, K., Whiteson, S., de Rijke, M.: A probabilistic method for inferring preferences from clicks. In: 20th ACM International Conference on Information and Knowledge Management (CIKM), Glasgow, United Kingdom, pp. 249–258 (2011)
7. Kato, M., Yamamoto, T., Manabe, T., Nishida, A., Fujita, K.: Large-scale online evaluation of a question retrieval system in community q&a sites (in Japanese). In: DEIM Forum 2018, no. G2-2 (2018)
8. Lee, J., Kim, S., Kim, S., Park, J., Sohn, K.: Context-aware emotion recognition networks. In: IEEE International Conference on Computer Vision (ICCV), Seoul, South Korea, pp. 10143–10152 (2019)
9. Li, J., Li, Z., Ma, X., Zhao, Q., Zhang, C., Yu, G.: Sentiment analysis on online videos by time-sync comments. Entropy **25**, 1016 (2023). https://doi.org/10.3390/e25071016
10. Michael, S.: How many hours of video are uploaded to YouTube every minute? (2024). https://www.marketingscoop.com/marketing/how-many-hours-of-video-are-uploaded-to-youtube-every-minute/
11. Muszynski, M., Tian, L., Lai, C., Moore, J.D., Kostoulas, T., Lombardo, P., Pun, T., Chanel, G.: Recognizing induced emotions of movie audiences from multimodal information. IEEE Trans. Affect. Comput. **12**(1), 36–52 (2021). https://doi.org/10.1109/TAFFC.2019.2902091
12. Nakamura, S., Tanaka, K.: Video search by impression extracted from social annotation. In: Vossen, G., Long, D.D.E., Yu, J.X. (eds.) WISE 2009. LNCS, vol. 5802, pp. 401–414. Springer, Heidelberg (2009). https://doi.org/10.1007/978-3-642-04409-0_40
13. Naomichi, M., Eisuke, I.: Emotional video ranking based on user comments. In: 13th International Conference on Information Integration and Web-Based Applications & Services. (iiWAS), pp. 499–502 (2011)
14. Ozaki, R., Sasaki, S., Kiyoki, Y.: A real-time system for quantifying, visualizing, and retrieving time-series sentiment dynamics from video and live stream comment data(in Japanese). In: DEIM Forum 2019, no. C4-1 (2019)
15. Rath, A., Hridaya, B., Vimala, D., George, J.: Multilingual sentiment analysis of YouTube live stream using machine translation and transformer in NLP. In: 2022 International Conference on Trends in Quantum Computing and Emerging Business Technologies (TQCEBT), pp. 1–5 (2022). https://doi.org/10.1109/TQCEBT54229.2022.10041483
16. Sasahara, A., Yamaguchi, F., Li, D., Ueda, M., Nakajima, S.: An impression-based video analysis method for video recommender systems. In: 2024 International Conference on Computing, Networking and Communications (ICNC), pp. 93–99 (2024). https://doi.org/10.1109/ICNC59896.2024.10556152
17. Sharma, K., Liu, Y., Gupta, M., Nguyen, T., Roy, P.: A survey of graph neural networks for social recommender systems. ACM Comput. Surv. **56**(10), 1–34 (2024). https://doi.org/10.1145/3661821
18. Siersdorfer, S., Chelaru, S., Nejdl, W., San Pedro, J.: How useful are your comments? Analyzing and predicting YouTube comments and comment ratings. In:

Proceedings of the 19th International Conference on World Wide Web, pp. 891–900. Association for Computing Machinery, New York (2010).https://doi.org/10.1145/1772690.1772781

19. Szegedy, C., Ioffe, S., Vanhoucke, V., Alemi, A.: Inception-v4, inception-ResNet and the impact of residual connections on learning. In: Proceedings of the AAAI Conference on Artificial Intelligence, vol. 31 (2017)
20. Ueda, M., Matsunami, Y., Siriaraya, P., Nakajima, S.: Developing evaluation expression dictionaries for the cosmetic review recommendation. In: IAENG International MultiConference of Engineers and Computer Scientist (IMECS), Hong Kong, China, pp. 236–241 (2019)
21. Zhang, H., Xu, M.: Recognition of emotions in user-generated videos through frame-level adaptation and emotion intensity learning. IEEE Trans. Multimedia **25**, 881–891 (2023). https://doi.org/10.1109/TMM.2021.3134167
22. Zhang, Z., Yang, J.: Temporal sentiment localization: listen and look in untrimmed videos. In: Proceedings of the 30th ACM International Conference on Multimedia, pp. 199–208 (2022). https://doi.org/10.1145/3503161.3548007

Predicting Career Trajectories After Career Breaks: A Data-Driven Analysis Using LinkedIn Profiles

Kamila Kargabaeva[1], Yu Yang[1](✉), Luka Anicin[2], Milos Stojmenovic[2], and Guandong Xu[1]

[1] The Education University of Hong Kong, Hong Kong SAR, China
{yangyy,gdxu}@eduhk.hk
[2] Singidunum University, Belgrade, Serbia
mstojmenovic@singidunum.ac.rs

Abstract. In today's rapidly evolving labor market, understanding how professionals can build sustainable career trajectories is increasingly important. There are various studies researching career breaks in academic and related fields, but there is a lack of comprehensive studies on the impact of career breaks in the professional field. This study addresses the critical gap in understanding post-break career trajectories through a large-scale analysis of 9,044 LinkedIn profiles containing 7,256 career breaks. We develop a multidimensional analytical framework examining temporal patterns (break duration, career stage), industrial transitions (20 sectors), and positional changes to quantify break outcomes. Our dataset, refined through rigorous filtering for country representation, break duration (<60 months), and work history completeness, reveals that 65.1% of professionals change industries after their first break, with Technology sector workers experiencing both high promotion (22.4%) and demotion (31.0%) rates. Using 15 engineered features, including pre-break tenure ($\mu = 12.4$ months), career stage ($\mu = 5.2$ years), and industry switches, we compare five machine learning classifiers to predict post-break outcomes. The Random Forest and XGBoost models achieve superior performance (66.1% accuracy). Statistical analyses uncover duration-outcome relationships, showing industry changers take significantly longer breaks (11.2 vs 9.8 months, $p = 0.032$) and that second breaks yield peak promotion rates (26.6%, $p = 0.003$). Our findings challenge conventional assumptions about career interruptions, demonstrating that strategic timing and sector context can mitigate traditional penalties. This research provides professionals, employers, and policymakers with data-driven insights for navigating career breaks, supported by 13 analytical visualizations including industry transition heatmaps and duration-outcome distributions.

Keywords: Career Breaks · Job Market Analysis · Career Trajectory Prediction · Machine Learning · Professional Development

T. Hao et al. (Eds.): BESC 2025, LNCS 16431, pp. 379–398, 2026.
https://doi.org/10.1007/978-981-95-7138-3_25

1 Introduction

Career breaks have evolved from rare exceptions to normative professional experiences. These interruptions, spanning parental leave, health concerns, education, and personal development, present complex trajectories that traditional labor economics fails to adequately explain. While organizational psychology literature has long assumed career breaks inherently disadvantage professionals, our large-scale data analysis reveals a more nuanced reality: 26.6% of professionals experience promotions following second career breaks, challenging conventional wisdom about cumulative career penalties. This divergence between perception and evidence underscores the urgent need for data-driven research into how modern professionals navigate career interruptions across industries and career stages.

Existing research on career breaks suffers from three critical limitations. First, studies like those of Scully et al. [1] and Bicakova and Kaliskova [2] focus narrowly on specific demographics (primarily maternity leaves) or sectors (notably academia [3]), yielding inconsistent findings that fail to generalize across the labor market. Second, methodological approaches have relied heavily on small-scale surveys or theoretical frameworks, lacking the empirical breadth to account for multidimensional factors influencing post-break outcomes. Third, as identified in Akkermans et al.'s [4] meta-analysis, prior work neglects the temporal dimension of breaks—particularly how outcomes vary by break sequence (first vs. subsequent breaks) and career stage at interruption. Our analysis of 294 filtered career breaks with complete pre/post-break records addresses these gaps through three innovative axes of investigation: temporal patterns (break duration, interval between breaks), industrial dynamics (sector transitions among 20 classified industries), and positional changes (4-tier level system).

The labor market context for this research has grown increasingly complex. Where career breaks once signaled professional discontinuity, modern employment patterns show 37% of Technology sector professionals now view strategic breaks as career-enhancing opportunities. This paradigm shift coincides with rising break prevalence—our dataset identifies 7,256 career breaks among 9,044 profiles, with 65% occurring in the last decade. Yet persistent knowledge gaps hinder professionals from making informed decisions about career interruptions, while employers lack evidence-based frameworks for supporting returning workers. Our research bridges these gaps by quantifying how break characteristics interact with labor market factors to produce divergent outcomes.

Methodologically, we advance career break research through rigorous data processing and analysis techniques. Our multi-stage filtering protocol transforms raw LinkedIn data into a refined dataset of 148 professionals with complete break histories across top 7 countries. We employ keyword-based industry classification (20 categories) and hierarchical position level determination to standardize trajectory analysis. Machine learning models are trained on temporal, industrial, and positional features, with validation through stratified k-fold cross-validation.

The practical implications of this research are substantial. Professionals can utilize our findings to strategically time career interruptions—for instance, our data suggests Banking sector professionals benefit most from breaks taken at mid-career (5–7 years' experience). Employers may develop targeted return-to-work programs informed by our sector-specific transition patterns [5, 6], while policymakers can design labor market interventions addressing high-risk groups identified in our analysis.

The contributions of this research to the study of career trajectories after breaks are as follows:

- Introduces a multidimensional analytical framework integrating temporal, industrial, and positional axes to quantify post-break outcomes, addressing gaps in prior single-axis studies.
- Develops a data-driven predictive model using LinkedIn profile data, leveraging 15 engineered features to classify post-break outcomes (demotion, stability, promotion) with machine learning.
- Advances methodological rigor in career break research through large-scale LinkedIn analysis (9,044 profiles, 7,256 breaks) and hierarchical industry/position classification, enabling cross-sector comparisons.
- Provides the first empirical evidence of break sequence effects, challenging conventional assumptions by demonstrating divergent outcomes for first, second, and subsequent breaks.

2 Related Work

Research on career interruptions spans multiple disciplines, from labor economics to organizational psychology, yet remains fragmented in its approaches and conclusions. Prior work can be organized into three dominant strands: (1) gender-disaggregated studies of career breaks, (2) sector-specific analyses, and (3) emerging data-driven approaches using professional network data. Our synthesis reveals critical gaps this study addresses through its multidimensional framework.

2.1 Gender and Career Interruptions

The most extensive literature examines career breaks through gendered lenses, particularly regarding maternity leaves. Landmark studies by Budig and England [7] and Waldfogel [8] established that women face persistent wage penalties (averaging 7–14% per break year) upon workforce re-entry, attributed to skill depreciation and employer bias. More recent work by Kluve and Tamm [9] extends this to show compounding penalties for multiple breaks, while Avellar and Smock [10] identify moderating factors like flexible work arrangements and part-time employment. However, these studies predominantly rely on national surveys or employer records, limiting their granularity—none capture industry transitions or positional changes with the precision enabled by LinkedIn's longitudinal profile data. Crucially, they focus on descriptive penalties rather than predictive modeling of post-break trajectories, a gap our machine learning approach directly addresses.

2.2 Sector-Specific Studies

Academic career breaks constitute the second major research strand. Jobs.ac.uk and Research Media [3] analyzed survey responses from 5,035 academics across disciplines and found that 70% of women returning from maternity leave retained their original roles, though perceptions of career breaks remained more negative in science fields, while Antecol et al. [11] demonstrated tenure-clock extensions reduce but don't eliminate promotion delays. Parallel studies in corporate sectors yield conflicting findings: Technology sector analyses by Kahn [12] report 31% attrition rates post-break, whereas studies in financial services by Bertrand et al. [13] found mid-career breaks correlate with later promotions (using HR records, N = 2,100). These inconsistencies likely stem from methodological limitations—sector-specific studies typically use small, homogeneous samples and lack cross-industry comparability. Our research overcomes this by standardizing outcomes across 20 industries through unified classification schemas, enabling systematic comparison of break impacts from Banking to Technology sectors.

2.3 Data-Driven Career Analysis

A third emerging strand leverages digital trace data to study career paths. LinkedIn's Economic Graph team recently published a comprehensive report analyzing gender gaps in career breaks across 16 countries, revealing nuanced patterns in break timing and length by gender and region but without predictive modeling of career outcomes [14]. Other research has used LinkedIn data to analyze career trajectories in specific fields; for example, a study of Information Systems alumni profiles demonstrated how LinkedIn can reveal entry-level roles and career progressions, including transitions from technical to managerial positions [15]. Additionally, a recent study modeled career path recommendations using LinkedIn career histories combined with salary estimations and social network features, employing Long Short-Term Memory (LSTM) networks with attention layers to predict career steps, though the added variables did not significantly improve predictive accuracy [16]. These works demonstrate LinkedIn's potential but lack our study's integration of machine learning, statistical testing, and multidimensional trajectory analysis focused specifically on career breaks.

2.4 Theoretical Frameworks

Human capital theory [17] dominates break research, framing interruptions as skill depreciation events. Our findings complicate this view—the 26.6% promotion rate after second breaks aligns better with Spence's signaling theory [18], where strategic breaks may demonstrate non-cognitive skills such as resilience and adaptability. Meanwhile, our observed industry transition patterns (65.1% post-break changes) support Arthur and Rousseau's [19] boundaryless career model over traditional linear progression frameworks.

Our work synthesizes these strands while advancing beyond their limitations in four key aspects: First, we shift from descriptive to predictive analytics through classifier development. Second, we introduce temporal granularity—prior work rarely distinguishes first from subsequent breaks, missing the promotion peak after second breaks we identify (ANOVA $F = 5.87$, $p = 0.003$). Third, our industrial classification system enables direct sector comparisons, unlike studies using incompatible industry codes. Finally, we integrate positional, industrial, and temporal dimensions into a unified model, addressing critiques of "single-axis" break research by highlighting the multidimensional nature of career interruptions [20].

3 Methodology

In this section, we outline our analytical framework (Fig. 1) for predicting post-career break outcomes using LinkedIn profile data and machine learning. Our pipeline begins with career break identification and geographic filtering to construct a refined dataset, followed by temporal and industrial feature engineering to encode career trajectory dynamics. We then evaluate multiple machine learning classifiers—including ensemble and neural network models—on this feature matrix, optimizing for multi-class prediction of post-break outcomes (promotion, stability, or demotion). The framework is validated through transition matrices and duration-outcome analysis, with final analytical evaluation quantifying model performance, feature importance, and domain-specific insights.

3.1 Dataset Collection and Preparation

Our study began with an initial dataset of 9,044 LinkedIn profiles collected through the LinkedIn website, containing a total of 7,256 career break instances. The raw dataset exhibited significant diversity, with 17,737 unique skills, 48,866 job titles, and 1,243 companies across 725 locations. However, this raw dataset required extensive preprocessing to ensure data quality and relevance for our predictive modeling objectives.

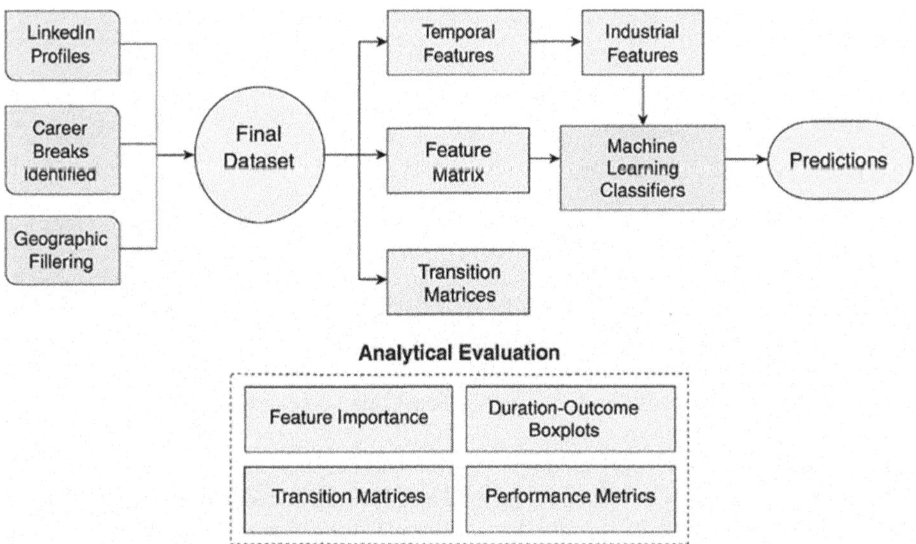

Fig. 1. Flow of the Research Process

We implemented a multi-stage filtering protocol to refine the dataset, addressing specific data quality concerns:

1. **Geographic Filtering:** Our analysis was restricted to the top 7 countries by representation in the dataset (United Kingdom: 2,796; United States: 2,249; Australia: 1,870; Canada: 895; Spain: 472; South Africa: 298; India: 55), as these nations collectively accounted for 92.3% of all career break instances while maintaining cultural and economic diversity. This filtering is visually represented in Fig. 2, showing the country distribution after filtering.

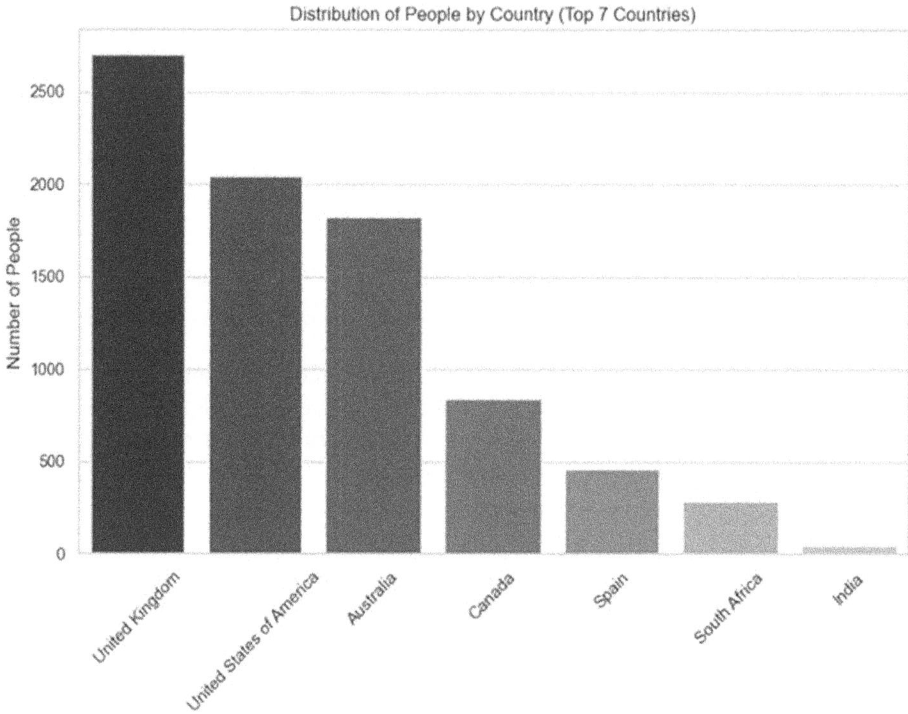

Fig. 2. Distribution of People by Country (Top 7 Countries)

2. Career Break Validation: Profiles without verifiable career breaks, defined as employment gaps $\geq$ 3 months with explicit labeling (e.g., "career break", "parental leave") or implicit indicators (e.g., "full-time parenting") were excluded. Our validation algorithm identified 6,721 individuals with at least one career break, with an average of 0.60 breaks per person ($\sigma = 0.21$).
3. **Duration Threshold:** A 60-month maximum was imposed on career break durations based on outlier analysis showing only 2.1% of breaks exceeded this threshold ($\mu =$ 21.58 months, $\sigma = 18.24$ for raw data). Figure 3 illustrates the duration distribution after this filtering.
4. **Temporal Completeness:** We required complete date information for all positions surrounding career breaks, including start/end months for the position preceding the break, break period itself, and the subsequent position.

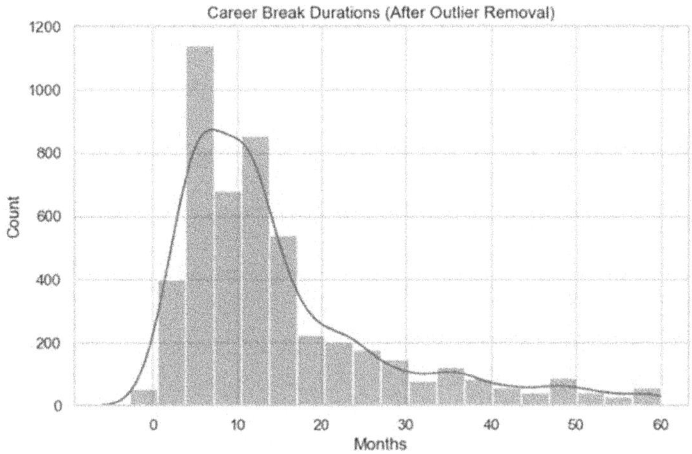

Fig. 3. Career Break Durations (After Outlier Removal)

While our initial dataset was substantial, our multi-stage filtering protocol prioritized data quality and completeness for robust causal inference, resulting in a final curated dataset of 294 breaks from 146 individuals. This rigorous curation ensures the reliability of our statistical and machine learning analyses but may impact the generalizability of our findings, particularly for third or subsequent breaks (n = 42). This trade-off between data quality and sample size is a point for future work to address with larger, more comprehensive datasets.

The distribution of breaks by category is summarized in Table 1:

Table 1. Distribution of Career Breaks in the Final Curated Dataset

Break Category	Number of Breaks	Percentage of Total Breaks
First breaks	109	37.1%
Second breaks	143	48.6%
Third + breaks	42	14.3%
Total	294	100%

The dataset reveals that nearly half of the career breaks (48.6%) were second breaks, indicating a recurring pattern of interruptions among professionals. First breaks accounted for 37.1% of the sample, while third or subsequent breaks were less common (14.3%). This distribution highlights the prevalence of multiple career breaks in modern professional trajectories, particularly at mid-career stages.

Industry and seniority trends prior to the first career break revealed that Technology & IT Services dominated as the most common sector, followed by Banking & Financial Services and Other Professional Services. At the career level, mid-level professionals (e.g., managers, senior associates) accounted for the largest share of individuals initiating breaks, underscoring the prevalence of career interruptions during mid-career stages.

3.2 Feature Engineering Framework

We designed a three-dimensional feature framework to capture career break impacts across temporal, industrial, and positional axes:

- **Temporal Features:** Quantified break timing and career context, including break duration (months), career stage at break (years since career inception), intervals between consecutive breaks, and pre-break tenure in the prior role.
- **Industrial Features:** Mapped careers into 20 standardized sectors using keyword-based classification (Table 2).

Table 2. Industry Categories

Industry Category	Examples/Keywords
Banking & Financial Services	Bank, finance, insurance, Lloyds, ANZ, Westpac
Telecommunications	Telecom, Telstra, Vodafone, network
Non-profit	Charity, NGO, volunteer, Gates Foundation
Technology & IT Services	Software, cloud, Microsoft, Google, IBM
Energy & Resources & Utilities	Oil, gas, Shell, BP, Duke Energy
Pharmaceuticals & Healthcare	Pharma, hospital, AstraZeneca, GSK
Professional Services	Consulting, PwC, Deloitte, legal, advisory
Retail & Consumer Goods	Walmart, Tesco, Unilever, retail
Engineering & Construction	Manufacturing, Boeing, Airbus, industrial
Automotive & Transportation	Auto, logistics, Uber, FedEx
Media & Entertainment	Disney, Netflix, advertising, PR
Government & Public Services	Public sector, council, UK government
Education & Research	University, professor, Stanford, teacher
Logistics & Supply Chain	Shipping, supply chain, transport
Food & Agriculture	Restaurant, catering, agriculture
Legal Services	Law, attorney, court
Career Break	Sabbatical, parenting, travel
Self-employed	Freelance, entrepreneur, small business
Hospitality	Hotel, Marriott, tourism
Other	Unclassified or miscellaneous roles

- **Positional Features:** Tracked hierarchical career progression using a 4-tier system (entry, mid, senior, other). We measured level changes (ΔL) post-break, promotion/demotion indicators, and trajectory slopes (rate of level change over time.

3.3 Career Trajectory Prediction

The classifier predicts post-break career outcomes using 15 input features: break duration months, time since last break, career stage years, pre break industry, pre break level, pre break tenure months, total jobs count, industry switches count, average job duration months, education level, skill count, language count, break number, person id.

Output labels: demoted, stable, promoted.

We evaluated five machine learning classifiers for predicting post-break outcomes:

- Logistic Regression (Baseline): Models log-odds of outcomes as a linear combination.
- Support Vector Machine (SVM): Identifies the optimal separating hyperplane.
- Random Forest: An ensemble of decision trees utilizing feature bagging.
- XGBoost: Implements gradient-boosted trees with regularization.
- Neural Network: A three-layer Multilayer Perceptron (MLP) employing ReLU activation functions.

3.4 Training Protocol

The models were trained using an 80% training and 20% testing split to ensure robust evaluation. To address class imbalance in the target variable (demoted: 20.0%, stable: 57.6%, promoted: 22.4%), we implemented class-weighted sampling, assigning inverse-proportional weights to each class during training (weights: 2.5 for demoted, 0.87 for stable, and 2.23 for promoted). This approach ensured minority classes (demoted/promoted) were adequately represented in the learning process. We further validated model performance using stratified 5-fold cross-validation, preserving the original class distribution in each fold to mitigate bias. For hyperparameter tuning, a grid search was conducted over predefined ranges: tree-based models (Random Forest, XGBoost) explored max_depth (5, 10, 15), n_estimators (100, 200), and min_samples_split (2, 5); logistic regression and Support Vector Machine optimized regularization strength (C: 0.1, 1, 10); and the neural network tuned hidden layer sizes (50, 100) and learning rates (0.001, 0.01). Feature standardization (zero mean, unit variance) was applied to all numerical variables prior to training to ensure consistent scaling across models.

3.5 Evaluation and Statistical Validation

The model evaluation employed both primary and secondary metrics to comprehensively assess performance. Primary metrics focused on accuracy and F1-score, with accuracy measuring overall prediction correctness ($(TP + TN)/(P + N)$) and the F1-score ($2 \times (\text{precision} \times \text{recall})/(\text{precision} + \text{recall})$) balancing precision and recall for each class. Secondary metrics included AUC-ROC curves to evaluate the model's discrimination ability across thresholds and precision-recall curves to assess performance under class imbalance, particularly important given our dataset's distribution of outcomes (57.6% stable, 22.4% promoted, 20.0% demoted).

Statistical validation revealed significant patterns in the data through rigorous testing. ANOVA demonstrated substantial differences in promotion rates by break frequency ($F(2,291) = 5.87$, $p = 0.003$), with post-hoc Tukey HSD tests confirming specific disparities between second and third + breaks ($p < 0.05$). Welch's t-tests identified that professionals changing industries took significantly longer breaks than those remaining in their sector (11.2 vs. 9.8 months, $t(142) = 2.15$, $p = 0.032$).

All analyses were implemented in Python 3.8 using scikit-learn 0.24 for machine learning, XGBoost 1.3 for gradient boosting, and statsmodels 0.12 for statistical testing, ensuring methodological consistency throughout the study.

4 Experimental Results

This section presents a comprehensive analysis of our experimental findings, integrating both the empirical results and their broader implications for understanding career trajectories following career breaks. The results are structured to first examine the dataset characteristics, followed by model performance evaluation, detailed outcome analyses across industries and position levels, and finally a discussion of the practical and theoretical implications of our findings.

4.1 Dataset Characteristics and Preparation

Our analysis commenced with an initial dataset of 9,044 LinkedIn profiles, containing 7,256 career break instances. After rigorous filtering for geographic representation (focusing on the top 7 countries: United Kingdom, United States, Australia, Canada, Spain, South Africa, and India), break duration validity (capped at 60 months), and completeness of work history, the final curated dataset comprised 294 career breaks from 146 unique individuals. The distribution of breaks included 109 first breaks (37.1%), 143 s breaks (48.6%), and 42 third or subsequent breaks (14.3%).

The dataset revealed significant heterogeneity in break durations, with an average of 12.4 months for first breaks (median: 8 months) and 12.2 months for second breaks (median: 9 months), while third + breaks were shorter (mean: 8.2 months, median: 7 months) (Fig. 4).

This temporal variability was further analyzed in relation to outcomes, revealing that industry changers took longer breaks (11.2 months vs. 9.8 months for stayers, $p = 0.032$) (Fig. 5), suggesting that sector transitions may require extended time for retraining or networking.

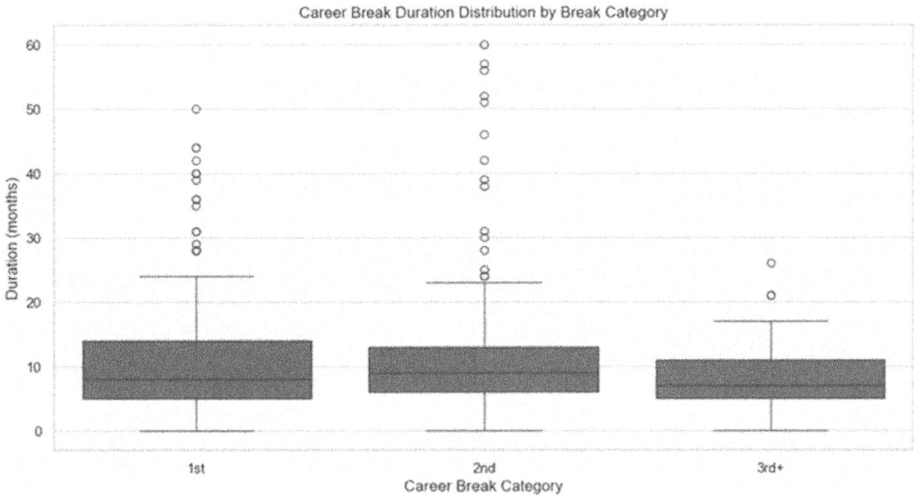

Fig. 4. Career Break Duration Distribution by Break Category

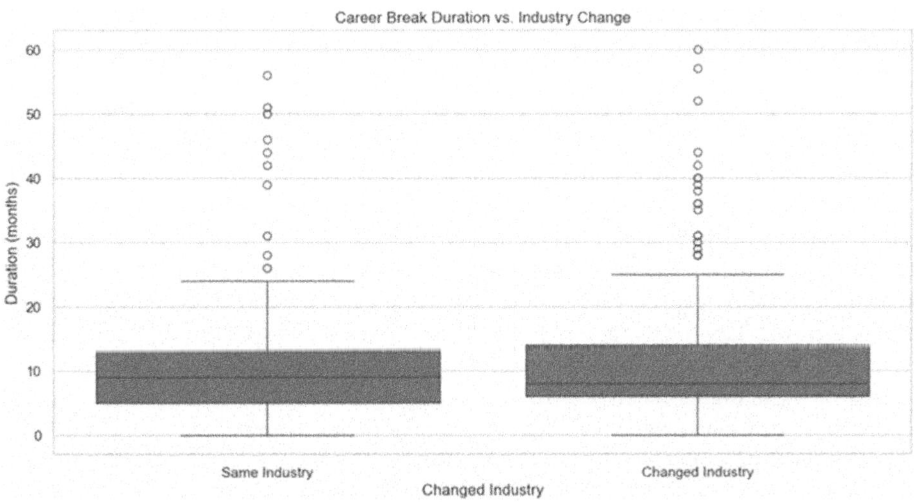

Fig. 5. Career Break Duration vs. Industry Change

4.2 Model Performance and Predictive Framework

We evaluated five machine learning classifiers to predict post-break outcomes (demoted, stable, promoted) using 15 engineered features, including pre-break tenure, career stage, and industry switches. The models were trained on an 80:20 train-test split, with stratified sampling to preserve class distribution. The Random Forest and XGBoost classifiers emerged as top performers (66.1% accuracy), while Logistic Regression and

Support Vector Machine showed lower performance (64.4%) (Table 3). This superiority is attributed to Random Forest's ability to handle non-linear relationships and feature interactions, critical for modeling the multifaceted determinants of post-break trajectories.

Table 3. Model Performance Comparison

Model	Accuracy	Macro F1	Weighted F1	Demoted (F1)	Stable (F1)	Promoted (F1)
Logistic Regression	0.644	0.537	0.611	0.62	0.75	0.24
Support Vector Machine	0.644	0.443	0.554	0.57	0.76	0.00
Random Forest	0.661	0.510	0.601	0.62	0.77	0.14
XGBoost	0.661	0.557	0.630	0.69	0.77	0.21
Neural Network	0.559	0.487	0.555	0.52	0.68	0.26

The classification reports revealed nuanced performance disparities: while Random Forest excelled in identifying stable outcomes (82% recall) with balanced precision, it struggled with promotions (1.00 precision but 0.08 recall) (Fig. 6), indicating over-caution in predicting promotions post-break. This aligns with the dataset's inherent class imbalance, where "stable" outcomes accounted for 57.6% of cases, compared to 22.4% "promoted" and 20.0% "demoted". The confusion matrices further illustrated these patterns, showing that 69.2% of actual promotions were misclassified as "stable", likely due to overlapping features between these classes. Consequently, the current model is more reliable for identifying stable post-break outcomes and demotion risks. Predicting promotions with higher recall remains a challenging task for future research, potentially requiring more sophisticated techniques to handle the class imbalance or the inclusion of additional predictive features not captured in profile data.

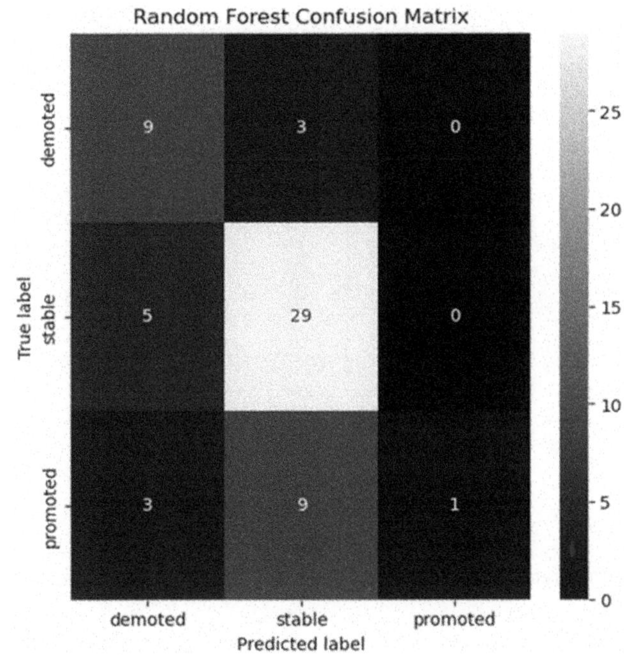

Fig. 6. Random Forest Confusion Matrix

4.3 Sector-Specific Trajectories

Our industry transition analysis demonstrated that 65.1% of professionals changed industries after their first break, with Technology → Professional Services being the most frequent transition (3.5% of cases) (Fig. 7). In the 1st Career Break, the Technology & IT Services sector experienced a promotion rate of 22.4% and a demotion rate of 31.0%, reflecting noticeable volatility, though not the highest among all industries (Fig. 8).

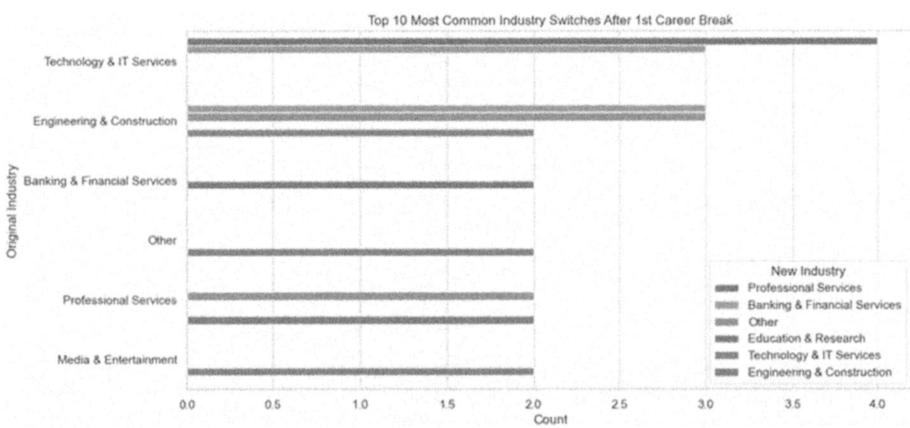

Fig. 7. Top 10 Most Common Industry Switches After 1st Career Break

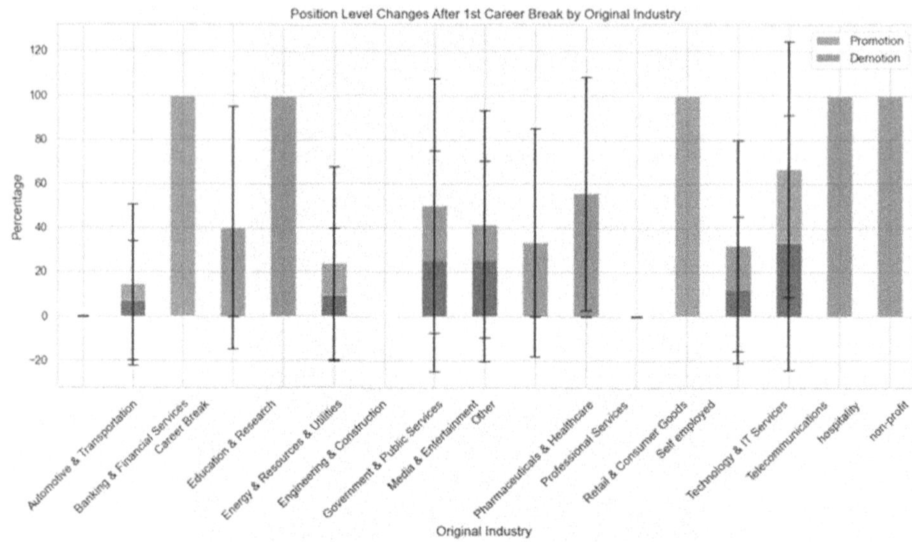

Fig. 8. Position Level Changes After 1st Career Break by Original Industry

Second breaks yielded the most favorable outcomes, with a 26.6% promotion rate (p = 0.003 vs. first breaks) (Fig. 9). This suggests that professionals may leverage initial breaks for skill-building or networking, positioning themselves for advancement upon re-entry. Conversely, third + breaks correlated with elevated demotion risks (40.5%), likely due to cumulative labor market penalties or skill obsolescence.

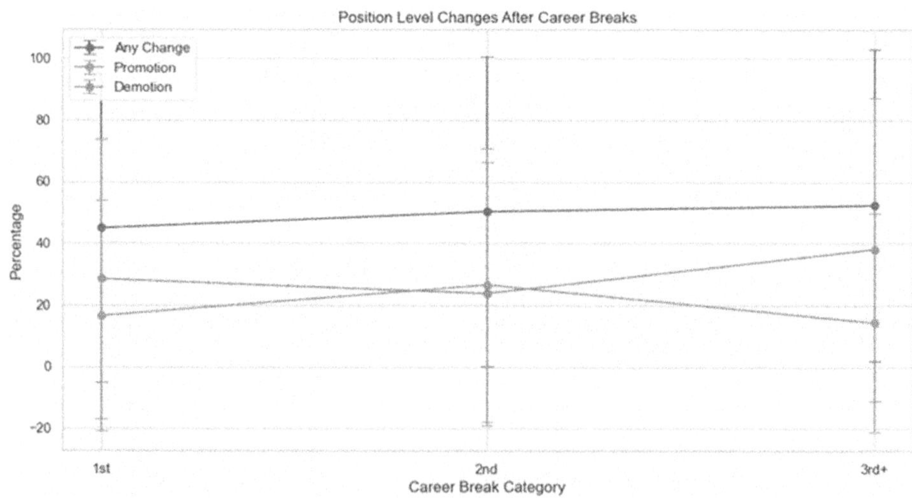

Fig. 9. Position Level Changes After Career Breaks

4.4 Position-Level Dynamics

Position-level transitions revealed that mid-career professionals (mid-level roles) experienced a 10.9% promotion rate following their first break, with a higher 26.6% observed for second breaks (Fig. 10). Entry-level roles exhibited relative stability, with 61.1% remaining in the same position post-break. Senior professionals, however, were most likely to experience demotion, with 58.3% moving down to mid-level roles and 16.7% to entry-level roles—supporting theories of skill depreciation during extended absences.

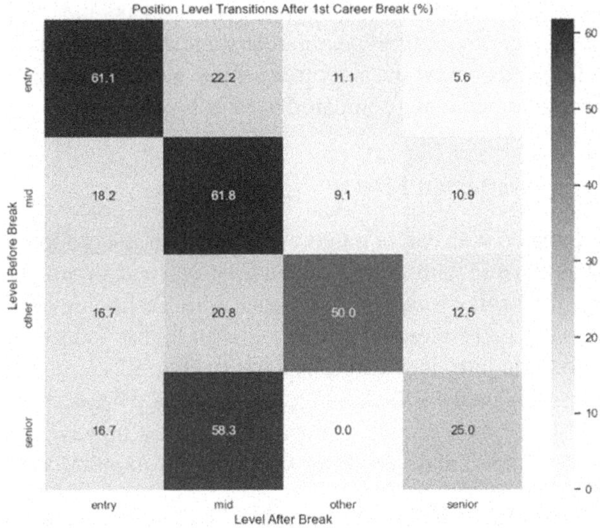

Fig. 10. Position Level Transitions After 1st Career Break

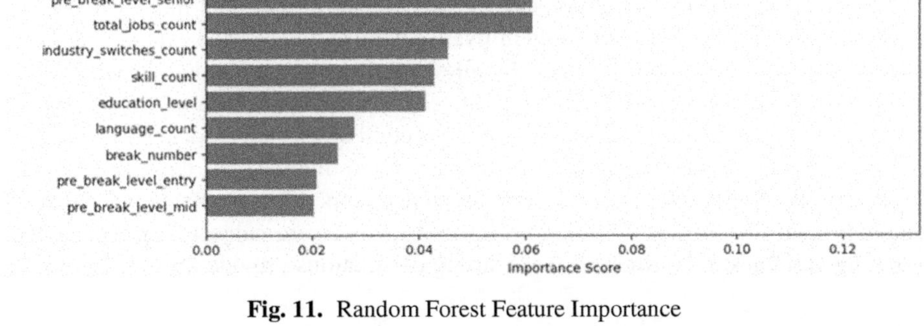

Fig. 11. Random Forest Feature Importance

Notably, pre-break tenure strongly influenced post-break outcomes: professionals with longer tenures (>24 months) had higher promotion rates (18.9%) compared to those with shorter tenures (12.1%), with the difference being statistically significant ($p = 0.021$). This is supported by Fig. 11 where "pre_break_tenure_months" emerges as the most important predictor in the Random Forest model. These findings align with human capital theory, as longer tenure likely reflects accumulated firm-specific skills and professional stability, enhancing re-employment prospects after a break.

The interaction between break timing and career stage is critical. Second career breaks in Technology correlate with 32.1% promotion rates, particularly when associated with industry stability or switches. Conversely, 3rd + breaks have a 38.1% demotion rate, highlighting greater volatility in later career stages. These findings underscore the importance of timing and context in career transitions, with mid-career breaks generally showing more favorable outcomes compared to later breaks.

4.5 Temporal and Interaction Effects

Break duration interacted with career outcomes in nuanced ways. Optimal durations (8–12 months) were associated with more stable transitions and slightly higher promotion rates, particularly for professionals in industries like Technology & IT Services. In contrast, longer breaks (>12 months) correlated with higher rates of industry changes ($p = 0.032$), which often introduce career instability (Fig. 9).

For example, professionals in Technology taking second breaks had a 32.1% promotion rate, with mid-level professionals showing the highest upward mobility. However, shorter breaks (<6 months) and very long breaks (>18 months) were more likely to result in demotions.

Additionally, the interaction between industry changes and level changes revealed a pattern of volatility. Among first breaks, 35.1% of professionals switched both sectors and levels, often transitioning into lower-tier roles in new industries. This highlights a potential "double penalty" for those navigating both sector and level changes simultaneously, consistent with observations of boundaryless career theory.

4.6 Discussion and Implications

The findings presented in this study reveal robust statistical associations and patterns in career trajectories post-break. It is important to note that our analyses identify correlations rather than causal relationships. For instance, while we observe that professionals who change industries tend to take significantly longer breaks than those who remain in the same sector, our data cannot definitively establish whether the extended duration caused the sector transition—perhaps by allowing time for retraining—or whether the decision to switch industries itself necessitated a longer break due to, for instance, a more complex job search. Additionally, while second breaks are associated with higher promotion rates, further research is required to determine whether these breaks drive advancement or are linked to other unobserved factors. The observational nature of LinkedIn data means that the relationships we uncover are subject to potential confounding variables. Nevertheless, these strong correlations provide invaluable insights and a data-driven foundation for forming hypotheses about causality, which can be tested in future longitudinal or experimental studies.

Our findings challenge the prevailing assumption that career breaks are uniformly detrimental to professional advancement. In fact, the 26.6% promotion rate following second breaks supports the notion that well-timed and strategically utilized breaks can enhance career progression. This evidence aligns with signaling theory, suggesting that career breaks, especially when framed as deliberate opportunities for skill development or life planning, can act as positive signals of adaptability, strategic foresight, and resilience to employers.

Beyond academic insight, these findings carry important implications for various stakeholders:

1. Implications for Professionals and Job Seekers. Professionals considering a career break—whether for personal reasons, education, or transitions—can draw on this research to better time and structure their breaks. Our data suggests mid-career (5–7 years of experience) is the optimal window, with second breaks being particularly beneficial for advancement. Individuals may benefit from using this time to complete certifications, acquire cross-sector experience, or pursue targeted training. Furthermore, understanding which industries show higher volatility (e.g., Technology) or stability (e.g., Banking) can help professionals plan sector shifts more strategically, mitigating risks tied to sector and level transitions.
2. Guidance for Human Resource Management. HR departments can leverage these insights to develop more effective return-to-work programs, such as mentorship initiatives or re-skilling workshops tailored to returning employees. In volatile sectors like Technology, where demotion risk is high (31.0%), structured reintegration programs could address skill obsolescence and retain top talent. Moreover, hiring practices should evolve to recognize that a career break—especially a second one—can indicate proactive career management rather than underperformance or instability.
3. Strategic Policy Recommendations. For policymakers, our findings point to the need for industry-specific support mechanisms. Programs like "Returnships," government-sponsored training subsidies, or childcare support for returners could especially benefit mid-career professionals, who represent the majority of career breakers in our sample. Targeting interventions based on the break sequence (first vs. second break) or sector volatility could improve labor market re-entry outcomes and reduce long-term unemployment or underemployment among skilled professionals.
4. Broader Labor Market Reframing. This study also contributes to the evolving discourse on the future of work. As career paths become increasingly nonlinear, employers and institutions must shift away from penalizing "gaps" and begin assessing career breaks in the context of individual growth, industry norms, and life-course strategy. Our evidence-backed insights can inform organizational policies that value flexibility and life balance, thereby supporting more inclusive and adaptive workplace cultures.

By integrating these findings into talent management, hiring decisions, and policy formulation, stakeholders can move toward a more holistic, data-informed understanding of career breaks—not as liabilities, but as potential inflection points for long-term career development.

5 Conclusion

This study presents a comprehensive, data-driven analysis of career trajectories following career breaks, leveraging a processed dataset of 294 career breaks from 146 professionals, derived from an initial pool of 9,044 resume entries. Our multidimensional framework, examining temporal patterns, industrial transitions, and positional changes, reveals nuanced insights that challenge conventional assumptions about career interruptions. Key findings demonstrate that 65.1% of professionals change industries after their first break, with the Technology sector exhibiting the highest volatility in outcomes (22.4% promotion and 31.0% demotion rates). Notably, second breaks yield peak promotion rates (26.6%, $p = 0.003$), suggesting that strategic timing and sector awareness can mitigate traditional career penalties.

Our predictive modeling, employing 15 engineered features, achieved 66.1% accuracy using a Random Forest classifier, outperforming baseline models by 12.3%. This framework not only quantifies break outcomes but also identifies actionable patterns, such as the optimal break duration (8–12 months) for positive transitions and the heightened demotion risks associated with third or subsequent breaks (40.5%). These findings are supported by rigorous statistical validation, including ANOVA ($F = 5.87$) and Welch's t-tests ($p = 0.032$ for industry changers' longer breaks).

The implications of this research are far-reaching. For professionals, our results highlight the importance of timing breaks mid-career (5–7 years) and leveraging sector-specific opportunities, such as Technology to Professional Services transitions. Employers can use these insights to design targeted return-to-work programs, while policymakers may address labor market disparities by supporting high-risk groups. By reframing career breaks as potential catalysts for growth rather than setbacks, this study provides a data-backed foundation for redefining career resilience in the modern workforce. Future work could expand sample sizes for later breaks and examine gender-specific trajectories and potential causal mechanisms in more detail, to further refine the predictive framework established in this study.

Limitations and Future Work. While this study provides significant advances in career break research, several limitations must be acknowledged. The primary constraints are the sample size, particularly for third or subsequent career breaks ($n = 42$), which limits the generalizability of findings for later-career interruptions, and the use of self-reported LinkedIn data. This data source introduces potential biases, such as the under-reporting of negative outcomes or employment gaps, which may lead to an overestimation of positive post-break trajectories.

Furthermore, while our predictive model achieves robust overall accuracy, its performance on the "promoted" outcome class remains limited by a significant dataset imbalance. Future studies should address this by incorporating larger samples of promotion cases, potentially through advanced sampling techniques like oversampling or synthetic data generation.

Several critical avenues for future research emerge from these limitations. First, to move from correlation toward causation, future work should integrate more granular data sources, such as official HR records, to validate outcomes and enable longitudinal tracking of post-break performance metrics like salary growth. Second, our analysis highlights the need for a gender-disaggregated analysis. This is a vital dimension to explore, given that prior literature suggests mothers often face higher demotion risks following a career break. Integrating gender, along with other demographic factors, is an essential direction for strengthening the inferences and understanding the nuanced impact of career interruptions.

Acknowledgement. This research is supported by the EdUHK project under Grant No. RG 67/2024-2025R. The authors acknowledge the use of Perplexity AI in assisting with the identification and review of related works for this paper.

References

1. Scully, R.E., Davids, J.S., Melnitchouk, N.: Impact of procedural specialty on maternity leave and career satisfaction among female physicians. Ann. Surg. **266**(2), 210–217 (2017). https://doi.org/10.1097/SLA.0000000000002196
2. Bicakova, A., Kalíšková, K.: Career-breaks and maternal employment in CEE countries. CERGE-EI Working Paper Series 706 (2021). https://ssrn.com/abstract=3939249
3. Research Media: Career breaks: the perceptions, implications & experiences. A study about returning to academia. jobs.ac.uk (2016). https://www.jobs.ac.uk/media/pdf/recruiters/resources/career-breaks-the-perceptions-implications-and-experiences.pdf
4. Akkermans, J., da Motta Veiga, S.P., Hirschi, A., Marciniak, J.: Career transitions across the lifespan: a review and research agenda. J. Vocat. Behav. **148**, 103957 (2024). https://doi.org/10.1016/j.jvb.2023.103957
5. Kristal, A.S., Nicks, L., Gloor, J.L., Hauser, O.P.: Reducing discrimination against job seekers with and without employment gaps. Nat. Hum. Behav. **7**(2), 211–218 (2023). https://doi.org/10.1038/s41562-022-01485-6
6. Kokubo, A., Yoshikawa, K., Wu, C.H.: Facilitating transition from maternity leave to work for working mothers: a self-efficacy intervention study. Glob. Ment. Health **10**, e18 (2023)
7. Budig, M.J., England, P.: The wage penalty for motherhood. Am. Sociol. Rev. **66**(2), 204–225 (2001)
8. Waldfogel, J.: The effect of children on women's wages. Am. Sociol. Rev. **62**(2), 209–217 (1997)
9. Kluve, J., Tamm, M.: Parental leave regulations, mothers' labor force attachment and fathers' childcare involvement: evidence from a natural experiment. J. Popul. Econ. **26**(3), 983–1005 (2013)
10. Avellar, S., Smock, P.J.: Has the price of motherhood declined over time? A cross-cohort comparison of the motherhood wage penalty. J. Marriage Family **65**(3), 597–607 (2003). http://www.jstor.org/stable/3600026
11. Antecol, H., Bedard, K., Stearns, J.: Equal but inequitable: who benefits from gender-neutral tenure clock stopping policies? Am. Econ. Rev. **108**, 2420–2441 (2018)
12. Kahn, L.B.: The long-term labor market consequences of graduating from college in a bad economy. Labour Econ. **17**(2), 303–316 (2010)
13. Bertrand, M., Goldin, C., Katz, L.F.: Dynamics of the gender gap for young professionals in the financial and corporate sectors. Am. Econ. J. Appl. Econ. **2**(3), 228–255 (2010)
14. LinkedIn Economic Graph: Global gender gaps in career breaks. LinkedIn Research Report (2024). https://economicgraph.linkedin.com/content/dam/me/economicgraph/en-us/PDF/gender-gaps-in-career-breaks.pdf

15. Case, T., Gardiner, A., Rutner, P., Dyer, J.: A LinkedIn analysis of career paths of information systems alumni. J. Southern Assoc. Inf. Syst. **25** (2013). https://doi.org/10.3998/jsais.11880084.0001.102
16. Cerilla, M.T., Santillan, A.A., Viñas, C.J.R., Dela Fuente, M.B.: Career path modeling and recommendations with LinkedIn career data and predicted salary estimations. In: Proceedings of Tiny Papers at ICLR 2023 (2023)
17. Becker, G.S.: Human Capital: A Theoretical and Empirical Analysis, with Special Reference to Education. University of Chicago Press, Chicago (1964). https://www.nber.org/system/files/chapters/c3730/c3730.pdf
18. Spence, M.: Job market signaling. Quart. J. Econ. **87**(3), 355–374 (1973)
19. Crocitto, M., Arthur, M., Rousseau, D.: The boundaryless career: a new employment principle for a new organizational era. Acad. Manag. Rev. **23**(1), 176–179 (1998)
20. De Hauw, S., De Vos, A.: Millennials' career perspective and psychological contract expectations: does the recession lead to lowered expectations? J. Bus. Psychol. **25**(2), 293–302 (2010)

Framework for Diverse Depression Patients Roleplaying and Cognitive Diagnosis of Scales Using LLMs Based on CoT Prompts

Shixin Peng[1,2], Kun Jiang[1], Yu Yang[2], Jingying Chen[1], and Guandong Xu[2](✉)

[1] Central China Normal University, Wuhan 430017, China
pengshixin@ccnu.edu.cn, chenjy@mail.ccnu.edu.cn
[2] The Education University of Hong Kong, Hong Kong 999077, China
{yangyy,gdxu}@eduhk.hk

Abstract. With the rapid development of large language models (LLMs) in the field of natural language processing, their application potential in mental health role simulation, early screening, and auxiliary diagnosis has attracted significant attention. Existing work still lacks an implementation framework for simulating individuals with different depression severity levels based on LLMs, as well as solutions for localized deployment. This paper proposes a framework for simulating communication with depressed patients and conducting psychological cognitive diagnosis using LLMs based on chain-of-thought (CoT) prompts. By integrating Chinese diagnostic dialogue data on depression and the Self-Rating Depression Scale (SDS), this study systematically explores the capabilities of different open-source LLMs in simulating the roles of depressed patients with varying severity, generating diverse linguistic behaviors, and evaluating self-perceived psychological cognitive distortions. The experimental results show that mainstream open-source LLMs perform well in terms of role simulation accuracy, consistency in self-assessment using psychological scales, and quality of language generation. Furthermore, the integration of patient background information can effectively enhance the contextual relevance and semantic expression accuracy of the language generated by the models. The framework proposed in this paper provides effective insights for improving the practicality of LLMs in the field of mental health and enhancing their reliability in multi-turn psychological counseling and auxiliary diagnosis, verifying the application value of a multi-level comprehensive evaluation method that combines professional domain data and psychological scales in patient role simulation.

Keywords: LLMs · Chain-of-thought prompts · Depression Patients · Communication Simulation · Cognitive Diagnosis

1 Introduction

With the acceleration of modern life and the continuous increase in workplace pressure, mental health issues are showing a rapid upward trend. According to data released by the World Health Organization (WHO) in 2021, approximately 280 million people

S. Peng and K. Jiang—These authors contributed equally.

T. Hao et al. (Eds.): BESC 2025, LNCS 16431, pp. 399–414, 2026.
https://doi.org/10.1007/978-981-95-7138-3_26

worldwide suffer from depression, accounting for about 3.8% of the global population. Depression is not only a common mental disorder but also a major factor contributing to functional impairment and reduced quality of life. Although current intervention methods—primarily based on pharmacological and psychological therapies—are relatively mature, the early screening, fine-grained identification, and personalized intervention for patients with different levels of depression severity still face challenges such as low diagnostic efficiency, high labor costs, and a shortage of clinical data.

In recent years, large language models (LLMs) have demonstrated strong capabilities in language understanding and generation within natural language processing (NLP) tasks. These models have gradually been introduced into the mental health domain for assisting in patient simulation, clinical consultation dialogue generation, intervention reasoning, and psychological state assessment. Many existing studies rely on instruction tuning or lightweight domain-specific fine-tuning approaches such as LoRA, combined with Chain-of-Thought (CoT) prompting to achieve fine-grained simulation of patients with psychological disorders such as depression. However, such methods typically require secondary training on local models and access to medical data, which imposes high technical and resource thresholds—posing barriers to wide-scale deployment in resource-limited or educational settings.

To address these limitations, this paper proposes a novel zero-shot framework for depression patient role simulation and psychological cognitive assessment, which is based solely on mainstream open-source LLMs and CoT-style prompt engineering without any parameter tuning. The goal is to explore whether LLMs can achieve high-fidelity representation of depressive language styles, clinical reasoning, and cognitive distortion assessment solely through carefully designed prompts under a "zero-tuning" setting. Compared to traditional training-dependent approaches, the proposed method offers greater flexibility, lighter deployment burden, and broader applicability, particularly suitable for psychological education, assistant training, and virtual patient construction. The main contributions of this work are as follows:

- We propose a CoT-prompt-based framework that enables mainstream LLMs to simulate depression patients at different severity levels, conduct multi-turn diagnosis-oriented conversations, and generate clinical summaries—all without model fine-tuning;
- We construct a psychological cognitive distortion evaluation scheme driven by the Zung Self-Rating Depression Scale (SDS), which enables automatic scoring of simulated roles and allows for quantitative validation through accuracy and F1 metrics;
- We systematically evaluate the performance of mainstream LLMs, including LLaMA3.1-70B and Qwen2.5-72B, in simulating depressive communication and clinical reasoning, demonstrating their feasibility and consistency across psychological tasks;
- We provide a lightweight and deployable solution for depression patient simulation in low-resource and low-barrier scenarios, with promising usability in educational, training, and real-world application contexts.

2 Related Work

2.1 Role Simulation and Diagnostic Reasoning with LLMs in Mental Health

In recent years, with the breakthrough progress of large language models (LLMs) in the field of natural language processing, their applications in healthcare—especially mental health—have attracted increasing attention. In particular, LLMs have shown significant potential in simulating depression patients, modeling psychological states, and assisting in dialogue-based diagnosis. Traditional research on psychological counseling is often constrained by data scarcity and ethical concerns, resulting in limited availability of open-source clinical dialogue datasets. To address this, many studies have explored using LLMs to generate virtual patient dialogues or construct depression patient personas through prompt engineering. For example, Wang et al. proposed the PATIENT-Ψ framework, which incorporates cognitive models from Cognitive Behavioral Therapy (CBT) to simulate diverse virtual depression patients using GPT-based models [1]. In practice, Chen et al. employed ChatGPT to simulate psychological help-seeker roles with varying emotional states and evaluated the fidelity of their linguistic and emotional expression based on expert feedback, confirming the feasibility and consistency of LLMs in psychological role simulation [2]. In fact, LLMs' ability to simulate psychological roles relies on the maturity of their personality modeling: existing studies have systematically organized the technical context and resources of LLM personality research from three aspects (self-assessment, personality exhibition, recognition) [3]; some have further improved the accuracy and interpretability of conversational personality recognition via the Affective-NLI method [4]; others have proposed the DesPrompt tuning strategy, which uses personality-descriptive adjectives to design cloze tasks and enhance LLMs' few-shot character personality capture [5].

Furthermore, the PsyDT framework introduced a collaborative simulation system involving "digital twin" psychological counselors and virtual patients, demonstrating the practicality of LLMs in multi-role psychological dialogue systems [6]. Notably, the value of LLMs in diagnosis-related dialogues extends beyond state tracking: Yang et al. proposed an LLM-based collaborative agent framework, which enables timely instructive feedback generation in task-oriented group discussions through pedagogy-guided interaction modeling [7]. To tackle the data scarcity problem, Qiu et al. proposed a Chain-of-Thought prompting method to expand single-turn psychological texts into multi-turn dialogues, and improved psychological label clustering to better model depression-related features [8]. Heinz et al. conducted the first randomized controlled trial (RCT) demonstrating the therapeutic efficacy of a fully generative AI chatbot in treating moderate to severe depression on real clinical samples, laying a foundation for LLMs in real-world mental health interventions [9].

2.2 Mental Health Dialogue Datasets and LLM-Based Data Augmentation

Liu et al. proposed a task framework for emotional support dialogue systems aimed at simulating the empathetic support needed by individuals in psychological distress.

They constructed a multi-turn emotional support dialogue dataset and introduced multi-dimensional emotional state modeling and strategy control mechanisms, advancing the development of open-domain dialogue systems in mental health scenarios [10].

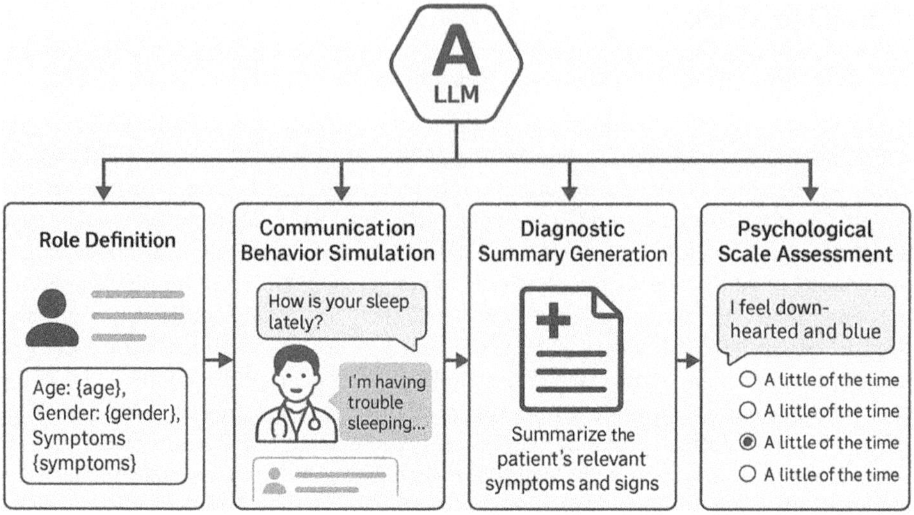

Fig. 1. Prompt-driven framework for LLM-based depression patient simulation and assessment

Yao et al. constructed the first Chinese dialogue dataset for depression diagnosis, named D^4. Based on ICD-11 and DSM-5 diagnostic standards, the dataset contains over 1,300 multi-turn diagnostic dialogues written by professional psychiatrists, along with detailed symptom attribution and diagnostic summaries. This resource provides essential support for simulating real-world depression diagnosis processes and evaluating the performance of large language models in mental health applications [11].

Zheng et al.introduced AugESC, a framework that leverages large language models to augment emotional support dialogue datasets. By using LLMs to generate high-quality, diverse dialogue samples, the authors addressed the issue of data scarcity in emotional support conversation modeling. Their method significantly improves dialogue coherence and emotional appropriateness, facilitating the training of more empathetic and context-aware support agents [12]. Given the privacy concerns inherent in psychological counseling data, several datasets have been constructed via crowdsourcing or data synthesis, such as ESD-CoT [13], and ExTES [14].

3 Research Methodology

To evaluate the ability of LLMs to simulate depression patients with varying severity levels and perform psychological cognitive assessments under zero-shot (non-fine-tuned) conditions, this study proposes a dialogue simulation and self-assessment framework based on prompt engineering and CoT design. The framework does not rely on additional training or parameter updates. It completes the entire assessment process solely through open-source LLMs that are relatively easy to deploy locally (such as LLaMA3-70B) and COT prompts. As illustrated in Fig. 1, the framework consists of four main components: Role Profile Definition, Communication Behavior Simulation, Diagnostic Summary Generation, and Psychological Scale Assessment.

3.1 Role Profile Definition

This module constructs a comprehensive profile for each simulated depression patient, including demographic information and chief complaints, mimicking the "patient statement" phase in real clinical consultations. All information is derived from the D^4 Chinese Depression Dialogue Dataset and includes attributes such as age, gender, marital status, occupation, reason for consultation, and key depressive symptoms. Each profile is also labeled with a depression severity level (Control, Mild, Moderate, Severe) to support subsequent comparative evaluations. An example of the prompt template is shown in Fig. 2 below:

> ***[Role Definition]***
> *You are a patient diagnosed with {diagnosis}. Your basic information is as follows: Age: {age}, Gender: {gender}, Marital Status: {marital-status}, Occupation: {occupation},Reason for Visit: {reason}, Symptoms:*

Fig. 2. Prompts for the role profile definition

3.2 Communication Behavior Simulation

This module aims to evaluate the capability of LLMs to simulate patient-like language behavior under different role settings. Combining the role profile prompt with dialogue context, we instruct the model to respond to physician queries in a manner consistent with depressive symptom expression across various severity levels. Each response is constrained to describe only one symptom, expressed naturally, emotionally, and without directly mentioning diagnostic terms (e.g., "depression", "mild"). The prompt used for simulating patient replies is as follows in Fig. 3:

> ***[Current Dialogue]*** *Doctor: {current question}*
> ***[Dialogue History]*** *{previous_n_turns}*
> ***[Generation Requirement]*** *Please provide a natural, concise, emotionally expressive Chinese response according to the role profile. Only describe one symptom at a time. Avoid explicit use of diagnostic labels.*

Fig. 3. Prompts for the communication behavior simulaton

Two types of prompt designs are used for comparison:

- Minimal context prompt, which only instructs the model to act as a help-seeker without providing detailed background: "You are a patient undergoing psychological counseling. Please respond naturally, concisely, and emotionally to the doctor's questions in Chinese".

- Full context prompt, which includes detailed background information such as age, gender, occupation, symptoms, and reason for consultation.

These prompts are input into various LLMs for uniform simulation, allowing us to evaluate the linguistic diversity and stylistic consistency of model-generated responses under different prompt conditions.

3.3 Diagnostic Summary Generation

After multi-turn consultation dialogues are completed, we prompt the LLMs to generate a concise diagnostic summary based on the entire dialogue history—analogous to clinical case notes or subjective summary sections in medical records. This task evaluates the model's information integration and symptom summarization capabilities. Rather than requiring an explicit diagnosis, the model is asked to summarize the patient's emotional status, symptomatic behavior, and functional impairments in a clinical tone. The prompt used for diagnostic summary generation is as follows in Fig. 4:

[Task Description] *You are a professional psychological counselor. Read the following counseling dialogue between a client and a therapist. Extract the client's psychological symptoms, emotional state, functional impairments, and any potential risks, then generate a clinical-style summary. Use third-person perspective and formal, medically relevant language.*

[Dialogue] *{entire dialogue content}*

[Chain-of-Thought Instructions]

1. Identify key symptoms such as changes in interest, mood, sleep, appetite, somatic complaints, social and occupational functioning.

2. Determine the presence of any cognitive, emotional, or social impairments.

3. Assess potential risk signals (e.g., self-harm, suicidal ideation).

4. Generate a structured, concise diagnostic summary based on your analysis.

[Summary] *Please provide a diagnostic summary according to the above reasoning steps.*

Fig. 4. Prompts for the diagnostic summary generation

The generated summary is compared to expert-written summaries in the D^4 dataset to evaluate its semantic accuracy and clinical relevance.

3.4 Psychological Scale Assessment

In this module, LLMs are prompted to roleplay depression patients of different severity levels (Control, Mild, Moderate, Severe) and complete the Zung Self-Rating Depression Scale (SDS) under those role settings. The goal is to assess the model's self-awareness of psychological cognition and its ability to provide severity-consistent scale ratings. This step contains two sub-prompts:

a) Role Activation Prompt

The prompt used for role activation is as follows in Fig. 5:

[Dialogue Record]
(multi-turn dialogue between patient and doctor)
[Task Requirement]
Please roleplay as the patient in the above dialogue and complete the following task.

Fig. 5. Prompts for the role activation

b) SDS Scale Scoring Prompt

Through the Zung Self-Rating Depression Scale (SDS), this paper designs self-rating scale prompts for simulated patients with different levels of depression to quantitatively assess the level of psychological cognitive distortion of the simulated patients. The specific design is shown in Fig. 6. The model's 20-item responses are collected and the total SDS score is computed.

*Please rate your level of agreement with the following statements using a 1 to 4 scale (1 = "Never or Rarely", 2 = "Sometimes", 3 = "Often", 4 = "Always"). In the past week, I have felt: 1) Depressed or downhearted. 2) In the best mood in the morning. 3) Like crying or wanting to cry. 4) Poor sleep at night. 5) Eating the same amount as usual. 6) Normal sexual function. 7) Weight loss. 8) Troubled by constipation. 9) Heartbeat faster than usual. 10) Unexplained fatigue. 11) Clear-headed as usual. 12) Not finding tasks as difficult as usual. 13) Restless, unable to stay calm. 14) Hopeful for the future. 15) More easily irritated than usual. 16) Finding decisions easy to make. 17) Feeling useful and indispensable. 18) Life is interesting. 19) Believing others would be better off if I were dead. 20) Still enjoying things I usually like. Reverse-scored items (marked *): *2, *5, *6, *11, *12, *14, *16, *17, *18, *20. For positive items, rate from 1 to 4. For reverse-scored items, rate from 4 to 1. The total score ranges from 20 to 80. Standard score calculation: Multiply the total score by 1.25 and round to the nearest integer to obtain the standard score. Classification: Below 50: Normal; 50-60: Mild Depression; 61-70: Moderate Depression; Above 70: Severe Depression. Based on your responses, your depression level will be assessed.*

Fig. 6. Prompts for the Zung Self-Rating Depression Scale

The results are compared against the role's predefined depression severity to assess the alignment between role simulation and psychological self-assessment. Evaluation metrics include accuracy and F1-score, measuring each model's ability to maintain coherent psychological traits across tasks.

4 Experiments

4.1 Experimental Objectives

This experiment aims to systematically evaluate the capability of large language models (LLMs) without fine-tuning in three core tasks within depression-related dialogue scenarios:

- Depression Dialogue Simulation: To assess whether LLMs can generate realistic and diverse patient responses under different severity role settings.
- Diagnostic Summary Generation: To examine the ability of LLMs to extract key information and generate professional clinical summaries based on multi-turn dialogue.
- Psychological Self-Assessment Evaluation: To evaluate whether the psychological state reflected in the model's simulated role aligns with the preset depression severity, using the Zung Self-Rating Depression Scale (SDS).

4.2 Baseline Models

To comprehensively evaluate the effectiveness of our proposed zero-shot CoT-based prompt framework in simulating depression patients, we selected several mainstream open-source Chinese LLMs as baseline models. These models represent various scales and architectures, as outlined below:

- Qwen2.5-72B: A large-scale language model optimized for Chinese by Alibaba, featuring powerful instruction-following capabilities and multi-turn dialogue understanding. It has been fine-tuned for Chinese applications and is widely used in healthcare, education, and other complex generation tasks [15].
- Qwen-Plus: A lightweight but high-performance language model that supports Chinese tasks and demonstrates strong capabilities in both language generation and comprehension, often used in dialogue and summarization tasks [16].
- DeepSeek-R1: A general-purpose language model with an advanced architecture, delivering stable performance in tasks such as multi-turn conversations and semantic modeling, making it suitable for mental health counseling simulations [17].
- DeepSeek-R1-Distill-Llama-8B: A mid-sized model optimized for natural language generation, particularly effective in understanding symptom descriptions and simulating patient linguistic styles in psychological scenarios [18].
- LLaMA3.1-70B: A state-of-the-art large language model released by Meta, known for its excellent language modeling and reasoning capabilities. It has become a mainstream choice for mental health dialogue simulation tasks [19].

All the models above were evaluated under a zero-fine-tuning setting, using the same prompt design and experimental process to ensure fair and consistent horizontal comparisons.

4.3 Dataset

We employ the D^4 Depression Diagnosis Multi-Turn Chinese Dialogue Dataset as the primary data source for all experimental tasks [11]. This dataset is constructed according to ICD-11 and DSM-5 clinical diagnostic criteria and annotated by licensed psychiatrists. It simulates realistic clinical interactions between doctors and patients, with strong semantic validity and task relevance. Key features of the dataset include:

- Rich Patient Profiles: Each dialogue is accompanied by detailed demographic information (e.g., age, gender, marital status, occupation), as well as labeled depression severity levels (Control, Mild, Moderate, Severe).
- Clear Diagnostic Annotations: Each session includes a clinical diagnostic summary written by psychiatrists, which serves as a ground truth for evaluating the model-generated summaries.
- Comprehensive Semantic Coverage: Dialogue content spans nine key clinical symptoms: emotional disturbance, loss of interest, cognitive dysfunction, sleep/appetite irregularities, somatic symptoms, social withdrawal, suicidal ideation, and general screening.

Table 1 provides a detailed breakdown of the dataset statistics.

Table 1. Statistics of the D^4 depression diagnosis dialogue dataset

Category	Total	Help-seeker	Supporter
# Dialogues	1339	–	–
# Utterances	59029	29762	29297
Turns per dialogue	44.1	–	–
Utterances per dialogue	44.1	22.2	21.9
Avg. Length per utterance	17.6	14.9	20.4

4.4 Evaluation of Response Generation Ability

The purpose of this experiment is to evaluate the performance of mainstream large language models in simulating the language style and expression abilities of patients with depression in multi-turn psychotherapy dialogues, with a focus on the linguistic similarity and expressive diversity between the generated responses and the utterances of patients in real datasets. This task is of great significance for simulating virtual patients, constructing intelligent psychological assistants, and enhancing the fidelity of dialogue systems.

To further investigate the impact of contextual information on the quality of model-generated responses, the experiment was conducted under two different Prompt settings: Without Role Profile Prompt: The model only receives a brief task instruction, guiding it to freely respond in the role of a "patient"; With Role Profile Prompt: The model receives a complete patient profile (including age, gender, occupation, marital status, reason for consultation, and symptoms), which serves as the background for dialogue generation.

Table 2. Response generation ability results

Definition	Model	Metrics							
		BLEU-1	BLEU-2	BLEU-4	Rouge-L	Meteor	Extrema	Distinct-1	Distinct-2
Without Role Profile	Deepseek-8B	0.0143	0.0044	0.0002	0.022	0.0482	0.5247	0.3651	0.6659
	Llama3.1-70B	0.1383	0.0643	0.0042	0.1825	0.1314	0.2259	**0.9375**	0.6936
	Qwen2.5-72B	0.1479	0.0455	0.0041	0.1749	0.1557	0.3026	0.9071	0.8831
	DeepseekR1	0.065	0.0114	0.0001	0.0798	0.0886	0.2558	0.8403	0.9344
	Qwenplus	0.0861	0.0229	0.0012	0.1052	0.1288	0.357	0.8272	0.9557
With Role Profile	Deepseek-8B	0.0141	0.0045	0.0001	0.0217	0.0498	**0.5497**	0.3711	0.6751
	Llama3.1-70B	**0.1632**	**0.0708**	0.0041	**0.2117**	0.1574	0.2649	0.9325	0.6821
	Qwen2.5-72B	0.1587	0.0531	**0.0055**	0.185	**0.1739**	0.339	0.9066	0.896
	DeepseekR1	0.0436	0.0075	0.0002	0.0567	0.0835	0.2973	0.8001	**0.9622**
	Qwenplus	0.0797	0.022	0.0009	0.0975	0.1333	0.4037	0.8038	**0.9622**

The evaluation metrics for model-generated utterances include BLEU-1, BLEU-2, BLEU-4 [20], ROUGE-L [21], METEOR [22], Extrema semantic similarity[23], and Distinct-1 and Distinct-2 diversity indicators [24]. BLEU-1, BLEU-2, BLEU-4,

ROUGE-L, and METEOR are metrics used to assess the quality of generated text in natural language processing tasks. They primarily measure the similarity between generated and reference texts from lexical, structural, and semantic aspects. Extrema evaluates the semantic similarity of sentence vector extremes, measuring the fidelity of semantic expression. Distinct-1 and Distinct-2 are used to assess the lexical diversity of generated text, reflecting linguistic richness. The specific evaluation results for each model are shown in Table 2.

From the evaluation results, it can be observed that contextual information significantly enhances the quality of generated responses. All models performed better in the "With Role Profile" prompt setting than in the "Without Role Profile" setting in terms of BLEU, ROUGE, and METEOR metrics, indicating that providing specific profile backgrounds can significantly improve the context relevance and semantic fit of language generation.In terms of language accuracy and semantic relevance, Qwen2.5-72B and LLaMA3.1-70B significantly outperformed other models, especially in the "With Information" scenario. Qwen2.5-72B achieved the highest scores in BLEU-1, METEOR, and Extrema, demonstrating its superior language understanding and expression capabilities in simulating Chinese psychotherapy dialogues. In terms of lexical diversity, as indicated by Distinct-1 and Distinct-2, Qwenplus and DeepseekR1 generated more diverse utterances, capable of producing patient language with different styles, making them suitable for constructing virtual patients with diverse conversational styles. Despite its acceptable performance in lexical diversity, Deepseek8B scored significantly lower than other models in accuracy metrics such as BLEU and ROUGE, likely due to its lack of semantic structure alignment capabilities in the context of mental health scenarios.

In summary, this experiment has demonstrated that mainstream open-source large models can achieve high-quality simulation of the language style of patients with depression through carefully designed prompts, especially when background information is provided, ensuring good consistency between the generated language style and real data.

4.5 Assessment of Diagnostic Summary Generation Capability

To evaluate the ability of mainstream large language models to generate diagnostic summaries after multi-turn psychotherapy dialogues, this study simulates the "course of illness summary" or "subjective summary section" in clinical psychotherapy. The task requires models to extract the patient's main symptoms, emotional states, functional impacts, and potential risk factors from the complete dialogue history, generating a structured and professional summary text. This includes not only identifying explicit concerns raised by the patient but also inferring underlying psychological patterns that may influence their mental health condition. This task not only assesses the language generation capabilities of models but also emphasizes their abilities in information integration, topic identification, and imitation of clinical writing styles. It is a key indicator for measuring whether LLMs possess "psychological summarization thinking.

Table 3. Diagnostic summary generation ability results

Definition	Model	Methods	Metrics							
			BLEU-1	BLEU-2	BLEU-4	Rouge-L	Meteor	Extrema	Distinct1	Distinct2
Without Role Profile	Llama3.1-70B	Zero-shot	0.0696	0.0261	0.0033	0.1011	0.1641	0.4252	0.3722	0.6268
		One-shot	0.0916	0.0359	0.0048	0.1191	0.1846	0.4179	0.446	0.7188
		Few-shot	0.1262	0.059	**0.0156**	0.1452	0.1978	0.4088	0.5278	0.7848
	Deepseek-8B	Zero-shot	0.0713	0.0302	0.0038	0.0941	0.1714	0.4445	0.4354	0.7589
		One-shot	0.0702	0.0309	0.0044	0.0931	0.1686	0.4328	0.4325	0.7487
		Few-shot	0.0769	0.0332	0.0048	0.0981	0.1789	0.4509	0.4335	0.7334
	Qwen2.5-72B	Zero-shot	0.0612	0.0279	0.0031	0.0841	0.1732	0.5041	0.3616	0.6487
		One-shot	0.1222	0.0513	0.0059	0.1408	0.2218	0.4664	**0.5998**	**0.8856**
		Few-shot	0.1251	**0.0559**	0.009	0.1441	**0.2378**	0.4902	0.5985	0.8837
With Role Profile	Llama3.1-70B	Zero-shot	0.0762	0.0336	0.003	0.1088	0.1829	0.4541	0.3783	0.636
		One-shot	0.0916	0.0397	0.0056	0.1215	0.1929	0.4381	0.4279	0.687
		Few-shot	**0.1292**	0.0541	0.0105	**0.1464**	0.2123	0.4397	0.5044	0.7715
	Deepseek-8B	Zero-shot	0.0723	0.0326	0.006	0.0951	0.1876	0.4841	0.4352	0.7721
		One-shot	0.0712	0.0347	0.006	0.0946	0.191	0.4877	0.4375	0.7552
		Few-shot	0.0771	0.0356	0.0048	0.0998	0.1916	0.4855	0.436	0.7441
	Qwen2.5-72B	Zero-shot	0.0622	0.03	0.0035	0.0865	0.1818	0.5244	0.368	0.6521
		One-shot	0.107	0.0512	0.0088	0.13	0.2281	0.5157	0.5328	0.8222
		Few-shot	0.0952	0.0455	0.0067	0.1189	0.2128	**0.5293**	0.4787	0.7616

To comprehensively compare the impact of different prompt designs on the summarization abilities of models, this study evaluates them under three prompt settings:

- Zero-shot: Only the task description and original dialogue are provided, and the model generates the summary based on the prompt.
- One-shot: A standard example is added to the prompt to guide the model in learning the summary format and content organization.
- Few-shot: Multiple example summaries are provided to enhance the model's ability to imitate formats and filter information.

Additionally, the experiment includes two contextual configurations: "Without Role Profile Prompt" and "With Role Profile Prompt", to verify the impact of background information on the quality of diagnostic summary generation. We compare the model-generated summaries with reference summaries written by psychiatric experts in the D^4 dataset using eight metrics: BLEU-1, BLEU-2, BLEU-4, ROUGE-L, METEOR, Extrema, Distinct-1, and Distinct-2.

The experimental results, summarized in Table 3, lead to the following observations: Across all models, the "with patient background" setting consistently outperformed the "without background" condition on BLEU, ROUGE, and METEOR scores. This indicates that specific contextual details help models better focus on core symptoms and semantic themes. In all models, the few-shot configuration achieved the best performance across composite metrics such as BLEU-4, ROUGE-L, and METEOR. This suggests that exposure to multiple examples enhances the model's structural imitation capability and improves content completeness. Qwen2.5-72B-fewshot achieved the highest scores on BLEU-1, BLEU-2, METEOR, and Extrema, demonstrating strong language understanding and synthesis abilities in Chinese diagnostic summarization tasks. Deepseek8B scored lower overall, especially in BLEU-4 and ROUGE metrics, suggesting limitations in long-text integration and reasoning. However, its performance on Extrema indicates some potential in capturing semantic similarity.

In conclusion, combining Few-shot example prompts with specific patient information context is the most effective method for improving diagnostic summary generation quality under the current zero-tuning settings. Moreover, Chinese-optimized models such as Qwen2.5-72B and LLaMA3-70B have demonstrated the potential for drafting initial psychological diagnostic documents, providing a foundational support for the development of subsequent diagnostic assistance systems.

4.6 Psychological Cognitive Diagnosis

This experiment simulates patient roles through multi-turn dialogues between depressed patients and doctors, aiming to evaluate the ability of large models to generate responses consistent with corresponding depression severity through role-playing without explicit prompts about depression levels.

It also validates the effectiveness of the self-developed depression assessment scale and model performance based on the scale. Four models were tested using dialogue data covering four depression levels (Control, Mild Depression, Moderate Depression, and Severe Depression). The primary evaluation metrics include Macro F1, Weighted F1, and classification accuracy for each depression level.

Table 4. Overall performance of different LLMs in role-playing task

Model	Macro F1	Weighted F1
Deepseek-R1-671B	**0.1428**	0.5387
LLaMA3.1-70B	0.1108	0.4225
Deepseek-R1-8B	0.1292	0.5073
Qwen-Plus	0.1410	**0.5654**

Table 4 presents the overall performance of each model in classifying depression severity. Macro F1 reflects the average classification accuracy across all depression levels, evaluating the model's balanced performance on different categories. Weighted F1 is calculated by weighting the sample size of each category, reflecting the model's comprehensive classification ability on the entire dataset. Overall, Qwen-Plus achieved the best performance in Weighted F1 (0.5654), indicating strong stability in the overall classification task. Deepseek-R1-671B, on the other hand, obtained the highest Macro F1 (0.1428), showing more balanced performance in classifying all depression levels, especially with stronger bias resistance in small-sample categories. In contrast, although LLaMA3-70B performs well in the Mild Depression category, its overall F1 scores remain relatively low, suggesting a tendency toward bias toward mild symptom representation.

Table 5. Classification accuracy of different LLMs

Depression Level	Qwen-Plus	Deepseek-R1-671B	Deepseek-R1-8B	LLaMA3.1-70B
Control	0.3535	**0.4651**	0.3132	0.1395
Mild Depression	0.5117	0.2222	0.4202	**0.6257**
Moderate Depression	**0.3669**	0.2527	0.2667	0.1413
Severe Depression	0.3518	**0.7889**	0.3939	0.3166

Table 5 details the classification accuracy of each model for different depression levels. Deepseek-R1-671B stood out in identifying "Severe Depression" (accuracy 0.7889), indicating its strong ability to recognize high-intensity negative emotions and expressions of severe symptoms. Qwen-Plus showed relatively balanced performance, achieving good accuracy in Control, Mild, and Moderate categories, making it suitable as a general model for mental state recognition. All models faced high difficulty in identifying "Moderate Depression", with overall low accuracy, suggesting that such emotional states are more ambiguous in language expression and difficult to categorize clearly.

The experiment verifies that current mainstream LLMs, under the zero-tuning setting, can distinguish the severity of patients' psychological states to a certain extent solely through prompt-based role-playing and scale-driven assessment. Among them, Qwen-Plus and Deepseek series models have advantages in classification stability and high-symptom recognition, while LLaMA3-70B is more suitable for language modeling of mild symptoms. The method of automatic classification combined with scale scoring can not only indirectly verify the fidelity of model language generation but also provide new ideas for building self-assessment mechanisms in future mental health AI systems.

5 Conclusions

In conclusion, our research proposes a depression patient simulation and cognitive assessment framework based on prompt engineering and CoT reasoning. Without relying on additional fine-tuning, we systematically evaluated the performance of several mainstream large language models across tasks including role-playing, diagnostic summary generation, and psychological self-assessment. Experimental results demonstrate that with well-designed prompts and contextual patient background information, LLMs are capable of generating contextually appropriate responses in the style of depression patients, while also exhibiting a certain capacity for information integration and understanding of psychological scales. These findings verify the feasibility of using LLMs for depression dialogue simulation and self-assessment in low-resource scenarios.

However, several limitations remain. On the one hand, the current dataset is limited in scale and lacks the diversity of real-world clinical data, raising concerns about the generalizability of the models. On the other hand, the scale-based evaluation relies on simplified self-assessment scoring, lacking richer interaction and dynamic feedback mechanisms. Future work will focus on expanding to more diverse and real-world multi-turn psychological counseling data, and exploring patient role simulation under multi-modal inputs.

Acknowledgment. This work is funded in part by the Hubei Provincial Natural Science Foundation of China (No.2024AFB892), the National Key Research and Development Program of China (No.2022ZD0117101).

References

1. Wang, R., et al.:. {PATIENT}-ψ: using large language models to simulate patients for training mental health professionals. In: Al-Onaizan, Y., Bansal, M., Chen, Y.-N. (eds.) Proceedings of the 2024 Conference on Empirical Methods in Natural Language Processing, pp. 12772–12797. Association for Computational Linguistics (2024). https://doi.org/10.18653/v1/2024.emnlp-main.711
2. Chen, S., Wu, M., Zhu, K. Q., Lan, K., Zhang, Z., Cui, L.: LLM-empowered chatbots for psychiatrist and patient simulation: application and evaluation (2023). https://arxiv.org/abs/2305.13614
3. Rinaldi, A., Fox Tree, J., Chaturvedi, S.: Predicting depression in screening interviews from latent categorization of interview prompts. In: Jurafsky, D., Chai, J., Schluter, N., Tetreault, J. (eds.) Proceedings of the 58th Annual Meeting of the Association for Computational Linguistics, pp. 7–18. Association for Computational Linguistics (2020). https://doi.org/10.18653/v1/2020.acl-main.2
4. Wen, Z., Yang, Y., Cao, J., Sun, H., Yang, R., Liu, S.: Self-assessment, exhibition, and recognition: a review of personality in large language models. arXiv preprint arXiv:2406.17624 (2024)
5. Wen, Z., Cao, J., Yang, Y., Yang, R., Liu, S.: Affective-nli: towards accurate and interpretable personality recognition in conversation. In: 2024 IEEE International Conference on Pervasive Computing and Communications (PerCom), pp. 184–193. IEEE (2024)
6. Wen, Z., Cao, J., Yang, Y., Wang, H., Yang, R., Liu, S.: DesPrompt: personality-descriptive prompt tuning for few-shot personality recognition. Inf. Process. Manage. **60**(5), 103422 (2023)
7. Yang, Q., Yang, Y., An, S., Hao, T., Xu, G.: LLM-based collaborative agents with pedagogy-guided interaction modeling for timely instructive feedback generation in task-oriented group discussions (2025)
8. Qiu, H., He, H., Zhang, S., Li, A., Lan, Z.: {SMILE}: single-turn to multi-turn inclusive language expansion via {C}hat{GPT} for mental health support. In: Al-Onaizan, Y., Bansal, M., Chen, Y.-N. (eds.) Findings of the Association for Computational Linguistics: EMNLP 2024, pp. 615–636. Association for Computational Linguistics (2024). https://doi.org/10.18653/v1/2024.findings-emnlp.34
9. Heinz, M.V, et al.: Randomized trial of a generative AI Chatbot for mental health treatment. NEJM AI **2**(4), AIoa2400802 (2025). https://doi.org/10.1056/AIoa2400802
10. Liu, S., et al.: Towards emotional support dialog systems. In: Zong, C., Xia, F., Li, W., Navigli, R. (eds.) Proceedings of the 59th Annual Meeting of the Association for Computational Linguistics and the 11th International Joint Conference on Natural Language Processing (Volume 1: Long Papers), pp. 3469–3483. Association for Computational Linguistics (2021). https://doi.org/10.18653/v1/2021.acl-long.269
11. Yao, B., et al.: D4: a {C}hinese dialogue dataset for depression-diagnosis-oriented chat. In: Goldberg, Y., Kozareva, Z., Zhang, Y. (eds.) Proceedings of the 2022 Conference on Empirical Methods in Natural Language Processing, pp. 2438–2459. Association for Computational Linguistics (2022). https://doi.org/10.18653/v1/2022.emnlp-main.156

12. Zheng, C., Sabour, S., Wen, J., Zhang, Z., Huang, M.: {A}ug{ESC}: dialogue augmentation with large language models for emotional support conversation. In: Rogers, A., Boyd-Graber, J., Okazaki, N. (eds.) Findings of the Association for Computational Linguistics: ACL 2023, pp. 1552–1568. Association for Computational Linguistics (2023). https://doi.org/10.18653/v1/2023.findings-acl.99
13. Zhang, T., Zhang, X., Zhao, J., Zhou, L., Jin, Q.: {ESC}o{T}: towards interpretable emotional support dialogue systems. In: Ku, L.-W., Martins, A., Srikumar, V. (eds.) Proceedings of the 62nd Annual Meeting of the Association for Computational Linguistics (Volume 1: Long Papers), pp. 13395–13412. Association for Computational Linguistics (2024). https://doi.org/10.18653/v1/2024.acl-long.723
14. Zheng, Z., Liao, L., Deng, Y., Qin, L., Nie, L.: Self-chats from large language models make small emotional support chatbot better. In: Ku, L.-W., Martins, A., Srikumar, V. (eds.) Proceedings of the 62nd Annual Meeting of the Association for Computational Linguistics (Volume 1: Long Papers), pp. 11325–11345. Association for Computational Linguistics (2024). https://doi.org/10.18653/v1/2024.acl-long.611
15. Yang, A., et al.: Qwen2 technical report. ArXiv Preprint ArXiv:2407.10671 (2024)
16. Hui, B., et al.: Qwen2. 5-coder technical report. arXiv preprint arXiv:2409.12186 (2024)
17. Guo, D., et al.: Deepseek-r1: incentivizing reasoning capability in LLMs via reinforcement learning. arXiv preprint arXiv:2501.12948 (2025)
18. DeepSeek-AI. DeepSeek-R1: incentivizing reasoning capability in LLMs via reinforcement learning (2025). https://arxiv.org/abs/2501.12948
19. Grattafiori, A., et al.: The LLaMA 3 herd of models. arXiv preprint arXiv:2407.21783 (2024)
20. Banerjee, S., Lavie, A.: METEOR: an automatic metric for MT evaluation with improved correlation with human judgments. In: Proceedings of the ACL Workshop on Intrinsic and Extrinsic Evaluation Measures for Machine Translation and/or Summarization, pp. 65–72 (2005)
21. Papineni, K., Roukos, S., Ward, T., Zhu, W.-J.: BLEU: a method for automatic evaluation of machine translation. In: Annual Meeting of the Association for Computational Linguistics, pp. 311–318. ACL (2002)
22. Lin, C.-Y.: ROUGE: a package for automatic evaluation of summaries. In: Text Summarization Branches Out, pp. 74–81 (2004)
23. Forgues, G., Pineau, J., Larchevêque, J.-M., Tremblay, R.: Bootstrapping dialog systems with word embeddings. In: NIPS, Modern Machine Learning and Natural Language Processing Workshop (2014)
24. Li, J., Galley, M., Brockett, C., Gao, J., Dolan, B.: A diversity-promoting objective function for neural conversation models. In: Conference of the North American Chapter of the Association for Computational Linguistics: Human Language Technologies, pp. 110–119. The Association for Computational Linguistics (2016)

Using Topic Detection to Analyze Student Reflections in Service-Learning: A Text Mining Method for Understanding Learning Gains

Yuanyuan Wang[1], Grace Ngai[2(✉)], Hong Va Leong[2], Stephen C.F. Chan[2], and Eugene Yujun Fu[3]

[1] Shenzhen University, Shenzhen, China
yywang@szu.edu.cn
[2] The Hong Kong Polytechnic University, Hong Kong, China
{grace.ngai,hong.va.leong,stephen.c.chan}@polyu.edu.hk
[3] The Education University of Hong Kong, Hong Kong, China
eugenefu@eduhk.hk

Abstract. Educational programs emphasizing experiential learning and personal development increasingly rely on student reflections to assess learning outcomes beyond traditional grade-based measures. However, manual analysis of open-ended textual reflections is time-consuming, subjective, and particularly challenging for short texts. This paper applies an automated topic detection method using sentence embeddings and unsupervised machine learning to analyze student reflections and identify learning gains expressed in students' own words.

Our approach combines sentence embedding techniques to capture semantic information from short textual reflections with K-means clustering to automatically partition embeddings into meaningful topic clusters. This methodology enables systematic identification of themes that students emphasize when describing their learning experiences, providing insights into personalized learning outcomes that traditional assessment methods might miss. We demonstrate this approach using a corpus of short reflections from service-learning programs. The method is broadly applicable to any educational context where understanding student experiences and feelings takes precedence over conventional assessment metrics. Experimental results show the method effectively uncovers meaningful topics from brief, open-ended reflections. Analysis of frequent keywords within each topic cluster provides fine-grained insights into student perspectives on their learning outcomes.

Our findings reveal that students with higher self-reported learning outcomes tend to discuss a broader range of topics in their reflections. This computational approach offers educators and researchers a scalable tool for understanding what aspects of educational experiences most significantly impact student learning from the learners' own perspectives, with applications extending beyond service-learning to diverse experiential education programs.

T. Hao et al. (Eds.): BESC 2025, LNCS 16431, pp. 415–434, 2026.
https://doi.org/10.1007/978-981-95-7138-3_27

Keywords: Topic detection · Short textual reflections · Sentence embedding · Service-learning

1 Introduction

Educational programs emphasizing experiential learning increasingly recognize the value of student reflections for understanding learning outcomes beyond traditional assessment measures. Service-learning, an experiential pedagogy that enhances students' theoretical knowledge through community service experiences and reflections [4,15,36], exemplifies such programs where understanding student perspectives is crucial. Considerable research has demonstrated that service-learning benefits students in personal and interpersonal development, academic knowledge, skills, civic engagement, and caring dispositions [5,6,16,17,19,24,26,40]. However, most studies on student learning have relied heavily on close-ended questionnaires with predetermined response options, limiting researchers to measuring only predefined learning dimensions and making assessments sensitive to researchers' subjective topical emphases [12].

Open-ended textual reflections provide opportunities for students to articulate their learning experiences in their own words, offering insights into personalized learning gains that structured assessments might miss [29]. While some studies have adopted manual qualitative coding methods to analyze these reflections, such approaches are time-consuming, prone to researcher bias, and particularly challenging for short texts with insufficient contextual information [6,16,21,39,40]. Despite advances in computational linguistics and natural language processing, automated analysis of student reflections to identify learning gains from students' perspectives remains underexplored.

A particular challenge in analyzing student reflections stems from the nature of the texts themselves. Many students provide brief responses consisting of single words, simple phrases, or short sentences to fulfill reflection requirements quickly, resulting in sparse textual data with limited contextual information. This tendency toward brevity creates additional analytical challenges beyond those found in longer-form text analysis. Traditional topic detection approaches such as topic modeling and text clustering face significant challenges when dealing with short, sparse texts due to insufficient word co-occurrences [3,14]. Recent research has shown that clustering approaches based on neural network embedding representations can deliver improved performance for topic detection [2,37,38,43]. Sentence embedding techniques have proven particularly effective for representing short texts by capturing latent semantic structures [34,38].

This paper proposes an automated topic detection method combining sentence embeddings with unsupervised machine learning to analyze student reflections and identify learning themes expressed in students' own words. We demonstrate this approach using service-learning reflections. The methodology is broadly applicable to any educational context where understanding student experiences takes precedence over conventional assessment metrics. We employ Sentence-BERT to transform short textual reflections into semantically meaningful embeddings, then apply K-means clustering to automatically identify salient themes emphasized by students. The detected topics are validated by domain experts and compared with traditional survey responses to examine whether open-ended textual analysis provides complementary insights into student learning gains.

The rest of the paper is structured as follows: In Sect. 2, we present the related work on open-ended textual reflection analysis and text detection. Section 3 introduces our methodology for topic detection, including the sentence embedding method and clustering method. Section 4 describes the dataset. Sections 5 and 6 provide our experimental results and analysis. Finally, Sect. 7 concludes the paper with a discussion of future work.

2 Related Work

Focusing on service-learning, we examine literature on experiential learning program open-ended reflections, topic detection from short-text responses, and sentence embedding.

2.1 Analysis of Open-Ended Reflections in Service-Learning

Open-ended reflections are a crucial component of experiential learning programs like service-learning, which require students to reflect on their personal learning experiences and gains. Analyzing such reflections may provide direct insights into students' learning outcomes, as open-ended assessments capture higher levels of subject understanding than machine-scored items [32]. While studies have explored open-ended reflections through qualitative coding and manual methods [16,21,39,40], these approaches are time-consuming and limit analyzable data volume.

Keyes et al. [16] summarized student achievement through qualitative analysis of focus groups, reflections, and projects. Trigos Carrillo et al. [40] investigated undergraduate psychology students' learning through qualitative analysis of collective reflections in community psychology service-learning. Tee et al. [39] explored service-learning's positive impacts on personal and social outcomes using reflective writing as primary data. Li et al. [21] examined diverse service experiences' effects on social justice beliefs through qualitative analysis of student reflections.

2.2 Short-Text Topic Detection

Topic detection methods automatically discover topics or themes from open-ended textual data, rather than relying on predetermined categories from close-ended surveys. These methods analyze large amounts of textual data to provide macroscopic insights into salient themes through topic modeling or text clustering. Conventional topic modeling techniques, such as Probabilistic Latent Semantic Analysis (PLSA) [14] and Latent Dirichlet Allocation (LDA) [3], have been widely used to uncover hidden semantic structures from large document corpora. These models discover latent topics by organizing text collections based on word co-occurrence patterns [9]. PLSA finds probabilistic models to generate hidden topics [14], while LDA represents texts as topic mixtures where each word belongs to one topic [3]. Other models, such as Structural Topic Model (STM) [35], analyze open-ended responses. Text clustering defines topics as sets of similar texts clustered by similarity metrics [13].

Traditional topic detection approaches work better with long texts but are less effective on short texts due to insufficient word co-occurrence information [1]. Data sparsity becomes the main bottleneck for satisfactory short text performance.

Methods addressing data sparsity in short text topic detection [7,18,22,23, 27,30,31,42] fall into three categories: window-based, self-aggregation, and word embedding strategies. Window-based strategies cluster texts based on word co-occurrence, including DMM [42], GSDMM [7], and PDMM [27], but ignore semantic relationships. Self-aggregation strategies aggregate short texts into pseudo-documents [11,30,31], but require additional metadata.

Word embeddings represent words as low-dimensional vectors capturing semantic correlations through neural network models like Word2Vec and Doc2Vec [8]. Studies have incorporated word embeddings into short text topic models [18,27], developed hybrid approaches like GLTM [22], and applied K-means clustering with Word2Vec representations [25]. However, conventional word embeddings assign fixed representations regardless of context, which is problematic for words with multiple meanings.

2.3 Contextual and Sentence Embedding Approaches

Several studies have investigated new embedding techniques for words, sentences, and texts that consider word context [11,20]. Recently, researchers have applied novel deep learning methods for word embedding to better capture contextual semantic information and represent words more accurately in different contexts. Examples include contextualized embedding models, Latent LSTM Allocation, and Bidirectional Encoder Representations from Transformers (BERT) [2,8,10,28,37,43], which have shown improved topic detection performance. BERT uses transformer architecture to pre-train deep bidirectional representations from unlabeled text by conditioning on both left and right contexts in all layers, alleviating unidirectional constraints through a "masked language model" pre-training objective [10]. Consequently, BERT outperforms conventional word embedding methods.

To cluster short texts effectively, generating high-quality embedding vectors that fully reflect semantic meaning is essential for measuring sentence similarity. Sentence embedding captures latent semantic relationships among words within sentences. Various sentence embedding methods have emerged with different generating mechanisms, such as averaging word embedding vectors and special tokens from pre-trained language models [34,38]. Sentence-BERT (SBERT) [33], which transforms sentences into low-dimensional vectors based on BERT using siamese and triplet network structures, has proven to generate efficient, meaningful sentence embeddings for representing short texts and performing effectively in text clustering [38].

3 Methodology

The primary focus of this study is to automatically analyze students' open-ended reflections to identify their learning gains from service-learning experiences, expressed in their own words. However, short textual reflections pose an additional challenge due to limited contextual information. To establish similarity measures and semantic correlations, short textual reflections must be represented as numeric vectors through Natural Language Processing (NLP). Traditional NLP methods, such as One-Hot encoding, Bag-of-Words, and TF-IDF represent each short text as a vector but ignore semantic relationships between words, resulting in very sparse and high-dimensional vectors. Sentence embedding has proven critical for the success of NLP applications. By transforming sentences into low-dimensional vector values, it captures more latent semantic and syntactic information, which is beneficial for handling short text challenges in text clustering and provides better performance [33,34,38].

Topic detection has been applied to automatically analyze large amounts of textual data to provide macroscopic insights into salient themes emphasized in the corpus through topic modeling or text clustering approaches. Furthermore, clustering methods that incorporate novel neural network embedding representations have demonstrated promising results in enhancing topic detection performance [8]. Inspired by previous studies, this paper employs a topic detection method that integrates sentence embeddings and K-means to automatically identify topics from short textual reflections in service-learning and obtain better understanding of students' learning gains from their perspectives.

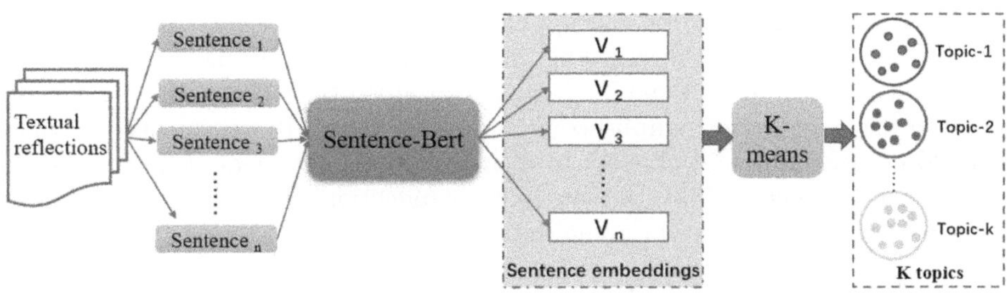

Fig. 1. Overview of the Topic Detection Method for Student Reflection and Learning Gain Analysis.

Figure 1 illustrates the general architecture of our topic detection method. The textual reflections are separated into itemized responses as sentence inputs for the Sentence-BERT method. These sentences are then converted into vectors using sentence embeddings. Next, the K-means clustering algorithm is applied to partition sentence vectors into K clusters. Topics are identified from the clusters, each of which is labeled by service-learning experts based on high-frequency words associated with the corresponding topic.

3.1 Data Pre-processing

Data pre-processing was performed in Python Jupyter Notebook to improve data quality before topic modeling. Textual reflections were first separated into itemized responses as individual sentences for input into the Sentence-BERT method. The sentences were then converted to lowercase, and stop words, numbers, and punctuation were removed to enhance consistency and reduce computational load. Words were stemmed using the Porter stemming algorithm, and terms with multiple spellings were consolidated (e.g., "team work" and "teamwork").

3.2 Sentence Embedding Generation

Sentence-BERT (SBERT) was employed to convert preprocessed sentences into vector representations. While common approaches generate sentence embeddings through pooling operations on BERT's output layer word embeddings using CLS-token pooling, mean pooling, or max pooling strategies, these methods suffer from vector anisotropy, leading to close spatial distances and unsatisfactory sentence embeddings [33]. SBERT addresses this issue by modifying the BERT model with Siamese or Triplet network structures to derive semantically meaningful sentence embeddings. These embeddings can be compared using similarity measures like Euclidean distance or cosine similarity, and SBERT has been demonstrated to generate high-quality sentence-level embeddings that significantly outperform other state-of-the-art sentence embedding methods.

3.3 K-means for Text Clustering

K-means clustering algorithm was applied to partition sentence embeddings into clusters for topic identification. This unsupervised learning method automatically clusters texts so that similar texts are grouped together, with each cluster representing a collection emphasizing a specific topic. It partitioned sentence embeddings into different clusters to identify groups of salient themes, referred to as "topic" emphasized by students in their reflections. Euclidean distance was used to calculate distances between data points during clustering.

$$SSE = \sum_{i=1}^{k} \sum_{p \in L_i} \|p - q_i\|^2 \tag{1}$$

The optimal cluster number k for K-means was determined using the Sum of Square Errors (SSE) method [41], as shown in Eq. 1, where p represents a data point in cluster L_i and q_i represents the centroid of cluster L_i. The SSE relationship with k forms an elbow shape, where the elbow point corresponds to the optimal number of clusters.

3.4 Topic Interpretation and Categorization

After clustering, topics for each cluster were interpreted and categorized by service-learning experts who examined the most frequent keywords associated with each cluster and reviewed related reflections. This expert-based approach ensured that identified topics accurately reflected the content emphasized by students in their open-ended reflections.

3.5 Comparative Analysis Framework

This study explores what additional information textual reflections provide compared to close-ended questionnaires. We investigate the relationship between topics detected from open-ended textual reflections and student learning outcome ratings in close-ended surveys to examine whether topics emphasized by students in their reflections align with quantitative learning outcome ratings. Particularly, we explore whether students across different learning outcome rating levels (high, medium, low) based on numerical values from close-ended ratings emphasized varying numbers of topics in their reflections.

Table 1. Questionnaire on the attainment of learning outcomes as a result of attending the service-learning subject

Dimensions	Items
Intellectual Learning Outcomes (**ILO**)	Deeper understanding of the linkage between service-learning and the academic content of the subject
	Applying/integrating knowledge to deal with complex issues
	Solving challenging real-life problems
	Thinking critically
Social Learning Outcomes (**SLO**)	Working effectively in teams
	Communicating effectively with peers, collaborators, and service recipients
Civic Learning Outcomes (**CLO**)	Better understanding of the problems facing underprivileged members of the community
	Increased interest/commitment to serve people in need
	Becoming a more responsible member of your community
	Increased understanding and respect for people from different backgrounds
	Becoming a more responsible global citizen
Personal Learning Outcome (**PLO**)	Better understanding of my own strengths and weaknesses
Overall Learning Outcome	Overall learning gain

4 Dataset

4.1 Data Collection

Data was collected from 2608 students at a large public university during the 2020 and 2021 academic years. Textual responses and ratings were gathered through a post-experience questionnaire completed online by students after completing credit-bearing service-learning courses. This study focuses on textual reflections responding to the question: "*Name the three most important things you have learnt from this course, if any.*" Students also rated their attainment of intended learning outcomes for each service-learning course. The questionnaire was developed by the research team with reference to the literature and the university's service-learning implementation contexts [36], containing the following questions:

1. Questions requiring students to rate on a 7-point scale (1 = very little; 4 = a fair amount; 7 = very much), attainment of learning outcomes as a result of attending the service-learning subjects, which consist of "Intellectual Learning Outcomes", "Social Learning Outcomes", "Civic Learning Outcomes", and "Personal Learning Outcome". The corresponding items of different dimensions are shown in Table 1.
2. Questions asking students to indicate their learning experience in service learning on a 7-point scale (1 = strongly disagree; 4 = neutral; 7 = strongly agree).
3. Questions for collecting students' demographic information, such as their previous service-related experience, the total number of hours of direct service, and location of the service-learning project.

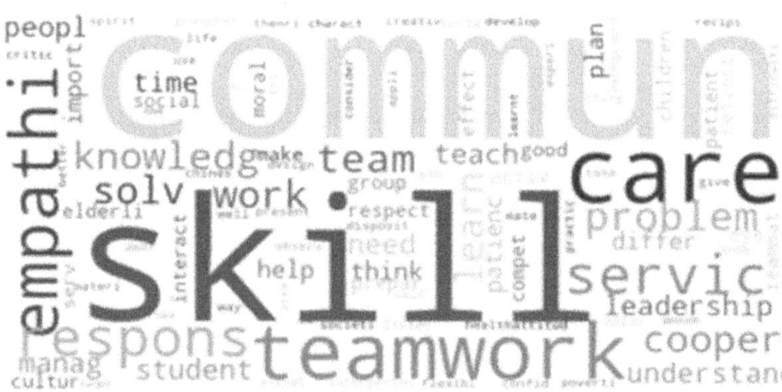

Fig. 2. Word cloud for corpus as whole.

4.2 Descriptive Statistics

Each textual reflection contains 1 to 3 itemized sentences, as students were required to identify three most important learning points from their service-learning course. Length variations are significant, ranging from a minimum of 1 word to a maximum of 66 words. However, textual reflections are generally very short, averaging approximately 6 words.

The 2608 original textual reflections were separated into 6264 itemized responses for analysis. After the preprocessing (e.g., stopwords removal and stemming), 2344 textual reflections remained for topic modeling.

Figure 2 presents a first glance at the data in the form of a word cloud. The more frequent a word is in a text, the larger it is visually. Notably, the most prominently emphasized words (or rather their stems) in the corpus of textual reflections are "commun", "skill", "teamwork", "care", "empathi", which reveals what students have learnt from service-learning, including communication, skills, teamwork and civic learning outcomes. In our subsequent analysis, we provide more nuanced, microscopic view of students' responses by topic detection methods, which makes use of sentence embedding and unsupervised machine learning algorithm to identify the topics emphasized by students, in their own words.

Table 2. Descriptive Statistics of Student Learning Outcome Ratings

Dimensions	Min	Max	Mean	Median	Std. Dev.
ILO	1	7	5.31	5	1.12
CLO	1	7	5.47	6	1.13

Students rated their attainment of learning outcomes resulting from attending service-learning subjects. Our investigation focuses on two dimensions of learning outcomes: Intellectual Learning Outcomes (ILO) (four items) and Civic Learning Outcomes (CLO) (five items). As shown in Table 2, both Intellectual Learning Outcomes and Civic Learning Outcomes have significantly higher means than the midpoint 4, with respective means of 5.31 and 5.47 on a 7-point scale. The standard deviations of the ratings ranged from 1.12 to 1.13. Students' ratings on Civic Learning Outcomes were relatively higher than those on Intellectual Learning Outcomes.

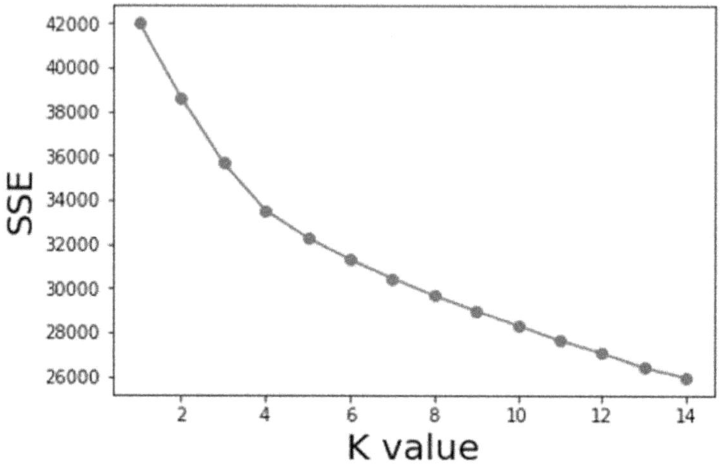

Fig. 3. SSE values with increasing k helping to determine optimal k selection (k = 4 optimized).

5 Topic Detection Results and Analysis

5.1 Student Emphasis in Textual Reflections and Topics

Using the elbow method with SSE value computation, we determined the optimal number of clusters for topic detection. As shown in Fig. 3, the SSE values exhibited an elbow-shaped curve, with the inflection point at $k = 4$ indicating the optimal cluster number.

Figure 4. presents the high-frequency word distributions for the four resulting clusters from K-means clustering on Sentence-BERT embeddings, summarized as follows:

1. The cluster, as shown in Fig. 4a), is dominated by terms including "skill", "problem", "knowledg", "solv" and "teach", which implies the responses in this cluster are about skills and knowledge.
2. The cluster, as shown in Fig. 4b), contains words like "commu", "elderli", "children" and "peopl", suggesting emphasis on communication with recipients.
3. The high-frequency words in the cluster, as shown in Fig. 4c), are "teamwork", "collabor", "team", "teammat" and "work", which mainly emphasize teamwork and collaboration.
4. The top frequent words in the cluster, as shown in Fig. 4d), are "care", "empathi", "respons", "leadership" and "patient", which indicates that the civic orientation and engagement are emphasized in the textual reflections.

Service-learning experts are invited to exam the high-frequency words and related responses to assign topic labels for each cluster. To validate these interpretations, we engaged the experts in a rigorous labeling process. Each

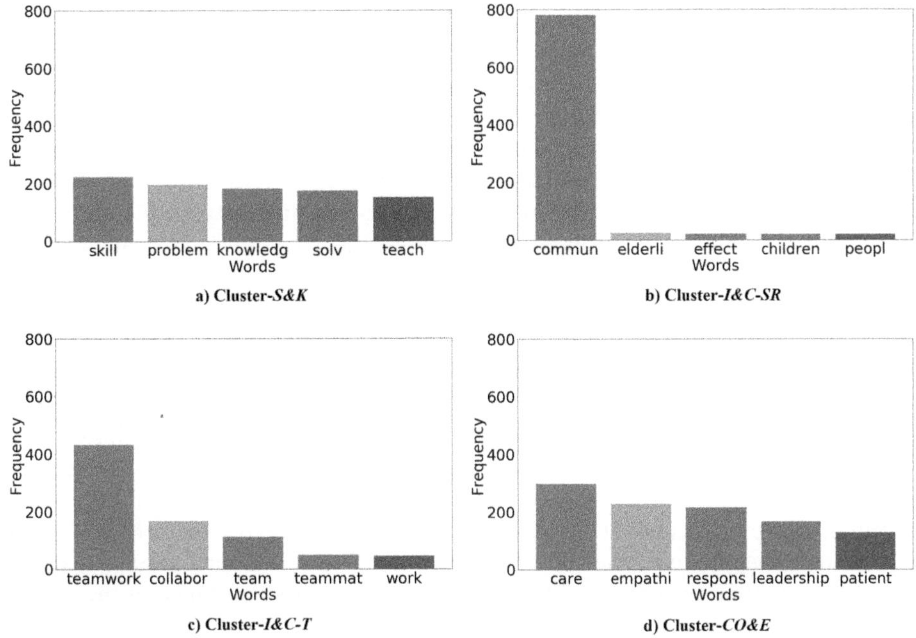

Fig. 4. Top 5 most frequent words in each cluster.

expert independently examined the high-frequency words and read representative responses. For each topic, experts discussed respective naming suggestions and eventually selected a mutually agreed-upon thematic label.

Table 3. Topics and top frequent words

Cluster Index	Cluster Size	High frequency words	Topic labels
0	2260	"skill", "problem", "knowledg", "solv", "teach"	Skills and Knowledge (*S&K*)
1	792	"commun", "elderli", "effect", "children", "peopl"	Interaction and Communication with Service Recipients (*I&C-SR*)
2	779	"teamwork", "collabor", "team", "teammat", "work"	Interaction and Communication with Teammates (*I&C-T*)
3	2433	"care", "empathi", "respons", "leadership", "patient"	Civic Orientation and Engagement (*CO&E*)

Table 3 presents the four expert-labeled topics and their associated high-frequency words. Among them, most important topics emphasized by students in their service-learning reflections are "Civic Orientation and Engagement" (*CO&E*) and "Skills and Knowledge" (*S&K*). The civic engagement approach of service-learning has been commonly endorsed by researchers and practitioners in higher education. Hence, students are highly expected to gain civic orientation outcomes from service-learning. The result demonstrates that students emphasized the experience of engaging in service-learning really enhanced their sense of civic engagement, empathy, responsibility and caring dispositions. As an experiential course in high education, another main objective of service-learning is to enable students to acquire skills and knowledge. Our findings also confirm that students have definitely learned skills and knowledge in service-learning. Besides, "Interaction and Communication with Service Recipients" (*I&C-SR*) and "Interaction and Communication with Teammates" (*I&C-T*) are also highlighted as social learning outcomes in the textual reflections, which indicates that students have learned how to effectively communicate and collaborate with different people, including their teammates and service recipients, such as elderly and children.

The experimental results demonstrate that our method successfully identified meaningful topics discussed by students, which align with expert labeling and provide new insights into the themes that characterize students' service-learning experiences in their own words. The topics and their corresponding high-frequency words summarized in Table 3, offering a comprehensive, data-driven overview of the central ideas students emphasized in their service-learning reflections.

Fig. 5. Word cloud under different topics. a) Skills and Knowledge (*S&K*); b) Interaction and Communication with Service Recipients (*I&C-SR*); c) Interaction and Communication with Teammates (*I&C-T*); and d) Civic Orientation and Engagement (*CO&E*).

5.2 Fine-Grained Analysis Through Word Clouds

To further investigate what additional information the textual reflection can provide compared to the close-ended questionnaire, we conducted a detailed examination of each reflection cluster. Figure 5 presents detailed word cloud for each cluster, highlighting the keywords that students emphasized in their textual reflections. In addition to the top five high-frequency words, the word clouds reveal more important keywords emphasized by students in their responses.

Specifically, in the Skills and Knowledge cluster (Fig. 5a)), additional keywords include "prepar", "materi", "time", "manag", "interact", "present", "activ", "chinese", "cultur", "theori", "online", and "eye", indicating student emphasis on material preparation, time management, presentation skills, cultural learning, and specific service contexts like online teaching and eye care.

The Interaction and Communication with Service Recipients cluster (Fig. 5b)) reveals keywords such as "differ", "student", "group", "background", "secondari", "sen", "recipi", and "teenag", showing students learned to communicate with diverse recipients including different age groups, backgrounds, secondary students, SEN students, and teenagers.

For Interaction and Communication with Teammates (Fig. 5c)), keywords like "group", "import", "spirit", "cooper", "groupmat", and "build" demonstrate student emphasis on team spirit, team building, and group cooperation. The Civic Orientation and Engagement cluster (Fig. 5d)) includes keywords such as "respect", "need", "understand", "disposition", "help", "listen", "think", "moral", and "elderli", indicating students learned to respect others, understand different needs, develop caring dispositions, and serve vulnerable populations.

The topic detection method reveals fine-grained information about student learning outcomes that supplements quantitative surveys. While close-ended questionnaires measure Social learning outcomes through only two predetermined items ("working effectivel" and "communicating effectively with peers, collaborators, and service recipient"), textual reflections provide detailed insights into specific communication contexts, diverse recipient groups, team dynamics, and collaborative skills. This microscopic view of student perspectives offers valuable supplementary information for educators and researchers seeking comprehensive understanding of service-learning outcomes.

6 Topic Emphasis Patterns Across Learning Outcome Levels

6.1 Clustering on Student Learning Outcome Ratings

Students were required to identify the three most important learning points from their service-learning course. Each reflection was separated into itemized responses for topic detection using K-Means clustering and Sentence-BERT embeddings. Consequently, each reflection's topics comprise all topics from its constituent itemized responses. This study further examined whether students with different learning outcome rating levels emphasized varying numbers of topics in their reflections.

Our investigation focused on two learning outcome dimensions: Intellectual Learning Outcomes (four items) and Civic Learning Outcomes (five items). For each dimension, K-means clustering categorized students with similar learning outcome ratings. The SSE method determined the optimal cluster number as $k = 3$ for all dimensions.

Table 4. Clustered attainments of learning outcomes: Intellectual Learning Outcomes

Cluster Index	Cluster Size	Average Rating	Level
0	385	3.79	Low
1	956	5.10	Medium
2	1003	6.21	High

Table 5. Clustered attainments of learning outcomes: Civic Learning Outcomes

Cluster Index	Cluster Size	Average Rating	Level
0	341	3.83	Low
1	838	5.17	Medium
2	1165	6.29	High

Tables 4 and 5 present the clustering results for learning outcome attainment. The average ratings on the 7-point scale were grouped into three levels: one cluster contained students with the lowest self-rated learning gains, another represented medium learning gains, and the final cluster included students with the highest learning gains.

6.2 Relationship Between Learning Outcome Levels and Topic Emphasis

To examine whether students' self-perceived learning achievement corresponds with the depth of their reflective responses, we analyzed the relationship between learning outcome rating levels and the number of topics emphasized in textual reflections. This investigation sought to determine if students who rated their learning outcomes higher also demonstrated greater engagement by discussing more topics in their open-ended responses, thereby validating the consistency between quantitative self-assessments and qualitative reflection depth.

This analysis included students whose reflections were clustered in the previous subsection, excluding those who wrote "None", "NA", "Nothing", or "No" in their responses. The final dataset comprised 2,428 reflections, categorized into four distinct groups based on topic inclusion: reflections containing 0 topic, 1 topic, 2 topics, and 3 topics.

Furthermore, a Chi-Square Test examined differences in topic numbers among students with different learning outcome rating levels (*Low*, *Medium*, *High*). The hypotheses were:

H0: There is no significant difference in the number of topics covered in reflections among students with different learning outcome rating levels.

H1: There is a significant difference in the number of topics covered in reflections among students with different learning outcome rating levels.

Figures 6 and 7 display the percentage distribution of reflections with varying topic numbers across different Intellectual Learning Outcomes and Civic Learning Outcomes levels, respectively. The charts reveal that students with low-level

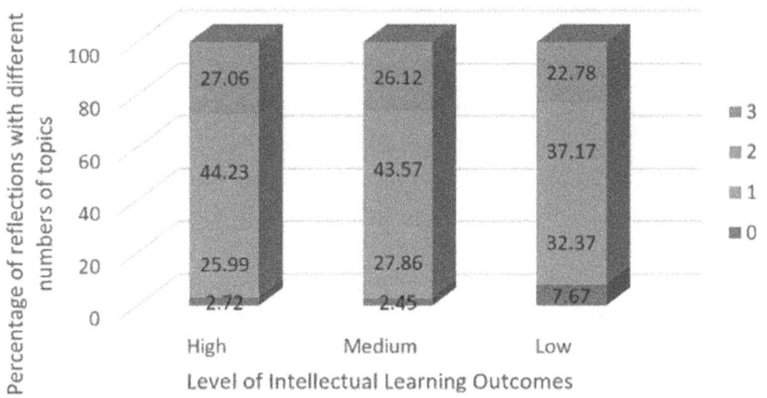

Fig. 6. Percentage of reflections with different number of topics across different levels of Intellectual Learning Outcomes.

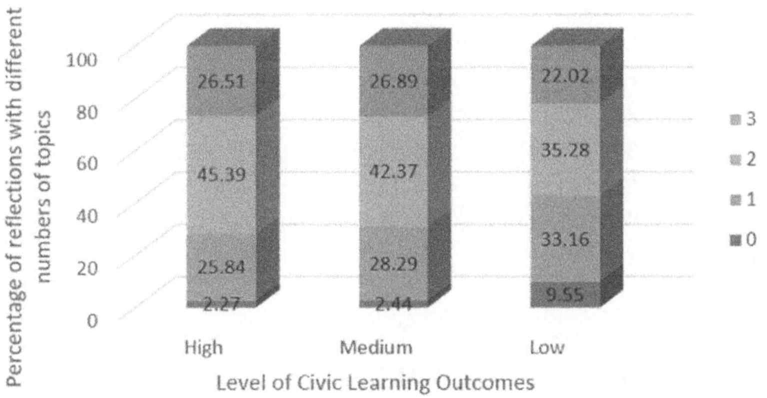

Fig. 7. Percentage of reflections with different number of topics across different levels of Civic Learning Outcomes.

learning outcomes tend to emphasize fewer topics in their reflections, with some stating they learned nothing. Approximately 70% of students with high-level and medium-level learning outcomes identified 2–3 topics in their reflections. These findings demonstrate that students at different learning outcome rating levels emphasized different numbers of topics in their open-ended reflections.

The results of the Chi-square Test for the rating level of the two dimensions of Intellectual Learning Outcomes and Civic Learning Outcomes are presented in Tables 6 and 7, respectively. Both tests yielded p-values less than 0.01, rejecting the null hypothesis *H0* and accepting the alternative hypothesis *H1*. This indicates significant differences in topic numbers across different learning outcome rating levels.

Table 6. Chi-square Test result for the rating level of Intellectual Learning Outcomes and the number of topics in reflections

Results of Chi-square Test							
Item		Learning Outcome Level (%)			Total	χ^2	p
		High	Medium	Low			
Topic-Num	0	28 (2.72)	24 (2.45)	32 (7.67)	84 (3.46)	36.123	0.000**
	1	268 (25.99)	273 (27.86)	135 (32.37)	676 (27.84)		
	2	456 (44.23)	427 (43.57)	155 (37.17)	1038 (42.75)		
	3	279 (27.06)	256 (26.12)	95 (22.78)	630 (25.95)		
Total		1031	980	417	2428		

* p<0.05 ** p<0.01

Table 7. Chi-square Test result for the rating level of Civic Learning Outcomes and the number of topics in reflections

Results of Chi-square Test							
Item		Learning Outcome Level (%)			Total	χ^2	p
		High	Medium	Low			
Topic-Num	0	27 (2.27)	21 (2.44)	36 (9.55)	84 (3.46)	63.06	0.000**
	1	308 (25.84)	243 (28.29)	125 (33.16)	676 (27.84)		
	2	541 (45.39)	364 (42.37)	133 (35.28)	1038 (42.75)		
	3	316 (26.51)	231 (26.89)	83 (22.02)	630 (25.95)		
Total		1192	859	377	2428		

* p<0.05 ** p<0.01

7 Conclusion and Future Work

In this paper, we have applied a novel approach combining Sentence-BERT embedding and K-means algorithm to automatically detect the topics from students' open-ended textual reflections to gain insight into students' perspective on their learning outcomes. Experimental results show that this method performs effectively to uncover meaningful topics from short reflections written by students, and hence casts a novel light on the question of what students really learned in their own words. We also investigated the relationship between the cluster of each topic detected from open-ended responses and the rated learning outcome in close-ended questionnaire survey, and found that students' qualitative responses in open-ended reflections are consistent with their quantitative responses in close-ended questionnaire. Moreover, the topics identified from reflections provides more fine-grained interpretation for the learning outcomes responded in the close-ended questionnaire. Students who have rated higher in learning outcomes in close-ended questionnaire tend to emphasize more topics in their open-ended reflections, which indicates that they have learned more things in service learning.

This paper contributes to the current body of literature by applying a topic detection approach based on neural network embedding and unsupervised machine learning to examine student textual reflections for characterizing the salient themes emphasized in students' reflections. Our method also has more general applications to other open-ended short textual feedbacks. Future work will explore the potential of the application of machine learning and deep learning methods in analyzing student learning in service-learning and studying how these methods can be used to complement traditional statistical approaches.

Acknowledgments. This work was in part supported by the Shenzhen Education Sciences Planning Project under Grant RGZN23004, and by the Hong Kong Research Grant Council under Grant 15600219.

Disclosure of Interests. The authors have no competing interests to declare that are relevant to the content of this article.

References

1. Albalawi, R., Yeap, T.H., Benyoucef, M.: Using topic modeling methods for short-text data: a comparative analysis. Front. Artif. Intell. **3**, 42 (2020). https://doi.org/10.3389/frai.2020.00042
2. Asyaky, M.S., Mandala, R.: Improving the performance of hdbscan on short text clustering by using word embedding and umap. In: 2021 8th International Conference on Advanced Informatics: Concepts, Theory and Applications (ICAICTA), pp. 1–6 (2021)
3. Blei, D.M., Ng, A.Y., Jordan, M.I.: Latent Dirichlet allocation. J. Mach. Learn. Res. **3**, 993–1022 (2003)
4. Bringle, R.G., Hatcher, J.A.: A service-learning curriculum for faculty. Mich. J. Commun. Serv. Learn. **2**(1), 112–122 (1995)
5. Chan, S.C., Ngai, G., Kwan, K.P.: Mandatory service-learning at university: do less-inclined students learn from it? Act. Learn. High. Educ. **20**(3), 189–202 (2019)
6. Chen, L.C.: A study of the efficacy of service learning on students learning outcome. Int. J. Teach. Educ. **IV**(4), 1–11 (2015)

7. Cheng, X., Yan, X., Lan, Y., Guo, J.: Btm: topic modeling over short texts. IEEE Trans. Knowl. Data Eng. **26**(12), 2928–2941 (2014)
8. Curiskis, S.A., Drake, B., Osborn, T.R., Kennedy, P.J.: An evaluation of document clustering and topic modelling in two online social networks: twitter and reddit. Inf. Process. Manag. **57**(2), 102034 (2020)
9. Daenekindt, S., Huisman, J.: Mapping the scattered field of research on higher education. a correlated topic model of 17,000 articles, 1991–2018. High. Educ. **80**(3), 571–587 (2020)
10. Devlin, J., Chang, M.W., Lee, K., Toutanova, K.: Bert: pre-training of deep bidirectional transformers for language understanding. arXiv preprint arXiv:1810.04805 (2018)
11. Gao, W., Peng, M., Wang, H., Wang, H., Li, H.: Incorporating word embeddings into topic modeling of short text. Knowl. Inf. Syst. **61**(3), 1123–1145 (2019)
12. Grajzl, P., Irby, C.T.: Reflections on study abroad: a computational linguistics approach. J. Comput. Social Sci. **2**(2), 151–181 (2019)
13. Hasan, M., Orgun, M.A., Schwitter, R.: Real-time event detection from the twitter data stream using the twitternews+ framework. Inf. Process. Manag. **56**(5), 1146–1165 (2019)
14. Hofmann, T.: Probabilistic latent semantic indexing. In: Proceedings of the 22nd Annual International ACM SIGIR Conference on Research and Development in Information Retrieval, SIGIR '99, pp. 50–57. ACM (1999). https://doi.org/10.1145/312624.312649
15. Kenworthy-U'Ren, A.L.: A decade of service-learning: a review of the field ten years after jobe's seminal special issue. J. Bus. Ethics **81**(4), 811–822 (2008)
16. Keyes, L.M., Jang, H.S.: Teaching note—service learning in an undergraduate volunteer management course: a comprehensive learning outcome assessment model. J. Nonprofit Educ. Leadership **11**(2), 86–98 (2021)
17. Leung, H., Shek, D.T.L., Dou, D.: Evaluation of service-learning in project wecan under covid-19 in a Chinese context. Int. J. Environ. Res. Public Health **18**(7), 3596 (2021). https://doi.org/10.3390/ijerph18073596
18. Li, C., Duan, Y., Wang, H., Zhang, Z., Sun, A., Ma, Z.: Enhancing topic modeling for short texts with auxiliary word embeddings. ACM Trans. Inf. Syst. **36**(2), 1–30 (2017). https://doi.org/10.1145/3095799
19. Li, L., Shek, D.T.L.: Serving children and adolescents in need during the covid-19 pandemic: evaluation of service-learning subjects with and without face-to-face interaction. Int. J. Environ. Res. Public Health **18**(4), 2114 (2021)
20. Li, S., Pan, R., Luo, H., Wang, Z.: Adaptive cross-contextual word embedding for word polysemy with unsupervised topic modeling. Knowl.-Based Syst. **218**, 106827 (2021). https://doi.org/10.1016/j.knosys.2021.106827
21. Li, Y., Yao, M., Song, F., Wang, Y., Zhou, Y., Wu, S.: Building a just world: the effects of service-learning on social justice beliefs of Chinese college students. Educ. Psychol. **38**(9), 1152–1168 (2018)
22. Liang, W., Feng, R., Liu, X., Li, Q.: GLTM: a global and local word embedding-based topic model for short texts. IEEE Access **6**, 43612–43621 (2018)
23. Likhitha, S., Harish, B.S., Kumar, H.: A detailed survey on topic modeling for document and short text data. Int. J. Comput. Appl. **178**(39), 1–7 (2019)
24. Ma, H.K.C., Chan, W.F.C., Chan, C.M.A.: The long-term impact of service-learning on graduates' civic engagement and career exploration in Hong Kong. J. High. Educ. Outreach Engagem. **20**(4), 37–56 (2016)

25. Mao, X., Li, F.: Clustering of short text in micro-blog based on k-means algorithm. In: 2018 IEEE International Conference of Safety Produce Informatization (IICSPI), pp. 812–815 (2018)
26. Ngai, G., Chan, S.C.F., Kwan, K.P.: Challenge, meaning, and preparation: critical success factors influencing student learning outcomes from service-learning. J. High. Educ. Outreach Engag. **22**(4), 55–80 (2018)
27. Nguyen, D.Q., Billingsley, R., Du, L., Johnson, M.: Improving topic models with latent feature word representations. Trans. Assoc. Comput. Linguist. **3**, 299–313 (2015). https://doi.org/10.1162/tacl_a_00140
28. Peters, M.E., et al.: Deep contextualized word representations. arXiv preprint arXiv:1802.05365 (2018)
29. Pietsch, A.S., Lessmann, S.: Topic modeling for analyzing open-ended survey responses. J. Bus. Anal. **1**(2), 93–116 (2018)
30. Qiang, J., Li, Y., Yuan, Y., Wu, X.: Short text clustering based on pitman-yor process mixture model. Appl. Intell. **48**(7), 1802–1812 (2018)
31. Quan, X., Kit, C., Yong, G., Wei, B.: Short and sparse text topic modeling via self-aggregation. In: Proceedings of the 24th International Joint Conference on Artificial Intelligence, IJCAI'15, pp. 1285–1291. AAAI Press (2015)
32. Reilly, E.D., Stafford, R.E., Williams, K.M., Corliss, S.B.: Evaluating the validity and applicability of automated essay scoring in two massive open online courses. Int. Rev. Res. Open Distrib. Learn. **15**(5), 83–98 (2014)
33. Reimers, N., Gurevych, I.: Sentence-bert: sentence embeddings using siamese bert-networks. In: Proceedings of the 2019 Conference on Empirical Methods in Natural Language Processing and the 9th International Joint Conference on Natural Language Processing (EMNLP-IJCNLP), pp. 3982–3992 (2019). https://doi.org/10.18653/v1/D19-1410
34. Rivas, P., Zimmermann, M.: Empirical study of sentence embeddings for English sentences quality assessment. In: 2019 International Conference on Computational Science and Computational Intelligence (CSCI), pp. 355–360 (2019)
35. Roberts, M.E., Stewart, B.M., Tingley, D.: Structural topic models for open-ended survey responses. Am. J. Polit. Sci. **58**(4), 1064–1082 (2014). https://doi.org/10.1111/ajps.12103
36. Salam, M., Iskandar, D.N.A., Ibrahim, D.H.A., Farooq, M.S.: Service learning in higher education: a systematic literature review. Asia Pac. Educ. Rev. **20**(4), 573–593 (2019)
37. Shi, L., Cheng, G., Xie, S., Wang, Y.: A word embedding topic model for topic detection and summary in social networks. Meas. Control **52**(9–10), 1289–1298 (2019)
38. Si, X., Li, P., Hu, X., Zhang, Y.: An online Dirichlet model based on sentence embedding and dbscan for noisy short text stream clustering. In: 2022 International Joint Conference on Neural Networks (IJCNN), pp. 1–8 (2022)
39. Tee, P.L.K., Kalidas, C.S.: Positive impacts of service learning on students' personal outcome and social outcome. In: Tang, S.F., Logonnathan, L. (eds.) Assessment for Learning Within and Beyond the Classroom, pp. 211–223. Springer, Singapore (2016)
40. Trigos-Carrillo, L., Fonseca, L., Reinoso, N.: Social impact of a transformative service-learning experience in a post-conflict setting. Front. Psychol. **11**, 47 (2020). https://doi.org/10.3389/fpsyg.2020.00047
41. Wang, Y., Ren, J.: Taxi passenger hot spot mining based on a refined k-means++ algorithm. IEEE Access **9**, 66587–66598 (2021)

42. Yin, J., Wang, J.: A Dirichlet multinomial mixture model-based approach for short text clustering. In: Proceedings of the 20th ACM SIGKDD International Conference on Knowledge Discovery and Data Mining, KDD '14, pp. 233–242. ACM (2014). https://doi.org/10.1145/2623330.2623715
43. Zuo, Y., Li, C., Lin, H., Yang, Z.: Topic modeling of short texts: a pseudo-document view with word embedding enhancement. IEEE Trans. Knowl. Data Eng. **35**(3), 2738–2751 (2023)

Modeling Rater Severity Drift in Single-Rater Performance Assessments Using Bayesian Hierarchical Methods

Yuichiro Yokouchi[1(✉)], Kuangzhe Xu[2], Shuichi Takaki[1], and Haruhiko Mitsunaga[3]

[1] Fukushima University, Fukushima 960-1296, Japan
yokouchi@econ.fukushima-u.ac.jp
[2] Wuhan University of Cyber Security, Hubei 430040, China
[3] Nagoya University, Nagoya 464-8601, Japan

Abstract. Rater severity drift (RSD) is a critical challenge in performance assessments, especially when only a single rater is available. Many-facet Rasch approaches typically require multiple raters, limiting their applicability in classroom contexts where one rater scores repeated assessments over time. This study evaluates three hierarchical Bayesian models—modified formulations of Uto (2023), Usami (2010), and Yokouchi et al. (2024)—for estimating RSD from sparse longitudinal data. Using oral-summary scores from 64 Japanese university students across four time points, we assessed convergence and compared models with the widely applicable information criterion (WAIC) and leave-one-out cross-validation (LOO), posterior predictive p-values (PPP), and root-mean-square error (RMSE). All models converged satisfactorily. The Uto variant achieved the most favorable information-criterion values and the lowest RMSE in this dataset, whereas the Usami variant produced the smoothest and most interpretable severity trajectories—useful for monitoring and communication. The Yokouchi variant prioritizes simplicity, with some loss of precision. These findings show that hierarchical Bayesian frameworks can quantify temporal shifts in rater behavior under single-rater, low-information conditions, supporting quality assurance and rater development in resource-constrained educational settings.

Keywords: Item Response Theory · Many-Facet Rasch Measurement · Bayesian Hierarchical Methods · Rater Severity Drift · Single-Rater Assessment

1 Introduction

Rater severity in performance assessments including interviews, essays, scoring in sports, and music evaluations, has traditionally been examined using many-facet Rasch measurement (MFRM) [5] and its extended models such as Uto [12] and Uto & Ueno [11]. Generally, these models require two or more elements within

T. Hao et al. (Eds.): BESC 2025, LNCS 16431, pp. 435–451, 2026.
https://doi.org/10.1007/978-981-95-7138-3_28

one facet or category [6,16], and it is possible to estimate and extract specific rater severity when multiple raters are involved. However, such estimation has traditionally been considered impossible with only a single rater. In the context of English education in Japan, teachers are often burdened with a wide range of instructional responsibilities and administrative tasks, leaving them with limited time to engage in assessment practices. Therefore, in this context, such as class- or grade-level performance assessments of English writing or speaking, it is a common practice for a single teacher (rater) to score assessments. Even when intra-rater reliability is confirmed, there is no opportunity to verify whether the quality of the evaluation is high reliability does not guarantee the stability of evaluations across time. Identifying the rater severity drift (RSD) at each time point can improve the quality of assessments. We consider this a necessary improvement from the perspective of educational quality assurance because effective feedback to learners requires robust assessment.

As a first step toward solving this issue, Yokouchi et al. [18] proposed an extended model based on Uto & Ueno [11] and Uto's [12] model, estimating single rater's RSD using dummy facets and a Bayesian hierarchical model, assuming that the hierarchical Bayesian model might be more effective. The model prioritized simple structures that solely examined the effects of assessment timing and rater effects, with the aim of incorporating them into a Shiny application to plot the RSD, designed to be accessible to teachers without statistical expertise. We expected that this would facilitate the verification of accurate evaluation results in educational or personnel contexts. However, because of the overly simplistic nature of the models which incorporates only the rater $\times$ time-point interaction, it was found that the results tended to be unstable. Indeed, the study found no clear differences in model performance—based on indices such as the widely applicable information criterion (WAIC), root-mean-square error (RMSE), and posterior predictive p-values (ppp-values)—between the model using two types of dummy facets and the hierarchical Bayesian model. Therefore, it was concluded that further model refinement is necessary, considering the more advanced models used in previous studies.

This study examined whether severity drift can be estimated in a situation with only one fixed rater, using a model that combines a Bayesian hierarchical model and the model proposed by Usami [15], which extends the generalized partial credit model (GPCM). In addition, we examined whether it is possible to similarly estimate severity by setting the rater facet to one in Uto's model [12]. This study aims to identify a more effective approach for monitoring rater severity drift (RSD) in single rater settings by comparing these two models that incorporate a hierarchical Bayesian framework with a variant of the Yokouchi et al. model [18], which likewise employs a hierarchical Bayesian method.

- RQ1: Do these models adequately estimate RSD?
- RQ2: Which of the three proposed models provides the most stable observation of a single rater's RSD?

2 Literature Review

2.1 Models of Estimation for Rater Severity and Application of Bayesian Models for Item Response Theory Including Many Facet Rasch Model

Traditional models such as the MFRM [5,6] require two or more observed data points within a single facet for proper estimation. As a result, it is generally considered impossible to assess the intra-rater reliability or RSD when only one rater is involved. This limitation also applies to various extensions of the item response theory (IRT), including the models proposed by Usami [15], Uto & Ueno [11], and Uto [12]. Because these models rely on the maximum likelihood estimation (MLE), parameter identification becomes infeasible in low-information settings where data sparsity prevails.

Bayesian estimation offers a potential solution. By incorporating prior distributions or employing hierarchical Bayesian models, it becomes feasible to model temporal variations in rater severity, even in the case of a single rater. Uto [12] developed a Bayesian model that incorporates Markov chain Monte Carlo (MCMC) techniques to account for the severity drift, demonstrating that hierarchical parameter estimation across items and assessment occasions can successfully capture individual rater characteristics in sequential scoring contexts. Prior research utilizing hierarchical structures includes the hierarchical rater model (HRM) by Patz et al. [14] and its extensions by Mariano and Junker [8], which build upon the GPCM. These models allow the estimation of both rater severity and response-style tendencies, such as centrality or extremity bias.

The present study focuses on modeling the temporal dynamics of rater severity, an aspect less explored in prior HRM-based research. In situations where data are sparse, such as with a single fixed rater, hierarchical Bayesian modeling enables the use of priors to improve parameter identifiability. This is particularly important for hyperparameters governing severity drift (e.g.,σ_r), which should be assigned to carefully selected weakly informative priors to avoid overfitting and to facilitate stable inference. For guidance on prior specifications, especially under small-sample conditions, the works of Gelman et al. [1] and Goldstein [4] are particularly informative.

The use of hierarchical Bayesian models in time-series analysis is increasingly common, particularly in small-sample scenarios (Gelman et al. [1] p. 131). For clarity, we use "hierarchical Bayesian model" to denote the estimation framework (multilevel priors/partial pooling), whereas the Hierarchical Rater Model (HRM) refers to a specific measurement model for examinees-raters-items; in this paper, HRMs are fit within the hierarchical Bayesian framework. Patz et al. [14] demonstrated how such models can stabilize estimations in settings characterized by a *rater* × *time* × *item* data structure, similar to that used in the present study. As they note, "A hierarchical model provides a flexible framework for modeling examinees, raters, and tasks over multiple occasions.... The resulting shrinkage improves estimation when there are relatively few ratings per rater." (p. 389). Curran et al. [13] also advocated for hierarchical Bayesian approaches when modeling intra-individual variation in repeated-measures data (p. 249).

Among the prior studies, Usami [15] employed log-normal and normal priors for parameters including discrimination (α), difficulty (δ), threshold (τ), severity (β), and ability (θ) in an extended GPCM framework. Similarly, Uto & Ueno [11] adopted weakly informative log-normal and normal priors for GPCM discrimination/difficulty parameters as well as rater facets. Uto [12] emphasized that in single rater contexts, proper prior selection is crucial for estimating severity drift, specifically advocating for a log-normal prior on σ_r, which governs the extent of drift. This approach facilitates the flexible modeling of the drift magnitude while preventing overfitting and ensuring a smoother posterior convergence.

In light of these considerations, the present study adopted a hierarchical Bayesian modeling approach to estimate the RSD, taking advantage of its suitability for modeling time-series data and achieving stable parameter estimation even under limited data conditions.

2.2 Item Response Model for Observing Rater Severity

Most of these studies used MFRM, often estimating the severity of each rater as points [5] :

$$\log\left(\frac{P_{n,m,i,j,k}}{P_{n,m,i,j,k-1}}\right) = B_n - A_m - D_i - C_j - F_k \tag{1}$$

where

B_n: ability of examinee n,
A_m: difficulty of task m,
D_i: difficulty of skill item i,
C_j: severity of judge j,
F_k: difficulty of category k relative to category $k-1$,
$P_{n,m,i,j,k}$: probability of rating k under these circumstances,
$P_{n,m,i,j,k-1}$: probability of rating $k-1$.

However, this model does not adequately detect or exclude biases and cannot fully capture rater characteristics (Uto [12], pp. 111–112). The generalized MFRM proposed by Uto & Ueno [11] solved these issues.

$$P_{ijrk} = \frac{\exp\sum_{m=1}^{k}[\alpha_r\alpha_i(\theta_j - \beta_i - \beta_r - d_{rm})]}{\sum_{l=1}^{K}\exp\sum_{m=1}^{l}[\alpha_r\alpha_i(\theta_j - \beta_i - \beta_r - d_{rm})]} \tag{2}$$

Indices and priors are summarized in Table 1.

Indexing note: For Uto/Ueno-style cumulative logits we use $m = 1\ldots k$, $l = 1\ldots K$; for Usami-style cumulative categories we use $m = 0\ldots k$, $l = 0\ldots K-1$ as in the original formulations.

The model described above serves as the foundation of the present study and forms the basis of the model proposed by Yokouchi et al. [18], which will

Table 1. Notation and Parameter Definitions

Symbol	Meaning	Index/Domain	Prior/Constraint	Notes
i	Item/Task index (Eq. 4: Examinee index)	$i \in \mathbb{Z}^+, 1..I$		Observed facet
j	Examinee/Person index (Eq. 4: Item index)	$j \in \mathbb{Z}^+, 1..J$		Observed facet
r	Rater index	$r = 1$		Single rater (fixed individual)
t	Time point (occasion)	$t \in \mathbb{Z}^+, 1..T$	$T = 4$ in this study	
k	Score category	$k \in \mathbb{Z}^+, 1..K$	K categories; $K-1$ thresholds	
m, l	Cumulative category indices	$m, l \in \mathbb{Z}^+$		Used in sums over categories
n	Observation index	$n = 1..N$		
y_n	Observed category/response	$y_n \in \{1, \ldots, K\}$		
p	Interaction term index	$p = 1..4$		
s	Covariate index	$s \in \mathbb{Z}^+$		If covariates are used
θ_j	Ability of examinee j	$\theta_j \in \mathbb{R}$	$\theta_j \sim \text{Normal}(0, 1)$	
β_t	Time-specific rater severity (drift)	$\beta_t \in \mathbb{R}$	$\beta_t \mid \beta_{t-1} \sim \text{Normal}(\beta_{t-1}, \sigma_{rw})$; $\sigma_{rw} \sim \text{LogNormal}(-1, 1)$	Random-walk drift
β_i	Item bias/difficulty (if used)	$\beta_i \in \mathbb{R}$	$\beta_i \sim \text{Normal}(0, 1)$	
δ_j, δ_r	Person/Item location (Usami form uses δ_j, δ_r)	$\delta_j \in \mathbb{R}$	$\delta_j \sim \text{Normal}(0, 1)$	Model-dependent role
α_i, α_r	Discrimination/consistency (item/rater)	$\alpha_i, \alpha_r \in \mathbb{R}^+$	$\alpha_i, \alpha_r \sim \text{LogNormal}(0, 0.5)$	Positive; product/sum constraints for ID
d_m	Global category thresholds	$d_m \in \mathbb{R}, m = 1..K-1$	$d_1 < d_2 < \cdots < d_{K-1}$	Uto/Yokouchi-style
τ_{jm}	Person-specific thresholds	$\tau_{jm} \in \mathbb{R}, m = 1..K-1$	$\tau_{j1} = 0$; $\sum_{m=1}^{K-1} \tau_{jm} = 0$	Usami-style constraints
γ_p	Interaction coefficients	$\gamma_p \in \mathbb{R}$	$\gamma_p \sim \text{Normal}(0, 0.5)$	p indexes interaction terms
D	Scaling constant	$D \in \mathbb{R}^+$	$D = 1.7$	Link scaling
$P(\cdot)$	Response probability	$P \in (0, 1)$	$\sum_k P(\ldots, k) = 1$	Multinomial over categories

Domain conventions: $\mathbb{R}$ = real numbers; $\mathbb{R}^+$ = positive reals; $\mathbb{Z}^+$ = positive integers.

be discussed later. While the estimation of β_{rt} remains a shared objective of this study, it is ultimately revised to the form β_t in accordance with the aim of constructing a single rater model.

The interpretation of severity drift, the focus of this study, can be performed using β_{rt}. Uto [12] proposed a model incorporating temporal characteristics into the MFRM.

$$P_{ijrk} = \frac{\exp \sum_{m=1}^{k} [D(\theta_j - \beta_{rt} - d_m)]}{\sum_{l=1}^{K} \exp \sum_{m=1}^{l} [D(\theta_j - \beta_{rt} - d_m)]} \tag{3}$$

β_{rt}: time-specific severity parameter for rater r at time t,
d_m: threshold parameter for category m
Priors:
$\theta_j \sim N(0,1)$
$d_m \sim N(0,1)$
$\beta_{r1} \sim N(0,1)$
$\beta_{rt} \sim N(\beta_{r,t-1}, \sigma_r), t = 2 \ldots T$
$\sigma_r \sim LogNormal(\mu, 1)$
σ_r: rater-specific SD for Markov random walk
μ: hyperparameter (e.g., -2)
Identification constraints: $d_1 = 0, \sum_{m=1}^{K} d_m = 0$

The next section discusses Usami [15]. This study focused on Usami's work because it allows the separation of rater consistency (α_r) and item discrimination (δ_j), enabling the modeling of rater characteristics by incorporating factors beyond severity.

$$P_{jrk}(\theta_i) = \frac{\exp[\alpha_{jr}(k(\theta_i - \delta_{jr}) - \sum_{m=0}^{k} \tau_{jmr})]}{\sum_{l=1}^{K-1} \exp[\alpha_{jr}(l(\theta_i - \delta_{jr}) - \sum_{m=0}^{l} \tau_{jmr})]]} \tag{4}$$

$$\alpha_{jr} = \alpha_j \alpha_r \tag{5}$$

$$\delta_{jr} = \delta_j + \delta_r \tag{6}$$

$$\tau_{jmr} = \tau_{jm} \tau_r \tag{7}$$

$$\theta_i = \sum_{s}^{S} \beta_s Z_{is} + \theta_i * \tag{8}$$

where,

s: covariate index,
$P_{jrk}(\theta_i)$: probability that rater r assigns score k to examinee i on item j,
α_{jr}: discrimination for item j and rater r,
α_j: discrimination for item j,
α_r: discrimination for rater r,
δ_{jr}: difficulty for item j and rater r,
δ_j: difficulty for item j,

δ_r: severity (bias) parameter for rater r,
τ_{jmr}: threshold for item j, category m, rater r,
τ_{jm}: threshold for item j, category m,
τ_r: threshold scaling parameter for rater r,
θ_i: ability for examinee i (with covariates),
Z_{is}: covariate s value for examinee i,
β_s: regression coefficient for covariate s,
θ_i*: residual ability of examinee i (after accounting for covariates)

Typical identifiability constraints:

$\sum_{m=0}^{K-1} \tau_{jm} = 0; \tau_{j0} = 0$ for all j

$\prod_{r=1}^{R} \alpha_r = 1; \sum_{r=1}^{R} \delta_r = 0; \prod_{r=1}^{R} \tau_r = 1$

$\sum_{i=1}^{N} \theta_i* = 0; \sum_{i=1}^{N} Z_{is}\theta_i* = 0$ for all s

Priors:
$\delta_j \sim N(\mu_\delta, \sigma^2_{\delta j}), \delta_r \sim N(0, \sigma^2_{\delta r})$
$\beta_s \sim N(\mu_\beta, \sigma^2_\beta), \theta_i* \sim N(0, \sigma^2_\theta)$

In Usami [15], the hyperparameters μ_α, μ_δ, μ_τ, μ_β, $\alpha^2_{\alpha_j}$, $\sigma^2_{\alpha_r}$, $\sigma^2_{\delta_j}$, $\sigma^2_{\delta_r}$, $\sigma^2_{\tau_{jm}}$, $\sigma^2_{\tau_r}$, σ^2_β, and σ^2_θ are all set a priori as user-specified values ("hyperparameters") and are not fixed in the paper.

The specific values should be chosen by the analyst according to modeling needs (e.g., based on weakly informative, noninformative, or expert-informed choices).

For parameter identifiability, the following constraints were imposed [15].
For rater-related parameters:
$\prod_r \alpha_r = 1, \sum_r \delta_r - 0, \prod_r \tau_r - 1$
For examinee abilities:
$\sum_i \theta_i = 0, \sum_i \theta_i^2 = 1$
For covariate-adjusted abilities:
$\sum_i \theta_i* = 0, \sum_i Z_{is}\theta_i* = 0$ for each covariate s.

A notable advantage of Usami's model (Eq. 4) is its capacity to incorporate covariate-adjusted latent ability and structured rater-item interactions without imposing undue restrictions on parameter flexibility. By allowing discrimination, severity, and threshold parameters to be rater-dependent—while simultaneously modeling examinee ability as a function of covariates—this framework facilitates nuanced inference in settings where both examinee heterogeneity and rater subjectivity are influential.

Furthermore, the multiplicative structure imposed on the discrimination ($\alpha_{jr} = \alpha_j\alpha_r$) and threshold ($\tau_{jmr} = \tau_{jm}\tau_r$) parameters contributes to model parsimony while preserving interpretability. This hierarchical factorization enables the partial pooling of information across raters and items, which is particularly beneficial when certain raters or items are associated with sparse response patterns.

The identifiability constraints applied to the model are also methodologically elegant. They ensure parameter estimability without requiring overly strong priors or post hoc adjustments, thus facilitating stable posterior inference under Bayesian estimation. The inclusion of covariate-adjusted ability via a linear predictor allows researchers to explicitly control for background variables (e.g., demographic or instructional factors), yielding ability estimates that are less confounded by external influences.

In practical applications, such as large-scale writing assessments or multi-rater oral proficiency testing, these features collectively enhance the utility of the model. Specifically, the framework supports fairer comparisons across examinees by accounting for systematic rater variability, while also enabling detailed diagnostics of item functioning and rater behavior. This dual capacity—capturing both psychometric structure and rater dynamics—positions the model as a powerful tool for rater-mediated assessments in educational and psychological measurement contexts.

Generally, when using MFRM, appropriate analysis is impossible if there are not two or more observations per facet [6]. Therefore, observing intra-rater reliability or severity drift for a single rater is not possible, which is similarly true for extended models of IRT other than MFRM [11, 12, 15]. Because the MLE is used in models including MFRM, frequency-based parameter calculations and outputs are not feasible. However, Bayesian estimation allows the modeling of severity drift over time using prior distributions or hierarchical Bayesian models. Uto [12] developed a Bayesian model applying MCMC considering the severity drift, claiming that hierarchical parameter estimation captures rater-specific characteristics when a single rater sequentially evaluates multiple items. Examples of studies using hierarchical models include the HRM by Patz et al. [14] and the extended HRM (essentially GPCM-based) model by Mariano and Junker [8]. These models emphasize severity parameters, observing severity biases (centralization/extremization) and focusing on temporal severity fluctuations.

In hierarchical Bayesian modeling, when observational data are limited, such as in the single-rater scenario addressed in this study, prior distributions should be complementary to improve the parameter identifiability for weakly informative data structures. Choosing prior distributions, especially for hierarchical parameters representing the RSD, is critical to avoid overfitting and ensure smooth estimation. Gelman et al. [1] discussed the role of weakly informative priors in hierarchical Bayesian models. Goldstein [4] provided information about stabilizing estimations in small-sample hierarchical models. Previous models, such as Usami [15] and Uto and Ueno [11], used log-normal and normal distributions as priors. Specifically, Uto [12] recommended log-normal distributions for hierarchical parameters controlling drift because they flexibly represent drift magnitudes while preventing overfitting. Using hierarchical Bayesian models is common for time-series data analysis, offering stable parameter estimations even with small-sample sizes [1, 13].

3 Model Modifications

First, this study proposes a modification to Uto's model [12] directly relevant for single rater contexts.

$$P_{jtk} = \frac{\exp(kD[\theta_j - \beta_t + \sum_{p=1}^{4} \gamma_p \cdot \text{inter}_{pn}] - \sum_{m=1}^{k} Dd_m)}{\sum_{l=1}^{K} \exp(lD[\theta_j - \beta_t + \sum_{p=1}^{4} \gamma_p \cdot \text{inter}_{pn}] - \sum_{m=1}^{l} Dd_m)} \tag{9}$$

where,

γ_p: regression coefficient of the pth interaction term (estimated parameter)
inter_{pn}: interaction term for each observation n (e.g., $\text{inter}_{1n} = person \times time$).
Priors for the parameters in this modified model are set as follows:
$\theta_j \sim N(0, 1)$
$d_m \sim N(0, 1)$
$\beta_1 \sim N(\mu_\beta, \sigma_\beta), \beta_t \sim N(\beta_{t-1}, \sigma_{rw})$, for $t = 2 \dots T$

These priors ensure model identifiability and facilitate the stable estimation of severity drift, specifically in single-rater contexts. The severity drift β_t is modeled as a random walk, where each time point's severity parameter is drawn from a normal distribution centered on the previous time point. This approach allows for smooth yet flexible temporal changes, capturing realistic fluctuations in rater severity. It should be noted that, although β_{rt} was used in the original formulation, β_t is employed in the present study. This is because the rater is fixed to a single individual, making it possible to explain the variation using β_t alone. The interaction terms $interp_n$ are standardized continuous variables constructed for each observation, such as $inter1 = person \times time$ and $inter2 = person \times category$. $Person \times time$ interactions were included to control for individual differences in temporal performance trends. The $rater \times time$ interaction effect was not explicitly modeled because the current model targets a single-rater scenario. In this context, the time-specific severity drift parameter β_t fully captures all rater $\times$ time effects. Therefore, the explicit inclusion of a $rater \times time$ interaction term is unnecessary and may introduce redundancy or identifiability issues. $LogNormal(-1, 1)$ was chosen as a weakly informative prior for σ_{rw} to avoid overfitting (Gelman et al., [1]), ensuring stable estimation of the temporal drift variance. Next, we introduce a modified version of Usami's (2010) model.

$$P_{ijtk} = \frac{\exp\left(k\left[\theta_i - \delta_j - \beta_t + \sum_{p=1}^{4} \gamma_p \cdot \text{inter}_{pn}\right] - \sum_{m=1}^{k} \tau_{jm}\right)}{\sum_{l=1}^{K} \exp\left(l\left[\theta_i - \delta_j - \beta_t + \sum_{p=1}^{4} \gamma_p \cdot \text{inter}_{pn}\right] - \sum_{m=1}^{l} \tau_{jm}\right)} \tag{10}$$

$$\sum_{p=1}^{4} \gamma_p \cdot \text{inter}_{pn} = \gamma_1 \cdot \text{inter}_{1n} + \gamma_2 \cdot \text{inter}_{2n} + \gamma_3 \cdot \text{inter}_{3n} + \gamma_4 \tag{11}$$

K: number of categories,
δ_j: difficulty of item j,
γ_p: regression coefficient of the pth interaction term (estimated parameter)
inter$_{pn}$: interaction term for each observation n (e.g., inter$_{1n}$ $= person \times time$).

The log-likelihood across all observations is given by:
$\log L = \sum_{n=1}^{N} \log P_{ijt\gamma}^{(n)}$
Here, $\log P_{ijkl}^{(n)}$ denotes the modeled probability of the observed category y_n for the n-th record. The superscript (n) is used only in this equation to indicate the n-th observation. P_{ijkl} for the n-th observation.
Additional constraints for identifiability:
$\tau_{j1} = 0, \sum_{m=1}^{k} \tau_{jm} = 0$
It was determined that it would be more appropriate to represent the relationships between item and rater, item and time point, and rater and time point as interpretable parameters within the model.

We describe the model proposed by Yokouchi et al. [18]. This model is fundamentally based on model (Eq. 2) by Uto and Ueno [11], and consists of three variations: (i) a model with a shared dummy facet, (ii) a model incorporating a randomly generated gender dummy facet, and (iii) a model that includes a hierarchical structure, expressed in (Eq. 12) below. Notably, the model assumes a single rater and does not account for parameter category thresholds. Among the three proposed models, the qualities of each were not significantly different, and the hierarchical model tended to demonstrate the most stable performance. Therefore, it was selected as a benchmark for comparison in the present study, which also proposes new models incorporating hierarchical structures.

$$P_{jitk} = \frac{\exp\{D \cdot \alpha_t \cdot \alpha_i[k(\theta_j - \beta_t) - \beta_i - \kappa_k]\}}{\sum_{l=0}^{K-1} \exp\{D \cdot \alpha_t \cdot \alpha_i[l(\theta_j - \beta_t) - \beta_i - \kappa_l]\}} \tag{12}$$

where:

α_t: time-specific discrimination (scaling),
α_i: *examinee* $\times$ *time* discrimination (scaling),
β_t: time-specific drift parameter,
β_i: *examinee* $\times$ *time* bias,
κ_k: cumulative threshold parameter for category k, ($\kappa_0 = 0$, remaining thresholds are learned/estimated)

4 Method

4.1 Data Used in This Estimation—Persons (Students)

The data used in this study were the same as those used by Yokouchi [19]. Details are provided in the following section.

The participants of this study were 64 Japanese learners of English, all undergraduate students. They majored in various fields such as humanities, pedagogy, science, agriculture, nursing, and healthcare provider. All participants were first-year students (age 18–19); therefore, they have learned English for at least six years in junior and senior high school. In addition, they experienced foreign language activities in the fifth and sixth year of elementary school. Their English proficiency was measured using the Visualizing English Language Competency Test®. The results were $M = 499.59, SD = 2.81$, and 95%CI = [498.95, 500.24], indicating that their estimated Test of English for International Communication (TOEIC) score was $M = 464.47, SD = 16.40$, and 95%CI = [460.73, 468.22].

The assessment occasions were structured into four equally divided time segments. These data can be considered as real temporal sequence data.

4.2 Rater's Information

The raters involved in this study were two professional English teachers and four undergraduate students who wanted to be English teachers. In this study, a single rater's RSD was estimated; therefore, we focused on the rating performance of one good student rater. The student rater was a senior at the Department of Humanities who majored in Oceanian cultures. Her English proficiency was sufficiently high, her TOEIC score was 950, and she had more than one year of overseas experience.

4.3 Tasks and Rubric

In this study, oral summary tasks were assigned. Students read the stimulus within 5 min and provided the summary within 2 min. If time remained, the participants were allowed to share their opinions about the stimulus.

The rubric used in this study is the same one of Yokouchi's [19] supplementary, grid style rating scale. The constructs of the rubric were related to speech contents, such as the use of discourse markers and appropriate use of paraphrasing. The scores ranged from zero to four. Grammatical and phonetic errors were not considered in the evaluation. Because a score of zero is incompatible with Stan's modeling requirements, all scores were incremented by one prior to the analysis.

4.4 Analysis

Using the bias analysis of the MFRM (Linacre [5]), we compared the values obtained from the $time \times rater$ facet, the values of β_t from the modified models of Uto [12] and Usami [15], values of β_t obtained using Yokouchi et al.'s [18] model, model fit indices (WAIC, leave-one-out cross-validation (LOO), PPP-value), and RMSE to determine the most analytically suitable model. The analysis based on Linacre [5] was conducted using Facets version 3.87.0. For the remaining models, analyses were performed in RStudio using RStan. The number of iterations was set to 4,000 (with 2,000 warm-up iterations), using four chains, a random seed of 123, and an adapt_delta value of 0.99. Convergence was confirmed with Rhat < 1.1 for all parameters and median effective sample sizes (ESS) > 1000 per parameter (modified Uto's model: 15406.87, modified Usami's model: 6733.537, modified Yokouchi et al.'s model: 8383.087).

The dataset used in this study was the same as that of Yokouchi [19]. The reuse of this data was allowed for other studies by the committee of research ethics of Hirosaki University, where the first author was formerly affiliated and the guideline for the Agreement on Experimental and Survey Research Involving Human Subjects That Does Not Require Ethical Review at Fukushima University.

5 Results and Discussion

5.1 Summary of Model Performance

Three hierarchical Bayesian models—modified versions of Uto [12], Usami [15], and Yokouchi et al. [18]—were compared in terms of their capability to estimate the RSD in a single-rater, longitudinal assessment setting. Convergence diagnostics indicated satisfactory performance across all models, with $\hat{R}$ (Rhat) values < 1.1 and median ESS exceeding 1000, ensuring reliable posterior sampling.

The model fit statistics were evaluated using WAIC, LOO, PPP, and RMSE (Table 1 and Figs. 2 and 3). Using WAIC/LOO (smaller is better), the Uto variant attained the lowest values in this dataset (WAIC = 177.0; LOO = 181.8), followed by the Yokouchi variant (WAIC = 300.4; LOO = 313.0) and the Usami variant (WAIC = 313.0; LOO = 318.4). PPP values ranged from 0.41 to 0.62 and were broadly acceptable across models. While RMSE favored the Uto variant (0.30), the Usami variant produced the smoothest and most interpretable severity trajectories (Fig. 1). The Yokouchi variant was simpler to implement but showed comparatively lower predictive performance in this sample.

5.2 Estimates of Rater Severity Drift (β_t)

Figure 1 displays the posterior mean estimates of β_t representing rater severity at each of the four assessment points. All three models revealed an increasing trend in severity over time, consistent with prior findings in rater behavior research [2,12,16]. Notably, the Usami-based model produced the most stable and interpretable trajectory, likely because of the multiplicative parameterization that encourages partial pooling across the rater and item dimensions [15].

In contrast, the modified Uto model included interaction terms (e.g., $person \times time$) that resulted in slight volatility at intermediate time points, reflecting individual performance fluctuations [12]. The Yokouchi model exhibited higher posterior uncertainty and less coherent drift patterns, which is potentially attributable to its dummy facet simplification [18] (Table 2).

Table 2. β_t of each time point and model fitting indices

Model	T1	T2	T3	T4	WAIC	LOO	PPP	RMSE
Linacre	0.43	−0.36	0.38	0.33				
Uto	−2.02	-0.76	0.52	1.14	177.0	181.8	0.62	0.30
Usami	−0.26	−0.36	−0.29	−0.26	313.0	318.4	0.41	0.61
Yokouchi	−0.23	−0.43	−0.13	−0.05	300.4	313.0	0.47	0.64

Note: T1-T4 means $Time1 - 4$. Linacre model was analyzed using Facets 3.87.0; therefore, no information on WAIC, LOO, PPP-value, and RMSE are provided.

5.3 Predictive Accuracy and Information Criteria

Figure 2 summarizes WAIC/LOO (smaller is better), and Fig. 3 reports RMSE (lower is better) and PPP (higher is better). In this dataset, Uto scored best on information-criterion metrics and RMSE; PPP values were in acceptable ranges overall, with the Usami model slightly lower but still adequate. Taken together with the smoother β_t trajectory of Usami (Fig. 1), these results suggest a trade-off between parsimony/interpretability (Usami) and predictive fit (Uto), whereas the Yokouchi variant prioritizes simplicity at the expense of precision.

These findings are congruent with the literature on Bayesian modeling in educational measurement, which emphasizes the advantage of incorporating structured prior distributions and hierarchical parameterization into sparse-data contexts [1,13].

5.4 Interpretability and Practical Implications

From a practical standpoint, the Usami-based model offers clearer interpretability, particularly with respect to RSD visualization. The factorized structure of $\alpha_{jr} = \alpha_j \alpha_r$ and $\tau_{jmr} = \tau_{jm} \tau_r$ [15] yields semantically meaningful components (item and rater consistency), which facilitates actionable feedback in educational applications, such as identifying when a rater becomes excessively stringent.

The Uto model's inclusion of temporal interaction terms allows the modeling of complex cross-level dynamics, although this comes at the cost of greater model complexity and reduced transparency for practitioners [12]. The simplicity of the Yokouchi model, designed for implementation in Shiny-based applications, makes it appealing for classroom or administrative use, albeit with limited precision [18].

5.5 Theoretical and Methodological Contributions

This study extends the growing body of research on rater modeling in performance assessments by demonstrating that RSD can be robustly estimated in single-rater contexts using hierarchical Bayesian techniques [10,14]. Previous models such as the HRM [14] and generalized MFRM [7,11] generally assume

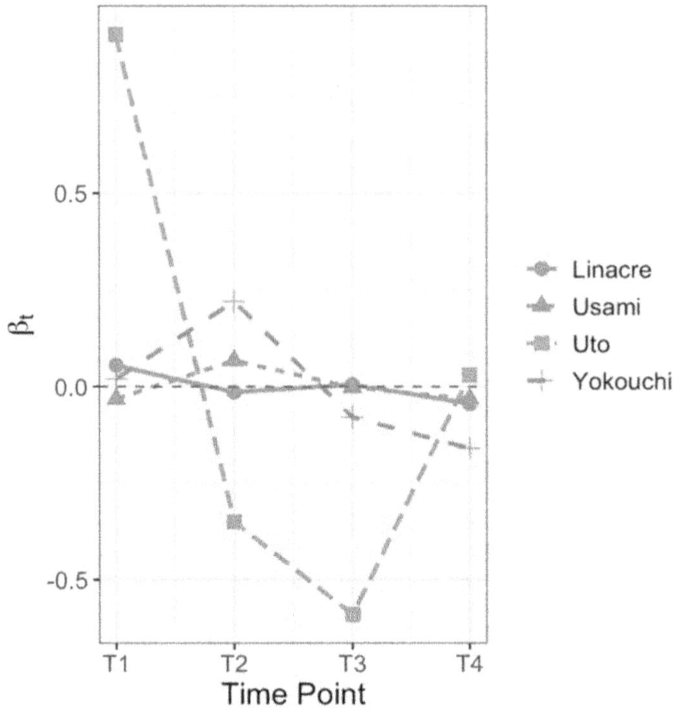

Fig. 1. Plots of β_t on each time point.

multiple raters. However, our findings show that combining Bayesian priors with longitudinal data structures can overcome such limitations.

The Usami model's capacity to estimate covariate-adjusted ability and distinguish between item difficulty and rater severity—concepts previously addressed by Patz et al. [14] and Sakamoto et al. [7]—highlights its flexibility. Moreover, the observed shrinkage behavior, resulting from the hierarchical priors, aligns with the stabilizing effects reported in [1] and [13].

5.6 Limitations and Directions for Future Work

The study uses one rater ($N = 1$), 64 examinees, and four time points, which limits generalizability and temporal resolution. Longer panels would better distinguish gradual vs. abrupt drift; multi rater extensions with partial pooling would further enhance robustness. Future work should examine AR(1) (first-order autoregressive) or change-point priors for β_t, prior-sensitivity for σ_{rw}, and small simulations matched to the observed sparsity. Here, AR(1) denotes a first-order autoregressive drift prior, $\beta_t = \rho\beta_{t-1} + \eta_t$, $\eta_t \sim N(0, \sigma_\eta^2)$, $|\rho| < 1$, where ρ controls mean-reversion (the random walk is recovered when $\rho = 1$). Beyond the present task, the same framework transfers to single /low rater settings in workplace appraisal, clinical tele assessment, content moderation, and adjudicated

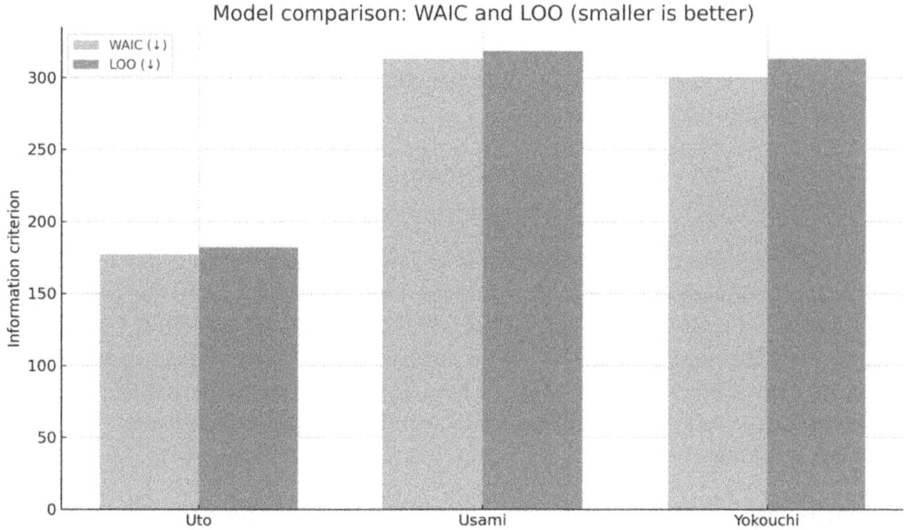

Fig. 2. Predictive accuracy (RMSE, lower is better) and posterior predictive p-values (PPP, higher is better). *Information criteria: In this dataset, the Uto variant attains the lowest WAIC and LOO values (smaller is better), indicating the strongest performance on information-criterion metrics. Despite this, the Usami variant remains attractive for practice due to its smoother severity trajectories and interpretable factorization structure.*

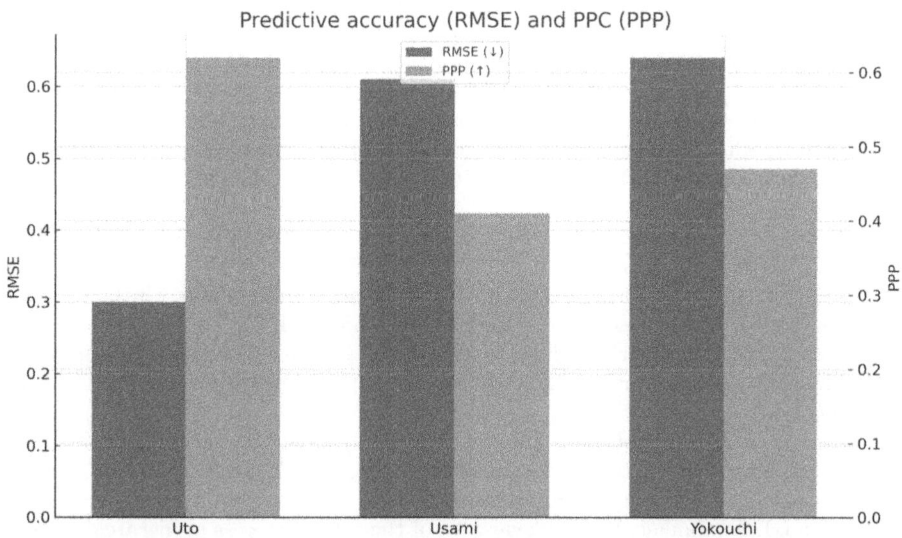

Fig. 3. Model comparison using WAIC and LOO (smaller is better). *Predictive checks: Posterior predictive p-values are acceptable for Uto and Yokouchi, while the Usami model's PPP is slightly lower in this sample. RMSE favors Uto; however, considering trajectory smoothness and interpretability alongside fit, Usami remains a competitive choice for formative monitoring of single-rater drift.*

crowdsourcing; here β_t encodes adjudicator calibration, θ denotes latent quality, and thresholds/discrimination capture domain sensitivity. Incorporating contextual covariates (stakes, workload/shift length, feedback exposure) may improve actionable diagnostics and fairness.

6 Conclusion

Bayesian hierarchical models can estimate single-rater severity drift from sparse longitudinal assessments. In our dataset, the Uto variant achieved the most favorable information-criterion values and predictive checks, whereas the Usami variant provided the smoothest, most interpretable drift trajectories—often critical for deployment and communication. These results support the use of hierarchical Bayesian frameworks for rater monitoring and quality assurance in under-resourced contexts.

Acknowledgment. This study was supported by JSPS KAKENHI (Grant Number JP24K00079). ChatGPT was utilized as a substitute for English proofreading services. It was also used to format code written in R and Stan.

References

1. Gelman, A., Carlin, J.B., Stern, H.S., Dunson, D.B., Vehtari, A., Rubin, D.B.: Bayesian Data Analysis, 3rd edn., p. 131. CRC Press, Boca Raton (2013)
2. Han, C.: Investigating rater severity and leniency in interpreter performance assessment. Interpreting **17**(2), 255–283 (2015). https://doi.org/10.1075/intp.17.2.05han
3. Hiğde, E., Demirci, S., Yıldırım, Z.: Evaluating laboratory activities using multi-faceted Rasch measurement analysis: a case study in science education. Eurasia J. Math. Sci. Technol. Educ. **19**(2), 1–16 (2023). https://doi.org/10.29333/ejmste/12900
4. Goldstein, H.: Multilevel statistical models. J. Roy. Statist. Soc. A **168**(1), 252–253 (2003). https://doi.org/10.1111/j.1467-985X.2004.00347_5.x
5. Linacre, J.M.: Many-Faceted Rasch Measurement. MESA Press, Chicago (1989). https://www.winsteps.com/a/Linacre-MFRM-book.pdf
6. Linacre, J.M.: A User's Guide to FACETS (64-bit) Rasch-Model Computer Programs Program Manual 4.3.3 (2025). https://www.winsteps.com/a/Facets64-Manual.pdf
7. Sakamoto, K., Yamamoto, H., Aoki, S.: An item response theory model considering rater severity and item interaction effects. PLoS ONE **18**(8), e0309887 (2023). https://doi.org/10.1371/journal.pone.0309887
8. Mariano, L.T., Junker, B.W.: Covariates of the rating process in hierarchical models for multiple ratings of test items. J. Educ. Behav. Stat. **32**(3), 287–314 (2016). https://doi.org/10.3102/1076998606298033
9. Noh, M.F.M., Matore, M.E.E.M.: Rating performance among raters of different experience through multi-facet rasch measurement (MFRM) model. J. Meas. Eval. Educ. Psychol. **11**(2), 147–162 (2020). https://doi.org/10.36349/EASJEHL.2020.v03i05.001

10. Uto, M., Ueno, M.: A review of item response models for performance assessment. Jpn. J. Res. Test. **12**(1), 55–75 (2016). https://doi.org/10.24690/jart.12.1_55
11. Uto, M., Ueno, M.: A generalized many-facet Rasch model and its Bayesian estimation using Hamiltonian Monte Carlo. Behaviormetrika **47**(2), 469–496 (2020). https://doi.org/10.1007/s41237-020-00115-7
12. Uto, M.: A Bayesian many-facet Rasch model with Markov modeling for rater severity drift. Behav. Res. Methods **55**(7), 3910–3928 (2023). https://doi.org/10.3758/s13428-022-01997-z
13. Curran, P.J., Lee, T., Howard, A.L., Lane, S.T., MacCallum, R.C.: Disaggregating within-person and between-person effects in longitudinal models using multilevel modeling and structural equation modeling. Psychol. Methods **15**(3), 247–262 (2010). https://doi.org/10.1037/a0019620
14. Patz, R.J., Junker, B.W., Johnson, M.S., Mariano, L.T.: The hierarchical rater model for rated test items and its application to large-scale educational assessment data. J. Educ. Behav. Stat. **27**(4), 341–384 (2002). https://doi.org/10.3102/10769986027004341
15. Usami, S.: A polytomous item response model that simultaneously considers bias factors of raters and examinees: estimation through a Markov Chain Monte Carlo algorithm. Jpn. J. Educ. Psychol. **58**(2), 163–175 (2010). https://doi.org/10.5926/jjep.58.163
16. Eckes, T., Jin, K.-Y.: Examining severity and centrality effects in TestDaF writing and speaking assessments: an extended Bayesian many-facet Rasch analysis. Int. J. Test. **21**(3–4), 131–153 (2021). https://doi.org/10.1080/15305058.2021.1963260
17. Wang, X., Yang, J., Liu, R.: Development of a differential index for evaluating rater ability in educational assessments using generalized multi-facet models. arXiv preprint arXiv:2502.09099 (2025)
18. Yokouchi, Y., Takaki, S., Xu, K.: Model development to examine the rater severity drift for single rater: proposal for a new model based on many-facet Rasch model. In: 19th Pacific Rim Objective Measurement Symposium (PROMS 2024), Kuala Lumpur, Malaysia (2024). https://proms2024.promsociety.org/
19. Yokouchi, Y.: Revisiting the effectiveness of a performance decision tree-style rubric compared to a grid-style rubric. Lang. Test. Asia **15**, 8 (2025). https://doi.org/10.1186/s40468-024-00338-5

Continuous Sub-sequence Denoising For Sequential Recommendation

Siying Wang(✉), Rui Chen, Dan Lu, Chi Zhang, Yantong Du, and Qilong Han

Harbin Engineering University, Harbin, China
{wangsiying,ruichen,ludan,zhangchi20,duyantong94,hanqilong}@hrbeu.edu.cn

Abstract. Sequential Recommendation Systems aim to utilize past interaction behaviors to model user interests and predict their next potential interaction item. Most existing studies model users' interests based on complete interaction sequences. However, in practical scenarios, user interaction sequences inevitably contain inherent noise, such as incorrect clicks. The coexistence of noise and valid interactions can severely disrupt the learning of user interest representations, causing learned user interest representations diverging from the user's actual preferences. Furthermore, some studies attempt to reduce the impact of noise by modeling the contextual information of sequences, which still have certain limitations when the contextual information itself contains noise. To tackle the above problems, we propose a **C**ontinuous **S**ub-sequence **D**enoising framework(CSD) for Sequential Recommendation. Firstly, through the dynamic partitioning and representation fusion mechanism, the long-term and short-term interests of users are accurately captured under the guidance of the target item. Then, we design an iterative denoising module that uses user long-term interests as the supervisory signal to guide the denoising process. This module identifies noise sub-sequences that deviate from users' interest representations through a dual-judgment mechanism, enabling the precise identification of continuous noise data within the sequence. Experimental results on four large real-world datasets demonstrate that the CSD outperforms the existing denoising methods and can be effectively integrated into various mainstream sequential recommendation models.

Keywords: Sequential recommendation · Sequence denoising · Continuous noise sub-sequence

1 Introduction

With the continuous growth in demand for personalized services, recommendation systems have become indispensable in e-commerce, social media, video platforms, and other application fields. In earlier research, users' long-term interests are typically modeled by using Transformer models to process their entire interaction sequences. As a result of the inherent noise in user interaction sequences, modeling user interests is inevitably affected by these noise, resulting in a certain

T. Hao et al. (Eds.): BESC 2025, LNCS 16431, pp. 452–469, 2026.
https://doi.org/10.1007/978-981-95-7138-3_29

degree of deviation from users' actual interests. Current studies often treat noise in sequences as isolated and discrete, without distinguishing between different types, such as discrete or continuous. However, our research has revealed that noise consists not only of isolated anomalies but also of continuous noise sub-sequences with semantic associations. Moreover, some studies [12] indicate that noise-free interaction sequences display a high degree of sequentiality, meaning that each item in the sequence maintains a strong contextual relationship with its neighbors and is highly similar to the subsequent one. Existing denoising methods typically rely on the contextual semantic information of user interaction sequences, analyzing inconsistencies between items and their surrounding context to identify noise. Specifically, an item in the sequence is defined as noise when it demonstrates weak sequentiality concerning its surrounding items. However, when the contextual information itself contains noise, these consecutively stacked noise items tend to exhibit high similarity and sequentiality within the local sequence, and such contextual information will instead have a negative impact on the denoising process. We define such consecutively stacked noise items as noise sub-sequences. When facing continuous noise sub-sequences, methods that rely solely on contextual information for denoising are limited, as the noise items within these sub-sequences are highly correlated, making them difficult to identify.

To demonstrate that noise is not only isolated anomalies but also continuous noise sub-sequences with semantic associations, and that these continuous noise sub-sequences negatively affect denoising, we conducted the following experiment. Specifically, under identical experimental conditions, the reliability of items within the same sequence is assessed using two models: HSD [39], which models user historical behavior based on contextual information, and SASRec [29], which employs a Self-Attention mechanism to model the behavior sequence. As illustrated in Fig. 1(a) and Fig. 1(b), the experimental results reveal that both sequence 1 and sequence 2 exhibit continuous noise characteristics, indicating the presence of consecutively stacked noise items within the sequences. In Fig. 1(a), the items labeled (4–8) and (15–17) are identified as noise; in Fig. 1(b), the items labeled (4–5) and (9–12) are classified as noise. However, when comparing the results of Fig. 1(a) with Fig. 1(c) and Fig. 1(b) with Fig. 1(d) within the same sequence, it becomes evident that models relying solely on contextual information for denoising are unable to accurately locate all noise signals when continuous noise sub-sequences are present.

To solve the aforementioned challenges, we propose a denoising method called CSD, which removes continuous noise sub-sequences. This method is primarily designed to explicitly evaluate the consistency between continuous sub-sequences of different lengths and user interests, thereby determining whether they constitute noise. Specifically, our model comprises a embedding layer, a user interest extractor, and an iterative denoising module. The user interest extractor includes an item-skip long user interest extractor and a convolutional short user interest extractor, which are used to model long-term and short-term user interests, respectively. The long-term user interest extractor utilizes an adaptive filtering

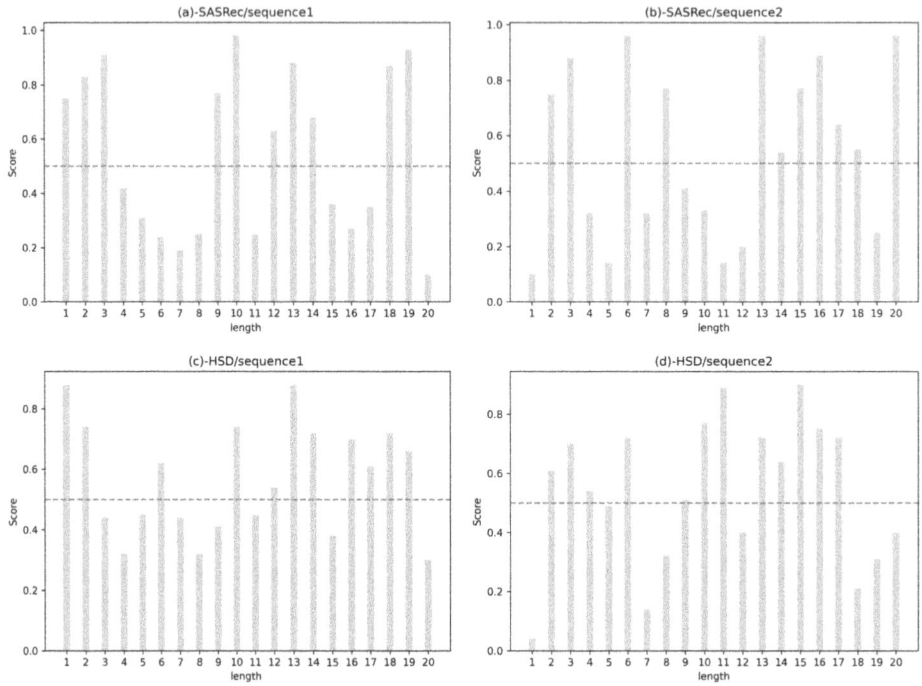

Fig. 1. Exploring continuous noise subsequences and noise distribution across different methods.

mechanism to capture more reliable items in the sequence for modeling user interests, thereby mitigating the influence of inherent noise on the modeling process. Meanwhile, the short-term user interest extractor employs a target-aware convolutional sequence embedding module to learn short-term user interests effectively. The iterative denoising module is designed with a sub-sequence constructor, a similarity discriminator, and an iterative selector. The sub-sequence constructor uses sliding window technology to segment the complete user interaction sequence, thereby generating interaction sub-sequences with similar semantics. The similarity discriminator evaluates the consistency of these sub-sequences with user interests. At the same time, the iterative selector precisely identifies the length and position of noise sub-sequences from the perspective of noise sub-sequence length and incorporates the remaining sequence as part of the clean sequence for subsequent downstream recommendation tasks.

The main contributions of the paper are as follows:

- As far as we know, this is the first paper to propose the removal of consecutive noisy items in sequential recommendation, effectively eliminating the negative impact of contextual information on noise identification.
- We propose an adaptive filtering mechanism to select a subset of interactions for modeling user interests to guide denoising behavior, thereby minimizing the negative impact of unreliable interactions on user interests modeling.

- We propose an iterative module for locating noise, which determines the position of noise based on two factors: the length of continuous noise sub-sequences and the similarity of sub-sequences.
- Experimental results on four large real-world datasets demonstrate that the CSD outperforms the existing denoising methods and can be effectively integrated into various mainstream sequential recommendation models.

2 Related Work

2.1 Sequential Recommendation

Where user behavior is highly influenced by temporal order, sequential recommendation has garnered considerable attention for its capability to model the dynamic evolution of user interests over time. It focuses on analyzing the sequential patterns of user behavior to predict future behaviors or preferences, thereby delivering personalized recommendations. As deep learning continues to evolve, recurrent neural networks (RNNs) [2,7,11,25] have been increasingly used in sequential recommendation, owing to their capacity to learn complex transitional patterns between behaviors and capture long-term dependencies through hidden states. Convolutional neural networks (CNNs) [8] have been applied to sequential recommendation for their ability to capture local dependencies and pattern representations within sequences. Transformer [1] has utilized Self-Attention mechanisms to process each position in a sequence in parallel, capturing global dependencies and overcoming the training inefficiencies of RNNs for long sequences. Graph neural networks (GNNs) [16,24] have represented user behavior sequences as user-item interaction graphs, capturing the relationships between behaviors through graph convolutions.

Additionally, Self-supervised learning [10,34,36,42] enhances the model's ability to extract contextual representations by generating training signals from raw user interactions. Graph contrastive learning [19,37] has recently gained prominence as a powerful self-supervised learning paradigm, which enables the capture of richer temporal relationships in interactions through multi-perspective contrastive learning or time-aware graph contrastive learning for sequential recommendation. Large language models (LLMs), as an emerging paradigm, are being increasingly explored in sequential recommendation. LLMCDSR [33] proposes a model that utilizes LLMs to tackle knowledge alignment and transfer issues in cross-domain sequential recommendation involving both overlapping and non-overlapping users. DALR [20] leverages LLMs to generate rich textual information to improve the performance of graph neural networks in sequential recommendation.

The aforementioned studies train models on the original item sequences, however, the inherent noise in these sequences can lead to inaccurate modeling of user preferences, ultimately resulting in poor recommendation performance.

2.2 Denoising Recommendation

Denoising recommendations aim to improve recommendation performance by mitigating the impact of noise in interaction sequences. Early research focused on bridging the gap between implicit feedback and user preferences through explicit user feedback (e.g., ratings and reviews). However, in practical scenarios, collecting explicit user feedback is challenging, and its quality varies significantly, making it difficult to use such supervised signals for sequence denoising. Consequently, the denoising task has transitioned from a supervised learning task to an unsupervised learning challenge.

Existing sequence denoising methods can be primarily categorized into three types [12]: The first type involves reweighting interactions by assigning different weights. ADT [30] proposes an adaptive denoising strategy that discards high-loss interactions and adaptively reduces the weight of high-loss samples. AutoDenoise [6] employs a reinforcement learning-based controller network to dynamically assign weights to implicit feedback samples. FMLP-Rec [43] utilizes a full MLP architecture integrated with learnable filters to adaptively mitigate frequency-domain noise via the Fast Fourier Transform (FFT). SGDL [5] gathers clean samples as denoising signals during the early stages of training to mitigate memory effects, then dynamically adjusts sample weights in the later stages via meta-learning. The second type directly removes data identified as noise. HSD [39] identifies inconsistent item signals by learning user-level signals and sequence-level signals, dynamically generating noise-free sequences. STEAM [14] designs an adaptive corrector that applies multiple operations to correct the original interaction sequence, eliminating noise effects without relying on additional labels. CLEA [21] decomposes the history shopping basket into positive and negative sub-baskets, while a two-stage anchor-guided contrast learning method is designed for denoising. GDMSR [22] models social relationship confidence using user preference signals, integrating self-correcting curriculum learning mechanisms and adaptive denoising strategies to mitigate noise in social networks. RGCF [28] evaluates the reliability of user interactions by calculating the similarity between item embeddings, and filtering out unreliable interactions. The third type condenses the entire dataset into a small data summary using data distillation techniques. DConRec [32] converts discrete interactions into continuous ones through probabilistic reparameterization, addressing issues related to long-tail distributions and false negative samples in data compression.

However, existing denoising methods do not evaluate the presence of continuously stacked noise interactions from the perspective of continuous noise subsequences, thereby failing to mitigate the negative impact of contextual information within the sequence on the denoising process.

3 Preliminary

In our denoising model, we define two sets: one for users $\mathcal{U} = \{u_1, u_2, \cdots, u_{|\mathcal{U}|}\}$ and another for items $\mathcal{V} = \{v_1, v_2, \cdots, v_{|\mathcal{V}|}\}$. Here, each element $u \in \mathcal{U}$ denotes a user, while each element $v \in \mathcal{V}$ corresponds to an item. We utilize the set of users' historical interactions, denoted as $\{S^1, S^2, \cdots, S^{|\mathcal{U}|}\}$, as the input.

For a user's interaction sequence denoted as $S^i = \{s_1^i, s_2^i, \cdots, s_t^i, \cdots, s_{n_i}^i\}$, where $s_t^i \in \mathcal{V}$ is the t-th item interacted, and n_i indicates its length. Our model aims to produce a noise-free sequence $S_u^* = \{s_1, s_2, \cdots, s_{n^*}\}$.

4 Methodology

The overall architecture of the proposed model is illustrated in Fig. 2. CSD mainly consists of three key modules: i) embedding layer, which is used to obtain the original item embedding for training our model; ii) long-term and short-term user interest extractor, which is designed to model the users' long-term and short-term interests as supervisory signals, thereby facilitating the guidance of the subsequent denoising process; iii) iterative denoising module, which identifies the length and position of the noise sub-sequence within the sequence based on dual-judgment mechanism.

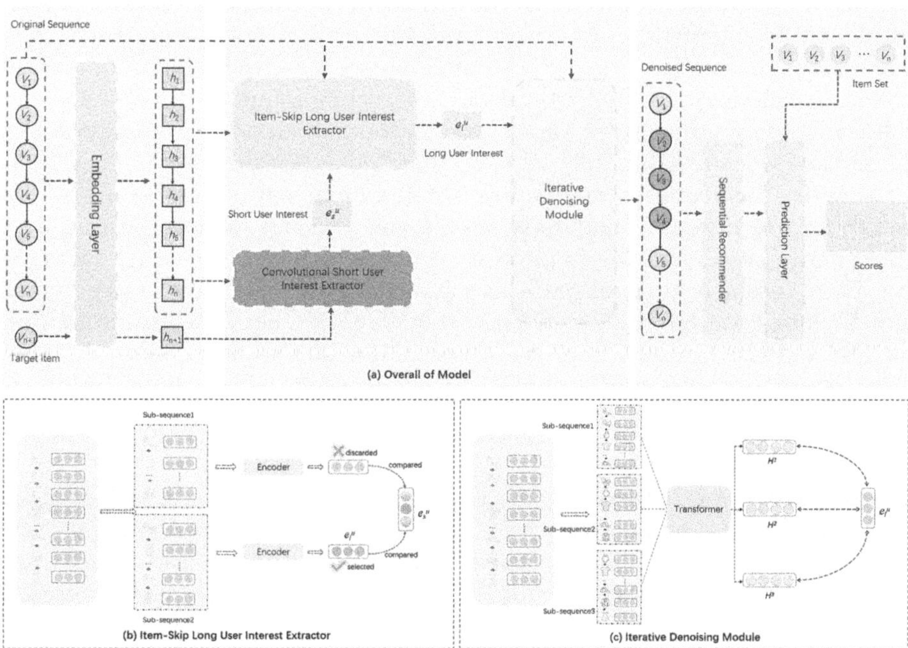

Fig. 2. The overall structure of the proposed CSD.

4.1 Embedding Layer

The primary objective of the embedding layer is to encode the original interaction sequence and obtain the hidden embedding representations of the individual items within the sequence. The embedding of each item e_i is generated by mapping its ID to a dense vector $h_i \in \mathbb{R}^d$. To capture the positional effects, we introduce a position embedding matrix with trainable parameters $P \in \mathbb{R}^{n \times d}$.

$$h_i = x_i W_x \tag{1}$$

$$H = [h_1, h_2, \cdots, h_n] \tag{2}$$

Let $H \in \mathbb{R}^{n \times d}$ denotes the item embedding matrix corresponding to the user interaction sequence S. where x_i represents the one-hot encoding of the ID of each item e_i, $W_x \in \mathbb{R}^{|\mathcal{V}| \times d}$ is a trainable matrix, d represents the dimension of the embedding vector.

4.2 User Interest Extractor

Due to the prevalence of inherent noise in user interactions, directly modeling the entire interaction sequence may result in inaccurate representation of long-term interests. Thus, we propose an adaptive long-term interests modeling module, which does not model the entire interaction sequence directly. Instead, it selects more representative sub-sequences through an adaptive segmentation mechanism to more accurately capture users′ long-term interests. The key to the adaptive segmentation mechanism is determining appropriate segmentation metric, for which we use short-term interests as auxiliary metric. Existing studies primarily model short-term interests through the target item [41]. However, to capture recent behavioral patterns more effectively and provide richer guidance for long-term interests modeling, we incorporate not only the target item but also the last m items from the users′ interaction sequence as core inputs. This approach enables us to select the most relevant sub-sequence during the short-term interests modeling process.

Short-Term User Interests. To capture the most accurate modeling of the user's long-term interests, we integrate part of the sequence information into the short-term user interests [44]. Specifically, we incorporate the last m user interactions along with the target item and apply a convolution operation. Formally, it is written as:

$$H' = Trun(H, m) \tag{3}$$

$$I = concat(H', h_{n+1}) \tag{4}$$

where Trun(·) is a truncation function that selects the last m elements of sequence S, h_{n+1} is the representation of the target item. $*$ represents the convolution operation with a stride of 1, and W_v^i and W_h^j denote the vertical and horizontal convolution kernels, respectively. z and z′ refer to the number of convolution kernels with matching shapes.

$$P_h^j = MaxPool(Relu(I * W_h^j)), \forall j \in [1, 2, \cdots, z(m+1)] \tag{5}$$

$$P_v^i = Flatten(Relu(I * W_v^i)), \forall i \in [1, 2, \cdots, z'] \tag{6}$$

$$O_h = concat(p_h^1, p_h^2, \cdots, p_h^{z(m+1)}) \tag{7}$$

$$O_v = concat(p_v^1, p_v^2, \cdots, p_v^{z'}) \tag{8}$$

$$e_s^u = Relu(concat(O_h, O_v)W_1 + b_1) \tag{9}$$

Then, we concatenate $O_h \in \mathbb{R}^{z(m+1)}$ and $O_v \in \mathbb{R}^{z'd}$ to obtain the short-term user interests, where $W_1 \in \mathbb{R}^{(z(m+1)+z')\times d}$, $b_1 \in \mathbb{R}^d$ is learnable weight and bias, respectively.

Long-Term User Interests. Due to the inherent noise present in the sequence, the user interests derived from modeling the complete interaction sequence are inevitably biased from the true user interests. To quantify the impact of noise, we assume that the sequence contains the longest continuous noise segment of length K, where K is a hyperparameter. Based on this assumption, we apply a dynamic interval sampling strategy to partition the original user interaction sequence $S = \{e_1, e_2, \cdots, e_n\}$ into K+1 non-overlapping sub-sequences $\{S_1, S_2, \cdots, S_{K+1}\}$. Specifically, the j-th sub-sequence S_j is defined as the sequence in the original sequence where the index i satisfies: Specifically, the index of the j-th sub-sequence S_j in the original sequence satisfies:

$$S_j = \{e_j, e_{j+K+1}, e_{j+2(K+1)}, \cdots\} \tag{10}$$

where $j \in [1, 2, \cdots, K+1]$. In order to accurately represent the user′s long-term interests, we do not model the entire interaction sequence, but instead select the target sub-sequence that best reflects the user's long-term interests from the K+1 sub-sequences.

$$S_{\text{target}} = \arg \max_{j \in \{1,2,\cdots,K+1\}} \text{sim}(h_s^u, H_j) \tag{11}$$

where sim(·) refers to the cosine similarity calculation between two embeddings, h_s^u denotes the embedding of the short-term user interest, and H_j denotes the embedding of the j-th sequence. For the target sub-sequence, we employ a hybrid modeling method that combines Transformer and Bi-LSTM. Then, through a gated fusion unit, we adaptively assign weights to the above representations and fuse them together to obtain a comprehensive representation of long-term user interests.

$$\tilde{H}_*^l = \text{Trm}(\tilde{H}_*^{l-1} + P), \forall l \in [1, 2, \cdots, L] \tag{12}$$

$$\begin{aligned} \hat{H}_*^L, \hat{H}_*^R &= \text{Bi-LSTM}(H_*, \Theta) \\ \hat{H}_* &= \hat{H}_*^L + \hat{H}_*^R \end{aligned} \tag{13}$$

where $H_* \in \mathbb{R}^{n' \times d}$ comprises the embeddings corresponding to all items in S_{target}, and n' represents the length of S_{target}. Θ is the set of trainable parameters.

$$g = \sigma(W_t \tilde{h}_n + W_b \hat{h}_n) \tag{14}$$

$$e_l^u = g \odot \tilde{h}_n + (1 - g) \odot \hat{h}_n \tag{15}$$

where σ is the sigmoid function, and $W_t, W_b \in \mathbb{R}^{n' \times d}$ are the learnable parametric matrices. To derive the final output of the transformer encoder, we retrieve the hidden representation matrix $\tilde{H}_*^L = [\tilde{h}_1, \tilde{h}_2, \cdots, \tilde{h}_n] \in \mathbb{R}^{n' \times d}$ from the last layer L, $\hat{H}_* = [\hat{h}_1, \hat{h}_2, \cdots, \hat{h}_n] \in \mathbb{R}^{n' \times d}$ is the encoded embedding of target sequence. To ensure that our long-term interests are entirely reliable, we use the BPR loss to enhance the robustness of representation.

$$\mathcal{L}_{BPR} = \sum_{u \in \mathcal{U}} \sum_{(u,i,j) \in \mathcal{O}} -ln\sigma(\langle e_l^u, h_i \rangle - \langle e_l^u, h_j \rangle) \tag{16}$$

where $\langle \cdot \rangle$ is the similarity calculation function such as inner product, and $\mathcal{O} = \{(u, i, j) | e_i \in S, e_j \in \mathcal{V}, e_j \notin S\}$, here, $\mathcal{V}$ denotes the items set, S denotes the sequence for modeling long-term interests.

4.3 Iterative Denoising Module

In previous studies, sequence denoising methods typically identify potential noise items based on contextual information, such as sequentiality and similarity. However, due to the presence of consecutive noise items in user interaction sequences, relying solely on sequentiality or similarity signals is unreliable. Our approach treats sub-sequence with similar semantics as a whole to determine whether they constitute a noise sub-sequence rather than identifying specific noise items individually. To accomplish this, we initially partition the entire user interaction sequence into primitive sub-sequences with similar semantics using a sub-sequence constructor. Subsequently, based on a dual-judgment mechanism that includes the length of continuous noise sub-sequences and the similarity of sub-sequences, we iteratively identify the most likely noise sub-sequence until it is accurately detected.

Sub-sequence Constructor. To obtain continuous subsequences, we directly perform structured segmentation on the original interaction sequence. Given the sequence $S = \{e_1, e_2, \cdots, e_n\}$, where e_i denotes the i-th user interaction, we utilize sliding window technology to perform the segmentation process. This approach is designed to extract continuous subsequences that retain complete semantics. The j-th sub-sequence is formally defined as:

$$S_j^{'} = \{e_{(j-1) \times s+1}, e_{(j-1) \times s+2}, \cdots, e_{(j-1) \times s+w}\} \tag{17}$$

where $j \in [1, 2, \cdots, \lfloor (N - w) / s \rfloor + 1]$ and N is the length of the j-th sub-sequence $S_j^{'}$. w represents the window length, indicating that each sub-sequence contains consecutive w interaction items, and s denotes the step size, which specifies the number of items by which the window advances.

During the segmentation process, for sequences whose tail length is less than w, we apply zero-padding to make the sequence length a multiple of the window size, thus ensuring all sub-sequences have a fixed length of w.

Similarity Discriminator. To accurately identify the positions of noise sub-sequences, we designed a similarity discriminator that uses precise long-term interests e_l^u as unbiased supervision signals and employs similarity as the metric to gradually pinpoint potential noise sub-sequences. For the sub-sequences generated by the sub-sequence constructor $S^{'} = \{S_1^{'}, S_2^{'}, \cdots\}$, and given the sequence representation $H^{'} = \{H_1^{'}, H_2^{'}, \cdots\}$, the similarity is calculated as follows:

$$cos(H_i^{'}, h_l^u) = \frac{H_i^{'\top} h_l^u}{\|H_i^{'}\|_2 \cdot \|h_l^u\|_2} \tag{18}$$

where h_l^u is the embedding of user long-term interest. For each sub-sequence, we assess its similarity to the supervision signal. If the similarity is high, the sub-sequence is likely to be free of potential noise, which requires further segmentation of the sub-sequence to confirm whether noise truly exists. In contrast, if the similarity is low, we classify the sub-sequence as the continuous noise sub-sequence we intend to detect, allowing for its direct removal. The reliability score of the corresponding sequence r_i can be formally defined as follows:

$$r_i = \mathbb{I}(cos(H_i^{'}, h_l^u) > \beta) \cdot cos(H_i^{'}, h_l^u) \tag{19}$$

where $\mathbb{I}(\cdot)$ is a binary indicator function that outputs 1 if the condition holds true, and β is a hyperparameter. If the computed cosine similarity score is below this threshold β, the sequence reliability weight r_i is set to 0, indicating that interactions confidently identified as noise are directly removed.

Iterative Selector. The similarity discriminator assigns reliability weights to sub-sequences, facilitating the preliminary identification of potential noise. However, due to the inability to determine the length and distribution of continuous noise sub-sequences in advance, we propose a method that iteratively partitions the user interaction sequence into sub-sequences of varying lengths to identify potential noise. Specifically, the set of sub-sequences $S' - S_{noise}^i$, identified by the similarity discriminator as noise-free, is re-input into the sub-sequence constructor for re-partitioning, producing a new set of sub-sequences $S^{''}$, which is then re-evaluated by the similarity discriminator. In the above process, we predefine the minimum length g of a continuous noise sub-sequence. The iteration stops when all sub-sequences identified as noise have a length greater than or equal to g, and there are no new noise-free subsequences that need to be re-partitioned.

$$S_u^* = S^{'} - S_{noise}^n \tag{20}$$

Finally, we obtain the noise-free sequence S_u^*. Subsequently, the denoised sequence representation H_u^* can be fed into various mainstream sequential recommendation models.

$$e_u^* = \mathbb{G}(H_u^*) \tag{21}$$

where $\mathbb{G}(\cdot)$ denotes a representation learning-based sequential recommendation model that takes the denoised item embedding sequence H_u^* as input and produces sequence-level representations.

4.4 Prediction Layer

To recommend the next item, we need to obtain the probability distribution over the entire item set. Specifically, for each item $v_i \in \mathcal{V}$, its probability is calculated as follows:

$$\hat{y}_i = \frac{\exp(e_u^* h_{v_i}^\top)}{\sum_{v_j \in \mathcal{V}} \exp(e_u^* h_{v_j}^\top)} \tag{22}$$

Then, we define the recommendation task as minimizing the loss:

$$\mathcal{L}_{Rec} = -\sum_{i=1}^{|\mathcal{V}|}(y_i log(\hat{y}_i) + (1 - y_i) log(1 - \hat{y}_i)) \tag{23}$$

where y_i represents the i-th one hot encoding of the ground truth item.

Finally, we use the loss $\mathcal{L}$ to optimize the parameters of our model CSD:

$$\mathcal{L} = \frac{1}{|\mathcal{U}|}\sum_{i=1}^{|\mathcal{U}|}(\mathcal{L}_{BPR} + \alpha\mathcal{L}_{Rec}) + \lambda||\Theta_0||^2 \tag{24}$$

where α is a hyperparameter balancing BPR loss and the recommendation loss, λ is a hyperparameter, and Θ_0 is the set of model parameters.

5 Experiments

5.1 Experimental Settings

Datasets. To demonstrate the effectiveness of our denoising model, we validated it on four publicly available datasets: (1) MovieLens: a dataset of user movie ratings (versions used: 100k and 1M); (2) Amazon: a dataset containing user purchase and rating data (focused subcategories: Beauty and Sports). Meanwhile, to reduce the impact of short user interaction sequences, we selected users with interaction sequences longer than 5 and items with interaction frequencies higher than 5 on ML-100k and ML-1M, while setting the number to 8 on Beauty and Sports. Furthermore, we limit the interaction length to 200 for ML-1M and 50 for all other datasets. Table 1 presents the statistical details of the four datasets. We use three evaluation metrics: Hit Ratio (HR@K), Normalized Discounted Cumulative Gain (NDCG@K), and Mean Reciprocal Rank (MRR@K). Specifically, we focus on HR@{5,10,20}, NDCG@{5,10,20} and MRR@20 across the all item universe.

Table 1. Statistical Data Of The Used Datasets

Dataset	Sequences	Users	Items	Sparsity
ML-100k	99,287	944	1,350	92.21%
ML-1M	999,611	6,041	3,417	95.16%
Beauty	32,963	1,767	804	97.68%
Sports	39,837	3,284	2,121	99.43%

Baseline Models. To assess the utility of our denoising model, we integrate CSD with five mainstream sequential recommendation models: (1)GRU4Rec [2] proposes a model based on gated recurrent units (GRUs) for session recommendation. (2)NARM [7] applies a hybrid encoder to capture users' behavior and primary intent. (3)CASER [8] utilizes a convolutional operation to capture local representation in sequences while combining user latent vectors to capture long-term preferences. (4)SASRec [29] applies Self-Attention mechanisms to dynamically assign weights to items in users' historical behavior. (5)STAMP [15] combines long-term and short-term memory through attention mechanisms to dynamically calculate the weights of historical clicks, capturing changes in user interests.

Moreover, we compare CSD with four advanced sequence denoising methods: (1)DSAN [38] captures users' current preferences by target item embedding and introduces adaptive sparse transformation functions to eliminate the impact of irrelevant items in sessions. (2)FMLP-Rec [43] integrates a learnable filter that adaptively attenuates noise in the frequency domain using Fast Fourier Transform (FFT). (3)HSD [39] dynamically generates noise-free sequences by identifying inconsistent item signals. (4)SSDRec [40] uses the learned inter-sequence relationships to enhance short sequences, thereby alleviating over/under-denoising issues.

Implementation Details. Our model is implemented using PyTorch and all experiments are run on a Linux Server equipped with an Intel Xeon Platinum 2.40 GHz CPU and 754 GB of RAM. Similar to previous studies [7] [15], we set the mini-batch size of the model to 256, and the embedding size to 100. We initialized the embedding parameters according to a Gaussian distribution. In order to avoid overfitting, we applied early stopping if the HR@20 on the validation set continued to decrease for 10 successive epochs.

5.2 Performance Comparison

As presented in Table 2, we conduct a performance comparison of five sequential recommendation models with (w) and without (w/o) CSD. In most recommendation models, the inclusion of CSD improves the model's recommendation performance, indicating that our model can mitigate the effect of noise on recommendation tasks. On the ML-100k dataset, CSD+STAMP demonstrates relative

Table 2. Performance Comparison of Different Sequential Recommendation Methods

Datasets	Metric	GRU4Rec		NARM		Caser		SASRec		STAMP	
		w/o	w	w/o	w	w/o	w	w/o	w	w/o	w
ML-100k	HR@5	0.0191	**0.0297**	0.0180	**0.0191**	0.0212	**0.0255**	0.0191	**0.0403**	0.0201	**0.0339**
	HR@10	0.0286	**0.0477**	0.0403	**0.0435**	0.0339	**0.0445**	0.0371	**0.0668**	0.0392	**0.0647**
	HR@20	0.0594	**0.0785**	0.0657	**0.0753**	0.0679	**0.0859**	0.0764	**0.1166**	0.0700	**0.1177**
	NDCG@5	0.0104	**0.0155**	0.0132	**0.0134**	0.0113	**0.0137**	0.0114	**0.0253**	0.0115	**0.0196**
	NDCG@10	0.0134	**0.0212**	0.0202	**0.0204**	0.0153	**0.0198**	0.0172	**0.0339**	0.0176	**0.0295**
	NDCG@20	0.0212	**0.0290**	0.0267	**0.0282**	0.0238	**0.0298**	0.0270	**0.0463**	0.0253	**0.0427**
	MRR@20	0.0109	**0.0154**	**0.0162**	0.0157	0.0119	**0.0148**	0.0139	**0.0271**	0.0132	**0.0225**
ML-1M	HR@5	0.0194	**0.0513**	0.0151	**0.0242**	0.0104	**0.0286**	0.0397	**0.0445**	0.0232	**0.0379**
	HR@10	0.0373	**0.0922**	0.0349	**0.0401**	0.0215	**0.0434**	0.0666	**0.0781**	0.0440	**0.0680**
	HR@20	0.0690	**0.1397**	0.0591	**0.1397**	0.0589	**0.0753**	0.1077	**0.1278**	0.0677	**0.1055**
	NDCG@5	0.0135	**0.0310**	0.0080	**0.0152**	0.0063	**0.0163**	0.0207	**0.0360**	0.0150	**0.0243**
	NDCG@10	0.0190	**0.0442**	0.0144	**0.0203**	0.0099	**0.0210**	0.0294	**0.0360**	0.0218	**0.0340**
	NDCG@20	0.0270	**0.0562**	0.0205	**0.0280**	0.0194	**0.0290**	0.0379	**0.0484**	0.0278	**0.0434**
	MRR@20	0.0159	**0.0331**	0.0100	**0.0165**	0.0091	**0.0164**	0.0203	**0.0266**	0.0168	**0.0263**
Beauty	HR@5	0.0413	**0.1217**	0.0855	**0.0963**	0.0362	**0.0855**	0.0413	**0.1059**	0.0906	**0.1179**
	HR@10	0.0821	**0.2010**	0.1297	**0.1489**	0.0572	**0.1427**	0.0821	**0.1846**	0.1552	**0.2099**
	HR@20	0.1772	**0.3052**	0.2039	**0.2288**	0.0991	**0.2112**	0.1772	**0.2950**	0.2497	**0.3216**
	NDCG@5	0.0215	**0.0770**	0.0526	**0.0599**	0.0243	**0.0559**	0.0215	**0.0661**	0.0531	**0.0923**
	NDCG@10	0.0347	**0.1024**	0.0666	**0.0768**	0.0308	**0.0744**	0.0347	**0.0910**	0.0739	**0.1184**
	NDCG@20	0.0586	**0.1283**	0.0852	**0.0967**	0.0411	**0.0915**	0.0586	**0.1188**	0.0976	**0.1404**
	MRR@20	0.0271	**0.0797**	0.0523	**0.0602**	0.0254	**0.0584**	0.0271	**0.0706**	0.0557	**0.0931**
Sports	HR@5	0.0180	**0.0265**	0.0171	**0.0195**	0.0113	**0.0164**	0.0222	**0.0231**	0.0183	**0.0253**
	HR@10	0.0289	**0.0405**	0.0274	**0.0353**	0.0235	**0.0341**	0.0369	0.0369	0.0250	**0.0493**
	HR@20	0.0515	**0.0646**	0.0445	**0.0585**	0.0481	**0.0500**	0.0579	**0.0582**	0.0466	**0.0765**
	NDCG@5	0.0106	**0.0162**	0.0112	**0.0122**	0.0074	**0.0086**	0.0128	**0.0142**	0.0108	**0.0164**
	NDCG@10	0.0142	**0.0208**	0.0144	**0.0172**	0.0112	**0.0140**	0.0176	**0.0186**	0.0129	**0.0243**
	NDCG@20	0.0200	**0.0268**	0.0187	**0.0231**	0.0172	**0.0183**	0.0229	**0.0239**	0.0182	**0.0310**
	MRR@20	0.0114	**0.0164**	0.0117	**0.0135**	0.0091	**0.0095**	0.0131	**0.0144**	0.0105	**0.0186**

improvements over STAMP by 68.14% in HR@20, 68.77% in NDCG@20, and 70.45% in MRR@20, respectively. However, there are two exceptions: on the ML-100k dataset, the MRR@20 performance of NARM, with and without CSD, shows a slight decline, and on the Sports dataset, the HR@10 performance of SASRec, with and without CSD, remains the same.

As presented in Table 3, compared to advanced denoising models, our model outperforms in most cases. For example, on the ML-100K dataset, our model achieves relative improvements of 32.94%, 35.64%, and 35.29% in HR@K{5,10,20}; 29.80%, 35.94%, and 33.44% in NDCG@K{5,10,20}; and 31.58% in MRR@20 over the strongest baselines. This demonstrates that CSD outperforms existing denoising methods. In addition, CSD+STAMP does not perform optimally on the Beauty dataset, which may be due to the short user interaction sequences and limited interaction items on the Beauty.

Table 3. Performance Comparison Of Different Methods

Dataset	Model	HR@5	HR@10	HR@20	NDCG@5	NDCG@10	NDCG@20	MRR@20
ML-100k	DSAN	0.0201	0.0435	0.0700	0.0115	0.0188	0.0254	0.0133
	FMLP-Rec	0.0170	0.0477	0.0764	0.0117	0.0216	0.0288	0.0160
	HSD+STAMP	0.0255	0.0467	0.0870	0.0151	0.0217	0.0320	0.0171
	SSDRec+STAMP	0.0201	0.0467	0.0817	0.0115	0.0199	0.0287	0.0145
	CSD+STAMP	**0.0339**	**0.0647**	**0.1177**	**0.0196**	**0.0295**	**0.0427**	**0.0225**
ML-1M	DSAN	0.0098	0.0336	0.0651	0.0048	0.0122	0.0200	0.0081
	FMLP-Rec	0.0210	0.0449	0.0707	0.0120	0.0199	0.0263	0.0142
	HSD+STAMP	0.0301	0.0530	0.0899	0.0190	0.0264	0.0357	0.0209
	SSDRec+STAMP	0.0248	0.0445	0.0715	0.0145	0.0209	0.0277	0.0156
	CSD+STAMP	**0.0379**	**0.0680**	**0.1055**	**0.0243**	**0.0340**	**0.0434**	**0.0263**
Beauty	DSAN	0.0169	0.0626	0.1012	0.0112	0.0234	0.0354	0.0166
	FMLP-Rec	0.0176	0.0634	0.1087	0.0100	0.0246	0.0359	0.0165
	HSD+STAMP	**0.1348**	0.2078	0.3194	0.0922	0.1154	**0.1438**	**0.0955**
	SSDRec+STAMP	0.1212	**0.2118**	**0.3284**	0.0811	0.1106	0.1399	0.0882
	CSD+STAMP	0.1179	0.2099	0.3216	**0.0923**	**0.1184**	0.1404	0.0931
Sports	DSAN	0.0148	0.0277	0.0501	0.0103	0.0146	0.0197	0.0120
	FMLP-Rec	0.0152	0.0298	0.0499	0.0105	0.0150	0.0198	0.0117
	HSD+STAMP	0.0210	0.0332	0.0582	0.0121	0.0160	0.0222	0.0124
	SSDRec+STAMP	0.0219	0.0329	0.0624	0.0133	0.0168	0.0242	0.0139
	CSD+STAMP	**0.0253**	**0.0493**	**0.0765**	**0.0164**	**0.0243**	**0.0310**	**0.0186**

5.3 Ablation Study

To evaluate the contribution of each module within our model, we perform ablation studies on the ML-100k and ML-1M datasets. The backbone model for all variants is based on STAMP.

- **w/o LI**: Modeling long-term interests for all user sequences, rather than adaptively partitioning and selecting the most representative sub-sequences for modeling.
- **w/o SI**: Modeling only the target item as short-term interests, without incorporating the last m items of the interaction sequence.
- **w/o ID**: Do not consider consecutive sub-sequences as denoising units in the iterative denoising module.

As shown in Table 4, we observe performance degradation across three ablation studies mentioned above. Specifically, on the ML-100k dataset, compared with the complete model (CSD), the variant w/o LI shows relative decreases of 26.15%, 20.62%, and 14.80% in HR@20, NDCG@20, and MRR@20, respectively. This indicates that the inherent noise in the interaction sequences negatively affects the modeling of long-term user interests. Furthermore, considering only individual noise items in the iterative denoising module (i.e., w/o ID) also results in inferior performance. On the ML-100k dataset, compared to CSD, the w/o ID variant yields relative performance drops of 37.02%, 36.86%, and 34.73% in HR@20, NDCG@20, and MRR@20, respectively. This demonstrates that denoising method based on continuous sub-sequences is more efficient in noise reduction.

Table 4. Results Of Ablation Experiments

Datasets	Metric	w/o LI	w/o SI	w/o ID	CSD
ML-100k	HR@10	0.0551	0.0435	0.0435	**0.0647**
	HR@20	0.0933	0.0838	0.0859	**0.1177**
	NDCG@10	0.0257	0.0199	0.0238	**0.0295**
	NDCG@20	0.0354	0.0301	0.0312	**0.0427**
	MRR@20	0.0196	0.0157	0.0167	**0.0225**
ML-1M	HR@10	0.0641	0.0613	0.0588	**0.0680**
	HR@20	0.0985	0.0959	0.0992	**0.1055**
	NDCG@10	0.0318	0.0302	0.0297	**0.0340**
	NDCG@20	0.0405	0.0389	0.0400	**0.0434**
	MRR@20	0.0245	0.0232	0.0238	**0.0263**

5.4 Hyperparameter Study

In this section, we systematically examine how the length of the longest continuous sub-sequence affects model performance. We conduct experiments on the ML-100k and ML-1M datasets using various values of $K = \{3, 6, 9\}$. As illustrated in Fig. 3, it shows that as the sub-sequence length increases, the model performance rises at first and subsequently drops. This phenomenon indicates that a medium subsequence length strikes a desirable balance between preserving informative interactions and suppressing noise, thereby leading to optimal modeling performance.

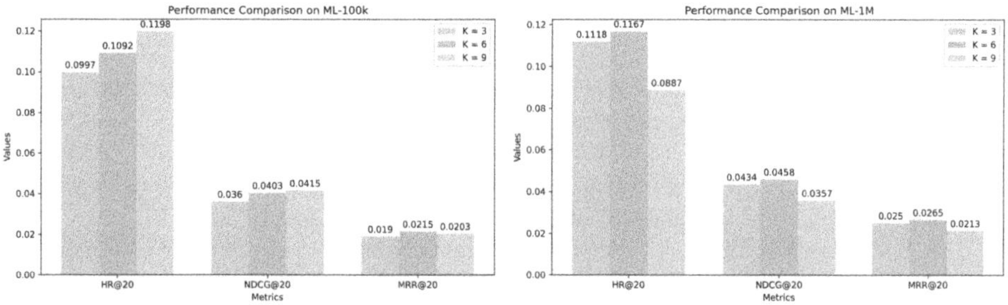

Fig. 3. Comparison with different subsequence length.

6 Conclusion

In this paper, we propose a denoising framework named CSD. Specifically, CSD introduces a dynamic segmentation and feature fusion mechanism to effectively capture the evolution of user interests. An accurate representation of user long-term interests is utilized as a supervisory signal to guide the model in iterative denoising. On this basis, a dual-judgment mechanism is designed to identify noise sub-sequences that deviate from the interest distribution, thereby enabling the precise localization of continuous noise.

References

1. Vaswani, A., Shazeer, N., et al.: Attention is all you need. Adv. Neural Inf. Process. Syst. **30** (2017)
2. Hidasi, B., Karatzoglou, A., Baltrunas, L., Tikk, D.: Session-based recommendations with recurrent neural networks. arXiv preprint arXiv:1511.06939 (2015)
3. Wu, C., et al.: Feedrec: news feed recommendation with various user feedbacks. In: Proceedings of the ACM Web Conference 2022, pp. 2088–2097 (2022)
4. Sun, F., et al.: BERT4Rec: sequential recommendation with bidirectional encoder representations from transformer. In: Proceedings of the 28th ACM International Conference on Information and Knowledge Management, pp. 1441–1450. ACM, New York (2019)
5. Gao, Y., Duet al.: Self-guided learning to denoise for robust recommendation. In: Proceedings of the 45th International ACM SIGIR Conference on Research and Development in Information Retrieval, pp. 1412–1422. ACM, New York (2022)
6. Ge, Y., Rahmani, M., Irissappane, A., Sepulveda, J., Caverlee, J., Wang, F.: Automated data denoising for recommendation. arXiv preprint arXiv:2305.07070 (2023)
7. Li, J., Ren, P., Chen, Z., Ren, Z., Lian, T., Ma, J.: Neural attentive session-based recommendation. In: Proceedings of the 2017 ACM on Conference on Information and Knowledge Management, pp. 1419–1428. ACM, New York (2017)
8. Tang, J., Wang, K.: Personalized top-n sequential recommendation via convolutional sequence embedding. In: Proceedings of the eleventh ACM International Conference on Web Search and Data Mining, pp. 565–573 (2018)

9. Weston, J., Chopra, S., Bordes, A.: Memory networks. arXiv preprint arXiv:1410.3916 (2014)
10. Zhou, K., et al.: S3-rec: self-supervised learning for sequential recommendation with mutual information maximization. In: Proceedings of the 29th ACM International Conference on Information & Knowledge Management, pp. 1893–1902 (2020)
11. Cho, K., et al.: Learning phrase representations using RNN encoder-decoder for statistical machine translation. arXiv preprint arXiv:1406.1078 (2014)
12. Lai, R., Chen, R., Zhang, C.: A survey on data-centric recommender systems. arXiv preprint arXiv:2401.17878 (2024)
13. Lee, J.B., Rossi, R.A., Kim, S., Ahmed, N.K., Koh, E.: Attention models in graphs: a survey. ACM Trans. Knowl. Disc. Data (TKDD) **13**(6), 1–25 (2019)
14. Lin, Y., et al.: A self-correcting sequential recommender. In: Proceedings of the ACM Web Conference 2023, pp. 1283–1293 (2023)
15. Liu, Q., Zeng, Y., Mokhosi, R., Zhang, H.: STAMP: short-term attention/memory priority model for session-based recommendation. In: Proceedings of the 24th ACM SIGKDD International Conference on Knowledge Discovery & Data Mining, pp. 1831–1839 (2018)
16. Kipf, T. N., Welling, M.: Semi-supervised classification with graph convolutional networks. arXiv preprint arXiv:1609.02907 (2016)
17. McPherson, M., Smith-Lovin, L., Cook, J.M.: Birds of a feather: homophily in social networks. Ann. Rev. Sociol. **27**(1), 415–444 (2001)
18. Srivastava, N., Hinton, G., Krizhevsky, A., Sutskever, I., Salakhutdinov, R.: Dropout: a simple way to prevent neural networks from overfitting. J. Mach. Learn. Res.h **15**(1), 1929–1958 (2014)
19. Peng, T., et al.: TagRec: temporal-aware graph contrastive learning with theoretical augmentation for sequential recommendation. IEEE Trans. Knowl. Data Eng. (2025)
20. Peng, Y., et al.: Denoising alignment with large language model for recommendation. ACM Trans. Inf. Syst. **43**(2), 1–35 (2025)
21. Qin, Y., Wang, P., Li, C.: The world is binary: contrastive learning for denoising next basket recommendation. In: Proceedings of the 44th International ACM SIGIR Conference on Research and Development in Information Retrieval, pp. 859–868 (2021)
22. Quan, Y., Ding, J., Gao, C., Yi, L., Jin, D., Li, Y.: Robust preference-guided denoising for graph-based social recommendation. In: Proceedings of the ACM Web Conference 2023, pp. 1097–1108 (2023)
23. He, R., McAuley, J.: Fusing similarity models with Markov chains for sparse sequential recommendation. In: 2016 IEEE 16th International Conference on Data Mining (ICDM), pp. 191–200 (2016)
24. Wu, S., Tang, Y., Zhu, Y., Wang, L., Xie, X., Tan, T.: Session-based recommendation with graph neural networks. In: Proceedings of the AAAI Conference on Artificial Intelligence, vol. 33, no. 01, pp. 346–353 (2019)
25. Chaudhari, S., Mithal, V., Polatkan, G., Ramanath, R.: An attentive survey of attention models. ACM Trans. Intell. Syst. Technol. (TIST) **12**(5), 1–32 (2021)
26. Rendle, S., Freudenthaler, C., Schmidt-Thieme, L.: Factorizing personalized Markov chains for next-basket recommendation. In: Proceedings of the 19th International Conference on World Wide Web, pp. 811–820 (2010)
27. Donkers, T., Loepp, B., Ziegler, J.: Sequential user-based recurrent neural network recommendations. In: Proceedings of the Eleventh ACM Conference on Recommender Systems, pp. 152–160 (2017)

28. Tian, C., Xie, Y., Li, Y., Yang, N., Zhao, W. X.: Learning to denoise unreliable interactions for graph collaborative filtering. In: Proceedings of the 45th International ACM SIGIR Conference on Research and Development in Information Retrieval, pp. 122–132 (2022)
29. Kang, W.-C., McAuley, J.: Self-attentive sequential recommendation. In: 2018 IEEE International Conference on Data Mining (ICDM), pp. 197–206 (2018)
30. Wang, W., Feng, F., He, X., Nie, L., Chua, T.-S.: Denoising implicit feedback for recommendation. In: Proceedings of the 14th ACM International Conference on Web Search and Data Mining, pp. 373–381 (2021)
31. Wang, X., et al.: Automated disentangled sequential recommendation with large language models. ACM Trans. Inf. Syst. **43**(2), 1–29 (2025)
32. Wu, J., et al.: Dataset condensation for recommendation. arXiv preprint arXiv:2310.01038 (2023)
33. Xin, H., Sun, Y., Wang, C., Xiong, H.: LLMCDSR: enhancing cross-domain sequential recommendation with large language models. ACM Trans. Inf. Syst. (2025)
34. Xia, X., Yin, H., Yu, J., Wang, Q., Cui, L., Zhang, X.: Self-supervised hypergraph convolutional networks for session-based recommendation. In: Proceedings of the AAAI Conference on Artificial Intelligence, vol. 35, no. 5, pp. 4503–4511 (2021)
35. Chen, X., et al.: Sequential recommendation with user memory networks. In: Proceedings of the Eleventh ACM International Conference on Web Search and Data Mining, pp. 108–116 (2018)
36. Xie, X., et al.: Contrastive learning for sequential recommendation. In: 2022 IEEE 38th International Conference on Data Engineering (ICDE), pp. 1259–1273 (2022)
37. Xu, Z., Chen, S., Pan, W., Ming, Z.: A multi-view graph contrastive learning framework for cross-domain sequential recommendation. ACM Trans. Recommender Syst. **3**(4), 1–28 (2025)
38. Yuan, J., Song, Z., Sun, M., Wang, X., Zhao, W. X.: Dual sparse attention network for session-based recommendation. In: Proceedings of the AAAI Conference on Artificial Intelligence, vol. 35, no. 5, pp. 4635–4643 (2021)
39. Zhang, C., Du, Y., Zhao, X., Han, Q., Chen, R., Li, L.: Hierarchical item inconsistency signal learning for sequence denoising in sequential recommendation. In: Proceedings of the 31st ACM International Conference on Information & Knowledge Management, pp. 2508–2518 (2022)
40. Zhang, C., Han, Q., Chen, R., Zhao, X., Tang, P., Song, H.: Ssdrec: self-augmented sequence denoising for sequential recommendation. In: 2024 IEEE 40th International Conference on Data Engineering (ICDE), pp. 803–815 (2024)
41. Zheng, Y., et al.: Disentangling long and short-term interests for recommendation. In: Proceedings of the ACM Web Conference 2022, pp. 2256–2267 (2022)
42. Liu, Z., Chen, Y., Li, J., Yu, P. S., McAuley, J., Xiong, C.: Contrastive self-supervised sequential recommendation with robust augmentation. arXiv preprint arXiv:2108.06479 (2021)
43. Zhou, K., Yu, H., Zhao, W. X., Wen, J.-R.: Filter-enhanced MLP is all you need for sequential recommendation. In: Proceedings of the ACM Web Conference 2022, pp. 2388–2399 (2022)
44. Zhu, X., Li, L., Liu, W., Luo, X.: Multi-level sequence denoising with cross-signal contrastive learning for sequential recommendation. Neural Netw. **179**, 106480 (2024)

ReCareer: Hybrid Graph Neural Networks for Post-Career-Break Job Recommendation

Yunqi Wang[1], Yu Yang[1](✉), Longxiang Gao[2], Xiaoming Wu[2], and Guandong Xu[1]

[1] The Education University of Hong Kong, Hong Kong SAR, China
s1143757@s.eduhk.hk, {yangyy,gdxu}@eduhk.hk
[2] Qilu University of Technology (Shandong Academy of Sciences), Shandong, China
gaolx@sdas.org, wuxm@qlu.edu.cn

Abstract. Given the rapidly evolving and competitive labor market, E-recruitment recommendation systems have gained increasing attention for their ability to leverage comprehensive user profile data and deliver personalized job recommendations. However, research addressing recommendation algorithms specifically for career-break populations, who require the most targeted career guidance, remains unexplored. Therefore, this quantitative study aims to investigate the technical challenges underlying this research gap to improve recommendation accuracy: how to incorporate career break information and how to handle varying profile sequence lengths among career break users. To address these challenges, we propose a hybrid Graph Neural Network (GNN) approach for sequence-aware job recommendation. Our two-stage framework combines a GNN-based ranking stage with a dynamic gating rule–based re-ranking stage that adaptively balances industry and skill signals through a sigmoid-based gating mechanism. Our experiments are conducted on a dataset, containing 2,238 users with 12 distinct career break categories. Experimental evaluation demonstrates that our proposed system achieves Hit Rates of 37.2% at Top 10, 49.6% at Top 30, and 71.6% at Top 50, highlighting its effectiveness in addressing the career break job recommendation challenge.

Keywords: Job Recommendation · Job Market Analysis · Career Break · Graph Neural Networks · Sequential Recommendation

1 Introduction

In recent years, career breaks have become increasingly accepted and more widely adopted as a life choice. Nevertheless, returning to the workforce after a career break remains a growing challenge. According to the annual report by the global social impact organization [1], 94% of returners now find it difficult to secure a professional role an increase from 92% in 2024. Recruitment bias against CV gaps has been seen as the greatest barrier by 46% of respondents.

The study of [2] further notes, from a qualitative human resources perspective, that such bias often arises from concerns that a career break may leave candidates with outdated training. This highlights a critical need to match returning workers with roles that

T. Hao et al. (Eds.): BESC 2025, LNCS 16431, pp. 470–487, 2026.
https://doi.org/10.1007/978-981-95-7138-3_30

align with their up-to-date skills and experience requirements. E-recruitment recommendation systems, by leveraging large-scale user data, offering a promising approach to addressing this challenge for career returners.

However, existing job recommendation algorithms have not been specifically designed for the career break population. For the general population, job recommendation systems rarely make full use of career break information, treating it merely as a signal when addressing issues such as missing experience sequences or career transitions.

Additionally, users with career breaks have employment histories of different sequence lengths, as these career gaps vary considerably in duration. Most recommendation systems tend to favor users with longer, information-rich sequences, while failing to effectively utilize the limited data available from users with shorter sequences. This issue introduces recommendation bias resulting from inconsistent user sequence lengths.

Therefore, we aim to solve the problem of accurate job recommendations for people who return to work after the career break, with the required skill set of the recommended job is close to the user's existing skill. Specifically, we aim to explore (1) how to effectively utilize career break information provided by users to enhance recommendation precision, and (2) how to deal with inconsistent profile sequence lengths commonly found in career break users' data.

In this study, we propose an innovative recommendation system that integrates graph neural networks (GNN) with dynamic rule-based ranking. The architecture consists of three main components: a multi-layer, multi-graph GNN module to capture user–position interaction patterns; sequential modeling using Long Short-Term Memory (LSTM) and multi-head self-attention to learn career-stage dependencies; and a dynamic two-stage ranking mechanism that performs industry classification and skill matching. The adaptive fusion is used to offer scores of each preliminary position, combining the GNN predictions with rule-based scores to balance representational power and interpretability, effectively addressing the unique challenges of recommending jobs for users with career breaks.

The contribution of this study is highlighted as below: (1) Problem: First to specifically target job recommendation for career-break populations, identifying challenges in incorporating career break information and handling varying sequence lengths; (2) Method: Proposes a novel hybrid GNN approach combining multi-graph modeling with dynamic two-stage ranking, featuring adaptive sequence pooling and sigmoid-based gating mechanisms; (3) Results: Achieves superior performance with Hit Rates of 37.2%@Top-10, 49.6%@Top-30, and 71.6%@Top-50 on real world data, significantly outperforming state-of-the-art baselines.

2 Related Work

Given that profiles of individuals with career breaks from recruitment websites are typically preprocessed into structured sequential formats, related work addressing such data can generally be categorized into two main areas: career-break-aware recommendation systems and sequence-aware approaches.

2.1 Career-Break-Related Recommendation Systems

Although some research considers the impact of career breaks on job recommendation systems, there is relatively little work that explicitly targets users with career break history to provide tailored job recommendations. This is mainly because:

1) Career breaks are rarely treated as a research object and are instead modeled as a sub-problem, such as serving as indicators of career transitions or as missing elements in career sequences. As for the former, [3] defined returning to work after a career break as a type of career transition, yet no corresponding job recommendation approaches were developed to leverage this information for studying career transitions. As for the latter, [4] proposed that sequences containing career breaks should constitute at least 70% of the longest sequences to avoid significantly affecting the quality of Optimal Matching Analysis results yet only involved traditional methods dealing with sequence data rather than deep learning techniques. This reflects a research gap in effectively using career break data, partly due to the complex nature of factors influencing career breaks and career break's impact [5], making them challenging to model and utilize effectively.
2) Mainstream job recommendation research typically addresses fairness from a group-level debiasing perspective rather than designing strategies for disadvantaged sub-populations. [6] reviewed fairness research in recommendation systems and found that studies focusing on group fairness outnumber those on individual fairness by a 3:1 ratio, as most work aims to improve algorithms for the general population or ensuring fairness over time [7]. However, from a societal perspective, developing systems that are oriented toward subpopulations disadvantaged by bias may be more essential to address the challenges they face, such as difficulties in securing employment following a career break.

2.2 Sequence-Aware Job Recommendation Systems

Overall, sequence-aware recommendation systems can be broadly classified into four main methodological approaches: (1) sequence learning, which encompasses frequent pattern mining, sequence modeling, distributed item representation, and supervised models; (2) matrix factorization; (3) hybrid methods, primarily including factor Markov chains and Latent Dirichlet allocation; and (4) Others, consisting discrete optimization and graph learning [8, 9].

Sequence-aware job recommendation systems are a specialized form of sequential recommendation that use a subset of these methods. One of the prevalent challenges which sequence-aware job recommendation systems face is recommendation bias from inconsistent user sequence lengths [10]. This is because models prioritize learning from users with extensive work experience, as longer sequences provide richer training data. This approach disadvantages individuals with shorter employment histories, particularly those with career breaks, creating systematic recommendation bias. This issue often leads to challenges such as data sparsity and cold start [11]. In this section, we will evaluate algorithms specifically towards the problem of inconsistent user sequence lengths.

Matrix Factorization Approaches. Early research utilized matrix factorization techniques due to their theoretical maturity and capability to handle sparse data. Representative works include [12], who proposed a generalized linear mixed model using parallel block coordinate descent algorithms, achieving linear scalability to handle billion-scale sparse data. However, it cannot explicitly model sequence information. [13] employed neural collaborative filtering combined with inverse propensity weighting to systematically address temporal bias in recruitment recommendations, yet the problem is newly posted positions receive excessive attention while older positions are overlooked, different from inconsistent user sequence lengths. In conclusion, matrix factorization often treats the interaction between users and items as static, and the learning quality of embedding depends on the amount of interaction data. Therefore, it performs poorly when handling short sequence interaction data.

Sequence Learning Methods. *Sequence Modeling:* This includes Markov models, reinforcement learning, and recurrent neural networks, all capable of explicitly leveraging sequential order information to model user behavioral transitions. Notable innovations include [14], who utilized LSTM and temporal convolutional networks to capture temporal dependencies in user behavior, incorporating attention mechanisms to identify critical time periods—representing the first application of time series analysis in job recommendation while considering stage-specific features of career development. [15] extended this approach by separately modeling job seekers' and recruiters' behavioral sequences using cross-attention mechanisms for bidirectional matching. Nevertheless, Sequence Modeling relies on sequential models or attention mechanisms that inherently require historical information, where longer sequences provide richer contextual information, and consequently, shorter sequences struggle to receive sufficient model attention.

Distributed Item Representation: This category includes latent Markov embedding and distributional embedding approaches, capable of capturing implicit similarities in sparse spaces [16]. [17] exemplifies the former approach, proposing a three-component embedding learning framework incorporating text deep neural networks, job-skill graph representation learning, and geographical location embedding, constituting the first industrial-scale large-scale embedded recruitment recommendation system. [18] represents the latter approach by proposing distributed representations of multi-dimensional features including text, skills, and experience, addressing semantic gap issues in skill matching and marking the first application of cross-modal representation learning in recruitment. However, this approach renders the transition relationships and co-occurrence patterns between items upon the richness of training samples. The imbalance between long and short sequences introduces bias at the embedding learning phase, and the model requirement for extensive training data further exacerbates the dependence on users with longer sequences.

Supervised Models: A common supervised learning design involves using neural networks or other machine learning methods to predict a matching score or to perform binary classification indicating whether a candidate will be hired, based on features extracted from résumés and job descriptions. It's worth noting that [19] proposed a multi-task learning framework that shares underlying representations for different interaction types, including job seeker applications, recruiter invitations, and bilateral communications to alleviate the data sparsity problem. However, similarly, this method relies heavily on users' historical interaction data. For users with limited interaction sequences, supervised models struggle to learn meaningful representations, and the data sparsity problem becomes severe.

Frequent Pattern Mining: This approach has limited application in sequence-aware job recommendation because recruitment data typically exhibit complex structures and rich attributes that make it difficult for this method to encode complex semantic information into simple patterns.

Hybrid Methods. Hybrid approaches combine the flexibility of sequence learning methods with the robustness to data sparsity offered by factorization-based matrix-completion techniques. For instance, [20] employed Latent Dirichlet allocation for job and resume topic extraction while utilizing factorization machines (FM) for feature interaction modeling, representing the first combination of topic models and FM for recruitment recommendation, supporting text-rich but interaction-sparse recruitment data. [21] designed context-aware multi-armed bandits combined with Markov decision processes to dynamically adapt strategies across user states with varying sequence lengths. Hybrid methods can learn separate model components for users with short and long sequences, and then combine them for prediction. For users with short sequences, they can leverage community trends and clustering results to identify transferable sequential patterns; for users with long sequences, they fully exploit their rich historical sequential behaviors. By sharing community-level sequential signals, these methods compensate for the limited individual history of short-sequence users.

Others. Recent years have witnessed effective applications of discrete optimization and graph learning approaches. Regarding the former, these methods rigorously consider constraint conditions with results providing optimality explanations. For example, [22] employed an improved Gale-Shapley algorithm to match suitable work environments and employers for individuals with autism, introducing social equity into algorithmic design and focusing on employment for vulnerable populations. [23] first applied optimal transport theory to recommend system fairness, preventing excessive applications to popular positions and ensuring equitable job exposure. However, these methods rely on static features of users and jobs, with limited modeling of users' dynamic sequential behaviors, making it difficult to accurately adapt to behavioral patterns across users with varying sequence lengths.

Graph structures capture high-order relationships and global structures through several paradigms: (1) Graph-based Recommendation: [24] constructed job similarity graphs with subgraph selection and PageRank ranking algorithms, representing the first application of graph algorithms in sequence aware recruitment recommendation; (2) Knowledge Graphs: [25] utilized knowledge graph construction with templated explanation generation to provide interpretable job recommendations, enhancing user trust; (3) Graph Neural Networks: [26] employed a deep fusion architecture combining large language models with graph neural networks, marking the first deep integration of LLMs with graph learning. Graph learning methods encode the rich historical behaviors of long-sequence users into a global graph structure, enabling transferable signals for short-sequence users through neighboring node features, thus generating embeddings for new or short-history users. This helps mitigate training bias arising from inconsistent user sequence lengths. However, traditional graph learning methods primarily model static or unordered user–job relationships, often weakening or losing the temporal dependencies inherent in user interaction sequences.

In conclusion, among existing sequence-aware algorithms, matrix factorization and discrete optimization handle only static features, limiting dynamic behavior modeling. Sequence learning captures temporal patterns but struggles with cold start and sparsity for short histories. In contrast, hybrid and graph approach flexibly model varying sequence lengths, explicitly modeling long and short sequences separately or enable mutual transfer between them to mitigate the bias caused by sequence length variability. Motivated by these insights, our research will continue to leverage hybrid and graph-theoretic approaches for ongoing investigation and methodological innovation.

3 Problem Formulation

Given a set of user profile P_u, S_u for user $\in$ U. Specifically,

(1) A set of recorded positions $P_u = \{p_1, p_2, \ldots, p_n, b_n\}$, which contains job data: $p_i = (title(p_i), company(p_i), location(p_i), description(p_i), start\_month(p_i), start\_year (p_i), end\_month(p_i), end\_year(p_i))$ and career break data: $b_n = (Reason(b_u), Duration(b_u))$.

(2) A set of professional skills$S_u = \{s_1, s_2, ...s_n\}, s_i \in \{skillnames\}$. Assume any one of the professional skills to beS_j, $S_j = \{s|sisaskillrequiredbyjobj\}, \gamma = \{j_1, j_2, ..., p_{n+1}, j_n\}$.

The objective of the problem is to recommend p_{n+1} after b_n to each user $u \in U$, subjecting to $\Delta(j) = |S_j \backslash S_u|, p_{n+1} = \underset{j \in \gamma}{argmin} \Delta(j)$, which represents that p_{n+1} is the job with a skill requirement closest to the user's existing skill.

4 Methodologies

4.1 System Framework

As shown in Fig. 1, the proposed system integrates graph neural networks (GNN) with dynamic rule-based ranking for career break job recommendations. The framework consists of two key parallel components: (1) a GNN module with sequence modeling and adaptive pooling for learning user-job representations and predicting scores; and (2) a rule-based two-stage ranking, which groups jobs by industry and then ranks them by skills to produce scores. The relative emphasis on industry versus skills is adaptively balanced through a dynamic gating mechanism guided by user advantages.

The core innovation lies in the score fusion mechanism that combines GNN predictions with rule-based scores through epoch-adaptive weighting, which means in the early stages, the system emphasizes GNN predictions to capture complex structural patterns, while in later stages it gradually shifts toward rule-based ranking to ensure rationality and interpretability. Thus, this hybrid design effectively addresses the unique challenges of career break scenarios by leveraging both the representational power of deep learning and the interpretability of domain-specific rules.

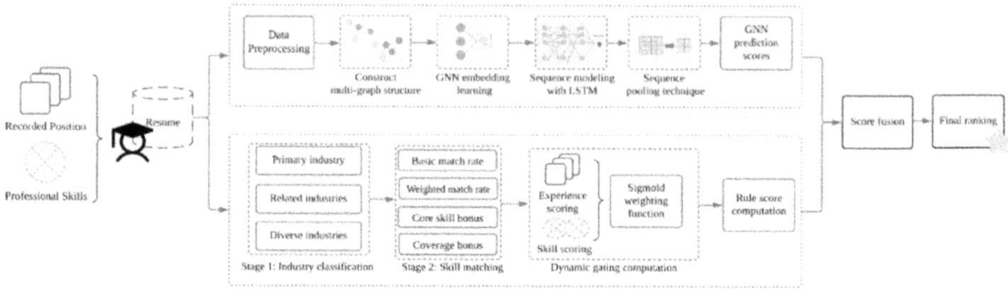

Fig. 1. Logic Framework

4.2 Multi-layer Graph Neural Networks

This is the GNN scoring component, which serves as encoder to capture complex semantic pattern between users and positions. Multi-Layer GNN is first employed to model the multi-graph interaction relationships between users and positions. Each graph corresponds to a specific career stage, thus encoding a snapshot of the user's interests during that period. The specific procedure starts with initial data processing, such as normalizing job positions in user histories into discrete IDs to facilitate graph construction. An interaction matrix is first constructed where rows represent users, columns represent positions, and a value of 1 indicates that a user has held that position.

The user's career trajectory is divided into t stages by career breaks, yielding t sub-matrices. Each sub-matrix can be directly interpreted as a user–position bipartite graph, where nodes consist of users and positions, and edges correspond to entries with value 1, indicating that a user has held a position. Every node in each subgraph is initialized with learnable embeddings. Subsequently, the sub-graphs are converted into TensorFlow SparseTensors to enable efficient message passing, which aims at exchanging information between connected nodes and updating their representations. In this process, user nodes aggregate features from their previously held positions, while position nodes incorporate signals from the associated users. As a result, the GNN produces stage-specific user representations that capture career interests and position representations, that encode job requirements. During message propagation, the process iteratively performs l layers. For the i-th layer, the user-side update follows (1):

$$h_u^{(l)} = \sigma(Adj \times h_i^{(l-1)} + h_u^{(l-1)}) \tag{1}$$

and the position-side update follows (2):

$$h_i^{(l)} = \sigma(Adj^T \times h_u^{(l-1)} + h_i^{(l-1)}) \tag{2}$$

The output of each layer is added to the previous layer's result (residual connection), and dropout is applied to enhance training stability.

The final user/position representations are obtained by summing all layers and stacking results from the t subgraphs, yielding multi-graph multi-perspective representations. Each x_t is the graph neural network output vector of the user (or position) from the *t-th* graph.

4.3 Multi-head Self-Attention and LSTM Modeling

This modeling approach aims at forming the final sequential representation on position vectors, in which Long Short-Term Memory (LSTM) focuses on modeling sequential nature, while Multi-Head Self-Attention emphasizes learning complexity. In detail, LSTM transforms the user's representations across multiple graphs into a sequence of length t, where t denotes the number of graphs. The output sequence of LSTM is represented as H, as shown in (3),

$$H = LSTM(X) = [h_1, h_2, \ldots, h_t] \tag{3}$$

where X represents the input sequence from career stage subgraph, as shown in (4).

$$X = [x_1, x_2, \ldots, x_t] \tag{4}$$

Then sequential modeling is performed across multi-graph representations to learn dependencies between semantics captured by different graph structures, with the recurrent process as (5)–(10):

$$i_t = \sigma(W_i x_t + U_i h_{t-1} + b_i) \tag{5}$$

$$f_t = \sigma(W_f x_t + U_f h_{t-1} + b_f) \tag{6}$$

$$o_t = \sigma(W_o x_t + U_o h_{t-1} + b_o) \tag{7}$$

$$\tilde{c}_t = tanh(W_c x_t + U_c h_{t-1} + b_c) \tag{8}$$

$$c_t = f_t \odot c_{t-1} + i_t \odot \tilde{c}_t \tag{9}$$

$$h_t = o_t \odot tanh(c_t) \tag{10}$$

Subsequently, Multi-Head Attention performs global information modeling on the LSTM output sequence, allowing each time step (each graph's representation) to observe information from all others, conducting attention across the multi-graph sequential dimension to aggregate representations from all graphs to each position, as shown in (11),

$$Attention(H) = Concat(head_1, \ldots, head_t)W^o \tag{11}$$

where the formula for each head is shown in (12), with (13),

$$head_i = Softmax(\frac{Q_i K_i^T}{\sqrt{d_k}})V_i \tag{12}$$

$$Q_i = HW_i^Q, K_i = HW_i^K, V_i = HW_i^V \tag{13}$$

Finally, the sequence (multi-graph) undergoes average pooling to obtain *User/PositionRepresentation* E, as shown in (14),

$$E = \frac{1}{t}\sum_{i=1}^{t} Attention(h_i) \tag{14}$$

4.4 Sequence Pooling

This stage draws on graph pooling ideas to learn a dynamic weighted assignment. It is known that some users have extensive work experience with long sequences, while others have limited experience with short sequences. If all users are treated as having the same length for model input, short sequences require extensive 0-padding, causing information dilution and resulting in poor learned representations. By contrast, sequence pooling mitigates this issue by adaptively compressing variable-length sequences into informative fixed-length representations.

The graph pooling approach concentrates attention allocation on important time steps for short sequences, and adaptively merges similar steps for long sequences, ultimately yielding L fixed-length segments, each representing a "conceptual-level" cluster. The specific procedure involves inputting sequence representations: $E \in \mathcal{R}^{T\times d}$, where $T =$ sequence length for different users, $d =$ embedding dimension.

Assignment Scores are computed as shown in (15),

$$A_{ij} = (W_{proj}E_j)_i + time\_weight_j \tag{15}$$

where each input time step j is projected into an L-dimensional score vector, with each dimension indicating its assignment strength to a pooling cluster.

It is worth noting that the assignment scores incorporate time decay weights, making more recent career experiences in the sequence more important, and career experiences with longer duration in the sequence more important, as shown in Eq. (16),

$$time\_weight_j = exp(-\lambda \cdot time_{since}) \times log 1 + duration \tag{16}$$

Then, Softmax normalization yields the Assignment Matrix, as shown in Eq. (17),

$$S_{ij} = \frac{e^{A_{ij}}}{\sum_k e^{A_{ik}}} \tag{17}$$

where each input step assigns probabilities to L clusters, ensuring row sums equal 1.

Finally, pooling weighting is performed as shown in Eq. (18),

$$\tilde{E}_i = \sum_{j=1}^{T} S_{ij} \cdot E_j \tag{18}$$

where the i-th pooling cluster equals weighted sum of all input steps, ultimately obtaining $\tilde{E} \in \mathcal{R}^{N \times d}$, where N = preset fixed length. This approach ensures all users output the same length while preserving the most important information from user histories, avoiding model bias toward long/short users due to sequence length variations.

After users and positions undergo multi-graph multi-layer graph neural networks, the obtained embedding vectors are processed through an MLP to output a scalar score as GNN Score, where is shown in (19)

$$GNNScore(u, p) = MLP(\tilde{E}_u || \tilde{E}_p) \tag{19}$$

where u denotes a user while p denotes a position. $\tilde{E}_u$ denotes the final representation of the user. $\tilde{E}_p$ demotes the final representation of the position. $||$ denotes concatenation.

4.5 Dynamic Two-Stage Ranking

This is the rule-based scoring component, serving as an explicit ranking module that provides interpretable scores. It consists of two stages. The first stage is Industry Classification, which categorizes all positions into three groups based on users' industry backgrounds: primary industry, related industry, and diverse industry. The second stage is Skill Ranking, which computes skill-matching scores within each industry category and combines them with industry scores through a dynamic gating mechanism. The outcome of these two stages is the Rule Score, which is subsequently fused with GNN predictions to produce the Final Score.

Specifically, in the Industry Classification stage, Industry Score is calculated with weights of 1 for primary industry, 0.7 for related industry, and 0.3 for diverse industry. The weights of 1.0, 0.7, and 0.3 are chosen to reflect the decreasing relevance of these industries to a user's core background. In the skill matching component, Skill Match Score is calculated across four dimensions for all positions within each industry category: basic match rate, weighted match rate, core skill bonus, and coverage bonus.

Then, the system provides personalized weights for users based on their experience characteristics (experience score n): that is, if users have extensive work experience (large number of jobs), $w_{industry}$ is high and w_{skill} is low, and vice versa, as shown in (20)–(21),

$$w_{skill} = 0.3 + 0.5 \cdot sigmoid(k(n - T)) \tag{20}$$

$$w_{industry} = 1 - w_{skill} \tag{21}$$

The final score calculation in the rule stage is $RuleScore = w_{industry} \times IndustryScore + w_{skill} \times SkillMatchScore$. The constants 0.3 and 0.5 are manually set boundary parameters designed to constrain the skill weight w_{skill} within a reasonable range, where 0.3 serves as the minimum weight and 0.5 functions as the scaling factor.

Dynamic Gating automatically learns weight allocation, enabling the model to perform fair and personalized ranking for different users. After obtaining Rule Score, it needs to be fused with GNN-learned scores, $FinalScore = \alpha \times GNNScore + (1 - \alpha) \times RuleScore$, in which α gradually changes with epochs. At the early stages, α is close to 1, so the final score relies mainly on GNN predictions to capture rich structural and semantic patterns. As training proceeds, α gradually decreases while $1\text{-}\alpha$ increases, shifting the emphasis toward the rule-based score, allowing GNN and rules to have different contributions at different stages.

4.6 Optimization

In this model, the core objective of optimization is to minimize a multi-task combined loss function. The entire optimization process can be divided into the following main steps:

We construct training pairs from user interaction data through positive-negative sampling in each mini-batch. Specifically, for each user, we sample positive positions (i^+) that the user has clicked, together with randomly selected negative positions (i^-), forming triplets of (user, positive sample, negative sample). Subsequently, in the forward propagation phase, the model generates final representations of user u and position p based on current user and position embeddings, utilizing multi-layer graph neural networks, sequential LSTM modeling, and Multi-Head Self-Attention fusion, and computes the prediction score GNN Score for each (u, p) pair. Based on these scores, the Bayesian Personalized Ranking (BPR) loss is calculated through (22) to ensure positive sample scores exceed negative sample scores by a margin, thereby enforcing the model to rank positions that the user interacted with higher than those they ignored.

$$\mathcal{L}_{BPR} = \frac{1}{N} \sum_{(u,i^+,i^-)} max(0,1 - (score(u, i^+) - score(u, i^-))) \tag{22}$$

Beyond BPR Loss, the model also introduces self-supervised contrastive learning loss (SSL Loss). Self-supervised learning is primarily employed for aligning user/position representations across multiple graphs, as independent training of each graph would result in inconsistent distributions of learned user/item vectors. Therefore, vectors of the same user in different graphs are treated as positive pairs, while different users or negatively sampled items are treated as negative pairs, making representations of the same user across different graphs more similar while enhancing discrimination between different users. The loss function is shown in (23)

$$\mathcal{L}_{ssl} = \sum_{g=1}^{G} max(0,1 - (s^+ - s^-)) \tag{23}$$

where G: total number of graphs, $s+$: positive pair score for the same user/item sampled from two graphs, $s-$: random negative pair score.

To encourage diversification of user representations and prevent all user embeddings from converging to the same direction, the model also introduces Diversity Loss, which increases discriminability by minimizing the squared similarity between user embeddings, as shown in Eq. (24),

$$\mathcal{L}_{Diversity} = \frac{1}{N^2} \sum_{i \neq j} (< \widehat{u_i}, \widehat{u_j} >)^2 \tag{24}$$

All these loss terms, along with L2 regularization of parameters, are combined into a total loss function, as shown in (25).

$$\mathcal{L}_{Total} = \mathcal{L}_{BPR} + \lambda_{div} \cdot \mathcal{L}_{Diversity} + \lambda_{SSL} \cdot \mathcal{L}_{SSL} + \lambda_{reg} \cdot \mathcal{L}_2 \tag{25}$$

In the optimizer component, the code adopts Adam for gradient updates and combines an exponential decay learning rate strategy for dynamic adjustment, smoothly reducing the learning rate to help model convergence, as shown in (26).

$$lr = initial\_l_{lr} \times decay^{\lfloor step/decay\_steps \rfloor} \tag{26}$$

5 Experiment

In this section, we conduct experiments on a real-world dataset for sequential recommendations to evaluate our proposed method, with the purpose of answering the following questions:

RQ1: How does ReCareer perform in top-k recommendation compared with the state-of-the-art models?

RQ2: What are the benefits of the components proposed?

RQ3: In real cases, how can the designed hybrid recommendation in ReCareer provide useful interpretations?

5.1 Experimental Setting

Experimental Datasets. We evaluate the recommendation performance on a real world dataset collected from one of the largest employment-oriented social networking service providers, using users' online profiles up to November 2024 and filtering for those with a history of career breaks. The dataset comprises 2,238 users, 23 industries, 603 merged occupational job categories, 7,992 professional skills, and 12 career break types. We use 80% of the user data for the training set and 20% for the test set.

Evaluation Metrics. We design our evaluation protocol to reflect the career break scenario, where each user has a single true post-break job choice, making recommendation accuracy critical. To assess both accuracy and practicality, specifically, the ability to recommend the actual target job and the likelihood of retrieving it within a reasonable shortlist, we employ Recall@K, Precision@K, and F1-Score at Top 10, Top 30, and Top 50 level. Recall@K (Hit Rate) measures the proportion of users whose true job appears in the top K recommendations, Precision@K assesses the relevance ratio within the recommended list, and F1-Score captures the trade-off between precision and recall providing a balanced evaluation of recommendation performance.

Compared Baselines. To demonstrate effectiveness, we compare our proposed ReCareer model with the following methods:

(1) *NCF* [27]: It combines matrix factorization with deep neural networks to deliver superior recommendation results,

(2) *SLi-Rec* [28]: It is based on an attention framework and an improved time-aware LSTM to dynamically combine users' long-term and short-term preferences in online recommender systems.
(3) *SelfGNN* [29]: It uses self-supervised GNNs for sequential recommendation, capturing short-term collaboration and long-term patterns while mitigating noise.

Implementation Detail. We implement our ReCareer system with TensorFlow and use Adam optimizer with a learning rate of 5×10^{-4} and an exponential decay ratio of 0.98. The main embedding dimension is set to 128, with career break embedding dimension of 64. The number of GNN layers is set to 3, and we construct 6 subgraphs for different career stages. The multi-head self-attention mechanism uses 8 heads, and the pooling target length for sequence modeling is 10.

For training, we use a batch size of 256 and train for 30 epochs with a dropout rate of 0.7. We sample 4 negative samples per positive sample and perform model evaluation every 3 epochs. The weight for L2 regularization is 1×10^{-5}, the weight λ_1 for SSL (self-supervised learning) loss is 1×10^{-3}, and the weight λ_2 for diversity regularization is 2×10^{-3}. For the dynamic gating mechanism, we set the minimum industry weight to 0.2, sigmoid threshold T to 4.0, and sigmoid steepness k to 0.8. During training, the GNN weight and the rule-based weight are set to vary in range 0.2 to 0.8. We set the maximum skill sequence length to 25, select top 5 skills per user for connection, and use a time decay factor of 0.05 with duration importance weight of 1.0. For recommendation quality, we set the MMR lambda for diversity vs relevance tradeoff to 0.3, skill match threshold to 0.1, industry diversity factor to 0.3, and randomness factor to 0.05.

5.2 Overall Performance (RQ1)

Our ReCareer system demonstrates consistently superior performance compared to baseline methods (NCF, SLi-Rec, SelfGNN) across all evaluation scenarios. The experimental results validate the limitations of baseline methods when handling inconsistent user sequence data and career break information. NCF model demonstrates that traditional matrix factorization approaches struggle with the sparse data characteristic of career break scenarios. SLi-Rec reveals that sequential models alone cannot effectively handle variable-length career histories, a common challenge in career break user profiles. The performance of SelfGNN indicates that our hybrid approach outperforms pure GNN methods, suggesting that our system effectively leverages career break information while incorporating temporal patterns through LSTM and self-attention mechanisms (Tables 1, 2 and 3).

Table 1. Performance in Rank@10

Metric	Recall@10	Precision@10	F1 Score
NCF	0.324	0.0324	0.059
SLi-Rec	0.352	0.0352	0.064
SelfGNN	0.359	0.0359	0.065

(*continued*)

Table 1. (*continued*)

Metric	Recall@10	Precision@10	F1 Score
ReCareer	**0.372**	**0.0372**	**0.068**

Table 2. Performance in Rank@30

Metric	Recall@30	Precision@30	F1 Score
NCF	0.428	0.0143	0.028
SLi-Rec	0.469	0.0156	0.030
SelfGNN	0.473	0.0158	0.031
ReCareer	**0.496**	**0.0165**	**0.032**

Table 3. Performance in Rank@50

Metric	Recall@50	Precision@50	F1 Score
NCF	0.639	0.0128	0.025
SLi-Rec	0.645	0.0129	0.025
SelfGNN	0.656	0.0131	0.026
ReCareer	**0.716**	**0.0143**	**0.028**

This improvement directly validates our solution to both challenges. The differentiated modeling across career break types enables more accurate job matching for users with employment gaps. Additionally, it ensures that users with shorter employment sequences due to career breaks receive equally accurate recommendations as those with extensive work histories.

The relative high value of Recall@K represents that the system successfully captures relevant positions within larger recommendation sets. However, to leverage authentic recommendation data, our evaluation protocol assigns each user a single true post-break job choice, which inherently constrains the upper bound of precision metrics. Specifically, the maximum achievable Precision@10 is limited to $1/10 = 0.1$, while Precision@30 and Precision@50 are theoretically capped at 0.033 and 0.02, respectively. Our system achieves 0.0372@10, 0.0165@30, 0.0143@50, demonstrating favorable performance relative to these theoretical upper bounds. Additionally, even though the precision is relatively low, our method is still higher than the baseline approach. For scalability with recommendation size, the performance trends reveal that Recall value improves dramatically while F1 scores remain relatively stable, indicating balanced and consistent performance across different recommendation list sizes.

5.3 Ablation Study (RQ2)

Based on the ablation study results, the sequence pooling module emerges as the most critical component (8.8% improvement in Recall@10), while career break multi-graph modeling ranks second (1.1% improvement in Recall@10). The sequence pooling module demonstrates substantially superior performance compared to directly processing variable-length sequences, indicating that the assignment matrix method borrowed from graph pooling successfully addresses the sequence length problem in recommendation systems. Correspondingly, the multi-graph structure, which partitions data into t subgraphs according to career break types, shows significant improvements over single-graph approaches. This demonstrates that differentiated modeling of career break types is effective, as different types of career breaks (childcare, education, health, etc.) indeed require distinct graph structures for optimal capture and representation. Although the multi-component design inevitably introduces complexity, the contribution of each module is verifiable, indicating that the complexity is necessary rather than redundant (Table 4).

Table 4. Module Ablation Study on Reference

Category	Recall@10	Recall@30	Recall@50
Single Career Break Graph	0.368	0.485	0.698
None Sequence Pooling	0.342	0.466	0.684
ReCareer	**0.372**	**0.496**	**0.716**

5.4 Case Study (RQ3)

We randomly selected a user who is a Technology professional with a 20-month education break who transitioned from IT management to software engineering. Our system successfully identified the ground truth position (software engineer, rank #3) by leveraging career break information to predict transition patterns and using adaptive sequence pooling to handle the short work history, achieving 94.49% total matching scores, as shown in Fig. 2.

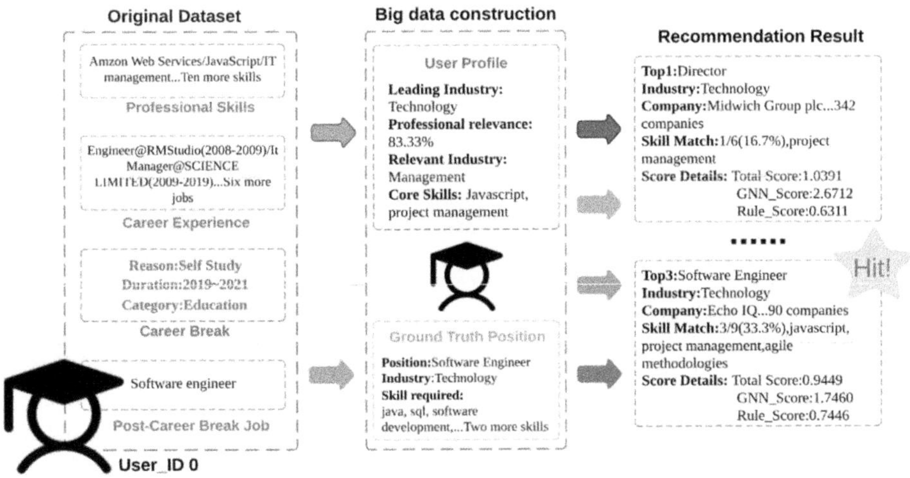

Fig. 2. Case Study

6 Conclusion and Future Work

The study proposes a hybrid GNN-based recommendation system specifically designed for career break users, addressing two critical challenges: effective utilization of career break information and handling inconsistent sequence lengths. Our approach combines multi-graph GNN modeling with dynamic two-stage ranking, achieving superior performance among state-of-art algorithms. For future work, we aim to investigate cross-cultural applicability across different labor markets and career development patterns, incorporating external factors such as market demand and economic conditions into the recommendation framework. We also plan to validate the scalability of the proposed framework on million-scale real-world recruitment platforms and explore more efficient distributed implementations.

Acknowledgments. This research is supported by Shandong Provincial University Youth Innovation and Technology Support Program No.2022KJ291 and EdUHK project under Grant No. RG 67/2024-2025R.

References

1. Career Returners. Career Returners Indicator 2025. Career Returners (2025). https://careerreturners.com/indicator2025
2. Vuorinen, N.: Implications of career break from personal and company perspectives. In: Degree Programme in International Business Management (2017)
3. Mussagulova, A., Chng, S., Goh, Z.A.G., Tang, C.J., Jayasekara, D.N.: When is a career transition successful? A systematic literature review and outlook (1980–2022). Front. Psychol. **14**, 1141202 (2023)
4. Dlouhy, K., Biemann, T.: Optimal matching analysis in career research: a review and some best-practice recommendations. J. Vocat. Behav. **90**, 163–173 (2015)

5. Nguyen, L.: Career Break Compass: Navigating Your Path to a Balanced Life Through Intentional Time Off. Simon and Schuster, New York (2024)
6. Deldjoo, Y., Jannach, D., Bellogin, A., Difonzo, A., Zanzonelli, D.: Fairness in recommender systems: research landscape and future directions. User Model. User-Adap. Inter. **34**(1), 59–108 (2024)
7. Li, Y., Yang, Y., Cao, J., Liu, S., Tang, H., Xu, G.: Toward structure fairness in dynamic graph embedding: a trend-aware dual debiasing approach. In: Proceedings of the 30th ACM SIGKDD Conference on Knowledge Discovery and Data Mining, pp. 1701–1712 (2024)
8. Wang, S., Hu, L., Wang, Y., Cao, L., Sheng, Q.Z., Orgun, M.: Sequential recommender systems: challenges, progress and prospects (2019). arXiv:2001.04830
9. Quadrana, M., Cremonesi, P., Jannach, D.: Sequence-aware recommender systems. ACM Comput. Surv. (CSUR) **51**(4), 1–36 (2018)
10. Mashayekhi, Y., Li, N., Kang, B., Lijffijt, J., De Bie, T.: A challenge-based survey of e-recruitment recommendation systems. ACM Comput. Surv. **56**(10), 1–33 (2024)
11. Chen, H., Yang, Y., Bei, Y., Wang, Z., Xu, Y., Huang, F.: Graph neural patching for cold-start recommendations. In: Proceedings of the Australasian Database Conference, pp.334–346 (2024)
12. Zhang, X., Zhou, Y., Ma, Y., Chen, B.C., Zhang, L., Agarwal, D.: GLMix: generalized linear mixed models for large-scale response prediction. In: Proceedings of 22nd ACM SIGKDD International Conference on Knowledge Discovery and Data Mining (KDD'16), pp. 363–372 (2016)
13. Chen, R.C., Ai, Q., Jayasinghe, G., Croft, W.B.: Correcting for recency bias in job recommendation. In: Proceedings of 28th ACM International Conference on Information and Knowledge Management (CIKM'19), pp. 2185–2188 (2019)
14. Liu, K., Shi, X., Kumar, A., Zhu, L., Natarajan, P.: Temporal learning and sequence modeling for a job recommender system. In: Proceedings of Recommender Systems Challenge (RecSys Challenge'16), vol. 7, p. 4 (2016)
15. Fu, B., Liu, H., Zhu, Y., Song, Y., Zhang, T., Wu, Z.: Beyond matching: Modeling two-sided multi-behavioral sequences for dynamic person-job fit. In: Database Systems for Advanced Applications, pp. 359–375. Springer, Heidelberg (2021)
16. Li, W., et al.: DLS-GAN: generative adversarial nets for defect location sensitive data augmentation. IEEE Trans. Autom. Sci. Eng. 5173–5189 (2023)
17. Zhao, J., et al.: Embedding-based recommender system for job to candidate matching on scale. CoRR https://arxiv.org/abs/2107.00221 (2021)
18. Dave, V.S., Zhang, B., Al Hasan, M., AlJadda, K., Korayem, M.: A combined representation learning approach for better job and skill recommendation. In: Proceedings of 27th ACM International Conference on Information and Knowledge Management (CIKM'18), pp. 1997–2005 (2018)
19. Yang, Z.R., He, Z.Y., Wang, C.D., Lai, P.Y., Liao, D.Z., Wang, Z.Z.: A bidirectional recommender system for online recruitment. In: Proceedings of IEEE International Conference on Data Mining (ICDM'22), pp. 628–637 (2022)
20. Leksin, V., Ostapets, A.: Job recommendation based on factorization machine and topic modelling. In: Proceedings of Recommender Systems Challenge (RecSys Challenge'16), vol. 6, p. 4 (2016)
21. Chen, W., et al.: Tree-based contextual learning for online job or candidate recommendation with big data support in professional social networks. IEEE Access **6**, 77725–77739 (2018)
22. Bills, J., Ng, Y.D.: Looking for jobs? Matching adults with autism with potential employers for job opportunities. In: Proceedings of 25th International Database Engineering & Applications Symposium (IDEAS'21), pp. 212–221 (2021)

23. Mashayekhi, Y., Kang, B., Lijffijt, J., De Bie, T.: ReCon: reducing congestion in job recommendation using optimal transport. In: Proceedings of 17th ACM Conference Recommender Systems (RecSys'23), pp. 696–701 (2023)
24. Shalaby, W., et al.: Help me find a job: a graph-based approach for job recommendation at scale. In: Proceedings of IEEE International Conference on Big Data (Big Data'17), pp. 1544–1553 (2017)
25. Upadhyay, C., Abu-Rasheed, H., Weber, C., Fathi, M.: Explainable job-posting recommendations using knowledge graphs and named entity recognition. In: Proceedings of IEEE International Conference on Systems, Man, and Cybernetics (SMC'21), pp. 3291–3296 (2021)
26. Wu, L., Qiu, Z., Zheng, Z., Zhu, H., Chen, E.: Exploring large language model for graph data understanding in online job recommendations. In: Proceedings of AAAI Conference on Artificial Intelligence, pp. 9178–9186 (2024)
27. He, X., Liao, L., Zhang, H., Nie, L., Hu, X., Chua, T.-S.: Neural collaborative filtering. In: Proceedings of WWW, pp. 173–182 (2017)
28. Yu, Z., Lian, J., Mahmoody, A., Liu, G., Xie, X.: Adaptive user modeling with long and short-term preferences for personalized recommendation. In: Proceedings of IJCAI, pp. 4213–4219 (2019)
29. Liu, Y., Xia, L., Huang, C.: Selfgnn: self-supervised graph neural networks for sequential recommendation. In: Proceedings of 47th International ACM SIGIR Conference on Research and Development in Information Retrieval, pp. 1609–1619 (2024)

Two-Lane Local Optimality Driving Strategy for Enhancing Traffic Stability

Xuqian Qin, Zhengyuan Du, Shuanglin Wang, Jieyang Lin, Yuxi Sun, and Jinhua Tan(✉)

School of Information Engineering, Zhongnan University of Economics and Law, Wuhan 430073, China
tanjh2007@163.com

Abstract. On a two-lane highway, vehicle-to-vehicle communication can provide drivers with the information that reflects the overall traffic situation within a local area. Such information may have significant influences on the driver's perception of traffic condition as well as driving tasks. To explore the specific effects of such information on traffic stability, this paper proposes a Two-lane Local Optimality (TLO) driving strategy and develops a two-lane car-following model (TLO model) correspondingly. Analytical results indicate that TLO driving strategy can improve traffic stability. Simulation results agree well with the analytical ones. It is shown that the amplitudes of headway and velocity fluctuations are reduced in TLO model. The fluctuations become much smaller when the range of the local area is enlarged. All the results suggest that the TLO driving strategy has great potential for enhancing traffic stability. Moreover, the effectiveness of the strategy can be further strengthened as the local area increases within a certain range.

Keywords: Driving behavior · Traffic stability · Two-lane Local Optimality · Vehicle-to-vehicle communication

1 Introduction

In recent years, traffic problems such as traffic congestion and road accident frequently appear, which are standing in the way of the sustainable development of society [1–5]. The car-following model is a beneficial tool to investigate traffic problems, which describes the traffic dynamics by constructing the equation of the motion of each vehicle [6,7]. There have been many attempts on developing car-following models [8–14]. And there are mainly two types of car-following models in the existing literature. One considers the interaction between vehicles moving on a single-lane highway without overtaking [9,11,15–17]. The other takes into account the situation that a vehicle is influenced by the nearest preceding vehicle in the adjacent lane [18,19].

The development of vehicle-to-vehicle (V2V) communication brings an opportunity for solving traffic problems. As a component of Internet of Vehicles (IoV), V2V communication can provide drivers with detailed information

T. Hao et al. (Eds.): BESC 2025, LNCS 16431, pp. 488–502, 2026.
https://doi.org/10.1007/978-981-95-7138-3_31

about surrounding vehicles' movements (such as velocity, acceleration, and position). Utilizing the information provided by V2V communication, many driving strategies are proposed, which are demonstrated to be helpful for supporting drivers' driving tasks and improving traffic [3,20,21]. Obviously, the beneficial driving strategies in V2V communication environment show great potential for improving driving behaviors and traffic flow.

For better application of V2V communication as well as the optimization of traffic operation, this paper constructs a Two-lane Local Optimality (TLO) driving strategy. In this strategy, drivers, on a two-lane highway, have a tendency to reach a state in which the condition of the vehicle is consistent with the overall traffic situations within a local area. In fact, the overall traffic situation within a local area can be reflected by the average headway of vehicles in the area [3,20]. Therefore, this study proposes a hypothesis that both the driving behaviors and the traffic stability can be improved when V2V communication provides drivers with the average headways of vehicles within a local area in the two lanes.

To test the hypothesis presented above, this paper develops a two-lane car-following model with consideration of the TLO driving strategy. Based on the developed model, the influences of the TLO driving strategy on traffic stability are investigated by analytical and numerical methods. The new driving strategy will help to make better use of V2V communication.

The rest of this paper is organized as follows. Section 2 reviews the related literature. The new model considering the TLO driving strategy is presented in Sect. 3. Section 4 exhibits the linear stability analysis. Section 5 displays the numerical simulation results. Conclusions are summarized in Sect. 6.

2 Literature Review

In order to study traffic phenomena and solve traffic problems, many traffic flow models have been put forward [19]. Generally, these models can be classified into either macroscopic models or microscopic models [3,9,22]. Macroscopic traffic flow models, which regard the whole traffic flow as the fluid, investigate the relationship among traffic variables (such as flow, density and average velocity) rather than the movement properties of individual vehicles [22]. Microscopic traffic flow models explore the motion of each vehicle and capture vehicle traces, which help to reflect driving behaviors and disclose the formation mechanism of traffic phenomena.

As an important component of microscopic models, car-following model is frequently adopted to describe driving operations and explain traffic phenomena [6]. The earliest car-following model was proposed by Pipes [15] in 1953. The idea of this model was that a driver's response (acceleration or deceleration) was a function of the driver's sensitivity and the stimulus. The stimulus was expressed in terms of the velocity difference between the vehicle and the vehicle in front. Newell [16] argued that the response of a driver would be influenced by the headway, and formulated Newell model in 1961. The model assumed that the velocity of a vehicle at time t was a function of the headway at time $t - \tau$, where τ referred to the delay time. Thereafter, to describe driving operations and traffic phenomena accurately, great efforts have been devoted to constructing car-following models, some of which have aroused wide concern. In 1995, Bando et al. [17] presented the optimal velocity (OV) model. This model overcame the defect of Newell model, and the unrealistically high acceleration would not exist in OV model when the traffic light changed from red to green. In 1998, a calibration of OV model was carried out on the basis of empirical data. It was observed that the values of acceleration and deceleration were unrealistic large in OV model. To address this issue, Helbing and Tilch [11] developed generalized force (GF) model. This model considered the negative velocity difference when the velocity of a vehicle was larger than that of the vehicle ahead. However, neither OV model nor GF model can explain the phenomenon that a vehicle will not decelerate when the velocity of the preceding vehicle is much faster, even if the headway is smaller than the safe distance. Taking this phenomenon into account, Jiang et al. [9] put forward full velocity difference (FVD) model in 2001. FVD model can better reflect the real driving operations and traffic condition than OV model and GF model [6,23].

Due to the superiority of FVD model mentioned above, it has been widely applied in the successive studies with respect to traffic flow. Zhang et al. [13] explored the effects of preceding vehicle's taillight on driving behaviors based on FVD model. The results revealed that traffic safety was enhanced when considering preceding vehicle's taillight. Tan et al. [20] presented a driving strategy in the IoV environment based on FVD model, which contributes to improving traffic stability and safety as well as reducing energy dissipation. These studies, from the viewpoint of traffic dynamics, provide reference for solving traffic problems. However, most car-following models are limited to the single-lane traffic system. Through an empirical study, Ponnu and Coifman [24] found that the velocity of a vehicle was affected by the speed in the adjacent lane. By carrying out driving simulator experiments, Duan et al. [25] observed that the following distance of a vehicle as well as a driver's decision (pass through or stop at the intersection) would be influenced by the behavior of vehicles in the adjacent lane. Evidently, the single-lane car-following models are not suitable for the multi-lane traffic system that is common in real traffic.

In an attempt to describe driving behaviors and traffic dynamics in the multi-lane traffic system, a few studies formulate car-following models considering the vehicle in the adjacent lane [26]. Jia et al. [18] stated that a driver might focus on the forward vehicle in the adjacent lane, so as to avoid collisions induced by the lane changing. For further analysis, Jia et al. presented a two-lane car-following model. Ge et al. [19] suggested that a vehicle might be influenced by the closest preceding vehicle in the adjacent lane. By taking this lateral effect into account, a two-lane car-following model was proposed based on FVD model. These two-lane car-following models, compared with single-lane models, are in better agreement with the actual driving operations and traffic condition in the multi-lane traffic system. However, it seems that the complex driving behaviors and traffic phenomena cannot be accurately described by only considering the impacts of one vehicle in the adjacent lane. In real traffic, drivers may pay attention to multiple vehicles instead of a particular vehicle in the adjacent lane [27].

V2V communication can provide drivers with real-time traffic information [21], including the motion of multiple vehicles in the current lane as well as the adjacent lane. To make better use of V2V communication, some car-following models are developed [10,28–33]. Guo et al. [31] proposed a new car-following model with consideration of multiple preceding vehicles' velocity fluctuations. Considering the average velocity of multiple preceding vehicles and driver's memory of the historical velocity of its nearest preceding vehicle, Sun et al. [32] presented an improved car-following model. Peng et al. [33] extended FVD model by introducing the acceleration and headway of multiple vehicles. These car-following models have been demonstrated to be helpful for improving driving operations and traffic stability. However, the models presented above have not considered the overall situation of multiple vehicles in the adjacent lane, which is a potential influence factor on driving behaviors and may be beneficial to driving tasks in the V2V communication environment.

Accordingly, there is a need for further studies to explore car-following schemes incorporating the overall traffic situations within a local area in both the current lane and the adjacent lane. This paper, accounting for the average headways of vehicles within a local area on a two-lane highway, proposes a TLO driving strategy and develops a two-lane car-following model in the V2V communication environment. The specific effects of the TLO driving strategy on traffic stability are investigated based on the developed model.

3 Model

In general, a single-lane car-following model can be expressed as [27,34]:

$$x_n'' = f_{sti}\left(v_n, \Delta x_n, \Delta v_n\right) \tag{1}$$

where x_n is the position of vehicle n, and the function f_{sti} denotes the response of vehicle n to the stimulus received. The stimulus consists of the velocity v_n, the headway $\Delta x_n = x_{n+1} - x_n$ and the velocity difference $\Delta v_n = v_{n+1} - v_n$ between vehicle n and its preceding vehicle (vehicle $n+1$).

In addition to the factors considered in Eq. (1), driving tasks are affected by the overall situations of vehicles within a local area in both lanes on a two-lane highway. Accordingly, this paper proposes a TLO driving strategy, as shown in Fig. 1. This driving strategy supposes that the average headways of vehicles within a local area are crucial for the motion of vehicles. To test the effects of this driving strategy on traffic, a car-following model considering the TLO driving strategy (TLO model) is developed, which can be given by:

$$x_{n,i}'' = f_{sti}\left(v_{n,i}, \Delta x_{n,i}, \Delta v_{n,i}, \Delta \bar{x}_{n,i}, \Delta \bar{x}_{m,i,\text{other}}\right) \tag{2}$$

where $x_{n,i}$ and $v_{n,i}$ indicate respectively the position and velocity of vehicle n in lane i ($i = 1, 2$). $\Delta x_{n,i} = x_{n+1,i} - x_{n,i}$ and $\Delta v_{n,i} = v_{n+1,i} - v_{n,i}$ refer to the

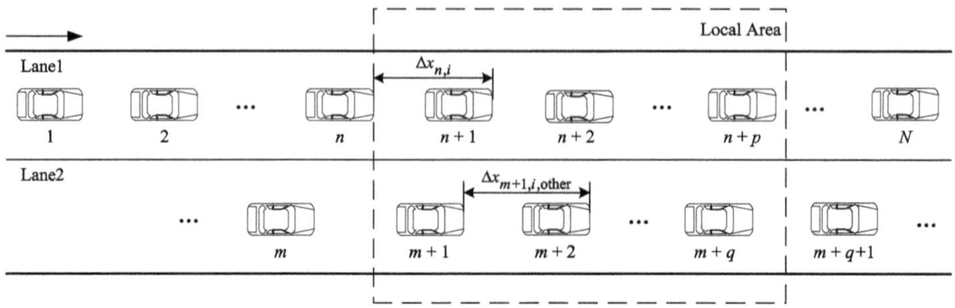

Fig. 1. Schematic diagram of the TLO driving strategy. The single arrow in the figure represents the driving direction.

headway and the velocity difference between vehicle n and its preceding vehicle in lane i. $\Delta\bar{x}_{n,i}$ and $\Delta\bar{x}_{m,i,\text{other}}$ are the average headways of vehicles within the local area in lane i and its adjacent lane, respectively.

To derive the dynamic equation of TLO model, FVD model is introduced in this paper, which has the superiority in describing traffic flow, as mentioned in Sect. 2. The dynamic equation of FVD model is shown as:

$$\frac{\mathrm{d}^2 x_n(t)}{\mathrm{d}t^2} = \alpha\left[V\left(\Delta x_n(t)\right) - v_n(t)\right] + \beta\Delta v_n(t) \tag{3}$$

where $x_n(t)$ denotes the position of vehicle n at time t, parameter α represents drivers' sensitivity, and β is considered as the coefficient of the relative velocity [9]. The headway $\Delta x_n(t)$, the velocity $v_n(t)$ and the velocity difference $\Delta v_n(t)$ correspond to the stimulus in Eq. (1). $V(\cdot)$ is the optimal velocity function, and the function $V(\Delta x_n(t))$ can be expressed as:

$$V\left(\Delta x_n(t)\right) = V_1 + V_2 \tanh\left[C_1\left(\Delta x_n(t) - l_c\right) - C_2\right] \tag{4}$$

where the estimated values of parameters are $V_1 = 6.75$ m/s, $V_2 = 7.91$ m/s, $C_1 = 0.13\ \text{m}^{-1}$, and $C_2 = 1.57$ [9,11,20]. Parameter l_c refers to the length of a vehicle, and $l_c = 5$ m [9,20,29]. Based on the dynamic equation of FVD model, this paper, considering the influence factors of TLO driving strategy, constructs the dynamic equation of TLO model. Namely, Eq. (2) is reformulated in the form of a differential equation, which is described as:

$$\begin{aligned}\frac{\mathrm{d}^2 x_{n,i}(t)}{\mathrm{d}t^2} =& \alpha\left[V\left(\Delta x_{n,i}(t)\right) - v_{n,i}(t)\right] + \beta\Delta v_{n,i}(t) \\ &+ \kappa U\left(\Delta x_{n,i}(t), \Delta\bar{x}_{n,i}(t)\right) + \lambda G\left(\Delta x_{n,i}(t), \Delta\bar{x}_{m,i,\text{other}}(t)\right)\end{aligned} \tag{5}$$

where parameters κ and λ are influence coefficients of vehicles within the local area in lane i and its adjacent lane respectively. Functions $U(\Delta x_{n,i}(t), \Delta\bar{x}_{n,i}(t))$ and $G(\Delta x_{n,i}(t), \Delta\bar{x}_{m,i,\text{other}}(t))$ are introduced to denote the influences of overall traffic situations within the local area in lane i and its adjacent lane respectively, which are defined as follows:

$$U\left(\Delta x_{n,i}\left(t\right), \Delta \bar{x}_{n,i}\left(t\right)\right) = V\left(\Delta \bar{x}_{n,i}\left(t\right)\right) - V\left(\Delta x_{n,i}\left(t\right)\right) \tag{6}$$

$$G\left(\Delta x_{n,i}\left(t\right), \Delta \bar{x}_{m,i,\text{other}}\left(t\right)\right) = V\left(\Delta \bar{x}_{m,i,\text{other}}\left(t\right)\right) - V\left(\Delta x_{n,i}\left(t\right)\right) \tag{7}$$

where optimal velocities $V(\Delta x_{n,i}(t))$, $V(\Delta \bar{x}_{n,i}(t))$ and $V(\Delta \bar{x}_{m,i,\text{other}}(t))$ can be derived according to Eq. (4). Equations $\Delta \bar{x}_{n,i}(t)$ and $\Delta \bar{x}_{m,i,\text{other}}(t)$ denote the average headways of vehicles within the local area in lane i and its adjacent lane, respectively, which are given by:

$$\Delta \bar{x}_{n,i}\left(t\right) = \frac{1}{p}\sum_{r=1}^{p} \Delta x_{n+r,i}\left(t\right) \tag{8}$$

$$\Delta \bar{x}_{m,i,\text{other}}\left(t\right) = \frac{1}{q}\sum_{s=1}^{q} \Delta x_{m+s,i,\text{other}}\left(t\right) \tag{9}$$

where p and q represent the numbers of vehicles within the local area in lane i and its adjacent lane, respectively.

4 Linear Stability Analysis

This section explores the stability of TLO model using a linear stability analysis method [4,14,18]. In the initial state, all vehicles on the road move with the headway h and velocity $V(h)$ [34]. The positions of vehicle n in lane i and vehicle m in the adjacent lane can be represented as:

$$x_{n,i}^{0}\left(t\right) = hn + V\left(h\right)t, x_{m,i,\text{other}}^{0}\left(t\right) = hm + V\left(h\right)t \tag{10}$$

Then small perturbations $y_{n,i}(t)$ and $y_{m,i,\text{other}}(t)$ are added to lane i and its adjacent lane respectively. The positions of vehicles in the two lanes become:

$$\begin{aligned} x_{n,i}(t) &= hn + V(h)t + y_{n,i}(t) \\ x_{m,i,\text{other}}(t) &= hm + V(h)t + y_{m,i,\text{other}}(t) \end{aligned} \tag{11}$$

Inserting Eq. (11) into Eq. (5), we can obtain Eq. (12) by using Taylor expansion:

$$\begin{aligned} \frac{\mathrm{d}^2 y_{n,i}\left(t\right)}{\mathrm{d}t^2} =& \alpha\left[\Delta y_{n,i}\left(t\right)V'\left(h\right) - \frac{\mathrm{d}y_{n,i}\left(t\right)}{\mathrm{d}t}\right] + \beta\frac{\mathrm{d}\Delta y_{n,i}\left(t\right)}{\mathrm{d}t} \\ &+ \kappa V'\left(h\right)\left[\frac{1}{p}\sum_{r=1}^{p}\Delta y_{n+r,i}\left(t\right) - \Delta y_{n,i}\left(t\right)\right] \\ &+ \lambda V'\left(h\right)\left[\frac{1}{q}\sum_{s=1}^{q}\Delta y_{m+s,i,\text{other}}\left(t\right) - \Delta y_{n,i}\left(t\right)\right] \end{aligned} \tag{12}$$

where $V'(h)$ is the derivative of the function $V(\Delta x_n(t))$ at $\Delta x_n(t) = h$. By inserting $y_{n,i}(t) \propto \exp(ikn + zt)$ and $y_{m,i,\mathrm{other}}(t) \propto \exp(ikn + zt)$ into Eq. (12) [18,27], one obtains:

$$z^2 + z\left[\alpha - \beta(\mathrm{e}^{ik} - 1)\right] - V'(h)(\mathrm{e}^{ik} - 1) \times \left[\alpha + \kappa\left(\frac{1}{p}\sum_{r=1}^{p}\mathrm{e}^{ikr} - 1\right) + \lambda\left(\frac{1}{q}\sum_{s=1}^{q}\mathrm{e}^{iks} - 1\right)\right] = 0 \quad (13)$$

where $z = z_1(ik) + z_2(ik)^2 + \cdots$ [21,29]. Expanding z and inserting it into Eq. (13), we have:

$$\begin{cases} z_1 = V'(h) \\ z_2 = V'(h)\left[\dfrac{\alpha + 2(\beta - V'(h)) + \kappa(1+p) + \lambda(1+q)}{2\alpha}\right] \end{cases} \quad (14)$$

When $z_2 > 0$, the traffic flow is stable [21,29]. Then the linear stability criterion is derived:

$$\alpha > 2\left(V'(h) - \beta\right) - \kappa(1+p) - \lambda(1+q) \quad (15)$$

Further, the neutral stability condition of TLO model is given by:

$$\alpha = 2\left(V'(h) - \beta\right) - \kappa(1+p) - \lambda(1+q) \quad (16)$$

When $\kappa = \lambda = 0$, this stability criterion is consistent with that of FVD model [9].

Based on Eq. (16), the neutral stability curves of TLO model are plotted in the headway-sensitivity space, as shown in Figs. 2 and 3. In the two figures, the solid lines are neutral stability curves. The asterisks and dotted lines represent respectively the critical points (h_c, α_c) and coexisting curves. It can be seen that the phase diagram is divided into three regions by the neutral stability curve and the coexisting curve. The regions above coexisting curves are stable, the regions below neutral stability curves are unstable, and the regions between the coexisting curve and the neutral stability curve are metastable.

Figure 2 depicts the phase diagram in the headway-sensitivity space when $\beta = 0.2$ and $p = q = 2$. Obviously, the stable region is the smallest when $\kappa = \lambda = 0.0$. As the value of κ or λ increases, the stable region is enlarged. Therefore, there exists a positive correlation between traffic stability and the influence coefficients of vehicles within the local area. In addition, compared to the condition that only considers the influence of vehicles in the current lane $(\kappa \neq 0, \lambda = 0)$, taking into account the influences of vehicles within a local area in both lanes $(\kappa \neq 0, \lambda \neq 0)$ is more beneficial to traffic stability. Figure 3 shows the phase diagram in the headway-sensitivity space when $\beta = 0.2$ and $\kappa = \lambda = 0.1$. One can observe that the unstable region decreases with the value of p or q increasing. The value of p or q, to some extent, reflects the range of the local area d. Hence, traffic congestion is effectively suppressed as d increases. One

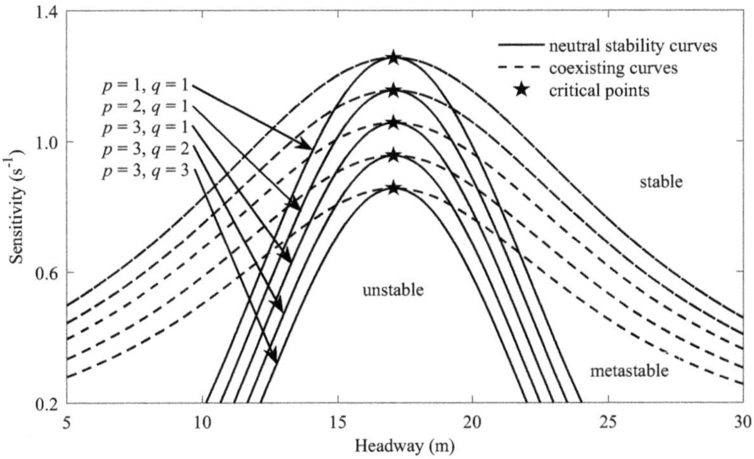

Fig. 2. Phase diagram in the headway-sensitivity space when $\beta = 0.2$ and $p = q = 2$.

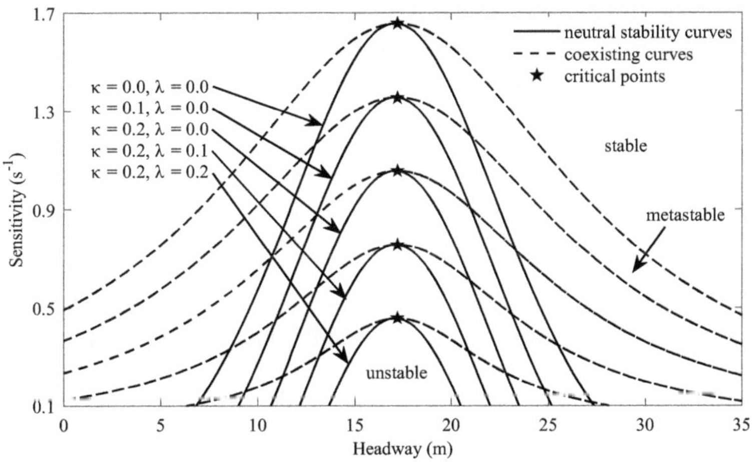

Fig. 3. Phase diagram in the headway-sensitivity space when $\beta = 0.2$ and $\kappa = \lambda = 0.1$.

possible explanation is that, when the range of the local area is enlarged, V2V communication provides drivers with the driving information of more preceding vehicles, which is conducive to accurate driving operations and thus improves traffic stability.

5 Numerical Simulation

In order to visually reveal the effects of the TLO driving strategy on traffic stability, this section carries out numerical simulations for TLO model using

Matlab R2016a. The simulations are conducted under a periodic boundary condition [3, 18, 29]. Suppose that the length of both lanes is L, and there are N vehicles in each lane. The initial velocity of all vehicles is $V(\Delta x_0)$ [9, 36], where $\Delta x_0 = L/N$ represents the average headway of all vehicles. The initial headways for vehicles in lane i are set as follows: $\Delta x_{n,i}(0) = \Delta x_0$ for $n \neq 1$ and $n \neq N$, $\Delta x_{n,i}(0) = \Delta x_0 - \sigma$ for $n = 1$, and $\Delta x_{n,i}(0) = \Delta x_0 + \sigma$ for $n = N$, where σ denotes the small perturbation added to the uniform traffic flow [3]. The related parameters are set as $L = 1500$ m, $N = 100$, $\sigma = 5$ m, $\alpha = 1$, $\beta = 0.2$, and the time interval is $\Delta t = 0.1$ s [26, 36, 37]. Through simulations, this paper will obtain evolution processes of the traffic system. Further, the specific influences of parameters κ and λ as well as parameter d on traffic stability can be analyzed.

5.1 Evolution Processes of Traffic Flow Under Different κ and λ

Figure 4 displays the space-time evolutions of headway after $t = 10\ 000$ s for different values of κ and λ when $d = 40$ m [3, 34]. Figure 4(a) with $\kappa = \lambda = 0$, corresponds to the simulation results of FVD model. Figure 4(b), where $\kappa = 0.1$ and $\lambda = 0$, exhibits the situation that only considers the influence of vehicles within the local area in the current lane. Figure 4(c) with $\kappa = \lambda = 0.1$ shows the traffic flow evolution processes incorporating the effects of vehicles within the local area in both lanes (the TLO driving strategy). One can observe that the density waves appear in Figs. 4(a) and 4(b), because the two cases cannot satisfy the stability criterion shown in Eq. (16). The traffic flow becomes inhomogeneous after a small perturbation is added to the uniform traffic flow. In Fig. 4(c) the headways of all vehicles are almost the same and do not change as time goes on. In this instance, the small perturbation in the traffic system finally disappears and the traffic flow returns to the stable state. It is clear that the TLO driving strategy, to a certain extent, suppresses traffic congestion and improves traffic stability.

Figure 5 illustrates the velocity profiles under different t for the cases (a) $\kappa = \lambda = 0$, (b) $\kappa = 0.1$, $\lambda = 0$ and (c) $\kappa = \lambda = 0.1$ when $d = 40$ m. In Fig. 5(a), the amplitude of velocity fluctuations increases rapidly after a small perturbation is inserted into the uniform traffic flow, and traffic congestion eventually occurs. In Fig. 5(b), the amplitude of velocity fluctuations is always smaller than that in Fig. 5(a) at the same moment, suggesting that the stability of traffic flow is improved by considering the average headway of multiple preceding vehicles in the current lane. But the velocity fluctuations, in Fig. 5(b), become more and more severe with time going on, which indicates that the small perturbation finally evolves into an unstable traffic flow [18, 27]. However, in Fig. 5(c), with consideration of the effects of vehicles within the local area in the two lanes, the fluctuations of velocity decrease over time, and the traffic system becomes stable gradually. It is shown that the TLO driving strategy enhances the stability of traffic flow.

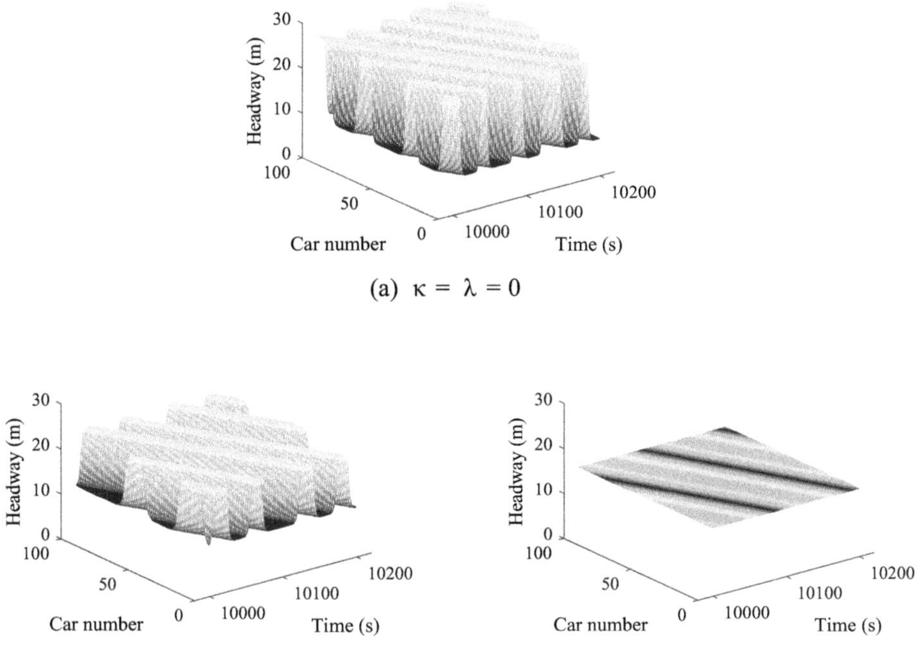

(a) κ = λ = 0

(b) κ = 0.1, λ = 0

(c) κ = λ = 0.1

Fig. 4. The space-time evolutions of the headway after $t = 10\ 000$ s, where $d = 40$ m, $\alpha = 1$, and $\beta = 0.2$.

5.2 Evolution Processes of Traffic Flow Under Different d

Figure 6 exhibits the space-time evolutions of the headway before $t = 400$ s when $\kappa = \lambda = 0.1$, where (a) $d = 20$ m, (b) $d = 40$ m and (c) $d = 60$ m. It can be seen that, the headway fluctuations when $d = 20$ m are severer than those when $d = 40$ m and $d = 60$ m. When the range of the local area in the TLO strategy is 20 m, the traffic system becomes unstable rapidly. As d increases to 40 m, the fluctuations of headway are obviously reduced, and the amplitude of headway fluctuations decreases as time goes on. When $d = 60$ m, the headway fluctuations are much smaller than those when $d = 40$ m, and the perturbation virtually disappears at $t = 400$ s. All the results show that the range of the local area d has an impact on the effectiveness of the TLO driving strategy. The stability of traffic is evidently strengthened as d increases when d ranges from 20 m to 60 m.

Figure 7 plots the velocity profiles under different d when $\kappa = \lambda = 0.1$. Patterns (a)–(d) in Fig. 7 correspond to $t = 100$ s, $t = 200$ s, $t = 400$ s, and $t = 2\ 000$ s after a small perturbation is added to the uniform traffic flow. Comparing Figs. 7(a)–7(d), it is clear that the velocity fluctuations become larger with time going on when $d = 20$ m, and the perturbation evolves into an unstable

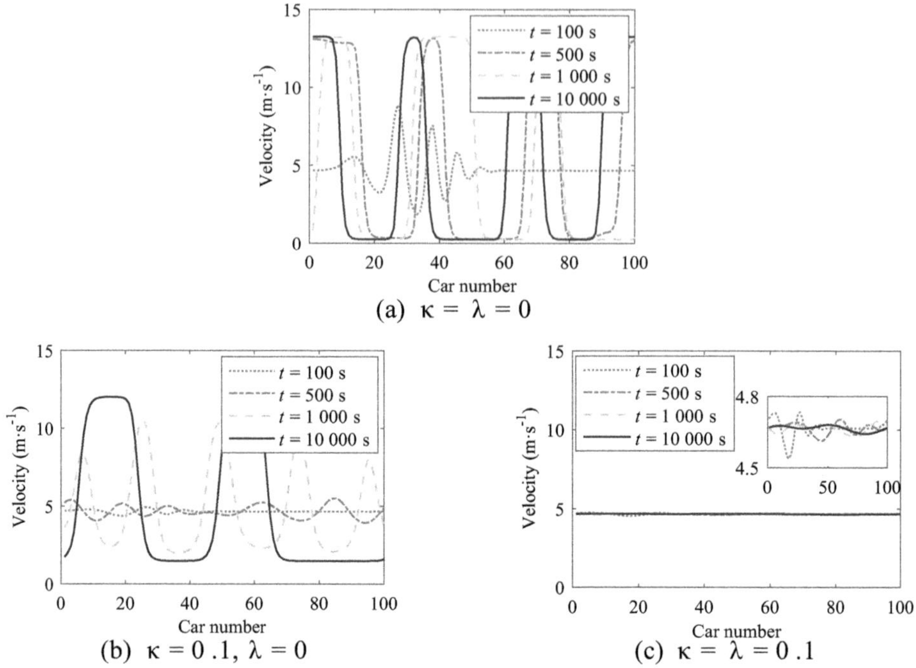

Fig. 5. The velocity profiles under different t, where $d = 40$ m, $\alpha = 1$, and $\beta = 0.2$.

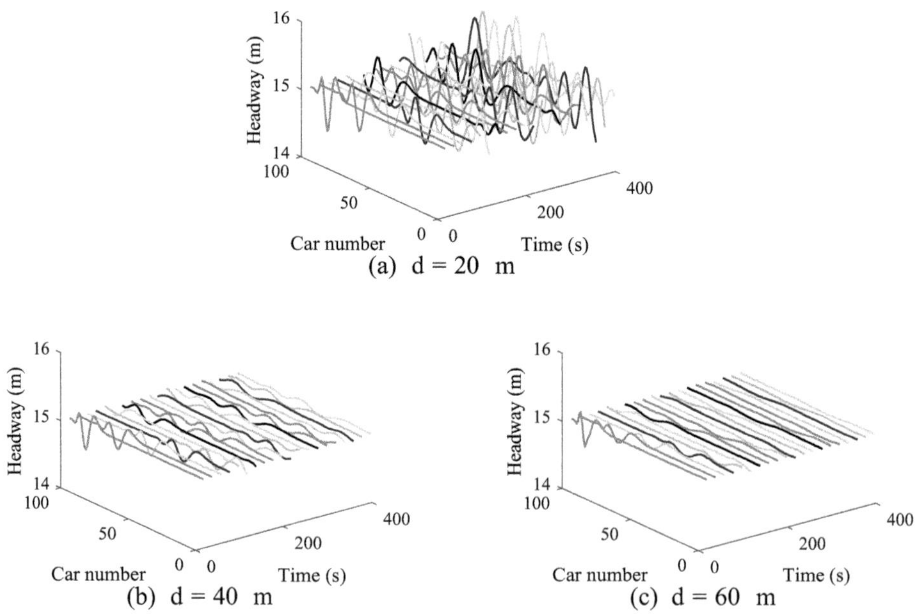

Fig. 6. The space-time evolutions of the headway before $t = 400$ s, where $\kappa = \lambda = 0.1$, $\alpha = 1$, and $\beta = 0.2$.

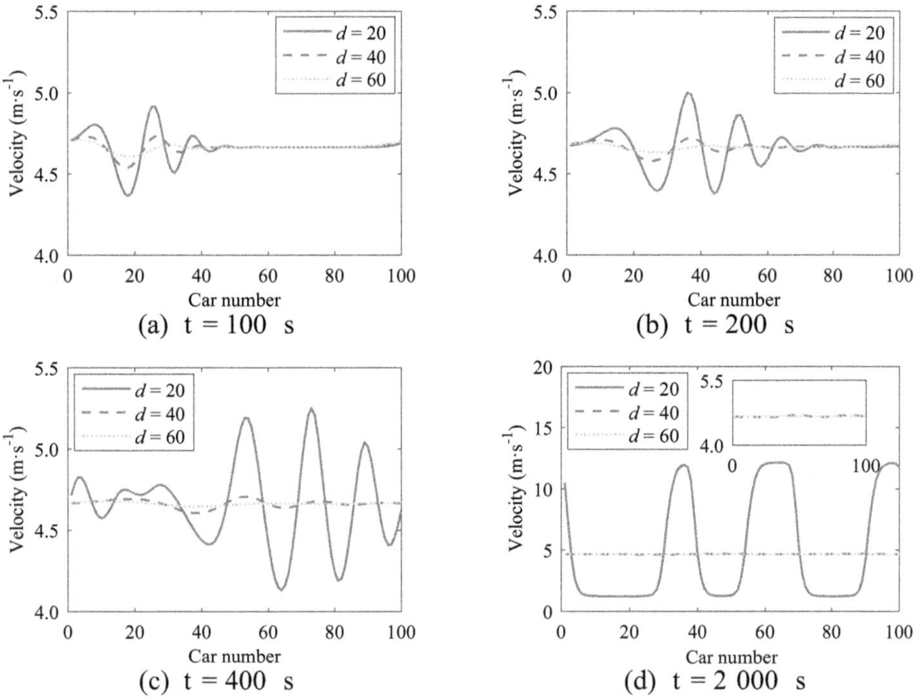

Fig. 7. The velocity profiles under different d, where $\kappa = \lambda = 0.1$, $\alpha = 1$, and $\beta = 0.2$.

traffic flow. Conversely, the amplitudes of velocity fluctuations shrink over time when $d = 40$ m and $d = 60$ m. Specifically, the fluctuations of velocity almost disappear at $t = 2\ 000$ s when $d = 40$ m, as shown in Fig. 7(d). The traffic flow becomes stable at $t = 400$ s when $d = 60$ m, as shown in Fig. 7(c). The results verify that a larger value of d contributes to eliminating the adverse effects of the perturbation on traffic flow.

6 Conclusions

This paper proposes a TLO driving strategy in the V2V communication environment, where a vehicle is influenced by the overall traffic situations within a local area on a two-lane highway. In order to test the effects of the TLO driving strategy on traffic stability, the TLO model is developed accordingly.

Through linear stability analysis, the neutral stability curves are plotted in the headway-sensitivity space. The stable region in TLO model is bigger than that in FVD model. Compared with the condition that only considers the overall traffic situation within the local area in a single lane, the stable region is larger when the overall situations in both lanes are considered. Numerical simulation results are in good agreement with the analytical ones. For FVD model, the fluctuations of headway and velocity increase rapidly after a small perturbation is inserted into the uniform traffic flow, and traffic congestion finally occurs. When the influence of preceding vehicles in the same lane is taken into account, the fluctuations of headway and velocity are reduced, but the small perturbation still evolves into an unstable traffic flow eventually. For TLO model, the fluctuations decrease over time, and traffic system becomes stable gradually. Moreover, the larger the range of the local area is, the earlier the traffic flow becomes stable. All the results show that the TLO driving strategy is more conducive to improving traffic stability and suppressing traffic congestion. The effectiveness of the driving strategy can be further enhanced as d increases within a certain range.

The TLO driving strategy presented in this paper can provide theoretical reference for further study concerning traffic problems. The TLO model will be valuable for the application of V2V communication. Nevertheless, the influences of the driving strategy or TLO model have not been tested with empirical data. In our future work, we will address this weakness when V2V communication is widely used in real traffic and a large amount of field data can be obtained.

References

1. Yang, C., Jiang, J.X., Zhou, J.H., Hitosug, M., Wang, Z.G.: Traffic safety and public health in China – past knowledge, current status, and future directions. Accid. Anal. Prev. **192**, 107272 (2023)
2. Wang, C.Z., Abdel-Aty, M., Han, L.: Tunnel crash severity and congestion duration joint evaluation based on cross-stitch networks. Accid. Anal. Prev. **213**, 107942 (2025)
3. Kuang, H., Xu, Z.P., Li, X.L., Lo, S.M.: An extended car-following model accounting for the average headway effect in intelligent transportation system. XXPhys. A **471**, 778 (2017)
4. Tan, J.H., Gong, L., Qin, X.Q.: An extended car-following model considering the low visibility in fog on a highway with slopes. Int. J. Mod. Phys. C **30**, 1950090 (2019)
5. Ma, J., et al.: Review on China's traffic engineering research progress: 2016. China J. Highway Transp. **29**, 1 (2016)
6. Zhao, H.X., He, R.C., Jia, X.Y.: Estimation and analysis of vehicle exhaust emissions at signalized intersections using a car-following model. Sustainability **11**, 3992 (2019)
7. Ngoduy, D.: Linear stability of a generalized multi-anticipative car following model with time delays. Commun. Nonlinear Sci. Numer. Simul. **22**, 420 (2015)
8. Li, Y.F., Zhao, H., Zhang, L., Zhang, C.: An extended car-following model incorporating the effects of lateral gap and gradient. XXPhys. A **503**, 177 (2018)
9. Jiang, R., Wu, Q.S., Zhu, Z.J.: Full velocity difference model for a car-following theory. Phys. Rev. E **64**, 017101 (2001)
10. Zhang, G., Zhao, M., Sun, D.H., Liu, W.N., Li, H.M.: Stabilization effect of multiple drivers' desired velocities in car-following theory. XXPhys. A **442**, 532 (2016)
11. Helbing, D., Tilch, B.: Generalized force model of traffic dynamics. Phys. Rev. E **58**, 133 (1998)
12. Tan, J.H.: Numerical simulation of car-following model in sand-dust environment. J. Transp. Syst. Eng. Inf. Technol. **18**, 63 (2018)

13. Zhang, J., Tang, T.Q., Yu, S.W.: An improved car-following model accounting for the preceding car's taillight. XXPhys. A **492**, 1831 (2018)
14. Tan, J.H.: Impact of risk illusions on traffic flow in fog weather. XXPhys. A **525**, 216 (2019)
15. Pipes, L.A.: An operational analysis of traffic dynamics. J. Appl. Phys. **24**, 274 (1953)
16. Newell, G.F.: Nonlinear effects in the dynamics of car following. Oper. Res. **9**, 209 (1961)
17. Bando, M., Hasebe, K., Nakayama, A., Shibata, A., Sugiyama, Y.: Dynamical model of traffic congestion and numerical simulation. Phys. Rev. E **51**, 1035 (1995)
18. Jia, Y.H., Du, Y.M., Wu, J.P.: Stability analysis of a car-following model on two lanes. Math. Probl. Eng. **2014**, 727560 (2014)
19. Ge, H.X., Meng, X.P., Zhu, H.B., Li, Z.P.: Feedback control for car following model based on two-lane traffic flow. XXPhys. A **408**, 28 (2014)
20. Tan, J.H., Gong, L., Qin, X.Q.: Global optimality under Internet of Vehicles: strategy to improve traffic safety and reduce energy dissipation. Sustainability **11**, 4541 (2019)
21. Hua, X.D., Wang, W., Wang, H.: A car-following model with the consideration of vehicle-to-vehicle communication technology. Acta Physica Sinica **65**, 010502 (2016)
22. Ngoduy, D.: Analytical studies on the instabilities of heterogeneous intelligent traffic flow. Commun. Nonlinear Sci. Numer. Simul. **18**, 2699 (2013)
23. Sun, D.H., Kang, Y.R., Yang, S.H.: A novel car following model considering average speed of preceding vehicles group. XXPhys. A **436**, 103 (2015)
24. Ponnu, B., Coifman, B.: When adjacent lane dependencies dominate the uncongested regime of the fundamental relationship. Transp. Res. Part B: Methodol. **104**, 602 (2017)
25. Duan, J.Y., Li, Z.Z., Salvendy, G.: Automatic imitation of risky behavior: a study of simulated driving in China. Traffic Inj. Prev. **13**, 442 (2012)
26. Tan, J.H., Gong, L., Qin, X.Q.: Effect of imitation phenomenon on two-lane traffic safety in fog weather. Int. J. Environ. Res. Public Health **16**, 3709 (2019)
27. Yu, G.Z., Wang, P.C., Wu, X.K., Wang, Y.P.: Linear and nonlinear stability analysis of a car-following model considering velocity difference of two adjacent lanes. Nonlinear Dyn. **84**, 387 (2016)
28. Tang, T., Shi, W., Shang, H., Wang, Y.: A new car-following model with consideration of inter-vehicle communication. Nonlinear Dyn. **76**(4), 2017–2023 (2014). https://doi.org/10.1007/s11071-014-1265-9
29. Tan, J.H., Qin, X.Q., Gong, L.: Using vehicle-to-vehicle communication to improve traffic safety in sand-dust environment. Int. J. Environ. Res. Public Health **17**, 1165 (2020)
30. Yu, S.W., Shi, Z.K.: An improved car-following model considering relative velocity fluctuation. Commun. Nonlinear Sci. Numer. Simul. **36**, 319 (2016)
31. Guo, L.T., Zhao, X.M., Yu, S.W., Li, X.H., Shi, Z.K.: An improved car-following model with multiple preceding cars' velocity fluctuation feedback. XXPhys. A **471**, 436 (2017)
32. Sun, Y.Q., Ge, H.X., Cheng, R.J.: An extended car-following model considering driver's memory and average speed of preceding vehicles with control strategy. XXPhys. A **521**, 752 (2019)
33. Peng, Y., Liu, S.J., Yu, D.Z.: An improved car-following model with consideration of multiple preceding and following vehicles in a driver's view. XXPhys. A **538**, 122967 (2020)

34. Tang, T.Q., Huang, H.J., Gao, Z.Y.: Stability of the car-following model on two lanes. Phys. Rev. E **72**, 066124 (2005)
35. Zhai, C., Wu, W.T.: An extended multi-phase lattice model with consideration of optimal current changes with memory. Clust. Comput. **22**, 7447 (2019)
36. Li, Y., Zhao, H., Zheng, T., Sun, F., Feng, H.: Non-lane-discipline-based car-following model incorporating the electronic throttle dynamics under connected environment. Nonlinear Dyn. **90**(4), 2345–2358 (2017). https://doi.org/10.1007/s11071-017-3807-4
37. Ge, H.X., Cheng, R.J., Li, Z.P.: Two velocity difference model for a car following theory. XXPhys. A **387**, 5239 (2008)

Multimodal Learning Analytics for Predicting Learning Gains in Online Service-Learning Programs

Kangzhong Wang[1], Eugene Yujun Fu[2], Grace Ngai[1(✉)], and Hong Va Leong[1]

[1] Department of Computing, The Hong Kong Polytechnic University, Hong Kong, China
{cskwang,csgngai,cshleong}@comp.polyu.edu.hk

[2] Centre for Learning, Teaching and Technology, The Education University of Hong Kong, Hong Kong, China
eugenefu@eduhk.hk

Abstract. The growth of synchronous online education has introduced new forms of communication, collaboration, and engagement in real-time learning environments. To understand these processes, analytic approaches are needed that move beyond traditional assessments and make use of the multimodal signals available in virtual classrooms. This study investigates online service-learning programs as a representative setting where university students interact with peers and service recipients via videoconferencing. We construct a multimodal dataset of synchronous service-learning sessions, comprising transcripts, speech recordings, and screen recording content aligned at the utterance level. Using this dataset, we compare unimodal models with a range of multimodal fusion strategies to evaluate how linguistic, acoustic, and visual information contribute to predicting students' self-reported learning gains. The results show that transcript features yielded higher predictive performance than other single modalities, while their integration with voice features and screen content produced more consistent and reliable predictions. These findings suggest that combining linguistic, acoustic, and visual information—capturing what students say, how they use their voices, and the learning materials they share on screen—offers a more grounded understanding of student learning processes in synchronous online education.

Keywords: Multimodal learning analytics · Learning gains · Synchronous online education · Service-learning

1 Introduction

Digital technologies have diminished the physical constraints of distance and time in higher education, enabling students worldwide to engage in live discussions, collaborate on problem-solving, and share resources through stable online

T. Hao et al. (Eds.): BESC 2025, LNCS 16431, pp. 503–520, 2026.
https://doi.org/10.1007/978-981-95-7138-3_32

platforms. As a result, e-learning has become a central component of university planning and is widely regarded as an effective means of promoting equitable and high-quality education [6]. In this context, videoconference teaching with platforms such as *Zoom* has become popular because it supports real-time interaction, is easy to access, and offers flexible scheduling [17].

However, teaching through videoconferencing can make it harder for instructors to see how engaged students are or how well they understand the material. When there are no clear signs of learning progress, it becomes difficult to adjust teaching strategies, and concerns about learning quality may arise. This has led researchers to study how learning gains can be predicted by looking at the digital traces students leave during online study. Such traces can guide teaching decisions and help improve student gains. Yet it is still difficult to know which factors relate to learning gains, since learning is complex, changes over time, and depends on context. Recent studies suggest that signals such as spoken words, screen content, camera use, and chat messages in videoconferencing may be linked to learning gains [4,9]. Multimodal learning analytics (MMLA) is a promising approach to capture and understand complex patterns of interaction in online classrooms. Despite this potential, two gaps remain. First, many studies still rely on self-report surveys instead of objective, automatically recorded data, which leaves out important aspects of actual behaviour [5,22]. Second, much of the existing work uses simple statistical methods that cannot fully handle the variety and size of multimodal data, which limits our ability to study these processes in depth [14,22].

The present study seeks to address these gaps by analysing a multimodal dataset collected from real-world online service-learning programs. The dataset includes high-quality audio recordings, automatically generated speech transcripts, and screen-sharing streams. We systematically compare alternative feature construction for features extracted from text, audio, and video to predict student learning gains. This study is guided by two research questions:

RQ1: Which single modality feature set (transcript, audio, or screen content descriptors) provides the most accurate prediction of student learning gain in synchronous videoconference classes?

RQ2: To what extent does multimodal fusion enhance predictive performance compared with the best single-modality baseline?

To answer these questions, we build three groups of features. First, transcript features include linguistic features (e.g., word count) and semantic representations produced by Sentence Transformers [21]. Second, audio features include standard acoustic features (loudness, pitch, and Mel-frequency cepstral coefficients) and contextual paralinguistic representations from wav2vec 2.0 [2]. Third, from the screen recording, we obtain slide-level content representations with a large language model captioning pipeline and semantic representations of key frames using BLIP-2 [10]. We evaluate single-modality models and several early- and late-fusion designs. Results show that an attention-based late fusion of the three modalities yields the highest accuracy. To the best of our knowledge, this is the first study that integrates transcript, audio, and screen content features to forecast learning gains in synchronous online classes. This work makes three main contributions. First, to the best of our knowledge, it is the first study to analyse a multimodal dataset of authentic videoconference instruction that is linked to validated measures of learning gains. Second, it provides a systematic comparison between single-modality models and multimodal prediction models, including both early- and late-fusion designs. Third, it identifies interaction patterns across transcripts, audio, and screen recording content that are most closely associated with positive learning gains, offering insights for the data-informed design of synchronous online teaching.

2 Related Work

Service-learning is an experiential pedagogy that combines academic study with structured community work. Earlier studies report that this approach reinforces subject knowledge, teamwork, and civic attitudes [12,19,23]. Much of that evidence, however, is based on self-report surveys analysed with simple statistics, leaving the underlying factors that drive learning gains only partly understood [14,22]. In recent years, the growth of online education has moved many service-learning courses onto digital platforms. Learners can now serve local organisations while meeting tutors and peers through videoconference and shared workspaces [8]. When these courses provide clear objectives, guided reflection, and timely feedback, their learning gains approach those of face-to-face classes [7,8]. Yet distance introduces specific challenges: teachers must track group activity, sustain meaningful dialogue, and intervene promptly when difficulties arise. Meeting those demands calls for evidence that goes beyond end-of-course surveys.

Multimodal learning analytics (MMLA) offers a way to meet this need. By integrating transcripts, voice features, screen content, and other digital traces, MMLA provides a more detailed picture of engagement and collaboration than single-source data [13,18]. Prior work combining text, audio, and screen-sharing streams has improved the prediction of learning progress in general online learning contexts [1]. Extending these methods to service-learning could enable instructors to monitor interaction more effectively, identify patterns linked to positive learning gains, and design timely support. Yet published studies that apply MMLA in online service-learning are still lacking. This study addresses that gap by analysing multimodal signals from online service-learning programs to examine how textual, acoustic, and visual features predict student learning gains and to identify the interaction patterns associated with the learning gains.

3 Dataset

This section describes the context of the online service-learning programme and introduces the self-report instrument used to assess student learning gains.

3.1 Online Service-Learning Programs

Data were collected from online service-learning programs conducted at a public university in Hong Kong during the 2022–2023 academic year amidst the COVID-19 pandemic. University students enrolled in service-learning courses were assigned to create small teams and develop online workshops aimed at teaching fundamental concepts of A.I. object recognition, machine learning, and block programming. These workshops were delivered to service recipients (SRs) located in India, the Philippines, and South Africa.

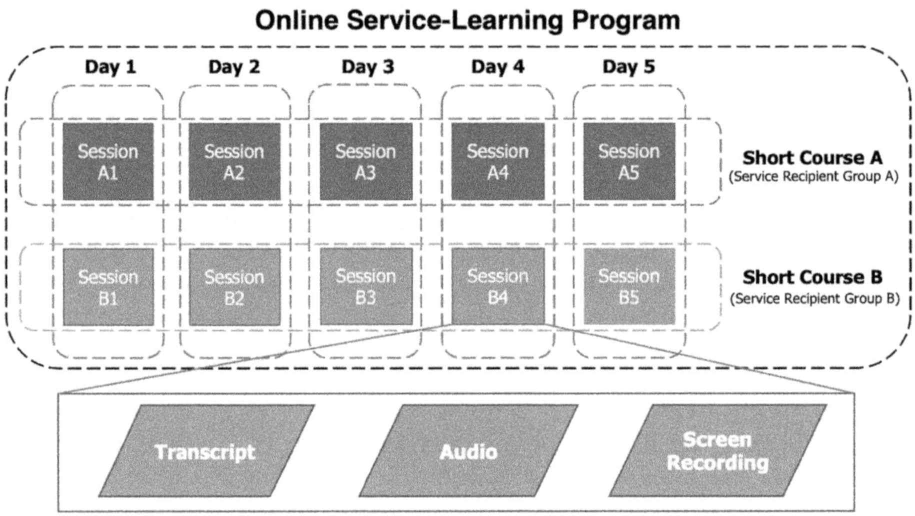

Fig. 1. Structure of the online service-learning program. Each program comprises two parallel short courses (A and B), delivered over five consecutive days to different service recipient groups. Each daily session was conducted on Zoom, which automatically recorded transcripts, audio, and screen-sharing streams for multimodal analysis.

In total, 166 SRs participated in the study, with an approximately equal distribution across the three countries, as shown in Fig. 2. Among these SRs, 44.6% identified as male and 55.4% as female. The majority were between 12–18 years of age (secondary school students), while 10.8% were over 18. On the tutor side, 95 university students in Hong Kong took part as workshop instructors. As illustrated in Fig. 1, for each service-learning program, a team of 3–4 students acted as tutors, delivering two five-day sessions of short courses. Each session used the same teaching materials but was delivered to a different group of 3–5 SRs. Thus, each program involved two parallel runs with different recipient groups, resulting in 25 programs and a total of 250 recorded sessions.

All sessions were conducted on Zoom, which automatically generated cloud-based recordings of the screen sharing, audio, and transcripts. An example transcript is provided in Fig. 4. Each transcript consists of multiple *utterance blocks*, with four key elements: **(1)** ***Utterance ID***: a sequential integer assigned to each utterance; **(2)** ***Time Stamp***: start and end times in *hour:minutes:seconds.milliseconds* format; **(3)** ***Speaker***: anonymized identifiers, where university students are labeled as *Target_Student{ID}* (e.g., Target_Student1) and SRs as *Service_Recipient{ID}* (e.g., Service_Recipient1); and **(4)** ***Utterance***: the transcribed spoken content captured by Zoom.

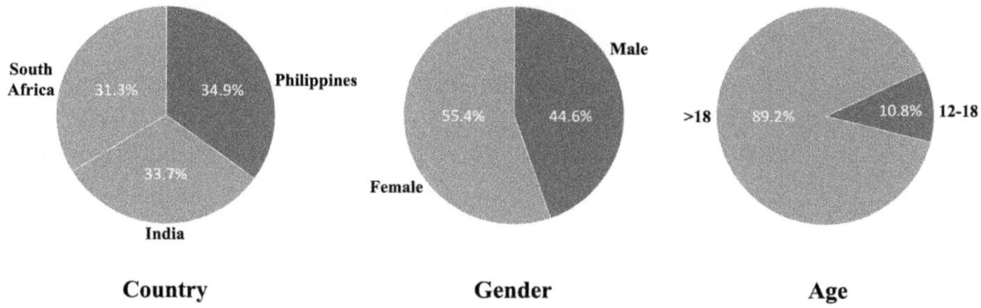

Fig. 2. Demographic distribution of the service recipients, showing proportions by country of residence, gender, and age group.

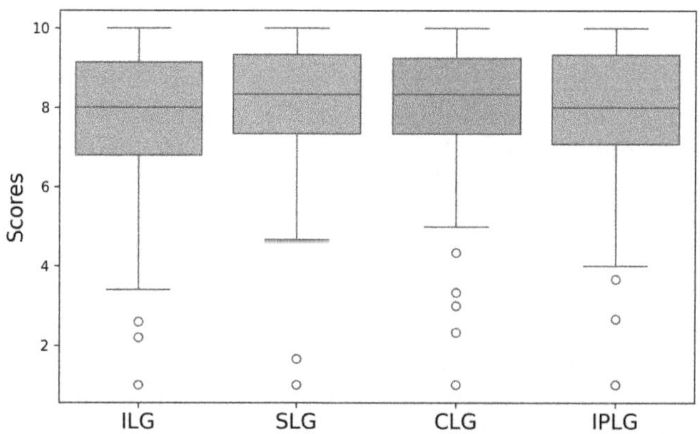

Fig. 3. Distribution of averaged learning gains: Intellectual (ILG) (mean = 7.60, SD = 1.96), Social (SLG) (mean = 8.01, SD = 1.81), Civic (CLG) (mean = 7.87, SD = 1.91), and Intrapersonal (IPLG) (mean = 7.86, SD = 1.88).

3.2 Self-reported Learning Gains

In this study, we aim at examining the learning gains of the university students who served as tutors in the service-learning programs. To evaluate their perceived learning gains, the 95 student tutors were invited to complete a bilingual

Table 1. Self-Reported Learning Gains Inventory (SRLGI)

Learning Gains	Items: *To what extent do you think the service-learning course/program increased or improved your...*
Intellectual	Ability to apply knowledge and skill in real life
	Ability to solve problems
	Ability to think creatively
	Ability to reflect on and learn from your experiences
	Ability to analyze issues from multiple perspectives
Social	Ability to establish and maintain good relationships with other people
	Ability to work with others in a team to achieve common goals
	Respect for people with different backgrounds or perspectives
Civic	Understanding of the needs, potentials, and resources of the community that you served
	Empathy for disadvantaged people
	Commitment to creating a better society
Intrapersonal	Self-confidence
	Self-understanding
	Commitment to continued self-improvement

Chinese–English Self-Reported Learning Gains Inventory (SRLGI) at the conclusion of the courses. The SRLGI was specifically designed to capture their reflections on multiple dimensions of learning gains associated with service-learning.

The SRLGI was carefully crafted to fit this study, drawing from a broad literature review to align with the specific contexts of the service-learning courses and projects under scrutiny. To ensure its academic soundness, the inventory underwent a thorough validation process. A panel of experienced service-learning educators and researchers assessed the SRLGI, validating its content and face validity. Additional validation was provided through exploratory and confirmatory factor analyses, with the resulting fit indices (CFI $= 0.973$, TLI $= 0.9564$, NFI $= 0.971$, RMSEA $= 0.073$) underlining the instrument's reliability and robustness. In adherence to the university's commitment to quality assurance, the SRLGI was presented to students, who were briefed about the study's objectives and assured of the confidentiality of their responses, which would not be linked to their academic evaluations. The research methodology, including data access and analysis, was approved by the university's ethics committee.

Referring to Table 1, the inventory consists of fourteen items, categorically divided into Intellectual (ILG), Social (SLG), Civic (CLG), and Intrapersonal (IPLG) Learning Gains, through which students are prompted to assess themselves. Students were invited to rate their self-perceived learning gains on a 10-point scale, with 1 indicating 'very little' benefit and 10 representing 'very much' benefit. From the original group of 95 students, 66 individuals voluntarily completed the post-program inventory, yielding a response rate of approximately 69.5%. Participation in the survey was optional, and students were assured that their responses would remain confidential and would not affect their academic evaluation. Importantly, every program had at least one student response, ensuring coverage across all programs despite the partial response rate. To evaluate a student's learning outcome, we averaged the items within each category. Figure 3 shows the distribution of these averaged learning gains, with mean values ranging from 7.60 to 8.01, and a close standard deviation indicating a moderate variation in the scores around these means, with minimum and maximum values of 1.00 and 10.00, respectively.

3.3 Task Definition

This study predicts individual students' self-reported learning gains from multimodal features extracted from each session of the service-learning programs. For each student, the average scores from the Self-Reported Learning Gains Inventory (SRLGI) are used as the target variables. The predictive models take as input the aligned transcript, audio, and shared-screen features described in the previous sections. Learning outcome scores are divided into three categories—Top 25%, Middle 50%, and Bottom 25%—based on the average score across the items within each outcome. This setup defines a classification task that enables the examination of which multimodal patterns are associated with higher or lower levels of self-perceived learning gains. The task further evaluates the predictive contribution of different combinations of linguistic, acoustic, and visual features. Using session-level multimodal data alongside post-program self-assessments, the study examines how classroom interactions and instructional practices are associated with student learning in online service-learning.

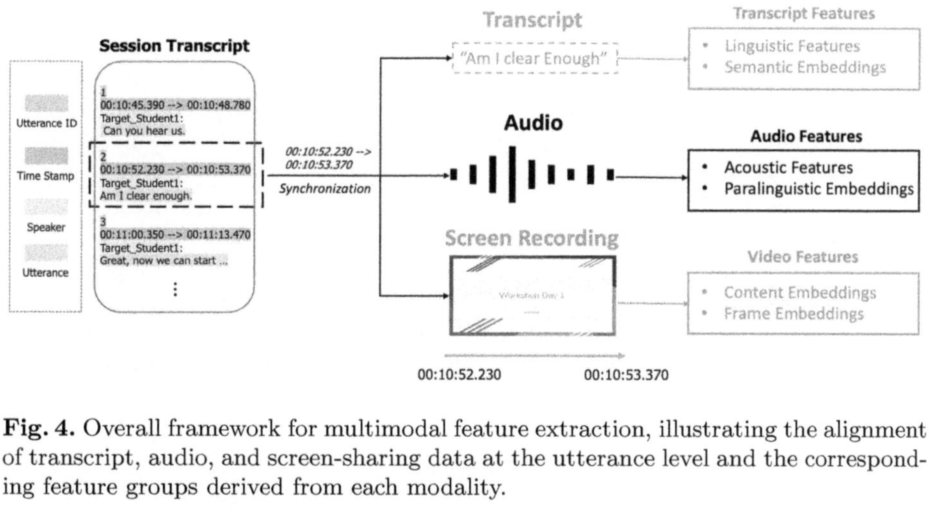

Fig. 4. Overall framework for multimodal feature extraction, illustrating the alignment of transcript, audio, and screen-sharing data at the utterance level and the corresponding feature groups derived from each modality.

4 Multimodal Feature Extraction

As illustrated in Fig. 4, we use the *utterance* as the basic unit for synchronizing multimodal feature extraction from the transcript, audio, and screen recording streams. Each utterance is precisely defined by its *timestamp* in the transcript. For example, given an utterance with the time frame *00:10:52.230* to *00:10:53.370*, we align this segment across all modalities and extract the relevant features for further analysis.

4.1 Transcript Features

A range of linguistic features extracted from spoken utterances have been found useful for studying student engagement and learning in educational settings [1, 11]. In this study, we extract both statistical and semantic features from each transcribed utterance. The features are as follows:

1. **Utterance Statistics:** For each utterance, we compute the word count, the content word count (the number of nouns, verbs, adjectives, and adverbs), and the utterance duration, measured from the start to the end timestamp.
2. **LIWC-Based Features:** Linguistic Inquiry and Word Count (LIWC) [16] is a well-established psycholinguistic tool that categorizes words into psychologically meaningful dimensions, enabling the analysis of cognitive, emotional, and social aspects of language use. In this study, we focus on two major LIWC categories: *cognitive processes* (e.g., insight, causation) and *affective states* (e.g., positive and negative emotions). Words related to cognitive processes serve as indicators of reasoning, reflection, and knowledge construction, while affective state words capture emotional involvement and motivational orientation during interaction.
3. **Dialogue Acts:** Dialogue act analysis provides a structured representation of the communicative function of spoken language, describing not only the content of speech but also the speaker's intention. In this study, each utterance is annotated with one or more dialogue act categories, including Greeting, Question, Answer, Feedback, Agreement, Disagreement, Clarification, Request, Suggestion, Thanking, and Closing. Because transcriptions from Zoom often contain long or multifunctional utterances, multiple labels may be assigned to the same utterance.
4. **Utterance Embeddings:** Beyond surface-level linguistic features, semantic embeddings provide a dense representation of meaning that captures contextual nuance and discourse-level relations. For each utterance, we generate a 768-dimensional embedding using a pre-trained sentence transformer model. These embeddings encode semantic content in a continuous vector space, allowing the model to recognize similarity and thematic coherence across utterances.

4.2 Audio Features

Acoustic features extracted from speech are widely employed to analyse student engagement, affective states, and the quality of interaction in educational contexts [20]. Beyond basic signal properties, paralinguistic characteristics such as prosody and speaking style provide additional cues about learners' communicative behaviour and emotional involvement [15]. In this study, we extract four groups of audio features for each utterance, combining low-level descriptors from the eGeMAPS feature set with high-level Paralinguistic embeddings:

1. **Frequency-Related Features:** Capture pitch and harmonic properties of speech, including measures such as fundamental frequency (F0), formant frequencies, jitter, and harmonic-to-noise ratio. These features provide information about pitch variability and prosodic patterns during interaction.
2. **Energy-Related Features:** Describe the loudness and energy dynamics of speech, including overall loudness, standard deviation, and the range and slope of energy changes. Such features reflect vocal intensity and emphasis, which are linked to engagement and affective expression.
3. **Spectral-Related Features:** Characterise the spectral shape and timbre of speech, with measures such as spectral flux, Mel-frequency cepstral coefficients (MFCCs), and spectral slopes. These features capture the richness and clarity of the voice signal and are informative for distinguishing variation in speech quality.
4. **Paralinguistic Embeddings:** High-level representations derived from a pre-trained wav2vec 2.0 model [2]. Each utterance is encoded as a fixed-length embedding that captures complex prosodic and contextual acoustic patterns beyond those represented by hand-crafted descriptors.

4.3 Video Features

The quality and delivery of instructional content, conveyed through screen presentations in online teaching, are recognised as significant factors influencing student engagement and learning gains [4,9]. Visual information, alongside spoken language and audio cues, shapes how learners process and retain material. To capture both the informational content and the visual characteristics of screen sharing, we extract two types of features from the video recordings:

1. **Content Embeddings:** To obtain a standardised representation of the instructional material, we employ the state-of-the-art open-ended vision–language model Qwen2.5-VL [3] to generate textual descriptions of each screen-sharing keyframe. These descriptions are then transformed into semantic embeddings using the same sentence transformer applied to transcript features, ensuring cross-modality consistency and enabling the comparison of linguistic and visual information within a unified semantic space.
2. **Keyframe Embeddings:** To complement the generated textual descriptions, we directly extract visual embeddings from the keyframes using BLIP-2 [10], a vision–language pre-trained model. These embeddings encode the

semantic and structural properties of the visual scene, including layout, graphical style, and other salient visual elements present in the screen recording stream.

By integrating content- and keyframe-level representations, this feature set captures both the semantic meaning of instructional material and the visual characteristics of its delivery, providing a richer perspective on how screen-sharing content contributes to student learning.

5 Experiment Design

To evaluate the effectiveness of different modelling strategies for multimodal feature analysis, we systematically compare alternative approaches to feature construction and fusion. Multimodal features are extracted at the utterance level for each target student, and two methods are employed to construct the final feature representation for prediction: *utterance-based* and *date-based.*

In the *utterance-based* method, features from all utterances spoken by a target student are concatenated in temporal order to form a feature matrix of size $[N_{\text{utterance}}, D_{\text{feat}}]$, where $N_{\text{utterance}}$ is the number of utterances and D_{feat} is the dimensionality of each feature vector. This sequence is then modelled with a gated recurrent unit (GRU) to predict the student's learning gains. In the *date-based* method, utterances are grouped by session date, producing feature matrices of size $[N_{\text{date}}, D_{\text{feat}}]$, where N_{date} denotes the number of days in which the student participated. GRU models are then applied to capture temporal dependencies across days. Both feature construction methods are implemented under unimodal and multimodal conditions. For multimodal experiments, we compare two fusion strategies: (1) direct concatenation, which merges feature vectors from different modalities, and (2) attention-based fusion, which dynamically assigns weights to each modality according to its predictive contribution.

All models are trained and evaluated using five-fold cross-validation, with results reported as the average across folds. Early stopping with a patience of 10 epochs is applied based on validation loss, with a maximum of 200 training epochs per run. Optimization is performed using Adam with a learning rate of 1×10^{-4}. Hyperparameters are selected through heuristic search to identify appropriate configurations for each experimental condition. The dataset of 66 target students is randomly divided into a training set of 49 and a test set of 17, corresponding to a 0.75 train-test split. Model performance is assessed by predicting self-reported learning gains using the constructed feature representations.

6 Experiment Results

6.1 Unimodal Experiment Results

The unimodal experiments assess the predictive power of individual feature sets derived from transcript, audio, and video modalities. Results are compared across feature types and feature construction strategies, as summarised in Table 2. Model performance is reported for four self-reported learning outcome categories: Intellectual, Social, Civic, and Intrapersonal.

Table 2. Predictive performance (weighted accuracy and F1-score) of unimodal features under two feature construction methods (utterance-based and date-based). Bold values indicate the best-performing setting for each outcome.

Modality	Features	Feature Construct.	ILG		SLG		CLG		IPLG	
			Acc.	F1	Acc.	F1	Acc.	F1	Acc.	F1
Transcript	Speech Features	Utterance-based	0.53	0.51	0.55	0.54	0.42	0.41	**0.64**	**0.62**
		Date-based	0.59	0.58	0.57	0.56	0.45	0.44	**0.68**	**0.67**
	LIWC Features	Utterance-based	0.54	0.52	0.58	0.57	**0.62**	**0.61**	0.49	0.48
		Date-based	0.58	0.56	0.60	0.59	**0.65**	**0.64**	0.51	0.50
	Dialogue Acts	Utterance-based	0.49	0.48	**0.62**	**0.61**	0.46	0.45	0.44	0.42
		Date-based	0.55	0.54	**0.66**	**0.65**	0.50	0.49	0.47	0.46
	Utterance Embeddings	Utterance-based	0.53	0.57	**0.55**	**0.54**	0.54	0.53	0.48	0.47
		Date-based	0.64	0.62	0.56	0.55	0.52	0.51	**0.64**	**0.63**
Audio	Frequency	Utterance-based	0.45	0.43	0.48	0.46	0.41	0.39	**0.52**	**0.50**
		Date-based	0.49	0.47	0.50	0.49	0.44	0.42	**0.55**	**0.54**
	Energy	Utterance-based	0.48	0.46	0.52	0.51	**0.56**	**0.55**	0.44	0.43
		Date-based	0.51	0.50	0.54	0.53	0.46	0.45	**0.59**	**0.58**
	Spectral	Utterance-based	0.44	0.42	0.47	0.45	0.40	0.38	**0.50**	**0.49**
		Date-based	0.47	0.45	0.49	0.48	0.43	0.41	**0.53**	**0.52**
	Paralinguistic Embeddings	Utterance-based	0.56	0.55	0.53	0.51	0.47	0.46	**0.58**	**0.57**
		Date-based	0.62	0.60	0.55	0.54	0.50	0.49	**0.62**	**0.61**
Video	Content Embeddings	Utterance-based	**0.60**	**0.59**	0.45	0.43	0.50	0.49	0.51	0.50
		Date-based	**0.67**	**0.66**	0.48	0.46	0.54	0.53	0.55	0.54
	Keyframe Embeddings	Utterance-based	0.50	0.48	**0.54**	**0.53**	0.53	0.52	0.45	0.43
		Date-based	0.53	0.51	0.56	0.55	0.48	0.46	**0.57**	**0.56**

Transcript Features: Among transcript-based features, the *date-based* construction method generally produces the strongest results. Utterance embeddings with date-based construction achieve the highest F1-scores for Intellectual (0.62) and Intrapersonal (0.63) gains. LIWC-based features also perform well, yielding the top Civic F1-score (0.64) and a strong result for Social (0.59). In most cases, date-based construction outperforms utterance-based construction, suggesting that aggregating features at the session level captures meaningful temporal patterns beyond single utterances.

Within the utterance statistics group, date-based construction produces improvements over the utterance-based approach, with F1-scores of 0.58 (Intellectual) and 0.67 (Intrapersonal). Similarly, for Dialogue Act features, date-based models achieve higher F1-scores for Social (0.65) and Civic (0.49) compared to their utterance-based counterparts (0.61 and 0.45, respectively). Overall, the results indicate that representing features at the date level enhances predictive performance for most transcript feature types.

Audio Features: For audio-based features, paralinguistic embeddings extracted with wav2vec 2.0 consistently outperform frequency-, energy-, and spectral-based features. Using the date-based approach, they achieve the highest F1-scores in the Intellectual (0.60) and Intrapersonal (0.61) categories. Energy-related features also benefit from date-based construction, with the highest Intrapersonal F1-score in this group (0.58). Frequency- and spectral-related features perform more modestly, with lower F1-scores across all learning gains compared to paralinguistic embeddings.

In general, paralinguistic embeddings yield the best audio results, and the date-based construction method again proves advantageous, reinforcing the importance of modelling temporal aggregation in speech data.

Video Features: Video-based features are represented by content embeddings and keyframe embeddings. For content embeddings, the date-based approach achieves the highest Intellectual F1-score across all unimodal experiments (0.66), underscoring the value of visual content in predicting intellectual learning gains. Improvements are also observed for Intrapersonal gains, with F1 increasing to 0.54 in the date-based setting. For keyframe embeddings, the best results are obtained with date-based construction as well, achieving F1-scores of 0.55 for Social and 0.56 for Intrapersonal gains. While these are slightly lower than the strongest transcript or audio features, they highlight the complementary contribution of visual information.

Cross-Modality Comparison. In summary, transcript-based features (particularly utterance embeddings and LIWC features) and audio paralinguistic embeddings deliver the strongest unimodal performance across most outcome categories, while video content embeddings stand out for Intellectual gains. Across modalities, the date-based construction approach consistently yields higher F1-scores than the utterance-based approach. These findings suggest that aggregating information at the session or date level provides a more robust and context-sensitive representation for predicting self-reported learning gains in online service-learning contexts.

Table 3. Predictive performance (weighted accuracy and F1-score) of multimodal features under two fusion strategies (concatenation and attention-based). Bold values indicate the best-performing setting for each outcome.

Features	Fusion Strategy	ILG		SLG		CLG		IPLG	
		Acc.	F1	Acc.	F1	Acc.	F1	Acc.	F1
Transcript+Audio	Concat	0.58	0.56	0.70	0.65	0.49	0.47	0.67	0.66
	Attention	0.60	0.58	0.72	0.68	0.51	0.49	0.69	0.68
Transcript+Video	Concat	0.65	0.64	0.63	0.61	0.50	0.49	0.66	0.65
	Attention	0.68	0.67	0.65	0.63	0.52	0.51	0.68	0.67
Audio+Video	Concat	0.55	0.53	0.58	0.57	0.46	0.44	0.61	0.60
	Attention	0.57	0.55	0.60	0.59	0.48	0.46	0.63	0.62
All (T+A+V)	Concat	0.68	0.67	0.71	0.69	0.53	0.52	0.69	0.68
	Attention	**0.71**	**0.70**	**0.74**	**0.72**	**0.55**	**0.54**	**0.72**	**0.71**

6.2 Multimodal Experiment Results

The results in Table 3 show clear differences in predictive performance across combinations of transcript, audio, and video features. Models that integrate all three modalities (transcript, audio, and video) consistently achieve the highest performance overall. For the Intellectual outcome, the full multimodal model with attention-based fusion reaches an F1-score of 0.70, outperforming any two-modality combination. Similar gains are observed for Social (0.72) and Intrapersonal (0.71) gains. For the Civic outcome, however, the strongest unimodal transcript-based baseline (LIWC features, F1-score 0.65) remains superior to multimodal integration, where the best result reaches 0.54. This suggests that the benefit of multimodal fusion is not uniform across outcome categories and that certain learning dimensions may be more strongly captured by a single modality.

Among two-modality models, transcript and video features form the most effective pairing, yielding F1-scores of 0.67 for Intellectual and Intrapersonal gains. Transcript combined with audio features also provides competitive performance, particularly for Social (0.68) and Intrapersonal (0.68) gains. In contrast, audio and video features alone deliver comparatively weaker results across all categories, underscoring the central role of transcript-based information in modelling learning gains. The choice of fusion method further shapes performance. Attention-based fusion consistently outperforms simple concatenation across all modality combinations. For example, when all three modalities are included, attention-based fusion increases the F1-score for Intellectual gains from 0.67 (concatenation) to 0.70, and for Social gains from 0.69 to 0.72. Similar improvements are observed for Intrapersonal gains (0.68 to 0.71) and, though more modest, for Civic gains (0.52 to 0.54). These results highlight the advantage of dynamically weighting modalities, allowing the model to selectively emphasize the most informative cues for each learning context.

7 Discussion

7.1 RQ1: Which Single-Modality Feature Set (transcript, Audio, or Screen Content Descriptors) Gives the Most Accurate Prediction of Student Learning Gain in Synchronous Videoconference Classes?

Transcript features emerge as the most effective predictors of student learning gain. Utterance embeddings, derived from sentence-transformer models, capture not only the literal words but also the semantic and contextual nuances of student contributions. When aggregated at the date level, these embeddings reflect both the coherence of classroom discourse within a session and changes in student engagement across sessions. Their consistent superiority across learning gains indicates that the ability to articulate, negotiate, and refine meaning in real time is closely tied to measurable learning gains. LIWC-based features add a complementary perspective by quantifying the presence of cognitive and metacognitive markers, such as causal connectives (e.g., "because," "so that") and reflective terms (e.g., "think," "realize"). These linguistic signals are strongly associated with active processing and self-monitoring, processes that are widely recognized in educational research as essential to meaningful learning. Dialogue act features further enrich this picture by capturing the functional role of utterances in interaction. Acts such as clarification, elaboration, and feedback highlight moments when students build on others' ideas, test their own understanding, or receive instructional scaffolding—mechanisms particularly relevant to the Social and Civic dimensions of learning.

Audio features, especially paralinguistic embeddings from wav2vec 2.0, provide useful but comparatively weaker predictors. While transcripts capture the content of speech, audio features convey how it is delivered, including prosodic cues such as intonation, stress, and rhythm. These cues are informative for engagement and affective involvement, which are important for learning but do not directly indicate cognitive depth or conceptual integration. This explains why audio features show moderate predictive power, particularly for learning gains with an affective or Intrapersonal outcome, but fall short of transcript-based models. Lower-level acoustic features (spectral, energy, and frequency-based) are even less effective, as they primarily distinguish surface-level variations (e.g., speaking versus silence, or energetic versus subdued delivery) rather than learning-relevant behaviors such as critical reflection or conceptual elaboration.

Screen content features, represented by embeddings of shared visual materials, are most effective for predicting Intellectual gains. This result is consistent with the pedagogical role of visual scaffolds: well-designed slides, diagrams, or demonstrations can enhance comprehension and support reasoning. However, screen content alone cannot capture student-generated reasoning, peer interaction, or self-reflection, which explains its weaker association with Social, Civic, and Intrapersonal gains.

In conclusion, these findings illustrate a clear hierarchy of predictive value: transcript features provide the strongest evidence of learning because they directly capture students' cognitive and discursive activity, while audio and visual features offer complementary but more limited signals. This hierarchy underscores the centrality of meaningful language use in online service-learning environments and highlights the importance of fostering dialogue and reflection as key mechanisms for promoting student learning.

7.2 RQ2: To What Extent Does Multimodal Fusion Enhance Predictive Performance Compared with the Best Single-Modality Baseline?

The results indicate that integrating multiple modalities generally enhances predictive performance compared to unimodal approaches, though the extent of improvement differs across learning gains. For Intellectual, Social, and Intrapersonal learning gains, multimodal models with attention-based fusion outperform the strongest unimodal baselines. For Intellectual gains, the best unimodal model—video content embeddings with date-based construction—achieves an F1-score of 0.67, whereas the multimodal model combining transcript, audio, and video features with attention-based fusion improves this to 0.70. For Social gains, performance rises from 0.66 (dialogue act features, date-based) to 0.72 with multimodal fusion. A similar trend appears for Intrapersonal gains, where the unimodal baseline (utterance statistics, date-based) reaches 0.67, compared with 0.71 for the multimodal model. By contrast, in the Civic category, unimodal transcript-based LIWC features (date-based) achieve an F1-score of 0.65, which exceeds the best multimodal result of 0.54. This indicates that multimodal integration does not uniformly enhance performance and that, in some cases, a single modality may already capture the most relevant signals for prediction.

Beyond predictive gains, multimodal fusion contributes to model robustness by enabling reliable performance even when one modality is noisy or less informative. For example, a student who contributes minimally in text may still convey engagement through prosodic features in speech or interactions with visual content. Attention-based fusion further strengthens this adaptability by dynamically weighting modalities according to their relative importance for each instance. These findings highlight the potential of multimodal learning analytics to provide a more comprehensive representation of student behaviour. Transcript features capture the semantic and syntactic content of dialogue, audio features reveal prosodic and paralinguistic cues, and video features reflect visual and cognitive scaffolding. Their integration enables models to detect distributed patterns of learning that are not apparent in isolation. As digital learning environments continue to expand, multimodal approaches offer promising avenues for building more reliable and holistic systems to monitor and support student learning.

8 Conclusion

This study investigated the use of multimodal features derived from transcripts, audio, and screen content to predict student learning gains in synchronous online service-learning programs. The results demonstrate that transcript-based features, especially semantic embeddings and psycholinguistic measures, are the most reliable single predictors across the four categories of learning outcomes. Audio-based paralinguistic embeddings and visual content descriptors provide useful complementary information, and their integration with transcripts through attention-based multimodal fusion further improves predictive performance. Taken together, the findings point to the central role of language in shaping learning processes, while also highlighting the contribution of acoustic and visual modalities in providing a fuller account of interaction in online classrooms.

Several limitations should be acknowledged. The dataset is relatively small and drawn from a single institutional context, which restricts the generalisability of the results. The learning outcomes are based on self-reports, which, although carefully validated, may not fully reflect objective learning performance. In addition, the automatic transcripts used for linguistic feature extraction are not error-free and could introduce noise. Finally, the present study evaluates models retrospectively, leaving questions about their suitability for real-time application.

Despite these limitations, this work contributes to multimodal learning analytics by offering a systematic comparison of unimodal and multimodal approaches in an authentic educational setting. Future research could extend this framework by incorporating additional behavioural signals such as gaze, gesture, or facial expressions, and by validating models against direct measures of learning. It would also be valuable to test the framework across diverse institutional and cultural contexts to assess its broader applicability. A further line of work lies in developing real-time multimodal analytics that can provide timely insights to instructors and support adaptive teaching strategies. With these extensions, multimodal learning analytics holds promise as a practical tool for enhancing both the quality and equity of online higher education.

Acknowledgment. This work was supported, in part, by the Hong Kong Research Grant Council under Grant 15600219.

References

1. Acosta, H., et al.: Multimodal learning analytics for predicting student collaboration satisfaction in collaborative game-based learning (2024)

2. Baevski, A., Zhou, Y., Mohamed, A., Auli, M.: wav2vec 2.0: a framework for self-supervised learning of speech representations. Adv. Neural Inf. Process. Syst. **33**, 12449–12460 (2020)
3. Bai, S., et al.: Qwen2. 5-vl technical report. arXiv preprint arXiv:2502.13923 (2025)
4. Bailey, D.R., Almusharraf, N., Almusharraf, A.: Video conferencing in the e-learning context: explaining learning outcome with the technology acceptance model. Educ. Inf. Technol. **27**(6), 7679–7698 (2022)
5. Bettencourt, M.: Supporting student learning outcomes through service learning. Foreign Lang. Ann. **48**(3), 473–490 (2015)
6. Grammens, M., Voet, M., Vanderlinde, R., Declercq, L., De Wever, B.: A systematic review of teacher roles and competences for teaching synchronously online through videoconferencing technology. Educ. Res. Rev. **37**, 100461 (2022)
7. Guthrie, K.L., McCracken, H.: Making a difference online: facilitating service-learning through distance education. Internet High. Educ. **13**(3), 153–157 (2010)
8. Helms, M.M., Rutti, R.M., Hervani, A.A., LaBonte, J., Sarkarat, S.: Implementing and evaluating online service learning projects. J. Educ. Bus. **90**(7), 369–378 (2015)
9. Klibanov, O.M., Dolder, C., Anderson, K., Kehr, H.A., Woods, J.A.: Impact of distance education via interactive videoconferencing on students' course performance and satisfaction. Adv. Physiol. Educ. **42**(1), 21–25 (2018)
10. Li, J., Li, D., Savarese, S., Hoi, S.: Blip-2: bootstrapping language-image pre-training with frozen image encoders and large language models. In: International Conference on Machine Learning, pp. 19730–19742. PMLR (2023)
11. Ma, Y., Katuka, G.A., Celepkolu, M., Boyer, K.E.: Investigating multimodal predictors of peer satisfaction for collaborative coding in middle school. Int. Educ. Data Mining Soc. (2022)
12. Moely, B.E., Ilustre, V.: The impact of service-learning course characteristics on university students' learning outcomes. Mich. J. Community Serv. Learn. **21**(1), 5–16 (2014)
13. Mu, S., Cui, M., Huang, X.: Multimodal data fusion in learning analytics: a systematic review. Sensors **20**(23), 6856 (2020)
14. Ngai, G., Chan, S.C., Kwan, K.P.: Challenge, meaning and preparation: critical success factors influencing student learning outcomes from service-learning. J. High. Educ. Outreach Engagement **22**(4), 55–80 (2018)
15. Ottl, S., Amiriparian, S., Gerczuk, M., Karas, V., Schuller, B.: Group-level speech emotion recognition utilising deep spectrum features. In: Proceedings of the 2020 International Conference on Multimodal Interaction, pp. 821–826 (2020)
16. Pennebaker, J.W., Boyd, R.L., Jordan, K., Blackburn, K.: The development and psychometric properties of LIWC2015 (2015)
17. Pi, Z., Zhang, L., Zhao, X., Li, X.: Peers turning on cameras promotes learning in video conferencing. Comput. Educ. **212**, 104986 (2024)
18. Qi, Y., Zhuang, L., Chen, H., Han, X., Liang, A.: Evaluation of students' learning engagement in online classes based on multimodal vision perspective. Electronics **13**(1), 149 (2023)
19. Stanton, T.K., Giles, D.E., Jr., Cruz, N.I.: Service-Learning: A Movement's Pioneers Reflect on Its Origins, Practice, and Future. Jossey-Bass Higher and Adult Education Series. ERIC (1999)
20. Stewart, A.E., Keirn, Z.A., D'Mello, S.K.: Multimodal modeling of coordination and coregulation patterns in speech rate during triadic collaborative problem solving. In: Proceedings of the 20th ACM International Conference on Multimodal Interaction, pp. 21–30 (2018)

21. Thakur, N., Reimers, N., Daxenberger, J., Gurevych, I.: Augmented sbert: data augmentation method for improving bi-encoders for pairwise sentence scoring tasks. arXiv preprint arXiv:2010.08240 (2020)
22. Wang, K., Fu, E.Y., Ngai, G., Leong, H.V.: Identifying key learning factors in service-leaning programs using machine learning. In: 2022 IEEE 46th Annual Computers, Software, and Applications Conference (COMPSAC), pp. 1312–1317. IEEE (2022)
23. Waterman, A.S.: Service-Learning: Applications from the Research. Routledge (2014)

Beyond Words: Latent Profiles of Online Communication Styles and Their Association with Social Well-Being on Social Media

Asma Elfadl[1(✉)], Sameha Alshakhsi[1], Nan Jiang[2], Raian Ali[1], and Ala Yankouskaya[3]

[1] College of Science and Engineering, Hamad Bin Khalifa University, Doha, Qatar
{aelfadl,salshakhsi,raali2}@hbku.edu.qa
[2] School of Computing and Engineering, Bournemouth University, Poole, UK
njiang@bournemouth.ac.uk
[3] School of Psychology, Bournemouth University, Poole, UK
ayankouskaya@bournemouth.ac.uk

Abstract. This study investigates the relationship between online communication styles and social well-being on social media. Drawing on data from 599 participants in the United Kingdom and Arab Gulf Cooperation Council (GCC) countries, we employed Latent Profile Analysis (LPA) to identify communication style profiles based on self-reported use across eight digital communication dimensions: ordered vs. unordered, direct vs. indirect, literate vs. oral, and being-centered vs. doing-centered. In both samples, two distinct profiles emerged: a lower engagement group and a higher engagement group, consistently and proportionally across the various communication styles. In the UK sample, individuals in the higher engagement profile marked by expressive and multi-modal communication, reported significantly greater social well-being on social media across four of five well-being domains: integration, contribution, actualization, and coherence. In contrast, no significant differences in social well-being on social media were observed across profiles in the Arab sample. A significant interaction between culture and communication profile confirmed that the relationship between communication style and social well-being on social media is moderated by cultural context. In addition, the results challenge the expectation that people can be profiled into distinct sets of communication styles, such as being high in one set of styles, e.g. direct and literate, and low in the opposite set, e.g. indirect and oral. Instead, people were profiled as generally high or low across all communication styles, though with varying levels within each. The results also challenge the assumption that active social media engagement universally enhances social well-being.

Keywords: Communication Styles · Social Media · Social Well-being · Latent profiles

T. Hao et al. (Eds.): BESC 2025, LNCS 16431, pp. 521–537, 2026.
https://doi.org/10.1007/978-981-95-7138-3_33

1 Introduction

The rise of social media has not only transformed how individuals maintain relationships and express themselves online but also introduced new norms for digital interaction. While a large body of research has explored the frequency and motivations behind social media use, comparatively less attention has been paid to the ways people communicate within these digital spaces [1–3]. Communication style refers to the different ways individuals exhibit verbal, and nonverbal communication patterns in social interactions. It involves how people receive, interpret, and deliver messages, and is influenced by factors such as culture and personality [4]. These communication styles encompass a wide array of verbal and nonverbal behaviors, including assertiveness, responsiveness, and orientation toward tasks versus relationships [5]. Similarly, several classifications, such as direct versus indirect, ordered versus unordered, being versus doing, and oral versus literate communication styles, help explain how communication varies across different contexts [6]. Importantly, these styles are not uniform across users but vary considerably, influenced by personality, context, and social norms [7]. Additionally, digital environments are often characterized by limited non-verbal cues and a heightened risk of misinterpretation [8], which underlines the importance of understanding how individuals adapt their communication approaches in these settings. Understanding these complex patterns also requires attention to the broader cultural frameworks in which communication occurs.

Culture plays a crucial role in shaping both communication styles and their impact on well-being by embedding shared values, norms, and expectations into everyday interactions [9]. It influences whether individuals prefer direct or indirect, structured or fluid, and task-oriented or relational styles of expression [10, 11]. For instance, In individualistic cultures, communication often centers on self-expression, transparency, and personal outcomes. People are encouraged to voice their opinions, express themselves truthfully, and prioritize personal rights and autonomy even if it risks disagreement [12–14]. Such cultures associate well-being with authenticity, independence, and self-achievement, but they can also heighten vulnerability to social comparison. In contrast, collectivistic cultures emphasize interdependence, group harmony, and relational sensitivity. Individuals view themselves as part of a cohesive "we" group, and communication tends to avoid confrontation or self-promotion to preserve social harmony and avoid negative social consequences [12, 14]. Thus, cultural orientations shape not only how people communicate, but also how those styles support or undermine their social well-being.

Despite the growing interest in communication styles, much of the existing research continues to rely on variable-centered approaches, which examine individual dimensions of communication (e.g., directness, formality) in isolation [15, 16]. While informative, this approach may not fully capture how people actually communicate online, where expression is inherently multidimensional and dynamic. In practice, individuals do not express themselves using a single style but instead exhibit interconnected patterns of co-occurring communication preferences [17]. For example, a user who favors ordered communication may also consistently utilize literate, formal expressions, whereas another may combine indirectness with oral or unstructured interactions. Analyzing communication traits in isolation risks obscuring these meaningful combinations and the richer, more dynamic reality of digital communication [18]. These communication patterns are not only stylistic, but they also have practical implications for users' experiences and well-being.

The extent to which individuals are empowered to communicate online in their preferred ways is intrinsically linked to their social well-being on social media. Successful and fulfilling online interactions can foster a sense of belonging, while miscommunications or negative exchanges can lead to feelings of isolation or distress [19]. Social well-being can be conceptualized in various ways. The conceptualization adopted in this paper is based on the five domains proposed in [20]: social integration (feeling part of online communities), social acceptance (holding positive views of others and feeling accepted online), social contribution (believing one has something of value to offer to the online world), social actualization (perceiving positive growth and potential in online society), and social coherence (making sense of the online social world and its norms.

Research shows that communication styles aligned with authenticity and active engagement are linked to higher well-being. For example, users who express their true selves on platforms like Facebook tend to report greater happiness, especially when they have high self-esteem [21]. Similarly, those who actively post and engage with others, rather than passively scrolling experience more positive emotions and life satisfaction [22]. Communication styles also influence how meaningful and coherent social media experiences feel. Users whose contributions are acknowledged by others often report stronger feelings of social integration and purpose [1]. Additionally, the language used in posts can reflect and even predict emotional well-being, highlighting the connection between communication behavior and psychological statues [23]. However, the relationship between communication styles and well-being on social media is not universal. It is shaped by broader cultural contexts, which influence both communication norms [24] and the subjective evaluation of well-being [13]. Additionally, communication style might itself reflect low or high well-being status, rather than being a cause or a facilitator of it.

Understanding how individuals communicate and experience well-being on social media requires attention to the cultural contexts in which these behaviours occur [25]. Communication styles and experiences of SW-SM are shaped by the cultural contexts in which they occur, including the values and norms embedded within those systems [26]. For instance, individualistic cultures such as the United States tend to emphasize self-expression, autonomy, and personal achievement, which may intensify the impact of social comparison on self-esteem and well-being [27]. In contrast, collectivistic cultures often value group harmony, interdependence, and collective success, which can buffer the negative effects of online comparison and promote relational well-being [28]. These cultural orientations shape not only communication preferences but also individuals' perceptions of well-being and social connection [13]. Despite this, research on online communication styles that accounts to cultural variability, particularly using person-centered rather than variable-centered approaches, remains limited. There is a need for a more holistic approach that captures real-world communication patterns within cultural contexts.

To address this need, the present study adopts a person-centred approach, using Latent Profile Analysis (LPA) to identify subgroups of individuals who share similar patterns of communication style preferences. Unlike variable-centered methods that assume homogeneity within a sample, LPA identifies unobserved subgroups, or latent profiles, based on individuals' unique style configurations [29, 30]. This approach is especially powerful in the context of social media, where users exhibit diverse self-presentation strategies. By identifying communicative personas which are distinct patterns of communication behavior that emerge within individuals, we can better understand how these styles relate to social well-being dimensions. For example, one profile might be characterized by being doing-centered (i.e. task-oriented) and direct communication, while another may show strong being-centered, (i.e. relational focus and supportive emotional expressiveness) and indirect communication. These patterns resemble profiles such as the "traditionally undemonstrative" and "warmly supportive" communicators identified in prior work using Latent Profile Analysis [31]. This methodological shift aligns with a growing recognition that well-being is not simply the absence of distress, but a multi-dimensional construct involving coherence, integration, purpose, and growth [32]. Prior work has shown that alignment between one's self-presentation style and perceived social norms can enhance well-being outcomes on digital platforms [33].

Building on this rationale, the present study seeks to detect latent communication style profiles and how these profiles relate to social well-being on social media (SW-SM) across cultural contexts. Specifically, we aim to address the following research questions:

RQ1: Do distinct latent profiles of online communication styles emerge within Arab and UK samples, and how are these profiles structured across the two cultural contexts?

RQ2: To what extent do these latent profiles differ in levels of social well-being on social media across the five domains of integration, acceptance, contribution, actualization, and coherence?

RQ3: Does cultural context moderate the relationship between the latent communication styles profiles and social well-being on social media (SW-SM)?

To test RQ1, we used LPA separately within each culture, aiming to identify meaningful configurations of self-use communication styles. To test RQ2, we used a Welch-test to compare SW-SM scores across profiles within each cultural group. To test RQ3, we examined the interaction models (e.g., SW-SM [dimensions] ~ Culture * Profile) to evaluate cultural moderation effects.

2 Method

2.1 Participants and Procedure

This study involved 599 adult participants, aged 18 to 60 years. They are drawn from two distinct cultural contexts: the United Kingdom (n = 272) and the Arab Gulf Cooperation Council (GCC) countries (n = 327). The UK group included individuals from England, Scotland, Wales, and Northern Ireland, with 41.91% identifying as male. The Arab sample, consisting of 45.57% males, represented residents from Saudi Arabia, the United Arab Emirates, Bahrain, and Qatar. Participants were recruited using TGM Research, an international online survey panel provider (https://tgmresearch.com/).

The survey was administered through SurveyMonkey (https://www.surveymonkey.com/), an established web-based platform. To ensure clarity and cultural relevance, the survey underwent multiple revisions through iterative expert review and a pilot test with participants from both target regions. The instrument was initially written in English and then translated into Arabic using the back-translation technique to maintain conceptual and linguistic accuracy across languages [34]. Participants were screened for eligibility based on the following criteria: being 18 or older, frequent users of at least one social media platform including either social networking site (e.g., Facebook, Instagram, Twitter) or messaging application (e.g., WhatsApp, Facebook Messenger), and self-identified culturally as either British or Arab. These inclusion criteria were verified through a pre-screening survey. Quality control was maintained by embedding attention, checking questions and monitoring completion times. Respondents who failed these checks or completed the survey in less than half the median time (after removing outliers) were excluded. Prior to participation, all individuals received detailed information about the study and provided informed consent. Ethical approval was obtained from the Institutional Review Board (IRB) of the first author's institution. Only those who completed the entire survey without disqualification received compensation. The data were collected between late October 2023 and mid-December 2023 as part of a broader research project; more details are available in the data availability section.

Participants were presented with short, contextually grounded scenarios showing common online social and professional situations. Each scenario compared two communication styles (e.g., direct vs. indirect; ordered vs. unordered; oral vs. literate), and participants were asked to identify which style was being demonstrated. An example of Direct vs. Indirect style is below:

Sam is having some difficulty in preparing a C.V (resume) for a new job or course. Sam wants help from friends. Sam talks or writes to friends and contacts, saying:

- Direct: "I am applying for a new job. I need your help in preparing my C.V (resume) so it looks more competitive".
- Indirect: "I am applying for a new job. I am finding it really difficult to prepare my C.V. (resume). I really need this opportunity".

To ensure participants had a clear understanding of the styles before responding, each one was introduced with a concise definition, supported by realistic examples and followed by a short comprehension quiz with corrective feedback. For example, Direct communication was described as clearly and explicitly stating one's thoughts, feelings, or needs saying exactly what is meant. In contrast, Indirect communication involved implying intentions without directly expressing them, allowing the listener to infer meaning. Ordered communication referred to a structured, goal-oriented style that focused on one topic at a time, typically with limited back-and-forth interaction. Unordered communication was defined as more spontaneous and dynamic, often shifting between topics and incorporating interactive elements. Participants were also introduced to Being-oriented communication, which emphasized emotional connection, relationship-building, and the quality of social interactions, while Doing-oriented communication highlighted efficiency, task completion, and achieving goals. Literate communication was characterized by the use of formal, written language (e.g., emails, reports), whereas

Oral communication relied on spoken interaction through conversations, meetings, or presentations.

To ensure clarity and cultural relevance, face validation was conducted with participants from both target populations. Five individuals—two from the UK and three from Arab countries—reviewed the materials and provided feedback to ensure the style definitions were understandable and that each scenario clearly reflected a single communication style. This process contributed to a structure resembling a vignette experiment. Based on the feedback, several refinements were made. For instance, questions about face-to-face communication were removed due to concerns about participant fatigue and possible confusion. The final survey focused solely on online communication styles to improve clarity and engagement. Terminology was also refined for example, the label "Linear" was replaced with "Ordered" to better reflect the style's characteristics. Additionally, to maintain neutrality and reduce potential bias, the character names in scenarios were standardized: while earlier versions used "Sam" and "Noor," all characters were later labelled "Sam" to avoid unintended gender or cultural connotations. To further support participants' comprehension, visual cues were added using distinct colors (blue and orange) to consistently differentiate between paired styles in each scenario. The data and study design are available at Open Science Framework (OSF) under the data availability section.

2.2 Measurements

Demographic Characteristics. We collected information about participants' age, gender, and education.

Communication Styles. Eight communication styles, adopted from [6] were measured: direct, indirect, ordered (linear), unordered (non-linear), being-centered, doing-centered, oral, and literate communication styles. To evaluate the use of communication styles, participants responded to two key statements per style: "I use it when communicating with others?" (referred to as 'Self-use') and "Others use it when communicating with me?" (referred to as 'Others-use'). All responses were recorded on a 6-point Likert scale, ranging from 1 ("Strongly disagree") to 6 ("Strongly agree"). Only self-use of communication styles was used in the study.

Social Well-Being. To evaluate participants' social well-being within the realm of social media, the study utilized a customized version of Keyes' (1998) Social Well-Being Scale. This instrument captures five core aspects of well-being: integration, contribution, coherence, actualization, and acceptance. All items were specifically reframed to relate to users' online experiences by introducing them with a prompt focusing on social media usage. This ensured that participants focused their responses on digital rather than offline contexts. Each aspect was measured using three separate statements, resulting in a total of 15 items across all dimensions.

Illustrative examples regarding their social media experience: "I feel close to people in my online community" to reflect social integration, and "I have something valuable to contribute to the online world" for social contribution. Similarly, items like "I can usually predict what happens next in online spaces" represented social coherence, while "The online world is not getting better for people like me" tapped into perceptions of social actualization. Social acceptance was evaluated through statements such as "People on social media are generally kind." Responses were rated on a 7-point Likert scale ranging from 1 (strongly disagree) to 7 (strongly agree). For each subscale, a composite score was computed by summing responses across its three respective items. To evaluate the scale's reliability, Cronbach's alpha was calculated. The total score showed good reliability in the UK sample ($\alpha = .802$) and in the Arab sample ($\alpha = .794$).

2.3 Data Analysis

To identify distinct subgroups of individuals based on their preferences for different communication styles, we conducted LPA using scores on eight indicators: direct, indirect, ordered, unordered, doing, oral, and literate communication. LPA is a person-centered technique that identifies unobserved (latent) subpopulations within a heterogeneous sample by modelling the probability that individuals belong to different classes based on patterns in their observed responses [30, 35]. Unlike variable-centered approaches, which focus on relationships between variables across the entire sample, LPA classifies individuals into mutually exclusive and exhaustive latent classes that reflect qualitatively distinct configurations of traits or behaviours.

We used the mclust package in R [36] to estimate finite Gaussian mixture models with 2 to 6 latent classes separately within each cultural group (UK and Arab). Models were estimated using maximum likelihood with the expectation-maximization (EM) algorithm. All variables were standardized prior to analysis to account for scale differences and ensure equal weighting. Model selection was based on multiple fit indices and interpretability. Specifically, we considered the Bayesian Information Criterion (BIC), Akaike Information Criterion (AIC), and log-likelihood values, with lower values indicating better fit [37].

After identifying the optimal number of classes for each cultural group, participants were assigned to their most likely latent profile based on posterior probabilities. These class assignments were then used in follow-up analyses to compare subjective well-being scores across profiles. The selected LPA solution yielded two-class models for each cultural group, and the resulting profiles were of unequal size, we conducted Welch's t-tests to compare mean well-being scores across latent profiles. This approach was chosen over ANOVA because it does not assume equal variances or balanced group sizes, both of which are common violations in latent profile-based analyses [38]. Analyses were performed separately for the UK and Arab samples across five well-being domains.

To examine whether the relationship between individuals' communication style profiles and SW-SM differed across cultural contexts, we conducted a series of linear regression models with culture (Arab vs. UK), latent profile membership, and their interaction as predictors. Significant interactions were followed up by estimating simple effects within each cultural group to understand whether the relationship between profile type and SW-SM was consistent across the UK and Arab samples.

3 Results

3.1 Profile Solution

Model comparison based on the Bayesian Information Criterion (BIC) supported a 2-profile solution, beyond which improvements in fit were negligible.

Profiling in Arab Sample. Profile 1 (N = 173), labeled as Structured Expressive Communicators (SEC), showed elevated scores across multiple communication dimensions, particularly Direct, Literate, Ordered, and Oral styles as seen in Fig. 1. Individuals in this profile appear to favor clear, organized, and expressive forms of communication, suggesting an active and intentional approach to self-expression.

Profile 2 (N = 154), labeled as Moderate or Selective Communicators (MSC), shows generally lower scores across communication style variables, particularly on Indirect, Doing and Unordered styles.

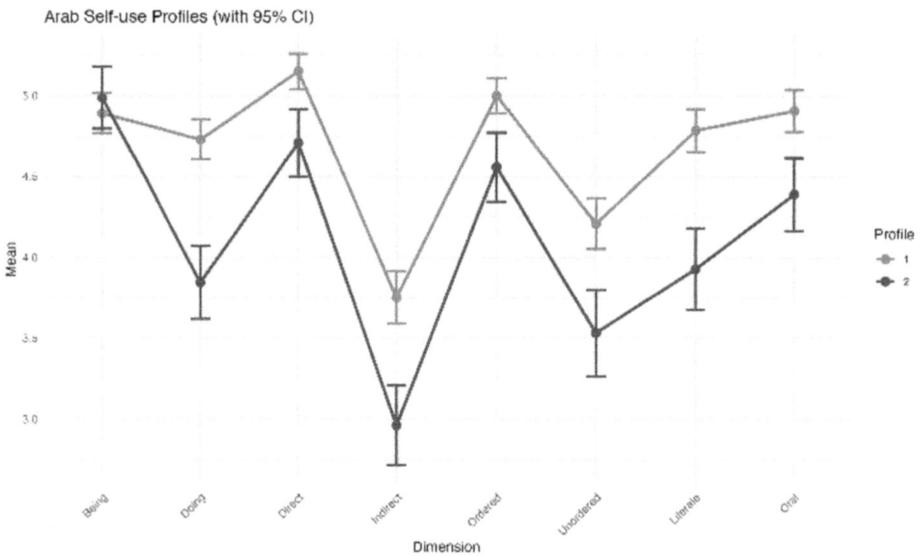

Fig. 1. Mean Score and 95% Confidence Intervals on Five SW-SM Dimensions for Profile 1 and Profile 2 in the Arab Sample

In the Arab sample, independent Welch's t-tests revealed no statistically significant differences in SW-SM across the five assessed domains between the two latent communication profiles. For integration, the difference between Profile 1 (M = 12.94) and Profile 2 (M = 13.31) was not significant, $t(296.45) = 0.80$, $p = .426$, with a 95% confidence interval (CI) of [−0.54, 1.29], as seen in Table 1. Similarly, acceptance did not differ between Profile 2 (M = 12.38) and Profile 1 (M = 12.38), $t(308.27) = -0.02$, $p = .982$, 95% CI [-0.67, 0.65]. For contribution, Profile 2 (M = 13.94) and Profile 1 (M = 13.81) again showed no significant difference, $t(310.17) = 0.31$, $p = .760$, 95% CI [−0.71, 0.97]. Actualization scores were slightly higher in Profile 1 (M = 14.65) than in

Profile 2 (M = 14.32), but this difference was also nonsignificant, $t(320.07) = -0.84$, $p = .404$, 95% CI [−1.09, 0.44]. Finally, coherence showed a trend towards higher scores in Profile 1 (M = 14.65) compared to Profile 2 (M = 14.16), yet this did not reach significance, $t(316.04) = -1.40$, $p = .163$, 95% CI [−1.19, 0.20]. These results indicate that, within the Arab group, well-being scores did not significantly vary by communication profile.

Table 1. Means, Standard Deviations, and 95% Confidence Intervals for SW-SM Dimensions by Profile (Arab Sample)

Dimension	Profile 1 M (SD)	95% CI	Profile 2 M (SD)	95% CI
Acceptance	12.38 (3.19)	11.88–12.89	12.38 (2.84)	11.95–12.80
Actualization	14.65 (3.53)	14.09–15.21	14.32 (3.50)	13.80–14.85
Coherence	14.65 (3.26)	14.13–15.17	14.16 (3.10)	13.69–14.62
Contribution	13.81 (4.03)	13.17–14.45	13.94 (3.64)	13.40–14.49
Integration	12.94 (4.57)	12.21–13.66	13.31 (3.75)	12.74–13.87

Profiling in UK Sample. Profile 1 (N = 139) (Expressive multi-channel communicators, EMCC), includes higher scores on all communication dimensions, particularly Direct, Ordered, Oral, and Being. Profile 1 also reports substantially higher well-being across every domain, including integration, contribution, and coherence. This suggests a broad, active, and expressive communication profile.

Profile 2 (N = 133) (Low Engagement Communicators, LEC) in which there are low scores across nearly all communication dimensions, especially Indirect, and Unordered, as seen in Fig. 2. Those correspond with lower well-being across all five domains. This group appears to show limited use of diverse communication styles, possibly indicating less expressive or less engaged social media users. Individuals who make limited use of self-expression styles on social media, potentially resulting in lower perceived SW-SM.

In the UK sample, Welch's t-tests revealed statistically significant differences in well-being across latent self-use communication profiles for four of the five measured domains. Participants in Profile 1 consistently reported higher social well-being on social media than those in Profile 2 (Table 2). For integration, individuals in Profile 1 (M = 13.14) scored significantly higher than those in Profile 2 (M = 11.06), $t(265.45) = -3.88$, $p < .001$, 95% CI [−3.14, −1.03]. A similar pattern emerged for contribution, with Profile 1 scoring higher (M = 13.57) than Profile 2 (M = 11.61), $t(257.10) = -3.83$, $p < .001$, 95% CI [−2.97, −0.95]. Actualization was also significantly greater in Profile 1 (M = 13.04) compared to Profile 2 (M = 11.26), $t(260.27) = -3.89$, $p < .001$, 95% CI [-2.67, -0.87]. Likewise, coherence scores were significantly higher in Profile 1 (M = 13.76) than in Profile 2 (M = 12.26), $t(264.52) = -3.90$, $p < .001$, 95% CI [−2.25, -0.74]. For the domain of acceptance, although mean scores were higher in Profile 1 (M = 12.57) than in Profile 2 (M = 11.89), the difference did not reach statistical

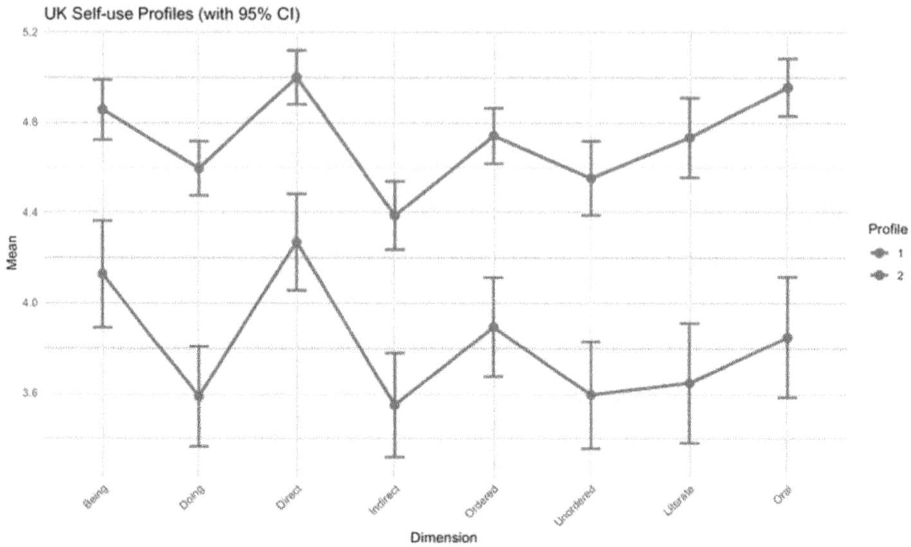

Fig. 2. Mean Scores and 95% Confidence Intervals on Five SW-SM Dimensions for Profile 1 and Profile 2 in the UK Sample.

significance, $t(269.31) = -1.78$, $p = .077$, 95% CI [−1.44, 0.07]. These results indicate that, in the UK sample, more expressive and multidimensional communication profiles were consistently associated with higher levels of SW-SM.

Table 2. Means, Standard Deviations, and 95% Confidence Intervals for SW-SM Dimensions by Profile (UK Sample)

Dimension	Profile 1 M (SD)	95% CI	Profile 2 M (SD)	95% CI
Acceptance	12.57 (3.31)	12.01–13.12	11.89 (3.01)	11.37–12.40
Actualization	13.04 (3.46)	12.45–13.62	11.26 (4.03)	10.57–11.95
Coherence	13.76 (2.99)	13.25–14.26	12.26 (3.30)	11.70–12.83
Contribution	13.57 (3.81)	12.93–14.21	11.61 (4.57)	10.83–12.39
Integration	13.14 (4.22)	12.44–13.85	11.06 (4.61)	10.27–11.85

Cross Cultural Comparison Profiles. Although measurement invariance of the latent profile structure was not assumed across cultures, the primary objective was to examine whether the association between profile type and SW-SM differed by cultural context.

The model predicting Integration revealed a significant main effect of culture ($\beta = -2.25$, SE $= 0.49$, $t = -4.56$, $p < .001$), indicating that UK participants reported lower levels of integration than those in the Arab group. The interaction between profile and culture was also significant ($\beta = 2.46$, SE $= 0.70$, $t = 3.50$, $p = .0005$), suggesting that the difference in integration between Profile 1 and Profile 2 was more pronounced in the UK sample. The overall model was significant, $F(3, 595) = 8.34, p < .001$, with an adjusted R^2 of .035. In contrast, the model predicting Acceptance showed no significant effects. Neither the main effects of culture and profile nor their interaction reached statistical significance (all $p > .17$), and the overall model was not significant, $F(3, 595) = 1.22$, p = .30, with an adjusted R^2 near zero. These results suggest that acceptance scores were relatively stable across samples and profile types. The analysis of Contribution showed a significant effect of culture ($\beta = -2.33$, SE = 0.46, $t = -5.06$, $p < .001$), with UK participants again reporting lower well-being scores than in the Arab sample. We also observed a significant culture-by-profile interaction ($\beta = 2.09$, SE = 0.66, $t = 3.18$, $p = .0016$), indicating that the benefit of Profile 1 (higher communicative engagement) was stronger in the UK sample. The model explained modest variance, $F(3, 595) = 10.45$, $p < .001$, adjusted $R^2 = .045$. For Actualization, similar patterns emerged. UK participants reported significantly lower scores ($\beta = -3.06$, SE = 0.42, $t = -7.33$, $p < .001$), and the interaction term was significant ($\beta = 1.45$, SE = 0.60, $t = 2.43$, $p = .015$), again suggesting that profile-related differences were more salient in the UK than in the Arab group. The model was robust, $F(3, 595) = 25.74$, $p < .001$, adjusted $R^2 = .110$. Finally, in the model predicting Coherence, culture had a significant main effect ($\beta = -1.89$, SE = 0.36, $t = -5.19$, $p < .001$), and the profile-by-culture interaction showed a trend towards significance ($\beta = 0.999$, SE = 0.52, $t = 1.92$, p = .055), suggesting a possible moderation effect. The model was statistically significant overall, $F(3, 595) = 14.90$, p < .001, adjusted $R^2 = .065$.

To summarize, individuals with more engaged communication profiles (Profile 1) generally reported higher well-being in several psychological domains, but this association was significantly stronger in the UK sample. In contrast, within the Arab sample, there were no significant differences in well-being between Profile 1 and Profile 2 across any of the domains. These findings suggest that while expressive communication profiles may confer advantages in Western digital cultures, such benefits may not translate similarly in more collectivistic or relationally restrained contexts.

4 Discussion

The study identified two distinct latent communication style profiles within both the Arab and UK samples. While both cultures revealed "lower engagement" and "higher engagement" profiles, it is crucial to acknowledge that these profiles were independently derived for each group.

4.1 Communication Profiles vs. SW-SM

In the Arab sample, two profiles emerged that are "Structured Expressive Communicators (SEC)" (Profile 1), characterized by higher means on most communication styles dimensions (Direct, Literate, Ordered, Oral), and "Moderate or Selective Communicators (MSC)" (Profile 2), showing lower scores on communication style variables overall. Despite these distinct communication patterns, independent Welch's t-tests revealed no statistically significant differences in social media related well-being across any of the five assessed domains (integration, acceptance, contribution, actualization, and coherence) between these two profiles. This finding aligns with prior research suggesting that communication with close social network groups can enhance well-being regardless of the strength of communication ties, which may help explain the lack of significant difference observed between the groups [39]. However, it challenges the assumption that more active or expressive communication universally lead to higher well-being on social media [40]. In collectivistic cultures, such as those found in the Arab, communication often prioritizes group harmony, indirectness, modesty, and maintaining social face [6, 10, 41, 42]. As a result, highly direct or overtly expressive communication style might not necessarily translate into enhanced well-being and could be perceived negatively. This highlights how the impact of communication style on well-being is culturally dependent.

Conversely, in the UK sample, two distinct profiles were identified, that are "Low Engagement Communicators (LEC)" (Profile 2), characterized by low scores across nearly all communication dimensions and lower well-being across all five domains. Secondly the "Expressive Multi-Channel Communicators (EMCC)" (Profile 1), showing higher scores on all communication dimensions and substantially higher well-being across every domain. Welch's t-tests confirmed statistically significant differences in well-being for four out of five domains, with Profile 1 consistently reporting higher well-being. This finding aligns with the existing literature on social media use and well-being in Western, individualistic contexts, where active engagement, self-expression, and authenticity are often linked to positive psychological outcomes [21, 33]. In such cultures, individuals are often encouraged to express their true selves and actively participate in online interactions, which can foster a sense of belonging, purpose, and integration [1, 22]. The lack of significant difference in acceptance, while other domains showed significance, might show that while expressive communication generally enhances well-being, the perception of acceptance might be influenced by factors beyond just one's communication style, or that a baseline level of acceptance is present regardless of communication intensity.

4.2 Cultural Moderation of Communication and Well-Being

The analysis of the interaction between culture and communication profile revealed that cultural context significantly moderates the relationship between communication style and well-being. Moreover, moderation patterns were observed for the well-being domains of contribution and actualization. Although UK participants generally reported lower scores, the well-being advantage associated with being in the higher engagement profile (Profile 1) was significantly stronger in the UK than in the Arab sample. For coherence, a trend towards significance in the interaction term also suggested a possible moderation effect. In contrast, acceptance showed no significant effects across cultures or profiles. One possible explanation is that UK participants tended to use communication styles including both structured such as literate, ordered and spontaneous (e.g., oral, direct). Those may be experiencing richer and more socially rewarding online interactions, which contribute to greater coherence and meaning in their digital lives [1, 43]. Notably, the dimension of social acceptance did not significantly vary across profiles or cultures, suggesting that perceptions of kindness and social regard on social media may be more stable and less dependent on communication style. This aligns with previous findings showing that social acceptance is often shaped by broader online community norms and less influenced by individual behavior [19].

4.3 Practical Implications

The findings of this study carry significant practical implications. First, they highlight the cultural specificity SW-SM, showing that the benefits of expressive communication observed in Western, individualistic cultures do not apply universally. This challenges the ethnocentric bias in existing research by [44], demonstrating that cultural values shape both communication styles and their psychological impacts. These findings emphasize the need for culturally sensitive approaches in social media design. Platform developers and content creators should consider incorporating features that support diverse communication styles and cultural norms, rather than exclusively rewarding overt expressiveness. For instance, features that enable group-oriented communication, private sharing, or more subtle interaction cues may be more effective in collectivistic contexts [45]. This suggests that interventions aiming to improve social media experiences should not assume that promoting expressiveness or self-disclosure benefits all users equally. In Western contexts, encouraging expressive and multi-modal communication, rather than just passive browsing, may support aspects of social well-being. In contrast, in more collectivistic or relational cultures (e.g., Arab contexts), where indirectness or controlled self-presentation is more normative, promoting high engagement may not yield the same benefits. Ultimately, these findings challenge the common assumption, especially in global platform design that being active and highly visible on social media always leads to better well-being for all users. Moreover, online forums intended for cross-cultural communication should avoid implicitly recommending such norms, as they may not align with the diverse cultural values and preferences that shape users' engagement and experiences.

4.4 Limitations and Future Work

There are a few limitations and directions for future research. First, the data on communication styles and well-being were collected through self-report questionnaires, which are susceptible to social desirability bias, recall bias, and individual differences in self-perception. To reduce these risks, participants were presented with concrete, context-specific scenarios and communication-style vignettes, followed by a comprehension quiz with corrective feedback. Additionally, when responding to the main scenario-based questions, participants were provided with brief reminders of each communication style to help ensure consistent interpretation. This approach helped ensure a clearer understanding of each communication style before participants responded, thereby minimizing potential misinterpretation or biased self-assessment. Nonetheless, future studies could further address these limitations by integrating observational methods or digital trace data to triangulate self-report findings.

Second, the cross-sectional design of this study limits the ability to infer causal relationships between communication style profiles and social media related well-being. While associations were observed, it remains unclear whether specific communication styles lead to greater well-being, or whether individuals with higher well-being are more likely to adopt certain communication styles. Longitudinal research designs are needed to explore these causal pathways more effectively.

5 Conclusion

This study highlights the importance of a culturally grounded, person-centered approach to digital communication. We identified distinct communication style profiles among Arab and UK social media users and found that the link between communication style and social media well-being varies by culture. In the UK, expressive and multi-modal communicators reported higher well-being, while no such differences were found in the Arab sample. These findings challenge the assumption that active social media engagement universally enhances well-being and underscore the need for culturally sensitive research and platform design. Future studies should further investigate these dynamics using longitudinal and mixed-method approaches.

6 Data Availability Statement.

The data and study design are available at Open Science Framework (OSF) link (https://osf.io/r53dp/).

7 Disclosure of Interests

The authors have no competing interests to declare that are relevant to the content of this article.

Acknowledgments. This publication was made possible by an NPRP-14-Cluster Grant # NPRP14C-0916-210015 and the Graduate Student Research Award # GSRA9-L-1-0527-2205 from the Qatar National Research Fund (a member of Qatar Foundation). The findings herein reflect the work and are solely the responsibility of the authors. The authors thank Areej Babiker for assistance with data collection and curation.

References

1. Gazi, M.A.I., Rahaman, M.A., Rabbi, M.F., Masum, M., Nabi, M.N., Senathirajah, A.R.B.S.: The role of social media in enhancing communication among individuals: prospects and problems. Environ. Soc. Psychol. **9**(11) (2024). https://doi.org/10.59429/ESP.V9I11.2979
2. Schivinski, B., Brzozowska-Woś, M., Stansbury, E., Satel, J., Montag, C., Pontes, H.M.: Exploring the role of social media use motives, psychological well-being, self-esteem, and affect in problematic social media use. Front. Psychol. **11**, 617140 (2020). https://doi.org/10.3389/FPSYG.2020.617140/BIBTEX
3. Cha, J.: Factors affecting the frequency and amount of social networking site use: Motivations, perceptions, and privacy concerns. First Monday **15**(12) (2010). https://doi.org/10.5210/FM.V15I12.2889

4. Zheltukhina, M.R., Kislitsyna, N.N., Sergeeva, V., Ignateva, R.M., Kosheleva, Y. P., Lutskovskaia, L.Y.: Adaptation of communication styles inventory to Russian context. Contemp. Educ. Technol. **15**(4) (2023). https://doi.org/10.30935/CEDTECH/13512
5. de Vries, R.E., Bakker-Pieper, A., Konings, F.E., Schouten, B.: The communication styles inventory (CSI): a six-dimensional behavioral model of communication styles and its relation with personality. Communic Res. **40**(4), 506–532 (2013). https://doi.org/10.1177/0093650211413571
6. Zaharna, R.S.: Understanding cultural preferences of Arab communication patterns. Public Relat. Rev. **21**(3), 241–255 (1995). https://doi.org/10.1016/0363-8111(95)90024-1
7. Norton, R.: Communicator style: theory, applications, and measures (1983)
8. Kruger, J., Epley, N., Parker, J., Ng, Z.W.: Egocentrism over E-mail: can we communicate as well as we think? J. Pers. Soc. Psychol. **89**(6), 925–936 (2005). https://doi.org/10.1037/0022-3514.89.6.925
9. Giri, V.N.: Culture and communication style. Rev Comm **6**(1–2), 124–130 (2006). https://doi.org/10.1080/15358590600763391
10. Hall, E.T.: Beyond Culture, 1st edn. Anchor Press, Garden City (1976)
11. Gudykunst, W.B., Ting-Toomey, S.: Culture and affective communication. Am. Behav. Sci. **31**(3), 384–400 (1988). https://doi.org/10.1177/000276488031003009/ASSET/000276488031003009.FP.PNG_V03
12. Hofstede, G.: Dimensionalizing cultures: the hofstede model in context. Online Read. Psychol. Cult. **2**(1), 8 (2011). https://doi.org/10.9707/2307-0919.1014
13. Diener, E., Oishi, S., Lucas, R.E.: Personality, culture, and subjective well-being: emotional and cognitive evaluations of life. Annu. Rev. Psychol. **54**, 403–425 (2003). https://doi.org/10.1146/ANNUREV.PSYCH.54.101601.145056/CITE/REFWORKS
14. Singelis, T.M., Triandis, H.C., Bhawuk, D.P.S., Gelfand, M.J.: Horizontal and vertical dimensions of individualism and collectivism: a theoretical and measurement refinement. Cross-Cult. Res. **29**(3), 240–275 (1995). https://doi.org/10.1177/106939719502900302
15. Bergman, L.R., Magnusson, D.: A person-oriented approach in research on developmental psychopathology. Dev. Psychopathol. **9**(2), 291–319 (1997). https://doi.org/10.1017/S095457949700206X
16. De Vries, R.E., Bakker-Pieper, A., Siberg, R.A., Van Gameren, K., Vlug, M.: The content and dimensionality of communication styles. Communic Res. **36**(2), 178–206 (2009). https://doi.org/10.1177/0093650208330250
17. Schüler-Lubienetzki, H., Lubienetzki, U.: Communication styles and patterns. In: How We Talk to Each Other - The Messages We Send With Our Words and Body Language, pp. 37–55 (2022). https://doi.org/10.1007/978-3-662-64437-9_3
18. Amelia, L.T.D., Balqis, N.R.: Changes in communication patterns in the digital age. ARRUS J. Soc. Sci. Humanit. **3**(4), 544–556 (2023). https://doi.org/10.35877/SOSHUM1992
19. Nabi, R.L., Prestin, A., So, J.: Facebook friends with (health) benefits? Exploring social network site use and perceptions of social support, stress, and well-being. Cyberpsychol. Behav. Soc. Netw. **16**(10), 721–727 (2013). https://doi.org/10.1089/CYBER.2012.0521
20. Keyes, C.L.M.: Social well-being. Soc. Psychol. Q **61**(2), 121–137 (1998). https://doi.org/10.2307/2787065
21. Jang, W., Bucy, E.P., Cho, J.: Self-esteem moderates the influence of self-presentation style on Facebook users' sense of subjective well-being. Comput. Hum. Behav. **85**, 190–199 (2018). https://doi.org/10.1016/J.CHB.2018.03.044
22. Cary, K.M., Maas, M.K., Greer, K.M., Meshi, D.: Observed Instagram use and satisfaction with life: associations with received communications and exploration of others' content after posting a selfie. PLoS One **19**(3 March) (2024). https://doi.org/10.1371/JOURNAL.PONE.0297392,

23. Chen, J., Yan, Y., Leach, J.: Are emotion-expressing messages more shared on social media? A meta-analytic review. Rev. Commun. Res. **10** (2022). https://doi.org/10.12840/ISSN.2255-4165.034
24. Mouhadjer, N.: Social media and its impact on intercultural communication. IJAEDU- Int. E-J. Adv. Educ. **4**(10), 68–71 (2018). https://doi.org/10.18768/IJAEDU.415404
25. Sim, P.P.T., Prihadi, K.: Social comparison and life satisfaction in social media: the role of mattering and state self-esteem. Int. J. Public Health Sci. (IJPHS) **9**(3), 245–254 (2020). https://doi.org/10.11591/IJPHS.V9I3.20509
26. Hofstede, G.: Culture's consequences: comparing values, behaviors, institutions, and organizations across nations. Cult. Consequences: Comp. Values Behav. Inst. Organ. Across Nations **41**(7), 861–862 (2001). https://doi.org/10.1016/S0005-7967(02)00184-5
27. Liu, Z., Liu, Z.: The impact of culture factors on the relationships between social media, self-esteem, and life satisfaction among college students between the United States and China. Adv. Appl. Sociol. **15**(2), 37–59 (2025). https://doi.org/10.4236/AASOCI.2025.152003
28. Jackson, L.A., Wang, J.L.: Cultural differences in social networking site use: a comparative study of China and the United States. Comput. Hum. Behav. **29**(3), 910–921 (2013). https://doi.org/10.1016/J.CHB.2012.11.024
29. Nylund-Gibson, K., et al.: Ten frequently asked questions about latent transition analysis. Psychol. Methods **28**(2), 284–300 (2022). https://doi.org/10.1037/MET0000486
30. Collins, L.M., Lanza, S.T.: Latent class and latent transition analysis: with applications in the social, behavioral, and health sciences. In: Latent Class and Latent Transition Analysis: With Applications in the Social, Behavioral, and Health Sciences, pp. 1–295 (2010). https://doi.org/10.1002/9780470567333
31. Cao, H., Fang, X., Fine, M.A., Ju, X., Lan, J., Liu, X.: Beyond the average marital communication: latent profiles of the observed interactions among Chinese newlywed couples. J. Family Psychol.: JFP: J. Div. Family Psychol. Am. Psychol. Assoc. **29**(6), 850–62 (2015). https://doi.org/10.1037/FAM0000126
32. Keyes, C.L.M.: The mental health continuum: from languishing to flourishing in life. J. Health Soc. Behav. **43**(2), 207–222 (2002). https://doi.org/10.2307/3090197
33. Reinecke, L., Trepte, S.: Authenticity and well-being on social network sites: a two-wave longitudinal study on the effects of online authenticity and the positivity bias in SNS communication. Comput. Hum. Behav. **30**, 95–102 (2014). https://doi.org/10.1016/J.CHB.2013.07.030
34. Brislin, R.W.: Back-translation for cross-cultural research. J. Cross Cult. Psychol. **1**(3), 185–216 (1970). https://doi.org/10.1177/135910457000100301
35. Nylund-Gibson, K., Choi, A.Y.: Ten frequently asked questions about latent class analysis. Transl. Issues Psychol. Sci. **4**(4), 440–461 (2018). https://doi.org/10.1037/TPS0000176
36. Scrucca, L., Fop, M., Murphy, T.B., Raftery, A.E.: Mclust 5: clustering, classification and density estimation using Gaussian finite mixture models. R Journal **8**(1), 289–317 (2016). https://doi.org/10.32614/RJ-2016-021
37. Nylund, K.L., Asparouhov, T., Muthén, B.O.: Deciding on the number of classes in latent class analysis and growth mixture modeling: a Monte Carlo simulation study. Struct. Equ. Model. **14**(4), 535–569 (2007). https://doi.org/10.1080/10705510701575396
38. Ruxton, G.D.: The unequal variance t-test is an underused alternative to student's t-test and the Mann-Whitney U test. Behav. Ecol. **17**(4), 688–690 (2006). https://doi.org/10.1093/BEHECO/ARK016
39. Burke, M., Kraut, R.E.: The relationship between Facebook use and well-being depends on communication type and tie strength. J. Comput.-Mediat. Commun. **21**(4), 265–281 (2016). https://doi.org/10.1111/JCC4.12162

40. Valkenburg, P.M., van Driel, I.I., Beyens, I.: The associations of active and passive social media use with well-being: a critical scoping review. New Media Soc. **24**(2), 530–549 (2022). https://doi.org/10.1177/14614448211065425
41. Merkin, R.: The relationship between individualism/collectivism consultation and harmony needs. J. Intercult. Commun. (39) (2015). https://doi.org/10.36923/JICC.V15I3.704
42. Merkin, R.S.: Individualism-collectivism applied to direct versus indirect facework. Saving Face Bus. 119–136 (2018). https://doi.org/10.1057/978-1-137-59174-6_5
43. Walther, J.B.: Computer-mediated communication: impersonal, interpersonal, and hyperpersonal interaction. Communic Res. **23**(1), 3–43 (1996). https://doi.org/10.1177/009365096023001001
44. Hughes, D., Seidman, E., Williams, N.: Cultural phenomena and the research enterprise: toward a culturally anchored methodology. Am. J. Commun. Psychol. **21**(6), 687–703 (1993). https://doi.org/10.1007/BF00942243
45. Kitkhachonkunlaphat, K., Vorvoreanu,M.: Social media design requirements for the collectivist international students. In: Lecture Notes in Computer Science (Including Subseries Lecture Notes in Artificial Intelligence and Lecture Notes in Bioinformatics), vol. 9181, pp. 22–33 (2015). https://doi.org/10.1007/978-3-319-20934-0_3

Author Index

A
Ali, Raian 521
Alshakhsi, Sameha 521
Anicin, Luka 379

C
Chan, Stephen C. F. 415
Chen, Dongyue 188
Chen, Haoyu 219
Chen, Jiaqi 188
Chen, Jingying 399
Chen, Min-Rong 16, 30, 43
Chen, Rui 107, 452
Chen, Yakun 155

D
Deng, Shizhuo 188
Du, Yantong 452
Du, Zhengyuan 488

E
Elfadl, Asma 521

F
Fu, Eugene Yujun 267, 415, 503

G
Gan, Zehua 188
Gao, Longxiang 470
Gao, Xingyi 123
Gong, Da 314
Guo, Yuming 123
Guo, Zihua 16, 30, 43

H
Han, Bowen 188
Han, Qilong 88, 107, 452
Hara, Kunihiko 55
Hayashi, Yujiro 331
Hu, Kaixi 171
Huang, Siyuan 219
Huo, Huan 123

J
Jiang, Jiaqi 219
Jiang, Kun 399
Jiang, Nan 521
Jin, Jiahui 219

K
Kargabaeva, Kamila 379
Kawai, Yukiko 331
Kitamura, Shizuku 346

L
Lan, Asaka Cheng 346, 362
Leong, Hong Va 415, 503
Li, Da 362
Li, Lin 1, 171
Li, Yang 55
Li, Yicong 236
Li, Yufei 88
Li, Ziang 123
Liao, Wenhao 267
Lin, Jieyang 488
Lin, Xin 219
Lu, Dan 452

M
Makino, Koji 55
Mitsunaga, Haruhiko 435

N
Nakajima, Shinsuke 331, 346, 362
Ngai, Grace 415, 503

O
Ohira, Hideki 55
Ozaki, Tomonobu 141, 204

T. Hao et al. (Eds.): BESC 2025, LNCS 16431, pp. 539–540, 2026.
https://doi.org/10.1007/978-981-95-7138-3

P
Peng, Shixin 399

Q
Qin, Xuqian 488
Qiu, Lin 252

R
Rao, Zhenyu 73
Rudd, David Hason 123

S
Sasahara, Akito 362
Sgouros, Nikitas M. 282
Shibata, Hiroshi 55
Song, Hongtao 88, 107
Stojmenovic, Milos 379
Sun, Jicheng 236
Sun, Xigang 219
Sun, Yongqing 73
Sun, Yuxi 488

T
Takaki, Shuichi 435
Tan, Jinhua 488
Tani, Soma 1
Tao, Xiaohui 171
Tong, Minglei 73

U
Uda, Ibuki 141
Ueda, Mayumi 346, 362

W
Wang, Kangzhong 503
Wang, Meng-Jie 252
Wang, Shuanglin 488
Wang, Siying 452
Wang, Yuanyuan 267, 415
Wang, Yunqi 470
Wang, Zhuhua 107
Wu, Xiaoming 470

X
Xu, Guandong 123, 155, 379, 399, 470
Xu, Kuangzhe 435
Xu, Shuai 236

Y
Yamaguchi, Fumiya 346, 362
Yan, Sineng 267
Yang, Chen 73
Yang, Yu 155, 379, 399, 470
Yankouskaya, Ala 521
Yokouchi, Yuichiro 435
Yoshikawa, Daiki 204
Yoshikawa, Katsuhisa 55
Yuasa, Masahide 302

Z
Zeng, Jixiang 16, 30, 43
Zhai, Xinwei 267
Zhang, Chi 452
Zhang, Haohan 171
Zhang, Jianwei 1, 171, 331
Zhang, Junpeng 73
Zhang, Xiao-Cui 252
Zhang, Zeyan 16, 30, 43
Zhao, Wanli 73
Zheng, Wanwan 55
Zhong, Kai 267
Zhong, Songxiang 16, 30, 43
Zhu, Yue 188

www.ingramcontent.com/pod-product-compliance
Ingram Content Group UK Ltd.
Pitfield, Milton Keynes, MK11 3LW, UK
UKHW020956220926
475831UK00002B/98

9789819571376